THE YEARBOOK OF CONSUMER LAW 2008

Markets and the Law

Series Editor:
Geraint Howells
Lancaster University, UK

Series Advisory Board:
Stefan Grundmann – Humboldt University of Berlin, Germany
Hans-W. Micklitz – Bamberg University, Germany
James P. Nehf – Indiana University, USA
Iain Ramsay – York University, Canada
Charles Rickett – University of Queensland, Australia
Reiner Schulze – Münster University, Germany
Jules Stuyck – Katholieke Universiteit Leuven, Belgium
Stephen Weatherill – University of Oxford, UK
Thomas Wilhelmsson – University of Helsinki, Finland

Markets and the Law is concerned with the way the law interacts with the market through regulation, self-regulation and the impact of private law regimes. It looks at the impact of regional and international organizations (eg EC and WTO) and many of the works adopt a comparative approach and/or appeal to an international audience. Examples of subjects covered include trade laws, intellectual property, sales law, insurance, consumer law, banking, financial markets, labour law, environmental law and social regulation affecting the market as well as competition law. The series includes texts covering a broad area, monographs on focused issues, and collections of essays dealing with particular themes.

Other titles in the series

Global Perspectives on E-Commerce Taxation Law
Subhajit Basu
ISBN 0 7546 4731 5

Fairness in Consumer Contracts
The Case of Unfair Terms
Chris Willett
ISBN 1 8401 4492 0

The Intersection of Rights and Regulation
New Directions in Sociolegal Scholarship
Bronwen Morgan
ISBN 0 7546 4982 2

The Yearbook of
Consumer Law 2008

Edited by
CHRISTIAN TWIGG-FLESNER
University of Hull

DEBORAH PARRY
Independent Consultant on Consumer Law, Hull

GERAINT HOWELLS
University of Lancaster

ANNETTE NORDHAUSEN
University of Manchester

ASHGATE

Published by
Ashgate Publishing Limited
Gower House
Croft Road
Aldershot
Hampshire GU11 3HR
England

Ashgate Publishing Company
Suite 420
101 Cherry Street
Burlington, VT 05401-4405
USA

Ashgate website: http://www.ashgate.com

British Library Cataloguing in Publication Data
The yearbook of consumer law 2008. - (Markets and the law)
  1. Consumer protection - Law and legislation
  I. Twigg-Flesner, Christian, 1975-
  343'.071

ISBN-13: 978 0 7546 7152 7

Printed and bound in Great Britain by TJ International Ltd, Padstow, Cornwall.

Contents

Contributors

Guido Alpa
Professor of Private Law, University of Rome 'La Sapienza'

Richard Bragg
Senior Lecturer in Law, University of Manchester, UK

Erika Budaite
Lawyer; formerly Research Fellow, British Institute of International and Comparative Law, London, UK

Mary Donnelly
Senior Lecturer in Law, University College, Cork, Ireland

Karen Gross
Professor of Law, New York Law School and President, Southern Vermont College, Bennington, Vermont, USA

Brian W. Harvey
Professor Emeritus, University of Birmingham, UK

André Janssen
Assistant Professor, University of Münster, Germany

Tatjana Jovanic
Lecturer, University of Belgrade, Serbia

Jens Karsten
EU Regulatory Affairs Adviser, Federation of European Direct Selling Association (FEDSA)

David Kraft
Lecturer in Law, University of Central Lancashire

Paul Edgar Micallef
Member, Malta Consumer Affairs Council

Hans-W. Micklitz
Professor of German and European Private and Economic Law, University of Bamberg, Germany and the European University Institute, Florence, Italy

James P. Nehf
Professor of Law and Cleon H. Foust Fellow, Indiana University, Indianapolis, USA

Luke Nottage
Senior Lecturer and Co-Director, Australian Network for Japanese Law, University of Sydney, Australia

Paraskevi Paparseniou
Lecturer in Civil Law, University of Athens, Greece

Udo Reifner
Professor for Commercial Law, University of Hamburg, and Director of Institute for Financial Services

Jac G.J. Rinkes
Professor of Private Law, Netherlands Open University and Professor of Consumer Law, Maastricht University, Netherlands

Roland Rowell
Legal Director, Legaleyes Limited, UK

Magdalena Sengayen
Research Officer in European Civil Liability Systems at the Centre of Socio-Legal Studies

Kate Tokeley
Senior Lecturer in Law, Victoria University, Wellington, NZ

Christian Twigg-Flesner
Senior Lecturer in Private Law, University of Hull, UK

Cees van Dam
Honorary Professor of European Private Law, Utrecht University, and Visiting Professor, Queen Mary, University of London

Eliza Varney
Lecturer in Law, Keele University, UK

Mike Varney
Lecturer in Law and Deputy Director of the Institute for European Public Law, University of Hull, UK

Fidelma White
Senior Lecturer in Law, University College, Cork, Ireland

Chris Willett
Professor of Consumer Law, De Montfort University, Leicester, UK

Joanna Wrona
On secondment to DG INFSO, European Commission; Member and former Head of Consumer Policy Unit, Office for Competition and Consumer Protection, Poland

The Future of Consumer Law

In early 2007, the first volume of the *Yearbook of Consumer Law* was published. The *Yearbook* is edited under the auspices of the Consumer Law Academic Network (CLAN), a cooperation of consumer law scholars lead by Geraint Howells (Lancaster), Annette Nordhausen (Sheffield), Deborah Parry and Christian Twigg-Flesner (Hull). The idea for the *Yearbook* emerged from a conversation Geraint Howells and I had some time ago, when we discussed the general state of consumer law scholarship in the UK and beyond. There are many scholars active in this field, but their work is often not that easy to access. It seemed to us that the reason for this is that, for some time, there had been no dedicated outlet for consumer law scholarship. Our intention was to fill that gap with an annual publication that would combine peer-reviewed scholarly articles and analysis of current developments. The response to our call for submissions to the first volume exceeded our expectations, not just in terms of the number of papers submitted, but also with regard to the quality of scholarship. This success did make us wonder whether we would be able to offer a second volume that would compare favourably to its predecessor, but as you are now holding that second volume in your hands, I am sure that you will agree with us that we had no reason to be worried. And, with an eye on things to come, at the time of putting the finishing touches to this volume, we were already in discussions with prospective contributors to the third volume. The *Yearbook* has therefore, we hope, filled the gap we identified, and will establish itself as a key publication in the area of consumer law scholarship.

Developments at the European level continue to shape consumer law in all the Member States of the European Union. In February 2007, the European Commission presented its *Green Paper on the Review of the Consumer Acquis* (COM(2006) 744, 8 February 2007) which may herald significant changes to the landscape of EU consumer law. Three contributions to this volume focus on aspects of EU consumer law: Jac Rinkes explores the current state of EU consumer law, whereas Guido Alpa comments on developments in European contract law generally. Hans Micklitz then examines the relationship between EU and domestic consumer law.

The impact of EU law on consumer law dominates other papers in this volume, too. Chris Willett analyses the role of general clauses in the regulation of fairness, using the example of services of general interest.

Changing the focus slightly, Cees van Dam and Erika Boudaite present an overview of the likely impact of the EC Directive on Unfair Commercial Practices on 25 of the EU's 27 Member States. Joanna Wrona, staying with the theme of unfair commercial practices, considers the regulation of covert advertising in the context of UK law.

One area in which the EU has made a significant contribution in recent years is Travel Law, and this *Yearbook* contains two significant contributions on this topic.

Mike and Eliza Varney critically analyse the regulation protecting air passengers, whereas Jens Karsten looks to the future with his paper on the forthcoming framework for a European law on passenger rights for sea and inland waterways transport. Although all forms of travel have a significant cross-border component, it is only now that a coherent EU framework in this area is beginning to emerge.

The *Yearbook* then turns to a number of regional developments. Paul Micallef talks about the challenges of developing a coherent consumer law in Malta. Evi Parpaseniou discusses the impact the EC Consumer Sales Directive has had on Greek consumer law. A significant contribution to consumer law scholarship is made by Fidelma White and Mary Donnelly, who are presenting the findings of an empirical study of the impact of information duties on consumers. Kate Tokeley then examines class actions in New Zealand. The final full paper is by Karen Gross, and discusses credit scoring.

This overview reveals that the *Yearbook* touches upon many different aspects of consumer law, reflecting the richness of the subject as an area of study and research. Our section on current developments continues this with a look at interesting developments both within particular jurisdictions and at the supranational level.

The work of CLAN has also continued, and during 2006, we organized two major conferences. The first, 'The Changing Face of UK Consumer Protection', was held at the University of Hull to mark the retirement from full-time academic life of my colleague and co-editor, Deborah Parry. Although no longer active at the University, Deborah continues her work as a consumer law scholar, and having acted as co-editor for this volume of the *Yearbook*, she will assume the managing editorship for the 2009 volume (with Annette Nordhausen as co-editor). This volume of the *Yearbook* features some of the papers from the conference in a special section. The event attracted over 80 delegates to Hull, and was sponsored by Domestic and General plc.

The British Institute of International and Comparative Law in London was the venue for an international conference on 'The Future of Consumer Law'. As is apparent to anyone with an interest in the subject, consumer law is now a mature area of law. Most jurisdictions have a reasonably well established body of law which falls broadly under this heading. Countries continue to identify new problems affecting consumers and develop responses designed to reduce any potential detriment. However, is it still possible to identify clear rationales for the adoption of consumer legislation? Is there still a need for a separate body of law called 'consumer law'? As consumer issues are increasingly factored into the development of legal frameworks in particular areas of law, do we still have a discrete area of 'consumer law'? And if there is, is it possible to identify a shift in the nature of consumer law, e.g., from a purely private-law approach to a regulatory approach? All these questions were considered in various ways during this conference. Some of the papers from this conference have been published (including the papers by Micallef and Gross in this volume), and we hope to feature a selection of others in the next volume of the *Yearbook*. But if one were to ask the general question of whether consumer law has a future, it seems to me that, based on the contents of this *Yearbook*, there can be no doubt that it does.

The editors are grateful to Julie Prescott for her assistance in preparing the manuscript, as well as to everyone at Ashgate involved in producing the *Yearbook*.

Christian Twigg-Flesner
Hull

Editors

Christian Twigg-Flesner, University of Hull
Deborah Parry, Independent Consultant on Consumer Law, Hull
Geraint Howells, University of Lancaster
Annette Nordhausen, University of Manchester

Editorial Board

Claire Andrews, Gough Square Chambers
Richard Bragg, Manchester University
Stephen Crampton, *Which?*
Cowan Ervine, Dundee University
Duncan Fairgrieve, British Institute of International and Comparative Law
Rod Freeman, Lovells
Suzanne Lace, OFCOM
Hans Micklitz, Bamberg University
James Nehf, Indiana University
Luke Nottage, Sydney University
Iain Ramsay, Osgoode Hall
Reiner Schulze, Münster University
Thomas Wilhelmsson, Helsinki University
Chris Willett, De Monfort University

Part 1: Articles 2008

1   European Consumer Law: Making Sense

Jac G.J. Rinkes[1]

1. Introduction

Careful examination of the European Commission's Action Plans regarding European Consumer Law over the past 30 years[2] makes at least one thing very clear: consumer protection is not merely one of the means of accomplishing an internal 'frontier-free' market: *it now exists in its own right*. The question, however, is whether Consumer Law is market behaviour law or law for the benefit of the consumer?[3] In an effort to bring European Consumer Law closer to the citizens, the Commission has laid down ten basic principles. With most of these we are familiar:

> ... buy what you want, where you want; if it doesn't work, send it back; know what you are eating; protection while on holiday; consumers should not be misled, and sometimes consumers change their mind. Comparing prices should be easy, contracts should be fair to consumers and effective redress should be available in cross-border disputes.

Apparently, this basic list leads Consumer Law back to the consumer. However, can consumers 'help themselves' with these principles? Lawyers will immediately comment that these general 'slogans' are not effective and lack legal certainty. The Commission appreciates this. In a footnote, we find an 'important legal notice': the principles are intended for information purposes only and do not constitute official guidance from the Commission on the interpretation of EU laws or policies. But how should consumers make sense of this in daily life?

My colleague, Schulte-Nölke, recently reviewed the situation with regard to European Consumer Law.[4] I cannot but agree with his assessment that, at present, a

---

1   Professor of Private Law, Netherlands Open University, Professor of Consumer Law, Maastricht University. Inaugural address on the acceptance of the chair in European Consumer Law at Maastricht University, 18 November 2005.

2   The first EEC preliminary programme for consumer protection and information policy dates from the 25 April 1975.

3   R.H. Stutterheim, *Recht voor de burger (law for the civilian)*, (Amsterdam, 2002). The application of rules promoting a free market requires complex legal reasoning, compare J. Borgesius, *Economisch ordeningsrecht en verzekeringsbedrijf (economic regulation and the insurance business)*, (Groningen, 2004), K.J. Cseres, *Competition Law and Consumer Protection*, (Utrecht/Deventer, 2005), departs from the perspective of law and economics, that is of justice, fairness, and reasonableness, on the one hand, and of efficiency, on the other.

4   H. Schulte-Nölke, 'Perspectives for the development of European consumer law',

conclusive, coherent corpus of European Consumer Law does not exist. European Consumer Law consists of individual pieces of legislation, whose number has increased over the course of many years under disparate political conditions; it lacks encompassing notions and structures, except – and up to a point – in specific categories, for instance in the case of the concept of 'consumer'. The exact definition of 'consumer' is unclear.[5] Inspired by the US Uniform Commercial Code, Klik[6] has questioned the feasibility of a consumer protection system *without* the use of the concept of 'consumer' and – looking at the consumers' counterpart – has asked whether we actually need the concept at all. It must be said: even in European Consumer Law, the concept is not always used. In the product liability directive, for example, the notion of 'consumer' is absent. There seems to be a hint of a consensus on a definition: a consumer is a natural person, acting for purposes outside his trade, business or profession. The definition is quite general, but in practice always limited to transactions covered by relevant EC legislation. The Court of Justice of the European Communities (CJEC) has its own views of the matter, so as to avoid, it seems, the question as to whether it should introduce its own consumer protection policy by protecting weaker parties in all cases.

2. The Nature of Consumer Law

Consumer interests are collective interests[7] with consumers being somewhat interchangeable: the United States Model regarding class actions opens the possibility of fluid class recovery. An interesting example of fluid recovery was the judgment,[8] passed by a California court at the end of a group action, brought by a passenger on behalf of the other members of the class, against the Yellow Cab Company. The company had increased its rates by modifying its meters in violation of a municipal ordinance, charging its passengers excessively. Since it was impossible to identify and compensate all injured passengers, the court ordered a fluid recovery: the defendant company had to charge a lower than normal rate until the illegal gains had been returned to the class of users.

Tijdschrift voor Consumentenrecht en Handelspraktijken (Netherlands Journal for Consumer Law and Trade Practices) (2005): 137–140, with many references.

5   M.B.M. Loos, Het begrip 'consument' in het Europese en Nederlandse privaatrecht (the definition of 'consumer' in European and Netherlands private law) WPNR 05/6638, p. 771–2.

6   P. Klik, 'The consumer in consumer law: who needs him? Some reflections on the consumer's counterpart', *Tijdschrift voor Consumentenrecht en Handelspraktijken*, (2005): 39–40.

7   Viewed from the public/private law dichotomy, the question has been raised whether the public, as consumers, have the right to be properly informed (as implied from the whole notion of consumer protection): G.H. Samuel, 'Ex facto ius oritur', *Civil Justice Quarterly*, (1989): 62–3.

8   *Daar v. Yellow Cab Co.*, 67 Cal. 2d 695, 63 Cal. Rprt. 724, 727, 433 p. 2d 732 (1967). The example is found in the European Consumer Law Group Report '*The need for group action for consumer redress*', ECLG/033/2005.

Consumer Law is not a simple legal area: there are at least three layers of relevant legislation: Community Law, Member State laws and the Common Frame of Reference and, possibly also, the Optional Instrument, as an emerging third layer.

Schulte-Nölke paints a dazzling prospect for Consumer Law: a spiral movement of mutual influences towards the upper levels of consumer protection offered by the existing spectrum. Consumer Law may be more colourful than one expected!

3. Consumer Law: Making Sense?

Today, I would like to take a closer look at this prospect: what is the true nature of European Consumer Law and does it make sense? This examination[9] seeks an answer to a question, which will have to explain everything that those engaged in the search take it to be the business of consumer law to explain.

Make no mistake; Consumer Law is serious business. It is an important and substantial part of the *acquis communautaire*. Current directives oblige Member States to ensure that producers and distributors comply with their obligations; Member States must define the duties, powers, organization and cooperation arrangements of competent authorities and, where applicable, rules on penalties must be implemented. The penalties provided for must be effective, proportionate and dissuasive.[10] This requirement is in conformity with CJEC case law: penalties for infringements must, in any event, be effective, proportionate and constitute a deterrent, see, for example, the *Yonemoto* case.[11] At issue in this case, which was about hydraulic press brakes in industrial machines, were rules regarding essential health and safety requirements. Member States are required, within the bounds of the freedom afforded them by Treaty provisions, to opt for the most appropriate forms and methods for ensuring the effectiveness of directives. Where a directive does not specifically provide a penalty for infringement or refers for that purpose to national laws, regulations and administrative provisions, the Treaty requires the Member States to take all measures necessary to guarantee the application and effectiveness of Community Law. Whereas the choice of penalty remains within their discretion, they must ensure in particular that infringements of Community law are penalized under conditions, both procedural and substantive, that are analogous to those applicable to infringements of similar national law. In any event, the penalty must be effective, proportionate and serve as a deterrent. Thus, France had to deal more strictly with vandalism: I am not referring to the present troubles, but to the problems in 1994 regarding French farmers who attacked Spanish transports of fruits and vegetables.[12]

---

9   B. Williams, *Truth and truthfulness*, (Princeton 2002), p. 257.

10   Article 7 Directive 2001/95/EC.

11   CJEC 8 September 2005, Case C–40/04 (*Syuichi/Yonemoto*).

12   CJEC 9 December 1997, Case C–265/95 (*Commission v. France*).

4. The Challenges of European Consumer Law

The history, achievements and ambitions of European Consumer Law have been thoroughly studied.[13] Consumer Law has been truly 'Europeanized'. Joerges states[14] that its proponents not only know and quote each other, they strive for a common cause. Their approaches, however, are different. Some, departing from the perspective of the consumer '*als passiver Marktbürger*', a passive participant in the internal market,[15] opt for a thematic description. Reich and Micklitz have thus developed Consumer Law doctrine beyond the original approach, which is described by Vivienne Kendall as: the exposure of the individual as a consumer to risks which face any of us in everyday life. There is no doubt that everyday life is full of risks, from the hazards of food and non-food products, as described by my colleague, Ellen Vos,[16] to minor consumer problems of a very specific nature. Anyone will appreciate that enjoying too much fast food is hazardous to your health, but does this imply that a consumer, who is overweight as a result of overindulging on hamburgers, is entitled to compensation from McDonald's? With the recent *Cheeseburger Act* of 20 October 2005, the US House of Representatives has denied claims from fat people against the fast-food industry. Close examination will reveal that many products are dangerous. For instance, in 2004, hospitals in the United Kingdom registered 7,093 casualties caused by Wellington boots. People wearing 'wellies' have slipped whilst walking and many have pulled a muscle when putting them on. Should there be a ban therefore on rubber boots?[17] Or can we expect detailed user manuals by the rubber-boot industry to inform consumers seeking 'informed consent', so as to avoid liability? There is a wider perspective: rubber-boots contain many chemicals and, when disposed of, present serious environmental hazards (and apparently jam waste incinerators).

Consumer Law presents legislators, courts and lawyers with problems of 'filling in' and 'leaving out': areas that have been regulated require unambiguous explanation and areas that have been left out – possibly in anticipation of future developments – present further difficulties: if things are left out, the explanation will be incomplete

---

13　　Chr. Joerges, 'The Challenge of Europeanization in the realm of private law: a plea for a new legal discipline', *Duke Journal of Comparative & International Law* 14, (2004):149. Since the 1920s, Duke University has rapidly developed: '(Michael) Few was convinced that the key to becoming a great university was to build a strong faculty. He embarked on a campaign to recruit the best professors with unheard of salaries. One leading Harvard psychologist was wooed by telegram with a remarkable offer. The Harvard professor quickly cabled back, 'I accept. Where is Durham?' S. Mansfield, *The richest girl in the world*, (New York, 1994), p. 104.

14　　Joerges, 'The Challenge of Europeanization in the realm of private law: a plea for a new legal discipline': 156, n. 15.

15　　N. Reich and H.-W. Micklitz, *Europäisches Verbraucherrecht*, (Nomos, 2003), p. 11.

16　　E.I.L. Vos, 'Overcoming the Crisis of Confidence: Risk Regulation in an enlarged European Union', Inaugural Lecture Maastricht University, 2004.

17　　With the potential risk of eliminating such fine events as welly-throwing (47.5 m for men, 39.6 m for women, *Guinness Book of Records 1978*, p. 229).

or unconvincing, or there is none.[18] Furthermore, in recent years, another dimension of European Consumer Law has contributed towards its importance. Since the 1970s, consumer protection constitutes both a functional need and a normative achievement.[19] Initially, the European Commission supported unambiguous and specific research activities and the formation of a European community of Consumer Law advocates. The private law community, however, generally responded for as long as was practically possible with benign neglect. The growing volume of European (consumer) law led to a profound change in attitude, according to Joerges:[20] 'the lamenting over the patchwork character of European legislative acts characterized by early initiatives in the realm of consumer protection was followed by a plea for nothing less than a European codification of private law'.

5. The Europeanization of Consumer Law

Although since the problems with the European Constitution[21] things seem to have cooled down to some extent, this dimension of European Consumer Law is a

---

18   Williams, p. 249–250.
19   Joerges, p. 156.
20   Joerges, id. See also Chr. Joerges, *On the Legitimacy of Europeanising Private Law: Considerations on a Law of Justi(ce)-fication (justum facere) for the EU Multi-level System*, METRO, Institute for transnational legal research, Maastricht 2003 (*Ius Commune Research School*). Legal diversity will remain part of Europe: J.M. Smits, *The Good Samaritan in European Private Law, On the Perils of Principles without a Programme and a Programme for the Future*, (Maastricht/Deventer, 2000), p. 46. The question whether a common civil code is needed has been fiercely debated (see also fn. 46): P. Legrand, 'Against a European Civil Code', *Modern Law Review* 60, (1997): 44 ff.; and see A. Watson, *Legal Transplants and European Private Law*, METRO, Institute for transnational legal research, Maastricht 2000 (*Ius Commune Research School*). The 'best practices' approach seems valuable: competing legal systems *in lieu of* a supranational system of private law, J.M. Smits, Europa en het Nederlands privaatrecht (Europa and Netherlands private law), *Nederlands Tijdschrift voor Burgerlijk Recht* (Netherlands Journal for Private Law) 10 (2004): 490–500, and H.-B. Schäfer, 'Direktiven als Ersatz für Humankapital: Empfehlen sich für Entwicklungs- und Transformationsländer präzise Rechtsnormen als für hochentwickelte Staaten?', *RabelsZ Bd.* 67 (2003): S. 550–80: *Polizeyrecht* (police laws) used to reign since the sixteenth century, for example: 'Nach einer Süddeutschen "Polizeyordnung" war es verboten, Fische auf einem Fischmarkt zu verkaufen, wenn sie nicht eine bestimmte Größe aufwiesen. Dieses Verbot kontrollierten die Polizeibeamten anhand von Schablonen mit realitätsgetreuen Abbildern der Fische in der zulässigen Minimalgröße. Diese wurde dann mit der Größe der Fische, die auf dem markt angeboten wurden, verglichen'(according to a police regulation from southern Germany it was prohibited to sell short measure fish at the local fish market; this provision was enforced by issuing police officers with true-to-life plates of each fish at the minimum length allowed), at 575.
21   For a holistic approach: D. Curtin, *Mind the Gap: the Evolving EU Executive and the Constitution*, Walter van Gerven Lecture (3), Leuven (*Ius Commune Research School*) 2004. Quite cautious on the question whether the Constitution could generate

strong and effective force in the process of Europeanization. A different question is whether this could lead to a return to orthodox supranationalism or to true European citizenship by empowering Member States to deal with the matter themselves.[22] Clearly, those engaged in legal research, legislation or legal practice must search for principles and provide procedures to organize interaction between political actors and courts at varying levels of governance, aimed at accompanying and legitimising social change.

Present day Consumer Law is everybody's business: Member States, the EU, professionals, courts, lawyers, consumer organizations, supervising authorities and consumers themselves. The European Commission has decided to abolish 15,000 of the 80,000 pages of EU-regulation: the *acquis communautaire* should become simpler, cheaper and more effective.[23] EU regulations will be more widely used as a unification tool; the use of directives should be limited.

Scholarly writers on European Consumer Law doctrine face the question of how to describe systematic aspects of this area of law in terms of *structure, outlook and concepts*. Trying to 'make sense' requires *accuracy and sincerity* and a willingness to appreciate what is real and what fantasy: what are people's perceptions and are these satisfied?[24]

6. The End of Consumer Law?

And the story goes on: Consumer Law is far from being complete. Hondius[25] has described the tendency to enlarge the substance of Consumer Law by calling attention for such other consumer concerns as discrimination, dumping, sustainable consumption and development, and environmental issues. This implies that Consumer Law could be embedded in legal areas quite different from private law. The recent changed approach to protecting consumer interests – through providing better information and enhanced control by supervising authorities – presents additional difficulties in developing a comprehensive theory of Consumer Law. Are we dealing with a 'command and control' consumer society, or does enforcement

---

or construct a sense of European solidarity in the longer term: G. de Búrca, *The EU Constitution: in Search of Europe's International Identity*, Walter van Gerven Lecture (4), Leuven (*Ius Commune Research School*) 2005.

22   Joerges 'The Challenge of Europeanization in the realm of private law: a plea for a new legal discipline': 196. On many classification fronts, Consumer Law, as a right-creating category, poses threats. Consumer rights are now sufficiently well established as to no longer requiring patronising treatment from private lawyers, compare G.H. Samuel, 'Consumer rights and the law of restitution', *Northern Ireland Legal Quarterly*, 38/4 (1987): 328-341, at 329.

23   Press Release 25 October 2005; see COM(2005) 456 final, Report from the Commission – First Annual Progress Report on European Contract Law and the *Acquis* Review, 23 September 2005.

24   Williams, pp. 131, 126, 256–7.

25   E.H. Hondius, *Kroniek Consumentenrecht (consumer law chronicle)*, (Nederlands Juristenblad – Netherlands Law Journal, 2004), pp. 1660–1671.

of existing rules suffice?[26] And how should the interests of commerce be protected? *'Das Sinken der Loyalität'* (customer loyalty decline) worries trade and industry: *'Es macht keinen Spaß mehr, zu verkaufe*n' (there is no more fun in selling) is the point of departure in Pinczolits' book *'Der befreite Vertrieb'* (The Enterprise Released).[27]

7. The Impact of Consumer Law

An investigation into the structure, outlook and concepts of Consumer Law should consider two basic questions: i) what is the common measure of Consumer Law? and ii) what is the true nature of Consumer Law? Is it a proper area of law or perhaps even a goal in itself? The investigation should focus on the development of Consumer Law and ultimately assess its impact.

At this point, I would like to give an example of the difficulties European Consumer Law. One of the major difficulties is the question of the *willingness* of all involved to deal comprehensively with an issue that is quite important to consumers. I am referring to the problems consumers encounter when entering into consumer credit agreements. Current European consumer credit legislation dates from 1987.[28] It has become outdated and fails to promote cross-border lending. Furthermore, the evolution and growth of the market for consumer credit requires legislative action. In its initial 2002 proposal,[29] the Commission had aimed at transparency where costs, terms and conditions are concerned. Consumers should be enabled to compare offers; moneylenders should assess the risks of lending consumers money: they should 'know their clients'. The Commission's proposal met with considerable resistance, whereupon the original proposal was reduced in scope and certain issues were left out. An example was the obligation for Member States to set up national consumer credit databases enabling creditors to identify consumers already in debt. This resulted in the amended 2004 proposal,[30] which, again, was not received with unanimous approval. For example, the European Consumer Law Group was not satisfied[31] with the directive's aim of harmonizing the field of consumer credit in full (maximum harmonization). Moreover, various types of credit were excluded, such as real estate/housing credit, operational leases, small credit agreements and very large ones. The decision to exclude investment credits (securities market) was

---

26   J.G.J. Rinkes, Handhaving van consumentenbelangen, een gemengd stelsel (enforcement of consumer interests, a mixed system), *Nederlands Tijdschrift voor Burgerlijk Recht* (NTBR Netherlands Journal for Private Law) 10, (2004): p. 509–514.

27   K. Pinczolitz, *Der befreite Vertrieb*, Campus Verlag, Frankfurt-New York, 2003), p. 41.

28   Directive 87/102/EEC, OJ 1987, L42/48, also published in H. Beale *et.al.*, (eds), *Fundamental texts on European Private Law*, (Oxford, 2003).

29   COM(2002) 443 final, V. Heutger, 'The Commission's revised proposal for a new EU Consumer Credit Law – strengthening cross-border trade?', *Tijdschrift voor Consumentenrecht en Handelspraktijken* , 3, (2005): 94–9.

30   COM(2004) 747 final.

31   European Consumer Law Group Report ECLG/030/2005.

particularly criticized: consumers who take out a credit in order to invest in the securities market deserve a degree of protection equal to that of regular consumers. The proposal has now been modified.[32] The new 2005 draft is the outcome of changes made on the basis of objections from and reflections by members of the European Parliament, the Council and as a result of consultations with stakeholders. The Commission expresses the hope that this will facilitate the proposal's adoption. However, the modified proposal continues to sway delicately between the business of consumer credit and protection of consumers, while there is the desire to establish the conditions for a genuine internal market for consumer credit and to increase competitiveness of EU creditors by enhancing competition and promoting product innovation.

The consumer should benefit from harmonized provisions, coupled with 'mutual recognition', in the area of retail financial services. For credit up to €50,000, the method for calculating the cost of credit is harmonized; consumers should receive information and have the right to terminate a credit contract if the related purchase is cancelled. Moreover, consumers will be afforded a cooling-off period of up to 14 days.[33]

The Commission[34] has stuck to its full harmonization approach, be it with a degree of flexibility for Member States in certain areas. Only those elements expressly dealt with in the text are fully harmonized, whereas such issues as joint and several liability are left to the national legal systems.

The proposed 'mutual recognition' provision poses additional difficulties: the European Consumer Law Group had warned that, for reasons of legal certainty, conflict of laws rules in Directives were not at all satisfactory. For a limited number of issues, the modified proposal complements full harmonization, which is to the benefit of consumers, with mutual recognition, thus helping consumer credit businesses. It is proposed that for an activity in a Member State other than the one in which they are established, creditors will only have to comply with legal requirements imposed by their Member State of origin (or its equivalent) and not with those set by the host Member State. In the area of contract law, this could lead to a different result than envisaged by Article 5 of the Rome Convention. An Article 5 situation would lead to the application of the law of the country in which the consumer has his habitual residence, but such a law may establish standards which, in relation to the equivalent standards applicable in the incoming creditor's home country, limit his activity, for instance by being higher than (or different from) those in his home country. In that event, the host Member State must ensure that these standards will not apply to the contract in areas referred to in the mutual recognition clause. Either the law chosen by the parties or, in the absence of such a choice, the requirements of the creditor's home country will continue to apply. If the credit agreement has a close link with the territory of one or several Member States, Member States must take the necessary measures to ensure that consumers do not lose the protection provided by this Directive when opting for the law of a third country as the law applicable to the

---

32   COM(2005) 483 final.
33   IP/05/1237.
34   COM(2005) 483 final, p. 7.

credit agreement. Not for the first time is European Consumer Law thus confronted with the principles of private international law with its own *desiderata* in relation to consumer protection.[35]

8. The Future of Consumer Law

On a more general note, the modified proposal for a directive on consumer credit makes manifestly clear that Consumer Law is about consumer protection in an internal market where conflicting interests and goals need to be reconciled. To achieve the optimum result, *willingness* on either side of the market is needed. However, who really wishes to foster the interests of consumers at a level equal to that of lobbying professionals? The legitimacy of EU proposals depends to a large extent on the system of consultation (comitology).[36] In the area of Consumer Law, however, consultation is at best an institutionalized dialogue without teeth.[37] How then must the spirit of the attempt at regulation of the European consumer credit market be assessed from the perspective of what is needed in terms of consumer protection? If the proposal is adopted, consumer credit law will be a 'blend' of European and Member State laws, enhanced by the principle of control by the creditor's country of residence.

On a more theoretical note, the question is whether European law that both establishes the conditions for a genuine internal market and ensures a high level of consumer protection can be approached through a coherent theory of Consumer *Law*.

The arguments for 'filling in', for instance, consumer protection in credit agreements should certainly be studied, but it quite often defies explanation why and how other aspects of consumer protection have been 'left out'.

---

35   CJEC 9 November 2000, Case C–381/98 (*Ingmar GB Ltd/Eaton Leonard Technologies Inc.*), see Th. M de Boer, 'Should harmonised or unified private law prevail over rules regarding conflict of laws? The Internet has led to unexpected problems in this field; transnational law may offer solutions', *Nederlandse Jurisprudentie* (Netherlands Law report) (2005): 332, compare G.-P. Callies, 'Transnationales Verbauchervertragsrecht', *RabelsZBd.* 68 (2004): S.244–287: 'Von einem transnationalen Verbauchervertragsrecht wird man im Ergebnis erst sprechen können, wenn sich die im Wettbewerb der verbraucherschützenden Zivilregimes herausprozessierenden best practices zu Prinzipien und Grundregeln grenzüberschreitender Verbaucherverträge verdichten, die die gesellschaftliche Praxis des Abschlusses solcher Verträge und die alternative Streitschlichtung tatsächlich anleiten, and – more ambitious – in 'Global German': Denn in Gegensatz zu den regional stark divergierenden Lösungen des mandatory consumer law bildet das facilitative consumer law gleichsam den Common Core der nationalen Verbauchervertragsrechte, für den sich der nötige rough consensus über Prinzipien eines Weltverbauchervertragsrechts mit Aussicht auf Erfolg besorgen läßt'.

36   M. De Witte and A. Vermeersch, *Europees consumentenrecht*, (Antwerp, 2004), p. 45, n. 252.

37   *Ibid.*, pp. 46–7.

9. Implementation of Consumer Law in the Member States

European Consumer Law may be somewhat haphazard, but the attitude taken by some Member States can be equally characterized as 'minimalist'. In some areas, maximum harmonization is successful – as seems to be the case with product liability – but then again it is a serious threat to the coherence of national law.[38] In others, maximum harmonization is undesirable because of differences in development of specific areas of trade and industry. Some areas of European Consumer Law, such as liability for services, are still a mystery.[39] European sale-of-goods law defines the rights of consumers up to a point, but in fact leaves much to the seller's discretion. Some parts of European unfair contract terms legislation are clear and directly applicable; others fail the test. The travelling consumer still faces difficulties in obtaining redress in case of disappointment and flying can still be hazardous. Certainty regarding cross-border financial services is incomplete and cross-border payments are still difficult to make and quite often costly. Consumers can expect enhanced duties of disclosure and information in relation to e-commerce, telecommunications, (health) insurance and energy supply, but how can they assess which offer suits them best? Unfair trade practices and anti-competitive behaviour may be dealt with by the Commission, but how can individual consumers enforce action by competent authorities and what will be the effect on individual contracts? Not all is lost, however. The benchmark of the expectations of the reasonably well informed and reasonably observant and circumspect average consumer still stands[40] and serves various purposes.

Pragmatism[41] apparently serves the European Court of Justice well when dealing with – for example – advertising cases. Very recently, Mars, not unknown in EC

---

38   E.H. Hondius, Kroniek algemeen (general survey), *Nederlands Tijdschrift voor Burgerlijk Recht* (Netherlands Journal for Private Law) (2005): 7. Compare, J.A. Jolowicz, 'The protection of the consumer and purchaser of goods under English law', *Modern Law Review* 92 (1969): 1-18 'the common understanding – for such I am sure it is – that it is the manufacturer and not the seller who is responsible if goods turn out to be unsatisfactory is reinforced in several ways by the facts of contemporary life which affects us all'.

39   'There is no such thing as a European policy on consumer service contracts', ECLG/040/05 (Micklitz). And,
      … the field of services which are relevant to consumers requires much more attention, at the national and at the European level. Parts of the work might probably be done in the groups of researchers who are discussing all over Europe what the *acquis communautaire* in European contract law is, or what a comparative analysis of national contract law might contribute to the envisaged Common Frame of Reference, but ECLG is calling for a launch of more consumer focused initiatives in the field of services.

40   CJEC 10 August 2002, Case C–299/99 (*Philips*), ECR I–5475, paras 59 and 63; however, see more recently CJEC 20 January 2005, Case C–464/01 (*Johann Gruber/ Bay Wa AG*), Loos, Privaatrecht actueel: WPNR 2005, 771–2; see on the notion of 'consumer' in (European) case law regarding commercial communication J.C. Kabel, *Rechter en publieksopvattingen: feit, fictie of ervaring? Over de beoordeling door de rechter van commerciële communicatie*, (Amsterdam 2005).

41   De Witte and Vermeersch, p. 76.

case law, disputed Nestlé's application for including one of its brands in a slogan. However, consumer expectations prevailed and Nestlé was granted the right to register its well known slogan 'Have a break, ... have a Kit Kat'.[42] And a little earlier, the Court had to decide[43] whether the Greek authorities were justified in regarding bread and bakery products that were either semi-baked or fully baked and frozen (the 'bake-off' method), as a complete process of preparing baking bread. The Commission held that 'bake-off' products were thus rendered less attractive to consumers compared to baked-off bakery products. Some products are attractive in other ways, for instance Worcester sauce, because of its distinctive colour. It starts losing much of its attractiveness, however, if the sauce has been dyed with the aid of chilli powder containing 'Sudan I', an unauthorized and hazardous colouring agent. The contaminated products were traced with difficulty: apparently, many processed products contain Worcester sauce. The problem here was that the United Kingdom provided information to other Member States via its website and not through the Rapid Alert System for Food and Feed (RASFF).[44] Furthermore, the information was not adequate to enable the other Member States to carry out investigations within their respective countries. This is but one example where the care taken and the methods used in protecting the interests of consumers leave much to be desired. In some instances, consumer protection policy can be self-deceiving or even result in fantasy: in trying to promote a life without tobacco, the Commission launched an EU wide TV advertising campaign that seeks to 'de-normalize' the deadly habit. The three adverts depict a teenager under pressure from his peers to start smoking, an adult smoker longing to quit and a non-smoker suffering other people's smoke at a party. However, in each ad, the smokers are pictured blowing on party whistles rather than smoking cigarettes.[45] It is expected that the sale of party whistles will rocket in the near future.

The 1993 Directive on the hygiene of foodstuffs is at the heart of a recent case before the European Court of First Instance, dealing with automatic vending machines. At issue, more specifically, was whether such machines may distribute chewing gum without wrappers.[46]

Furthermore, in Case C–324/05,[47] the Court had to decide whether the Court of First Instance was correct ('wishful thinking'?) in assuming that the smoking public in question was particularly alert and would readily distinguish between the tobacco trade marks 'Turkish Blend' and 'Turkish Power'. The main argument was that 'it is not established that consumers are more attentive when buying cigarettes than when buying groceries or other consumer goods'.

---

42 CJEC 7 July 2005, Case C–353/03.
43 OJ re Case C–82/05, CJEC 16 April 2005, Case C–82/05.
44 Memo/05/62, 24 February 2005.
45 IP/05/606.
46 CJEC 24 November 2005, Case C–366/04 (Opinion 28 July 2005).
47 CJEC 26 November 2005, Case C–324/05.

10. Is European Consumer Law Necessary, Logical and Transparent?

This brief survey shows that any investigation into the area of Consumer Law should take into account the difficulties in identifying attitudes, desires, the spirit of the attempt, the care taken and methods used, pragmatic issues, wishful thinking and, sometimes, even fantasy. Schulte-Nölke was spot on with his colourful description of the future of Consumer Law!

In order to make sense of European Consumer Law, specific issues should be addressed: is European Consumer Law necessary, logical and transparent? Are the measures taken practical, flexible, consistent and coherent? How effective is Consumer Law and how is its effectiveness for the average consumer to be measured? As Bossuet has said: '*comme chacun raisonne à sa mode, la loi deviendroit arbitraire*' (when everyone reasons according to his will, the law becomes arbitrary).[48]

11. Is European Consumer Law Necessary?

I will first address the question of *whether European Consumer Law is at all necessary*. Consumer protection is commonly associated with the concepts of justice and justified interests and with the desire to remove inequalities between parties. The needs of commerce had to adapt to the growth and power of an interest group that has given new impetus to the traditional civil/commercial law distinction while at the same time calling it into question. This new interest group is *the consumer*. Perhaps the greatest influence of consumer pressure has been felt in relation to the principle of freedom of contract. As a result of this, some areas of contract, in which there had been frequent abuse of consumer interests, are now governed by statute. Moreover, consumer influence is making itself felt in case law: the courts are now more prepared to consider the status of the parties in certain kinds of contract and tort cases and more inclined to decide liability in terms of policy, whereby a distinction is made between business-to-consumer and business-to-business relationships.

The starting point for consumer protection is the imbalance, from both a legal and economic perspective, between professionals and consumers. Legislation may be

---

48 Œvres de Bossuet, *tome XXIII* (Versailles, 1816), p. 539. The question presupposes that all European consumers will benefit from uniformity and is reminiscent of the development of unified private international law: 'Communauté juridique, cela voudrait-il dire, peut-être, communauté de droit (non)? Ou du moins seulement communauté de principes juridiques importants (cela non plus, assurément)?' E. Frankenstein (later of Zionist fame), 'Tendances nouvelles du Droit International Privé', *Recueil des Cours* III, (1930): 241, at 261. More balanced with regard to Von Savigny, and certainly with more vision, Meijers remarks: 'L'histoire nous a appris dans quelle mesure la jurisprudence est conservatrice et ne veut rien savoir des savants, and la tradition continue à être une force réelle qu'on ne peut combattre avec success qu'en recherchant ses sources et en démontrant que les raisons d'être d'autrefois n'existent plus', E.M. Meijers, 'L'histoire des principes fondamentaux du Droit International Privé a partir du Moyen Age, spécialement dans l'Europe occidentale', *Recueil des Cours*, III, (1934): 543, at 672.

helpful: parasitic interest rates (usury), unfair contract terms, unfair selling methods and trade practices are primarily of a legal nature.

12. Protection of Weaker Parties?

Protection of the weaker party plays an important role: arguably, this concept could be one of the few really new and innovative principles of justice and fairness in private law. The question has been raised[49] as to whether the premise of the weak consumer is correct: '*les consommateurs sont-ils en position de faiblesse*? (are consumers in a weak position?)' This benchmark will cause problems. Straetmans[50] quotes Calais-Auloy in pointing out that '*faiblesse*' (weakness) is a contamination of '*faire blesser*' (to hurt) and '*faible*'(weak), and this could be very close to being '*débile*'(id.): '*En protégeant le plus faible, on finit par l'excuser de son étourderie et de sa négligence: on finit par lui donner une mentalité d'assisté. En voulant le protéger contre sa faiblesse, on risque de perpétuer cette faiblesse*' (in the end, protection of the most vulnerable persons excuses their thoughtlessness and negligence: in the end, they will acquire an attitude of expecting to be relieved in all events, with the risk of enhancing their weakness). From this perspective, the best approach would be to recognize 'collective interest' as the correct basis for consumer protection.

13. The Ultimate Goal of Consumer Protection

Ultimately, consumer protection and Consumer Law should contribute towards a better society. Consumers and professionals establish their own rules in their economic relationships. Consumers quite often lack bargaining power in individual transactions. As a result of the consumer movement, Consumer Law is primarily focused on restoring the balance between weak and strong market players. A second (logical) aim is to regulate markets: dealing with problems and conflicts and preventing distortions through legislation, self-regulation and free competition. Consumer Law has thus developed at two distinct levels: an individual and a collective level.

14. Future Policy Issues

The time has come for a closer look at future EU consumer policy. Consumer protection is an area of law under construction, a dynamic area, which is continually influenced by social and economic circumstances.[51] How should policymakers deal

---

49   G.H. Samuel and J.G.J. Rinkes, *Contractual and non-contractual obligations in English Law*, (Maastricht/Nijmegen, 1992), p. 91.

50   G. Straetmans, *Consument en markt*, (Antwerp, 1998), p. 54.

51   *Nederlands Tijdschrift voor Burgerlijk Recht* (NTBR *Netherlands Journal for Private Law*) 10, (2004). Van Schaick has pointed out that consumer weakness and legislative action to redress this (mainly in private law) are exponents of a tendency to consider the *subjective* perspective of private law, A.C. van Schaick, *Contractsvrijheid en nietigheid*, (Tilburg/Zwolle, 1994), p. 200.

with it? There are no simple and straightforward answers: effective enforcement of consumer protection laws is inherently difficult.[52] While consumer protection laws apply to millions of daily commercial transactions, consumers and businesses do not always grasp them. The increasingly complex nature of transactions and the availability to do business through the Internet, although increasing much desired cross-border trade, are crucial obstacles to efficient consumer protection. In this respect, the Commission has focused on better consumer redress by tackling unfair commercial practices at the sharp end of the infringement spectrum. Furthermore, the Commission is trying to improve individual access to justice by facilitating alternative dispute resolution schemes and developing tools for the national courts to actively promote mediation. At a more practical level, the Commission has investigated the challenges regarding consumer information. A case in point is labelling, which is now under pressure from the deregulation movement. It admits that answers are not yet available; the appropriate questions may not yet have been asked.[53] Regarding consumer information, statutory provisions could be in the public interest as they would ensure such basic policy objectives as health and safety, and the protection of financial interests. Information, as an advertising and marketing vehicle, is equally important. And finally, consumers should benefit from free choice and from being able to compare offers available in the marketplace.

How, though, should we understand consumer perception and attitude with regard to information? The recently published[54] Health and Consumer Policy Strategy refers to consumer information as one of its main objectives. It attempts, in effect, to maximize the synergy between health and consumer policy. The Strategy proposes as a common objective the protection of citizens (not: 'consumers'!) from risks and threats beyond the control of individuals that cannot effectively be tackled by individual Member States. Secondly, the Strategy should enhance the ability of citizens to take better decisions with regard to their health and their interests as consumers. Finally, mainstream health and consumer policy objectives should be present in all Community policies. Specific consumer objectives include the desire to both ensure a common high level of protection of all EU consumers against risks and threats to their safety and their economic interests, regardless of where in the EU they live, travel or buy things, and increase consumers' capacity to promote their own interests: in other words, helping consumers to help themselves. This new approach has raised some existential (essential) questions for European Consumer Law:[55] what is the relationship between consumer policy and internal market policy? Can this issue be debated openly?[56] Furthermore, although a one-sided internal market approach could yield more goods and services to consumers, would

---

52   ECLG/030/2005.
53   Commissioner Kyprianou, Speech 05/237. See on consumer redress also OECD
      workshop document 19–20 April 2005, *Background Report* [2005] *OECD Workshop
      on Consumer Dispute Resolution and Redress in the Global Market Place.*
54   Commissioner Kyprianou, Speech on labelling, 05/266.
55   COM(2005)115 final.
56   ECLG/036/05 (Weatherill).

this be detrimental to consumer protection standards? Is the new consumer policy sufficiently flexible and effective?

15. Concluding Remarks

This inaugural lecture began with the question of whether Consumer *Law can be made sense of*. That consumer *protection* makes sense is undisputed, be it that trade and industry commonly approach the need for consumer protection from a rather selfish perspective: to make a profit *and* at the same time deal with consumer concerns.[57] In order to 'make sense' of Consumer Law two questions have been asked: (1) what is the common measure of Consumer Law, and (2) what is the true nature of Consumer Law?

To start with the second question: Consumer Law is an instrument to protect reasonable expectations of honest men regarding their health, safety and economic interests in a European or, for that matter, global marketplace. Determining the common measure of Consumer Law proves more difficult. Studies investigating the feasibility of a proper 'Consumer Code' or a European Civil Code have revealed[58] the importance of Consumer Law in determining such private law principles as 'good faith' and 'fair dealing'. At the same time, they expose its weakness in formulating clear and predictable rules and concepts, for example, the concept of 'consumer' or even 'citizen' as the addressee of legislation. The 'common measure' of Consumer Law is that it *is* common (shared by all) and applicable to all persons at any given time. Although difficult to define, it is readily recognizable and is closer to everyday life than most private law. However, Consumer Law seems to be drifting away from its roots. These days, it is virtually all about transparency of markets, consumer information and market behaviour. Many important areas of consumer protection are nowadays not recognizable as such, since they are buried, for instance, in telecommunication law or in rules regarding liberalization of energy markets. In some instances, they have gone 'underground': how should consumers appreciate, for example, that rules regarding financial services are actually strongholds of Consumer Law?

Consumer Law centres on information, authority and control, but in enforcing it a powerful interest group seems to have been overlooked: consumers themselves. European Consumer Law has become a vortex[59] of general and specific policy issues, the consumer movement, consumer policy related to other policies, competition policy and other issues, having evolved at different levels of legislation. Consumers – and all others involved – have to make sense of it all. Enforcement authorities, cooling-off periods, improved consumer information, consultation, access to justice and (alternative) dispute settlement may carry the day; but ultimately '*Verbraucheraufklärung macht nur Sinn, wenn man explizit die Verbraucherrechte*

---

57   ECLG/036/05.
58   Hondius, Kroniek algemeen, NTBR 2005/7, 311 and id. The notion of Consumer: European Union versus Member States, Sydney Law Review [Vol. 28:89 2006). See the Canadian Consumer Protection Act (2002) for an interesting example.
59   See for example, ECLG Compilation 2003–4.

darstellt. Nur so ist in diesem weitem Feld auch ein Fortschritt für den Bürger erreichbar' (consumer elucidation will only make sense if consumer rights are made explicit. This is the only way improvements can be made in this broad field).

In conclusion, there is one thing, therefore, that would boost consumer confidence in the achievements of the internal market: European Consumer law should be made simpler and more readily accessible. As earlier stated, Consumer Law is serious business. It should provide directly applicable uniform rules in lieu of 'harmonized harmonization directives'. These should be easily enforceable. Furthermore, consumers should be able to take legal action. Market authorities are in a position to impose dissuasive penalties and/or institute low cost proceedings before the ordinary courts, at low costs, in the general interest. Consumer organizations should be equally empowered. Small claims are no small beer. Consumers must learn to help themselves. Admittedly, I am fighting *pro aris et focis*,[60] but a European Consumer Code *would* make sense.

---

60   For my hearth and home, literally: for his altars and fires.

2 The Future of European Contract Law: Some Questions and Some Answers

Guido Alpa

1. Introduction

I would like to put some of the answers to a questionnaire, submitted by the Italian Bar Council to Italian lawyers, in a wider context and to touch on some aspects of the problems that the questionnaire itself refers to and which would also be worth discussing in the perspective of the practice of law.

Although the questionnaire does not radically question whether or not to begin the process of constructing a European Contract Law, one senses many reservations in discussions with lawyers who are involved in this theme. The reservations are varied; many fear that the introduction of uniform regulations may undermine the application of domestic ones. It is also feared that new regulations in the contracts sector may involve radical choices, starting over 'from scratch' and therefore unplanned and inevitable costs, such as extra study; as skills and experience already acquired may not, in themselves, be enough to form the set of notions and tools needed by a genuinely 'European' lawyer. Others fear a loss of their indirect advantage, thanks to the pre-eminence of one legal system over another or of one language over another – positions of advantage that would be reduced if all lawyers in a European context were subject to the arm's length principle.

These fears, doubts and scepticism are not only widespread in the field of legal practice: they reflect doubts and criticism that is also widespread in academic circles.

The basic questions on 'European Contract Law' were formulated with the usual perspicacious pragmatism of Roy Goode, at a conference:[1] 'Is there a problem with European Contract Law? Are the solutions proposed to resolve it appropriate?'

(i) Do We Need a European Contract Law?

The question regards European contract law in the sense of a harmonized or codified contract law. Many scholars have tried to provide an answer and, given the vast amount of literature on the subject, we cannot say who are more numerous: the

---

1   First published in *Ius Commune Lectures on European Private Law* 8 Maastricht, METRO, (2003) and then collected in a volume edited by F.W. Grosheide and E. Hondius, *International Contract Law. Articles on Various Aspects of Transnational Contract Law, 2003* (Intersentia, 2004), at p. 309.

supporters of European contract law, or the supporters of the current situation, which brings with it the approval of tradition, and favours diversity. In this case numbers certainly do not decree who is right and who is wrong. What does is the weight of arguments, their persuasiveness and rationality. We must first, however, clear up some perplexities.

The first arises from the connection between the construction of a European contract law and the choice of an *applicable law* for negotiation between parties. If everything could be resolved by applying the regulations of private international law to establish the law of the contract, the problem of European contract law would simply not arise. However, the problem does exist and it is different from a simple 'choice of law'.[2]

What is under discussion is not which law is applicable, because a 'model code' established at a European level could also become the law chosen by the parties and applied to their contract. On the contrary, the rules of private international law do not function so simply and the choice of the applicable law could be imposed by one party on another. Furthermore, what we want to avoid is the real aim of private international law: not choosing between laws, but *establishing a single law for everyone*. Or least building a solid, minimal base on which to set special rules that do not disappear into space, but have a 'safety network' around them, a way to interpret and apply them correctly and in a uniform manner to all countries that are members of the European Union (EU).

The second perplexity regards the 'beauty' or 'inalienability' of diversity: the assumption of 'the virtue of diversity' has become a cliché.[3]

Once again we are outside our area and this is not the problem to resolve. Comparison is like a mine, knowing how to compare is a great quality and using the results of comparison is a great wealth, but this science (or method) does not come into play in our case. We do not want to ignore, or even worse, emarginate national traditions and the origins of national legal culture. The great codes are the history of our legal systems and the *grands arrets* have marked their evolution. We are considering how to act in order that goods and services can circulate on the basis of *uniform* rules, not rules that are '*different*' amongst themselves. Furthermore, if we accepted only the advantages of diversity (in rules) there would be no need for conventions, multilateral agreements or even the so called uniform law.

And so is there a need for a European Contract Law?

---

2   See G. Alpa and M. Andenas, *Fondamenti del diritto privato europeo,* (Milan, 2005), II, Ch. 1.

3   See G. Wagner, 'The Virtues of Diversity in European Private Law', in J. Smits (ed.), *The Need for a European Contract Law. Empirical and Legal Perspectives,* (Groningen/ Amsterdam, 2005), p. 3; E. McKendrick, 'Harmonisation of European Contract Law: The State We Are In', in S. Vogenuaer and S. Weatherill (ed.), *The Harmonisation of European Contract Law. Implications for European Private Laws, Business and Legal Practice,* (Oxford and Portland, Oregon, 2006), p. 28.

(ii) A Critique of Uniform Contract Law from the Point of View of Business Relationships

As I previously stated, the question has been gracefully posed by a distinguished scholar of business law and *lex mercatoria*, Sir Roy Goode. It closely follows one of the basic questions posed by one of the founders of comparative law in the United Kingdom, Harold C. Gutteridge: 'Is there a problem?' Are the solutions suggested to resolve it appropriate?'

In order to answer the first question, Goode uses the same starting point as several institutions and study groups. He believes that the starting point for the construction of harmonized contract law (or even codified law) at a European level is incorrect. In other words, he believes that whoever supports the view that differences, currently in existence between national systems of contract and business law, damage trade, have not yet listed the reasons for these disadvantages and, furthermore, there is no evidence that business operators have ever complained about them. Multinational companies are used to using national regulations that are different and these differences only appear when national laws impose imperative regulations; otherwise, if rules can be deviated from, companies can prepare standardized contract forms for every legal system in which they carry out their activity.

Goode's criticism is also aimed at those who argue that transnational purchases of goods and services by consumers would be made easier by uniform contract law, for which there is no concrete evidence: it is merely hypothetical that success in business depends on the awareness (or otherwise) that consumers have of the law that can be applied to the contract.

In order to answer the second question, Goode maintains that a binding code for the parties involved would not be the best solution to the problem. A code presupposes that the Member States have a common social, cultural and economic background, but this connective framework does not yet exist. It cannot be said, either, that there are more similarities than differences between legal systems, or that the European Commission has the time or the technical skill to achieve this aim, or that study groups dedicated to this theme are legitimized to impose rules on operators. A democratic process requires all market actors to be involved, together with evaluations of a political nature that first need to mature elsewhere.

Goode adds the problem of language to all these difficulties. Translation implies choices of a conceptual nature and the end result is to invent an *ad hoc* language, in order to draw up texts that are acceptable to all. However, it is legal science that would suffer most, as all publications would have to be rewritten and a comparison of contract law would also be gravely damaged.

According to his conclusions, it does not mean that a 'model code' is not to be hoped for but, in Goode's opinion, the indispensable condition is that the parties involved choose its application, according to the rules of private international law.

In just a few sentences Goode summarizes a trend that is sceptical of (when not opposed to) the harmonization and codification of European contract law, in which many studies, carried out using different methods, converge. However, his position is not drastically negative, as he admits both the usefulness of a process of codification and its functionality, if the end result arises from free choice between the parties of the contract.

The disadvantages of harmonization have been studied in depth by Ewan McKendrick,[4] according to whom it is extremely difficult to achieve unanimous consensus on editing a uniform text on contractual law and the effects of its application might not bring the advantages that supporters of this initiative forecast. Furthermore, the range of choice that national systems offer to contract parties that want to carry out a business operation is such that a decision to harmonize contractual law would decrease this choice. The argument over competition between legal systems is one which is very important to many scholars of comparative law.

Further arguments against establishing a European contract law come from lawyers who work in situations where several legal systems exist side-by-side, due to multilingualism or the existence of different nationalities (for example, in Belgium, Scotland and England or the Autonomous Communities of Spain) and from lawyers who apply methods of economic analysis to law as a solution to this problem.

(iii) A Critique of Legislative Intervention

Among the many, interesting ideas that have arisen, there is also one, cloaked in deep scepticism, which sees in the 'European' code the illusion of reacting to the process of globalization (which is now irreversible in terms of timescales, methods and territorial borders) by preserving values and techniques of contractual law that are destined to be overwhelmed by supranational practices. Furthermore, this illusion is eroded not only at the highest level – that of the regulations of world globalization – but also at lower levels, given that, in many countries, contractual law also has regional origins and is no longer subject to the rigours of state law but is in competition with it. The codification of a European contract law would, therefore, be in conflict with globalized law and would inevitably be defeated by it and, with be in conflict with local laws, as it would represent authoritarian and anti-pluralist tendencies.[5]

This line of thought is shared by those who believe that only the *lex mercatoria* – obviously the new *lex mercatoria* – would be able to provide for the economic needs of the market.[6] These are joined by the critiques of those who conceive a contract not as the simple 'legal guise' of an economic operation but as the conventional means of realising private interests that the legislator can enrich with social content. So the discussion returns to the political not technical concepts of 'contract', 'freedom of contract', 'private autonomy' and of the role of the legislator and the judge in controlling the conduct of the parties to the contract, and of the aim, form and content of their transactions.

---

4   McKendrick, 'Harmonisation of European Contract Law: The State We Are In'.
5   N. Irti, *Nichilismo giuridico*, (Rome-Bari, 2004).
6   F. Galgano, *La globalizzazione nello specchio del diritto,* (Bologna, 2005).

(iv) A Critique of the Compression of the Situation's Spontaneous Evolution

In this area of liberal thought, there are those in favour of the natural evolutions of systems, as a solution to the most critical situations that derive from the applications of directives and the preservation of domestic principles that are by now out of date. Competition between legal systems, updating national systems on the basis of uniform rules set down by some sectors, such as that of international sales, imitating or transplanting principles worked out *ab externo* in order to render law uniform, would also be factors that came closer to national rules and would not require incentives or impositions from the Community legislator.

An attempt has been made to answer all these arguments in various works in favour of a 'model code' of European contract law:[7] in other words, a harmonization of regulations in European transnational contractual relationships would, in my opinion, bring far greater advantages that the disadvantages outlined above.

2. What Costs Might the Drawing up of European Contract Law Entail?

Many arguments in favour, or against, harmonising European contract law or rendering it uniform, have their basis in an economic analysis of law. These arguments are, however, not founded on concrete economic data or on research carried out 'in the field'. These arguments are rational, in that there is the common conviction that it is currently not possible to establish if it is more advantageous to maintain the existing situation or if it is more advantageous to change the system, by passing from a polycentric normative model to a centralized one, on the basis of economic analysis.

The perspective of economic analysis of the process of creating European contract law is the basis upon which contributions from some scholars with different scientific and cultural backgrounds, as well as from different countries, converge.[8] Some believe that rules of private international law and conventional rules – such as those included in the 1980 Rome Convention – lead to uncertainty in the choice of applicable law and, as a result, to costs that should be avoided.[9] However, the answer to this does not appear to be rendering them uniform, but rather offering the parties

---

7　See G. Alpa and M. Andenas, 'Harmonisation and Codification in European Contract Law', p. 149; E. Hondius, 'Towards a European Civil Code, International Contract Law', in *International Contract Law. Articles on Various Aspects of Transnational Contract Law, 2003*, at p. 147; A. Hartkamp, *Principles of Contract Law*, in A. Hartkamp *et al.* (eds), Towards a European Civil Code, 2nd edn, Nijmegen 1998, p. 171; W.H. Hesselink, 'The Ideal of Codification and the Dynamics of Europeanisation: The Dutch Experience', in Vogenauer and Weatherill (ed.), *The Harmonisation of European Contract Law. Implications for European Private Laws, Business and Legal Practice,* at p. 39.

8　Smits (ed.), *The Need for a European Contract Law. Empirical and Legal Perspectives.*

9　For example, see Wagner, 'The Virtues of Diversity in European Private Law', at p. 14.

greater freedom in their choice of applicable law. The 'virtues of diversity' are all oriented towards increasing contractual freedom, rather than imposing a binding choice on the parties. Only the harmonization of consumer contract law is to be wished for, even if a 'European contract law code' of an optional nature is, overall, also acceptable.[10]

As it is impossible to calculate the costs and benefits of harmonization[11] the way forward is to compare different solutions. Opting for change could, (in the opinion of H. Wagner[12]) result in costs of a political nature, lead down a different path to that originally planned and achieve results that are less satisfactory than forecast. In contrast, the existing situation allows us to choose a preferable situation, encourages efficient competition between legal systems and would reduce costs linked to bureaucracy to a minimum.

The same economists are also aware of the fact that 'legal diversity' creates costs: firstly, costs of acquiring information needed to choose the applicable law and therefore to adapt the drafting of the contract to be signed. There are costs from legal action arising from the application of one's own rules to different legal systems and costs that arise from contracts exposed to the uncertainty of continual changes in the contract law of different systems. There are also costs that arise from the legal administration systems that change from country to country.[13]

With the awareness that diversity creates costs, the solution of harmonization appears, at first sight, to be the remedy for all ills. However, it is rejected because it, in turn, generates costs linked to agreements and therefore a step by step approach is considered 'more desirable'.[14] This approach does not have the ambitious aim of drawing up a 'complete' code of European contract law, but aims to first resolve normative controversies arising from cross-border operations, through uniform rules and then to promote the convergence of civil procedure systems in order to improve the administration of justice in a European context.

From the 'behavioural' point of view, it is thought that operators do not see the need for change and that a spontaneous convergence of rules relating to contracts is, therefore, preferable.

Acquis is also not considered the best method for achieving this aim. Some believe that instead of harmonization, it generates diversity, and uncertainty rather than uniformity of interpretative choice.[15] This occurs for various reasons: (i) directives aim for minimal harmonization and the Community legislator leaves the Member States free to fill in the gaps, or to raise the standard of protection for interests to be safeguarded, or to make additions to the approved base texts, so that in national legal systems, EU-derived rules do not correspond perfectly; (ii) the interpretation of directives and norms to be implemented varies, because they contain

---

10   *Ibid.*, p. 16.
11   *Ibid.*, p. 19.
12   *Ibid.*, p. 39.
13   *Ibid.*, p. 44.
14   *Ibid.*, pp. 44–5.
15   J. Smits, *The Need for a European Contract Law. Empirical and Legal Perspectives,*
      at p. 164.

general clauses, vague expressions and generic terms. They, therefore, legitimize the attribution of different meanings to the same rules in different legal systems (iii) *acquis* is fragmentary, it touches marginal sectors or aspects and directives are not coordinated.

However, if drawing up a code that is 'imposed on the parties' appears fairly undesirable, the solution as a whole is a kind of 'model code' chosen by the parties as the contract law.[16]

At the end of the day, even those who argue in terms of an economic analysis of law come to the conclusion that a model code is preferable to the current situation.

3. Who is Legitimized to Draw up a 'European Contract Code'?

This question has been considered mainly by British and Italian scholars, but for somewhat different reasons.

Amongst British scholars, this problem has been studied by Stephen Weatherill.[17] He underlines that, in the three Communications of the Commission (2001, 2003 and 2004 respectively) that make up the development of this growing discipline, this question has remained in the background, almost obscured by other themes, even though this is a crucial problem of a 'constitutional' nature, because it directly affects the competence and, therefore, the legitimization of community bodies to deal with the issue. This competence is exercised under the principle of 'common rules for a common market' and began with the harmonization of some rules in certain sectors of consumer contract law. His opinion is that the same Article 153 of the EEC Treaty, by which the Community undertakes to protect the interests of consumers (including their economic interests), could not be the basis of legitimisation; and neither could Article 95 of the Treaty, which refers to Article 153. In other words, radical innovation of a legislative nature, such as drawing up common regulations for contracts in general, could only be the task of the legislating body and be confined only to sectors in which the Union has a precise competency (such as in the area of consumer rights).

Despite the doubts that have arisen, a conference was organized at Oxford by Stephen Weatherill and Stefan Vogenauer, dedicated to evaluating the answers to a questionnaire on this very theme, which had been sent to business people and to organizations representing them, and on the opportunity of constructing a European private law. What strongly emerged was the desirability of uniform regulations in contracts for transnational relations.[18] The fields of application of these general regulations should, according to the survey, be limited to contractual relations with consumers and aimed at improving *acquis*.

---

16   *Ibid.*, p. 179.
17   'Constitutional Issues – How Much is Best Left Unsaid?' in Vogenauer and Weatherill, (ed.), *The Harmonisation of European Contract Law. Implications for European Private Laws, Business and Legal Practice*, p. 89; and S. Vogenauer and S. Weatherill, *The European Community's Competence to Pursue the Harmonisation of Contract Law – an Empirical Contribution to the Debate*, Groningen/Amsterdam 2005, p. 105.
18   Vogenauer and Weatherill, *ult.cit.* p. 117.

The question has arisen amongst Italian scholars of competence, not only under the profile of textual legitimacy (derived from the EEC Treaty), but of legitimacy of a political nature, regarding the introduction at a European level of a 'code of contract law'. The assumption of the critique is based on the fact that the expression 'code' and the idea of a 'code', at least in continental European culture, implies a constitutive process, a basis of consensus and a pre-eminent role in the sources of law and the pillars of the legal system, which cannot be entrusted to a Community body (that is technically incapable of drawing it up) nor delegated to external research centres or to simple checks conducted on exponents of stakeholders. A subject like this should be decided by Member States with the contribution of European citizens.[19]

The problem, therefore, moves away from the technical and into the political dimension.

4. Which Values Should a 'European Contract Code' Incorporate?

Italian scholars were the first to discuss this aspect of the problem. It was followed by a debate that went far beyond the confines of Italy and a group of scholars even felt the need to sign a 'manifesto' entitled 'Giustizia sociale nel diritto contrattuale europeo';[20] and the comments of Somma: 'Scienza giuridica, economia e politica nella costruzione del diritto privato comunitario'.[21] Within such a multifaceted scenario, we can only identify some of the guidelines that mark the territory and the extent of the debate.

(i) A Critique of 'Ordoliberalism'

According to a part of Italian legal literature (one which expresses the view of the great majority), the current proposals for a contract code, or even for simple preparatory documents for a contract code, restatements, or lists of principles, would have the serious defect of favouring only technical or formal aspects rather than codifying regulations aimed at protecting *citizens'* rights. This method is, therefore, opposed at the outset. *Acquis* is assumed as a given right and the values on which *acquis* is based are also taken for granted, without considering that the sector of consumer interests is only a small part of the area of contract law and that a European citizen cannot be reduced to the mere level of a consumer. The values shared by the European Constitution and by the Treaty of Nice are totally different. They show a European citizen whose personal values are protected, rather than those of the market (even if this emphasis is sometimes considered insufficient).

These dangerous characteristics of a 'market-centred' legal system are insisted upon by those who have shown that, through European contract law, they would like to codify directives aimed at liberalising the market at a general level. This would

---

19   See S. Rodotà, in *Codici*, (Milan, 2003).
20   'Social Justice in European Contract Law: A Manifesto', *European L.J.*, 10/6, (2004): 653.
21   In *Riv.crit.dir.priv.*, (2006), n. 2; ID., *Diritto comunitario v. Diritto comune europeo*, Turin, 2003.

favour the interests of professional operators, rather than those of European citizens (who would be reduced to the simple role of consumers of goods and services). European contract law, in the form of *acquis*, already serves these interests. This operation would expand this line of thought to all contract law, sacrificing the values and interests of the European 'citizen'. In the experience of various countries, constitutional law and ordinary law, together with legislative action and doctrinal proposals, have enriched contract law as a stimulus for economic development, but also as a representation of individual values in negotiations between private parties. Criticism of the legislative method of standardization through single directives and criticisms regarding *acquis*, are multiplied in considering the possibility (which is here totally denied) of an 'amorphous', 'technically neutral' codification of contract law, which would have ideological connotations, as it would be aimed at protecting the interests of businessmen.

The 'Manifesto', which includes some criticisms by Italian authors, points out the lack of democracy in the process of constructing contract law. It demands greater social justice than that provided by *acquis* or any other current proposal, according to which just protecting some consumer rights (even at a less strong level) could in itself satisfy the need for a 'fair contract law'. Furthermore, the 'Manifesto' underlines the danger that a *reductio ad unum* of contractual regulations, which are today a great resource of the rich diversity of national cultures, would end up flattened by bureaucratic language in a dull, 'watered down' version of the depth and meaningfulness of centuries-old traditions and of dynamic systems.

We can go further: it has been pointed out how changeable (that is inspired by different degrees of intervention and different spheres of action) is the *welfarism* of *acquis* and of EU rules related to contracts. We can distinguish: (a) a model aimed at rationalising the functioning of the market and promoting the autonomy of the parties, mainly by imposing duties to give information; (b) a model aimed at correcting market dynamics in order to make professional behaviour acceptable, by using rules of fair dealing; (c) a model aimed at creating forms of distributive justice, which protect weaker parties and interfere with the content of the contract; (d) an egalitarian-type model of distributive contract law aimed at protecting certain categories of 'weak parties'; (e) a model for action aimed at protecting parties that find themselves in particular difficulty, as in the case of '*force majeure*'; (f) a model aimed at protecting public interests such as the environment or fundamental rights. The answer to these varied techniques of intervention presupposes that the legislator has a freedom of action that would be seriously limited by a European Civil Code.[22]

(ii) A Critique of 'Contractual Justice'

On the other hand, many legal experts believe that a model code should enhance freedom of contract, not contain mandatory rules, not impose contractual terms or types, but resolve only the simplest questions of interpretation of the words used

---

22   T. Wilhelmsson, 'The Ethical Pluralism of Late Modern Europe and Codification of European Contract Law', in Smits (ed.), *The Need for a European Contract Law. Empirical and Legal Perspectives*, p. 138.

in directives and leave the parties with maximum room for inventiveness, ability, competence and economic power. According to this idea, no regulations should be included for business-to-business (B2B) relations, while some regulations of merely elementary protection should be included in business-to-consumer (B2C) relationships.[23]

In every legal system there is a trend not only towards increased contractual justice in consumer contracts (to eliminate unfair terms and asymmetry of information) but also greater contractual justice in B2B contracts (to eliminate the abuse of economic dependence or the abuse of dominant positions).

(iii) A Critique of Code-Based Fundamental Rights

Those who care about the social dimension of the rules of European contract law put their trust in fundamental rights, to give an ethical base to regulations that would otherwise only be the result of an academic exercise. Most lawyers think in this way, not only because of the current relevance (acquired from the western model) of fundamental rights, but also because their application to relationships between private parties is the common experience of all national legal systems. There are, however, some people who challenge the feasibility of an organic system of fundamental rights and therefore do not believe that they can form the connective framework of a contract law code.[24]

It is therefore unthinkable that the values contained in the Treaty of Nice should not be applied to contractual relations and that a 'model code' should not be coordinated with a constitutional European dimension.

5. How Should a 'European Contract Code' Be Drawn Up?

There are those who believe that the sun has set on the idea of a nineteenth century code and that it cannot and *should not* be proposed again in a society such as ours, where law is necessarily fragmentary. There is no longer a coherent system of ethical values on which a uniform and systematic list of regulations can be founded. Each legal system is divided into blocks of regulations that mediate between conflicting interests. A legal system must necessarily be 'flexible' and would find it difficult to stand the straightjacket of codification, even if applied only to the contracts sector.[25]

The controversy over the modern relevance of codes has no basis in the initiatives of EU bodies. Not only because the Commission has changed direction in its works and has greatly circumscribed the objectives to achieve (even if the European Parliament continues to call the set of uniform regulations that it wants to introduce a 'code') but also because, even if we are dealing with a 'code', the end result of

---

23   See U. Perfetti, in AA.VV. *Diritto privato europeo,* Quaderni del Consiglio nazionale forense, 2005, edited by G. Alpa.

24   Wilhelmsson, 'The Ethical Pluralism of Late Modern Europe and Codification of European Contract Law', p. 141.

25   *Ibid.,* p. 130.

Transparency of terms is promoted by the UTD. The general unfairness test (which applies to the subsidiary terms of the contract) makes a term unfair if 'contrary to the requirement of good faith it causes a significant imbalance in the parties' rights and obligations to the detriment of the consumer'.[47] It appears, then, that in order to be unfair a term must satisfy two requirements: it must cause a significant imbalance in rights and obligations to the detriment of the consumer *and* it must violate the good faith requirement.[48] It seems likely that a term will often fail the significant imbalance/detriment limb of the test where it deviates (in favour of the supplier) from the default position that would otherwise apply, for example, by adding to the obligations or liabilities that would otherwise be owed by the consumer or reducing the obligations or liabilities that would otherwise be owed by the supplier.[49] In addition, a term will tend to fail the significant imbalance/detriment limb of the test where it allows for compromise of the reasonable expectations of the consumer, for example, by allowing for variation (to the detriment of the consumer) of the performance obligations of either party when this is not what the consumer would have expected given the way in which the basic agreement was presented to him.[50] The issue then is whether there has been a violation of the good faith requirement. This seems to depend upon a combined analysis of the substantive features of the term and questions of procedural fairness (Recital 16 to the Preamble to the UTD

---

47   Article 3(1) and on all of the following issues in relation to transparency see C. Willett, *The Development of Fairness in Consumer Contracts*, (Aldershot, Ashgate, 2007), Chs 5 and 6.

48   This is not the only view of the test, but certainly seems to be the view with the greatest degree of support. In particular see *Director General of Fair Trading* v. *First National Bank* [2001] 3 WLR 1297, Lord Bingham at 1307–8 and Lord Steyn at 1313. For a range of views as to the test see the discussion by R. Brownsword, G. Howells and T. Wilhelmsson, 'Between Market and Welfare', in C. Willett, (ed.), *Aspects of Fairness in Contract*, (London, Blackstone 1996), p. 25 at pp. 31–3 and M. Chen-Wishart, *Contract Law*, (Oxford, OUP, 2005), pp. 475–6.

49   This would be consistent with the idea (common in civilian codes) that the background default rules represent what is 'fair' or in good faith. On this see M. Tenreiro, 'The Community Directive on Unfair Terms and National Legal Systems', *European Review of Private Law*, 3 (1995): 273, at 279; and see the position in Greece, (CLAB, 000302) where the measure of fairness said to be deviation from substantive and basic evaluations of the law. This appears to be the approach of the Office of Fair Trading in the UK. It has been said that: 'The OFT's starting position in assessing the fairness of a term is ... normally to ask what would be the position for the consumer if it did not appear in the contract ... . Where a term changes the normal position seen by the law as striking a fair balance it is regarded with suspicion' (Office of Fair Trading, *Unfair Contract Terms Guidance* (2001) (Introduction), p. 2). For further support for the idea that default rules are the basic benchmark of fairness under the test of unfairness see S. Grundman, 'The General Clause or Standard in EC Contract Law Directives', in S. Grundman and D. Mazeaud, (eds), *General Clauses and Standards in European Contract Law*, (The Hague, Kluwer Law International, 2006), p. 141, at pp. 144–8.

50   The indicative list of terms that may be regarded as unfair contains many examples of terms allowing the trader to vary his own performance or vary the performance required of the consumer: see, for example, paras 1(g), (j), (k) and (l).

describes the question of good faith as involving an 'overall evaluation of the different interests involved', this appearing to cover both substantive and procedural matters). It seems likely that the UTD intended that of primary importance among such procedural matters is the issue of transparency; so that transparency is usually necessary for a term to pass the good faith limb of the test, even if it is not always sufficient.[51]

So, in relation to subsidiary terms, the unfairness test probably provides a very important role for transparency. However, there is room for improvement in the approach to the transparency of subsidiary terms. First of all, there should be a much clearer indication in the legislation as to what transparency involves and that transparency is indeed a primary requirement if terms are not to fail the test of unfairness. At present, the basic test of unfairness itself makes no reference to transparency and we have to deduce the makeup and relevance of transparency by looking at other provisions in the legislation and considering the broader picture. The indicative list of terms that may be regarded as unfair describes a term 'irrevocably binding the consumer to terms with which he had no real opportunity of becoming acquainted before the conclusion of the contract'.[52] This clearly goes to the *availability* of terms. However, it is less obvious that it includes questions as to the language used, the size of print, structuring, cross-referencing, highlighting particularly important/detrimental terms etc. Of course, it can be argued that all such factors affect whether the average consumer can genuinely become acquainted with terms. But this assumes that 'acquainted' can be equated with 'genuinely understand', rather than simply 'be aware of and read'. Then, quite separate from the test of unfairness, there is the requirement that written terms be in 'plain and intelligible language' and that if there is doubt as to the meaning of a term the interpretation

---

51   If terms could always be saved on the basis of transparency this would be problematic given what we have already noted about the limited impact that transparency is likely to have in relation to subsidiary terms. The position has not been made clear, either in the UK, by the House of Lords, or at ECJ level. However, it certainly seems to be accepted by most academic commentators that terms can be unfair on purely substantive grounds, irrespective of whether they are transparent. Hugh Beale has said that:

I suspect good faith has a double operation. First it has a procedural aspect. It will require the supplier to consider the consumer's interests. However, a clause which might be unfair if it came as a surprise may be upheld if the business took steps to bring it to the consumer's attention and to explain it. Secondly, it has a substantive content: some clauses may cause such an imbalance that they should always be treated as being contrary to good faith and therefore unfair.

(See H. Beale, 'Legislative Control of Fairness: The Directive on Unfair Terms in Consumer Contracts', in J. Beatson and D. Friedmann, (eds), *Good Faith and Fault in Contract Law*, (Oxford, OUP, 1995), p. 232, at p. 245). This was cited with approval by Peter Gibson in the Court of Appeal in *Director General of Fair Trading* v. *First National Bank* [2000] 2 All ER 759 at 769.

52   Paragraph 1(i).

consumers (B2C). This goes for Austria, Belgium, Denmark, Germany, Greece, Hungary, Lithuania, Luxembourg, and Sweden.

Austria: Act against Unfair Competition (Bundesgesetz gegen den unlauteren Wettbewerb, UWG)   In Austria the law on unfair commercial practices is codified in the UWG which contains a general clause (§ 1 UWG) and provisions on specific issues (§§ 2 onwards UWG) as well as an authorization of more detailed regulations (§§ 31(2) and 32 UWG). The UWG protects fairness in competition as a whole. Although it is not specifically aimed at protecting consumers, the modern view of this statute is that it has a protective function in B2C relationships, at least if they have an implication on competition between businesses.[31]

Belgium: Act on Commercial Practices and Consumer Information (Loi sur les pratiques du commerce et sur l'information et la protection du consommateur) (1991) (LPC)   The central pillar of the Belgian legal framework is the LPC. This Act pursues both to protect both business and consumer with a large set of rules and two general clauses. The first rule refers to fair competition in commercial relations (Article 93 LPC) and the second to consumer protection and information (Article 94 LPC). In addition to the LPC there are many other acts and regulations on specific issues.[32]

Denmark: Marketing Practices Act (MPA) (Markedsfoeringsloven) (1974)   The Danish MPA constitutes the core of the Danish legal framework regarding unfair commercial practices. It regulates marketing activities from private business. Its purpose is twofold: to protect consumers from unfair market behaviour and to protect competitors against acts of unfair competition. The MPA contains two general clauses: Section 1 sets out the principle of 'good marketing practices' and s. 2 concerns misleading advertising. These general provisions serve as an umbrella and are supplemented by a number of special provisions in the MPA as well as by special legislation (concerning specific marketing practices, specific products and specific media).[33]

Germany: Act against Unfair Competition (Gesetz gegen den unlauteren Wettbewerb) (1909)   For almost a century the central pillar of the German legal framework in the field of fair trading rules was the Act against Unfair Competition of 7 June 1909 (Gesetz gegen den unlauteren Wettbewerb) ('UWG'). This Act contained a general clause prohibiting any competitive behaviour which is contra bonos mores (against good morals) (§ 1 UWG).

In 2004 a new Act against Unfair Competition entered into force. § 3 of the Act provides a general clause prohibiting unfair commercial practices. This clause is supplemented by a list of unfair acts of competition in § 4 UWG, such as regarding unreasonably manipulating or exploiting consumers, surreptitious advertising, sales

---

31   Schulze and Schulte-Nölke, p. 12.
32   *Ibid.*
33   *Ibid.*, pp. 12–13.

promotions, competitions, draws and prizes, and so on. To a great extent the new Act codifies and systematizes the case law of the German court decided under the old Act. One of the changes is the introduction of a de minimis threshold in § 3 of the new Act and the introduction of a claim to skim unlawful profits (§ 10 UWG).

Greece: Act against Unfair Competition (1914)   The strong links in the early twentieth century between German and Greek law were also expressed in the fact that the Greek followed the German example in the Act against Unfair Competition of 27 January 1914 (Act 146/1914). The Act contains a general clause (Article 1) which prohibits competitive behaviour that is *contra bonos mores*. The general clause is supplemented by specific provisions on misleading advertising, liquidation and end of season sales and so on. In addition to this, Article 9 of the Act 2251/1994 on Consumer Protection regulates various forms of unfair, misleading and comparative advertising.[34]

Hungary: Act on the Prohibition of Unfair and Restrictive Market Practices   Act LVII of 1996 on the Prohibition of Unfair and Restrictive Market Practices contains a general clause on unfair commercial practices with a view on the interests of the undertakings as well as on the interest of consumers. This Act applies to the market conduct of natural persons and legal entities, as well as of unincorporated business associations. Article 2 prohibits carrying on economic activities unfairly, in particular, in a way violating or jeopardising the lawful interests of competitors or consumers, or in a way breaching the requirements of business integrity. Hence, this general clause applies to B2B, as to B2C.[35]

Lithuania: Act on Consumer Rights Protection   Lithuanian law did not hold a general statutory framework on unfair commercial practices. For a claim against an unfairly acting business, the consumer had to rely on the general tort law provisions and on the specific rules regarding specific practices.

This situation will change with an amendment to Act on Consumer Rights Protection. Article 6 of this Act sets forth the principle of fair commercial practice. It expressly states that sellers and service providers must obey fair commercial practice while offering and providing goods and services to the consumers. Goods and services have to be offered in a proper manner that consumer could clearly understand the commercial nature of such an offer.[36]

Luxembourg: Act Regulating Certain Commercial Practices and Unfair Competition (Loi du 30 juillet 2002 réglementant certaines pratiques commerciales et sanctionnant la concurrence déloyale) (2002)   The core of Luxembourg's unfair competition law is contained in the Act on Certain Trade Practices and Unfair Competition which also contains the implemented Directives 84/450/EEC and 97/55/EC. Article 14(a) contains a general clause on unfair trade practices directed exclusively at

---

34   *Ibid.*, pp. 13–14.
35   Z.K. Suhajda and S. Lendvai, Hungary, in Van Dam and Budaite, p. 76.
36   S. Katuoka, Lithuania, in Van Dam and Budaite, p. 123.

competitors. Consumer protection is considered as a kind of reflex of competition law. The general clause is complemented by provisions on advertising, sale at a loss, competitions/lotteries and pyramid selling which are – unlike the general clause – not limited to competitors but also cover B2C transactions.[37]

Sweden: Marketing Act (Marknadsföringslagen) (1995)   The Swedish Marketing Act of 27 April 1995 (Marknadsföringslagen 1995:450) contains a broadly formulated general clause (s. 4), a small general clause on misleading advertising (s. 6) and a number of special provisions. These special provisions concretize the general rule for various factual situations. Violation of a special rule can give rise to an obligation to pay damages but – contrary to other legal systems – a violation of general clause cannot. The Swedish Act protects both consumers and competitors but, a modern touch, it expressly and primarily addresses consumers. Section 1 puts the concept of combating unfair commercial practices within a broader concept to promote interest of consumers and of trade and industry in connection with the marketing of products.[38]

(iii) Statutory Framework: Combination of Acts

In seven Member States the framework to regulate commercial practices is divided over several Acts, such as the Commercial Code, the Act on Consumer Protection, or the Competition Act. In these countries, the general provisions of the Civil Code (or the Law of Obligations) can play an additional role. This goes for Czech Republic, Estonia, Finland, Latvia, Poland, Slovakia, and Spain.

Czech Republic: Commercial Code, Chapter V, Act on Consumer Protection, Civil Code   Unfair commercial practices are dealt with in general terms in § 44–52 Commercial Code. § 44(1) contains the general clause on unfair commercial practices as well as a list of different categories of unfair competition (§ 44(2)). The following provisions specify these various categories.

The Act on Consumer Protection deals in more detail with some kinds of unfair competitive conduct. It is not related to economic competition but, for instance, to the information that must be provided to the consumer, a prohibition of misleading the consumer and so on) and provides for administrative supervision and administrative sanctions, whereas the emphasis in the Commercial Code is on the private enforcement by harmed consumers or businesses.

A third legal instrument regarding unfair commercial practices is the Civil Code. On one hand it is applied as a *lex generalis* as regards the Commercial Code (see § 1(2)), on the other hand it contains general provisions on the liability for damage (§ 415 ff CC).[39]

---

37   Schulze and Schulte-Nölke, pp. 14–15.
38   *Ibid.*
39   M. Malacka, Chech Republic, in Van Dam and Budaite, p. 35.

Estonia: Consumer Protection Act (Tarbijakaitseseadus), Competition Act (Konkurentsiseadus), Law of Obligations (Võlaõigusseadus)   Estonian law contains two important instruments to regulate unfair commercial practices. Firstly, the Consumer Protection Act (Tarbijakaitseseadus), the purpose of which is to safeguard consumer rights (§ 1(1)) and to regulate the offering and sale, or marketing in any other manner, of goods or services to consumers by traders, to determine the rights of consumers as the purchasers or users of goods or services, and to provide for the organization and supervision of consumer protection and liability for violations of this Act (§ 1(2)).

Secondly, § 50(2) of the Competition Act (Konkurentsiseadus) prohibits unfair competition. Unfair competition is defined as '... dishonest trading practices and acts which are contrary to good morals and practices' (§ 50(1)). The scope of this Act is to ensure the proper functioning of the market and thus to safeguard competition in the interest of free enterprise upon the extraction of natural resources, manufacture of goods, provision of services and sale and purchase of products and services, and to prevent limitation of competition in other economic activities.

Finally, the Law of Obligations Act (Võlaõigusseadus) contains general provisions which may be applicable as regards unfair commercial practices such as the rules regarding damages and the principle of good faith (Article 6). This is, however, only a supporting argument and no independent basis for legal action as regards a trader.[40]

Finland: Consumer Protection Act, Unfair Trade Practices Act   Finnish law contains two main legal instruments as regards unfair commercial practices. The Consumer Protection Act applies to offering, selling and other marketing of consumer goods and services by business to consumers. It is aimed to prevent undue influence on the decisions of consumers to guarantee the provision of essential information by tradesmen.

The Unfair Trade Practices Act, however, aims at the protection of traders and of fair trading as a whole and thus to prevent commercial practices which may harm competition and competitors.

Both Acts are supplemented with sector-specific legislation, which is aimed at regulating and restricting the marketing of particular products (for example, Alcoholic Beverages Act, Tobacco Act and specific provisions concerning TV advertisements).

Each of the Acts contains a general clause prohibiting unfair commercial practices, be it that in the Consumer Protection Act the point of view of consumers is decisive and in the Unfair Trade Practices Act the point of view of other tradesmen.[41]

Latvia: Competition Act, Consumer Right Protection Act   Article 11 of the Competition Act holds that the violation of unfair commercial practices rules creating a hindrance, restriction or distortion of competition, shall be deemed to be unfair competition.

---

40   K. Käsper, Estonia, in Van Dam and Budaite, pp. 62–3.
41   Schulze and Schulte-Nölke, p 13.

According to Article 17 of the Consumer Right Protection Act, a manufacturer, seller or service provider is obliged to provide the consumer with true and complete information regarding the quality, safety, price, guarantee and the possibilities for guarantee service, directions regarding use, the name (firm name), given name, surname and address of the manufacturer, seller or service provider regarding the goods or services offered, indicating such information in the labelling, the attached instructions for use, the technical certificate or in other written information in respect of such goods or services.[42]

Poland: Act on Combating Unfair Competition; Civil Code   The Act on Combating Unfair Competition of 16 April 1993 regulates acts of unfair competition, such as misleading and aggressive conduct of 'traders'. The aim of the Act is to prevent and fight unfair competition in the interest of the public, traders, customers and in particular the consumers (Article 1). Although the consumers are mentioned as protected persons, they are unable to take a case to the court on the basis of the provisions of this Act. However, it is possible for them to use other provisions such as Article 388 Civil Code (referring to the law of contractual obligations and regulating undue influence/exploitation) and Article 5 Civil Code (referring to the general 'abuse of rights' – the use which is contrary to the socio-economic aim of the right and the principles of social cooperation). Proceedings based on the Act on Combating Unfair Competition can also be commenced by certain bodies or organizations representing consumer interests.

The Act refers to 'acts of unfair competition', which have been defined as acts contrary to legal provisions or the principle of good faith, threatening or infringing the interests of other traders or the customers (Article 3.1). The Act regulates specific examples of such conduct – misleading indication of the company, misleading or untruthful indication of the geographic origin of the goods or services, misleading description of goods or services, inciting rescission or failure to fulfil a contract, counterfeiting products, criticising or unfair praises, unfair or prohibited advertising, organising a snowball system of sale of goods (under certain conditions), lottery sales (under certain conditions), some free gifts, consortium-type organizations aimed at buying rights, movable or immovable goods or services. The Act on the Protection of Competition and Consumers mentions misleading or unfair advertising as an example of a practice which infringes collective interests of consumers (Article 23(a)(2)).[43]

Slovakia: Commercial Code, Act on Consumer Protection, Civil Code   Unfair commercial practices are dealt with in general terms in §§ 44–52 Commercial Code. § 44(1) contains the general clause on unfair commercial practices as well as a list of different categories of unfair competition (§ 44(2)). The following provisions specify these various categories.

The Act on Consumer Protection deals in more detail with some kinds of unfair competitive conduct. It is not related to economic competition but, for instance,

---

42   S. Grebe, Latvia, in Van Dam and Budaite, pp. 98–9.
43   M. Sengayen, Poland, in Van Dam and Budaite, p. 176.

to the information that must be provided to the consumer, a prohibition on misleading the consumer and so on) and provides for administrative supervision and administrative sanctions, whereas the emphasis in the Commercial Code is on the private enforcement by harmed consumer or business.

A third legal instrument regarding unfair commercial practices is the Civil Code. On one hand it is applied as a *lex generalis* as regards the Commercial Code (see § 1(2)), on the other hand it contains general provisions on the liability for damage (§ 415 ff CC).[44]

Spain: Act on Unfair Competition (Ley de Competencia Desleal); Act on Consumer Protection (Ley General para la Defensa de los Consumidores y Usuarios)   Spanish law provides for a combination of legal instruments to regulate unfair commercial practices. The most important statute is the Ley de Competencia Desleal (Ley 3/1991). Consumer protection rules can be found in the Ley General para la Defensa de los Consumidores y Usuarios (Ley 26/1984) and the Ley General de Publicidad (Ley 34/1988) regulates advertising. Also, the Spanish autonomous regions (Communidades Autónomas) are entitled to enact rules as regards unfair commercial practices.

The Act on Unfair Competition protects both competitors and consumers whose interests are directly affected by unfair competitive behaviour. Article 5 holds that any behaviour is unfair, if it objectively violates the principle of good faith. This Act contains several special provisions concerning specific behaviour which do not require individual investigation as to whether there has been a contravention of the principle of good faith.[45]

(iv) No Statutory Framework but General Rules in the Civil Code

Six Member States do not have a statutory framework aimed at regulating unfair commercial practices. Private law protection against unfair competition in these countries is, apart from specific legislation, based on the general contract law and tort law clauses in the Civil Codes. This goes for France, Italy, Malta, the Netherlands, Portugal, and Slovenia.

France   The general rules of the Code civil regarding the conclusion of contracts (Art. 1108 onwards, Code civil) play an important role in regulating pre-contractual transparency and fairness. In addition, a lack of transparency in the pre-contractual stage may constitute a civil wrong to which the general rules of tort law are applicable (Articles 1382 and 1383 Code civil). Based on these rules the courts have also developed the concept of unfair competition ('concurrence déloyale'), according to which a business whose commercial freedom is harmed by a competitor may obtain a cease and desist order and damages for a loss suffered.[46] Besides these general rules

---

44   Malacka, pp. 196–7.
45   Schulze and Schulte-Nölke, p. 14.
46   C. van Dam, *European Tort Law* (Oxford, 2006), nr. 712.

in the Code civil the Code de la Consommation contains fairness and transparency provisions aiming at the protection of consumers.[47]

Italy   Competition is mainly controlled by constitutional principles and by the Codice civile. For the most part, trading rules are derived from the concept of professional fairness contained in Article 2598 Codice civile, which also contains a general clause (Article 2598 No. 3) and represents the most important provision connected with unfair practices. Article 2598 No. 3 states that acts of unfair competition are committed by any person who directly or indirectly makes use of any other means not in accordance with the principles of professional fairness, which would be likely to damage the business of others. This article is deemed to solely protect the interests of competitors.[48]

Malta   There is no general legal framework as regards unfair commercial practices but there are various laws dealing directly or indirectly with certain practices that might be considered as unfair.

A damages claim for unfair commercial practices can be based (both by a consumer and a trader) on the general tort law provisions if it can be shown that there was a fault on the part of the trader and that damage was suffered as a result of such practices (Articles 1031–33 Civil Code). A person is deemed to be at fault if he does not use the prudence, diligence or attention of a bonus paterfamilias. The same goes for someone who voluntarily or through negligence, imprudence or want of attention, commits any act or omission constituting a breach of the duty imposed by law.

An example of specific legislation can be found in the Articles 32–7 Commercial Code (Chapter 13 of the Laws of Malta), prohibiting various forms of unfair competition between traders such as the use of names or marks that might create confusion with other names or marks, the use of false indications of origin of goods, or disseminating information that is prejudicial to other traders. Such practices carry a civil law sanction in the form of damages, a penalty or an injunction. These provisions are aimed to protect other traders rather than consumers.[49]

Netherlands   There is no general structure of legislation on unfair competition or unfair trade practices in the Netherlands. Unfair competition rules can be found in a variety of legal and self-regulatory instruments, whereas the general principles of unfair competition are derived from the general clause in the Civil Code concerning the law of tort (Article 6:162 Burgerlijk Wetboek). The case law regarding unfair commercial practices is developed on the basis of the violation of 'unwritten law' as provided for in the general clause (Article 6:162(2)).[50]

---

47   Schulze and Schulte-Nölke, p. 12.
48   *Ibid.*, p. 15.
49   P.G. Xuereb and E. Buttigieg, Malta, in Van Dam and Budaite, pp. 152–3.
50   Schulze and Schulte-Nölke, p. 15.

Portugal   Portuguese law in the area of unfair commercial practices is highly fragmented. Fair trading is not governed by a general statutory framework but by a large number of specific rules. There is especially strong regulation in the areas of advertising and intellectual property.

Article 260 Industrial Property Act (Codigo da Propriedade Industrial) holds a general clause on unfair trade practices supplemented by a non-exhaustive list of examples. However, the scope of this clause is limited. It requires a competitive relationship and additionally a close similarity in commercial activities between the parties. Hence, it only applies in B2B and not in B2C relations.

The Law for Consumer Protection (Lei da Defeso do Consumidor) focuses on information requirements and advertising. Regarding advertising, the Portuguese constitution provides for the consumer's general right to information and prohibits hidden, indirect or fraudulent advertising.[51]

Slovenia   There is no specific legislation in Slovenia governing fairness of commercial practices. Instead, the issue of unfair commercial practices is addressed in a piecemeal manner by a number of laws regulating various aspects of fairness in commercial transactions.

The Protection of Competition Act is the most general in its scope but its primary purpose is not the protection of consumers in business transactions. Rather, the main aim of the Act is to ensure fairness between competitors by safeguarding against distortions in the market caused by competitive advantages gained by businesses using unfair commercial practices.

Accordingly, the economic interests of consumers are only indirectly protected from unfair B2C commercial practices; their interest is only protected if unfair competition as between businesses can be shown to have occurred. This means that for damages actions consumers have to rely on the general tort law provisions in the Civil Code.[52]

(v) No General Framework and no General Rules: Common Law

Three Member States do not have a statutory framework aimed at regulating unfair commercial practices. Private law protection against unfair competition in these countries is, apart from specific legislation, based on the piece meal tort rules of the common law. This goes for Cyprus, Ireland and the United Kingdom.

Cyprus   There is no general comprehensive statutory framework as regards unfair commercial practices. There are, however, various specific legislative provisions, dealing directly or indirectly with practices, which might be considered as unfair. In addition, self-regulation is a method of control of unfair commercial practices in Cyprus. Also, the fairness of commercial practices may be challenged under common law. An unfair commercial practice may constitute a breach of contract in

---

51   *Ibid.*, p. 16.
52   A. Stanic, Slovenia, in Van Dam and Budaite, p. 226.

appropriate cases or duress or undue influence as well as other tortuous claims, such as passing off or injurious falsehood depending on the nature of the case.[53]

Ireland Irish law does not contain comprehensive legislation in the area of unfair commercial practices. Fair trading rules can be found in the common law, and in a number of statutes and statutory instruments.[54]

United Kingdom English law does not recognize a concept of unfair competition or a general rule governing the fairness of commercial practices. The courts have been reluctant to develop a general principle of unfair competition, despite the accession of the UK to the Paris Convention bringing along the obligation to assure to nationals of other countries effective protection against unfair competition. The subject matter is dealt with in more than one hundred Acts and Statutory Regulations, as well as in self-regulatory Codes of Conduct and tort law precedents. The most important applicable torts are passing off, defamation and malicious falsehood.[55] In *Moorgate Tobacco* v. *Philip Morris* Deane J. stated that the phrase 'unfair competition' has been used to 'describe what is claimed to be a new and general clause of action which protects a trader against damage caused either by "unfair competition" generally or, more particularly, by the misappropriation of knowledge or information in which he has a quasi-proprietary right'.[56]

(vi) Conclusion

Looking at the various ways the legal systems have regulated commercial practices, there are in fact three categories to be distinguished.

At one end of the spectrum are the most comprehensive statutory frameworks aiming at regulating commercial practices. They can be found in the Germanic,[57] Eastern-European[58] and Nordic systems.[59] Within this category, there are differences in legislative technique, in the sense that some countries have adopted a one statute for all approach (s. 2.2) and others have divided the rules on unfair commercial practices over two or three statutory instruments (s. 2.3). However, there does not seem to be a strong difference between these approaches if it comes to regulating conduct. The difference is more a matter of legislative technique than a matter of principle as regards regulating conduct. What they have in common is that the

---

53   A. Katsis, Cyprus, in Van Dam and Budaite, p. 8.
54   Schulze and Schulte-Nölke, p. 16.
55   *Ibid.*
56   The need for more general guidance is apparent from the core principles of the Department of Trade and Industry (DTI), that consumers should see 'truthful advertisements', 'clear, helpful and adequate pre-contractual information' as well as 'clear, fair contracts'.
57   Germany, Austria, Greece.
58   Czech Republic, Estonia, Hungary, Latvia, Lithuania (in the near future), Poland, and Slovakia. An exception is Slovenia.
59   Denmark, Sweden, Finland.

political will to regulate commercial practices (rather than leave it to the courts and the market) was strong enough to enact a statutory framework in this respect.

At the other end of the spectrum, the island states (United Kingdom, Ireland and Cyprus) have taken the loosest approach.[60] As countries with a common law tradition, they only regulate specific situations and do not hold overarching general rules or general Acts. Here, the corrections to market failures are approached in a more pragmatic way, leaving more space for the protection of the freedom of trade.

In the middle are the remaining Western-European countries which are partly French orientated. They do not have general statutes regulating commercial practices but they rely on specific provisions and on the general provisions in the Civil Code.[61] Important exceptions in this area are, however, Spain, Belgium and Luxembourg, the latter being closer to the Germanic approach.

The obvious starting point in all European economies is the freedom of trade and the freedom of competition. All countries recognize that, although much is allowed in this respect, competition and trade needs to be fair, both towards other traders and towards consumers. A parallel can be drawn between sports competition and economic competition. Both areas accept competition as a useful and beneficial incentive for action and therefore emphasize the value of the freedom to act. Protection of competitors' or opponent's interests only comes into play in case of unfair conduct according to the characteristics of the competition.[62]

The common starting point of all European economies is emphasized by the fact that all Member States hold a body of statutory rules regarding specific commercial practices. The differences between the Member States are gradual rather than a matter of principle. However, from a harmonization point of view these differences are far from negligible. They are reflected in the way market behaviour is regulated in the Member States. Generally, it can be said that the looser the statutory framework, the more emphasis will be put on the freedom of trade. For example, the common law does not know a general principle of fair trading and applies a piecemeal approach in order to limit the freedom to trade. It formulates exceptions only for certain specific cases of unfair trading practices that are likely to hinder competition.[63] On the other hand, German law takes fair trading as the starting point and the general rule of its statutory framework.

Another difference worth mentioning is that in economic tradition: whereas the old Member States have always embraced a (social) market economy, most of the new Member States were for decades strongly influenced by socialist politics and the accompanying collective rather than individual approach in regulating market behaviour. Most of these countries have adopted a more general statutory framework for regulating commercial practices.

It is the aim of the UCPD to eliminate these differences between the Member States as regards the regulation of commercial practices. The Directive provides for

---

60   Cyprus, Ireland and United Kingdom (but not Malta).
61   France and Italy, and, more at a distance from the French Code, the Netherlands and Portugal.
62   Van Dam, *European Tort Law*, nr 809–1.
63   De Vrey, pp. 279–281.

an overarching set of rules of market behaviour in the relation between business and consumers. This approach is familiar to 16 of the 25 Member States. These countries will have to fine-tune their legislation in order to make it compatible with the content of the Directive. The other nine Member States will have to introduce a (more) comprehensive statutory framework on the regulation of commercial practices in order to implement the Directive.

A comprehensive statutory framework aiming at regulating commercial practices, as embodied in the Directive, can contribute to a more visible life of the principle of fair trading within the legal systems and its content stronger impregnated in the legal minds. It can also encourage the development and elaboration of the principle of fair trading throughout the European Union.

3. Scope of the National General Clauses

(i) Introduction

Article 5 is the central provision of the UCPD and provides for a grand general clause and two small general clauses. The grand clause of Article 5(1) holds that 'Unfair commercial practices shall be prohibited'. Article 5(2) provides that a commercial practice shall be unfair if '(a) it is contrary to the requirements of professional diligence, and (b) it materially distorts or is likely to materially distort the economic behaviour with regard to the product of the average consumer ...'. Besides this general clause, two small general clauses outlaw commercial practices that are misleading (Articles 6–7) and aggressive (Articles 8–9). These general clauses are supplemented by an Annex blacklisting 31 commercial practices (23 misleading practices and eight aggressive ones).

In most Member States, the fairness of commercial practices is governed by general clauses. For a few countries this is the general tort law rule, but the vast majority knows a general clause that specifically relates to commercial practices. These clauses will be analysed in this section. Obviously, Member States that do not provide for a general clause on fair commercial practices (Cyprus, France, Ireland, Malta, the Netherlands, Portugal, and the United Kingdom) will not appear in this section.

(ii) Member States Holding One General Clause

Austria, Czech Republic, Denmark, Germany, Greece, Hungary, Italy, Latvia, Lithuania, Luxembourg, Poland, Slovakia, Spain, and Sweden hold a general clause as regards unfair commercial practices.

(1) Austria
§ 1 Bundesgesetz gegen den unlauteren Wettbewerb:

Any person who acts contra bonos mores in business dealings for a competitive purpose shall be liable to proceedings for a restraining injunction and damages.

Additionally, there is a small general clause on misleading advertising in § 2(1) UWG. It consists of a formulation in general terms ('Any person who, in the course of business activity and for purposes of competition, makes deceptive statements concerning business matters ...') and contains a list of unfairness categories by way of example.[64]

(2) Czech Republic
§ 44(1) Commercial Code:
Unfair competition is conduct in an economic competition, which is contrary to the *bonos mores* of the competition and is capable of harming other competitors or consumers. Unfair competition is prohibited.[65]

(3) Denmark
Section 1 Markedsfoeringsloven:
This Act shall apply to private business activities and to similar activities undertaken by public bodies. Such activities shall be carried on in accordance with good marketing practices.[66]

(4) Germany
§ 3 Gesetz gegen den unlauteren Wettbewerb:
Acts of unfair competition which are liable to have a more than insubstantial impact on competition to the detriment of competitors, consumers or other market participants, are prohibited.
§ 1 Gesetz gegen den unlauteren Wettbewerb:
This Act intends to protect competitors, consumers and other market participants from unfair competition. At the same time it intends to protect the public interest in undistorted competition.

(5) Greece
Article 1 Act Against Unfair Competition prohibits any competitive behaviour that is *contra bonos mores*.[67]

(6) Hungary
Article 2 Act on the Prohibition of Unfair and Restrictive market Practices:
It is prohibited to conduct economic activities in an unfair manner, in particular in a manner violating or jeopardising the lawful interests of competitors and consumers, or in a way which is in conflict with the requirements of business integrity.[68] This Act applies both to B2B and B2C relations.

---

64   Schulze and Schulte-Nölke, p. 17.
65   Malacka, p. 28.
66   Schulze and Schulte-Nölke, pp. 12–13 and 18.
67   *Ibid.*, p. 19.
68   Suhajda and Lendvai, p. 29.

(7) Italy

Article 2598 No. 3 Codice civile:

Acts of unfair competition are committed by any person who directly or indirectly makes use of any other means not in accordance with the principles of professional fairness, which would be likely to damage the business of others.[69]

This article is deemed to solely protect the interests of competitors.[70] Consumer protection rules are to be derived from the general tort law rules.

(8) Latvia

Article 18 Competition Act:

Actions that violate regulatory enactments or the fair practices of commercial activities and which have created or could create a hindrance, restriction or distortion of competition, shall be deemed to be unfair competition.[71]

(9) Lithuania

Draft Article 6 Act on Consumer Rights Protection (pending before Parliament):

Sellers and service providers must obey fair commercial practice while offering and providing goods and services to the consumers. These have to be offered in such a way that the commercial nature of the offer is clear to the consumer.[72]

(10) Luxembourg

Article 14 Loi réglementant certaines pratiques commerciales et sanctionnant la concurrence déloyale:

Any act by any person exercising a commercial, industrial, artistic or liberal activity, contrary to honest practices in commercial, industrial, artistic or liberal matters or to contractual engagement, which removes or tries to remove a part of the clientele from their competitors or from one of them or which is detrimental to, or intends to be detrimental to their competitive capacity is unfair.[73]

This general clause addresses competitors and consumer protection. The general clause is complemented by provisions on advertising, sale at a loss, competitions/ lotteries and pyramid selling which are – unlike the general clause – not limited to competitors. These specific provisions also cover business-to-consumer transactions.[74]

(11) Poland

Article 3.1 Act on Combating Unfair Competition prohibits unfair competition, including misleading and aggressive conduct of traders. Acts of unfair competition

---

69   Schulze and Schulte-Nölke, p. 19.
70   *Ibid.*, p. 15.
71   Grebe, pp. 29–30.
72   Katuoka, p. 30.
73   Schulze and Schulte-Nölke, pp. 19–20.
74   *Ibid.*, p. 14.

are acts contrary to legal provisions or the principle of good faith, threatening or infringing the interests of other traders or the customers.[75]

(12) Slovakia
§ 44(1) Commercial Code:
Unfair competition is conduct in an economic competition, which is contrary to the *bonos mores* of the competition and is capable of harming other competitors or consumers. Unfair competition is prohibited.[76]

(13) Spain
Article 5 Act on Unfair Competition (Ley de Competencia Desleal):
Any behaviour objectively violating the principle of good faith is unfair.[77]

(14) Sweden
Section 4(1) Marketing Act (Marknadsföringslagen):
Marketing must be compatible with good marketing practice and also in other respects be fair towards consumers and businessmen.[78]

(iii) Member States Holding Two General Clauses

Belgium, Estonia, Finland, and Slovenia, hold two general clauses as regards unfair commercial practices.

(15) Belgium
Article 93 Act on Commercial Practices and Consumer Information (Loi sur les pratiques du commerce et sur l'information et la protection du consommateur):
Any act contrary to fair commercial practice by which a seller harms or may harm professional interests of one or several other sellers is prohibited.
Article 94 Act on Commercial Practices and Consumer Information (Loi sur les pratiques du commerce et sur l'information et la protection du consommateur):
Any act contrary to fair commercial practice by which a seller harms or may harm the interests of one or several consumers is prohibited.[79]

The two general clauses differ only with regard to the damage or potential damage to be proven (damage to other sellers in Article 93 and to consumers in Article 94). The notion of 'fair commercial practices' is the same.[80]

(16) Estonia
Article 12 Consumer Protection Act (Tarbijakaitseseadus):

---

75   Sengayen, p. 30.
76   Malacka, p. 30.
77   Schulze and Schulte-Nölke, p. 20.
78   *Ibid.*, pp. 20–21.
79   *Ibid.*, p. 17.
80   *Ibid.*, Belgian Report, 4.

The offering and sale of goods and services to consumers shall follow good trade practice and be honest with regard to the consumers.
§ 50 Competition Act (Konkurentsiseadus):

> (1) Unfair competition includes dishonest trading practices and acts which are contrary to good morals and practices.
> (2) Unfair competition is prohibited.[81]

(17) Finland
Section 1 Consumer Protection Act:
No conduct that is inappropriate or otherwise unfair from the point of view of consumers shall be allowed in marketing. Marketing that does not convey information necessary in respect of the health or economic security of consumers shall always be deemed unfair.
Section 1.1 Unfair Trade Practices Act:
Good business practice may not be violated nor may practices that are otherwise unfair to other entrepreneurs be used in business.[82]

(18) Slovenia
Article 13 Competition Act:
Unfair competition is to be understood as an act contrary to good business practices which causes or is likely to cause damage to another market participant.
Article 25 Consumer Protection Act:
A business which sells goods or provides services to consumers has to do so in a manner which is not contrary to good business practices.[83]

(iv) Conclusion

Consequences of the choice for a general clause in the Directive:
General clauses as such are not unknown in European Community law. In the adjacent area of competition law, Article 82 EC holds a general clause prohibiting the abuse of a dominant market position.[84] This general clause is followed by four categories of situations of which such abuse may consist.[85] In this sense, there is a parallel with

---

81   Käsper, p. 29.
82   Schulze and Schulte-Nölke, p. 18.
83   Stanic, p. 31.
84   Article 82 ECL 'Any abuse by one or more undertakings of a dominant position within the common market or in a substantial part of it shall be prohibited as incompatible with the common market in so far as it may affect trade between Member States'.
85   '... (a) directly or indirectly imposing unfair purchase or selling prices or other unfair trading conditions; (b) limiting production, markets or technical development to the prejudice of consumers; (c) applying dissimilar conditions to equivalent transactions with other trading parties, thereby placing them at a competitive disadvantage; (d) making the conclusion of contracts subject to acceptance by the other parties of supplementary obligations which, by their nature or according to commercial usage, have no connection with the subject of such contracts.'

the construction in the UCPD with its general clause supplemented by an Annex of 31 practices which are deemed to be unfair. The application of Article 82, however, has been very complicated and it is clear from the outset that the application of the general rule in the UCPD will be far from easy either.

The general clause of Article 5 simply bans unfair commercial practices. Such a general rule suggests unity but in fact it does not give the courts much guidance. This lack of specificity is partly made up for by the list of 31 concrete commercial practices which are deemed to be unfair. Since also misleading and aggressive practices are governed by more specific general clauses (Articles 6–9), the general clause of Article 5 will usually be the port of last rather than of first resort. In this respect the maxim holds that the general clause only applies if there is no special provision covering the particular case (*lex specialis derogate legi generali*). This maxim does not only apply within the framework of the Directive but in Community law generally. This means that more specific Community rules (or applicable specific national rules for that matter), such as in European Directives regarding distance selling, doorstep selling, (misleading) advertising and the like have precedence over the general rules of the Articles 5–9 of the Directive (see Article 3(4) of the Directive).[86]

The general clause introduced in the UCPD will replace the existing divergent general clauses in the Member States and define a common EU wide framework. It is, however, doubtful whether this general clause will considerably simplify the legislative environment in which traders and consumers operate.[87] Indeed, the upside of a general clause is the flexibility needed to adapt decisions to new unfair trading practices. The downside is, however, a lack of legal certainty which can only be provided by case law over a longer period of time. Moreover, it is unlikely that the ECJ will or even can provide the clear guidance necessary to create a level playing field. The experiences with the concept of the average consumer (s. 1.2) have shown that the Court is increasingly inclined to confine itself to questions of interpretation and to delegate more detailed decisions of application to the national courts, thus leaving space for cultural, social and linguistic differences in what can be considered to be an application of the principle of subsidiarity. The division of competence between the European and the national courts is, however, far from crystal clear.[88]

---

86   See, for example, for an overview of the extensive Community rules on advertising: J. Kabel, 'Swings on the Horizontal: The Search for Consistency in European Advertising Law', *Iris Plus* 2003–8: 2–8.

87   De Vrey, pp. 65–6, is more optimistic about the effects of the general rule.

88   Ohly, 'Towards a Harmonised European Unfair Competition Law? Comments on the Proposal for a Directive on Unfair Commercial Practices', p. 7; Stuyck, Terryn and Van Dyck, 'Confidence Through Fairness? The New Directive on Unfair Business-to-Consumer Commercial Practices in the Internal Market': 138–9, the latter pointing out that as regards interpretation of the blacklist the ECJ will decide itself since unfairness in the sense of the blacklist does not suppose an examination of the concrete circumstances. More generally, they criticize the regulatory approach of the Directive, advocate an approach more closely to the *Lamfalussy Report* as regards the regulation of the European securities markets; *ibid.*, 144–7.

B2B and B2C protection

The concept of unfair competition entered the international scene with the Paris Convention for the Protection of Industrial Property of 1883. This Convention contains a general clause in s. 10bis(2) and three more specific provisions (against the creation of confusion, the discrediting of competitors through false allegations and the misleading of the public) but the scope of this Convention and of other Conventions on more specific issues (for example TRIPS) is limited to acts of competition between competitors. Consumer interests entered the international stage only some time after World War II.

In the 1970s consumer protection became one of the official policies of the European Community[89] and this reflected the growing importance of the European consumer at a national level. At a European level, this resulted in a considerable number of consumer protection directives, such as the Directive on Misleading Advertising in 1984.[90] The UCPD can be considered as the culmination of this policy.[91] However, the scope of the Directive is completely opposite to that of the Paris Convention in that its scope is limited to consumer protection and that it does not offer protection in B2B situations – some exceptions aside which have been pointed out in s. 1.2.

Also at a national level, the focus has shifted in order to include consumer protection. For example, the starting point for German unfair competition law was to enforce the '*bonos mores*' of the marketplace. This criterion has recently been replaced by the criterion of 'unfairness'. Although this is a quite similar criterion its scope is not confined to what is fair according to the 'best market practices' in a specific branch of producers, but to what is deemed to be fair or unfair in the eyes of the public.[92] Also recent acts such as in Sweden, Denmark, and Belgium illustrate the shift to the inclusion of consumer protection, providing for a more progressive model of combined competitor and consumer protection law.[93]

---

89   The EEC Summit in Paris of October 1972 is generally considered to be the starting point for the European Community's consumer policy; the participants declared '… à renforcer et à coordonner les actions en faveur de la protection des consommateurs'. See PE 31.196/Ann./déf., 16 (http://aei.pitt.edu/1112/01/Paris_72_summit_ep_report. pdf). The entry into force of the Maastricht Treaty in 1993 conferred explicit legislative competence on the EC as regards consumer protection. According to Article 153(3)(b) the Community may adopt measures which support, supplement and monitor the policy pursued by the Member States in order to promote the interests of consumers and to ensure a high level of consumer protection. This puts the EC in a secondary position to the Member States in matters of consumer protection.

90   Also the European Commission's Green Paper, *Damages Action for Breach of the EC Antitrust Rules*, 19 December 2005, COM(2005) 627 final, takes a combined consumer-business interest approach.

91   See Micklitz, 'A General Framework Directive on Fair Trading', p. 43 who argued in 2004 '… that a European legislative framework [on fair trading] has to pay tribute to the rise of consumer protection in recent decades'.

92   De Vrey, p. 279.

93   De Vrey, p. 278.

In most Member States holding one general clause, this clause applies to both unfair B2B and B2C practices. In Member States with two general clauses, one applies to B2B and one to B2C practices. The consequences of the Directive's B2C approach are that the first group of Member States will have to split their general clause into two: one European B2C clause and one national B2B clause. The second group will have to adapt their general clause relating to B2C relations.

The limited approach of the Directive was obviously not a matter of principle but of practicality. It was considered to be politically too complicated to combine both strands of commercial practices. The Directive is rather to be seen as a first step to a general legal framework for regulating commercial practices because a broadening of the current Directive is on the European Commission's agenda as set out in Recital 8 (s. 1.2). It provides the Commission with the task to carefully examine the need for Community action in the field of unfair competition beyond the remit of this Directive and, if necessary, make a legislative proposal to cover these other aspects of unfair competition. In the meantime, it is not excluded that the current Directive can contribute to a kind of harmonization of B2B situations if Member States choose to apply the Directive standard to the B2B situations which are covered by national law.

4. Content of the National General Clauses

(i) Introduction

In a fast changing world, general clauses are indispensable. As the Commission pointed out in the Green Paper on Consumer Protection, a high degree of specificity quickly becomes obsolete as rogue traders will find new methods.[94] In the same Green Paper the Commission pointed out that the general clause was to be understood as being based on legal models such as 'fair commercial practices' or 'good market behaviour', but it would imply a general test not to engage in unfair commercial practices.[95] In the final version of the Directive, Article 5(1) prohibits unfair commercial practices, whereas Article 5(2) holds that a commercial practice shall be unfair if:

(a) it is contrary to the requirements of professional diligence, and
(b) it materially distorts or is likely to materially distort the economic behaviour with regard to the product of the average consumer whom it reaches or to whom it is addressed, or of the average member of the group when a commercial practice is directed to a particular group of consumers.[96] Hence, the Directive contains a double standard: first, professional diligence, and second that the practice materially distorts the consumer's economic behaviour.

---

94   COM(2001) 531, 2 October 2001, para. 2.2.
95   Radeideh, p. 259.
96   Article 5(3) provides a specific rule for commercial practices which are likely to materially distort the economic behaviour of a group of particularly vulnerable consumers because of their mental or physical infirmity, age or credulity.

Professional diligence is defined in Article 2(h), stating that 'the standard of special skill and care which a trader may reasonably be expected to exercise towards consumers, commensurate with honest business practices and/or the general principle of good faith in the trader's field of activity'. Compliance with codes of conduct can be taken into account when assessing whether the requirements of professional diligence are infringed but this cannot be decisive.[97] This diligence standard does not apply to misleading and aggressive practices (Articles 6–9).

The notion 'material distortion of the consumer's economic behaviour' is defined in Article 2(e) as 'the ability to make an informed decision is appreciably impaired, thereby causing the consumer to take a transactional decision that he would not have taken otherwise'. The requirement of material distortion does not apply as regards the commercial practices which are blacklisted in Annex I to the Directive and which are deemed to be unfair *per se*.[98]

How does the Directive's double standard relate to the ones that are currently applicable in the Member States? Two major categories can be distinguished in this regard. In nine countries the notion of good trading practices or *bonos mores* applies as standard (s. 4.2). In nine other countries applying a general rule, notions like honesty, fairness, good morals, good faith and business integrity are being used.

(ii) Good Trading Practices (bonos mores)

(1) Austria
§ 1 UWG:
Any person who acts *contra bonos mores* in business dealings for a competitive purpose shall be liable to proceedings for a restraining injunction and damages.

(2) Czech Republic
§ 44(1) Commercial Code:
Unfair competition is conduct in an economic competition, which is contrary to the *bonos mores* of the competition and is capable of harming other competitors or consumers. Unfair competition is prohibited.

(3) Denmark
Section 1 MPA:
This Act shall apply to private business activities and to similar activities undertaken by public bodies. Such activities shall be carried on in accordance with good marketing practices.

---

97   Stuyck, Terryn and Van Dyck, 'Confidence Through Fairness? The New Directive on Unfair Business-to-Consumer Commercial Practices in the Internal Market': 137, arguing that these codes can have potential anti-competitive effects and are not always established in the general interest but sometimes merely in the interest of the sector concerned.

98   Critical about this concept is Radeideh, pp. 261–5.

(4) Estonia
Article 12 Consumer Protection Act (Tarbijakaitseseadus):
The offering and sale of goods and services to consumers shall follow good trade practice and be honest with regard to the consumers.
§ 50 (1) Competition Act (Konkurentsiseadus):
Unfair competition is defined as 'dishonest trading practices and acts which are contrary to good morals and practices'.

(5) Finland
Chapter 2, Section 1 CPA:
No conduct that is inappropriate or otherwise unfair from the point of view of consumers shall be allowed in marketing.
Section 1.1 UTPA:
Good business practice may not be violated nor may practices that are otherwise unfair to other entrepreneurs be used in business.

(6) Greece
Following the example of German law, the Greek codification contains a general clause (Article 1), which prohibits any competitive behaviour that is *contra bonos mores*.

(7) Slovakia
§ 44(1) Commercial Code:
Unfair competition is conduct in an economic competition, which is contrary to the *bonos mores* of the competition and is capable of harming other competitors or consumers. Unfair competition is prohibited.

(8) Slovenia
Article 13 Competition Act:
Unfair competition is an act contrary to good business practices which causes or is likely to cause damage to another market participant.
Article 25 Consumer Protection Act:
A business which sells goods or provides services to consumers has to do so in a manner which is not contrary to good business practices.

(9) Sweden
Section 4(1) Marketing Act:
Marketing must be compatible with good marketing practice and also in other respects be fair towards consumers and businessmen.

(iii) Other References: Honesty, Fairness, Good Morals, Good Faith and Business Integrity

(10) Germany
§ 3 Gesetz gegen den unlauteren Wettbewerb:

Acts of unfair competition which are liable to have a more than insubstantial impact on competition to the detriment of competitors, consumers or other market participants, are prohibited.

(11) Hungary
Article 2 Competition Act:
It is prohibited to conduct economic activities in an unfair manner, in particular in a manner violating or jeopardising the lawful interests of competitors and consumers, or in a way which is in conflict with the requirements of business integrity.

(12) Italy
Article 2598 No. 3 Codice civile:
Acts of unfair competition are committed by any person who directly or indirectly makes use of any other means not in accordance with the principles of professional fairness, which would be likely to damage the business of others.[99]

(13) Latvia
Article 18 Competition Act:
Actions that violate regulatory enactments or the fair practices of commercial activities and which have created or could create a hindrance, restriction or distortion of competition, shall be deemed to be unfair competition.

(14) Lithuania
Draft Article 6 Act on Consumer Rights Protection (pending before Parliament):
Sellers and service providers must obey fair commercial practice while offering and providing goods and services to the consumers.

(15) Luxembourg
Article 14 LPC:
Any act by any person exercising a commercial, industrial, artistic or liberal activity, contrary to honest practices in commercial, industrial, artistic or liberal matters or to contractual engagement, which removes or tries to remove a part of the clientele from their competitors or from one of them or which is detrimental to, or intends to be detrimental to their competitive capacity is unfair.

(16) Poland
Article 3.1 Act on Combating Unfair Competition prohibits unfair competition, including misleading and aggressive conduct of traders. Acts of unfair competition are acts contrary to legal provisions or the principle of good faith, threatening or infringing the interests of other traders or the customers.

(17) Portugal
Article 260 CPI:

---

99   Schulze and Schulte-Nölke, p. 19.

Any person acting in the course of business activity and trying to cause a loss to anyone, or to get an illegitimate gain for himself or for a third party is deemed to be acting unfair if his behaviour is in breach of rules or of honest trade practices.

(18) Spain
Article 5 LCD:
Any behaviour objectively violating the principle of good faith is unfair.

(iv) Conclusion

When defining unfair commercial practices most general clauses refer to good trading practice, in particular, to *bonos mores* of the competition (Austria, Czech Republic, Germany, Greece and Slovakia), to good business, trade and marketing practice, fairness, honesty and good morals (Denmark, Estonia, Finland, Germany, Luxembourg, Portugal, Slovenia, Sweden), to the principle of good faith (Poland, Italy and Spain) and to business integrity (Hungary). In countries in which the general rules of the Civil Code apply, the standard is, for example, '*faute*' in France and '*onrechtmatigheid*' (unlawfulness) in the Netherlands.

The national general clauses do not refer to the standard of professional diligence. Indeed, it has been rightly argued that it is not appropriate to relate the standard for commercial practices to diligence. What is at stake in commercial practices is not so much a standard of diligence (just as it is not appropriate to require people playing sports to behave diligently, see s. 2.6) but of fairness, good business practice or lawfulness.[100] Although the Directive's terminology is not very fortunate, it is not to be expected that it will as such have a considerable impact on the content of the rule.[101] Of more importance are the political, economic and cultural traditions in striking a balance between free and fair competition. For example, in the UK the emphasis has traditionally been more on freedom and in Germany more on fairness. A comparison can be drawn with the European-wide divergence in interpreting the concept of good faith.[102] More generally, Collins rightly said: 'No doubt there is much common ground between the different jurisdictions, but at the boundaries of permitted trading behaviour there are likely to be many disagreements about how to draw the line between unfair sharp practice and merely efficient marketing techniques.'[103]

The second leg of the standard (whether the practice materially distorts or is likely to materially distort the economic behaviour with regard to the product of the average

---

100   Ohly, p. 8. In this respect it can be argued, perhaps slightly paradoxically, that the extensive self-regulatory rules in the United Kingdom may serve as an inspiration for interpreting and concretising the general rule.
101   Compare in this respect for instance the change in the German statutory wording from conduct *contra bonos mores* to unfair competition which, according to the German Ministry of Justice, was not supposed to lead to any change in the content: see Schulze and Schulte-Nölke, p. 19.
102   R. Zimmermann and S. Whittaker, *Good Faith in European Contract Law* (Cambridge, 2000).
103   See also Collins, 'EC Regulation of Unfair Commercial Practices', p. 40.

consumer, according to Article 5(2)(b) neither has a link with the Member States' general clauses. This is not surprising since the standard is formulated in purely economic terms. However, it can be argued that in national law this requirement is disguised in the legal requirements of causation and damage.

An important question in this respect is whether the courts will consider this latter requirement as a *de minimis* rule (which means that the courts should not interfere with practices that harm nobody)[104] or whether it will be given a broader meaning. The latter seems to be more likely but it will not be easy to assess whether a practice materially distorts the consumer's economic behaviour. Moreover, the two legs of the standard cannot be easily separated and it has been rightly argued that there is only a thin line between 'persuasion' and 'appreciable impairment' and that the national courts in Europe will come up with diverging interpretations.[105]

The requirement of material distortion is directly linked to the concept of the average consumer of Article 5(2)(b). The higher the level of the 'average consumer' – that is the more informed, observant and circumspect he is supposed to be – the lower the protection provided and vice versa. More generally, the concept of the 'average consumer' is fuelled by the theory, or rather the belief, that informed choices lead to efficient choices ensuring maximization of consumers' collective interests.[106] More empirical evidence is needed as to what the factual influence of information is on the efficiency of consumers' choices and whether consumers need more protection than just being properly informed.[107]

The advantage of the Directive's terminology is that it is new: it does not have clear links with the existing Member States' terminology. This provides for a 'neutral' start for the new general standard. At the same time, however, it is conceivable that the national courts will be inclined, at least initially, to look at the new standard through their old national spectacles. In this respect, it will be hard to change trained legal minds. And whereas it is hardly feasible for the ECJ to give more than general guidance (see s. 1.2), the new standard is liable to maintain divergence as regards the application of the European standard for fair commercial practices. This might

---

104   In this sense Ohly, p. 8, probably inspired by the German *§ 3 Gesetz gegen den unlauteren Wettbewerb:* 'Acts of unfair competition which are liable to have a more than insubstantial impact on competition to the detriment of competitors, consumers or other market participants, are prohibited.'

105   Stuyck, Terryn and Van Dyck, 'Confidence Through Fairness? The New Directive on Unfair Business-to-Consumer Commercial Practices in the Internal Market': 126–7.

106   Stuyck, Terryn and Van Dyck, 'Confidence Through Fairness? The New Directive on Unfair Business-to-Consumer Commercial Practices in the Internal Market': 108 and 122, on the differences between the outcome of empirical research and the description of the vulnerable consumer in Article 5(3) of the Directive. See with regard to the 'information belief', for example, Case C–362/88 (GB-INNO BM) [1990] ECR 667, and the Communication from the Commission to the European Parliament, the Council, the Economic and Social Committee and the Committee of the Regions on Consumer Policy Strategy 2002–2006 (COM(2002) 208 final).

107   Also critical about the information paradigm are, for example, Howells and Wilhelmsson, 'EC Consumer Law: Has it come of age?': 370 ff.

also go for those blacklisted commercial practices in the Annex that are vaguely formulated.[108]

5. Concluding Remarks

This chapter has provided an overview of the current national laws on unfair commercial practices throughout the European Union and their relation with the upcoming UCPD. It has been illustrated how diverse the current national approaches are and how the rules to be implemented create a new standard and structure.

It was pointed out in s. 2 how the statutory frameworks of the Member States as regards commercial practices differ. The Directive does not aim to bring harmony in this respect because the Member States are free to choose the statutory instruments to implement the Directive. In a number of Member States, the Directive will not even be visible as such if the provisions are to be inserted in various existing Acts.

Section 3 showed that the UCPD runs counter to two important features of the current national laws. On one hand, the UCPD forces common law countries to adopt a general clause on unfair commercial practices and on the other it forces most civil law countries to split their rules on unfair commercial practices into two categories: one for B2B and one for B2C situations. The latter does not make a lot of sense, the more so since the Misleading and Comparative Advertising Directive was aimed at protecting traders and consumers and is partially amended by Article 14 UCPD in order to limit applicability to traders' interests. Also, consumer protection and competitor protection can be considered to be two sides of the same coin because many practices affect consumers and competitors alike.[109] However, it has also been pointed out that feasibility has remained over desirability.

Section 4 has shown that the content of the Directive's general rule in Article 5 represents a new approach which does not have an explicit parallel in the Member States. The advantage is that the standard is not prejudiced towards one or more national standards. The downside is that the development of the content of the rule starts from scratch and that it will take time, not only to develop this content but also to make it an instrument to create a level playing field. Furthermore, the risk involved in this new approach is that the national courts will initially be inclined to fall back on the old national standards with which they are familiar.

This chapter has illustrated the huge and complicated task for the national legislators to implement the Directive into national law and for the European Commission to supervise this process. The character of maximum harmonization does not give the legislators much manoeuvring space whereas many Member States have a long standing and elaborate national tradition in the area of regulating

---

108   Stuyck, Terryn and Van Dyck, 'Confidence Through Fairness? The New Directive on Unfair Business-to-Consumer Commercial Practices in the Internal Market': 130 ff, who also argue more generally that the interplay between the different levels of prohibitions (grand general clause, small general clauses and the blacklist) will lead to problems and diversity.

109   Ohly, 'Towards a Harmonised European Unfair Competition Law? Comments on the Proposal for a Directive on Unfair Commercial Practices', p. 5.

unfair commercial practices. The implementation process is, of course, much more complicated because this paper only highlighted a few aspects of it.

After the implementation is completed, the problems will only have begun. It will be interesting to see how the national courts are going to deal with the challenge of applying the Directive. This does not only go for those courts which are used to their own former general rule, but also and particularly for courts which are not used to applying a general rule in this area at all.

6   Covert Advertising – The Notion and Regulation in the UK

Joanna Wrona[1]

1. Introduction

The traditional forms of advertising no longer influence consumer choices to the extent required by companies' marketing strategies. Consumers have got used to advertising gimmicks and ignore them. In order to remedy this, marketing experts try to convey their commercial messages by other, more sophisticated instruments. Covert advertising[2] is one of them. It has become a more common advertising technique during the last two decades, although its use is as old as advertising history itself.

Like misleading advertising, covert advertising is detrimental to consumers, because it deprives them of information necessary to take conscious economic decisions.[3] It influences their minds and choices without them being aware of this fact. It must be agreed that nowadays almost everyone has accepted the widespread presence of advertisements. However, no one likes to be deceived, especially by commercial communications.

Various countries have dealt with this problem in different ways. The regulation of advertising in general is one of the areas where the discrepancies between continental law and common law countries are most clearly visible.[4] These discrepancies are also very apparent in the area of hidden advertising regulation.

The regulation of advertising in civil law countries traditionally forms the part of the unfair competition law.[5] The assumption that unfair advertising constitutes an

---

1   Joanna Wrona until March 2007 was the head of the Consumer Policy Unit in the Office for Competition and Consumer Protection in Poland (now delegated to the European Commission as a national expert), working for a doctorate in the field of 'hidden advertising'. This chapter is a result of the research she carried out in 2005/2006 as a British Chevening Scholarship holder at Lancaster University.

2   One can also refer to this form of advertising as 'hidden' or 'disguised' advertising.

3   On the role of reliable information in advertising see S. Weatherill, 'The Role of the Informed Consumer in European Community Law and Policy', *Consumer Law Journal*, 2, No. 2 (1994): 49; R. Rijkens and G.E. Miracle, *European Regulation of Advertising. Supranational Regulation of Advertising in the European Economic Community,* (North Holland, 1986), pp. 22–3.

4   R.D. Petty, 'The Law of Misleading Advertising: An Examination of the Differences Between Common and Civil Law Countries', *International Journal of Advertising*, 15 (1996): 33.

5   On the origins of unfair competition law and the unfair competition regimes in the EU Member States see F. Henning-Bodewig, *Unfair Competition Law. European Union and Member States*, (The Hague 2006).

act of unfair competition is derived from the fact that advertising does not function in a competitive way because it very often excludes or distorts the information that consumers need to take their economic decisions.[6] These countries distinguish a few types of unfair advertising, hidden advertising being one of them, next to misleading advertising, suggestive advertising or advertising interfering with privacy.[7] The banning of the above mentioned forms of unfair advertising, as with the banning of any other acts of unfair competition, is usually derived from the general clause of unfair competition that resembles the clause contained in Article 10 bis of the Paris Convention.[8] Considering the unfairness of any act of competition it refers to acts 'contrary to honest practices in industrial and commercial matters,' thus relying on very vague notions.

In contrast, the notion of unfair competition, including unfair advertising, is alien to the common law countries (for example the UK and Ireland, as well as to Malta and Cyprus). They have never decided to legislate on the matters of unfair competition, claiming that it is very difficult to define 'unfairness' of commercial activity since one can only rely on the criteria based on ethical assumptions that are elusive and subjective.[9] They regulate only on matters of 'truthfulness' (misleading and deceptive advertising) since this concept is objectively verifiable to them. The questions of unfair commercial practices, including unfair advertising, are left to self-regulation that is more flexible, especially as regards the interpretation of the law. Moreover, common law countries do not have a legal background, precedents, case law, that would enable their national courts to apply the concept of unfair advertising in particular situations.[10]

The above mentioned discrepancies between civil and common law countries made it impossible to harmonize the rules on unfair advertising on the EU level. Although such attempts were taken on few occasions, they always met strong opposition, especially on the part of the UK. The first such attempt was made in the 1960s when the Commission requested Professor Eugen Ulmer, from the Max Planck Institute in Munich, to carry out a study on unfair competition regimes in

---

6   E. Belate, 'Unfair advertising and comparative advertising: A fighting place for a new consumer policy', in E. Belate (ed.), *Unfair Advertising and Comparative Advertising,* (Louvain-la-Neuve, 1988), p. 4.

7   Some continental law countries, mostly Scandinavian countries, have adopted yet another model of protection against unfair advertising based on specific legislation related more generally to combating unfair marketing practices and focused to a larger extent on consumer protection, for example, the Finnish Unfair Trade Practices Act (1978) and Consumer Protection Act (1978).

8   The Paris Convention for the Protection of Industrial Property (1883).

9   D.J. Harland, 'The legal concept of unfairness and the economic and social environment: fair trade, market law and the consumer interest', in E. Belate (ed.), *Unfair Advertising and Comparative Advertising,* (Louvain-la-Neuve, 1988), pp. 13–52.

10   For more information on the topic see G. Howells, 'UK' in H.-W. Micklitz and J. Keβler, (eds), *Marketing Practices Regulation and Consumer Protection in the EC Member States and the US,* (Baden Baden, 2002), p. 260; R. Lawson, 'Advertising: the legal framework', in J. Mitchell, (ed.), *Marketing and the Consumer Movement,* (London, New York, 1978), p. 205 or Henning-Bodewig, pp. 137–45.

different Member States. It formed the basis of the preliminary draft of a Proposal for a Council Directive Concerning the Approximation of the Laws of the Member States on Unfair Trade Practices – Misleading and Unfair Advertising.[11] However, this draft and its later versions did not find the required agreement among the Member States – mostly due to British opposition, rejecting the possibility to legislate on unfairness issues. Finally, it was limited only to the regulation of misleading and, at a later stage, comparative advertising,[12] thus abandoning the regulation of unfair advertising as a whole.[13]

After the failure to harmonize unfair competition and unfair advertising rules on the basis of Professor Ulmer's proposal, another attempt was made recently. This time European legislators chose another, wider approach, trying to harmonize not just unfair competition but unfair commercial practices throughout the EU. The proposed Directive that was adopted as the Directive 2005/29/EC on Unfair Commercial Practices (UCPD)[14] was based on the proposal for a general legislative framework on fair trading,[15] prepared by a team of academics[16] in 2000. It was built on a general clause of fair trading, referring in particular to the unfairness of commercial communications which are not recognizable as such (thus covert), especially through subliminal advertising.[17] However, the final text of the UCPD

---

11   Document No. XI/C/94/75-E.

12   Directive 84/450/EEC relating to the approximation of the laws, regulations and administrative provisions of Member States concerning misleading advertising, OJ 1984, L250/17 and Directive 97/55/EC amending Directive 84/450/EEC concerning misleading advertising so as to include comparative advertising, OJ 1997, L290/18.

13   For more on the attempts to harmonize the unfair competition law on the basis of the Ulmer's study, see F. Henning-Bodewig 'History, features and prospects of the Commission proposal of directive on unfair and comparative advertising', in E. Belate (ed.), *Unfair Advertising and Comparative Advertising,* (Louvain-la-Neuve, 1988), pp. 225–37 and generally on the harmonization of unfair competition law in the EU: G. Schricker, and F. Henning-Bodewig, 'New initiatives for the harmonization of unfair competition law in Europe', *European Intellectual Property Review*, 24, Issue 5, (2002): 271–6.

14   Directive 2005/29/EC concerning unfair business-to-consumer commercial practices in the internal market and amending Council Directive 84/450/EEC, Directives 97/55/EC, 98/27/EC and 2002/65/EC and Regulation (EC) 2004/2006, OJ 2005, L149/22.

15   Study on the feasibility of a General Legislative Framework on Fair Trading by the Institut für Europäisches Wirtschafts und Vebraucherrecht e.V for Health & Consumer Protection DG, November 2000; available at: http://www.europa.eu.int/comm/consumers/cons_int/safe_shop/fair_bus_pract/studies_en.htm.

16   F.A. Baumann, G. Howells, J. Keßler, H.-W.Micklitz, M. Radeideh, N. Reich, J. Stuyck and D. Voigt.

17   The wording of the proposed general clause was the following:
(1) Unfair commercial communication is prohibited;
(2) Particularly unfair is commercial communication, which unduly interferes with the freedom and the autonomy of market participants be they competitors or final consumers and which impedes market transparency;
(3) Particularly unfair is commercial communication which is not recognizable as such, in particular through subliminal advertising.

did not follow this path and eventually only one form of covert advertising – the advertorial – was mentioned explicitly in the Annex 1 to the Directive, as one of many forms of unfair commercial practices that are considered to be unfair in all circumstances.

Eventually then, unfair advertising is still not covered by EU harmonized rules on advertising. Consequently, hidden advertising, as one of its forms, is not prohibited per se by the EU law. One can only find scattered provisions banning some types of hidden advertising.[18] Except for these specific provisions, the regulation of this type of advertising is left to the discretion of Member States. This is also the case of the UK, whose regulation of covert advertising is the subject of the present analysis.

2. The Notion of Covert Advertising

In order to analyse the British approach to covert advertising, one has to understand what is meant by this term. Covert advertising, as a form of unfair advertising, is the notion that has been defined by the civil law countries. It signifies a statement encouraging the purchase of goods and services that gives the impression of neutral information, thus misleading consumers as to its character. At an EU level, the term did not appear until the late 1960s when the European Commission launched the already mentioned debate on the draft directive on unfair advertising, including among other matters, disguised advertising. Although the final Directive on Misleading Advertising did not refer to the notion of hidden advertising, one could claim that the prohibition of hidden advertising can be derived from the wording of this Directive. This statement seems to be proved by the Council minutes of the adoption of the Directive. Although they are not binding, they indicate that the Directive could be read as to include covert advertising. One can come to this conclusion, after reading the following lines: 'The Council and the Commission agree that the following in particular may be deemed "misleading advertising" within the meaning of the Directive ... c) advertising which is not easily recognizable as advertising.' This argument can also be strengthened by the answer that EC Commission gave to the European Parliament during the process of the adoption of the said Directive. It concerned the question whether publicity articles (advertorials) can be covered by the provisions of the Directive. The Commission replied that the definition of advertising in the Directive was sufficiently wide to include cases where advertising was misleading because it was disguised as editorials or reports.[19] Although this

---

18   These rules can be found in the Television without Frontiers Directive (Directive 89/522/EEC on the coordination of certain provisions laid down by Law, Regulation or Administrative Action in Member States concerning the pursuit of broadcasting activities, OJ 1989, L298/23), the E-Commerce Directive (Directive 2001/31/EC on certain legal aspects of information society services, in particular electronic commerce, in the Internal Market [Directive on electronic commerce], OJ 2000, L178/1) and the Unfair Commercial Practices Directive 2005/29/EC.

19   'EEC Round up', *Advertising Law and Practice*, 1, No. 2, December (1984): 34.

approach is contested by some lawyers and academics,[20] it cannot be unequivocally excluded.

The term 'covert advertising,' although phrased in a slightly different way, was brought again to the attention of EU legislators in the text of Directive 89/522 EEC on 'Television without Frontiers'. This time it was not based on the unfair competition rationale, but referred to the consumer's right to information. Instead of the term 'covert' or 'hidden' advertisement, the Directive referred to 'advertisements not recognizable as such' or 'not identifiable as such'. It sought to ensure that consumers were not misled as to whether they are watching a programme or advertisement. Thus, it introduced an obligation, placed on broadcasters, to separate clearly programmes from advertisements. It also explicitly banned covert advertising in radio and TV – the so-called 'surreptitious advertising' – defined as 'representation in words or pictures of goods, services, the name, the trade mark or the activities of a producer of goods or a provider of services in programmes when such representation is intended by the broadcaster to serve advertising and might mislead the public as to its nature'. The definition further specifies that such representation is considered to be intentional in particular if it is done in return for payment or for similar consideration covering also product placement. The Directive also addressed a specific type of advertising that cannot be recognized as such, namely subliminal advertising.

Indirectly, the notion of advertisements not recognizable as such appears again in Directive 2001/31/EC on Electronic Commerce and Directive 2005/29/EC on Unfair Commercial Practices. The first requires commercial communications (advertisements being one of them) to be clearly recognizable as such,[21] while the UCPD explicitly bans one of the practices of hidden advertising – the advertorial.[22]

Yet, one would not be able to find the definition of hidden advertisement in any of the above mentioned EU laws.[23] Neither is it present in the law of the common law countries, including the UK. The term 'covert advertising' does not mean much to an English lawyer. It is rather the 'EC' English translation of the French 'la publicité clandestinne' or 'la publicité cachée' or the German 'Getarnte Werbung'.

However, one should not assume that what, in civil law countries, is meant as the practice of covert advertising is not at all covered by any type of control in the UK. After a thorough analysis, we have ascertained that covert advertising is regulated under English law and, in particular, by self-regulatory provisions in almost the same way as in civil law countries. In order to describe this commercial practice one

---

20   See R. Lawson, 'The legal control of unfair advertising in the United Kingdom', in E. Belate (ed.), *Unfair Advertising and Comparative Advertising,* (Louvain-la-Neuve, 1988), pp. 69–80.

21   For more on the EU rules as regards information obligations in e-commerce law, see G. Howells, and A. Nordhausen, 'Information obligation in the EC E-Commerce Law', in R. Nielsen, S.S. Jacobsen, and J. Trzaskowski, (eds), *EU Electronic Commerce Law,* (Copenhagen, 2004), pp. 52–3.

22   Annex 1 defines the practice as follows: 'using editorial content in the media to promote a product where a trader has paid for the promotion *without making that clear* in the content or by images or sounds *clearly identifiable by consumers* (advertorials).'

23   Apart from the definition of 'surreptitious advertising' placed in 'the Television without Frontiers' Directive.

should not simply refer to the notion of 'covert' or 'hidden' advertising but use the term present in the EC law, namely 'advertising not recognizable' or 'not identifiable as such'. This kind of formulation is closer to the common law, than the one referring to hidden techniques, because it does not imply a relationship with unfair competition that is unfamiliar to the English legal system. Instead, it puts an emphasis on the right of the consumer to be fully informed and the advertiser's obligation not to mislead consumers as to the character of the commercial communication. This is because, in civil law countries, the hidden advertisement is considered to be a practice of unfair competition, while in English law this is rather a type of misleading advertising. One can come to this conclusion on the basis of adjudications of the self-regulatory body (The Advertising Standards Authority – ASA)[24] and interpretations given by the public authority enforcing the advertising law (the Office of Fair Trading – OFT). The possibility to take proceedings for the breach of rules on the clear designation of advertisements on the basis of the provisions on misleading advertising is feasible, as long as one can prove the misleading character of the covert advertising.[25]

When it comes to the definition of covert advertising (advertising not recognizable/ not identifiable as such) one cannot find it either in statutory or self-regulatory rules. However, on the basis of particular cases that will be presented in the following sections, we can define it as 'an advertisement that influences consumers' economic choices without them being aware of it and thus misleading consumers as to its character'. As to specific examples of covert advertising, one should distinguish practices that are explicitly banned by law, for example product placement, undue prominence, subliminal advertising and other forms of broadcast covert advertising stemming from the breach of the rule of clear separation of programmes and advertisements. Moreover, there are other types of covert advertising that are not regulated by law, but by self-regulation. As an example, one should mention advertising features in media (especially press) not marked as such (so-called 'advertorials') and all forms of direct marketing advertisements not identifiable as such.

In order to define the above mentioned types of covert advertising and describe their regulation, it is helpful to look first at the whole system of advertising control in the UK.

3. The Regulation of Covert Advertising in the UK

The regulation of advertising in the UK is based on two pillars: common law and self-regulatory rules contained in the codes of good practice, elaborated by the advertising industry. Only at a second level should one mention statutory law and administrative control and, most recently, also the mediate form between administrative and self-

---

24   For example 'The Authority considered that the e-mail was misleading because its format and content did not make clear that it was a marketing communication', *Phone Direct,* 1 October 2003 or '... the advertisement was misleading because it did not make it clear it was an advertisement feature', *Raylene Van Worth t/a Winning Lottery Secrets,* 3 August 2005.

25   This kind of interpretation, although not binding, was indicated by the OFT officials.

regulatory control – co-regulation.[26] The most characteristic feature of English advertising regulation is, then, the lack of complex regulation and the major role played by self-regulation.

The statutory law related to advertising is scattered around more than 100 different pieces of legislation, referring to very narrow fields, for example consumer credit, medicines or food law.[27] It is very characteristic of the English legal system that relies on statutory acts regulating narrow fields of law rather than acts of horizontal nature, characteristic for civil law countries (for example civil codes, penal codes or unfair competition acts based on general clause).[28] On the other hand, there are English codes of conduct that resemble closely legal acts of civil law countries, because they are more general than English statutory law and thus, reminiscent of continental general clauses.

4. Statutory Law

As to statutory law in the field of advertising, one needs to distinguish the law of a general nature and the specialized law. The first category consists of two pieces of legislation that contributed to the creation of the extensive case law concerning misleading and deceptive advertising,[29] namely: The Trade Descriptions Act 1968 and The Control of Misleading Advertisements Regulations 1988 (CMARs).[30] The first constituted for many years the main legal basis for legal suits in the area of advertising, supporting the private law remedies, like passing off action in tort, that could not be used in case of some dishonest practices. The Act defines the notion of advertisements very broadly (s. 39) covering catalogues, circulars and price lists.

---

26   Under co-regulation the regulatory role is shared between the government and an industry body. It is usually effected through legislative reference or endorsement of a self-regulatory body competent in the relevant field. Typically it involves a code of practice (formulated in consultation with the government), breaches of which are enforced by sanctions imposed by a relevant industry or professional organization (with the possibility of administrative support). For a general insight into the differences between co-regulation and self-regulation see: G. Howells, 'Co-regulation's Role in the Development of European Fair Trading Laws', in H. Collins, (ed.), *The Forthcoming EC Directive on Unfair Commercial Practices. Contract, Consumer and Competition Law Implications,* (The Hague, 2004), pp. 119–29; L. Sendon, 'Soft law, Self-regulation and Co-regulation in European Law: Where do they meet?', *Electronic Journal of Comparative Law,* 9.1, (2005); available at: www.ejcl.org.

27   Except for The Control of Misleading Advertisements Regulations 1988, also other, more specialized pieces of legislation refer to matters of advertising, for example: The Consumer Credit (Advertisements) Regulations 2004, (S.I. 2004/1484), The Banking Act 1987 (Advertisements) Regulations 1988, (S.I. 1988/645), the Food Labelling Regulations 1996, (S.I. 1996/1499) or Medicines (Advertising) Regulations 1994, (S.I. 1994/1932).

28   R. Lawson, 'The legal control of unfair advertising in the United Kingdom', p. 205.

29   For a more detailed analysis see C.J. Miller, B.W. Harvey and D.L. Parry, *Consumer Law and Trading Law: Text, Cases and Materials,* (Oxford, 1998), pp. 601–71.

30   S.I. 1988/915.

However, it does not deal with the unfairness categories, and thus it does not refer to unfair or hidden advertising.

Another piece of legislation – (CMARs) – was introduced as an implementation of the EU Directive 84/450/EC on Misleading Advertising. It does not refer to unfair and hidden advertising either, although on the condition that covert advertising misleads consumers, it could also be used to combat these kinds of advertising practices. The Regulations (Regulation 2) define 'advertisement' in a way uniform throughout the EU, as meaning any form of representation which is made with connection to trade, business, craft or profession in order to promote the supply or transfer of goods or services, immovable property, rights or obligations. The enforcement of Regulations is ensured by the OFT – the body of administrative control competent in the field of competition and consumer protection and also the public enforcer in the field of advertising. However, since the coming into force of the Enterprise Act 2002, the OFT, on the basis of Part 8, performs its tasks with the help of other bodies, like the trading standards departments and consumer organizations. Yet, as will be shown later on, the public enforcement role is rather to support the self-regulatory control in the field of advertising than playing the main role in the enforcement of advertising rules.

In addition to the two above mentioned pieces of legislation in the area of advertising, one should also mention two pieces of legislation of more specialized nature: the Communications Act 2003, that deals with television and radio advertising, and the Electronic Commerce (EC Directive) Regulations 2002[31] that concern electronic commercial communications. The enforcement of the above mentioned advertising law is ensured either by the OFT (the Electronic Commerce (EC Directive) Regulations 2002) or by the communications market regulator – the Office of Communications (Ofcom).

The Communication Act 2003 is the Act that created Ofcom.[32] The Act commissioned the regulator (s. 319) to set and review the standards for the content of programmes that appear in television and radio services. Those standards, according to s. 319(2)(h) and (l) should ensure, among other things, that the inclusion of advertising which may be misleading, harmful or offensive is prevented and that there is no use of techniques which exploit the possibility of conveying a message to viewers and listeners, or of otherwise influencing their minds, without them being aware, or fully aware, of what has occurred (the so-called subliminal advertising techniques). In setting those standards, the Communications Act 2003, required that Ofcom take into account the desirability of maintaining the independence of editorial control over programme content (s. 319(4)(f)). Fulfilling this statutory obligation, Ofcom set the appropriate code – the Ofcom Broadcasting Code,[33] which came into force in May 2005. Ofcom is responsible for supervision of the code and, in cases of non-compliance by broadcasters, can use a series of legal instruments, the most severe of them being fines and the suspension or revocation of licences. The

---

31   S.I. 2002/2013.

32   Ofcom replaced two separate bodies: the Radio Authority and the Independent Television Commission (ITC).

33   It can be found at: www.ofcom.org.uk.

Ofcom Broadcasting Code is equivalent then to statutory law. It contains binding legal rules, established in response to statutory delegation (the Communications Act) and is enforced by the public body – Ofcom.

The Code prevents covert advertising by two sets of provisions, namely rules on clear separation of advertisements and programmes (ss 9 and 10) and a ban on subliminal advertising (s. 2, rule 2.12). The first requirement gives rise to other obligations and bans placed on broadcasters, for example, prohibition of undue prominence of products and services, prohibition of product placement and separation of sponsorship messages from programmes. They all aim at ensuring that consumers are aware whether they watch a programme or an advertisement and are not mislead with this respect.

Another form of hidden advertising banned by statutory provisions is electronic advertising not recognizable as such. This ban can be found in the Electronic Commerce (EC Directive) Regulations 2002. The Regulations refer to the notion of a commercial communication, understood as any form designed to promote, directly or indirectly, the goods, services or image of any person pursuing a commercial, industrial or craft activity or exercising a regulated profession, other than certain excepted communication. Advertising is also covered by the above definition. The Electronic Commerce (EC Directive) Regulations 2002 regulate covert advertising by providing for clear identification of commercial communications so that consumers are aware of their marketing character (Regulation 7). Moreover, they require unsolicited commercial communications to be clearly and unambiguously identifiable as commercial communications as soon as they are received (Regulation 8). The implementation of these rules is enforced by the OFT, trading standards departments and, in Northern Ireland, the Department of Enterprise, Trade and Investment.

5. Self-regulation

As has been mentioned, it is the self-regulatory system that plays the major role in the regulation of advertising in the UK. The advertising industry is proud of that fact, since it means a victory of business voluntary rules over burdensome legal restraints.[34] Although one can also find many critical comments concerning the effectiveness of self-regulatory controls in the field of advertising, concerning mostly poor records of enforcing the standards against the members of the codes not complying with them,[35]

---

34   S. Groom, 'United Kingdom', in J.R. Maxeiner and P. Schotthöfer (eds), *Advertising Law in Europe & North America*, 2nd edn, (The Hague, 1999), p. 469.

35   For more detailed analysis of advantages and disadvantages see S. Locke, 'Self-regulation in advertising', *Consumer Policy Review*, 4/2 (1994): 111; B. Middleton and D. Rodwell, 'Regulating advertising – time to get tough?', *Consumer Policy Review*, 8/3 (1998): 88; A. Wilson and R. McArthur, 'Fair Trading', *Consumer Policy Review*, 8/4 (1988): 138; J.F. Pickering and D.C. Cousins, 'The Benefits and Costs of Voluntary Codes of Practice', *European Journal of Marketing*, 16/6 (1982): 31.

it is considered to be the largest, the most active and the best financed self-regulatory system in the world.[36]

It is based on two bodies: the Committee of Advertising Practice (CAP), called into being in 1961 by the Advertising Association, and its executive – the Advertising Standards Authority (ASA). The CAP is a body that comprises of business associations active in media and advertising field. It is composed of two committees: broadcast and non-broadcast, whose members come from the different fields of advertising industry. Another body – the ASA – is responsible for the enforcement of advertising rules and its credibility in this field is ensured by its independence from the industry. This is guaranteed by the fact that two-thirds of its members are from outside the business.

Until recently, the ASA's sole responsibility was non-broadcast advertising. Its effectiveness in this field had been appreciated by Ofcom which, in 2004, commissioned the ASA to perform some of its statutory competences in the field of control of the content of broadcast advertising. Ofcom was convinced that with the growth of digital communication, the number of cases dealt with by Ofcom would increase to the extent that it was wiser to share its competencies with other experienced bodies.[37] Due to the said transfer, the self-regulatory bodies now form a 'one-stop shop' for all advertising issues and complaints. It makes it much more convenient for consumers, who do not need to inquire which body is responsible for particular complaints they wish to lodge. As to competitors' complaints, they are at first dealt with by CAP.

The ASA performs its duties on the basis of the codes of practice, elaborated by the CAP. It administers and enforces three codes of good practice in the area of advertising: one on non-broadcast advertising – the British Code of Advertising, Sales Promotions and Direct Marketing, and two codes on broadcast advertising – the Broadcast Committee of Advertising Practice (BCAP) Television Advertising Standards Code and BCAP Radio Advertising Standards Code. All the codes, both broadcast and non-broadcast, contain a provision which sounds like an unfair advertising clause found in civil law countries, since it states that all marketing communications should be legal, decent, honest and truthful.[38] Additionally, the BCAP Television Advertising Standards Code, in Rule 6.1, requires that 'advertisements must not cause serious or widespread offence against generally accepted moral, social, cultural standards, or offend against public feeling'. These kinds of formulations allow for their flexible interpretation and the possibility of verifying advertisements as to their decency and honesty, which is excluded from legal control.

---

36   J.J. Boddewyn, *Advertising self-regulation and outside participation. A multinational comparison* (Westport, 1988), p. 267.

37   *Ofcom's decision on the future regulation of broadcast advertising*, Ofcom, 17 May 2004.

38   Rule 2.1 of British Code of Advertising, Sales Promotions and Distance Marketing; Rule 1 of the BCAP Radio Advertising Standards Code and Foreword to the BCAP TV Advertising Standards Code.

The oldest CAP code – the British Code of Advertising, Sales Promotions and Direct Marketing – dates back to 1961[39] and is of the most general nature. It relates to advertisements in newspapers, magazines, brochures, leaflets, circular, mailings, e-mails, fax transmissions, catalogues, follow-up literature and other electronic and printed material; posters, cinema and video commercials, online advertisements and other advertisements in non-broadcast electronic media. It contains a group of provisions ensuring that consumers are not exposed to hidden advertisements. They aim to protect consumers against non-identifiable marketing practices. The most important is Rule 22.1 which requires marketers, publishers and owners of other media to ensure that marketing communications are designed in a way that makes it clear that they are marketing communications. The same applies to unsolicited commercial e-mails that should be identifiable as such without the need to open them. Moreover, Rules 23.1 and 2 refer explicitly to marketing communications placed in magazines and newspapers that may be confused with editorial content, known as advertising features or advertorials. Marketers and publishers are thus obliged to mark clearly this kind of advertisements, for example by heading them with words 'Advertising feature'. The lack of designation may lead consumers to believe that they are reading an objective article. This kind of practice is very often used, not only in press, but also in specialist books (for example, medical books) and academic reports.

The field of television and radio advertising, in addition to the mentioned codes, is ruled by other self-regulatory rules, namely: Advertising Guidance Notes, Rules on the Scheduling of Television Advertising, the Code for Text Services and Guidance on Interactive Television.[40] These codes and rules have co-regulatory character since they are set and enforced both by CAP and ASA, with Ofcom retaining some control over them. Additionally, although Ofcom does not set the standards and does not handle consumer complaints about advertising content, it has retained the right to veto standards set in the code if it considers that they may be put at risk. It also monitors the system, by means of its own official with an observer status in the Advertising Advisory Committee (the Broadcast CAP expert body that was set in January 2005 and contributes to setting of the CAP's rules and policies). Ofcom has also retained some enforcement powers in the situations when instruments used by the ASA are not sufficient. If this is the case, the ASA may refer the matter to Ofcom, which can impose further sanctions, including fines and even revocation or termination of a broadcaster's licence.

The broadcast advertising codes and rules also regulate covert advertising by providing for the separation of advertisements and programmes in television and radio services. They are to be found in three documents: BCAP Radio Advertising Standards Code, BCAP Television Advertising Standards Code and the Rules on the Scheduling of Television Advertisements. In order to fulfil the obligation on the clear separation of advertisements and programmes they also provide for separate definitions of advertisements in radio and television. The BCAP Radio Advertising Standards Code defines advertising as any item, including spot advertisements and

---

39   Now in its 11th edition.
40   The texts of all the codes and rules can be found at: www.asa.org.uk.

promotions with advertisers, which are broadcast in return for payment or other valuable consideration to a licensee or which seek to sell to listeners any products or services. BCAP Television Advertising Standards Code considers advertisement as any publicity by advertisers in breaks during or between the programmes, irrespective of whether the payment is made. BCAP Radio Advertising Standards Code sets the principle of transparency and clear separation of advertising in s. 2. It underlines that advertising should be clearly distinguishable from programming. It obliges the licensees to ensure that consumers are not misled as to whether they listen to a programme or an advertisement. In order to fulfil this obligation, advertisements that have similar style and format to programme editorial should be separated from programming by a means such as a jingle, a station indent or by scheduling in the middle of a break. The same rules apply to radio stations' advertisements about their own commercial activities. Because it is even more probable that this type of advertising could be taken by consumers for a part of editorial content, stations should pay special attention to clear distinction of their own advertisements. They should also be very careful about using expressions and sounds typical for news bulletins in advertisements so as listeners can easily recognize them as advertisements. Consequently, radio presenters and newsreaders may voice advertising messages only if such advertisements are clearly distinguished from programme content (Rule 24); neither can they personally endorse products or services in advertisements presented on stations on which they appear (Rule18).

Similar limitations are imposed on licensed television stations by the BCAP Television Advertising Standards Code. Rule 2.1 of the Code requires clear distinction between programmes and advertisements so as viewers know, at all times, whether they watch programming or advertisements. In ambiguous cases, when such a separation may not be visible to viewers, advertisements should be identified as such on the screen. Moreover, according to Rule 2.1.1, advertisements may not use expressions reserved for important news and public service announcements, for example, a newsflash, or make use of a situation or style reminiscent of a programme. They should neither refer to themselves as programmes nor feature anyone who regularly presents news or current affairs on television. All these conditions aim at ensuring that consumers are not confused as to what they are watching. Additionally, the Television Code refers to subliminal advertising which, according to Rule 5.4.5, is prohibited. This type of covert advertising is thus banned both by statutory and co-regulatory rules.

The third document, that forms the basis of the co-regulatory system governing broadcast advertising – BCAP Rules on the Scheduling of Television Advertising – concerns particular separations of advertisements and programmes, namely limitations on the appearance of certain persons in advertisements and programmes. These limitations, like in previous cases, are justified by the concern that consumers could be confused as to whether they watch a programme or an advertisement. Thus, advertisements featuring a very well known person (film/sport/music star and so on) or a very well known presenter, or leader of the programme must not be scheduled in breaks in, or adjacent to, that programme (Rule 4.2.7).

Except for the rules on covert advertising stemming from the statutory and self-regulatory provisions, one should also mention the rules established by the British

National Union of Journalists (NUJ). Although it is quite difficult to find any sign of their enforcement, it is still worth noting that journalists themselves set ethical rules for their activity. In June 2004, the NUJ adopted a Code of Conduct and, in September 2004, Ethical guidelines for PRs.[41] Provisions of the Code are quite vague, however they tackle an issue of journalist independence from commercial influences. Rules 8 and 12 state that journalists should not allow any inducements influencing performance of their professional duties. They should neither, by statement, voice or appearance, endorse by advertisement, any commercial product or service. Besides, Ethical guidelines refer explicitly to advertorials. They do not disapprove of this kind of practice, as long as the advertising features are clearly identified as such. Unfortunately, there is no access to information on the enforcement of the above mentioned rules so it is hard to judge whether they are complied with by journalists and PR specialists.

From the above description of regulatory framework, one can realize that although there is no general ban on covert advertising, there exists a quite extensive set of rules concerning this type of advertising. They are, in large part, enforced by self-regulatory bodies that, in cases of non-compliance by advertisers, may refer the matter to the public body for application of stronger sanctions. The complex enforcement structure, illustrated in the next section, proves that both administrative and self-regulatory measures can coexist successfully, to the benefit of consumers and the market.

6. Enforcement of the Self-Regulatory Rules

It is the ASA that enforces the rules contained in the self-regulatory codes. It monitors the application of the codes and once it finds out its rules are violated it requests the advertiser to change or withdraw an advertisement. However, most of its investigations are carried out on the basis of the consumer complaints that can be lodged with the ASA free of charge, including online. Once the ASA establishes that the advertisement constitutes a serious breach of the rules, after carrying out a formal investigation, it issues an adjudication, committing the advertiser to change or withdraw the advertisement. The adjudications are published on the ASA website. Publication of the ASA's decisions, although seemingly constituting a very soft means of enforcement, is a very effective mechanism, since advertisers will always try to avoid bad publicity for their business. To enforce its adjudications the ASA possesses powers that range from seeking assurances as to future compliance, through ruling out eligibility for industry award competitions, to a system of Ad alerts (the refusal of media owners and broadcasters to run the advertisement in question) or the revocation of some benefits (for example, Royal Mail discounts). If the advertisers' breaches are notorious and continuous, and they refuse to cooperate with ASA, the Authority can refer a matter to either the OFT (non-broadcast advertising) or Ofcom (broadcast advertising).

---

41   Both documents can be found on NUJ web page: www.nuj.org.uk.

In the field of non-broadcast advertising, the ASA's role is bigger than in the field of broadcast advertising, since it is the only enforcer of the rules, while in the field of broadcast advertising the enforcement powers are shared with Ofcom, in a co-regulatory system. The enforcement procedure usually finishes with an ASA adjudication. However, if the ASA refers the matter to the OFT, the Office may use its tools of administrative control with respect to misleading and comparative advertising. As regards cases of covert advertising, this public body can enforce the rules only when it can be proved that this kind of advertising misleads consumers. In practice, it is usually the case.[42]

The OFT may apply to the court for an enforcement order against any person responsible for the publication of misleading advertising.[43] Non-compliance with the court's enforcement order is considered as contempt of court,[44] which constitutes a serious breach, for which high fines can be imposed or even imprisonment.[45]

Although the OFT's enforcement role is substantial, it needs to be underlined that the role of public enforcer is rather to support and reinforce existing advertising controls, than to replace them. This fact is also confirmed by the provisions of the Control of Misleading Advertising Regulations that indicate that administrative control should not be initiated unless other channels (for example, self-regulatory control) have been used (Regulation 4).

Except for the above mentioned possibility of action on the part of the OFT, the ASA's position is also reinforced by the fact that its decisions are subject to judicial review. This fact was confirmed in the case *R.* v. *Advertising Standards Authority, ex parte Insurance Services plc*,[46] where the court held that ASA adjudications are judicially reviewable because the Authority serves public law function, otherwise performed by OFT. Normally, the cases that happen to be subject of OFT procedures do not go further than the OFT level,[47] however on a few occasions ASA rulings were subject to court litigation and courts respected the ASA's decisions.[48]

---

42   Most of the ASA's adjudications on covert advertising justify the breach of the code by referring to the misleading character of those practices, (for example, faxes) were 'misleading because they were not identifiable as marketing communication', 'mailing masqueraded as personal correspondence and was therefore misleading', 'the leaflet was misleading because it was not clear that it was an advertisement'.

43   The procedure is based on Part 8 of the Enterprise Act 2002. There is also the separate injunction procedure under Regulation 5 of CMARs, which is the process the OFT normally uses.

44   The Contempt of Court Act 1981 ('CCA 1981').

45   G. Crown, *Advertising Law and Regulation* (London, 1998), pp. 155–9.

46   (1989) 133 Sol Jo 1545, QBD.

47   G. Howells and S. Weatherill, *Consumer Protection Law*, 2nd edn, (Aldershot, 2005), p. 426.

48   *R.* v. *ASA, ex parte SmithKline Beecham plc.*, [2001] EMLR 23; *R.* v. *ASA, ex parte Charles Robertson (Developments) Ltd, The Times*, 26 November 1999; *R.* v. *Advertising Standards Authority, ex parte DSG Retail Ltd, CL*, April 1997, 461; *R.* v. *Advertising Standards Authority, ex parte Vernons Organisations* [1992] 1 WLR 1289; *Director General of Fair Trading* v. *Tobyward Ltd* [1989] 2 All ER 266.

Self-regulation is also supported by the administrative control exercised by the OFT in the field of electronic commercial communications (e-mails, pop-ups, banner advertisements). However, in the area of electronic communications not recognizable as such, there is a lack of practical cases enforced by the OFT. This may be due to the fact that most of the cases of unsolicited e-mails and commercial communications not recognizable as such are dealt with by the ASA and do not go further than this.

In the field of broadcast advertising, broadcasters' and advertisers' compliance with the rules on advertising and covert advertising is, in the first place, ensured by the obligation, stemming from the licence, to pre-clear all the advertisements in advance of their transmission. This can be done by the Radio Advertising Clearance Centre (RACC), the Broadcast Advertising Clearance Centre (BACC), or the British Television Shopping Association (BTSA). It proves to be quite a good means of ensuring compliance, since many advertisements are stopped already at this stage. Additionally, the licence places another requirement on broadcasters, namely to comply with the directions made by the ASA. The ASA can, for example, demand that an advertisement is changed prior to further broadcast or instruct the broadcaster to restrict the transmission according to its guidelines or even cease the broadcasting of the advertisement. Once the ASA realizes that its enforcement powers in the field of broadcast advertising are not sufficient, it can forward the case to Ofcom. The communications regulator may use different kinds of sanctions, from softer ones, like a formal reprimand, to more burdensome ones, such as a fine, a warning about possible revocation of the licence or, eventually, the termination of the licence. That means that Ofcom acts only in the last resort, when the ASA's powers are not sufficient and there is a need for stronger, administrative sanctions.

The described system, where strong self-regulation is supported by statutory law and public enforcement, represents a very unique example of advertising control. Its effectiveness can be judged on the basis of the practical examples and issued adjudications that are going to be presented in the next section.

7. Different Types of Covert Advertising

Already this general framework, within which covert advertising is regulated and enforced, gives us an idea of how common the practices of hidden advertising can be. After having analyzed the extensive case law in this area, one could be even more surprised by the regularity with which advertisers, advertising agencies, publishers and broadcasters breach the rules on the clear distinction of advertisements.

8. Hidden Advertisements and Direct Marketing

The oldest breaches of the rule on the clear identification of advertisements concern practices of direct marketing.[49] The British Code on Advertising, Sales Promotions and Direct Marketing requires, in Rule 22.1, that all marketing communications are designed and presented in such a way that it is clear they are marketing communications. From the ASA's adjudications, it can be seen that this rule especially has been often contravened by marketers active in the field of direct marketing, namely leaflets, circulars, brochures and so on. Since consumers have got used to this form of advertising, very often they do not pay any much attention to it or simply throw the advertisements away. That is why marketers have started to introduce new techniques, bringing consumer attention to advertised goods and services. One of them relies on the presentation of the commercial material as an official letter from a public institution, for example, the Royal Mail,[50] the NHS,[51] the police,[52] government or local government bodies.[53] Consumers are then convinced that the correspondence received is important, so they open and read it, whereas if they were aware it was only a commercial communication, they would not probably pay any attention to it. As an example illustrating this practice, we can cite a case *LA Fitness* concerning an advertisement for gym membership which was placed underneath the windscreen wiper of the car and looked like a parking ticket.

Another way of hiding the commercial character of an offer is to make it look like a public notice or announcement.[54] In the *Ray Sayers Insulation & Preservation* case, a home insulation company distributed circular titled 'Public Notice' and 'Notification of works', which gave an impression of an official notice and thus misled consumers as to its genuine character. However, in another case – *Chrysalis Radio, t/a Galaxy 106.4*,[55] the similar content of an advertisement was not considered sufficiently misleading to uphold the consumer's complaint. The ASA argued, that although in fact, at the first sight one could consider that the advertisement looked like a public notification, since it was headed 'Notice of Jury Service', the way of its distribution (on the street, by people wearing radio station clothing) and its content (logo of the radio station clearly visible) did not allow one to suppose that it could confuse consumers as to its character. It shows that, while assessing the case, the ASA takes into consideration not only the content of the letter, but all the accompanying circumstances.

---

49   For the purposes of this paper I have analyzed the ASA's adjudications from the years 1990–2005. However, the increase of cases of hidden advertising is clearly visible only from the year 1995 onwards.

50   *Mediaprom Ltd, t/a The National Award Fund,* 12 October 2005.

51   *Hospital Information Services* 14 September 2005; *Aviva plc., t/a Norwich Union Healthcare,* 6 July 2005.

52   *LA Fitness,* 23 March 2005; *Unicorn Fitness & Leisure Centres,* 4 February 2004.

53   *Scutari Projects Ltd, ASA Monthly Report,* 41, October 1994.

54   *Ray Sayers Insulation & Preservation,* 9 July 2003; *British Telecommunications plc.,* 16 July 2003.

55   *Chrysalis Radio, t/a Galaxy 106.4 ASA Monthly Report,* 111, August 2000.

Advertisers may also try to confuse consumers as to the genuine aim of their correspondence by appealing to human feelings. For example, the ASA recorded a few cases where advertisements were disguised as Valentine's cards[56] or Christmas cards.[57] Other advertisements tried to attract consumers' attention by referring to health concerns, for example, hearing[58] or x-ray tests (like in the case *Aviva plc., t/a Norwich Union Health*,[59] where the insurance company sent round a circular resembling X-ray results). In another case, *Aviva plc., t/a Norwich Union Healthcare*,[60] the same company advertised its insurance plan giving access to private health care, as opposed to NHS services, where people had to queue for a long time to get the operation. Since it looked like information on NHS waiting times in particular hospitals, it was confusing for consumers.

Another covert advertising technique, used in direct marketing messages, aims at distressing consumers making them feel in danger, for example, of robbery.[61] To distress consumers the communications resemble invoices to be paid,[62] parking tickets,[63] and speeding notifications[64] or represent images causing fear (for example an image of a black bottle marked with the word 'POISON' and a skull and crossbones.) [65] Characteristically, the ASA did not consider the latter direct mail as not recognizable as such, because it took into account that it was sent only to business clients of this financial company, and one could expect a higher degree of awareness from professionals. The same approach was applied by the ASA in few more cases, including ones where the target group consisted of lawyers or people at managerial positions.[66]

Marketers very often apply one more method to disguise advertising character of direct mailing, namely they give it an image of private correspondence. This is done by a series of means, for example, using handwriting and personal expressions, such as 'Dear John, I am leaving you (...)' or 'Help me please ...'; [67] or by sending series

---

56   *Jaguar Car Ltd*, 26 May 2004; *Prudential Plc.*, 5 May 2004; *Legal & General Assurance Society Ltd, ASA Monthly Report*, 3, August 1991; *Barclays Bank plc., ASA Monthly Report*, 88, September 1998.

57   *Telecom Plus Plc.*, 2 June 2004.

58   *Hidden Hearing Ltd*, 24 August 2005.

59   *Aviva plc., t/a Norwich Union Health*, 26 May 2004.

60   *Aviva plc., t/a Norwich Union Healthcare*, 6 July 2005.

61   *Bels Ltd, ASA Monthly Report*, 29, October 1993; *Banham Patent Locks Ltd, ASA Monthly Report*, 20 January 1993; *System & Security Bristol Ltd, ASA Monthly Report*, 37, June 1994.

62   *Waldermann Publishers*, 30 November 2005; *Simpsons, ASA Monthly Report*, 104, January 2000; *ZD Internet Magazine, ASA Monthly Report*, 71, April 1997; *Damart Group*, 8 June 2005; *Redcats (Brands) Ltd, t/a Empire Stores*; 27 July 2005.

63   *NGM Professional Valeting Services, ASA Monthly Report*, 94, March 1999; *Smartpark Ltd, ASA Monthly Report*, 71, April 1997.

64   *Toyota (GB) Ltd, ASA Monthly Report*, 108, May 2000; *Konica Minolta Printing Solutions UK Ltd*, 26 November 2003.

65   *Sovereign Finance, ASA Monthly Report*, 68, January 1997.

66   *Times Newspapers Ltd, t/a Times, ASA Monthly Report*, 104, January 2000; *G. Neil Companies, ASA Monthly Report*, 114, November 2000.

67   *Potterton Myson Ltd, ASA Monthly Report*, 82, March 1998; *NSPCC, ASA Monthly*

of postcards with content that could indicate that they are holiday postcards from friends.[68] What is surprising is that this method of hidden advertising is very often used by car producers and dealers.[69] Messages, disguised as personal correspondence, also happened to be sent by fax, which was the case in *Herbalife*,[70] where the firm sent, by fax, handwritten messages encouraging people to buy its products, in order to help them lose weight. They were formulated in a way that one could think they were recommendations from a friend.

There are still many more examples of hidden advertising applied by direct marketing companies, like the use of messages handwritten on self-adhesive notes,[71] disguising advertisements for lotteries as official or personal letters[72] or others. Yet, the great majority of the ASA's adjudications, based on the breach of Article 22.1 of the Code, show only a fragmented picture of the phenomenon, because many cases are solved in an informal way. On the other hand, the language used by the ASA in its adjudications is quite soft. We could doubt whether it is discouraging enough for entrepreneurs so that they do not repeat the same practices in future.[73] However, it must be remembered that the rules we are talking about are voluntary, thus one could argue that the sanctions for breaching them should not be the same as for the breach of law.[74]

9. Advertorials

Another, quite common, form of hidden advertising – the advertorial – is characteristic of press advertisements.[75] In the UK, it is better known under the term 'advertisement

---

Report, 94, March 1999; *New World Cassettes, ASA Monthly Report*, 28, September 1993.

68   *Fiat Auto (UK) Ltd, ASA Monthly Report*, 59, April 1996.

69   *Ford Motor Company Ltd*, 10 November 2004; *Volkswagen Group Ltd, t/a SkodaAuto*, 3 November 2004; *Toyota (GB) Ltd, ASA Monthly Report*, 108, May 2000; *Volkswagen Group United Kingdom Ltd, t/a Skoda UK, ASA Monthly Report*, 111, August 2000; *Crompton & Holt, ASA Monthly Report*, 1, June 1991; *Fiat Auto (UK) Ltd, ASA Monthly Report*, 59, April 1996.

70   *Herbalife (UK) Ltd*, 10 November 2004.

71   *Science International, t/a Science Magazine, ASA Monthly Report*, 107, April 2000; *Teamstar Group, ASA Monthly Report*, 105, February 2000.

72   *Mediaprom Ltd, t/a The National Award Fund*, 12 October 2005; *Hospital Plan Insurance Services*, 22 December 2004.

73   The Authority uses in its adjudications the following expressions: '(ASA) ... told the advertisers not to use the approach again,' '... welcomed the advertisers' assurance that they would not repeat it ...', '... asked the advertisers to take more care in future', '... told the advertisers to ensure future, similar advertisements made clearer that the message was an advertisement', and so on.

74   On the other hand many academics express the need for a reform of self-regulatory controls that would include among other things imposition of sanctions for the breach of advertising codes; for more detailed analysis see B. Middleton and D. Rodwell, 'Regulating advertising – time to get tough?': 88–92.

75   For more on the topic: T. Wilhelmsson, *The Consumer's Right to Knowledge and the*

feature'. An advertisement feature is an advertisement, presented in a way that it could be taken for an editorial part of the newspaper or magazine. It is usually formulated as an objective article, on the basis of which, readers could expect to receive neutral information. Its presentation can confuse consumers, since very often advertorials are not clearly separated, as required, from the editorial section of press material. A very important criterion for distinguishing advertorials is their dissemination 'in exchange for a payment or other reciprocal arrangements'.[76] In practice, cases of arrangements, other than payment, are much more common than payment itself. Under the term 'other arrangements' we can understand, for example, a reciprocal arrangement between a magazine and a taxi company, where the publisher of the magazine offers to advertise the taxi company, and in exchange the latter advertises the magazine on the outside of the cars.[77] Another important criterion for falling within the scope of the Code is the control over the editorial content. The CAP and the ASA have powers over advertorial arrangements only if they are controlled by marketers. When the publisher has overall control over the content of advertorial, the ASA does not interfere with this kind of editorial decisions. However, when it is the marketer who has the right to final approval of the text, or at least can influence its shape to a significant extent, then this kind of advertisement feature will fall under the CAP Code.

Advertisement features are generally allowed and do not constitute a breach of Rule 23.2 of the British Code of Advertising, Sales Promotions and Direct Marketing, as long as they are clearly recognizable as such, for example, they are headed 'advertisement features' or 'sponsored article'. However, it is a fact that many advertisers try to hide the commercial character of their offer under the image of an article that is sanctioned.

In order to understand better the whole mechanism of advertorial arrangements one should have a look at characteristic cases adjudicated by ASA. The case *Killi's for Kleaners*[78] serves as an excellent example of the reciprocal agreements between the publisher and advertiser, where there is no exchange of money. In the magazine *Grapevine Property & Business* there appeared an advertisement for Killi's for Kleaners vacuum cleaner shop, that was headed 'Death by Hanging' and was formulated as a story about Hungarian spies. Just at the end of the story there was a mention (entangled in the content of the story) about the said vacuum cleaners. The advertiser claimed that it was not an advertisement, since he had paid for an advertisement on another page, and the magazine invited him to write a story based on his experiences and allowed him to include a reference to the paid-for advertisement. For the ASA it was obvious that the article formed a part of reciprocal arrangement between the two parties and was, therefore, an advertisement.

Press, in T. Wilhelmsson, S. Tuominen, H. Tuomola, (eds), *Consumer Law in the Information Society*, (Dordrecht, 2001), pp. 375–6.

76   Rule 23.1 of the British Code of Advertising, Sales Promotions and Direct Marketing.

77   CAP Help Note on Advertisement Features, October 1995, revised March 2003.

78   *Killi's for Kleaners, ASA Monthly Report*, 100, September 1999.

The act of writing the article in exchange for payment was the subject of a very significant ASA decision in the case *Metrocrest Ltd, t/a Coarse Fisherman.*[79] The issue that was raised there concerned articles in a professional magazine for fishermen that were written by journalists, paid for their specialist knowledge in the field. They tried to recommend the best products for fishing and at the same time presented their photographs. Complainants objected that the articles written by these journalists constituted, in fact, an advertisement of the mentioned products that was not identified as such. The ASA could not require clear distinction of the articles, because they did not fulfil the criteria of advertisement features, for two important reasons: they were not paid-for articles (there was no kind of arrangement between the firms mentioned in those articles and the publisher) and the publisher maintained control over the editorial content of these articles.

To illustrate another important characteristic of advertorials, namely the requirement of marketers' and not publishers' control over editorial content, one may refer to the case *French Duncan Chartered Accountants.*[80] It concerned an advertisement feature in the regional press – 'Professional Brief' – which consisted of a series of articles by different companies. According to the publisher, they 'contributed editorial content to the publishers' titles on newsworthy subjects on which they were experts'. The publishers claimed that they had editorial control over those articles and they charged sponsoring companies only nominal fees, to cover the cost of the staff time. However, although the publishers exerted some editorial control over the content of the columns, the content was provided by advertisers. Moreover, the columns were published in exchange for payment. These arguments were convincing enough to consider the columns as advertisement features, and thus require their clear designation.[81]

Very often, we do not realize that all kind of ratings of for example, banks, supermarkets and so on can also be found to constitute an advertisement feature that should be clearly identified as such. This was the case in *Associated Newspapers Ltd, t/a Mail on Sunday*[82] where the Mail on Sunday published a double-page advertisement headlined 'essential web guide', which, to readers, looked like the newspaper's suggestion of the best web pages, but, in fact, it was a paid-for advertisement, which should have been clearly marked as such.

Advertisements in newspapers and magazines may also be hidden by means of heading them as a 'public notice' or giving the impression of an official statement.[83]

79   *Metrocrest Ltd, t/a Coarse Fisherman, ASA Monthly Report,* 113, October 2000.
80   *French Duncan Chartered Accountants & Newsquest (Herald & Times) Ltd,* 1 September 2004.
81   The criteria of editorial control over the content of advertisement features was also the subject of the following cases: *Erdic UK Ltd,* 11 August 2004; *Weston Financial Group Ltd, Weston Financial Services Ltd, ASA Monthly Report,* 109, June 2000.
82   *Associated Newspapers Ltd, t/a Mail on Sunday, ASA Monthly Report,* 109, June 2000.
83   *Downs Insulation Ltd, ASA Case Report,* 6, November 1991; *Yohden Hall Nursing Home; ASA Case Report,* 17, October 1992; *Dundee Upholstery, ASA Monthly Report,* 52 September 1995; *Newark & Sherwood District Council, ASA Monthly Report,* 37, June 1994; *Nottinghamshire County Council, ASA Monthly Report,* 40, September

Sometimes this type of behaviour constituted a clear abuse of the term, like in the case where the advertisers used the headline 'Public Notice' to advertise furniture sales[84] or a double glazing company.[85] Similar to direct marketing advertisements, it happens that press advertisers try to take advantage of the good or bad reputation of public institutions (for example, the NHS)[86] or make advertisement features look like editor's announcements or notices.[87]

Advertorials may also appear as wraps over the front cover of newspapers. In many cases, those wraps are just one big advertisement, but hardly ever they are identified as such, which was the basis for a number of the ASA's adjudications.[88] In fact, they very often copy the format of the newspaper, which makes them even harder to distinguish as advertorials.

One should also mention cases where consumer complaints highly underestimate consumers' skills to distinguish advertisements from editorial material. The example of *D.C. Thomson & Company Ltd, Kellog Company of GB Ltd*[89] demonstrates this. The advertisement in this children's magazine was clearly headed as 'Advertisement', but still the complainants claimed that, to a child, it was not clearly differentiated from the editorial content of the comic. The ASA noted, however, that except for the clear headline, the advertisement was separated from the editorial content by a straight, coloured border and the company logo was also clearly visible. Consequently, the ASA could not agree with the complainants. In other cases adjudicated by the ASA, similar factors, namely the clear separation of advertisements from editorial content and a clear company logo on the advertisement, were considered to be sufficient to identify an advertisement feature as such.[90]

In all cases where the ASA considered that advertorials were not clearly recognizable as such, thus misleading consumers, advertisers[91] were instructed to mark clearly their advertisements in future as 'sponsored articles' or 'advertisements features'. Besides, in the area of covert advertising, the ASA did not need to use strict sanctions. Many complaints were solved at the very early, informal stage. In

---

1994; *Sureclaim Ltd*, 18 February 2004.

84 *Dundee Upholstery, ASA Monthly Report*, 52, September 1995.
85 *MV Building Contracts Ltd*, 30 June 2004.
86 *News Group Newspapers, Norwich Union Healthcare Ltd, ASA Monthly Report*, 27, August 1993.
87 *Flex Training Ltd, Times Newspapers Ltd, t/a the Sunday Times, ASA Monthly Report*, 88, September 1998; *First Mortgage Securities, ASA Monthly Report*, 53, October 1995; *Clear Communications, ASA Monthly Report*, 106, March 2000.
88 *Crocfords Health & Fitness Club, ASA Monthly Report*, 82, March 1998; *Mark-One Minicabs, ASA Monthly Report*, 31, December 1993; *Express Newspapers Plc., ASA Case Report*, 28, September 1993.
89 *D.C. Thomson & Co. Ltd, Kellogg Company of GB Ltd, ASA Monthly Report*, 85, June 1998.
90 *British Tobacco Co. Ltd, ASA Monthly Report*, 87, August 1998; *Walkers Snack Foods Ltd, ASA Monthly Report*, 60, May 1996; *London Borough of Croydon, ASA Monthly Report*, 71, April 1997.
91 It should be mentioned that advertisers share the responsibility for clear designation of advertorials with advertising agencies and publishers.

cases adjudicated by the ASA, advertisers and publishers were usually willing to cooperate, so it was sufficient to instruct them to take more care in future.

10. Covert Advertising in the Cinema

Advertising in cinemas is covered by the same rules on the recognition of advertisements as direct mail and press advertising, namely Rules 22.1 and 23.1–2 of the British Code of Advertising, Sales Promotions and Direct Marketing. However, covert advertising in this type of media is not as common as in other media. It is not quite clear whether this is due to the very thorough pre-clearance of cinema advertisements[92] or to some other reason.

The fact is that there is just one substantial ASA adjudication on the matter. It concerns the case *Transport for London*,[93] where the company, in order to 'encourage motorcyclists to ride defensively and drivers to look more carefully' presented in the cinemas, live drama that highly distressed viewers. Because the presented scene looked real, consumers complained that the live drama could not be easily recognized as an advertisement. The ASA noted that, although the performance was publicized by notice on the cinema's door, it could be easily overlooked by viewers. It required Transport for London to make the relevant announcement just before the start of the live drama.

11. Covert Advertising – Mobile Phone Messages

Mobile phones, in particular text messages and voicemail, have recently become more and more popular means of advertising goods and services. The rules of the British Code of Advertising, Sales Promotions and Direct Marketing also apply to this kind of advertising, including the rules on clear identification of advertisements. Yet, there are not many ASA adjudications concerning messages and voicemails that are not clearly recognizable as advertisements. This may result from the fact that advertisers use more classic ways of advertising their goods or services and do not resort to hidden forms of advertising. It could also be due to the willingness of telecom companies to cooperate with ASA and thus most of the cases are resolved by informal means. On the other hand, the recorded rogue practices are caused not by telecom companies themselves, but by third party companies who buy the right to use their network.

Still, two adjudications should be mentioned here. One, in the case *Eidos Interactive*,[94] concerned a text message suggesting that the recipient of the message should report to his local army recruitment centre immediately for his second tour of duty and only in the end lines was the genuine identity of the advertiser – Computer Games Company – identified. The ASA noted that the message could distress recipients, since until the very end it could not be recognized as advertisement. The

---

92   Copy Panel of the Cinema Advertising Association.
93   *Transport for London,* 28 May 2003.
94   *Eidos Interactive Ltd,* 14 November 2001.

second advertisement[95] was sent by a voicemail message. It promoted a new movie and started with a man drawing his breath, who then tried to convey a commercial message, in between breathing heavily and screaming. The ASA was convinced that although at the end of the message it was clear that it constituted an advertisement, the fact should be made clear to listeners much earlier. In both cases, it required the advertisers not to repeat the practice and to ensure future advertisements were better distinguished as such.

12. Covert Advertising in Internet

Advertising not recognizable as such may appear on the internet under two forms: unsolicited electronic communications and online advertisements in paid-for space, including banner and pop-up advertisements. Both forms are subject to self-regulatory (British Code of Advertising) and statutory provisions (the Electronic Commerce (EC Directive) Regulations 2002 and Privacy and Electronic Communications (EC Directive) Regulations 2003).[96] However, while the ASA has adjudicated on many occasions on the issue of hidden advertising on internet, that has not been the case with the OFT. So far, it has not taken any action concerning Articles 7 and 8 of the Electronic Commerce Regulations. This may stem from the fact that it is the ASA that deals, in the first place with consumer complaints, including with regard to clear identification of commercial communications, sent by mail or placed online. None the less, this sphere of activity is also quite new to ASA. Control over internet advertisements was added to ASA's competences only in 1995 and the first adjudication concerning an online advertisement was issued in 2000. It concerned the company *LineOne*[97] that advertised an internet service provider in the form of a banner that appeared once as one was reading the financial web sites. Since the advertisement said 'ISP Upgrade' and showed a progress bar, it could suggest that it was some notice of a computer system. Moreover, if one tried to click on the 'cancel' button, the result was the same as clicking on the 'ok' button: redirection to the advertiser's webpage. The advertisement was obviously considered as not clearly identifiable as such and the ASA requested the company to introduce the necessary changes. Since then, until the end of 2002, the ASA noted six breaches of the CAP Code with regard to advertising which, however, did not require issuing of any adjudications.[98] They all concerned banner advertisements.

---

95 *Twentieth Century Fox Home Entertainment Ltd,* 12 February 2003.

96 The Privacy and Electronic Communications (EC Directive) Regulations 2003 regulates in Regulation 22 the use of electronic mail for direct marketing purposes, establishing an opt-in option for these kinds of communications, while the Electronic Commerce Regulations 2002 reflects the generally applied opt-out option, requiring however from entrepreneurs clear identification of unsolicited commercial communications as soon as they are received (Regulation 8).

97 *LineOne, ASA Monthly Report,* 108, May 2000.

98 *Compliance Report. Internet Banner and Pop-up advertisements Survey 2002.* http://www.asa.org.uk/NR/rdonlyres/CF839AFD-FFD3-4C98-BF83-231958BB97F2/0/upl_15.pdf.

Recently one more adjudication with regard to covert advertising was given in case *Freeserve plc*.[99] It related to the search listings results from an internet service provider that did not make clear to internet users that they were ranked according to the amount of money the sponsors paid, and not according to their relevance to the search term. This information was only given to internet users when they clicked on the hyperlink, at the foot of each sponsored result. In fact, the search listings results constituted hidden advertising of the sponsoring firms. In consequence, the ASA asked Freeserve to ensure clear identification of the above mentioned advertisements in future.

Another form of conveying advertising messages on the internet is via e-mail. Unsolicited e-mails, in general, pose quite a serious problem with respect to the protection of consumer rights. The e-mails that pretend to be private correspondence and only after reading them, turn out to have commercial character are one of the most common breaches of the British Code of Advertising. They are either titled in a very familiar way ('Hiya', 'hello' and so on),[100] or suggest they are private correspondence by use of other instruments. Sometimes they also try to attract internet users' attention by threatening them.[101]

The above mentioned examples show that one cannot generalize while assessing compliance with the rules on clear recognition of online advertising. For, we are faced with very distinct advertisers' behaviour. While online advertising does not pose major problems with regard to the clear identification of marketing communications, that is not the case with unsolicited commercial communications sent via e-mails. First of all, there is an abundance of complaints about this type of advertising; second, it is very difficult to make the advertisers cooperate with the ASA. Usually they do not even answer the ASA's inquiries, so in the end, the Authority has to resort to ad alerts. These do not seem to be a very effective means of enforcing the self-regulatory rules in this area of advertising, mainly because it is very often impossible to identify those responsible for the breach of the rules.

13. Covert Advertising in Radio and Television

Radio and television advertising is nowadays still the most common way of promoting products and services. It is also the only type of advertising that is regulated both by binding and self-regulatory rules, in a co-regulatory scheme.

The leading principle of broadcast advertising is the clear separation of advertising and editorial material. This principle has been ever present in regulation since the first commercial appeared on the UK's television screens in 1955.[102] It was the Television Act 1954 (Schedule 2, Rule 1) that introduced this principle. At the moment, it stems from a few documents: the Communications Act 2003 and The Ofcom Broadcasting Code, as well as from the BCAP Television Advertising

99   *Freeserve plc.*, 16 June 2004.
100   *Business in a Box,* 17 December 2003; *Phone Direct,* 1 October 2003.
101   *Premier Direct UK Ltd*, 19 November 2003.
102   Ofcom Consultation Paper on *Product Placement,* 19 December 2005, p. 1.

Standards Code, the BCAP Radio Advertising Standards Code and the BCAP Rules on the Scheduling of Television Advertisements.

In order to enforce the above mentioned principle, it is important to define the notions of 'programme' and 'advertisement'. It is not difficult to find a definition of the latter. Except for the Control of Misleading Advertising Regulations, it is separately defined in the Radio and TV Advertising Codes.[103] Yet, it is much more difficult to set the borders of 'the programme'. We cannot really find the answer to where the programme begins and where it ends, in any Act or Code. The definition of programme included in s. 405 of the Communications Act 2003 is even more misleading, since 'programme' is understood there to include also advertisements. Although such a broad definition aims to ensure that the broadcasting of advertising falls within the regulatory system, it does not make it easy to enforce properly the rules on the clear separation of advertising.[104] However, where there is a need to differentiate between the advertisements and programmes, the Communications Act 2003 does so by setting the provisions which specifically exclude advertising from the definition of programme.[105] It may suggest that, in fact, there is a distinction between the editorial and commercial content of the programmes. It is also confirmed by Ofcom (before, the Independent Television Commission) and ASA decisions on the unclear separation of advertisements and programmes. For example, in June 2005, Ofcom issued a decision against Video Interactive Television Plc., in respect of its service Channel U,[106] concerning the breach of the rules on the clear separation of advertisements and programmes. Channel U, following the advertising break and immediately preceding the Hip-Hop 'Honeyz' video, broadcasted a promotion of the same group, featuring Snoop Dog. Ofcom considered it a breach of, binding at that time, Rule 2.1.1 of the Advertisements Standards Code. For this and other breaches of rules on advertising, the broadcaster was fined £18,000. Ofcom does not have to resort to such severe sanctions in all cases. As has already been mentioned, it happens only when the breaches are serious and broadcasters do not want to cooperate with the enforcer. Thus, in another case, also concerning the separation principle,[107] Ofcom limited itself to the publication of the statement of findings in the Ofcom Advertising Complaints Bulletin. The case related to the programme 'Your Guide to a Beautiful Body' broadcast at Life TV that looked like a programme but contained a number of advertisements for beauty products and services. Because it was the first contravention of the rules by this station and the station was willing to introduce the necessary changes to its programme, Ofcom's approach was softer than in the previous case.

---

103   These definitions were described in the section on 'The regulation of covert advertising in the UK'.

104   L. Woods, A. Scheuer, *Advertising frequency and the Television without Frontiers Directive, European Law Review*, 29, (2004), p. 372.

105   For example ss 278 and 390 of the Communications Act 2003.

106   Ofcom Content Sanction Committee decision *Video Interactive Television Plc.*, 21 June 2005.

107   *Your Guide to a Beautiful Body*, Life TV, *Ofcom Advertising Complaints Bulletin*, 17 February 2004.

The predecessor of Ofcom in the field of television advertising – the Independent Television Commission (ITC) – also issued few interesting decisions concerning clear separation of commercial and editorial material, two of them concerning the crawler messages presented during a programme. One appearing on a Pakistani channel, during a cricket match, consisted of expressions of luck sent by different restaurants,[108] while the Danish channel used the scrolling text at the bottom of the screen to advertise Canal+ services during a Premier League Football match.[109] In both cases, the crawler messages constituted clear breach of the separation principle. The third ITC decision with respect to a breach of the same rule related to an advertisement of Subaru cars during the Channel 4 programme 'Driven'. Similar breaches of rules appeared also as regards interactive television services.[110] Since this is a quite new area of activity, both the ITC and now the ASA issued guidelines on this type of services.[111] They also refer to the separation principle.

What is striking in all the cases is that the only sanction applied was the publication of the ITC's findings in the ITC Complaints Report. It proves that enforcement of the separation principle is quite soft and one can wonder whether it is really effective. The number of cases related to this matter may allow us to doubt it.

In order to ensure that the border between programmes and advertisements is not blurred, the BCAP Codes and Rules have introduced rules concerning the presence of radio and television presenters in advertisements broadcast on the same channel, as well as the presence of famous personalities in advertisements adjacent to the programme in which they appear. The application of these rules can be presented in a few examples of the ASA's decisions. In 2005, the ASA objected to the radio advertisement of *Smile Teeth Whitening Studios*[112] where the famous presenter of Radio LBC news endorsed in an advertisement, presented on the station, the Smile Studios. Similarly, the ITC noted the breach of the clear separation of rules by the television station, Meridian,[113] that broadcasted an advertisement for Cornhill Insurance, featuring two news presenters in a setting resembling a news programme. The announcement of the advertising offer also looked like a news report.

As to the breach of rules on the actor/artist presence in advertisements adjacent to the programmes in which they appear, the ITC (later the ASA) issued more then 40 decisions on the matter.[114] Because in all these cases broadcasters were willing to cooperate and not to repeat the practices in future, the ITC limited itself to the publication of findings. On the one hand, it is understandable that more severe sanctions might not have been necessary; on the other hand, one can also have the

---

108   ITC Television Advertising Complaints Reports, 1 October 2001; *ITC Television Advertising Complaints Reports,* 1 April 2000.
109   *ITC Television Advertising Complaints Reports*, 31 March 2003.
110   *ITC Television Advertising Complaints Reports*, 1 June 2002 and 12 May 2003.
111   Guidance to Broadcasters on the regulation of the interactive television services: http://www.asa.org.uk/NR/rdonlyres/D41345A2-31B5-4149-879B-69A08A64879C/0/BCAP_Guidance_on_Interactive_TV.pdf.
112   *Smile Teeth Whitening Studios, ASA Broadcast Adjudications*, 19 October 2005.
113   *ITC Television Advertising Complaints Report*, 1 July 2000.
114   *ITC Television Advertising Complaints Reports*, 2000–2003 and ASA Adjudications online.

impression that the enforcement policy run by the ITC may have even encouraged advertisers to commit further breaches of the rules.

The principle of clear separation of commercial and editorial material gives rise to other more specific rules relating to the presentation of branded products in television and radio programmes. One can distinguish two substantial sets of provisions: rules on undue prominence and product placement. Undue prominence signifies the presence of, or reference to a product or service (including company names, brand names, logos) in a programme, where there is no editorial justification for this kind of practice.[115] The manner in which a product or service appears or is referred to in a programme is also considered as a practice of undue prominence, for example, showing a product in close-up or from an angle, which displays the branding to best advantage, or for any significant length of time. Under any circumstances the manner in which the product is presented or referred to can be subject to negotiations with the supplier. The point is that no impression of external commercial influence on the editorial process can be created.[116] However, since brands are an integral part of our times it is inevitable that they will appear at least in certain types of programmes. This explains why in few cases one can find an editorial justification for the appearance of brands, for example, in sport or music programmes.[117] Nonetheless, even in these programmes, this flexibility cannot be abused, which was proved by the ITC decision from 1999,[118] when the ITC fined MTV station £40,000 for the undue prominence of products during a programme run by the station.

The practice of undue prominence is quite common in different kind of competitions organized by television and radio stations. While presenting sponsors of the awards, the broadcasters show or mention sponsors' branded products, in a way that breaks the rules on undue prominence. This was the case of the television station ITV (Granada) that was fined by ITC £500,000 for repeated practices of undue prominence of products in its programme *This Morning*.[119]

The most recent case of undue prominence was adjudicated by Ofcom, on the basis of Rule 8.4 of Ofcom's Programme Code and concerned the programme *The Richard and Judy Show*, run by Channel Four.[120] The programme quite openly advertised the energy drink Red Bull. The station claimed that presentation of the brand was inevitable in order to give consumers reliable information on the benefits of caffeine. Since the breach was considered to be serious and the station had already received an ITC warning with regard to the same breach of broadcasting rules in

115   Rule 10.4 of the Ofcom Broadcasting Code.
116   *Guidance Note on Rule 16 Undue Prominence*, The ITC Rules Concerning Advertiser Involvement in Programmes, Autumn 2000.
117   More exceptions, for example, the National Lottery, are described in *Guidance Note to section 10 of Ofcom Broadcasting Code*, Issue 4, 5 December 2005 (www.ofcom.org.uk).
118   ITC News Release 59/99.
119   ITC News Release 82/94 and the ITC Programme Complaints and Interventions Report (Oct-Dec 1994).
120   Channel Four Television Corporation, Ofcom Content Sanctions Committee Decision, 3 August 2005.

its programme, Channel Four was fined £5,000 for giving undue prominence to a commercial product and directed to broadcast Ofcom's statement of finding in a form and at a time determined by Ofcom.

Although, the above mentioned decisions show that competent authorities enforce the relevant rules aimed at ensuring the clear separation of programmes and advertisements, one can have an impression that the number of detected breaches constitutes just a very small fraction of all the breaches. Even less attention is paid to the practices of product placement[121] that have not been subject to any decisions, either by the ITC or by Ofcom. Product placement is now prohibited by the Ofcom Broadcasting Code (Rule 10.5), which defines it as 'the inclusion of, or reference to, a product or service within a programme in return for payment or other valuable consideration to the programme maker or broadcaster'. This prohibition stems from the provisions of the Television Without Frontiers Directive that had to be incorporated into UK law. The European prohibition of product placement stands in contrast to the very liberal American approach. It seems that, in a global environment, when American films and programmes reach us every day, it is not feasible and practical to enforce the prohibition of product placement. The same conclusion has been recently drawn by the European Commission, which presented a draft law aiming at the partial liberalization of the rules on product placement.[122] This initiative encouraged Ofcom to start a debate on the controlled introduction of product placement into certain genres of programmes on commercial stations.[123] Ofcom experts are convinced that the total prohibition of product placement in television programmes is no longer proportionate to the potential detriment it seeks to prevent, the more so as consumers generally accept product placement, as long as the transparency principle is abided by. Some of them are even convinced that it is allowed under the present rules.[124] According to the consultation paper, product placement could be allowed just on commercial stations. It means that people, who are not willing to watch programmes including this type of advertising, could still choose public channels. Moreover, product placement would not be acceptable in news or current affairs programmes, religion and children's programmes. The principle of transparency would be ensured by the requirement of clear identification of product placement at the beginning of the programme.

Neither the European Commission's nor Ofcom's proposal concerns undue prominence – the notion very close to product placement. However, Ofcom's consultation paper poses a question whether the concept of 'undue prominence' should be retained in a regulatory regime permitting product placement. If so,

---

121 'Now you see it ...', *The Independent*, Media Weekly, Monday 12 December 2005.

122 Proposal for a Directive of the European Parliament and the Council amending Council Directive 89/522/EEC and Commission Staff working document annex to the Proposal for a Directive of the European Parliament and the Council amending Council Directive 89/522/EEC – Impact Assessment – Draft Audiovisual Media Service Directive {COM(2005) 646} http://www.europa.eu.int/comm/avpolicy/regul/regul_en.htm#4.

123 *Product Placement. A consultation on issues related to product placement,* Ofcom, 19 December 2005.

124 *Section 5, Viewer reaction, ibid.*, pt. 5.1–5.18.

the only rationale for maintaining the prohibition of undue prominence would be editorial integrity, not the need for clear distinction between programme and advertising content, since this is also the only rationale for maintaining the ban on product placement.[125]

It seems that the proposed changes to the present regulatory system are a much better solution, than maintaining the present, fictional situation where everyone pretends that this phenomenon does not exist in English media sector while, at the same time, it can be easily proved that companies regularly pay for the covert promotion of their products.[126]

Similarly, English law maintains (Rule 2.12 of the Ofcom Broadcasting Code) an artificial ban on subliminal advertising. Subliminal advertising is considered to be a technique which exploits the possibility of conveying a message to viewers or listeners, or otherwise influencing their minds, without them being aware or fully aware of what has occurred (for example, images of very brief duration).This ban is artificial, because no one has ever spotted this type of advertising.

Subliminal advertising is also prohibited by self-regulatory rules. However, neither Ofcom, responsible for the enforcement of the Broadcasting Code, nor the ASA, responsible for enforcing the rules of the BCAP TV Advertising Standards Code, have ever issued any decision with respect to subliminal advertising or initiated any relevant proceedings. One can come to the conclusion that these rules are even more outdated then the rules on product placement.[127] On the other hand, it is difficult to predict whether the absence of the prohibition would not cause the widespread use of this type of advertising technique.

14. Conclusions

The above analysis of English law and soft law on covert advertising proves that, although one cannot find a general ban on this type of advertising, the existing framework of rules prevents the same kind of rogue advertising behaviours as do the continental systems. Yet, English legislators do not use the term 'covert advertising,' which in civil law systems represents an act of unfair competition. Instead, regulating the same kind of rogue practices, they refer to advertising not recognizable or not identifiable as such.

Another important characteristic of the British system on covert advertising is the role played by self-regulation. While civil law countries regulate the issues of unfair advertising by statutory means, relying mostly on the provisions of laws on combating unfair competition or more generally unfair trading practices, the English system relies much more on self-regulation and co-regulation and, to a lesser extent, on statutory acts. The control performed by the self-regulatory body (the ASA), in particular in the field of press and direct mail advertising, turns out to be more effective than administrative controls could be. It is undoubtedly due to the more flexible rules

---

125   *Section 6, Options and issues, ibid.*, pt. 6.24–6.29.
126   'Now you see it ...', *The Independent*, Media Weekly, Monday 12 December 2005.
127   This opinion was also shared by Ofcom experts, during the meeting on the 13 December 2005.

applied in the self-regulatory proceedings. It also seems that the protection offered by the voluntary rules is not worse than that offered by public bodies, although many EU countries, where self-regulation does not really play any role, would fear that this kind of control would lack independence from business. It is not really the case in the UK. One could rather have the impression that administrative controls, carried out by Ofcom (before, the ITC and the Radio Authority) are too soft for companies breaching the broadcasting rules, especially the rules resulting from the separation principle. On the other hand, it must be seen that some of the current provisions, for example, prohibition of product placement and subliminal advertising, might be outdated already. Regulators are aware of this fact and try to apply moderate instruments to the above mentioned types of advertising.

The overall picture of covert advertising control in the UK looks then relatively good although one cannot overlook its most important weakness – the softness of applied sanctions. This concerns both the ASA's and public bodies' sanctions.

7   Grounded? Air Passenger Rights in the European Union

Eliza Varney[1] and Mike Varney[2]

1. Introduction

The introduction of Regulation 261/2004[3] is destined to make a significant impact on consumer protection in the aviation sector. When the Regulation came into force on the 17 February 2005, Jacques Barrot, European Commission Vice-President responsible for transport, argued: 'The boom in air travel needs to be accompanied by proper protection of passengers' rights. This is a concrete example of how the Union benefits people's daily lives. Competitiveness and competition in the air sector go hand-in-hand with guaranteed passengers' rights.'[4]

There is no doubt that the enactment of the Regulation is likely to lead to significant benefits for consumers, and expands the rights which were previously available to those who were denied boarding, or suffer long delays or flight cancellations. Air carriers have seen a vast expansion in passenger numbers over the past 20 years, and the implementation of Regulation 261/2004 appears to offer a timely intervention into the market for air travel in order to secure a basic corpus of rights for all consumers using a carrier based in the European Union (EU), or flying from an EU airport.

The Commission has endeavoured to publicize the existence of the Regulation, and the rights enumerated therein, aggressively. The Commission's website contains a leaflet[5] and a poster,[6] which are designed to inform passengers of the rights given

---

1   Lecturer in Law, School of Law, Keele University.

2   Lecturer in Law and Deputy Director of the Institute for European Public Law, Law School, University of Hull. We would like to extend our thanks to Tony Dugdale, Kelvin Johnstone, Gary Wilson, Christian Twigg-Flesner and the anonymous referee for reading a draft of this article. The usual disclaimer applies.

3   Regulation 261/2004 of the European Parliament and of the Council of 11 February 2004 establishing common rules on compensation and assistance to passengers in the event of denied boarding and of cancellation or long delay of flights, and repealing Regulation (EEC) No. 295/91, [2004] OJ L46/1.

4   European Commission Press Release IP/05/181, 16 February 2005. Available at: http://europa.eu.int/rapid/pressReleasesAction.do?reference=IP/05/181&format=HTML&aged=0&language=EN&guiLanguage=en (last accessed 11 August 2006).

5   European Commission (2005) *Air Passenger Rights* Brussels: European Commission. Available at: http://ec.europa.eu/transport/air/rules/rights/doc/2005_01_19_apr_leaflet_en.pdf (last accessed 11 August 2006).

6   European Commission (2005) *Air Passenger Rights* Brussels: European Commission. Available at: http://ec.europa.eu/transport/air/rules/rights/doc/2005_01_19_apr_

to them by the new legislation. Furthermore, Article 14 of the Regulation obliges air carriers to display posters alerting passengers to the existence of these rights at the check-in desk, and to distribute written details of the rights to all of those who are denied boarding, or suffer long delays or cancellation of their flights.

These measures should do much to empower the air passenger, securing new levels of comfort and compensation to those suffering disruption and disappointment at the airport. The realities may not, however, be so straightforward. The Regulation is designed to strike a balance between the perceived economic realities of the airline market on the one hand, and the need for consumer protection on the other. In order to strike this balance, air carriers are offered the opportunity to avoid liability for denied boarding or cancellations in some situations. The way in which these circumstances have been defined differs, depending on whether the compensation claim is for denied boarding (where there are a number of defences outlined in Article 2(j) of the Regulation) or for cancellation (where the airlines may refuse payment of compensation where 'extraordinary circumstances' led to the cancellation in accordance with Article 5(3)). We will argue below that these defences, while necessary, are not spelled out with a sufficient degree of precision to offer either passengers or airlines sufficient certainty upon which to base their decisions over complaints handling. An additional problem is posed by the absence of any rules in the Regulation which distinguish between cancellations and long delays. This distinction is crucial, as the Regulation makes no provision for the payment of compensation in the event of long delays, but does do so in the case of cancellations. Later in this paper, we identify some of the difficulties which have been caused by this failure to include such a distinction in the legislation.

A further difficulty which we highlight lies in the means of enforcement. It is well known that by virtue of Article 249 of the EC Treaty, Regulations are directly applicable in Member State law, and so anyone who feels that their rights under the Regulation have been breached might take civil action in order to gain redress. In many cases, it seems that the Regulation is hoping to avoid the need for legal action, as Article 16 of the Regulation places Member States under an obligation to designate a body responsible for ensuring that the Regulation is enforced.[7] In many cases, it appears that the potential for passengers to ensure effective redress of disputes without recourse to the courts is minimal. This situation is regrettable, but is perhaps unsurprising, as the Regulation does not have the support of the aviation industry, which launched a legal action challenging the validity of the Regulation.[8] Both the traditional 'full service' scheduled airlines, and the low-fare airlines have

---

poster_en.pdf (last accessed 11 August 2006).

7   See the decisions in Case C–453/99 *Courage* v. *Bernard Crehan* [2001] ECR I–6207 and Case C–253/00 *Muñoz* [2002] ECR I–7289, where the European Court of Justice (ECJ) suggests that private enforcement of obligations created by Regulations plays an important role in upholding Community law, particularly where other measures of monitoring and enforcement of the rights granted therein have failed.

8   Case C–344/04 *R (On the Application of the International Air Transport Association and European Low Fares Airline Association)* v. *Department of Transport* (decided on 10 January 2006), *The Times*, 16 January 2006 [hereafter *R (On the Application of the IATA and ELFAA)* v. *Department of Transport*].

condemned the regulation through their respective trade associations.[9] Such a situation was never likely to lead to a spirit of cooperation between the EU and the airlines on this issue, and it seems likely that the airlines will seek to adopt an expansive reading of the defences provided in the Regulation and to exploit any uncertainties in the wording of the Regulation to maximum possible effect.

In this chapter we will discuss and analyse the key provisions of the Regulation, with the hope of casting some light on major issues of controversy which have arisen and uncertainties which have been highlighted in the first few months of the Regulation coming into force. Our primary focus will be on 'scheduled' flights, whether 'full service' or 'low-fare', rather than charter flights. It is likely that clearer interpretation of the various provisions contained in the Regulation will only be forged in the furnace of experience, but we aim to offer an insight into some of the major issues which have arisen through an examination of the relevant case law which has been decided up to now, alongside a consideration of the relevant economic and social factors which seem likely to inform future decisions over the operation of the Regulation. Through this analysis we hope to highlight the practicalities and realities which must influence the operation of the Regulation in this time of considerable change in the aviation industry, where increased competition, and a breaking down of traditional business models have fundamentally changed the structure and operation of the European aviation market.

(i) Compensation Rights for Air Passengers under Regulation 261/2004

Prior to the adoption of Regulation 261/2004, passengers were entitled to assistance under Regulation 295/91[10] only in the event of denied boarding and only if the flight was operated by a scheduled airline.[11] The assistance was in the form of reimbursement or re-routing, meals and hotel accommodation, and compensation between €150–300, depending on the length of the flight.[12] Regulation 261/2004 has a much wider scope, protecting passengers affected not only by denied boarding, but also by cancellations or long delays. The Regulation applies to all airlines (both scheduled and non-scheduled[13]) operating from airports in the EU, and to EU airlines

---

9   International Air Transport Association (2005) *EC Regulation 261/2004 on Denied Boarding Compensation* Montreal: IATA. Available at: http://www. iata.org/whatwedo/government_industry/EU_regulation_261.htm (last accessed 11 August 2006). See also European Low Fares Airline Association (2005) *ELFAA Announce Legal Challenge of Punitive EU Legislation on Air Passenger Compensation for Cancellations and Long Delays* Brussels: ELFAA. Available at: http://www.elfaa.com/documents/ELFAA-4May2004-ELFAAannouncelegalchallengeofpunitiveEUlegislationonAirPassengerCompensat_001.pdf (last accessed 11 August 2006).

10 Council Regulation (EEC) No. 295/91 of 4 February 1991 establishing common rules for a denied boarding compensation system in scheduled air transport, [1991] OJ L36/5.

11 Article 1, Regulation 295/91.

12 Article 4(2), Regulation 295/91.

13 Non-scheduled flights include 'charter' flights.

operating from third countries to EU airports.[14] The measures are no longer confined to scheduled services, possibly as a response to the blurring of the distinction between scheduled and non-scheduled airlines.[15] Affected passengers may be entitled to reimbursement or re-routing,[16] refreshments and hotel accommodation,[17] and in the event of denied boarding and cancellations, passengers may also receive compensation between €250–600, depending on the length of the flight.[18]

The higher levels of compensation under the current provisions were seen as a necessary step to address the practice of overbooking, where airlines issue more tickets than available seats in an aircraft.[19] In 2002, over 250,000 passengers in the EU were prevented from boarding their intended flight as a result of this practice.[20] Airlines generally overbook flights to prevent the situation where seats in an aircraft are left empty by passengers who fail to check-in, or who have a flexible ticket which allows them to opt for a different flight.[21] As the European Commission indicates, increased levels of compensation are necessary in order to address the 'scale of the problem' created by overbooking, rather than the actual commercial practice.[22] Compensation at 'dissuasive' levels was envisaged to act as a deterrent against those airlines which engage in the practice.[23]

According to Article 2(j) of the Regulation, passengers who have been denied boarding may not be able to claim compensation if the decision of the airline can be justified on 'reasonable grounds'. These grounds include 'reasons of health, safety or security, or inadequate travel documentation'.[24] However, the Regulation is silent in defining these terms. A narrow reading of these terms would seem to suggest that 'safety' or 'security' reasons for denying boarding relate to the potential threat that could be posed by a particular person, although the text of the Regulation does not exclude a broad reading of these provisions. If, for example, an airline has to replace an aircraft with a smaller aircraft from its fleet due to 'safety' concerns caused by

---

14   Article 3(1), Regulation 261/2004.

15   Recital 5 and Article 2(a), Regulation 261/2004.

16   Article 8, Regulation 261/2004.

17   Article 9, Regulation 261/2004.

18   Article 7, Regulation 261/2004.

19   COM(2000) 365 *Communication from the Commission to the European Parliament and the Council Protection of air passengers in the European Union* Brussels: European Commission, at para. 32. Available at: http://europa.eu.int/eur-lex/lex/LexUriServ/site/en/com/2000/com2000_0365en01.pdf (last accessed 11 August 2006).

20   COM(2005) 46 *Communication from the Commission to the European Parliament and the Council – Strengthening passenger rights within the European Union* Brussels: European Commission, at para. 12. Available at: http://eur-lex.europa.eu/LexUriServ/site/en/com/2005/com2005_0046en01.pdf (last accessed 11 August 2006).

21   *Ibid.*

22   *Ibid.*, at para. 13.

23   European Commission Press Release IP/04/98, 26/01/2004. Available at: http://europa.eu.int/rapid/pressReleasesAction.do?reference=IP/04/98&format=HTML&aged=0&language=EN&guiLanguage=en (last accessed 19 May 2006).

24   Article 2(j), Regulation 261/2004.

technical problems and, as a result, has to deny boarding to a number of passengers who cannot be accommodated within the smaller aircraft, there is the potential that airlines would rely on a broad reading of Article 2(j) in order to refuse the payment of compensation to these passengers.

Airlines may also be required to pay compensation in the event of cancellations, unless passengers have been informed of the cancellation two weeks in advance, or have been offered satisfactory re-routing where the arrival is no later than 2–4 hours from the time of arrival in their original itinerary (depending when the notice of cancellation is given).[25] The same amount of compensation applies as in the case of denied boarding.

The measures protecting passengers who have suffered disruption were expected to provide 'a *substantial* increase in the level of compensation',[26] which took into account the inconvenience suffered as a result of denied boarding and cancellations.[27] However, the figures referred to in Article 7(1) of the Regulation are much lower than originally suggested under the proposals for the Regulation.[28] While the proposals referred to figures between €750–1500,[29] the final text of the Regulation provides for compensation between €250–600, depending on the length of the flight.[30] One of the reasons for the lower figures referred to in the final text of the Regulation is to ensure that airlines are not overburdened by the provision requiring the payment of compensation. As the Economic and Social Committee indicated, high levels of compensation could hinder the potential for airlines to make profits and this may have the greatest impact on low-cost airlines.[31]

While the Regulation makes provisions for the payment of compensation in the event of cancellations, no compensation is required for passengers affected by long delays. The Regulation provides no guidance on how to distinguish between a cancellation and a long delay, nor does it indicate a maximum time limit where the failure to provide a flight no longer constitutes a 'delay' and is considered to be a 'cancellation'. In the absence of such indication, airlines may be tempted to deny claims for compensation from passengers that reached their destination later than it was originally scheduled, by classifying such disruption as a 'long delay'.

---

25 Article 5(1)(c), Regulation 261/2004.

26 COM(2000) 365 above, n. 17, at para. 14 (emphasis added).

27 *Ibid.*

28 European Commission (2002) *Proposal for a Regulation of the European Parliament and of the Council establishing common rules on compensation and assistance to air passengers in the event of denied boarding and of cancellation or long delay of flights*, [2002] OJ C103 E/225. Available at: http://europa.eu.int/eur-lex/pri/en/oj/dat/2002/ ce103/ce10320020430en02250229.pdf (last accessed 11 August 2006).

29 *Ibid.*, at Article 7(1).

30 Article 7(1), Regulation 261/2004.

31 Economic and Social Committee (2002) *Opinion on the 'Proposal for a Regulation of the European Parliament and of the Council establishing common rules on compensation and assistance to air passengers in the event of denied boarding and of cancellation or long delay of flights'* [2002] OJ C241/29, at para. 3.3. Available at: http://europa.eu.int/eur-lex/pri/en/oj/dat/2002/c_241/c_24120021007en00290033.pdf (last accessed 11 August 2006).

Passengers seeking compensation for cancellations may face an additional hurdle in Article 5(3) of the Regulation. According to this provision, airlines are not required to pay compensation if a flight has been cancelled due to 'extraordinary circumstances'. Yet, the Regulation provides no clear guidance as to the meaning of such circumstances and there is a risk that airlines will adopt a broad definition of this provision in order to refuse passengers their request for compensation. A particular difficulty is posed by the question whether airlines should have to pay compensation for cancellations caused by technical problems.

Initially, the proposal for the Regulation stated in Recital 7 (now Recital 12) that compensation does not have to be paid 'when the cancellation occurs in exceptional circumstances beyond the responsibility of an air carrier or that of its subcontracting agent'.[32] A similar wording was provided in Article 1 of the proposal (now Article 1(b)), which stated that the Regulation aims to protect passengers when '… their flight is cancelled, except for reasons beyond the responsibility of an air carrier or that of its subcontracting agent'.[33] This seemed to imply that airlines could not refuse to pay compensation for matters falling within their responsibility and under this wording, airlines would find it difficult to rely on the 'extraordinary circumstances' defence in the case of cancellations caused by technical problems.

Further amendments to the Regulation replaced the reference to 'exceptional circumstances beyond the responsibility of the air carrier' with provisions on '*force majeure*'.[34] This was designed to bring more clarity to the circumstances where airlines were not responsible for cancellations.[35] Under Recital 8(a) of the amended proposal for the Regulation (now Recital 14), such circumstances included 'shortcomings in security or in safety despite due care and full compliance with safety and security standards'. The reference to 'due care' and 'full compliance' with standards of security and safety placed a heavy onus on the airlines seeking to rely on this provision as a defence for cancellations caused by technical problems. Article 1(b) of the amended proposal for the Regulation referred to the application of the Regulation to cancellations, 'except for reasons of *force majeure*', while Article 2(ha) defined '*force majeure*' as 'unusual and unforeseeable circumstances beyond the control of the party by whom it is pleaded, the consequences of which could not have been avoided even if all due care had been exercised'.[36] Airlines that had to cancel flights due to technical problems would have found it difficult to rely on this defence in order to refuse the payment of compensation.

---

32   European Commission (2002) above, n. 26.
33   *Ibid.* A similar wording was provided also under Article 10 of the Proposed Regulation.
34   European Commission (2003) *Amended proposal for a Regulation of the European Parliament and of the Council establishing common rules on compensation and assistance to air passengers in the event of denied boarding and of cancellation or long delay of flights* [2003] OJ C71 E/188. Available at: http://europa.eu.int/eur-lex/ pri/en/oj/dat/2003/ce071/ce07120030325en01880197.pdf (last accessed 11 August 2006).
35   *Ibid.*
36   *Ibid.*

The reference to '*force majeure*' has been abandoned in the final text of the Regulation. Article 2(ha) of the amended proposal has been taken out, without being replaced by a definition of 'extraordinary circumstances'. Unlike the original proposal, which referred to 'circumstances beyond the responsibility of the air carrier',[37] and the amended proposal, which referred to 'unusual and unforeseeable circumstances beyond the control of the party by whom it is pleaded',[38] the final text of the Regulation opts for a more ambiguous wording. According to Article 5(3), airlines are not required to pay compensation if the cancellation was caused by 'circumstances which could not have been avoided if all reasonable measures had been taken'. Yet, no guidance is provided on determining what could amount to 'reasonable measures'. The same degree of uncertainty is reflected in Recital 12, which mirrors almost entirely the ambiguity of Article 5(3).

Recital 14 of the Regulation makes reference to the provisions on 'extraordinary circumstances' under the *Convention for the Unification of Certain Rules for International Carriage by Air* (Montreal Convention)[39] and provides examples of such circumstances: 'Political instability, meteorological conditions incompatible with the operation of the flight concerned, security risks, unexpected flight safety shortcomings and strikes that affect the operation of an operating air carrier.'[40]

However, the term 'safety shortcomings' is undefined and it is unclear whether unexpected technical problems which led to the cancellation of flights would always amount to 'extraordinary circumstances', allowing airlines to refuse the payment of compensation. The final text of the Regulation left out the reference to 'shortcomings in security or in safety, despite due care and full compliance with safety and security standards', as previously provided in the amended proposal for the Regulation.[41] Instead, the Regulation provides a more ambiguous wording, where airlines could potentially rely on the 'extraordinary circumstances' defence, even if the cancellation was caused by matters within their control and for which they should have taken appropriate measures to avoid disruption.

A similar degree of ambiguity is present also in Recital 15 of the Regulation. As in the case of Article 5(3) and Recitals 12 and 14, this provision fails to cast any light on what might constitute 'reasonable measures' that could have prevented the cancellation:

> Extraordinary circumstances should be deemed to exist where the impact of an air traffic management decision in relation to a particular aircraft on a particular day gives rise to a long delay, an overnight delay, or the cancellation of one or more flights by that aircraft,

---

37   European Commission (2002) above, n. 26, Article 1.
38   European Commission (2003) above, n. 32, Article 2(ha).
39   *Convention for the Unification of Certain Rules for International Carriage by Air* (Montreal Convention) 1999, approved by Council Decision 5 April, [2001] OJ L 194/38. Available at: http://ec.europa.eu/transport/air/rules/rights/doc/convention_ montreal/l_19420010718en00390049.pdf (Last accessed 11 August 2006).
40   Recital 14, Regulation 261/2004.
41   European Commission (2003) above, n. 32, Recital 8(a).

even though all reasonable measures had been taken by the air carrier concerned to avoid the delays or cancellations.[42]

Rather than attempting to define 'extraordinary circumstances' in the preamble of the Regulation, a preferable approach would have been to clarify the meaning of these terms in the list of definitions provided in Article 2 of the Regulation. Unlike the definition of 'denied boarding' in Article 2(j) (which provides examples of 'reasonable grounds' to deny boarding, under which airlines are not bound to pay compensation), the definition of cancellations in Article 2(1) provides no such examples. By their very nature, 'extraordinary circumstances' will be impossible to define exhaustively. However, the current ambiguity on the meaning of such circumstances may be detrimental for consumers, and it is very likely that in the absence of greater clarification from the European Court of Justice (ECJ), the industry will adopt a broad interpretation of these terms.

2. The Airline Industry's Challenges to Regulation 261/2004

The adoption of Regulation 261/2004 has not been welcomed by the airline industry, which launched a challenge to the validity of the Regulation in April 2004.[43] The action was brought by the trade associations of the traditional scheduled airlines (International Air Transport Association – IATA)[44] and the low fares airlines (European Low Fares Airline Association – ELFAA).[45] While ELFAA contested all aspects of the Regulation, IATA challenged only the provisions on cancellations and long delays, but chose not to contest the measures on denied boarding.[46]

Most of the grounds of the consolidated challenge brought by IATA and ELFAA referred to the scope of the 'extraordinary circumstances' defence, which is available under the Regulation only for compensation claims in the event of cancellations.[47] Firstly, the airline industry expressed dissatisfaction with the absence of such a defence in relation to long delays. Under the Regulation, airlines are required to assist passengers affected by long delays,[48] even if the delay has been caused by matters outside the control of the airline, such as bad weather conditions. As provided in Article 6(1) of the Regulation, the assistance must be provided in the form of refreshments and hotel accommodation when necessary, and in the case of delays of over five hours, the airline must also provide reimbursement of the fare paid or re-routing.

---

42   Recital 15, Regulation 261/2004.
43   *R (On the Application of the IATA and ELFAA)* v. *Department of Transport* above, n. 6.
44   IATA (2005) above, n. 7.
45   ELFAA (2005) above, n. 7.
46   IATA (2005) above, n. 7. See discussion in P. Phillips, 'Low air fares grounded?', *Legal Week* 7(36) October (2005): p. 18.
47   Article 5(3), Regulation 261/2004.
48   Article 6, Regulation 261/2004.

The airlines argue that these requirements are not consistent with the Montreal Convention.[49] According to Article 19 of this Convention, airlines are not liable for damages caused by the delay, if they have taken 'all measures that could reasonably be required to avoid the damage' or 'it was impossible for ... them to take such measures'.[50] In addition, Article 22 of the Convention imposes a limit on the amount of compensation that may be payable by an airline in the event of a delay, while Article 29 limits the liability of the airlines in actions for damages. On the other hand, Article 6 of the Regulation makes no reference to limitations on liability or to an 'extraordinary circumstances' defence, and the airlines perceive this to be inconsistent with the Montreal Convention.[51] This claim has been dismissed by the ECJ, which distinguished between damages which might be accrued by individual passengers as a result of their individual circumstances, and damages that are common to all passengers, which include the trouble and inconvenience suffered as a result of a delay.[52] According to the ECJ, the Montreal Convention is concerned only with damages accruing to individuals, while Regulation 261/2004 requires compensation for all passengers left grounded as a result of a delay. Given the different objectives of these instruments, the ECJ found no incompatibility between Article 6 of the Regulation and the Montreal Convention.[53]

Some commentators have expressed unease with this approach adopted by the ECJ, arguing that it relies on an artificial distinction between 'individualized' and 'standardized' damages.[54] While commentators were resigned to the fact that the ECJ was never likely to find against the validity of the Regulation, they argued that a preferable approach would have been to justify the provision of care for long delays as part of the 'social duty' of the airlines towards passengers who are facing disruption.[55] The emphasis on social obligations would have been in line with the opinion of Advocate General Geelhoed,[56] who argued that Regulation 261/2004 complemented the rights available to passengers under the Montreal Convention by ensuring a minimum level of protection to passengers affected by disruption.[57]

49　See above, n. 37.

50　Article 19, Montreal Convention.

51　*International Air Transport Association* v. *Department of Transport*, Detailed Statement of Grounds (Incorporating Statement of Facts relied on), High Court of Justice, at paras 4(a) and 19–42 [hereafter IATA Statement of Grounds]. Available at: http://www.iata.org/NR/ContentConnector/CS2000/Siteinterface/sites/whatwedo/file/statement_of_grounds.pdf (last accessed 11 August 2006).

52　*R (On the Application of the IATA and ELFAA)* v. *Department of Transport*, para. 43.

53　*Ibid.*

54　J.Y. Gilg, 'How Airlines affected by ECJ Compensation Ruling', Lexis Nexis, Legal Analysis, 17 January (2006) (citing Richard Gimblett, partner at Barlow Lyde Gilbert).

55　*Ibid.*

56　*Ibid.* See Opinion of Advocate General Geelhoed (delivered on 8 September 2005) Case C–344/04 *R (On the Application of the IATA and ELFAA)* v. *Department of Transport*, [hereafter Opinion of Advocate General Geelhoed].

57　Opinion of Advocate General Geelhoed, above, n. 54, paras 42–45.

According to the Advocate General, these measures must be provided 'regardless of whether there is damage',[58] and represent 'rules of a public nature'.[59]

Another area in which IATA and ELFAA were dissatisfied with the absence of an 'extraordinary circumstances' defence is the provision of care in the event of a cancellation. While such a defence is available for compensation claims under Article 5(3) of the Regulation, airlines are under an absolute obligation to assist passengers affected by cancellations through the provision of meals, refreshments and hotel accommodation when necessary.[60] Although the initial drafts of the Regulation comprised an 'extraordinary circumstances' defence for the provision of care following a cancellation,[61] this was removed by the Conciliation Committee at a later stage. The ECJ concluded that the removal of the 'extraordinary defence' for the provision of care in the event of cancellations was valid.[62]

The claimants also contested the Regulation on grounds of uncertainty.[63] IATA and ELFAA point towards an apparent inconsistency between Recitals 14 and 15 of the Regulation (which limit or exclude the liability of the airlines for events caused by 'extraordinary circumstances') and Articles 5 and 6 of the Regulation (which impose a requirement of care, even if the events were outside the control of the airline).[64] According to IATA's submission, the recitals reflected the Commission's views on these issues and the text of the Regulation failed to take into account these views.[65] This submission was rejected, given that recitals are merely designed to provide an explanation for the actual content of the Regulation and are not legally binding.[66]

Further grounds of challenge included the claim that the measures prescribed by the Regulation for assisting passengers do not comply with the principle of proportionality.[67] According to this principle, community measures must be 'appropriate for the objective pursued' and 'must not go beyond what is necessary to achieve'.[68] The measures imposed by Regulation 261/2004 in the event of delays and cancellations are alleged to be disproportionate to the objectives pursued by the measures for assisting passengers affected by these events.[69] The airlines argue that the removal of the 'extraordinary circumstances' defence for the provision of care

---

58   *Ibid.*, at para. 47.
59   *Ibid.*, at para. 48.
60   Article 5(1), Regulation 261/2004.
61   Article 5, Common Position (EC) No. 27/2003 of 18 March 2003, [2003] OJ C125 E/64. Available at: http://europa.eu.int/eur-lex/pri/en/oj/dat/2003/ce125/ce12520030527en00630071.pdf (last accessed 11 August 2006).
62   *Ibid.*, at paras 62 and 63.
63   IATA Statement of Grounds above, n. 49, paras 4(c) and 53–58.
64   *Ibid.*, at para. 55.
65   *Ibid.*, at para. 54.
66   *R (On the Application of the IATA and ELFAA)* v. *Department of Transport*, para. 76. See Case C–155/04 *Alliance for Natural Health and Others* [2005] ECR I–6451 at para. 91.
67   IATA Statement of Grounds above, n. 49, paras 4(d) and 59–60.
68   Case C–210/00 *Käserei Champignon Hofmeister* [2002] ECR I–6453, para. 59.
69   IATA Statement of Grounds above, n. 49, para. 4(d).

was an unnecessary step, which is not likely to lead to a reduction in the number of passengers affected by disruption.[70] The ECJ addressed this challenge by determining the objectives of the Regulation and assessing whether the measures adopted by the Regulation are appropriate in achieving these objectives.[71] While the airlines' submission concentrated on the objective of reducing the number of cancellations and long delays through preventive measures, the ECJ perceived this as merely a secondary objective of the Regulation.[72] The primary aim of the Regulation is to protect passengers affected by denied boarding, cancellations and long delays, and to provide them with immediate assistance that would reduce the inconvenience caused by these events.[73] In light of these factors, the imposition of a requirement to provide care for passengers regardless of the cost of the ticket and without the possibility to rely on an 'extraordinary circumstances' defence is not disproportionate to the objectives of the Regulation.[74] As indicated by Advocate General Geelhoed: 'It is logical that there is no exception to the obligation to provide assistance and care in situations where passengers are confronted with delays or cancellations ... Lack of information could easily lead to an abuse of the extraordinary circumstances derogation, leaving the passengers uncared.'[75]

One of the key arguments in ELFAA's submission was an alleged discrimination against low-cost airlines, as the Regulation imposes the same level of obligation on both traditional scheduled airlines and low-cost airlines.[76] ELFAA also pointed out that the airlines often compete on shorter routes with other means of transport such as trains, coaches and ferries, but there are no similar obligations of care and assistance imposed on providers of these means of transport.[77] In their view, this is in breach of the principle of equality and non-discrimination, which requires that 'comparable situations must not be treated differently ... unless such treatment is objectively justified'.[78] The ECJ refused to consider different modes of transport as 'comparable', given that the location of the airports and the baggage check-in and reclaim brings an added level of inconvenience for passengers denied boarding, or affected by cancellations or long delays.[79] Furthermore, the ECJ declined to distinguish between traditional scheduled and non-scheduled airlines on the level of assistance that should be provided for passengers. The level of inconvenience caused by cancellations or long delays is similar for all passengers, irrespective of the price paid for the ticket.[80]

---

70 *Ibid.*, at paras 4(d), 59 and 60.

71 *R (On the Application of the IATA and ELFAA)* v. *Department of Transport*, para. 82.

72 *Ibid.*, at paras 82–83.

73 *Ibid.*

74 *Ibid.*, at paras 84–86.

75 Opinion of Advocate General Geelhoed, above, n. 54, at para. 125.

76 ELFAA (2005) above, n. 7.

77 *R (On the Application of the IATA and ELFAA)* v. *Department of Transport*, para. 94.

78 *Ibid.*, at para. 95. Reference is made to Case C–210/03 *Swedish Match* [2004] ECR I–11893, para. 63.

79 *R (On the Application of the IATA and ELFAA)* v. *Department of Transport*, paras 96–97; Case C–249/95 *SAM Schiffahrt and Stapf* [1997] ECR I–4475, para. 34.

80 *Ibid.*, at para. 98.

The action brought by IATA and ELFAA, contesting the validity of Regulation 261/2004, was dismissed on all grounds. Yet, approximately one year after this action had been launched in the High Court, this Regulation was at the centre of another challenge launched by the airline industry. In April 2005, the European Regions Airlines Association (ERA) has filed a complaint to the European Ombudsman, against the European Commission's actions for publicising passenger rights under Regulation 261/2004.[81] ERA alleged that the European Commission's posters and leaflets[82] informing passengers of their rights in the event of denied boarding, cancellations or long delays, provide consumers with misleading information.[83] It is notable that these posters do not contain any reference to the 'extraordinary circumstances' defence for compensation claims in the event of cancellations.[84] By refusing to withdraw or correct these allegedly misleading posters, the European Commission is arguably in beach of Article 11 (fairness), Article 12 (courtesy) and Article 17 (reasonable time-limit for taking decisions) of the *Code of Good Administrative Behaviour.*[85] The decision of the European Ombudsman in this matter is pending.[86]

The challenges brought by the airline industry against Regulation 261/2004, and the Commission's endeavours to publicize the rights granted therein, have wide implications and reflect a limited spirit of cooperation between the industry and the EU. These actions also highlight the weight placed by the industry on having an 'extraordinary circumstances' defence. Under the current framework, this defence is available only for compensation claims for passengers affected by cancellations.[87] In the absence of clear guidance on the appropriate use of Article 5(3) of the Regulation, it is likely that the airlines will seek to adopt an expansive reading of this defence, potentially transforming it into an escape route from compensation claims.

---

81   'European Regions Airlines Association Complaint of Maladministration against the European Commission', Complaint No. 1475/2005/IP. See discussion in S. Dolan, 'EC Aviation Scene: Compensation for Denied Boarding, Cancellation and Delay', *Air and Space Law* 30(4/5) (2005): 367–369.

82   See above, ns 3 and 4.

83   See ERA Press Release 'ERA takes EC to European Ombudsman', 6 April 2005 [hereafter ERA Press Release 6 April 2005]. Available at: http://www.eraa.org/news/erapressreleases/050406april.php (last accessed 11 August 2006).

84   Article 5(3), Regulation 261/2004. See 'ERA Submission to Ombudsman regarding EC Opinion on Maladministration Complaint', 21 November 2001, p. 4. Available at: http://www.eraa.org/intranet/documents/22/587/051121extBeaumontresponsetoECopinion.pdf (last accessed 11 August 2006).

85   ERA Press Release 06/04/2005 above, n. 81. The *Code of Good Administrative Behaviour* is available at: http://www.euro-ombudsman.eu.int/code/pdf/en/code2005_en.pdf (last accessed 11 August 2006).

86   Decisions of the European Ombudsman can be found at: http://www.euro-ombudsman.eu.int/decision/en/default.htm (last accessed 11 August 2006).

87   Article 5(3), Regulation 261/2004.

3. Costs Imposed by the Regulation – Excessive or Not?

We have noted above that the 'extraordinary circumstances' defence is not well defined in the Regulation. The interpretation of the Regulation which is ultimately adopted by national regulators and courts may rest in some respects on the ability of the airlines to demonstrate that they have made reasonable endeavours to avoid the cause of the disruption. We have noted above that Article 2(j) of the Regulation provides a defence to the payment of compensation for denied boarding where such boarding is denied on 'reasonable grounds'[88] and Article 5(3) offers a similar opportunity to airlines where compensation would otherwise be payable for flight cancellations, but only where the airline can demonstrate that 'extraordinary circumstances' led to the cancellation.

The compensation provisions in the Regulation are certain to impose costs on all airlines which were not previously accrued. The UK's Regulatory Impact Assessment (RIA) of the Regulation[89] suggests that the costs which are imposed by the Regulation vary according to the business model adopted by the airline concerned. For the traditional, 'full service'[90] carriers, it is possible that the Regulation will impose greater costs because they engage in the practice of overbooking and increased compensation will have to be paid to those denied boarding due to this reason. In addition, they will suffer extra costs due to the requirement that passengers be compensated for cancellations and offered care where long delays arise. Although the costs of this have not been calculated precisely, the UK RIA suggests that the cost will be the equivalent of £1 per one way ticket, if these costs were to be passed on to the consumer in their entirety.[91]

In the *IATA* case, discussed above, ELFAA suggested that the Regulation discriminated against low-fare carriers by imposing a greater burden on their activities than is imposed on the activities of full-fare airlines. It is difficult to determine whether or not this is the case, as the manner in which full-fare airlines operate tends to be different from the business model adopted by low-fare carriers. For example, low-fare airlines do not engage in the practice of overbooking, so they would incur only minimal costs from the provisions on denied boarding, although they would face the costs of compensation for cancelled flights, which the Department for Transport[92] estimate as being around €1 per one way flight.[93] It is far more difficult to ascertain the costs imposed by the duty to care for passengers who

---

88　See above, n. 22 and accompanying discussion for a detailed analysis of this provision.

89　Department for Transport (2005) *Final RIA on the Enforcement of Council Regulation 261/2004 in the UK* London: Department for Transport. Available at: http://www.dft. gov.uk/stellent/groups/dft_aviation/documents/pdf/dft_aviation_pdf_037808.pdf (last accessed 11 August 2006).

90　A definition adopted by M. Franke, 'Competition between Network Carriers and Low-Cost Carriers – Retreat Battle or Breakthrough to a New Level of Efficiency?', *Journal of Air Transport Management* 10 (2004): 15.

91　Department for Transport, above, n. 87, p. 14.

92　*Ibid.*

93　This would accord to around £0.67 on 11 August 2006.

are affected by long delays, as this is dependent on a variety of factors, including the availability of alternative flights to offer to passengers, and the 'load factor', or number of passengers as a percentage of the available seating capacity, of each flight. At the time of the Department for Transport RIA, no figures were available for the costs which might be imposed by this requirement. There are, of course, no defences to the obligation to provide care, meaning that this will be a definite cost imposed by the Regulation in all circumstances.

It may be that in certain cases, the low-fare airlines will feel a greater impact than full-fare airlines. The Department for Transport's RIA suggests that in some cases, the high 'load factors' of the low-cost airlines, combined with the low-profit margins on each flight, could lead to flights which are delayed resulting in significant losses for the airlines concerned. It is evident that low-cost airlines and full-fare airlines operate different business models.[94] Full-fare airlines tend to operate what is known as the 'hub and spoke' model – where one airport is operated as a base of the great majority of the airline's operations.[95] Under this business model, the approach is to offer services between a variety of destinations and the 'hub' airport. Some passengers will be travelling only from the point of origin to the 'hub', but many will be 'transit' passengers, transferring to another flight operated by either the same airline or another in order to reach a destination further on. These passengers are often transferring to a 'long haul' flight to a destination outside of the EU, where profitability is often stronger than on 'short haul' intra-European routes.[96] The 'full-fare' industry is also characterized by certain other factors, including high frequency

---

94   See Franke, 'Competition between Network Carriers and Low-Cost Carriers – Retreat
      Battle or Breakthrough to a New Level of Efficiency?', and N. Dennis, 'Changes to
      the Intra-EU Operations of Traditional Carriers', (2005) Paper given at the German
      Aviation Research Society Workshop, 21/22 November 2005, German Aerospace
      Centre (DLR), Cologne. Available at: http://www.garsonline.de/Downloads/051121/
      Dennis%20-%20Paper.pdf (last accessed 11 August 2006). We would like to thank Dr.
      Dennis for his permission to quote from this paper. See also R. Doganis, *The Airline
      Business*, 2nd edn, (London 2006): Ch. 6.
95   Examples include London Heathrow for British Airways, Amsterdam Schipol for
      KLM and Vienna International for Austrian Airlines.
96   Franke, 'Competition between Network Carriers and Low-Cost Carriers – Retreat
      Battle or Breakthrough to a New Level of Efficiency?', and R. Doganis, *Flying Off
      Course: The Economics of International Airlines*, 3rd edn (London, 2002): Ch. 5.

of flights,[97] load factors on each flight which are below those of low-cost operators[98] and the average aircraft utilisation per day is lower than for low-fare airlines.[99]

Low-fare airlines tend to offer a 'point-to-point' service, where they do not have one large base from which they operate the majority of their services. Instead, the network that they operate links two destinations directly, and there is little or no possibility of 'transit' at the destination airport.[100] In some cases, the flight frequency between the destinations tends to be lower,[101] and both load factors[102] and aircraft utilisation[103] tend to be higher than in the case of full-fare airlines.

The ECJ rejected these arguments in the *IATA* case, but did not really deal with ELFAA's arguments regarding the difference of its members when compared with full-fare airlines.[104] Although there are undoubtedly differences between the 'hub and spoke' and 'point-to-point' structures, there is some evidence that the distinction between the operations of the full-fare and low-cost carriers is disintegrating as full-fare carriers adapt their business model in order to reduce costs.[105] Given that this is the case, and the Department for Transport's RIA seems to suggest that the costs imposed on low-fare airlines are not significantly greater than on full-fare airlines

---

97   Dennis, 'Changes to the Intra-EU Operations of Traditional Carriers', s. 3.

98   According to the Association of European Airlines' figures (which account for many of the European full-fare airlines), the average passenger load factor for 2005 was 76 percent, whereas the passenger load factor for Ryanair in the same period was 84 percent and easyJet's was 85.2 percent. See Association of European Airlines (2006) *AEA Monthly Traffic Snapshot* Brussels: AEA. Available at: http://www.aea. be/AEAWebsite/Presentation_Tier/Pr_GroupMenuItem.aspx?NodeID=rootMenu403 (last accessed 11 August 2006), Ryanair Holdings Plc. (2005) *Annual Report and Accounts 2005* Dublin: Ryanair, p. 10 and easyJet plc., (2005) *Annual Report and Accounts 2005* Luton: easyJet plc., p. 8 respectively for the sources of this information. It is important to note that due to the different accounting period adopted by the companies, and the lack of monthly information on passenger load factors produced by low-fare airlines, that the period over which the average passenger load factor has been calculated will differ slightly. For an overview of the impact of these load factors on airline costs see Doganis, *The Airline Business*, p. 178.

99   Doganis, *The Airline Business*, pp. 170–71.

100   There is, of course, nothing to stop passengers from organising their own 'transit' from one low-fare airline flight to another, although this will involve the collection of luggage and checking in afresh at the intermediate airport.

101   Dennis, 'Changes to the Intra-EU Operations of Traditional Carriers'. Doganis argues that these lower frequencies are not always typical of the activities of low-fare airlines. See Doganis, *The Airline Business*, p. 168, where he suggests that frequency is equally important to the low-fare model.

102   See above, ns 96–97 and associated text.

103   See Doganis, *The Airline Business*, p. 170.

104   See IATA, above, n. 49, para. 94.

105   See Franke, 'Competition between Network Carriers and Low-Cost Carriers – Retreat Battle or Breakthrough to a New Level of Efficiency?', Dennis, 'Changes to the Intra-EU Operations of Traditional Carriers' and K.J. Mason, 'Observations of Fundamental Changes in the Demand for Aviation Services', *Journal of Air Transport Management* 11 (2005) 19.

(though the costs as a proportion of the fare might be greater), it may be that ELFAA's case was unfounded.

The second complaint raised by ELFAA suggested that the Regulation infringes the principle of equal treatment because it imposed costs on the airline industry which were not imposed on other means of transport, such as road and rail. Once again, the ECJ rejected these complaints relatively briefly,[106] without deep analysis. If we delve deeper into the Commission's competition law decisions in the field of air transport, we can see that economic research conducted by the Commission in previous cases concerning the aviation industry supports the ECJ's conclusion. In its decisions in *Air France/KLM*[107] and *AUA/Lufthansa*,[108] the Commission engaged in research on the potential for road or rail to offer an adequate substitute for air travel. It found that there were two markets for air travel – one was 'time sensitive' – travellers for whom time was of the essence, and who used air travel because of the time savings regardless of the price premium, and the other for those (often leisure travellers) whose journeys were not 'time sensitive', and who were more readily influenced by price differences. In the *AUA/Lufthansa* case, the Commission found that there were relatively few routes where rail or road travel would have been considered to be an acceptable substitute for 'time sensitive' passengers,[109] whereas there were some further routes where passengers who were not 'time sensitive' might consider rail or road travel to be an acceptable substitute, particularly if road or rail offered significant cost savings. The probability, however, is that for the vast majority of intra-EU travel, very few consumers would consider road or rail to be an adequate substitute for air travel, particularly where long distances are to be travelled.

The *Air France/KLM* decision appears to affirm the previous research in the *AUA/Lufthansa* decision. The only rail travel deemed to offer an effective substitute to air travel on the routes between Paris and Amsterdam is the high speed Thalys network, and this is only the case for those passengers who are not 'time sensitive'.[110] Given that this route operates over a specific high speed network, it seems most unlikely that most other rail services, with the possible exception of the Eurostar service between the South-East of England and Brussels and Paris, will be seen as adequate substitutes by the vast majority of passengers.

In addition to these observations, it is notable that the Commission is presently examining the scope for a Regulation similar to Regulation 261/2004 for the international rail transport industry.[111] This would place the two industries on an equal footing in terms of consumer protection, although the realities of the market for air transport render it unlikely that rail travel will offer a credible alternative for

---

106   *R (On the Application of the IATA and ELFAA)* v. *Department of Transport*, paras 93–99.

107   COMP/M.3280 *Air France/KLM*.

108   COMP/37.730 *AuA/Lufthansa* [2002] OJ L242/25.

109   *Ibid.*, Table 1.

110   *Air France/KLM*, above, n. 119, paras 69–76.

111   COM(2004) 143 *Proposal for a Regulation of the European Parliament and of the Council on International Rail Passengers' Rights and Obligations* Brussels: European Commission. Available at: http://www.europa.eu.int/comm/transport/rail/package2003/doc/com143-en.pdf (last accessed 11 August 2006).

many travellers, particularly where the intra-EU travel is over a long distance, or is undertaken for business purposes. In these circumstances, the low-cost airlines compete only with the full-fare airlines, though the distinction between these two business models, particularly on short haul European routes, is becoming increasingly blurred.

Under these circumstances, ELFAA's claims do not appear to be well grounded in economic analysis. There is no doubt that the Regulation imposes extra costs, but the RIA which was carried out by the Department for Transport does not suggest that these costs are borne disproportionately by low-cost airlines. In fact, some may argue that the low-cost airlines' networks extend only within Europe, and quite often only within the boundaries of the EU, so similar costs will be imposed on all players within this market, whereas full-fare airlines might face competition from players based overseas, who only face these costs on any leg of the journey which originates from an EU airport. As such, there is a risk that full-fare airlines might face costs which are not borne in their entirety by competitors on long haul routes. Insofar as costs are imposed by the Regulation, it seems that impact on the cost of tickets is relatively small, and will be borne equally by all low-cost carriers.

Some might argue that Regulation 261/2004 is a paternalistic device which ought not to have been promulgated. Prior to the coming into force of the Regulation, many airlines had Codes of Practice on compensation, and the Association of European Airlines, which represents many of the major European full-fare carriers, also adopted a Code of Practice which some of its members implemented.[112] In addition to these Codes of Practice, the Association also produces information about punctuality and reliability of its members' services from a number of major airports situated in the EU's Member States.[113] If the punctuality of services and recompense that might be offered for disruption to flight plans is particularly important to some consumers, it is arguable that there is adequate information available for them to make a choice over which carrier to use on these grounds. We do not have any data available which give an indication of the importance which air passengers accord to such information, but we might be dubious that significant numbers of passengers would discriminate between competing airlines on the basis of the information provided. In particular, the 'time sensitive' passengers that we identified above are most likely to choose the quickest means of travel between two airports, and non-time sensitive passengers are more likely to be concerned with price. ELFAA, the representative of low-fare airlines, does not appear to provide such information, perhaps as an acknowledgement that the provision of such information can often be costly.[114]

---

112   Association of European Airlines (2001) *European Airlines Make Commitment on Customer Service* Brussels: AEA. Available at: http://www.aea.be/AEAWebsite/datafiles/cust_svc_comm.pdf (last accessed 11 August 2006).

113   This date forms a part of the AEA's Consumer Report. This documentation is available at: http://www.aea.be/AEAWebsite/Presentation_Tier/Pr_GroupMenuItem.aspx?NodeID=rootMenu425 (last accessed 11 August 2006).

114   See A.I. Ogus, *Regulation: Legal Form and Economic Theory* (Oxford, 2004), (Reprinted Edition): pp. 38–41 and W.K. Viscusi, *et al., Economics of Regulation and Antitrust* 3rd edn, (Cambridge, Mass., 2002): pp. 755–57.

Viscusi *et al.,* make the point that 'If individuals differ in their tastes and the willingness to bear risks, then information provides consumers with the ability to make these market judgments and to choose the level of risk that is most efficient given their own preferences'.[115]

A regulatory approach based on provision of information is adopted in the USA, where there is a degree of legislative protection for those passengers who are denied boarding due to overbooking,[116] but all other matters, including delays and cancellations are not subject to any legal regulation. Instead, the Department of Transportation produces a monthly *Air Transport Consumer Report,*[117] which gives a detailed breakdown of the performance of each of the major airlines operating in the USA, combined with details of the number of complaints referred to the Department of Transportation for investigation in a number of predefined categories. These publications are accompanied by a website with advice for air passengers, informing them that it might be wise to check airlines' policies on this issue before booking, and also highlighting the fact that 'some airlines, often those charging very low fares, do not provide any amenities to stranded passengers'.[118] In all circumstances apart from where a passenger has been denied boarding, the approach taken in the USA is reliant on the provision of information to consumers rather than the creation of legal rights. This is in contrast to the position in Europe after the adoption of Regulation 261/2004. It is evident from the challenge to the Regulation in the *IATA* case that the airlines would have preferred the continuation of a regime based on informal Codes of Practice and the provision of information to be continued in the EU.

The difficulty with adopting an approach based on information and consumer choice is that there appears to be no guarantee that consumers will act rationally on the provision of such information,[119] even where they make sufficient endeavours to seek out such information. This situation is described by economists as one where consumers operate in a state of 'bounded rationality', that is that '… the capacity of individuals to receive, store and process information is limited'.[120] Furthermore, it is arguable that the provision of information by a government agency, or by an industry association, is often not well enough publicized to make a significant impact on consumers' decisions. While these are not decisive argument for adopting a form of mandated regulation setting out minimum standards, they do cast some doubt over the effectiveness of informational regulation in many situations.

It is evident, however, that Regulation 261/2004 was born out of a policy choice, rather than any persuasive economic evidence. This seems to be outlined by the

---

115   Viscusi *et al.,* p. 755.

116   See Title 14 of the Code of Federal Regulations (Air and Space Law), pt 250.

117   The reports can be found at: http://airconsumer.ost.dot.gov/reports/index.htm (last accessed 11 August 2006).

118   US Department of Transportation (no date) *Fly Rights: a Consumer Guide to Air Travel* Washington: Department of Transportation (Online) Available at: http://airconsumer. ost.dot.gov/publications/flyrights.htm#delayed (last accessed 11 August 2006).

119   See B.L. Lipman, 'Information Processing and Bounded Rationality: A Survey', *Canadian Journal of Economics* 28 (1995): 42 and P.E Earl and J. Potts, 'The Market for Preferences', *Cambridge Journal of Economics* 28 (2004): 619.

120   Ogus, *Regulation: Legal Form and Economic Theory,* p. 41.

Commission's Communication during the process of promulgation of the Regulation. In this document, it was argued that there were a number of reasons why enhanced consumer protection was necessary for the aviation industry:

> ... a passenger depends heavily on the efficiency and good will of the airline when things go wrong, for example when flights are delayed or cancelled and baggage lost or damaged. He or she will probably be unable to make other arrangements because of financial commitments already made, the difficulty of finding alternative flights or the sheer impracticality of using other forms of transport like the train or the car.[121]

The Commission also called on support from the EC Treaty, noting that Article 153 EC highlights consumer protection as an avowed goal of the Community. This position has been strengthened by the adoption of the EU's Charter of Fundamental Rights, where Article 38 appears to reinforce the Union's commitment to securing effective mechanisms for consumer protection. As we have noted above, it is possible to envisage a system of regulation based on information for consumers, rather than on legal obligation on the part of the airlines, but this approach was not followed. Ultimately, regulation such as that created by Regulation 261/2004 is the outcome of political choices, and, in this context, it seems to be agreed that a cost of around £1 per one way ticket is not excessive if it offers air passengers a greater degree of protection from disruption to their travel plans.

4. Interpretation of the Regulation – 'Reasonable Measures' and 'Extraordinary Circumstances'

We noted above that under Article 5 of the Regulation, airlines might offer a defence to the obligation to pay compensation for cancellation of a flight under the Regulation if 'extraordinary circumstances' arise, and airlines have taken 'reasonable measures' to avoid the cancellation. In such circumstances, no compensation will be payable to passengers who are affected by the cancellation. The inclusion of such a defence is logical. All air passengers are aware of the fact that in certain situations, particularly where weather conditions or air traffic control issues intervene, disruption to flights is inevitable and there is little that the airline companies can do to avoid this. A potential difficulty arises under the Regulation, as the precise scope of the extraordinary circumstances defence is never 'fleshed out'. Recitals 14 and 15 outline certain issues, in particular weather conditions, security risks, 'unexpected flight safety shortcomings', strikes and decisions made by air traffic controllers which lead to cancellations which are all considered to fall within the definition of 'extraordinary circumstances'. It is not clear whether the circumstances outlined in Recitals 14 and 15 of the Regulation characterize those where an absolute defence might be put forward to deny compensation, or whether these must be balanced with the measures which airlines have taken to avoid disruption in the event of such circumstances arising.

---

121   COM(2000) 365 above n. 17, p. 6.

For example, in the case of poor weather, strikes and decisions made by air traffic controllers, it would seem that there are no 'reasonable measures' which the airline could adopt to avoid disruption. If the weather in a particular area is unfit to allow the airline to carry on its ordinary operations, then its fleet is effectively grounded. Although the position in regard to industrial action is slightly less clear,[122] it is evident that if the airline's crews are unwilling to work, then it is impossible for it to operate its flights.[123] The same considerations would seem to apply to security risks, as the decision over whether a flight might be operated due to security concerns is usually outside the airline's control. As such, it seems that if airlines can raise any one of these defences, then it is likely that a claim for compensation can be denied.

The key focus of the discussion in this area appears to rest on how courts and regulators should interpret the requirement to take 'reasonable measures' to avoid disruption. It is possible to argue that any disruption, of whatever kind, could be treated as avoidable – in general, safety shortcomings will be caused either by defects with a particular aircraft, or by a crew shortage which leads to a flight being cancelled. If airlines are required to take measures in order to avoid such cancellations, it seems to be logical to argue that there should be a degree of overcapacity within their fleet and crew scheduling, in order to allow for backup if any such difficulty arises. If the 'reasonable measures' defence is frequently adopted by airlines a number of difficult interpretive questions might arise. We noted above[124] that there are distinct business models in the aviation industry. These differences might be considered in order to determine whether an airline took 'reasonable measures' in order to avoid disruption. As an example, does a full-fare airline's lower aircraft utilisation and higher concentration of activities in one 'hub' airport mean that the requirement that reserve aircraft are available to replace those with technical faults is more onerous than that which is incumbent on low-fare airlines?

Furthermore, is it reasonable for a complainant to argue that full-fare airlines should be expected to have a larger complement of reserve crew members to cover for staff illness, given the differences in the business model that these airlines operate? It seems that such arguments might be more difficult to sustain given the increasing convergence of business models, but it is evident that such disputes might still arise. It appears evident that full-fare airlines might be in a better position to avoid the

---

122 A particular issue to consider is whether all industrial action can be characterized as a 'strike' for the purposes of the Regulation. In most European states workers and their Trade Unions must fulfil a variety of legislatively mandated steps before a strike protected by law can be taken. There is no doubt, however, that the impact of industrial action such as that taken by British Airways' ground staff as a part of the dispute between Gate Gourmet and its workers had a significant impact on British Airways' ability to operate its services. At a purely legal level, however, there is no doubt that this industrial action did not constitute a legally protected strike for the purposes of Section 238A of the Trade Union and Labour Relations (Consolidation) Act 1992.

123 It is notable that there are no defences available to airlines for the obligation to provide care and assistance found in Article 9 of Regulation 261/2004. As a result, airlines which are unable to operate services in a sustained period of industrial action will face considerable costs for the care of those passengers who are stranded.

124 See above, ns 93–101 and associated text.

expense imposed by the obligation to provide care, such as refreshments and hotel accommodation, by virtue of their higher flight frequencies and lower passenger load factors. These observations are, at least at present, all based in hypothetical situations, as there are few cases which offer any concrete guidance on the precise scope of the 'reasonable measures' defence.

What is clear, however, is that the potential for airlines to raise the arguments outlined above does little to aid certainty in the application of the Regulation. There is a risk that an expansive interpretation of 'extraordinary circumstances', combined with the potential for dispute over whether airlines have taken reasonable measures, will act to deny compensation in many cases. It is evident that there was a need to provide the potential for airlines to deny certain claims for compensation which were truly unavoidable, but the current wording of the provisions leaves scope for considerable uncertainty over the extent to which airlines can claim that they took 'reasonable measures' to avoid cancellations or delays. Such uncertainty seems likely to be exacerbated by the differences in business models and practices adopted by airlines. These differences are most readily demonstrated by the differing business models operated by full-fare and low-fare airlines.

These issues seem to bear heavily upon the consumer's ability to gain the compensation provided for in the Regulation. From this perspective, the ability of the consumer to make a claim for compensation, and the ease and effectiveness of the mechanisms provided for claiming such redress, will be crucial. It is to this issue that we now turn.

5. Rights without Remedies? Enforcement of Rights under the Regulation

(i) Enforcement by the Regulator – Is the UK's Approach Effective?

The enforcement of the rights enshrined in the Air Passenger Rights Regulation is unusual, in the sense that it might come from two sources. First, the European legislators chose to enact the legislation as a Regulation, which is directly applicable in national law under Article 249 of the EC Treaty. As such, passengers who are in dispute with airlines are free to bring a legal action directly in the courts of a Member State in order to claim the refunds and compensation to which they believe that they are entitled. In addition to this 'self-enforcement', a system of monitoring and enforcement by a state regulator is also provided for in Article 16(1), which states that:

> Each Member State shall designate a body responsible for the enforcement of this Regulation as regards flights from airports situated on its territory and flights from a third country to such airports. Where appropriate, this body shall take the measures necessary

to ensure that the rights of passengers are respected. The Member States shall inform the Commission of the body that has been designated in accordance with this paragraph.

Article 16(2) then moves on to create a mechanism for dealing with passenger complaints, where passengers may complain either to the body designated under Article 16(1) or an alternative body designated by a Member State. Finally, Article 16(3) provides that any sanction for infringements of the Regulation must be 'effective, proportionate and dissuasive'. This creation of a two-pronged method of challenge for passengers who believe that they have been wrongly denied the rights contained in the Regulation is quite different from the scope of the previous Regulation which did not provide for any particular means of redress, thus leaving passengers wishing to receive compensation with only one option – that of pursuing an airline in court. The shortcomings of this method seem to be acknowledged by the UK's Air Transport User's Council in its response to the consultation on the promulgation of the EC's Draft Regulation on Enforcement of Consumer Protection,[125] when it noted that 'Individual UK consumers already have access to the courts under Small Claims procedures. The process nevertheless discourages many complainants from seeking resolution in the courts'.[126]

The inclusion of Article 16 in the Regulation seems to reflect a desire on the part of the EU legislators to ensure redress for passengers without the need for recourse to formal legal action. This view is reinforced by the Commission's Press Release on the day when the Regulation came into force, where it was stated that 'The new Regulation … requires each State to set up an independent body responsible for dealing with passengers' complaints and any disputes they may have with airlines, which will help to avoid long and expensive court cases'.[127] The approach adopted in the Regulation seems to be a logical one, particularly given that the volume of complaints is likely to be high, and that the subject matter of each complaint will be relatively similar. The realities of the implementation of Article 16 do not, however, inspire confidence in the system. Member States have adopted differing approaches to the implementation of the provisions, and the likelihood of the authority designated under Article 16 achieving redress for the consumer may vary significantly.

Redress through the courts, while always possible, is more attractive in some states than in others. In England and Wales, it is relatively simple for a small claim, such as the ones which will arise under Regulation 261/2004 to be brought, and the costs imposed on a claimant are relatively small. Even though this is the case, the relatively small amount of money at stake in many cases, combined with the uncertainties thrown up by the 'extraordinary circumstances' defence in compensation

---

125   This provision has now been adopted as Regulation 2006/2004 of the European Parliament and of the Council of 27 October 2004 on Co-operation Between National Authorities Responsible for the Enforcement of Consumer Protection Laws [2004] OJ L364/1.

126   Air Transport User's Council (2003) *DTI Consultation on Draft EC Regulation on Consumer Protection Co-operation* London: AUC, p. 2. Available at: http://www.caa.co.uk/docs/306/Consumer%20Protection%20Cooperation.pdf (last accessed 11 August 2006).

127   European Commission Press Release IP/05/181 above, n. 2.

claims will make the pursuit of an airline in the courts unattractive other than for the most tenacious claimant. It is clear that even if an aggrieved consumer takes the step of pursuing an airline in the County Court under the small claims procedure,[128] there is little certainty of outcome due to the lack of binding precedent at the present time.

The alternative route for grievance redress lies in recourse to the regulator nominated in Article 16 of the Regulation. In the case of the UK, this obligation is split, with the Civil Aviation Authority[129] acting as the enforcement body for the purposes of Article 16(1), and the Air Transport User's Council[130] acting as the body to which consumers might make a complaint regarding a breach of the Regulation. The AUC is a non-statutory body, with no enforcement powers of its own, and acts primarily as a mediator between the consumers and the airline which is subject of the complaint. In its most recent Annual Report, the AUC states that 'We were content with the Government's division of responsibilities as proposed in the consultation paper as we considered that the AUC and CAA were best placed to receive individual complaints and enforce the Regulation respectively'.[131]

The relationship between the AUC and the CAA in relation to the issue of enforcement seems to be rather unclear. The AUC has not made it clear how many complaints it must receive before it refers an airline to the CAA for enforcement, and there are no figures available at the present time which give information about the number of referrals made to the CAA for enforcement, or the number of actions brought by the CAA in order to enforce compliance with the Regulation. There is, in fact, little information about the approach of the AUC and the CAA to the enforcement of the Regulation – although a Memorandum of Understanding[132] between the CAA and the Department for Transport gives a hint of the approach that might be taken in cases of breach. The scheme of the UK complaints system is made clear by paragraph 2 of the MoU, which states:

> Once the Regulation enters force, the AUC will be responsible for dealing with all initial complaints from dissatisfied passengers. Where the AUC is unable to secure a satisfactory resolution to a passenger's complaint or identifies a trend of apparent non-compliance by an airline, the matter will be referred to the CAA to consider further action.

Due to its non-statutory nature, the only means available to the AUC to facilitate a resolution of a breach of the Regulation is to write to the airline concerned on

---

128   The small claims procedure or 'Small Claims Track' in the courts of England and Wales is governed by Part 27 of the Civil Procedure Rules.

129   Hereafter, 'CAA'.

130   Hereafter, 'AUC'.

131   Air Transport User's Committee (2005) *Annual Report 2004 – 2005* London: AUC, p. 12. Available at: http://www.caa.co.uk/docs/306/AUC%20report%20for%20web.pdf (last accessed 11 August 2006).

132   Civil Aviation Authority (2005) *Memorandum of Understanding between the Department for Transport and the Civil Aviation Authority* London: CAA. Available at: http://www.caa.co.uk/docs/148/DBC%20MOU%20-%2016%20February%202005.pdf (last accessed 11 August 2006) [hereafter 'MoU'].

behalf of the passenger. At this stage the airline concerned will not be referred to the CAA for enforcement action, and it seems to rest with the aggrieved passenger to write to the AUC once again if the initial contact between the AUC and the airline is unsuccessful. It is unclear what approach will be adopted by the AUC at this point – will it write to the airline once again, or consider making a referral to the CAA? Whatever approach the AUC decides to take, it seems obvious that the airline concerned will have to be given the opportunity to respond and this is likely to extend the process over some months. Once a reference is made to the CAA, either in an individual case where the AUC considers there to be a breach, or where there is evidence of a sustained pattern of non-compliance, then paragraphs 3 and 4 of the MoU set out the CAA's approach: in the first place to negotiate with the airline concerned in order to achieve compliance, and if this fails, to consider a prosecution in accordance with the provisions of the UK's implementing legislation.[133] The maximum penalty which might be imposed if the court convicts an airline is a fine not exceeding Level 5 on the Standard Scale.[134]

An examination of the legislation which empowers the CAA to enforce the Regulation, along with the Memorandum of Understanding between the Department for Transport and the CAA suggest that the enforcement measures are not always likely to be successful. In Ayers and Braithwaite's seminal work on regulation[135] they argue that regulators should act as 'benign big guns' – that is:

> ... regulatory agencies are often best able to secure compliance when they are benign big guns. That is, regulators will be more able to speak softly when they carry big sticks (and crucially, a hierarchy of lesser sanctions). Paradoxically, the bigger and the more various are the sticks, the greater the success regulators will achieve by speaking softly.[136]

It is evident from the MoU that the intention of the CAA is to deal with most cases in negotiation with the airlines, rather than pursuing prosecutions. When it is necessary for the CAA to invoke its power of sanction, it is notable that a prosecution will lead to what is a relatively small fine for a large airline. In its RIA which accompanied the enactment of the Regulations, the Department of Transport considered that the adoption of administrative sanctions, such as the suspension or revocation of the airline's operating licence would be '... wholly disproportionate to the "offence" of failure to comply with one of the provisions of the Council Regulation'.[137] It may be, however, that in order to combat sustained non-compliance, the availability of a more radical sanction than a prosecution which may lead to a fine could have been

---

133 The CAA's powers in this respect were enacted by The Civil Aviation (Denied Boarding, Compensation and Assistance) Regulations 2005, S.I. 2005/975 [hereafter 'the Regulations'].

134 At the present time, Level 5 on the Standard Scale is £5000. The scales are to be found in s. 37 of the Criminal Justice Act 1982, as amended by s. 17(2) of the Criminal Justice Act 1991.

135 I. Ayers and J. Braithwaite, *Responsive Regulation: Transcending the Deregulation Debate,* (Oxford, 1992).

136 *Ibid.,* at p. 19.

137 Department for Transport, above, n. 87, p. 5.

a useful tool in the CAA's armoury of enforcement measures. It is true to say that a suspension or revocation of the airline's operating licence would constitute an extreme step for the regulator, but in the case of continued failure to comply with the terms of the Regulation, the potential to invoke such a measure may ensure future compliance with the requirements of the Regulation. As it presently stands, though the CAA is technically in a position to bring a separate prosecution for each infringement of the Regulation, this seems unlikely from the position adopted in the MoU.

Even if the Department for Transport did not wish to adopt administrative penalties such as the potential to suspend or revoke the airline's operating licence, it may have been possible to adopt a system of penalties which gave greater protection to passenger's rights and ensure a greater likelihood of redress for those complaining to the regulator. The Republic of Ireland's implementing legislation serves as an example.[138] This legislation nominates the Commission for Aviation Regulation as the body to receive complaints from passengers. Under this model, there is no separation between the body which deals with complaints, and the body with enforcement powers. The Irish legislation is interesting because it appears to give the Commission for Aviation Regulation greater powers and potential to ask the courts for assistance than is the case for the CAA in the UK. In particular, paragraph 4 states:

> Where the Regulator considers either on its own initiative, or following a complaint from a passenger that an operating air carrier is infringing the Parliament and Council Regulation, it may issue to the carrier a direction to cease the infringement and to comply with any instructions contained in the direction.

Where the airline fails to comply with the direction given by the regulator[139] then paragraph 5 gives the court a number of options:

> Where an operating air carrier to whom a direction has been issued does not comply, or has failed to comply, with the direction, the Regulator may, not earlier than one month after considering any representations and having replied to them, apply to the appropriate court for an order directing such compliance. The court may make such order as it sees fit.[140]

---

138   Irish S.I. 274/2005 – The European Communities (Compensation and Assistance to Air Passengers) (Denied Boarding, Cancellation or Long Delay of Flights) Regulation 2005.

139   It is notable that para. 4 gives the airline concerned the opportunity to make representations to the regulator, and for the direction to be modified or rescinded after these representations have been made.

140   Paragraph 6 of the legislation offers the court an opportunity to impose a fine on the airline. Where cases are heard in the District Court (and the vast majority would be under the terms of para. 2 of the legislation), the fine is not to exceed €6,348.69. See: http://oasis.gov.ie/justice/courts/district_court_civil_juris.html (last accessed 11 August 2006).

This approach offers greater flexibility than the measures adopted in the UK. In particular, it appears that the Commission for Aviation Regulation is able to offer complainants a degree of redress from the airline concerned, as it might order compensation to be paid, or refunds to be given which could then be enforced through the seeking of a court order. In the UK, the CAA is unable to offer such a guarantee. Though it seems most likely that an airline which has been fined for non-compliance would then offer redress to the passengers who were the source of the original complaint,[141] the only way to ensure that compensation or refunds are received in the UK is for a passenger to take action in the County Court under the small claims procedure and receive judgment in their favour.

Of course, though the Irish solution seems to offer a more satisfactory route for the redress of complaints by the regulator, the only proof of this will be demonstrated by the successful operation of the complaints system. For the present time, a search does not reveal any case brought by the regulator under these provisions, and there are no reports from the regulator on the operation of the Irish system, so we cannot be sure that the system is operating any more effectively than that in the UK. Nevertheless, an inspection of the Irish provisions suggests that the system which has been implemented is closer to that envisaged by the Commission when the Regulation was promulgated.

(ii) Enforcement by the Courts

In the UK, passengers seeking to enforce their rights under Regulation 261/2004 may still have no realistic alternative other than to resort to legal action. While the Regulation requires the enforcement bodies to apply 'effective, proportionate and dissuasive' sanctions[142] against non-compliant airlines, the reality presents a different picture. The CAA (the body set up to enforce the Regulation in UK) has so far brought no action against non-compliant airlines and has adopted instead a 'light touch' regulatory approach.[143]

In the presence of a weak enforcement body, consumers whose rights under the Regulation have been breached are drawn into taking the matters in their own hands. In February 2006, David Harbord brought a successful claim in the Oxford County Court against Thomas Cook, for the failure of the airline to compensate him for the cancellation of a flight from Stansted to Vancouver.[144] Thomas Cook initially argued

---

141   This may, however, not be the case. According to the MoU between the CAA and the AUC, it is most likely that action will only be taken where there is evidence of a repeated pattern of non-compliance. In cases where there are many complaints, it may not be practicable for the airline to revisit each case and offer each passenger redress accordingly.

142   Article 16(3), Regulation 261/2004.

143   B. Webster, 'How passengers beat airlines over cancelled flight', *The Times*, 2 February 2006. Available at: http://www.timesonline.co.uk/article/0,,2-2020733,00.html (last accessed 11 August 2006).

144   *David Harbord* v. *Thomas Cook Airlines and Another*, Case 5QZ54903, 30 January 2006, Oxford County Court (unreported) [hereafter *Harbord*].

that the flight was not cancelled but merely delayed for twenty-four hours.[145] The airline stated that passengers were offered a flight from Manchester to Vancouver, which had the same flight number as the original flight, and that passengers were offered transportation from Stansted to Manchester.[146] The distinction between a delay and a cancellation is crucial, as Regulation 261/2004 makes no provision for the payment of compensation in the event of long delays. Yet, the Regulation provides no assistance on how to distinguish between a long delay and a cancellation. In rejecting the arguments put forward by Thomas Cook, Judge Jenkins indicated that the transfer of a flight from the south-east to the north-west of the country, as well as the twenty-four hour difference between the original time of departure and the actual flight, were more indicative of a cancellation rather than a delay.[147]

In the event the flight was classified as a 'cancellation', Thomas Cook argued that no compensation should be payable to the claimant, as the cancellation was due to 'extraordinary circumstances'.[148] The airline attempted to rely on Recital 14 of the Regulation, which defines such circumstances to include 'unexpected flight safety shortcomings'. The technical failure that ultimately led to the cancellation of the flight had occurred only three times before.[149] In addition, Thomas Cook argued that it should not be expected to keep a backup aircraft for such occurrences, as it was 'uneconomic' to do so.[150] Yet, the aircraft affected by the technical problem was not the particular aircraft allocated for Mr. Harbord's flight, but merely an aircraft out of the defendant's fleet.[151] The court found this to be too imprecise and preferred to adopt a more restrictive interpretation of Recital 14 applicable only to the particular aircraft allocated to the claimant's flight. Judge Jenkins found the narrow interpretation of the 'extraordinary circumstances' defence to be in compliance with the general objective of the Regulation to protect the interest of consumers.[152]

A similarly successful claim had been brought a month earlier in the Carmarthen County Court against easyJet, following the cancellation of a flight from Rome to Bristol.[153] These claims brought by consumers under the small claims procedure ensure justice on a case by case basis. So far, litigation has been limited to the County Court level, from which an Article 234 reference, which could bring about important clarifications, is unlikely to materialize. For future passengers affected by cancellations, the ambiguity regarding the interpretation of the 'extraordinary circumstances' defence still persists. In a climate where airline groups advise their members to 'make their own judgement' when interpreting ambiguous provisions

---

145   *Ibid.*, para. 1.

146   *Ibid.*, para. 2.

147   *Ibid.*, para. 4.

148   *Ibid.*, para. 1.

149   *Ibid.*, para. 3.

150   *Ibid.*, para. 5.

151   *Ibid.*

152   *Ibid.*, para. 6.

153   M. Brignall, 'New hopes for air passengers as the grounded fly high in court'. *The Guardian* 4 February 2006, referring to the successful claim brought against easyJet by Philip Adams and Sylvia Duffy. Available at: http://money.guardian.co.uk/travel/money/story/0,,1701667,00.html (last accessed 11 August 2006).

of the Regulation,[154] it is very likely that the 'extraordinary circumstances' clause will be at the centre of many more disputes. It is, however, disappointing that the new regulatory framework under Regulation 261/2004 failed to meet one of its key objectives: that of limiting the need for consumers to resort to individual litigation.[155]

The interpretation of the 'extraordinary circumstances' clause has featured highly on the agenda of the European Commission's meeting with National Enforcement Bodies in April 2006. As the Commission acknowledged:

> The notion of 'extraordinary circumstances' ... is often used by carriers when flights are disrupted. The existence of such circumstances can only be judged on a case by case basis by National Enforcement Bodies. While the right to a safe flight prevails in all circumstances, the notion of 'extraordinary circumstances' should not be used as a pretext for diminishing consumer protection.[156]

One potential difficulty for consumers seeking to enforce their rights is to find out the actual reason for the cancellation, as airlines could be tempted to justify cancellations with reasons that are likely to exonerate them from paying compensation.[157] Unless the Regulation makes provisions for increased transparency in the form of a duty on the airlines to disclose to the enforcement body the reason for each cancellation, consumers are likely to be left vulnerable, and the grounds on which to take legal action are likely to be rather uncertain.

6. Conclusion

This article has analysed the provisions of Regulation 261/2004 as they apply to operators of scheduled flights, be they 'full-fare' or 'low-cost'. In doing so, we have suggested that there is a risk that the Regulation, combined with the process of implementation in the UK, creates a range of rights without providing for effective remedies. In particular, the Regulation itself is vague on issues such as what will constitute 'extraordinary circumstances' determining when compensation will not be paid. Furthermore, though Article 16 of the Regulation appears to envisage that passengers should be able to seek redress without the need to go to court, the UK's method of implementation appears to place the greatest focus on the small claims procedure as the means for passengers to seek redress.

As we have noted above, placing the onus on passengers to seek compensation through legal action is likely to reduce the effectiveness of the Regulation. In reality,

---

154   ERA Press Release 06/04/2005 above, n. 81, p. 3.
155   European Commission (2005) 'The EU strengthens Air Travellers' Rights' 17 February 2005. Video available at: http://ec.europa.eu/comm/transport/air/index_en.htm (last accessed 11 August 2006).
156   European Commission Press Release IP/06/177, 16/02/2006. Available at: http://europa.eu.int/rapid/pressReleasesAction.do?reference=IP/06/177&format=HTML&aged=0&language=EN&guiLanguage=en (last accessed 11 August 2006).
157   Brignall, 'New hopes for air passengers as the grounded fly high in court'.

the sums involved are relatively small in the majority of cases, and the viability of a claim for compensation is made most uncertain by the vagaries of the 'extraordinary circumstances' test contained in the Regulation. Under these circumstances, it appears unlikely that large numbers of passengers who are denied compensation will actually pursue the airline concerned in court, which frustrates the intention of the Commission when it put the Regulation forward. Although there is little evidence available at present to indicate that the approach adopted in the Republic of Ireland has operated to secure passengers' rights more effectively, the actual method of implementation appears to be closer to the original intent of the Community legislator. As such, the system of enforcement in the UK is in need of reform in order to ensure that passengers are able to enforce any redress to which they may be entitled.

Some provisions of Regulation 261/2004 are also open to criticism. In particular, we have placed focus upon the difficulties caused by the 'extraordinary circumstances' defence provided for in Article 5(3) of the Regulation, which offers a very broad opportunity to airlines wishing to avoid the payment of compensation for cancelled flights. It is possible to argue that one means to ensure more effective operation of the Regulation would be to see that it is amended to include an Annex, indicating the circumstances that could/could not be considered to be 'extraordinary' for the purposes of the Regulation.[158] While an exhaustive list of such circumstances would be unfeasible and undesirable (due to the need to preserve a certain degree of flexibility), the inclusion of this Annex would be beneficial in clarifying the potential classification of cancellations caused by technical difficulties. Although this approach might be regarded as somewhat eccentric by some, particularly as it may be difficult to enumerate what circumstances cannot constitute 'extraordinary circumstances', given that cases brought in the County Court under the small claims procedure do not create precedent, and the AUC do not publish their decisions in the cases which are referred to them by consumers, it is difficult to see how else greater certainty can be injected into the process. Furthermore, the adoption of such an Annex would ensure a more uniform application of the Regulation throughout Europe, rather than each regulator or court in each Member State adopting a differing interpretation of 'extraordinary circumstances'.

Without some of these changes, it seems likely that the Regulation will not live up to its initial promise. At present, many passengers in the UK are likely to be deterred by the need to take action in the County Court in order to secure the compensation due, and the uncertain interpretation of the 'extraordinary circumstances' defence make the enforcement of such rights excessively difficult in the majority of cases.

---

158   This could be akin to the Annexes of 'blacklisted' and 'greylisted' terms to be found in Directive 93/13/EEC of 5 April 1993 on Unfair Terms in Consumer Contracts [1993] OJ L95/29.

8   European Passenger Law for Sea and Inland Waterway Transport

Jens Karsten[1]

1. Introduction

The rise of passenger law Regulations in EC transport law is one of the most dynamic consumer policy developments in recent years. This process has gathered momentum in 2007 with the adoption of a Railway Passenger Regulation – thereby leaving the confines of air transport law – and with the further pursuance of parallel passenger initiatives for other modes of transport and their inter-modal use. Of these other projects, the pending proposal for a maritime and fluvial passenger Regulation is a very significant one, not least because of its contribution to the growth of European private law, including private international law. Different from transport literature, consumer law writing has tended to neglect this area, and this paper shall attempt to start to fill this gap by looking at the different layers of regulation (international, nascent European and, in two examples, national) for passengers boarding vessels. It concludes with an overview of private international law and passenger rights.

2. The Aircraft Has Landed: The Advent of Non-Aviation Passenger Regulations

As it stands in the EU statute book in 2006, European passenger law looks like a section of air transport law. The relevant convention and Regulations according to this survey tally ten key pieces of legislation: the Montreal Convention,[2] the Computer Reservation Systems (CRS) Regulation[3] (partly also applicable on rail), the Denied Boarding Regulation,[4] the Air Carrier Liability Regulation,[5] the Air Carrier Insurance

---

1   LL.B. (Frankfurt am Main 1994), LL.M. in European Law (University of Nottingham 1996), German Bar Exam (Wiesbaden 1999).

2   Convention for the Unification of Certain Rules for International Carriage by Air of 28 May 1999 (OJ L194, 18 July 2001, p. 39).

3   Regulation (EEC) No. 2299/89 on a code of conduct for computerised reservation systems (OJ L220, 29 July 1989, p. 1), as amended by Regulation (EEC) No. 3089/93 (OJ L278, 11 November 1993, p. 1) and Regulation (EC) No. 323/1999 (OJ L40, 13 February 1999, p. 1).

4   Regulation (EC) No. 261/2004 establishing common rules on the compensation and assistance to passengers in the event of denied boarding and of cancellation or long delay of flights, and repealing Regulation (EEC) No. 295/91 (OJ L46, 17 February 2004, p. 1).

5   Regulation (EC) No. 2027/97 on air carrier liability in the event of accidents (OJ L285,

Regulation,[6] the Air Fares Regulation[7] and its proposed recast,[8] the Aviation Blacklist Regulation,[9] the Persons with Reduced Mobility in Air Transport Regulation[10] and the new Block Exemption,[11] based on the Air Transport Competition Regulation.[12]

In 2007, this focus on aviation will change, as this paper attempts to demonstrate. Most importantly, it will see the adoption of the Regulation on International Rail Passengers' Rights and Obligations. The Regulation notably imposes rules on passenger information as well as assistance to persons with reduced mobility (PRM) and incorporates international transport law (CIV 1999[13]) in the *acquis*

---

17 October 1997, p. 1), as amended by Regulation (EC) No. 889/2002 (OJ L140, 30 May 2002, p. 2).

6   Regulation (EC) No. 785/2004 on insurance requirements for air carriers and aircraft operators (OJ L138, 30 April 2004, p. 1).

7   Regulation (EEC) No. 2409/92 on fares and rates for air services (OJ L240, 24 August 1992, p. 15).

8   Proposal for a Regulation on common rules for the operation of air transport services in the Community [recast] (COM(2006) 396 final of 18 July 2006. See also Commission press release IP/06/1010 of 18 July 2006 'More competition and better quality: European Commission wants to strengthen the Single Market for Aviation' and MEMO/06/294 of the same day 'Proposed Regulation of the European Parliament and the Council on common rules for air services in the European Union'.

9   Regulation (EC) No. 2111/2005 on the establishment of a Community list of air carriers subject to an operating ban within the Community and on informing air transport passengers of the identity of the operating air carrier, and repealing Article 9 of Directive 2004/36/EC (OJ L344, 27 December 2005, p. 15); Corrigenda (OJ L186, 7 July 2006, p. 60 and OJ L189, 12 July 2006, p. 27).

10   Regulation (EC) No. 1107/2006 concerning the rights of disabled persons and persons with reduced mobility when travelling by air (OJ L204, 26 July 2006, p. 1).

11   Commission Regulation (EC) No. 1459/2006 on the application of Article 81(3) of the Treaty to certain categories of agreements and concerted practices concerning consultations on passenger tariffs on scheduled air services and slot allocation at airports (OJ L272, 3 October 2006, p. 3).

12   Council Regulation (EEC) No. 3976/87 on the application of Article 85(3) of the Treaty to certain categories of agreements and concerted practices in the air transport sector (OJ L374, 31 December 1987, p. 9), as last amended by Regulation (EC) No. 411/2004 (OJ L68, 6 March 2004, p. 1).

13   The *Convention relative aux transports internationaux ferroviaires* (COTIF or Berne Convention concerning International Carriage by Rail of 9 May 1980, amended by the Vilnius Protocol of 3 June 1999) includes in its Appendix A 'Uniform Rules concerning the Contract for International Carriage of Passengers and Luggage by Rail'. This 'CIV 1999' entered into force 1 July 2006. Ratified by Austria, Belgium, Bulgaria, Czech Republic, Denmark, Finland, France, Germany, Hungary, Latvia, Lithuania, Luxembourg, The Netherlands, Poland, Portugal, Romania, Slovakia, Slovenia, Spain and the United Kingdom. Greece applies the CIV 1999 without having ratified it (Source: OTIF, http://www.otif.org).

communautaire. Proposed as part of the Third Railway Package[14] in 2004,[15] it has reached the stage of its Second Reading, with a Common Position adopted in 2006[16] and is close to adoption after a conciliation agreement reached in June 2007.[17] The Railway Passenger Regulation is set to become the first non-air law component in its own right in the body of Community passenger law.

But the year in which this Yearbook is published will also witness EC lawmakers embarking on legislation for the protection of maritime and fluvial passengers. In this case too, the incorporation of an international transport convention requires the European regulator to reflect on what should and could be done for the passenger boarding a ship in Europe. Community law is therefore set to reach beyond safety regulation and competition policy in maritime passenger transport and to endorse a liability regime that will – like almost all of the proliferating passenger Regulations – substantially add to the body of European private law. Consumer lawyers should do their share of thinking too, as they otherwise risk missing out on the emergence of the novel concept of an inter-modal 'EC passenger law' as an entire new and fairly independent segment of consumer legislation.[18] So while it is somewhat unusual for a Yearbook to speculate on *de lege ferenda* rules in the regulator's pipeline (although international law provides *de lege lata* for a sufficiently elaborated scaffolding), it is timely to fill the current void in consumer academic writing on the consumer dimension of maritime and fluvial passenger law. Because when the aircraft lands (or the seaplane waters), it should have a cushioned landing.

This chapter serves as an introduction to (1) the EC law on passenger safety in sea transport, (2) the Athens Convention as amended and (3) the proposed Regulation aiming to incorporate the convention (and to do something more for the passenger). It also provides (4) a review of other projects currently being prepared to strengthen the protection of rights of passengers travelling by sea or inland waterway in the EU. It finally (5) provides an overview over EC private international law in relation to passenger law. With a view to this year's EU presidencies of Germany and Portugal, references to national law are limited to these countries that incidentally present unique, if far from perfect, concepts for maritime passenger protection. As an initiation for consumer lawyers, the paper intends to highlight the necessity of

---

14 Commission press release IP/04/291 of 3 March 2004 'With a quality European railway system the aim, the Commission is proposing the opening up of the market for international passenger services in 2010'.

15 COM(2004) 143 final of 3 March 2004.

16 Common Position adopted by the Council with a view to the adoption of a Regulation on international rail passengers' rights and obligations of 24 July 2006 (OJ C289E, 28 November 2006, p. 1).

17 European Parliament press release 'Parliament and Council reach agreement on third rail package' of 21 June 2007. Compare also para. 54 of the 18-months Programme of the German, Portuguese and Slovenian Presidencies of 21 December 2006 that vows to bring the proposal to a conclusion.

18 J. Karsten, 'Passengers, Consumers, and Travellers: The Rise of Passenger Rights in EC Transport Law and its Repercussions for Community Consumer Law and Policy', *Journal of Consumer Policy*, 2, (2007): 117–136.

observing the advent of passenger Regulations, typified here by maritime and fluvial passenger protection.

3. Passenger Safety in Sea Transport

A major incentive for tackling, above all, passenger safety at sea by means of EC transport legislation was the sinking of the ferryboat *Estonia* in 1994, which caused the death of 852 people. The number of casualties makes this single incident Europe's worse transport disaster. While the 1996 Stockholm Agreement,[19] concluded in direct response to this tragedy, remained an instrument of regional, northern European cooperation,[20] the Community was almost as quick (and sometimes quicker) to adopt measures for the improvement of safety conditions on board passenger ships, thereby adding to the existing framework established by SOLAS,[21] SAR[22] and other instruments of international maritime law.[23] Regulation (EC) No. 3051/95 on the safety management of roll-on/roll-off (ro-ro) passenger ferries,[24] Directive 98/18/EC on safety rules and standards for passengers ships,[25] Directive 98/41/EC on the registration of persons sailing on board passenger ships operating to or from ports of the Member States of the Community,[26] Directive 1999/35/EC on a system of mandatory surveys for the safe operation of regular ro-ro ferry and high-speed passenger craft services,[27] and Directive 2003/25/EC on specific stability requirements for ro-ro passenger ships[28] are all expressions of a firm commitment to make maritime passenger transport safe. Declarations of political intent may date

---

19 Stockholm Agreement Concerning Specific Stability Requirements for Ro-Ro Passenger Ships undertaking Regular Scheduled International Voyages Between or to or from Designated Ports in Northwest Europe and the Baltic Sea of 28 February 1996.

20 Denmark, Finland, Germany, Ireland, the Netherlands, Norway, Sweden and the United Kingdom are signatory States; all but Norway are EU members.

21 International Convention for the Safety of Life at Sea of 1974.

22 International Convention on Maritime Search and Rescue of 1979.

23 Announced in the Council Resolution on the safety of roll-on/roll-off passenger ferries of 22 December 1994 (OJ C379 31 December 1994, p. 8). IMO Briefing 47/2006 of 27 November 2006 'New passenger ship safety standards set for adoption at IMO's Maritime Safety Committee'.

24 OJ L320, 30 December 1995, p. 14. Amended by Regulation (EC) No. 179/98 (OJ L19, 24 January 1998, p. 35), Regulation (EC) No. 1970/2002 (OJ L302, 6 November 2002) and Regulation (EC) No. 2099/2002 (OJ L324, 29 November 2002, p. 1).

25 OJ L144, 15 May 1998, p. 1. Amended by Directive 2003/24/EC (OJ L123, 17 May 2003, p. 18) and Directive 2003/75/EC (OJ L190, 30 July 2003, p. 6).

26 OJ L188, 2 July 1998, p. 35.

27 OJ L138, 1 June 1999, p. 1. See also Commission Decision of 5 August 2003 on compliance of the fire-extinguishing system used on the ro-ro ferry 'Finnsailor' (IMO No. 8401444) with Council Directive 1999/35/EC (OJ L198, 6 August 2003, p. 17).

28 OJ L123, 17 May 2003, p. 22, amended by Directive 2005/12/EC (OJ L48, 19 February 2005, p. 19).

back earlier[29] but the *Estonia* disaster, together with the sinking of the *Herald of Free Enterprise* in 1987 and the *Express Samina* in 2000, made and still make a powerful case for tough EC measures.

4. The Athens Convention

Compared to this avalanche of European safety regulation, establishing a (private law) liability regime for passengers is a slow process. Setting up an international framework on passenger rights in sea transport was first attempted in the 1960s. The International Convention for the Unification of Certain Rules Relating to Carriage of Passengers by Sea and Protocol of 29 April 1961 had few adherents among States,[30] and its update[31] never even entered into force. More successful was the subsequent Athens Convention relating to the Carriage of Passengers and their Luggage by Sea of 13 December 1974 (abbreviated by the International Maritime Organization (IMO)[32] as 'PAL') that, with 32 signatories,[33] entered into force on 28 April 1987 (and its protocol of 19 November 1976 on 30 April 1989).[34] Its 1976 protocol established a fault-based liability regime, in which the carrier can limit his liability to up to 46,666 SDR (Special Drawing Rights),[35] approximately 58,400 Euros[36] per passenger in case of death and personal injury. In the consumer *acquis*, it is mentioned in the Package Travel Directive as one of the conventions limiting a travel organizer's or retailer's liability for failure to perform or improper performance of the services involved in the package.[37] But ratification amongst EU Member States was limited to just six States (2002).[38]

---

29   Council Recommendation 78/584/EEC on the ratification of conventions on safety in shipping of 26 June 1978 (OJ L194, 19 July 1978, p. 17), Resolution of the Council and of the representatives of the Governments of the Member States, meeting within the Council of 19 June 1990 on improving passenger ferry safety (OJ C206, 18 August 1990, p. 3), Council Resolution of 8 June 1993 on a common policy on safe seas (OJ C271, 7 October 1993, p. 1).

30   The Convention entered into force on 4 June 1965. Amongst EU Member States, only France signed the Convention but withdrew from it in 1975.

31   International Convention for the Unification of Certain Rules Relating to Carriage of Passengers by Sea of 27 May 1967.

32   IMO is a sub-organization of the United Nations (http://www.imo.org).

33   Status as at 31 October 2005. According to IMO, the contracting States represent together 38.64 percent of world tonnage.

34   Twenty-five contracting States representing 38.36 percent of world tonnage (status as at 31 October 2005).

35   A unit of account defined by the International Monetary Fund (IMF). The daily conversion rates for SDRs can be found on the IMF website (http://www.imf.org).

36   Value as of 16 October 2006.

37   Recital 19 of the preamble to Directive 90/314/EEC on package travel, package holidays and package tours (OJ L158, 23 June 1990, p. 59).

38   Belgium, Greece, Ireland, Luxembourg, Spain and the United Kingdom according to the Maritime Passenger Safety Communication (COM(2002) 158 final (p. 9, n. 17)). According to the *Comité Maritime International* (http://www.comitemaritime.org),

A seventh Member State, Germany, was rather idiosyncratic in accommodating the Athens Convention 1974. The first peculiarity is that the former German Democratic Republic (GDR) ratified the Convention in March 1989, which was still binding for its territory after reunification, but with the reservation that it would only apply to transport of foreigners on German vessels and Germans on foreign vessels.[39] Transport of German citizens on German ships is thus exempted, while the notions of 'German citizen' and 'German vessel' are limited to those persons and ships with their permanent residence respectively registered in the territory of the former GDR.[40] West Germany, on the other hand, did not accede to the Convention but voluntarily implemented its provisions in 1986 with higher compensation levels than those laid down in international law.[41] Hereafter, the Annex to § 664 of the *Handelsgesetzbuch* (HGB or Trade Act) established a fault-based liability regime within the liability limits prescribed by the Convention on Limitation of Liability for Maritime Claims of 19 November 1976 (LLMC), as later amended by protocol of 2 May 1996,[42] (§§ 486 to 487e HGB). Since reunification in 1990, these West German rules have been exempted from applying on citizens and companies of the eastern part of the country 'insofar its application is incompatible with commitments of public international law the GDR has assumed',[43] that is, where the Athens Convention 1974 applies. This could, in the event of an accident of a ferry sailing from Rostock carrying East, West and non-Germans, lead to legal quandaries of significant proportions, especially as German legal doctrine is divided over this question.[44]

The second peculiarity is West German law itself. The mentioned Annex to § 664 HGB transposes the Athens Convention 1974 in sixteen provisions[45] that, five years after the introduction of the Euro as legal tender, still refer to the Deutschmark as the currency. True, where reference is made to national currency units, these references shall be read as references to the Euro unit according to the respective conversion rates[46] but it is still a most unusual exception in today's German legislation. The

         Estonia, Latvia and Poland have also joined.

39   *Gesetzblatt der DDR* 1989 II 33 (Legal Gazette of the GDR 1989, Series II, p. 33).

40   P. Mankowski, *Seerechtliche Vertragsverhältnisse im Internationalen Privatrecht*, (Tübingen, 1995), pp. 417–420.

41   *Zweites Seerechtsänderungsgesetz* of 25 July 1986 (BGBl. I 1120) (Second Act amending the Law of the Seas 1986 (Federal Law Gazette 1986, Series I, p. 1120)).

42   Text available from IMO (http://www.imo.org). Protocol of 1996 in force since 13 May 2004.

43   Continued application according to the Reunification Treaty of 1990 (BGBl. 1990 II 889, Anl. I Kap. III Sachgebiet D Abschn. III Nr. 1 lit. b). Compare *Bundesgerichtshof* (Federal Supreme Court) decision of 12 July 2005 (VI ZR 83/04, BGHZ 163, 351 = NJW 2006, 1271).

44   G.B. Czerwenka, 'Passagierschaden im Binnenschiffsverkehr', *Neue Juristische Wochenschrift*, 18, (2006): 1250–2.

45   H. Hopperdietzel, 'Die Haftung bei der Veranstaltung von See- und Flussreisen', *ReiseRecht aktuell*, 5, (2005): 194 at 196–8.

46   Article 14 of the Regulation (EC) No. 974/98 on the introduction of the Euro (OJ L139, 11 May 1998, p. 1), as last amended by Regulation (EC) No. 1647/2006 (OJ L309, 9 November 2006, p. 2).

intricacies of Germany's law are only likely to be sorted out by the intervention of Community law, superseding national rules.

Portugal, which is not party to the Athens Convention, provides a semiautonomous legal framework for maritime passengers by virtue of Law-Decree No. 349 of 1986 on transport contracts for maritime passengers.[47] The Law-Decree intends to complement international law on 'maritime passenger transport contracts'[48] in force in Portugal (Article 2).[49] But it thereby effectively creates an original concept of (private law) passenger protection. Article 14(1) of the Law-Decree (*responsabilidade por danos pessoais*) makes 'the carrier liable for damages suffered by the passenger from the ship, during the voyage, and also for those [damages] occurring from the start of boarding until the end of disembarking, no matter from which port the vessel sailed and no matter the ports of stop-over'. According to Article 14(2) it is 'for the damaged party to prove that the carrier either did not comply with any of the prescribed requirements of the previous Article [security requirements of Article 13] or that the event causing the damage resulted from fault of the carrier or his servants'. Article 15(1) (*responsabilidade por acontecimentos de mar*) renders 'the carrier liable for damages suffered by the passenger following the sinking, collision, explosion or burning of the ship'. It 'falls on the carrier to prove that the events referred to in the previous paragraph do not result from his fault or the fault of his servants' (Article 15(2)). Article 16(2) of the Law-Decree determines that damages can only be claimed up until two years after the event; a provision that corresponds with Article 13 of the Annex to § 664 HGB.

The protocol of 29 March 1990 to the 1974 Athens Convention with just five contracting States never had sufficient support for entering into force as it did not, in the eyes of many States, provide for a sufficiently high level of compensation. The Commission expressed its discontent with this liability regime in its Maritime Passenger Safety Communication of March 2002[50] whilst outlining the features of more adequate rules for maritime passenger transport, both international and European. In the autumn 2002 then, in an attempt to remedy the failures of its predecessors, inspired by the Montreal Convention[51] and with the aim of truly arriving at the establishment of an international liability regime, a diplomatic conference held under

---

47   Decreto-Lei n. 349/86, de 17 de Outubro, relativo ao contrato de transporte de passageiros por mar (Diário da República I Série – N. 240 – 17 October 1986, p. 3150).

48   Defined in Article 1 (Noção/Notion) as 'A maritime passenger transport contract is such where one party takes responsibility in relation to the other party to transport the latter by sea for monetary recompense'.

49   Article 2 (Direito aplicável/Appliable law) reads: 'This contract is regulated by treaties and conventions in force in Portugal and, in subsidiarity, by the provisions of the present law.'

50   Communication on the enhanced safety of passenger ships in the Community (COM(2002) 158 final of 25 March 2002), pp. 8–15.

51   B. Kröger, 'Passenger Carried by Sea – Should they be granted the same rights as airline passengers?' *CMI [Comité Maritime International] Yearbook 2001*, (2001), pp. 244–252.

the auspices of IMO, critically commented on by Soyer,[52] succeeded on 1 November 2002 in updating the Athens Convention by a protocol.[53] The new convention as amended by the 2002 London Protocol will replace the 1974 convention,[54] which is henceforth renamed 'Athens Convention relating to the Carriage of Passengers and their Luggage by Sea 1974, as last amended by the London Protocol 2002' (hereinafter the 'Athens Convention 2002'). These are – in an overview and without claiming to provide a profound analysis – its key provisions.

(i) Bodily Harm

The Athens Convention 2002 introduced two tiers of liability for a carrier for loss suffered as a result of the death or personal injury of a passenger which is attributable to an incident related to shipping activity. Under the newly introduced Article 3(1), damage caused by the operation of a ship – so-called 'shipping incidents' defined in Article 3(5)(a) – are made subject to a strict liability regime up to a limit of 250,000 SDR or 312,875 Euros (first tier). The carrier can exempt himself from liability should he prove that the shipping incident resulted from belligerent activities or a natural disaster or was intentionally caused by a third party. If the loss exceeds this limit, the carrier is further liable under Article 7(1) up to a limit of 400,000 SDR (or 500,600 Euros, that is, more than eight times the amount of the 1974 convention) unless he can prove that the incident that caused the loss occurred without his fault or neglect, thus reversing the burden of proof between the strict liability limit and the maximum liability limit (second tier). Even higher liability limits can be adopted nationally (Article 7(2)).[55] These limits set maximum limits, empowering – but not obliging – courts to compensate up to these limits. Obviously, liability under Article 3(1) is transport focused and refers to ferries and steamboats but including cruise ships as means of transport with leisure elements not included or ranking second. They find their justification in the risks inherent to shipping, where the scope for passengers to control events is very limited.

Wholly different from the regime applicable to shipping incidents, Article 3(2) maintains the fault/negligence-based liability of the 1974 convention for other types of personal injury or damage incurred on board and not caused by a shipping incident. Accordingly, the burden of proving of fault or neglect lies with the claimant

---

52   B. Soyer, 'Sundry Considerations on the Draft Protocol to the Athens Convention Relating to the Carriage of Passengers and Their Luggage at Sea 1974', *Journal of Maritime Law and Commerce*, 33, No. 4, (2002): 1–22.

53   IMO Briefing 34/2002 of 1 November 2002 'Liability limits for ship passengers raised with new Athens Convention, compulsory insurance introduced'.

54   The 2002 Protocol will enter into force twelve months after being accepted by ten States. Amongst EU Member States, Finland, Germany, Spain, Sweden and the United Kingdom have signed until September 2006. According to the *Comité Maritime International* (http://www.comitemaritime.org), Latvia has already acceded to the Protocol.

55   This 'opt-out' clause enables State parties to retain or introduce higher limits of liability (or unlimited liability) in the case of carriers or insurers who are subject to the jurisdiction of their courts.

passenger. This rule is leisure focused and refers to ships, and especially cruise ships, more as 'floating hotels' and only in the second instance as means of transport. They therefore find their justification in a comparison with the law on travel and tourism. The risks to which the passenger is exposed on a cruise are seen as no greater than in a land based resort. Passengers therefore bear more responsibility for events on board.[56]

Liability under Article 3(1) and (2) is backed by Article 4*bis*(1) introducing an obligation for carriers who actually perform the whole or a part of the carriage (the performing carrier is defined in Article 1(1)(c)) to take out compulsory insurance to cover passenger claims. However, with a ceiling of compulsory insurance of 250,000 SDR, it is effectively limited to cover for strict liability claims only (as well as negligence based 'leisure' liability within this limit). Nor does this duty extend to cover for loss or damage of luggage (liability under Article 3(3) and (4) discussed below). Article 4*bis* paragraphs (2) to (8) (and the Annex to the Athens Convention 2002, which constitutes an integral part of the convention (Article 1*bis*)) elaborate on the form of financial security certificates and the process of their issue. Article 4*bis*(9) deals with mutual recognition for certificates issued by parties to the convention. What is very important is the provision that in civil procedure, passengers, as claimants for compensation covered by insurance, are permitted to take direct action against the insurer (Article 4*bis*(10)). Such action therefore largely puts responsibility for claims in the hands of the insurer. Article 4*bis* paragraphs (12) to (15) deal with specific State party obligations to enforce these rules, while generally, several layers of control are designated the responsibility for watching over these insurance requirements, principally ship owners, classification societies and flag State administrations,[57] as well as the port State.[58]

Clearly, the purpose of making insurance compulsory is to ensure that funds are available to compensate passengers against becoming victims of bodily harm during a maritime journey. Shipping insurance is mostly provided by P&I [Protection & Indemnity Insurance] clubs. These are mutual funds providing cover against third

---

56   Soyer, 'Sundry Considerations on the Draft Protocol to the Athens Convention Relating to the Carriage of Passengers and Their Luggage at Sea 1974': 6.

57   Directive 94/57/EC on common rules and standards for ship inspection and survey organizations and for the relevant activities of maritime administrations (OJ L319, 12 December 1994, p. 20), as amended by Directive 97/58/EC (OJ L274, 7 October 1997, p. 8), Directive 2001/105/EC (OJ L19, 22 January 2002, p. 9) and Directive 2002/84/EC (OJ L324, 29 November 2002, p. 53). Also compare Article 94 of UNCLOS 82 (United Nations Convention on the Law of the Sea of 10 December 1982). Commission press release IP/06/1369 of 12 October 2006 'Maritime Safety: the Commission reviews the classification societies'.

58   Port State control for Europe and the North Atlantic is regulated by the Paris Memorandum of Understanding (http://www.parismou.org) and, for the Community, by Directive 95/21/EC on port State control of shipping (OJ L157, 7 July 1995, p. 1), as amended by Directive 98/25/EC (OJ L133, 7 May 1998, p. 19), Directive 98/42/EC (OJ L184, 27 June 1998, p. 40), Directive 1999/97/EC (OJ L331, 23 December 1999, p. 17), Directive 2001/106/EC (OJ L19, 22 January 2002, p. 17) and Directive 2002/84/EC (OJ L324, 29 November 2002, p. 53).

party liabilities and expenses arising from owning ships or operating ships as principals. They seem worried about the sheer scale of the obligation. In the case of a 3,000 passenger cruise ship, compulsory insurance coverage will be no less than 750 million SDR. This, insurers say, will strain insurance capacities (the 'amount issue') and explains the keen interest in adding reservations excluding war and terrorism during the ratification process of the Athens Convention 2002 (the 'war risk issue'). These concerns have already led the *Rapporteur* of the European Parliament's Committee on Transport and Tourism (TRAN) to suggest that regular ferry lines operating domestically should be given a supplementary deadline of two years after the entry into force of the Athens Regulation in order to allow the insurance market to adapt.[59] It was requested that the phrases 'act of war, hostilities, civil insurrection' (Article 3(1)(a)) and 'wholly caused by an act or omission done with the intent to cause the incident by third party' (Article 3(1)(b)) should be interpreted as including 'terrorism' in order to exclude liability for such acts. The website of the IMO Correspondence Group on Provision of Financial Security in Respect of Passenger Claims[60] provides rich background material for this debate.

The IMO Assembly asked the IMO Legal Committee (LEG) to deal with these remaining issues to facilitate ratification.[61] Answering this request, this committee adopted in its 92nd session of 19 October 2006 the text of a reservation, intended for use as a standard reservation, to the Athens Convention 2002 and guidelines for the implementation of the Athens Convention 2002.[62] These guidelines are expected of having the effect of qualifying some of the provisions of the Athens Convention 2002 as they allow for limitation of liability in respect of claims relating to war or terrorism. The aim is to unblock the ratification process for the Athens Convention 2002 which is slow, in part, due to concerns relating to the ability of the insurance market to provide compulsory cover up to the general limits established under the new convention and its ability to provide insurance cover for injury and damage arising out of acts of terrorism. The text of the agreed reservation states that the government concerned reserves the right to and undertakes to limit liability to 250,000 SDR in respect of each passenger on each distinct occasion, or 340 million SDR overall per ship on each distinct occasion. This relates in particular to war insurance which, under the guidelines, shall cover liability, if any, for loss suffered as a result of death or personal injury to a passenger caused by (a) war, civil war, revolution, rebellion, insurrection, or civil strife arising therefrom, or any hostile act by or against a belligerent power, (b) capture, seizure, arrest, restraint or detainment, and the consequences thereof or any attempt thereat, (c) derelict mines, torpedoes, bombs or other derelict weapons of war, (d) act of any terrorist or any person acting maliciously or from a political

---

59   MEP Paolo Costa, chairman of the TRAN Committee, has been appointed *Rapporteur* to prepare the European Parliament's position on the proposal. His draft report was published on 22 September 2006 and was debated on 10 October 2006.

60   http://folk.uio.no/erikro/WWW/corrgr/index.html (visited 22.12.2006).

61   IMO Assembly Resolution A.998(24) of 1 December 2005 'Protocol of 2002 to the Athens Convention: Reservation concerning the issue and acceptance of insurance certificates with special exceptions and limitations'. See also the minutes of the 91st session of the IMO Legal Committee of April 2006 (LEG 91/4/1).

62   IMO Circular Letter No. 2758 of 20 November 2006.

motive and any action taken to prevent or counter any such risk, and (e) confiscation and expropriation. A Commission Staff Working Document on compensation for terrorist-related damage has accordingly been drawn up.[63]

(ii) Non-Corporal Damage

While the provisions above deal with bodily injury and harm, liability for loss of or damage to luggage, defined in Article 1(7) to include pecuniary loss resulting from late re-delivery to the passenger, distinguishes between cabin luggage and other luggage (a generic definition of luggage is contained in Article 1(5)). In the case of cabin luggage, that is, items in possession of the passenger and under his/her control (Article 1(6)), liability of the carrier is fault-based, while fault or neglect is presumed if the loss is caused by a shipping incident (Article 3(3)). If other luggage is lost or damaged, the carrier is liable unless he can prove that the incident which caused the loss (not just shipping incidents but any incident, irrespective of its nature) occurred without his fault or negligence, thus reversing the onus of proof (Article 3(4)).

Article 8 establishes limits for loss or damage to luggage and vehicles (vehicles count as luggage under Article 1(5)). Under the convention, cabin luggage can be compensated up to a limit of 2,250 SDR (2,815 Euros). Vehicles (including luggage carried in or on the vehicle) have a liability cap of 12,700 SDR (15,894 Euros). Any other luggage is limited to 3,375 SDR (4,224 Euros). Deductions of 330 SDR (413 Euros) for vehicles and 149 SDR (186 Euros) for other luggage are possible under Article 8(4). Valuables are subject to a special regime under Article 5.

Pursuance of damages for both bodily harm and non-corporal damage are subject to a time-bar of two years according to – a rather complex – Article 16 of the convention.[64]

(iii) EC Reception

With a few exceptions below, this paper does not attempt to explain in more detail the new Athens Convention's concept of liability. That has been done more competently by, for instance, Soyer,[65] and Czerwenka[66] and IMO itself. What matters for the reception of international transport law in Community legislation is that for

---

63   SEC(2007) 377 of 16 March 2007.

64   Compare with limitation of actions rules of Article 60 of CIV 1999, Article 35 of the Montreal Convention and Article 30 of the *Convention internationale relative au contrat de voyage* (CCV) of 1970. Also see European Parliament Resolution with recommendations to the Commission on limitation periods in cross-border disputes involving injuries and fatal accidents of 31 January 2007 (European Parliament press release of 1 February 2007 'Limitation periods for cross-border disputes over accidents – MEPs say harmonization needed').

65   Soyer, 'Sundry Considerations on the Draft Protocol to the Athens Convention Relating to the Carriage of Passengers and Their Luggage at Sea 1974'.

66   G.B Czerwenka, 'Das Protokoll von 2002 zum Athener Übereinkommen von 1974 über die Beförderung von Reisenden und ihrem Gepäck auf See', *ReiseRecht aktuell*, 4, (2003): 158–161.

the first time in this UN organization's history, an IMO convention is open for the signature of 'regional economic organizations' such as the EC. Unsurprisingly, the Commission was enthusiastic about the prospect of both to sign the 2002 convention and to announce its transposition into Community law.[67] A proposal for a Council Decision concerning the conclusion of the Athens Convention 2002 was duly presented[68] but, in particular due to unresolved questions surrounding the status of Gibraltar, without much progress having been achieved ever since. In the accompanying Communication to this proposal, as well as in the preceding Maritime Passenger Safety Communication,[69] the Commission pointed out that ratification by the EC was indispensable because parts of the amended convention belonged to the exclusive competence of the Community, which therefore required it to become a contracting party before Member States could do so. This refers to Articles 17 and 17*bis* of the Athens Convention 2002 that provide rules on the jurisdiction and the recognition and enforcement of judgments that differ from the 'Brussels I' Regulation and thus the Community's private international law rules (discussed below). But this argument has not as yet led to the convention's ratification.

It took three years to expire between the conclusion of the IMO conference on the London Protocol and 23 November 2005 when the Commission adopted its Third Maritime Safety Package.[70] The package, that comprises seven legislative measures, aims above all at safety in maritime transport and the prevention of oil spills of the kind suffered after the shipwrecking of the oil tankers *Erika* and the *Prestige*. But among these measures are two proposals that:

> ... are aimed at improving the quality of the overall framework of liability and damage repair in the event of an accident. This involves incorporating the provisions of the Athens Convention 2002 into European law in order to extend the protection – introduced by this convention – to cover all passengers on ships in the Union, including intra-European maritime and inland waterway traffic. The aim is also to make ship owners act more responsibly, and to oblige them to take out an insurance policy or other financial security for third-party damage.[71]

While the proposal for a Directive on the civil liability and financial securities of ship owners[72] cannot be discussed here, the planned incorporation of the Athens Convention 2002 deserves close attention.

---

67   Commission press release IP/03/884 of 24 June 2003 'Commission proposes to accept IMO's passenger liability rules'.
68   COM(2003) 375 final of 24 June 2003.
69   Communication on the enhanced safety of passenger ships in the Community (COM(2002) 158 final of 25 March 2002), p. 14.
70   Commission Communication 'Third package of legislative measures on maritime safety in the European Union' (COM(2005) 585 final of 23 November 2005).
71   Commission press release IP/05/1457 of 23 November 2005 'Stringent measures to guarantee the safety of maritime transport.' See also MEMO/05/438 'Third Maritime Safety Package' of the same day.
72   COM(2005) 593 final of 23 November 2005.

5. The Athens Regulation

The proposal for a Regulation on the liability of carriers of passengers by sea and inland waterway in the event of accidents[73] aims to integrate the Athens Convention 2002 almost *tel quel* into Community law. The 'Athens Regulation,' as the proposal may therefore be called, chooses to incorporate the entire text of the convention *verbatim* by reproducing a consolidated version of the London Protocol in its Annex. From the issues covered, it is linked to the Air Carrier Liability Regulation,[74] but its copy/paste approach compares more to the incorporation of the CIV 1999[75] into Annex I of the amended railway passenger proposal.

In the ongoing legislative procedure, the Committee of the Regions (CoR) was the first EU institution to comment formally on the Third Maritime Package in its opinion of 15 June 2006,[76] in which it also expressed its views on the Athens Regulation. The Economic and Social Committee (EESC) followed in its Opinion of 13 September 2006.[77] The European Parliament is set to follow in a first reading of the proposal. The responsible TRAN Committee is currently debating a draft report,[78] and the Committee on Legal Affairs (JURI) has also been asked for an opinion.[79]

The *en bloc* incorporation of the Athens Convention 2002 in EC law ensures that the ECJ can interpret the Athens Convention 2002 in a uniform manner – which international law does not currently allow for. This implies that the Court will acquire jurisdiction over the meaning of one of the many other notions of 'passenger' in Community law: '"Passenger" means any person carried in a ship, (a) under a contract of carriage, or (b) who, with the consent of the carrier, is accompanying a vehicle or live animals which are covered by a contract of carriage of goods not governed by this Convention' (Article 1(4) of the Athens Convention 2002).

As it happens, this is not the same definition as is used for maritime safety purposes, where Article 2(b) of Directive 2003/25/EC[80] defines 'passenger' as 'every person other than the master and the members of the crew or other person employed or engaged in any capacity on board a ship on the business of that ship and other than a child under one year of age'. This is similar to Article 2(c) of Directive 1999/35/EC,[81] which says that '"a passenger" is every person other than: (i) the master and

---

73   Proposal for a Regulation on the liability of carriers of passengers by sea and inland waterways in the event of accidents (COM(2005) 592 final of 23 November 2005); *Etude d'impact approfondie* (impact assessment only available in French) SEC(2005) 1516 of the same day.

74   Note 5 above. The Commission directly links both acts in its Maritime Passenger Safety Communication (COM(2002) 158 final of 25 March 2002), pp. 8 and 10.

75   Note 13 above.

76   OJ C229, 22 September 2006, pp. 38 *et seq.* (pp. 48–9).

77   OJ C318, 23 December 2006, pp. 195–201.

78   Note 59 above.

79   MEP Piia-Noora Kauppi is *Rapporteur* for the opinion of the Committee on Legal Affairs (JURI). Her draft opinion was published on 26 June 2006 and was debated on 2 October 2006.

80   Note 28 above.

81   Note 27 above.

the members of the crew or other persons employed or engaged in any capacity on board a ship on the business of that ship, and (ii) a child under one year of age'. Yet it is different to Article 2 (1ˢᵗ indent) of Directive 98/41/EC,[82] reading '"persons" shall mean all people on board irrespective of age'. Such dissimilarities are unfortunately the rule in passenger law but should eventually be replaced by common notion of 'passenger'.[83]

Beyond and above incorporation as the main effect of the proposed Regulation, a number of adaptations original to the Commission proposal each need to be explained, referring to: (1) extending the scope of application to domestic traffic, (2) extending the scope of application to inland waterways, (3) removing the possibility for Member States to fix limits of liability higher than those provided for in the Convention, (4) compensation for damage or loss of mobility equipment/medical equipment belonging to a passenger with reduced mobility, (5) offers for advance payment, as provided for in the air and rail sectors, and (6) offers of pre-journey information.

(i) Domestic Transport and Extraterritorial Scope

While the Athens Convention 2002 applies to international carriage only, the Athens Regulation will also apply to sea transport within a single Member State (national carriage). This comprehensiveness had always been the aim of the Commission and the case for it was convincingly argued in the relevant Communication.[84] The extension to domestic transport is certainly necessary if the Regulation is meant to create a level playing field for sea transport in the Community. Also, peculiarities like the continuing two-standard regime in the eastern part of Germany, as described above, cannot be maintained. Most importantly, it would be impossible to explain rationally the reason for making an unfavourable differentiation in compensation between a passenger suffering a loss while travelling by sea from, for instance, Calais to Dover (international) and a passenger travelling from Lisbon to the Azores (domestic), even though the Portuguese route is far longer. This element of the Athens Regulation therefore seems straightforward and has been accepted by the European institutions that have already dealt with the proposal in the legislative procedure. As a tool to allow carriers and insurers to adapt to the enhanced requirements, the TRAN Committee's Rapporteur has suggested giving a supplementary deadline of two years for regular ferry services (not cruise ships) before the Athens Regulation becomes fully applicable.[85] The JURI Committee's draftswoman has remarked that as far as

---

82   Note 26 above.

83   See: Karsten, 'Passengers, Consumers and Travellers: The Rise of Passenger Rights in EC Transport Law and its Repercussions for Community Consumer Law and Policy': 131.

84   Maritime Passenger Safety Communication (COM(2002) 158 final of 25 March 2002), p. 13.

85   Note 59 above.

small carriers operating in domestic waters are concerned, special attention should be paid to the cyclical nature of their activities (referring to seasonal variations).[86]

An extraterritorial extension already stemming from the convention is that a passenger also benefits from the protection under the Regulation if he or she has purchased their tickets in Europe even though the journey itself takes place outside the Community's waters (Article 2(1)(b) of the Athens Convention 2002). Thus, when a cruise takes place in, for instance, the Caribbean and on board a ship flying the flag of a non-European country (or a State not party to the convention), the passenger is still covered when the contract of carriage has been concluded in an EU Member State. The same effect for fluvial shipping is given by Article 2(b) of the Athens Regulation, which would extend the application of Community law to extra-European inland waterways, such as the Nile or the Volga.

(ii) Inland Waterways

Some more explanation is needed to justify the second major extension. While the convention is limited to sea transport, the Athens Regulation intends to widen its application to cover carriage by inland waterway. This policy choice responds, one may assume, to the general tendency to align the law of the seas and the law governing inland waterways. The 'fresh water = salt water' approach (which requires the proposal to be jointly based on Articles 71(1) and 80(2) EC Treaty) seems enticing, as in both cases passengers cross water, thus, in theory, taking the risk of drowning. Applying the same set of rules would seem to have the further advantage of avoiding further fragmentation in an already transport-mode centred EC passenger law. However, if applied without some necessary adaptations, such an approach would run the risk of creating unwanted difficulties in the application of the Athens Regulation while ignoring the different pedigree of inland waterway law and governance. The right approach for the Athens Regulation concerning inland waterways therefore requires elaboration in a separate chapter, which follows below.

(iii) Advance Payments

Article 5 of the Athens Regulation requires the carrier to make an advance payment on the passenger's claim in case of death or personal injury 'sufficient to cover immediate economic needs, within 15 days from the identification of the person entitled to damages'. This provision is nearly identical to Article 5 of the Air Carrier Liability Regulation and Article 13 of the Commission railway passenger proposal, now Article 12 of the amended proposal. Unlike under the Athens Convention 2002, which makes him subject to passenger claims (Article 4(1) second sentence of the convention), the performing carrier (Article 1(1)(b) of the convention) or any other person potentially responsible is not made liable by the Regulation, which seems to limit the passenger to just one debtor. This could change in the final version of the law.

---

86   Note 79 above.

In the event of death, this advance payment shall not be less than a forfeiture sum of 21,000 Euros. In air transport, the advance payment in the event of death is 16,000 SDR (20,024 Euros) and in rail transport it is also proposed to be set at 21,000 Euros (which would mean total approximation between the three modes of transport should air law eventually switch to the single currency). The practical problem that arises here is that the forfeiture sum cannot be paid to the passenger (who will be dead) but must be made to 'the person entitled to damages', a notion no more closely defined in the Athens Regulation. The analogous application of Article 2(1)(c) of the Air Carrier Liability Regulation could be helpful here, as it is more precise in saying, in conjunction with Article 5 of that Regulation, that the payment should be made to the 'person entitled to claim in respect of that passenger, in accordance with applicable law'. Depending on the outcome of the application of private international law on the applicable law on succession, whose harmonization is currently subject to a consultation procedure,[87] this would most likely be the person liable to bear the expenses of the funeral and the person who loses his or her maintenance through the death of the passenger. Nevertheless, in trans-border cases in particular, it can be difficult to determine the beneficiary (inheritor) of the lump sum advance payment, though this could be facilitated by a 'European certificate of inheritance'.[88]

Paragraphs 3 of both the air and the rail provisions provide that 'an advance payment shall not constitute recognition of liability and may be offset against any subsequent sums paid on the basis of this Regulation, but is not returnable'. This does not apply in cases of exoneration (in air transport specified in Article 20 of the Montreal Convention), that is, where the damage was caused by the negligence or fault of the passenger, or where the person who received the advance payment was not the person entitled to compensation (a *sui generis* case of unjustified enrichment). Not including such a clause in the Athens Regulation must be interpreted as recognition of the application of the convention's own rules on contributory fault (the notion of 'contributory fault' is defined in Article 6 of the Athens Convention 2002), while the rules for unjustified enrichment are determined by Article 10 of Regulation (EC) No. 864/2007 on the law applicable to non-contractual obligations[89] ['Rome II'] which expressly includes 'payment of amounts wrongly received'.

---

87   Green Paper 'Succession and Wills' (COM(2005) 65 final of 1 March 2005). EESC Opinion of 26 October 2005 (OJ C28, 3 February 2006, p. 1). European Parliament resolution with recommendations to the Commission on succession and wills of 16 November 2006: Recommendation 7 (on the European certificate of inheritance).

88   Point 5 of the Green Paper (previous note).

89   OJ L 199, 31.7.2007, p. 40. Prepared by COM(2003) 427 final of 22 July 2003 (Commission press release IP/03/1068 of 22 July 2003 'The Commission adopts a proposal for a Regulation on the law applicable to non-contractual obligations ("Rome II")'. Modified by COM(2006) 83 final of 21 February 2006 (Commission press release IP/06/168 of 15 February 2006 'Commission's modified proposal on cross-border disputes is key element in achieving a European area of justice'). Now close to adoption (Common Position adopted on 25 September 2006 (published OJ C289E, 28 November 2006, p. 68) followed by Commission Communication (COM(2006) 566 final of 27 September 2006) and the European Parliament legislative resolution of 18 January 2007).

The EESC is in favour of Article 5 of the Athens Regulation but wishes to limit advance payments to strict liability (Article 3(1) of the convention) cases.[90] The JURI Committee's draftswoman shares this view. Advance payments would accordingly only be paid after shipping incidents.

(iv) Freezing the Ceiling of Liability and Thawing Limits for PRMs

Article 4(1) of the Athens Regulation bars EU Member States as State parties to the convention from individually raising liability limits above the levels foreseen under international law. Article 7(2) of the Athens Convention 2002 otherwise offers this option[91] but according to the proposal, fixing higher levels requires a legislative amendment of the Athens Regulation. This thereby erects an effective barrier against national over-compensation – a phenomenon known as 'gold-plating' in EC consumer law – in the field of passenger protection and provides a level playing field and legal security for carriers throughout the Community.

While the Athens Regulation therefore freezes the ceiling of liability, it was inspired by the amendment to the railway passenger proposal[92] to exceed the liability limits of Article 8(1) of the convention of 2,250 SDR/2,815 Euros for damage to cabin luggage (defined in Article 1(6) of the convention, for which the carrier is liable under Article 3(3)) in the specific case of compensation of damage or loss of mobility equipment/medical equipment of PRMs (Article 4(2) of the Regulation). While approving the intention pursued by this clause (caring for the special needs of PRMs), three problems need to be pointed out that arise in the context of its inclusion.

The first relates to the exact meaning of such clauses in passenger Regulations. Article 4(2) of the Athens Regulation reads: 'In the event of total or partial destruction or loss of or damage to mobility equipment/medical equipment belonging to a passenger with reduced mobility, the compensation is equivalent, at the maximum, to the replacement value of the equipment.'

This wording suggests that only the 'replacement value' of the PRM equipment would impose a ceiling of liability. A horizontal view on EC passenger law shows that, although clearly pursuing a similar purpose, the wordings differ. Still similar appears Article 22 of the amended railway passenger proposal that says that no financial ceiling applies to lost or damaged PRM equipment.[93] But Article 12 of the PRMs in Air Transport Regulation is just making a general statement on the right for

90   OJ C318, 23 December 2006, point 4.6.6.
91   Note 55 above.
92   See the Communication accompanying the maritime passenger proposal (COM(2005) 592 final of 23 November 2005, p. 9).
93   Article 22 on 'Compensation in respect of mobility equipment of other specific equipment' of the amended railway passenger proposal (n. 15 above) reads: 'If the railway undertaking is liable for the total or partial loss of, or damage to, mobility equipment or other specific equipment used by persons with reduced mobility, no financial limit shall be applicable.' This provision seems to refer to Article 34 CIV 1999 providing for a compensation cap of 1,400 SDR for hand luggage.

compensation, referring to the different layers of air transport regulation.[94] However, taking into account the common objective pursued by these clauses – financial compensation for lost and damaged equipment – it should thus be assured that no specific sum apart from the replacement value of the lost and the repair costs of the damaged PRM equipment should be recoverable, while any more far reaching liability would be excluded. While this is a first attempt at measuring their impact, the debate is just starting about the exact meaning of PRM liability rules. In the long run, the result of the study on compensation thresholds for damaged or lost equipment and devices belonging to air passengers with reduced mobility[95] that the Commission has tendered will compare existing national (EU Member States and overseas), Community and international regulations defining the liabilities of airports and airlines. When the Commission reports on this study to the European Parliament and the Council early in 2008,[96] the ensuing discussion should open, one would hope, the possibility to clarify Article 12 of the PRMs in Air Transport Regulation and similar clauses like Article 4(2) of the Athens Regulation, and improve their drafting to bring them up to standard for private law legislation.

The second problem arises when enquiring whether this PRM clause actually just adds to the standard of protection offered by the convention outside the coordinated field of international law (like the clause on advance payments) or whether it modifies it against binding international rules.[97] Advance payments under the Regulation, we have seen, are partial payments on an overall claim that does not in its entirety exceed the limits established by the convention. However, payments for broken PRM equipment above the ceiling of Article 8(1) of the convention would exceed internationally agreed ceilings. While advance payments are made for bodily harm suffered, for which Article 7(2) of the convention allows State parties to be more generous, the PRM clause relates to non-corporal damage for which no such flexibility exists. Indeed, strict adherence to international law would require the Community to seek an international agreement on higher limits for PRM equipment for which Article 23 of the Athens Convention 2002 institutes a special procedure.[98] The time-bar instituted by Article 23(7), however, pre-empts any action before May 2008. It would therefore have to be a political decision to go ahead with PRM protection at European level, which would expose discrepancies with international law – a risk that may still be worth taking.

---

94   Article 12 of the PRMs in Air Transport Regulation (n. 10 above) reads: 'Where wheelchairs or other mobility equipment or assistive devices are lost or damaged whilst being handled at the airport or transported on board of aircraft, the passenger to whom the equipment belongs shall be compensated, in accordance with rules of international, Community and national law.' This provision arguably refers to Article 22(2) of the Montreal Convention, which provides for a compensation cap of 1,000 SDR.

95   OJ S111–118193 of 14 June 2006.

96   This was announced on 30 November 2005 in the course of the negotiation process (see previous note: Tender Specifications, point 1.2 referring to the *traveaux préparatoires* on the PRMs in Air Transport Regulation).

97   EESC Opinion, OJ C318, 23.12.2006, p. 200, point 4.6.7.

98   Compare the 'review of limits' procedure of Article 24 of the Montreal Convention.

The third problem, specific to maritime law, occurs because the Athens Regulation omits any statement on a precise notion of 'PRM' for the purposes of this clause. This is because EC maritime passenger law provides for a particularly broad definition of 'persons with reduced mobility' in Article 2(w) of Directive 98/18/EC on safety rules and standards for passenger ships.[99] Accordingly, a PRM is 'anyone who has a particular difficulty when using public transport, including elderly people, disabled persons, persons with sensory impairments and wheelchair users, pregnant women and persons accompanying small children'. Is the carrier obliged to compensate for the broken pram of a perfectly healthy child pushed by a parent of equally good physical condition? Doubtless the pram is 'mobility equipment' of 'a person accompanying small children'. This example certainly overstretches the notion of PRM for the purpose of Article 4(2). Thus, in order to avoid unwarranted or indeed frivolous compensation claims, the clear and narrow definition of PRM used in parallel passenger instruments should be preferred. This says that:

> 'PRM' means any person whose mobility when using transport is reduced due to any physical disability (sensory or locomotory, permanent or temporary), intellectual disability or impairment, or any other cause of disability, or age, and whose situation needs appropriate attention and adaptation to his or her particular needs of the service made available to all passengers.[100]

It is worth mentioning that Portuguese law went ahead with a PRM policy with Law-Decree No. 123 of 1997, later amended by virtue of the transposition of Directive 98/18/EC and its amendments by Law-Decrees No. 180 of 2003 and No. 210 of 2005.[101]

(v) Pre-Journey Information

Article 6 of the Athens Regulation on information to passengers also compares to pre-journey information required for other transport modes. The clause says that,

> the carrier, the performing carrier [*defined in Article 1(1) of the Athens Conventions 2002*] and/or tour operator [*not defined in the Regulation*] shall provide to the passengers, prior to their departure, information regarding their rights under this Regulation, in particular on the limits of compensation for death, personal injury or loss and damage of luggage, on their right of direct action against the insurer or the person providing financial security and on their entitlement to an advance payment. This information shall be provided in the most appropriate format.

The TRAN Committee's *Rapporteur* is in favour of upholding the provision 'but it would have to be in line with what has been done in other transport modes', while 'the content of obligation to inform could be made more precise later on (attached

---

99   OJ L144, 15 May 1998, p. 1, as amended (n. 25 above).
100   Article 2(a) of the PRMs in Air Transport Regulation and Article 3(17) of the amended railway passenger proposal (Common Position).
101   Decreto-Lei n. 123/97, de 22 de Maio, Decreto-Lei n. 180/2003, de 14 de Agosto, Decreto-Lei n. 210/2005, de 6 de Dezembro.

to the ticket (general sales conditions) and/or inserted in brochures'. Article 6 and the Annex of the Air Carrier Liability Regulation and Article 3 of the Commission railway passenger proposal, now Article 7 of the amended railway passenger proposal, could be taken as models. Beyond this, the railway proposals make the effort to explain to the unfamiliar reader the notion of 'tour operator,' which is a defined concept borrowed from the Package Travel Directive[102] – something which the Athens Regulation should perhaps do too. Inspiration for 'the most appropriate format' of passenger information could also come from the CVN Convention, whose Article 3(2) on transport documents stipulates that 'the ticket shall show the name of the carrier and shall indicate by the endorsement "CVN applicable" that, notwithstanding any clause to the contrary, the contract is subject to the provisions of this Convention'.[103] An issue which is not addressed is the one of in which language the information notice has to be issued, which in trans-border transport would often be an indispensable precondition for conveying information to passengers. This point often seems to be overlooked. A search of EC consumer law most notably turns up a general Commission document of 1993,[104] a Council document of 1998 on operating instructions[105] and a range of ECJ rulings mostly related to labelling,[106] from which one may deduct the principle that information notices shall drafted in 'a language easily understood by the consumer'. However, the exact meaning of such a notion for passenger law would still need to be elaborated.

(vi) Conclusion: Athens Regulation Can Be Improved

While all the elements are there in the proposal for up to date maritime passenger protection, there is still a margin to improve the wording of the Athens Regulation in the legislative procedure. Although the debate on the maritime passenger proposal/ Athens Regulation is embedded in the discussion on the Third Maritime Package, which naturally focuses on other, in particular environmental issues, this must not impede the drafting of sound passenger rights legislation with a view also for more cohesion between the different modes of transport.

---

102   Article 2(2) of Directive 90/314/EEC (n. 37 above).

103   For a comparison with national law see Articles 3 to 6 of the Law-Decree No. 349 of 1986 (n. 47 above).

104   Commission Communication concerning language use in the information of consumers in the Community (COM(93) 456 final of 10 November 1993).

105   Council Resolution of 17 December 1998 on operating instructions for technical consumer goods (OJ C411, 31 December 1998, p. 1).

106   *Piageme I* (Case C–369/89, *Groupement des Producteurs, Importateurs et Agents Généraux d'Eaux Minérale Etrangères (Piageme)* v. *Peeters NV* (1991) ECR I–2971); *Schott* (Case C–51/93, *Meyhui* v. *Schott Zwiesel Glaswerke* (1994) ECR I–3879); *Piageme II* (Case C–85/94, *Groupement des Producteurs, Importateurs et Agents Généraux d'Eaux Minérale Etrangères (Piageme)* v. *Peeters NV* (1995) ECR I–2955); *Goerres* (Case C–385/96, *Criminal proceeding against Hermann Josef Goerres* (1998) ECR I–4431); *Colim* (Case C–33/97, *Colim* v. *Bigg's Continent Noord* (1999) ECR I–3175); and *Geffroy* (Case C–366/98, *Criminal proceedings against Yannick Geffroy and Casino France SNC* (2000) ECR I–6579).

6. Maritime Transport Service Quality

After tackling safety issues and liability/insurance, the Commission is currently forging the third prong of Neptune's trident of maritime passenger protection. The ambition is to make sea travel more attractive by 'improving the quality of services provided and strengthening the protection of passengers' rights to raise them to the levels currently enjoyed by the users of other means of transport'. This statement stems from the ongoing consultation on sea passenger rights[107] that has the dual focus of, firstly, the protection of the rights of PRMs during a journey by sea and, secondly, the rights of passengers in the event of disruption, namely denied boarding, interruption, delay or cancellation of a journey by sea.[108] The consultation paper includes a questionnaire enquiring about the necessity and possible shape of regulation. The outcome of this consultation has recently been published.[109] But the findings of a study that should shed light on the needs of maritime passengers[110] (soon to be supplemented by a study on citizens' needs[111]) are, as yet, not available. It is therefore too early to conclude that legislation will flow from this initiative. But recurring passenger issues have been raised and it would not be surprising eventually to learn that it has been concluded to allow maritime passengers the protection that users of other transport services enjoy.

7. Inland Waterways

The proposed Athens Regulation suggests that passengers boarding vessels cruising on inland waterways should enjoy a level of protection equal to passengers travelling on seagoing vessels. It thereby follows a general tendency to approximate the law governing fluvial shipping to maritime law. But it also represents quite a bold extension of EC law into this area. So far, Community law in relation to fluvial transport has essentially been limited to rules on market opening, ship safety and boatmasters'

---

107 Commission staff working paper: 'Strengthening the protection of the rights of passengers travelling by sea or inland waterway in the European Union' – Public consultation document of the Directorate General for Energy and transport of 13 January 2006.

108 For a comparison with national law see Articles 9 to 12 of the Portuguese Law-Decree (n. 47 above).

109 Summary of contributions published on 6 December 2006: http://ec.europa.eu/transport/maritime/rights/doc/2006_03_30_consultation_summary_contributions_en.pdf (visited 22 December 2006).

110 Study 'Analysis and assessment of the level of protection of passenger rights in the EU transport sector'.

111 Invitation to tender concerning a public consultation with citizens on passengers' needs for maritime transport and international coach transport (OJ S128–136075 of 8 July 2006).

qualifications[112] and, most recently, a Directive on technical requirements for inland waterway shipping.[113]

EC law is a relatively recent addition to the long-established 'Rhine system', or *acquis rhénan* that was developed by the much older river commissions responsible for the management of Europe's main waterways. The Central Commission for Navigation on the Rhine (CCNR),[114] set up by the Mannheim Convention of 17 October 1868, is the oldest still existing form of institutionalized European cooperation, and indeed the world's most ancient international body. The CCNR's twin, the Danube Commission, founded in 1948,[115] succeeds the European Danube Commission created 1856 after the Crimean War (the first 'European Commission').

Efforts are being undertaken to reinforce cooperation between the river commissions and the EU[116] but these do not, at least for the time being, specifically mention passenger's interests. Indeed, until the publication of the proposal for the Athens Regulation, neither the Commission in a recent consultation[117] nor the OECD-sponsored European Conference of Ministers of Transport[118] seemed to place any emphasis on passenger rights. However, that should not necessarily be interpreted as a manifest lack of interest in the issue.

Regulators of inland waterways will be conscious of the fact that the transport conventions drafted by the United Nations Economic Commission for Europe[119]

---

112   For an overview, consult the Commission's 'Inland Waterway Transport' website: http://ec.europa.eu/transport/iw/index_en.htm (visited 22 December 2006). Latest addition to Community law on internal waterways: Directive 2005/44/EC on harmonised river information services (RIS) on inland waterways in the Community (OJ L255, 30 September 2005, p. 152), with corrigendum (OJ L344, 27 December 2005, p. 52), Regulation (EC) No. 1365/2006 on statistics of goods transport by inland waterways and repealing Council Directive 80/1119/EEC (OJ L264, 25 September 2006, p. 1) and Directive 2006/87/EC laying down technical requirements for inland waterway vessels and repealing Council Directive 82/714/EEC (OJ L389, 30 December 2006, p. 1).

113   European Parliament press release of 5 July 2006 'Inland waterway vessels – technical requirements'.

114   http://www.ccr-zkr.org.

115   The Danube Commission (http://www.danubecom-intern.org) was founded by the Belgrade Convention regarding the Regime of Navigation on the Danube of 18 August 1948.

116   The Commission Communication on the promotion of inland waterway transport 'NAIADES' – An integrated European Action Programme for inland waterway transport (COM(2006) 6 final of 17 January 2006) considers adhesion of the EC to the Rhine and the Danube Commissions (p. 12). See also Commission press releases IP/03/315 of 5 March 2003 'Inland waterways: European Commission signs co-operation agreement with Central Commission for Navigation on the Rhine', IP/03/1293 of 26 September 2003 'The EU should be actively involved in issues regarding navigation on the Rhine and the Danube' and the EESC Opinion on 'The institutional framework for inland waterway transport in Europe' (OJ C185, 8 August 2006, p. 101).

117   Commission Consultation: An Integrated Action Programme for Inland Waterway Transport of 14 July 2005.

118   http://www.cemt.org.

119   http://www.unece.org.

aiming to address passenger concerns remain dead letter. These are the UN-ECE Convention relating to the Limitation of the Liability of Owners of Inland Waterway Vessels of 1 March 1973 (CLN) and the UN-ECE Convention on the Contract for the International Carriage of Passengers and Luggage by Inland Waterway of 6 February 1976 (CVN), each with protocols dated 5 July 1978. Neither of them has entered into force due to an insufficient numbers of ratifications. The fault-based CVN, however, comes closest to what one could imagine becoming a project for an EC law instrument. It provides detailed rules on carrier liability for personal injury of passengers and damage and loss of their luggage, including rules for legal actions to enforce claims under the CVN.

(i) Strasbourg Convention

The only instrument of international law that has become effective for countries adjacent to the Rhine and Moselle (not the Danube) is therefore the Strasbourg Convention on the Limitation of Liability of Owners of Inland Navigation Vessels of 8 November 1988 (CLNI),[120] a modernized version of the unsuccessful CLN. Its contracting parties[121] have consented to a liability regime similar to the (maritime) LLMC,[122] although with lower, inflexible liability constraints. Article 7 of the CLNI limits passenger claims for loss of life or personal injury to 60,000 SDR, compared to 175,000 SDR under the LLMC 1996 and 250,000 (400,000) SDR under the Athens Convention 2002. Recognising the gap between the CLNI and the LLMC, the CCNR is negotiating an adjustment of the present CLNI limits, but it appears that this is confined to compensation for the loss caused by inflation (apart from modifying the CLNI to allow for accession of the countries of the Danube Convention – notably Romania and Bulgaria on the eve of their accession to the EU).

Now, according to the Athens Regulation, this amount would be increased more than four times over and balloon to a quarter of a million SDR for strict liability only.[123] Such an increase risks to overburden the financial resources of fluvial shipping, as it operates with much smaller vessels (and values) than maritime transport and the insurance is organized in a different way from seagoing ships. Some criticism of this proposed arrangement has already been hinted at by the CoR in its opinion on the Third Maritime Package, which 'asks the Commission to clarify the definition of inland waterway and advises it less extensive measures would suffice here'.[124] In the further legislative procedure, the EESC is hinting these problems[125] while the TRAN Committee's *Rapporteur* believes that the extension of the Athens Convention 2002

---

120   Authentic in French, German and Dutch, but not in English. The convention entered into force on 1 September 1997.
121   Ratified by Germany, Luxembourg, The Netherlands and Switzerland. Belgium and France have signed but not ratified.
122   Note 42 above.
123   It is uncertain whether Article 19 of the Athens Convention 2002 ('Other conventions on limitation of liability') can be interpreted as applying, considering also in that it refers to liability for seagoing ships.
124   OJ C229, 22 September 2006, p. 38, point 6.2.
125   OJ C318, 23 December 2006, p. 195, point 4.6.8.

to inland waterways is feasible and that the insurance market has the capacity to insure these types of risks with a reasonable extra cost for the passenger. In order to allow operators of fluvial shipping and the insurance market to adapt, a supplementary deadline of four years for applying the Athens Regulation would suffice.[126]

Nevertheless, the combined application of the Athens Convention 2002 and the CLNI would not necessarily be irreconcilable as they determine liability caps differently. While the CLNI puts forth a global limit on all liability claims, the Athens Convention 2002 provides a limit per passenger. However, the question of the proportionality of the financial arrangements of the Athens Regulation for inland waterway passenger transport will certainly need to be discussed in the legislative process, along with the general compatibility of the Athens Regulation with the *acquis rhénan* and the spirit of cooperation between the EC and the river commissions. Merely suggesting a four year term for the insurance market to adapt is perhaps insufficient to deal with the complexity of the issues raised.

Turning to national law applying the CLNI, it is perhaps interesting to note that Germany considers sea and fluvial shipping a similar case for passenger protection, albeit differentiating in the limits of liability due to the country's commitments in public international law. The relevant German law was drafted in the aftermath of the death of 19 people in 1984 when the launch *Martina* sank in Hamburg harbour. According to the rules in force at the time of the disaster, the liability of the ship owner was limited to the value of ship and cargo. A global liability cap was introduced in the law of 1986[127] to replace this completely inadequate regime. Henceforth, the *Binnenschiffahrtsgesetz*[128] (Inland Waterways Navigation Act of 1895) refers in § 77(1) for the transport of travellers and their luggage to § 664 HGB on maritime passengers. This, we have seen above, was Germany's adaptation of the Athens Convention before the London Protocol. Liability limits are however not those transposing the LLMC (§§ 486 to 487e HGB) but §§ 4 to 5m of the *Binnenschiffahrtsgesetz* and § 5e(1) No. 1 and § 5k in particular.[129] This deviation from the maritime regime stems from the fact that Germany is party to the Strasbourg Convention.[130] Now, with the proposed Athens Regulation, this combined approach has become Commission policy, as the future Regulation is designed to cover essentially all passengers boarding a vessel and crossing water.

(ii) The Athens Regulation and Fluvial Shipping

With the reservations expressed above, it is certainly sensible to care for consistency of regulation between two modes of transport that have much in common and to align Commission initiatives to national precedence. Also, establishing a separate,

---

126   Note 59 above.
127   Note 41 above.
128   Gesetz betreffend die privatrechtlichen Verhältnisse der Binnenschiffahrt vom 15. Juni 1895.
129   Hopperdietzel, 'Die Haftung bei der Veranstaltung von See- und Flussreisen': 195.
130   German ratification published in the Federal Law Gazette 1998 Series II, p. 1643.

inland waterway 'Loreley Regulation,'[131] perhaps in the form of a resuscitated CVN, is potentially more difficult to achieve then the extension proposed by the Athens Regulation. The fate of the CVN seems to show that States with an interest in fluvial shipping have little desire to bind themselves by a separate international regime for passenger rights in fluvial transport. Moreover, considering that these Member States already cooperate in river commissions, a singular legislative initiative could also be questioned under the Treaty's subsidiarity clause Article 5(2) EC,[132] while it would be constitutionally intriguing to look at the river commissions as some sort of enhanced cooperation[133] with third party participation.[134] To the advantage of the passenger, the Athens Regulation brushes off these subtleties with the momentum provided by the Athens Convention's incorporation.

But perhaps this brush is too rough. Applying the Athens Convention 2002 in the Annex of the Athens Regulation on fluvial shipping can prove to be tricky without adaptations. Plainly, the terminology of some provisions designed to suit sea transport does not fit inland waterway transport. The notion of 'ship,' for instance, is defined by the Convention as a 'seagoing vessel, excluding an air-cushion vehicle.'[135] Yet a riverboat will hardly ever be 'seagoing' because it is not constructed to brave ocean waves. What it should have is a navigability licence that gives evidence of its safety features and for which common rules exist at Community level.[136] It is therefore better to refer to the first sentence of Article 1(2)(b) CLNI to find a suitable definition of 'inland navigation vessel'.[137] Another example for incongruence is 'contract of carriage' which is defined as an agreement on 'the carriage *by sea* of a passenger'.[138] Staying with terminological problems, it is also clear that the 'Certificate of insurance or other financial security' mentioned in the Annex of the Athens Convention 2002, even if attached 'for reference purposes only',[139] is difficult to use without replacing the maritime vocabulary by terms common to fluvial shipping. But while

---

131   The Loreley is a rock towering over the Rhine where it forms a canyon between Bingen and Koblenz which according to legend is inhabited by a beautiful girl combing her hair. Ferrymen watching her were supposed to be distracted by the sight and neglect to look out for the rocks underneath the water's surface, thereby sinking their boats and drowning. The Loreley became the subject of poetic works in European literature in German (Clemens Brentano, Heinrich Heine, Erich Kästner) and French (Guillaume Apollinaire: La Loreley). Perhaps an apt label for fluvial passenger law.

132   Article I–11(3) of the Constitutional Treaty.

133   Articles 43 to 45 EU respectively Articles II–416 to II–423 of the Constitutional Treaty.

134   Switzerland is party to the Mannheim Convention; Serbia to the Belgrade Convention.

135   Article 1(3) of the Athens Convention 2002.

136   Directive 76/135/EEC on reciprocal recognition of navigability licences for inland waterway vessels, as amended by Directive 78/1016/EEC.

137   '"Vessel" shall mean an inland navigation vessel and shall also include hydrofoils, ferries and small craft but not air-cushion vehicles […].'

138   Article 1(2) of the Athens Convention 2002 (emphasis added).

139   COM(2005) 592 final of 23 November 2005, Communication introducing the maritime passenger proposal, p. 10, contradicting Article 1*bis* of the Athens Convention 2002 that states that the Annex 'constitutes an integral part of the convention'.

this appears to be hair-splitting, the really difficult question lurks again behind the compatibility of the Athens Convention 2002 on liability ceilings and compulsory insurance with the CLNI.[140] It is better that it should be beyond doubt that the (soon to be amended) Strasbourg Convention, which is binding for those Member States that have acceded to it, enjoys precedence over the Athens Convention 2002 where it applies. This is a significant point where the proposal for the Athens Regulation can still be improved.

8. Private International Law

Passenger transport crosses intra-Community borders (borders between Member States) and borders between the Community and third countries. The conflicts of law that arise from the internationality of transport services are resolved with the tools of an increasingly Europeanized private international law (PIL). In order to establish what law applies to a contract of passenger carriage – maritime or other – or to a loss suffered by a passenger, and to determine the competence of the tribunals of a certain country to judge a passenger case, reference has to be made to Community legal instruments. These are notably the 1980 Rome Convention on the law applicable on contractual obligations[141] (likely to be replaced by the Regulation on the law applicable to contractual obligations ['Rome I']);[142] Regulation (EC) No. 864/2007 on the law applicable to non-contractual obligations ['Rome II'];[143] Regulation (EC) No. 44/2001 on jurisdiction and the recognition and enforcement of judgements in civil and commercial matters[144] ['Brussels I'] (which outside Denmark has already

---

140   Article 19 of the Athens Convention 2002 ('Other conventions on limitation of liability') says that 'this Convention [the Athens Convention 2002] shall not modify the rights or duties of the carrier, the performing carrier, and their servants or agents provided for in international conventions relating to the limitation of liability of the owners of *seagoing ships* [emphasis added]'.

141   Convention on the law applicable to contractual obligations of 19 June 1980, as amended by the first and second protocol (consolidated version published in OJ C334, 30 December 2005, pp. 1–27).

142   COM(2005) 650 final of 15 December 2005. EESC Opinion (OJ C318, 23 December 2006, p. 56).

143   Note 89 above.

144   OJ L12, 16 January 2001, p. 1, amended by Regulation (EC) No. 1496/2002 (OJ L225, 22 August 2002, p. 13), Regulation (EC) No. 1937/2004 (OJ L334, 10 November 2004, p. 3) and Regulation (EC) No. 2245/2004 (OJ L381, 28 December 2004, p. 10).

replaced the 1968 Brussels Convention[145]); and the Lugano Convention concluded with EFTA-States,[146] as interpreted by the ECJ.[147]

As a rule, the consumer-specific provisions of these instruments do not extend to passengers. According to 'Brussels I' and 'Rome I' (assuming the latter is adopted as proposed), passenger contracts are 'contracts of carriage' and, if concluded outside a package tour in the sense of the Package Travel Directive, do not qualify as consumer contracts (Article 15(3) of 'Brussels I' and Article 5(3)(b) of 'Rome I'). This is irrespective of the private, non-professional character the passenger's journey may have or any other consideration that would take into account any intrinsic 'weaker party' status of the passenger.[148] This distinction between consumers and other passengers, it seems, has never really been made an issue and, if questioned, has been laconically excused with reference to the need for uniform rules in mass transactions such as for international transport.[149] The Schlosser Report[150] gave the following justification:

> The reason for leaving contracts of transport out of the scope of the special consumer protection provisions in the 1968 Convention is that such contracts are subject under international agreements to special sets of rules with very considerable ramifications, and the inclusion of those contracts in the 1968 Convention purely for jurisdictional purposes would merely complicate the legal position.

From the existence of these 'special sets of rules with very considerable ramifications,' it has further been concluded that the relative similarity of protective standards synchronized by transport law conventions makes the choice of law less significant. The passenger would find similar protection in the law of any country.[151] This latter argument will become compelling for intra-Community transport once the protective standards really had been aligned between Member States by virtue of

---

145   Convention of 27 September 1968 on jurisdiction and the enforcement of judgments in civil and commercial matters (consolidated version published in OJ C27, 26 January 1998, p. 1).

146   Lugano Convention on jurisdiction and the enforcement of judgments in civil and commercial matters of 16 September 1988 (OJ L319, 25 November 1988, p. 9). On the competence of the Community to conclude the new Lugano Convention, see the Opinion 1/06 of the Court (Full Court) of 7 February 2006. EFTA-States are Iceland, Liechtenstein, Norway and Switzerland (http://www.efta.int).

147   On the question of the Court's jurisdiction, see the Commission Communication 'Adaptation of the provisions of Title IV of the Treaty establishing the European Community relating to the jurisdiction of the Court of Justice with a view to ensuring more effective judicial protection' (COM(2006) 346 final of 28 June 2006).

148   Compare Recital 3 of the preamble to the railway passenger proposal as amended (Common Position).

149   Mankowski, *Seerechtliche Vertragsverhältnisse im Internationalen Privatrecht*, p. 393.

150   Report by Professor Peter F. Schlosser on the 1978 Accession Convention (OJ C59, 5 March 1979, pp. 71–150 (p. 119, para. 160)).

151   Mankowski, *Seerechtliche Vertragsverhältnisse im Internationalen Privatrecht*, pp. 394–5.

the adoption of passenger rights Regulations for the main modes of transport. Until such time however, it is worth asking whether the level of synchronization achieved by international law really is that satisfactory and whether the application of the law the carrier chooses would not potentially disadvantage the passenger (realistically, the carrier is the party who exercises the freedom of choice of law, rather than the passenger). Given that PIL in its distinction between consumer affairs and transport law is entrenched in its patterns and thus unlikely to grant the passenger consumer-like status in any future amendment, it is therefore even more important to adopt EC passenger legislation such as the Athens Regulation, which would thus make PIL less relevant.

How the EC-PIL instruments operate in practice (or would operate when adopted) shall now be outlined with special reference to maritime and fluvial passenger issues.

(i) Brussels I

As stated in its official title, 'Brussels I' informs litigants where to file a lawsuit and how to have a judgment recognized and enforced following such proceedings. Transport and insurance is subject to a number of specific provisions in 'Brussels I' that direct the pursuance of passenger claims to the Member States' judiciaries, that is, ordinary courts.[152]

Obviously, the (plaintiff) passenger may bring a case directly against the (defendant) carrier according to the general rules of the Regulation and *vice versa*. This will not be further explained here. But being able to turn to the insurer of the carrier may be essential for finding a solvent debtor and thus ensuring the enforceability of a passenger claim. In the event that the carrier is (voluntarily) insured against the risk that a passenger holds against him, Articles 8 to 14 (Articles 7 to 12(a) of the Brussels Convention) determine the jurisdiction for direct action against the insurer. Accordingly, a passenger can sue the insurer either in the courts of the Member State where the insurer is established or 'domiciled' (Article 9(1)(a)) or, as the passenger is the plaintiff of the case and beneficiary of the insurance policy, in his or her own country of residence (Article 9(1)(b)). The latter option, which will usually be more convenient for the passenger, is one of the changes introduced by the Regulation in comparison to its predecessor Brussels Convention.

If, on the other hand, the carrier's activity is covered by a (compulsory) liability insurance, his insurer may be sued not only in the jurisdictions applicable to voluntarily insurance, but also in the courts of the Member State where the harmful event occurred (Article 10) or, if feasible under the *lex fori* (the law of the court), in the country where the passenger has brought a case against the insured carrier (Article 11(1)).

Within the ambit of passenger law, these provisions are mandatory in the sense that it is not possible to depart *ex ante* from these provisions by agreement between carrier and passenger. This stipulation prevails against the exemptions from the

---

152   For arbitration and mediation the Regulation does not apply (Article 1(2)(d) 'Brussels I,' identical with Article 1 No. 4 Brussels Convention).

rule: although Article 13(5) would principally allow for agreements relating to an insurance contract in so far as it covers one or more of the risks set out in Article 14, Article 14 defines these risks narrowly to limit this discretion in the interest of passengers. Accordingly, Article 14(1) for goods in transit essentially excludes 'loss or damage to passengers' baggage' where the transit is commercially conducted by seagoing ships (but not inland vessels) and aircraft (not trains or coaches).

This distinction between passengers of different modes of transport may become a topic for the implementation report due under Article 73 also to be published in 2007. Article 14(2) on liability arising out of the use or operation of a ship or aircraft excludes 'bodily injury to passengers or loss of or damage to their baggage' (but not, for instance, damage due to delay). For maritime transport, Article 7 of 'Brussels I' (Article 6(a) Brussels Convention) finally clarifies that the court determined by the Regulation in liability cases is also competent to rule over claims for limitation of such liability.

How do these rules relate to rules on jurisdiction, recognition and enforcement in international transport conventions? Insofar as Member States have ratified a convention before the adoption of 'Brussels I' (as it might be the case with some States and the CIV 1999), the earlier one prevails according to Article 71 of the Regulation. Insofar as a convention has been concluded after 'Brussels I' (as in the case of the Athens Convention 2002), the Community has exclusive competence for jurisdiction, recognition and enforcement of judgments. So the EC must either be party to the convention or entitle Member States to ratify the convention in the Community interest. If this is the case, the international agreement will prevail over 'Brussels I'. A specific Community act of transposition is not then actually necessary. Where the Community has adopted such an act anyway – whether for transparency or other reasons (like in the case of the Athens Regulation) – the EC instrument should correspond with international law. In any event, the plaintiffs could rely on and invoke the convention's law and its prevalence over 'Brussels I'.

For maritime passenger transport, the future Athens Regulation would, within its scope of application, modify 'Brussels I'. The (incorporated) Athens Convention 2002 provides for specific rules on jurisdiction (Article 17) and recognition and enforcement (17*bis*).[153]

According to Article 17(1), the passenger can choose between four different jurisdictions for bringing a claim in a carrier liability case (liability of the carrier (Article 3) and performing carrier (Article 4)). These are the State either of (a) permanent residence or principal place of business of the defendant, (b) departure or that of the destination according to the contract of carriage, (c) the domicile or permanent residence of the claimant, if the defendant has a place of business and is subject to jurisdiction of that State, or (d) where the contract of carriage was made, if the defendant has a place of business and is subject to jurisdiction of that State. Article 17(2) gives the same choice to the passenger suing the carrier's insurer directly, according to Article 4*bis*(10). Article 17(3) allows passenger and carrier to choose a competent court of arbitration after the occurrence of the incident.

---

153   Soyer, 'Sundry Considerations on the Draft Protocol to the Athens Convention Relating to the Carriage of Passengers and Their Luggage at Sea 1974': 17–18.

Article 17*bis* obliges State parties to recognize judgments 'given by a court with jurisdiction in accordance with Article 17 which is enforceable in the State of origin where it is no longer subject to ordinary forms of review'. Exceptions exist for judgments obtained by fraud and where the defendant was not given reasonable notice and a fair opportunity to present his or her case (Article 17*bis*(1)). Otherwise, the judgment shall be enforceable in each State party as soon as the formalities required in that State have been complied with, while the formalities shall not permit the merits of the case to be re-opened (Article 17*bis*(2)).

Between EU Member States, continued application of the regime for recognition and enforcement established by 'Brussels I' is assured by virtue of the disconnection clause Article 17*bis*(3), that is, a clause that allows State parties to continue to apply their own rules in contravention of international law. Problems may arise due to the disconnection clause's inbuilt limitation of uncertain scope, which requires that the rules of 'Brussels I' only prevail 'provided that their effect is to ensure that judgments are recognized and enforced *at least to the same extent* as under Article 17*bis*(1) and (2)' [emphasis added]. This wording creates some uncertainty as to the applicable rules. Certain however is that both 'Brussels I' and an incorporated Athens Convention 2002 overrule and supersede national rules such as Article 20 of the Portuguese Law-Decree No. 349 of 1986 (*Tribunal competente*) that provides for own rules for the jurisdictions of courts.

Other transport conventions also provide for rules on jurisdiction. In railway passenger transport, Article 57(1) ('Forum') of CIV 1999 stipulates that

> … actions based on these Uniform Rules may be brought before the courts or tribunals of Member States [*of CIV*] designated between the parties or before the courts or tribunal of the Member State on whose territory the defendant has his domicile or habitual residence, his principal place of business or the branch or agency which concluded the contract of carriage. Other courts or tribunals may not be seized.

This PIL clause, which deviates from 'Brussels I,' is omitted from Annex I of the railway passenger proposal as amended by the Common Position (which otherwise proclaims adherence to international law). This presents a dilemma for the 20 EU Member States which have ratified CIV and are bound by it. Article 42 COTIF 1999 only allows declarations and reservations to the Convention when they are 'expressly provided for by the provisions themselves', which is not the case with Article 57 CIV. The relationship between the *lex specialis* CIV and 'Brussels I' will thus have to be worked out in application of Article 71 of the 'Brussels I' Regulation.

Article 33 of the Montreal Convention ('Jurisdiction'), which provides for a specialized regime for air passenger transport, poses no such problems because, being incorporated into the *acquis*, it is *lex specialis* in relation to 'Brussels I'. One relatively passenger-friendly provision however is Article 33(2), newly introduced in comparison to the Warsaw Agreement, which gives the passenger an additional forum in which to sue, but only for bodily injury and not, for instance, for loss or damage to baggage or damage due to delay (perhaps only an editorial omission).

(ii) Rome I

De lege ferenda – that is, according to law as it ought to be – 'Rome I' would tell passenger/carrier litigants what law applies to the contract of carriage. Should the pending proposal[154] become law and supersede the Rome Convention, its Article 4(1)(c) would, in the absence of an express choice of law, determine that 'a contract of carriage shall be governed by the law of the country in which the carrier has his habitual residence'. Knowing that for companies, 'habitual residence' is their 'principal establishment' (Article 18(1)),[155] the result would be that passenger contracts would be governed by a law which, in cross-border travel, would mostly be a contract law to which the passenger is unaccustomed.

Even if the passenger was a consumer, that is, a natural person acting outside his or her professional sphere (Article 5(2)),[156] this rule would not change if the person is not a package tourist (Article 5(3) No. 2), that is, a person acquiring a transport/accommodation combination forming a 'travel package' according to Article 2(1) of Directive 90/314/EEC.[157]

In maritime transport, such status of a passenger can, at times, be difficult to determine. There might be no argument to say that a ferry passenger hiring a deckchair with his ticket is not a package tourist, despite the leisurely appearance he or she might give. But to find a straightforward answer would be more complicated in the case of the passenger travelling overnight who might rent a cabin when also buying a travel ticket. This would seem to be a transport/accommodation combination, although the transport service, not the accommodation, would still form the main element of the contract. Perhaps it is helpful to draw a parallel here with night trains and sleeping-car compartments. In an everyday understanding, the person using these services is still just a train passenger and not a package tourist. In this interpretation, only cruise ship travels are travel packages and covered by EC law on travel and tourism.

(iii) Rome II

'Rome II', the tort law complementary to 'Rome I', tells the person who has sustained damage (that is, the passenger) and the person claimed to be liable (that

---

154   Note 142 above.

155   Compare Article 23(1) of 'Rome II'.

156   Article 5(2)(first sub-para.) of the 'Rome I' proposal says that it 'shall apply to contracts concluded by a natural person, the consumer, who has his habitual residence in a Member State for a purpose which can be regarded as being outside his trade or profession with another person, the professional, acting in the exercise of his trade or profession'.

157   Note, however, that the notion of 'consumer' in package travel is wider than the standard formula (Article 2(4) of Directive 90/314/EEC).

is, the carrier) which country's law applies should the passenger be killed or hurt or his or her baggage be damaged or lost. It covers fault-based tort law, but also obligations based on rules imposing strict liability. 'Rome II' establishes the *lex loci damni* principle enshrined in its Article 4(1), that is, the law of the place (country) applies where the damage is sustained (see also Recitals 16 to 18 of the preamble). Direct actions against the insurer of the person liable are possible under Article 18, provided that the law applicable to the tort or to the insurance contract allows for such actions. Direct actions are for instance permitted by Article 4*bis*(10) of the Athens Convention 2002, as already shown above.

9. Towards 2009

It will be interesting to observe the ratification process of the Athens Convention 2002, the advances of the German and the Portuguese EU presidencies concerning the proposed Athens Regulation and whatever other proposals the Commission may make further to consultations and studies. But it is no guessing game to predict that at the end of the current political cycle of the Commission and European Parliament in 2009, a mixed audience of transport and consumer lawyers will look upon one (or perhaps more) maritime passenger Regulation(s) that will make further inroads into European private law. Combined with PIL Regulations, this emerging legislation will provide for a fairly complete set of European law on passenger issues, directly applicable with the same wording in 27 Member States and with the European Court of Justice as the final arbiter for all interpretative disputes. Also bearing in mind that an estimated 400 million plus passengers pass through European ports every year who will be increasingly aware of their rights, it is timely to prepare for the advent of EC maritime and fluvial passenger law.

9 The Future of Consumer Law: Reflections on a Regulatory Framework for a Small Island State

Paul Edgar Micallef[1]

1. Introduction

Consumer law is a dynamic area of law and consequently needs continuously to be kept under review if it is to be responsive to the changing requirements of the modern market. In this paper the focus is on what I believe should be the changes to Maltese consumer law. I strongly contend that there are various matters that need to be addressed if the existing legal framework is to respond to the continuous changing environment of consumer affairs in Malta. These, notably, include improving the existing regulatory setup and the enforcement tools available, which have not always proved to be effective and revising certain parts dealing with substantive law issues.[2] In this paper, I focus on what I consider to be the more crucial areas that need to be addressed and suggest some changes.

As a small country, Malta cannot ignore certain realities conditioned, in part, by the limitation of human and financial resources, coupled with the fact that, geographically, Malta is a small island in the middle of the Mediterranean. Time and again, the Maltese Government has opted to implement legislative measures that might suit the needs of much larger countries like the United Kingdom, but were not necessarily the optimum solution for Malta. The classical example, that typifies such an approach, is in the regulation of utilities, where the Maltese Government opted to create separate sector-specific regulators as distinct from having a comprehensive regulatory authority for all utilities, a route followed by many of the larger EU Member States but, significantly, not by some of the smaller Member States.[3]

In many instances the approach taken by the Maltese Government was, with some modifications to adapt to local legislative requirements, to emulate the approach taken by other countries. This does not mean that the Maltese Government has always slavishly copied what other countries do. There have been some instances, albeit few

---

1   Dr. Micallef is a member of the Consumer Affairs Council and chief legal adviser with the Malta Communications Authority. This paper reflects only his personal views.
2   After-sales services is a case in point.
3   The Maltese Government had actually proposed a single utility regulator in 1999 but the idea was subsequently discarded. See White Paper *Privatisation – A Strategy for the Future*, Ministry of Finance, November 1999. It is relevant to note that two of the smallest EU member states, Luxembourg and Latvia, actually had sectoral utility regulators and subsequently opted for a single utility regulator.

and far between,[4] where the Maltese Government took some interesting and, at times original, initiatives as a means of safeguarding and promoting consumer rights. Generally, however, the Maltese Government has been content with following the footsteps of other countries. To some degree, this is understandable given that Malta, unlike larger countries, does not have the resources to undertake in depth research leading to the formulation of detailed legislative measures specifically intended to cater for Maltese domestic requirements. Time and again the approach adopted was to look at what other countries have done in a given area and copy those measures into domestic law.

If anything the accession on the 1 May 2004 of Malta as a full Member State within the EU, has reduced the possibility of the Maltese authorities devising tailor made 'original' domestic legislative measures, given that after that date Malta, as a Member State of the EU, is required to abide with the EU consumer protection *acquis*, ensuring that the various applicable directives are transposed as part of national law. The impact of the EU on Maltese consumer law has been in evidence since at least 1990 when Malta applied to join the EU. Indeed, even before the date of accession, a good part of the then existing EU consumer protection *acquis* had already been transposed into Maltese law.[5] This is a reality that cannot be ignored and EU consumer policies will, at least for the foreseeable future, continue to be the basis of most Maltese consumer laws.

2. Consumer Law in Malta So Far

In discussing the future of consumer law in Malta, one must factor in the legislative and political history of Malta. The legal tradition of Malta is, to some extent, unique since Maltese law has been subjected to both Continental Civil law and Anglo–Saxon law, legal influences that are the result of the proximity to Italy and the close inevitable cultural ties with this country,[6] and of the British colonial rule that came to an end with political independence in 1964. In addition, as has already been observed, a more recent important political milestone in the history of Malta, that has impacted on the content of Maltese legislation and, for the foreseeable future, should continue to do so in a significant way, was the membership of Malta within the EU.

---

4   Two such instances are, respectively, the rights granted to recognized consumer associations under the Consumer Affairs Act whereby associations that satisfy certain criteria are entitled to be so recognized and consequently to certain rights at law including, notably, the right to request the issue of compliance orders under the Act; and the creation of the Consumer Claims Tribunal, providing consumers with a quick, cheap and efficient means of redress in relation to disputes with traders involving small monetary claims.

5   The notable exception was the Consumer Credit Directive which was only transposed in March 2005, following the enactment of the Consumer Credit Regulations as per Legal Notice 84 of 2005.

6   Until 1934 Italian was one of the official languages and was used by the legal profession and by the Maltese Courts. After that date, Italian was replaced by Maltese, which is now the national language, whilst English enjoys the status of an official language.

When drafting legislation, especially in the sphere of public law, to some extent Malta has always looked at the wealth of the legal knowledge of the United Kingdom and to a lesser degree of other British Commonwealth countries and of Ireland.[7] With membership in the EU, there has been a shift in the approach adopted by the Maltese Government since many Maltese laws are now EU inspired, implementing requirements established in the applicable EU directives. This is also the case with Maltese consumer law, with the bulk of consumer laws introduced since the early 1990s being enacted to implement various EU consumer protection related directives.

Consumer policy and legislation in Malta is not, however, solely driven by the requirement to abide with and implement the applicable EU *acquis*. Equally, if not more, important is the need to ensure that consumer rights in Malta are adequately protected. The measures introduced over the years by different Maltese Governments indicate a degree of political and social sensitivity to cater for this consideration. In some instances, the Maltese Government was not simply content in introducing the minimum requirements as set down by the various EU directives but opted to go beyond those minimum requirements. Examples include the provisions on unfair terms and on sales of goods to consumers under the Consumer Affairs Act,[8] and the Timeshare Promotion (Licensing of OPC Representatives) Regulations.[9]

Consumer law in Malta does not have a long history. Until the early 1980s consumer law did not even have an identity of its own. Until then there were various laws dealing with different aspects of consumer protection. Several parts of the Civil Code[10] dealt, and still do, with matters that intimately relate to consumer law including torts and quasi-torts, the rights and obligations of sellers and buyers, and contracts of letting and hiring.[11] The Civil Code, however, nowhere granted any specific rights to

---

7   In recent years the legislative experience of Ireland has been an important source for Malta more so as a model in implementing certain EU directives given similar public law traditions.

8   Under Articles 44–7 of Part VI of the Consumer Affairs Act the concept of unfairness is extended to terms 'individually negotiated', whereas under Part VIII of the Act there are wide ranging requirements about the minimum information that a trader must include in a commercial guarantee and about the obligations, onerous on traders, with regard to the provision of replacement parts and repair services.

9   See Legal Notice 209 of 2004 which came into force on the 25 May 2004. These regulations regulate the conduct of what are described as 'outside promotional contacts' and aim to prohibit aggressive marketing practices by timeshare salespersons which have, in past, caused considerable harm to the timeshare industry in Malta and go beyond the measures stated in the Council Directive 94/47/EC dealing with timeshare. The measures in the Directive are implemented in a separate set of regulations under the Protection of Buyers in Contracts for Time Sharing of Immovable Property Regulations. See also P.E. Micallef, 'The Regulation of Timeshare under Maltese Law', *Travel Law Journal*, Issue 2 (2005): 76–84.

10   The Code, enacted in the latter part of the nineteenth-century, was in line with the civil law traditions of Malta and was modelled on the Code Napoleon.

11   See Civil Code, Title II subtitle II, Title IV subtitles IV and V and Title IX thereof. These provisions are still in place and still apply to consumers provided they do not detract from the more specific rights that consumers enjoy under consumer law. See

the figure of the 'consumer'. Indeed the word 'consumer' was not even used in the Code.[12] Other laws included the Weights and Measures Ordinance,[13] and the Food, Drugs and Drinking Water Act,[14] the Code of Police Laws[15] and the Criminal Code,[16] which laws similarly focused on specific matters relating to consumer protection without referring specifically to the 'consumer'.

The beginning of the 1980s saw some interesting, if somewhat sporadic, developments in the sphere of consumer protection. The first, albeit small step, was taken in 1981, with the enactment of the Consumer Protection Act. This was a very short law with a somewhat grandiose and misleading title, giving the impression of being a general law on consumer protection when, in actual fact, this law consisted of only seven provisions, the purpose of which was to protect recognized consumer associations from ruinous libel lawsuits when making *bona fide* public statements.[17] In the mid-1980s two other laws, namely the Trade Descriptions Act which law in substance was based on the United Kingdom Trade Descriptions Act of 1968, and the Door-to-Door Salesmen Act, were enacted to address specific issues relating to consumer protection. The latter law is noteworthy in that, for the first time in Maltese consumer law, a law was, in part, modelled on an EU consumer protection directive.[18]

The turning point in the history of consumer legislation was the publication by Government of a White Paper on Consumer Protection in 1991.[19] Until then consumer protection was dealt with in a piecemeal fashion, focusing on specific issues and lacking a general comprehensive and coordinated approach, with a myriad of different public authorities, including the Department of Public Health, the Commissioner of Police, the Director of Trade, the tourism authorities[20] and the

---

    Articles 55 and 92 of the Consumer Affairs Act.

12   With one exception, the Civil Code has never featured in the context of the implementation of consumer protection measures. The only instance was when the period of remedies available in context of latent defects in movables was extended from one month to six months, this as part of the measures approved by Parliament in 1994 when enacting measures to complement the Consumer Affairs Act.

13   The Weights and Measures Ordinance was replaced by the Metrology Act.

14   This law was repealed and replaced by the Food Safety Act.

15   Parts IX, X and XI of the Code which respectively deal with Hotels and other Lodging Houses, Shopkeepers and other Traders, and the requirement of licences in respect of certain trades. Some of these provisions have since been repealed.

16   See Titles VI and IX which deal with crimes against public trade and crimes against property and public safety.

17   This law was repealed with the coming into force of the Consumer Affairs Act in 1996.

18   At that stage, Malta had not yet expressed any intention of joining the EU, however the drafters of that law opted to model certain provisions on Council Directive 85/577/ ECC of 20 December 1985.

19   White Paper: *Rights for the Consumer*, August 1991. A second White Paper: *Fair Trading the next step forward...*, was published in 1993 and included a draft of the Consumer Affairs Act.

20   The nomenclature of regulatory authorities responsible for tourism has changed over the years. In 1991 the competent authority was the Department of Tourism, now this

Malta Board of Standards, being separately responsible for the administration of various laws relating directly or indirectly to some aspect of consumer protection.

In the 1991 White Paper the Government, for the first time, undertook a fairly wide ranging review of the laws[21] that, until that date, dealt with some aspect of consumer protection, proposing new measures to deal with consumer protection in a comprehensive manner. The White Paper proposed a new regulatory body – the Consumer Protection Council – and new laws on consumer related issues ranging from the prohibition of unfair terms and misleading advertising to product liability and product safety.[22] Significantly, the White Paper also suggested there should be a single comprehensive law on consumer protection and a small claims court,[23] proposals that, to some degree, were subsequently taken up.

The next step was the enactment, in 1994, of the Consumer Affairs Act.[24] The purpose of this law was primarily to have in place the regulatory structures to deal with consumer affairs and to lay down the foundations for the gradual enactment of different measures relating to substantive consumer law, either by amending the Consumer Affairs Act or by subsidiary legislation promulgated by the Minister responsible for consumer affairs, by virtue of his powers under this Act. The Consumer Affairs Act provided for the establishment of the office of the Director of Consumer Affairs, with the responsibility of ensuring compliance with the provisions of the Act and other consumer related laws,[25] empowering him with enforcement tools;[26] the setting up of the Consumer Affairs Council composed of persons coming from both the business and the consumer lobbies, with the role of advising Government on consumer policies; and of the Consumer Claims Tribunal, an adjudicative forum to hear and determine disputes between consumers and traders involving small monetary values. In addition, the Act included a separate part dealing with the role of voluntary consumer associations, granting associations that satisfy certain criteria, rights at law in order to facilitate their task in protecting and promoting consumer interests.[27]

---

role has been assumed by the Malta Tourism Authority.

21   Not all areas were dealt with. There were, for example, no proposals relating to package travel or timeshare.

22   Page 7 onwards of the White Paper.

23   See *ibid.*, at p. 32.

24   Act No. XXVIII of 1994 which was published on 2 December 1994 and all the provisions of this Act came into force on 23 January 1996.

25   Notably the Weights and Measures Ordinance, the Trade Descriptions Act and the Door-to-Door Salesmen Act. The responsibility for the Weights and Measures Ordinance was subsequently transferred to the Malta Standards Authority.

26   These tools included the faculty of issuing 'public warning statements' and requiring traders to give written undertakings where there has been a breach of certain provisions.

27   This part of the Act improved upon the provisions of the former Consumer Protection Act by establishing clear criteria at law on the basis of which associations are entitled to be recognized as 'registered consumer associations' by the Consumer Affairs Council.

In 2000 the Government, in line with its endeavours to implement the various EU consumer protection directives, undertook a major overhaul of the Consumer Affairs Act, amending this Act by adding new parts relating to the use of unfair terms in consumer contracts, misleading and comparative advertising, product liability, and the sale of goods to consumers, whilst empowering the Director of Consumer Affairs with the faculty of issuing compliance orders, either of his initiative or at the request of a 'qualifying body',[28] against any person acting in breach of the Consumer Affairs Act or of any regulations made thereunder. In addition, as part of these changes, the Government amended the Door-to-Door Salesmen Act[29] and the Malta Travel and Tourism Services Act.[30]

Subsequently various regulations were promulgated under the Consumer Affairs Act primarily in order to implement other consumer related EU directives which had not as yet been transposed under Maltese law. These included the Distance Selling Regulations, the Consumer Affairs Act (Price Indication) Regulations, and the Consumer Credit Regulations.[31] Another important law enacted in compliance with EU consumer *acquis* was the Product Safety Act,[32] enforced by the Director of Consumer Affairs.

On the structural side, even if not reflected at law, in 2001 Government took the administrative decision to amalgamate the Office of Fair Competition and the Office of the Director of Consumer Affairs in one single new public agency called the Consumer and Competition Division with the Director General of this division exercising the dual roles of the Director of the Office of Fair Competition and of the Director of Consumer Affairs. The functions of the Division are broadly spread through three directorates namely policy and regulatory services, operations, and information and client services, with all three directorates, in varying degrees, dealing with both consumer and competition issues.[33]

Not all laws implementing the EU consumer protection directives, or which are intended to protect consumers, have been enacted within the framework of the Consumer Affairs Act or are administered or enforced by the Director of Consumer Affairs. Hence, issues related to the travel and leisure industry, notably package travel and timeshare, are dealt with by regulations issued under the Malta Tourism and Travel Services Act.[34] Other laws relating to consumer protection issues not

---

28   'Qualifying body' includes registered consumer associations and any other body designated as such by the Minister responsible for consumer affairs.

29   The title of this law was changed to 'Doorstep Contracts Act'.

30   The Malta Travel and Tourism Services Act was amended in order to give the Minister responsible for tourism the *vires* to introduce regulations relating to timeshare.

31   These regulations were promulgated respectively by Legal Notices 186 of 2001, 283 of 2001 and 84 of 2005.

32   See Chapter 427 of the Laws of Malta.

33   There is a fourth directorate – the Support Services Directorate – that deals with corporate matters including human resources and finance of the Division.

34   See Legal Notice 157 of 2000 entitled the 'Package Travel, Package Holidays and Package Tours Regulations', Legal Notice 269 of 2000 entitled the 'Protection of Buyers in Contracts for Time Sharing of Immovable Property Regulations' and Legal Notice 299 of 2004 entitled 'Timeshare Promotion (Licensing of OPC Representatives)

dealt by or under the Consumer Affairs Act include the Manufacture of Medicinal Products for Human Use Regulations,[35] enforced by the Licensing Authority; the Distance Selling (Retail Financial Services) Regulations,[36] enforced by the Malta Financial Services Authority; the Civil Aviation (Denied Boarding Compensation and Assistance to Passengers) Regulations,[37] enforced by the Director of Civil Aviation; and the Electronic Commerce Act,[38] enforced by the Malta Communications Authority.

3. The Regulatory Framework – Identifying and Addressing the Shortcomings

(i) The Roles of the Director of Consumer Affairs and of the Sector-Specific Regulators

Given the myriad of the issues that impact on consumers including product safety, public utility regulation, standards, financial services and general commercial activities, it is fairly obvious that consumer protection, even in a small country like Malta, can never realistically be the exclusive responsibility of a single public authority. This consideration does not mean that there should not be a focal organization with a general remit to ensure that consumer interests are safeguarded, whilst at the same time having in place sector-specific regulatory authorities with a remit to deal with consumer issues related to their sectors of responsibility. In part this is reflected in the approach taken by the Maltese legislator, with the establishment of the post of Director of Consumer Affairs who has a 'general' consumer protection remit, and of a number of other public authorities with sector-specific expertise empowered to enforce certain aspects relating to consumer protection falling within their respective areas of responsibility.

In a relatively short time span following the establishment under the Consumer Affairs Act of the post of Director of Consumer Affairs in 1996, various sector-specific regulatory authorities with a remit to deal with certain areas relating to consumer protection came into being.[39] As the various structures set up under the Consumer Affairs Act[40] and the different sector-specific regulatory authorities started to function, the overall regulatory consumer protection framework in time started to manifest various shortcomings. In the main these shortcomings relate to the overlap and lack of clarity of the roles of the Director of Consumer Affairs on the one hand,

---

Regulations'.
35   See Legal Notice 143 of 2004.
36   See Legal Notice 36 of 2005.
37   See Legal Notice 297 of 2005.
38   See Chapter 426 of the Laws of Malta.
39   Between 1999 and 2000 the Malta Tourism Authority, the Malta Standards Authority, the Malta Communications Authority and the Food Safety Commission, all with a remit in some aspect impinging on consumer protection, came into being.
40   Apart from the post of the Director of Consumer Affairs, the Act also provides for the establishment of the Consumer Affairs Council, the Consumer Claims Tribunal and regulates the role of registered consumer associations.

and of the sector-specific regulatory authorities on the other hand, coupled with the apparent lack of strong, active regulatory action intended to protect consumer rights. In part this situation occurs because it is not always clear with which competent regulatory authority certain complaints should be lodged. Moreover, in some instances, issues arising out of the same complaint contravene different consumer laws enforced by different authorities. For example, the use of an unfair term in a timeshare agreement may contravene both the Protection of Buyers in Contracts for Time Sharing of Immoveable Property Regulations, enforced by the Malta Tourism Authority, and Part VI of the Consumer Affairs Act,[41] enforced by the Director of Consumer Affairs.

In yet other instances, matters are further compounded by the dependency of sector-specific regulators – especially the public utility regulators – on the intervention of the Director of Consumer Affairs, where there are alleged breaches of consumer law that impact users negatively. Primarily, this occurs because the sector-specific regulators have limited or no powers at law to intervene under the Consumer Affairs Act or under the regulations made thereunder. Hence, in the electronic communications sector, one of the stated primary objectives at law of the Malta Communications Authority (MCA) is to ensure 'a high level of protection for consumers in their dealings with suppliers ...' and to promote 'the provision of clear information, in particular requiring transparency of tariffs and conditions for using publicly available electronic communications services'.[42] Yet, notwithstanding these laudable objectives, the MCA has no authority to intervene in consumer disputes involving the sectors it regulates where such disputes involve an alleged breach of the provisions of the Consumer Affairs Act or any of the regulations made thereunder, notably with regard to disputes about the use of unfair terms in consumer contracts and the use of misleading and comparative advertising. In a recent case that related to the communications sector, involving the use of unfair terms by a cable television company, the MCA was unable to intervene directly to curb the use of such terms, because the only competent enforcement authority under the Consumer Affairs Act is the Director of Consumer Affairs. The end result in this instance was that the MCA, notwithstanding its competency and specialized knowledge of the sector, was unable to intervene directly. Consequently, the issue had to be referred to the Director of Consumer Affairs who, whilst having the powers at law to intervene, did not have the required sector-specific expertise to be able to intervene effectively.

In a small jurisdiction like Malta, the reference from one public authority to another hardly makes sense and certainly does not augur well for an effective and quick response in dealing with such disputes, more so when in such instances *prima facie* the sector-specific authority is generally more *au courant* in the intricacies

---

41   Articles 44 to 49 of Part VI of the Consumer Affairs Act prohibit the use of unfair terms in contracts between consumers and traders.

42   See Electronic Communications (Regulation) Act, Articles 4(c)(ii) and (iv). In the case of the MRA there is no similar objective clause under the Malta Resources Authority Act. However, as is the case with the MCA, consumers look towards the MRA for its intervention with regard to disputes that arise concerning energy and water service providers.

involved and in the measures that can be best adopted in curbing the alleged abuse of the applicable consumer law provisions. Clearly one of the issues that must be addressed is to ensure that such disputes are investigated and determined by the public authority that is best versed in the particulars of the issues involved. Complementary to this consideration, the said public authority must be adequately empowered at law and resourced to undertake such a regulatory task. This must be the point of departure in the regulation of any given consumer issue. If the attaining situation is allowed to continue, it will mean that consumers will continue to be faced with a situation where non-compliance of consumer legislation, in many instances, has to be referred to the Director of Consumer Affairs, rather than to the competent sector-specific authority having the required expertise and knowledge of the issues that need to be investigated.

There are various options available to address this situation. One option, which would not necessitate any amendments to the applicable legislation, is for the Director of Consumer Affairs to enter into a memorandum of understanding with each sector-specific regulator, establishing how each authority will act when faced with an issue which potentially infringes both consumer laws enforced by the Director and the legislation enforced by the sector-specific regulator. Complementary to such a measure, each sector-specific regulator can also be designated as a 'qualifying body' by the Minister responsible for consumer affairs under the Consumer Affairs Act.[43] This would signify that each sector-specific regulator would be entitled to avail itself of the procedures under Part IX of the Consumer Affairs Act and accordingly request the Director of Consumer Affairs to issue a compliance order with regard to infringements of the Consumer Affairs Act or any regulations made thereunder. Such an approach, however, only partially ensures that there is effective enforcement, since the sector-specific regulator remains dependent on the Director of Consumer Affairs for the initiation of corrective enforcement procedures. Such a situation is conducive to unnecessary bureaucratic cross-references from one regulatory authority to another.

Another, possibly more practical, option is for the Consumer Affairs Act to be amended, enabling the Minister responsible for consumer affairs to authorize sector-specific regulators to exercise some of the powers that the Director has under that Act, notably the power to issue compliance orders under Part IX of the Act, with, however, the obvious limitation that the exercise of such powers would be restricted to the sectors falling within the remit of the sector-specific regulator concerned. Such a measure would enable the sector-specific regulator to investigate and take the appropriate regulatory measures in cases involving, for example, the use of unfair terms or misleading advertising in the sectors falling under the remit of that regulator and where, to date, the regulator was unable to act of its own accord, precisely because it was not authorized to do so under the Consumer Affairs Act.

This option would necessitate the inclusion of rules determining how the Director and the sector-specific regulator are to operate in such instances so as to ensure that matters are done in a coordinated fashion. Alternatively, a memorandum of understanding can be entered into between the Director and each sector-specific

---

43   See Consumer Affairs Act, Article 2 and Article 94 onwards.

regulator.[44] Furthermore, if sector-specific regulators are empowered to exercise the same powers that the Director has under the Consumer Affairs Act, then it is imperative that the said regulators are also empowered to utilize the same enforcement tools available to the Director of Consumer Affairs under the Consumer Affairs Act, including the issuance of public warnings statements and of compliance orders, and requiring undertakings from persons who act in breach of the law.[45]

(ii) The Existing Setup and the Enforcement Tools Available – Do They Suffice to Ensure Effective Consumer Protection?

The present setup of a Government department, headed by the Director of Consumer Affairs, operating as part of an umbrella organization – the Consumer and Competition Division[46] – lacks the desired flexibility to act autonomously from Government; and is not perceived by stakeholders generally as being adequately resourced to undertake the lead role in regulating consumer affairs in Malta. This perception is evidenced by the few instances of enforcement action taken by the Director, especially in recent years, with the substantial increase in consumer legislation including the enactment of laws regulating unfair terms, advertising and other commercial practices. With the increase in the number of laws, one would have expected a more proactive and visible presence in regulating abuses in the market. This, however, has not materialized. Equally disturbing is that there has been scarce recourse by consumers to the civil remedies available to them under the Consumer Affairs Act, particularly in contesting one-sided contracts littered with blatantly unfair terms, or the utilization of the rights safeguarding the rights of consumers when purchasing goods.[47]

Whilst there is no doubt that the enforcement tools under the Consumer Affairs Act can be improved upon, to date these tools have been scarcely, if at all, used. Ultimately, one cannot really criticize the ineffectiveness of the existing enforcement tools simply because these have rarely been used and therefore put to the test. There appear to be various reasons for this situation. In the first instance, the Director of Consumer Affairs is not adequately resourced to ensure that he is able to fulfil his mandate at law with a reasonable degree of success. The main focus of the work undertaken since the inception of the office of the Director of Consumer Affairs has been two fold – consumer education and the handling of consumer complaints. Not enough human and financial resources have been dedicated to the surveillance of the market and to the investigation of alleged breaches of consumer law. Whilst

---

44   In the United Kingdom, for example under the Unfair Terms in Consumer Contracts Regulations 1999, the Office of Fair Trading and various sectoral regulators may apply to the Courts for the issue of an injunction to prohibit the use of an unfair term. These regulations require a sectoral regulator to notify the Office of Fair Trading if it has agreed to consider a complaint under these regulations.

45   See Consumer Affairs Act, Articles 8, 13 and 94 onwards.

46   The Division seeks to combine competition and consumer regulation, with the Director General of the Division assuming the roles of both Director of Consumer Affairs and Director of the Office of Fair Competition.

47   See respectively Articles 44–7 and Articles 72–81 of the Consumer Affairs Act.

this shortcoming can, in part, be resolved administratively, one cannot ignore the fact that if the Consumer Affairs Act were to be amended to provide for a robust and independent consumer protection authority with its own budget and resources, then such an authority would be in a better position to fulfil the currently onerous mandate on the Director of Consumer Affairs.

There is also room for substantial improvement with regard to the present enforcement regime. The Consumer Affairs Act and the other laws enforced by the Director of Consumer Affairs[48] are characterized by the fact that non-compliance with the requirements under these laws, in most instances, constitutes a criminal offence, which, in turn, entails the initiation of criminal proceedings conducted by the Director.[49] To date there has been no initiation of such criminal proceedings by the Director for any alleged breach of any of the provisions of the Consumer Affairs Act. One reason for this apparent lack of inaction is that the burden of proof in criminal proceedings is more onerous than in civil proceedings. Moreover, criminal proceedings are conducted before the Court of Magistrates, which is a court of general jurisdiction with no perceived specialization in consumer law. The non-existence of a properly resourced enforcement unit would appear to be another determining factor for this sorry state of affairs.

It is pertinent to note that, apart from the initiation of criminal proceedings, the Director, under the Consumer Affairs Act, has access to other tools. These tools include the issue of public warning statements in the media about goods that are unsatisfactory or dangerous, or services supplied in an unsatisfactory manner, or about trading practices detrimental to consumers. In doing so the Director can also mention by name the persons involved, provided that in doing so he adheres to the principles of fairness and objectivity.[50] Another tool, which the Director has, is the faculty to seek written undertakings from traders who allegedly commit a breach of regulations made under the Consumer Affairs Act or of the provisions of Article 9 of that Act. One evident shortcoming with respect to this particular measure is that the faculty of requesting an undertaking is limited only to certain provisions of consumer law.[51] There is no reason why the faculty of requiring an undertaking should not be extended to all the consumer laws enforced by the Director.

What is, or should be, the most effective tool[52] in the armoury of the Director is that he is empowered, either of his initiative or at the written request of a 'qualifying

---

48 Laws falling under this category include the Trade Descriptions Act, the Doorstep Contracts Act, the Product Safety Act, the Distance Selling Regulations, the Consumer Affairs Act (Price Indication) Regulations and the Consumer Credit Regulations.

49 See Consumer Affairs Act, Article 13.

50 *Ibid.*, Article 8. The Director, when issuing such warnings, must act with the concurrence of the Consumer Affairs Council and is exempt from liability in relation to any such warnings provided that in issuing such warnings the Director acts in good faith.

51 In August 2006 the Consumer Affairs Act was amended, in part to address this shortcoming, by extending the application of this article to Articles 44 to 50 of the Act and to the Doorstep Contracts Act. Regrettably, this measure, however, was not being extended to other provisions of the Act including Articles 51, 52 and 53 which deal with specific unfair commercial practices and to the Trade Descriptions Act.

52 To date the power to issue compliance orders has never been utilized, notwithstanding

body',[53] to issue a compliance order on any person, requiring that person to comply with any measures specified in the order or to cease and desist from committing any offences against the Consumer Affairs Act, any regulations made under that Act or any other consumer protection law designated by the Minister.

What is particularly significant in the context of the issue of compliance orders is that the Director, in relation to the use of unfair terms, can also require the person acting in breach of the provisions of the Consumer Affairs Act regulating unfair terms, to incorporate such terms in the relevant consumer contract as the Director considers 'to be necessary for the better information of consumers, or for preventing a significant imbalance between the rights and obligations of the parties, and this to the benefit of consumers'.[54] The Consumer Affairs Act further provides that a compliance order, unless contested, comes into immediate effect and any non-compliance with such an order is a criminal offence under the Act.[55] To date, however, these enforcement tools have rarely, if ever, been used.

There is room for substantial improvement in the enforcement tools currently available to the Director. One measure that should be implemented, as part of any future amendments to the Consumer Affairs Act, is the inclusion of administrative fines in lieu of, or concurrent with, the criminal penalties already in place punishing instances of non-compliance with the provisions of the Consumer Affairs Act. This is a long overdue measure, which should have been included in the first instance when the Consumer Affairs Act was first enacted in 1994. At that time, there was some criticism from the business lobby that equating non-compliance with consumer law as a crime would be counterproductive and that breach of consumer laws should never be punishable as a criminal offence.

Whilst not necessarily agreeing with the business lobby, inflicting criminal sanctions if there is non-compliance with a provision of consumer law should, in most cases, other than instances involving public safety and excessive fraudulent practices, be done away with. Limiting sanctions for non-compliance with consumer law primarily to criminal penalties has not proven to be effective, given the failure of the competent authorities to prosecute successfully traders under the provisions of the Consumer Affairs Act, thereby effectively rendering compliance with the provisions of that law a dead letter. The Courts, in most instances, would generally be reluctant to inflict criminal penalties in cases, for example, involving misleading advertising. Conversely, it is submitted that the Courts would be less reluctant to impose administrative fines for infringements of consumer law.

A compliance regime, reinforced with the imposition of proportionate administrative fines if there is a breach of the applicable provisions, should prove to be more effective. In the first instance, the degree of the burden of proof in such

---

       that this measure has been on the statute books for well over four years.

53   Under Article 2 of the Consumer Affairs Act a 'qualifying body' is defined as being a registered consumer association and any other body whether constituted in Malta or otherwise as the Minister after consulting the Consumer Affairs Council, may designate in the Government Gazette.

54   Consumer Affairs Act Article 94(1)(a)(ii).

55   *Ibid.*, Article 106.

instances would be less than that required under criminal law – where one must prove beyond 'reasonable doubt' that a breach of the law has been committed. In addition, in introducing a regime of administrative fines one can consider empowering the Director to impose such administrative fines where the amounts involved are relatively small. In doing so, the offending party would have the right to contest such fines before an independent tribunal. If the fine is not contested, or if the decision of the Director imposing the fine is confirmed on appeal, then the fine becomes an executive title recoverable as a civil debt by the Director. This system has already been used with success in other sectors, notably in the regulation of financial services and more recently in the communications sector.[56]

In any event, irrespective of the enforcement tools that the Director has at law, it is imperative to emphasize that such amendments to the law alone will not lead to an improvement in effectively ensuring compliance with consumer law. Any such changes must be complimented by a willingness by Government to strengthen the competent consumer regulatory authority with such human and financial resources as will enable such an authority to fulfil its mandate at law to safeguard consumer rights and ensure compliance with consumer law. If this is not forthcoming then any amendments, however wide ranging, will be futile and illusory.

(iii) A New Regulatory Setup?

In 1996 the establishment of the post of Director of Consumer Affairs and of the Consumer Affairs Council under the Consumer Affairs Act was, with some justification, seen as a significant step forward in protecting the rights of consumers. Until then there was no one public regulatory authority responsible for consumer affairs. The setting up and commencement of operations of these two bodies, therefore, marked an important milestone in fostering the protection of consumer rights in Malta. Now, ten years down the line, this regulatory framework needs to be re-evaluated in the light of the developments that have occurred since then.

The regulatory framework, as it subsequently evolved with the enactment of new consumer laws and with the emergence of various sector-specific regulatory authorities, some having a limited role in the context of the protection of consumer rights, has not always proved to be effective in ensuring that consumer rights are safeguarded. Issues that were perhaps not so evident or crucial when the structures set up under the Consumer Affairs Act started to operate in 1996 or which arose later, including significantly the autonomy of the Director, the effectiveness of the enforcement tools available and the overlap of jurisdiction with sector-specific authorities, now need to be tackled with some urgency, if there is to be an effective regulatory framework, which is responsive to an continuously changing market environment, which as time passes is becoming more and more sophisticated and complex.[57]

---

56   See Fines and Penalties for Offences Regulations issued under the Financial Institutions Act, and Articles 31–3 of the Malta Communications Authority Act.

57   A case in point is the regulation of transactions over the internet. Until some years ago, the use of internet as a medium to conduct consumer transactions did not exist. Now it

The Maltese legislator, in many instances, when creating the existing regulatory framework, looked at the experience of larger countries, notably the United Kingdom and, to a lesser degree, Ireland. This has in turn led to the creation of a number of sector-specific regulatory authorities modelled on counterpart authorities in other countries. In doing so, it does not appear that there was enough in depth discussion about the various alternative regulatory solutions that could be adopted. In particular, it appears that not enough consideration was given to the specific requirements of a small country with limited human and financial resources, as is the case with Malta. Time and again the approach taken by the Maltese legislator was to copy the regulatory models adopted in other, larger countries, with little thought to the feasibility of devising home-grown regulatory solutions suited to the specific needs of a small island state like Malta. There have been a few isolated instances where, initially, Government seemed intent on proposing regulatory models designed specifically to take into account the particular requirements conditioned by the size and resources of Malta.[58] These proposals, however, invariably fell by the wayside, and the regulatory models of much larger countries were instead copied and adopted.

The responses to the 1991 White Paper, *Rights for the Consumer*, and subsequently the debate in Parliament during the discussion of the Consumer Affairs Act in 1994, all failed to query whether there should be a regulatory model tailor-made for the specific needs of Malta, with both the respondents to this White Paper and the members of Parliament seemingly content with the regulatory structures that were being proposed. In this context, it is of interest to note that the 1991 White Paper had proposed a public authority entitled 'Consumer Protection Council' exercising executive powers in relation to the enforcement of consumer laws.[59] However, subsequently when the Consumer Affairs Act was enacted in 1994, the renamed Consumer Affairs Council was given only an advisory role with the executive regulatory functions being the responsibility of the Director of Consumer Affairs. This signified a noticeable change; given that in the 1991 White Paper Government had proposed that the executive functions should be entrusted to a body – the Consumer Protection Council – which would function with some degree of autonomy from Government, whereas under the Consumer Affairs Act the executive functions were given to a public officer, the Director of Consumer Affairs, directly answerable to Government.

In the light of what has been stated above, two distinct considerations emerge. The first is that the present regulatory setup needs to be revisited. This cannot be accomplished simply by administrative intervention,[60] but also requires a radical rethinking about the soundness of the current setup and the active consideration

---

is increasingly becoming one of the more popular means of undertaking transactions.

58 A case in point was the proposal for an economic multi–sectoral utility regulator in the White Paper: *Privatisation: A Strategy for the Future*, Ministry for Finance, December 1999. Government subsequently decided not to take up this proposal and instead created separate utility regulators.

59 See 1991 White Paper pp. 5 onwards.

60 Namely, by providing additional resources to strengthen the office of the Director of Consumer Affairs.

of other viable options, if there is to be a robust and effective consumer protection regulatory framework. The second consideration is that, irrespective of whether one decides to retain the present regulatory framework or opt for some other option, the enforcement tools must be re-evaluated and substantially improved upon, to ensure that there are effective means of ensuring compliance with the substantive provisions of consumer law.

It is relevant, at this juncture, to consider briefly a proposal made by the Maltese Government in 1998, whereby a draft Bill was circulated for consultation with the various stakeholders proposing the establishment of an 'Authority for Fair Trading and Consumer Affairs'.[61] In this Bill it was envisaged that the proposed authority would be responsible overall for both competition and consumer protection, and would include amongst its members a chairperson responsible for the general administration of the Authority, two ex-officio members being the Consumer Ombudsman and the Director of Fair Trading[62] and six other members representing specific interest groups including the private sector and consumers. Among the functions of this Authority was the safeguarding of fair competition practices and of the general interests of consumers and the investigation of restrictive or anticompetitive practices. The Consumer Ombudsman had the core function of investigating complaints by consumers and of exercising the functions carried out by the Director of Consumer Affairs.[63]

One interesting measure, proposed in this draft Bill, was the faculty of the Authority to appoint 'regulators' in order to assist the Authority in 'the better performance of its functions'. The idea was to assign to such regulators the responsibility of monitoring and keeping under review specific issues identified by the said Authority. It appears that these regulators would, in all instances, operate under the aegis of the Authority, whilst having access to the resources of the Authority. The proposals in this draft Bill were not, however, taken forward since, in the interval, a general election was called and there was a change in administration, with the new Government deciding not to proceed with these legislative changes.

Whilst there was room for improvement in the proposals made in this draft Bill, it is regrettable that this legislative initiative was not explored and taken forward. Some of the proposals, particularly that of having in place an autonomous authority, were a step in the right direction, given that, significantly, there was recognition of the importance of having a comprehensive regulatory structure enjoying some degree of autonomy in the exercise of its functions.

The above mentioned legislative amendments, proposed in 1998, indicate the way forward if there is to be an effective and comprehensive regulatory framework.

---

61 This draft law was never formally published in the Government Gazette. The Bill was overtaken by events as, in the interval, a general election was called and there was a change of Government. The proposals in the Bill were consequently not pursued.

62 The Consumer Ombudsman would be the executive head of the unit responsible for administering consumer laws, the Director of Fair Trading the executive head of the unit responsible for competition issues.

63 Draft Bill entitled 'The Authority for Fair Trading and Consumer Affairs Act, 1998', Clauses 4 onwards.

In doing so, however, one cannot ignore the current framework and existing realities. For a small country like Malta, the ideal solution would be to converge the regulation of consumer and competition issues in a single public authority acting autonomously from Government. Such a solution would bring with it certain benefits, not least that consumers and traders alike would have one focal point of reference and issues of jurisdiction between one authority and another would, hopefully, become history. Available human and financial resources would, moreover, be concentrated in one functional body and would ensure that necessary regulatory measures are taken in a coordinated fashion. In practice, however, taking such a proposal forward would bring an upheaval requiring the dismantling of the various existing executive posts and of existing regulatory bodies, including the post of Director of Consumer Affairs and the separate utility regulators. This, in turn, would necessitate the amendment of various laws relating to consumer affairs, competition and utility regulation. This, however, is not an impossible task and should be considered as a long term objective in relation to which discussion should be initiated now.

In the short to medium term, other measures can be taken. The post of Director of Consumer Affairs and the Consumer Affairs Council should, ideally, be merged into one umbrella organization rather than, as is the case at present, having two bodies working closely with but separately from each other. The idea of the present setup was, in part, to have a regulatory framework, whereby the executive role is performed by the Director of Consumer Affairs, whilst the Council acts as a semi-autonomous consultative body advising and commenting about policies adopted by Government that impact consumers. In reality, things have not worked out as was originally envisaged. The Council is inadequately resourced and, in many instances, has not been able to take a lead role on issues impacting consumers.[64] In the 1998 draft Bill, referred to above, it was suggested that a new authority should be created with the notable innovation that this authority would be composed of a board with responsibility for both consumer affairs and competition. One substantial difference with the present setup is that the board of the proposed authority would establish the policies, which the executive officers of the authority would then implement.

Such an option should be actively reconsidered. It is suggested that, similar to what was proposed in 1998, Government should establish an authority headed by a policymaking board composed of persons coming from different interest groups, with the executive functions being performed by a director acting in accordance with the policies determined by the Authority. Ideally, such an Authority should be answerable directly to Parliament rather than to a specific Minister, with the members of the Authority being appointed by the President of Malta rather than by a particular Minister.[65] Such a measure would, to some extent, serve to give the Authority some degree of visible autonomy in the conduct of its business, whilst ensuring that it is directly accountable to the highest elected organ of the State. In the past, there have been instances where the competent regulatory authorities were reluctant to

---

64   The Council is made of part time appointees and has no professional staff.
65   The members of the Consumer Affairs Council are all directly appointed by the
      Minister whereas the Director of Consumer Affairs is appointed by Government from
      amongst members of the public service.

intervene because of political considerations, including the impact of regulatory intervention on sensitive commercial interests of Government. Whilst a public authority should, when exercising its functions, act with due regard to the policies of the administration of the day, it should also, on the other hand, be guaranteed sufficient flexibility to ensure that it is able to effectively fulfil its role as the guardian of consumer rights and fair trading in the market. It is suggested that making such an authority answerable to Parliament, rather than to a specific Minister, would go some way towards achieving such a purpose.

Ultimately, irrespective of the routes that may be followed in shaping the future of the overall consumer protection regulatory framework, the point of departure should, in any event, be fashioned on basic cardinal principles to enable the designated authority to fulfil its role effectively. These principles include autonomy from all stakeholders, including government, to ensure that the regulatory body has the requisite flexibility in monitoring and regulating the market; clarity of jurisdiction, eliminating as far as is reasonably possible overlap of roles between different regulatory bodies; and adequate and effective enforcement tools. If these are not adequately catered for, then any future changes will fail to achieve the desired goal of having in place a solid regulatory framework responsive to the task of safeguarding the rights of consumers in the market.

4. The Adjudicative *Forae* – Creating Specialized Tribunals

(i) Consumer Claims Tribunals – A Partial Success?

An important facet of consumer affairs is to ensure that are in place tribunals that have the necessary expertise to deal with issues that may arise under consumer law. Consumer law, especially in recent years, has grown in importance, stature and complexity. If quality justice is to be meted out, especially in those cases where issues that impact consumers in general are being contested, then it is imperative that the legislator ensures that there are in place tribunals which are composed in such a manner as to ensure that those who are responsible for determining consumer law disputes, have the requisite in depth knowledge of the applicable legislation and, where appropriate, are supported by economic, commercial and other specialized experts.

Until now the focus of the Maltese legislator has been in ensuring that consumers have access to tribunals whereby disputes with traders which involve relatively small monetary values, can be heard and determined in a reasonably short time, at little expense to the consumer and in an informal manner. To some extent, this goal has been achieved even if there is room for improvement. The idea of creating a specialized 'small claims' or 'consumer claims' tribunal was first raised in the 1991 White Paper.[66] Subsequently, in 1994, the Maltese legislator established a Consumer Claims Tribunal that started to operate in 1996.[67]

---

66 See White Paper 1991 at p. 31 onwards.

67 The Tribunal was set up under the Consumer Affairs Act of 1994 and started to function with the coming into force of the Act on 23 January 1996, with the first cases being submitted a few weeks after that date.

This Tribunal is an alternative forum to the ordinary courts, before which Tribunal a consumer can refer a dispute with a trader for adjudication.[68] The Tribunal is composed of a single arbiter and hears and determine disputes between consumers and traders, provided the monetary value in dispute does not exceed Lm 1,500.[69] In addition the arbiter may award up to Lm100 for 'any pain, distress, anxiety and inconvenience' suffered by the consumer. The issues in dispute are decided according to the substantive merits and justice of the case and in accordance with equity. A case once decided can then be enforced as if it is a decision given by an ordinary court.[70] When hearing a case the arbiter has the faculty to regulate the proceedings before the Tribunal as he considers best suited to the ends of justice, provided that in doing so he acts according to the rules of natural justice. The arbiter is not bound to give 'extensive reasons for his decisions' and it is enough for him to list the main points on which his decision is based.[71] A decision of the Tribunal can only be contested before the Court of Appeal if it is shown that the Tribunal acted contrary to the rules of natural justice and such action prejudiced the rights of the appellant.[72]

The Tribunal has now been functioning for more than ten years. To some degree one can, with some justification, state that the Tribunal does provide an alternative means of dispute resolution that in many respects, as far as consumers are concerned, is preferable to recourse before the ordinary courts. The costs involved are relatively minimal, the procedure is informal and the law grants the arbiter the required flexibility in regulating how cases are heard.

Over the years, however, some problems have emerged. One problem, directly related to the popular favourable perception of many consumers of the Tribunal as an effective means of redress, is that the Tribunal is taking some time to dispose of claims filed before it,[73] because of the increase in its workload. The situation can be easily remedied, at least for the immediate future, simply by the appointment of another arbiter.

Another, more serious shortcoming, that cannot readily be rectified by administrative intervention relates to the difficulties that consumers face in enforcing decisions given in their favour by the Tribunal. There have been a number of instances, involving relatively small monetary amounts, where traders blatantly

---

68   A consumer has the option of either taking his claim before the ordinary courts or else before the Consumer Claims Tribunal. Conversely, the trader against whom the claim is being made, does not have the faculty of requesting that a claim made before the Tribunal be referred to the ordinary courts unless it is clear that the Tribunal does not have the requisite jurisdiction to determine the suit. See Consumer Affairs Act, Article 20(2).

69   See Consumer Affairs Act, Article 16 onwards. See also P.E. Micallef, 'Making Consumer Redress a Reality: the Consumer Claims Tribunal and the Rights of Consumer Associations under Maltese Law' (2002), New Zealand Business Law Quarterly pg. 432-441.

70   Consumer Affairs Act, Article 25(3).

71   *Ibid.*, Article 23.

72   *Ibid.*, Article 22.

73   There is at present only one part-time arbiter. There have been repeated calls on Government to appoint at least one other arbiter to ease the existing caseload.

refuse to comply with the decisions given by the Tribunal. Though consumers can enforce such decisions as if these were decisions given by an ordinary court, in practice doing so means that a consumer will, in most instances, need to engage the services of a lawyer to prepare the required applications to the court for the issue of executive warrants to enforce the decision of the Tribunal. In doing so consumers will provisionally incur more expenses to recover what, in most instances, are relatively small sums of money. Many consumers faced with such a situation decide not to proceed any further, since they consider that the effort and costs involved to conclude matters are invariably disproportionate to the amounts which they want to recover.

This sorry situation merits an equitable solution to ensure that the redress mechanism offered through the medium of the Consumer Claims Tribunal remains an attractive proposition to those consumers who have valid claims and who wish to pursue these. The obvious solution is to reform the existing means of enforcing tribunal decisions. Measures which should form part of such a solution include minimizing the reliance of consumers on the intervention of lawyers by simplifying the paperwork involved, by having easy to complete forms and delegating court or tribunal officers with the task of assisting consumers in taking forward the processing of the enforcement of final tribunal decisions. Another aspect would be to revise the costs involved to the extent that these are proportionate to the amounts being recovered. Regrettably, if no measures are taken in the near future, the confidence of consumers in the efficacy of the Consumer Claims Tribunal as an effective means of redress will diminish and undermine what has, to date, in many respects proved to be one of the positive salient features of consumer law in Malta.

(ii) The Case for a Specialized Market Court

Whilst on the level of disputes involving small monetary values, the Consumer Claims Tribunal has been operating for quite some years with some success, providing consumers with access to a specialized forum, conversely there has been no proposals about the feasibility of having in place a specialized tribunal to hear and determine consumer protection related issues where the amounts or interests involved are substantial or where an interested party can contest measures taken by the Director of Consumer Affairs under consumer legislation.

At present, a breach of the Consumer Affairs Act which constitutes an offence is prosecuted by the Director before the ordinary courts of criminal jurisdiction. If an interested party wishes to contest a compliance order issued by the Director under the Consumer Affairs Act, this may then be contested before the Court of Magistrates in its civil jurisdiction, whereas if a dispute arises between a consumer or trader in relation to some aspect of consumer law and the monetary value exceeds Lm 1,500, then the competent adjudicative tribunals are the ordinary courts of civil jurisdiction.[74] In all these instances, litigation is heard before a single magistrate or

---

74 This would then vary according to the values in contestation. If the value is between Lm 1,500 and Lm 5,000 the case would be heard by the Court of Magistrates, if the

judge sitting in a court of criminal or civil jurisdiction depending on the nature of the proceedings.

At a time when consumer law is gradually becoming more focused and complex, the Maltese legislator should actively consider having in place a specialized tribunal to determine such consumer law issues. It is important, first, to establish precisely what the role of such a tribunal should be and then to consider the options and how such a tribunal should be composed, taking into account the requirements of the existing situation in Malta. Ideally, such a tribunal should be able to take on a dual role of deciding both private consumer law disputes, and compliance issues relating to enforcement action and decisions taken by the Director of Consumer Affairs. At this juncture, it is important to emphasize that the changes in reviewing the existing adjudicative process should be complemented with other legislative changes including implementing an administrative fines regime, in lieu of the present system of criminal penalties for most infringements of consumer law. Part of the remit of a new specialized tribunal should include the right of aggrieved persons to contest, before such a tribunal, an administrative fine imposed upon them.[75]

How then should such a tribunal be composed and what should its remit be? Should it be limited to issues arising under the consumer laws enforced by the Director of Consumer Affairs or should its remit be wider and extend to consumer protection related laws enforced by other public authorities? And finally, should such a tribunal also have jurisdiction to determine competition issues? In answering these questions, the practical considerations that are specific to Malta must be factored if, ultimately, the right solution is to be identified. In this context the experience of the Scandinavian 'market courts', which tribunals enjoy a fairly wide ranging remit to determine issues relating to different aspects of consumer and competition law, may serve as a model for the establishment of a similar tribunal under Maltese law.[76] However, in a small country which already has a considerable number of specialized tribunals,[77] it is more logical to consider if such a task can be undertaken by an existing tribunal by extending its remit, rather than creating a new one and adding to myriad of tribunals that already exist.[78]

---

value exceeds Lm 5,000 then the competent forum would be the First Hall of the Civil Court.

75   Whilst most infringements of consumer law would be sanctioned by the imposition of administrative fines, some instances, such as threatening the Director or his officers in the exercise of their duties, would, because of their nature, still remain criminal offences and would be prosecuted before the Court of Magistrates sitting as a court of criminal judicature. See Consumer Affairs Act, Article 105.

76   Hence under Finnish law the Market Court has jurisdiction to decide disputes relating the decisions taken by the Finnish Competition Authority and by the Finnish Consumer Ombudsman in relation to certain laws including the Finnish Unfair Business Practices Act.

77   There are over a hundred specialized tribunals. In a consultation paper, published in 2005, Government said that it was reviewing the role of some of these tribunals and considering the feasibility of introducing a system of administrative courts. To date, however, no further more detailed proposals have been made by Government.

78   There are, for example, 103 different administrative tribunals.

A more practical solution would be to revisit the role of the Commission for Fair Trading, the competition tribunal set up under the Competition Act.[79] This Commission is composed of a magistrate, an economist and a certified public accountant appointed by the President of Malta acting on the advice of the Prime Minister. It determines competition law issues that are referred to it in accordance with the Competition Act, including issues relating to abuse of dominance and prohibited agreements or practices. The remit of the Commission could be extended to any litigation that may arise under the Consumer Affairs Act, including the right to contest decisions taken by the Director of Consumer Affairs and disputes that many arise between a consumer and a trader, where the amount exceeds the monetary jurisdiction of the Consumer Claims Tribunal. On a more ambitious and wide ranging level, the Commission could, in the longer term, assume the roles of the two utility appeals boards currently operative in the communications and resources[80] sectors, whereby any decisions taken by the Malta Communications Authority and the Malta Resources Authority can be contested before the Commission. This is, of course, a tall order which, however, if there is the requisite willingness by Government to move forward in this direction, is not impossible to implement. The obvious benefit is that there would be one tribunal dealing with most, if not all, of the issues relating to consumer and competition law, eliminating to some extent the undesirable situation of different adjudicative tribunals dealing with different aspects of consumer and/or competition law in an uncoordinated fashion, with the latent confusion that such a situation can lead to.

If such an option is taken forward, then the composition of the Commission of Fair Trading would have be changed to ensure that the Commission has a wider range of expertise to deal with the variety of issues that may be referred to it for its judgment. In this context, one useful measure successfully used is that relating to the composition of the Competition Appeal Tribunal in the United Kingdom, where the President of that Tribunal selects the members who are to form part of the Tribunal according to the issues involved in each appeal lodged before the Tribunal.[81] The Commission could be similarly composed with the Chairman of the Commission selecting the other two members of the Commission depending on the issues in dispute. Initially, the jurisdiction of the Commission could be extended to litigation under the Consumer Affairs Act and then gradually extended to other laws, including contestation of regulatory decisions taken by sector-specific regulators, such as the Malta Communications Authority or the Malta Tourism Authority.[82]

---

79   See Competition Act, Article 4.

80   'Resources' under the Malta Resources Authority Act refers to energy, water and minerals.

81   The Competition Appeal Tribunal has a list of members with expertise in different areas. The President of the Tribunal selects two persons from this list to sit on any given appeal together with a chairman. See http://www.catribunal.org.uk/about/personnel. asp, and the 'Competition Appeal Tribunal – Guide to Proceedings', October 2005.

82   This Authority enforces various consumer laws including those that regulate timeshare and package travel.

5. The Rights That Consumer Associations Have Under Maltese Law – Has Enough Been Done?

Consumer associations enjoy some important rights under Maltese law. If an association satisfies the criteria[83] stated under the Consumer Affairs Act, then it is entitled to request that it is recognized by the Consumer Affairs Council as a 'registered' consumer association and accordingly entitled to the rights that such an association enjoys under Maltese law. Significantly such rights include exemption from liability at law in respect of any communication or statement that is *bona fide* and is intended 'for the better information, education or protection of consumers',[84] and the faculty to request the Director of Consumer Affairs to issue a compliance order on any person acting in breach of the Consumer Affairs Act or another consumer law enforced by the Director.[85]

The perennial problem that has always undermined the effectiveness of such associations in Malta is that, though they enjoy some significant rights at law, in practice, because of lack of financial and human resources, most of these rights have rarely, if ever, been exercised. This is an ongoing problem that has plagued the consumer movement from the very beginning when the first association was set up in the early 1980s. New legislative measures that may mitigate such a situation include the exemption or reduction of any tribunal or court registry fees that a consumer association has to pay when taking legal proceedings to protect the general interests of consumers, and the deposit of fines collected by the competent regulatory authorities, from persons who act in breach of consumer law, in a fund the purpose of which would be to support the financing of registered consumer associations.[86] However, ultimately the core of the problem lies with the lack of support by consumers in Malta in fostering such associations. Until there is a wide ranging public consciousness of the need to support such associations by joining and actively participating in their work, the contribution of such associations towards the wellbeing of consumers in Malta will continue to be minimal.

6. The Immediate Future

It is unlikely that anything like the initiatives taken in the early 1990s and the subsequent legislative measures enacted in 2000 will be emulated in the foreseeable

---

83   See Consumer Affairs Act, Article 28.

84   *Ibid.*, Article 36.

85   *Ibid.*, Article 96. A registered consumer association is automatically considered a 'qualifying body' and therefore entitled to request the issue of such orders under Part IX of the Consumer Affairs Act. See also Micallef, 'Making Consumer Redress a Reality: the Consumer Claims Tribunal and the Rights of Consumer Associations under Maltese Law': 441 onwards.

86   These two measures were actually proposed in a model law for the protection of consumer rights in Latin American. See International Organisation of Consumers Unions (now Consumers International) 'The Consumer: Proposals for Protection', 1994, regional office of IOCU in Chile, Articles 49 and 50.

future. The impetus for change in consumer law now appears to be tied solely to the implementation of the measures being enacted by the EU. There appears to be little willingness by Government to undertake domestic legislative initiatives in the sphere of consumer protection, if not to comply with EU requirements. Such a situation, whilst regrettable, means that the consumer lobby in Malta must focus at least part of its energy towards acting in closer harmony with other similar bodies in the EU and endeavour to influence the EU Commission in ensuring that the consumer interest is adequately factored in any future policies that impact on consumers.

Overall, to date EU consumer policies, and the consequential transposition of the various applicable directives, have had a salutary impact on consumer rights in Malta, prompting various important domestic legislative measures supportive of such rights. However, recent developments in EU consumer policy do not necessarily augur well for the future of consumer protection in Malta. The prime reason for such concern is the change in priorities of the EU, typified by the elimination of the faculty of EU Member States to introduce legislative measures in favour of consumers that go beyond the measures stated in consumer protection directives. This is in order to ensure harmonisation throughout the internal market at the cost of prohibiting Member States to have in place measures that go beyond those established in the directives.

This is a trend which appears to have commenced with the directive on unfair commercial practices[87] and which may also be reflected in the amendments to the directive on credit agreements for consumers once these amendments are finally approved.[88] The impression one gets, if such a trend continues, is that the consumer lobby in Malta – weak as it is – will be fighting a rearguard action, simply to keep the existing measures in place and to counter the negative impact on national legislation as a result of this new creeping horizontal approach adopted by the EU where, regrettably, it seems that consumer protection interests play second fiddle to internal market considerations.

Until now compliance with EU consumer related directives was always viewed as one of the positive aspects of Maltese membership of the EU, since membership meant that Government had to implement certain consumer protection measures which would not have necessarily been readily implemented had Malta not been a member of the EU. Now, however, there is the distinct possibility that Malta

---

87   Directive 2005/29/EC of the European Parliament and of the Council of 11 May 2005 on unfair commercial practices. See also paper by G. Howells entitled 'Unfair Commercial Practices Directive – A Missed Opportunity?' presented during the conference organized by the Malta Consumer Affairs Council and the International Association of Consumer Law, March 2006, http://www.mcmp.gov.mt/pdfs/consumers/Mar05Seminar/Geraint_Howells.pdf.

88   The proposed Directive to replace the Directive 87/102/EEC (as amended) on credit agreement for consumers envisages a similar measure, doing away with the faculty under the existing directive of enabling Member States to implement more favourable measures in support of consumers. See COM (2002) 443 final, Proposal for a Directive of the European Parliament and of the Council on the harmonisation of the laws, regulations and administrative procedures of Member States concerning credit for consumers, draft article 30.

may, in the not too distant future, be required to review, if not outright delete, those legislative measures that actually go beyond the minimum established by the various EU consumer protection directives. This is a step in the wrong direction.

The next step on the legislative agenda of Government is the implementation of the EU Unfair Commercial Practices Directive.[89] This will necessitate, as a minimum, amending the Consumer Affairs Act[90] and possibly other consumer laws.[91] In the process of examining how this directive should be implemented, one hopes that Government will take a broad approach and consider other amendments to the Consumer Affairs Act and other consumer laws, undertaking a general review of consumer law, as was previously done in 1991 when Government published its proposals for a comprehensive legal regime to regulate consumer rights.[92] It is still not too late in the day[93] for Government to make its proposals for a wide ranging review of consumer law as suggested in this paper. The deadline for the implementation of the Unfair Commercial Practices Directive is, however, not that far off. Government should, therefore, without any further delay, initiate a consultation process with all stakeholders, circulating its proposals as to how it intends to implement the Directive. As part of this process, Government should also include its proposals about how it intends to strengthen the existing compliance measures under the Consumer Affairs Act, notably the enforcement tools and the judicial review of decisions taken under that Act. One augurs that Government will not simply content itself with transposing the directive but will look beyond and propose measures which attempt to improve upon the existing regulatory framework.

---

89   Directive 2005/29/EC of 11 May 2005 on unfair business to consumer commercial practices in the internal market. Member States are required to publish the laws necessary to comply with this Directive by the 12 June 2007.

90   The Directive for example requires changes to misleading and comparative advertising which is regulated by Articles 48 to 50 and Article 94 of the Consumer Affairs Act.

91   Such as the Distance Selling Regulations and the Distance Selling (Retail Financial Services) Regulations, which respectively transpose the EU Directives 97/7/EC and 2002/65/EC which directives are amended by the Unfair Commercial Practices Directive.

92   White Paper: *Rights for the Consumer*, August 1991.

93   This article was written in April 2006.

10 The Legal Rights of the Consumer in Cases of Lack of Conformity of Goods with the Sale Contract and His/Her Contractual Rights According to Guarantee Statements

Paraskevi Paparseniou[1]

1. Historic Review

Ancient Greece is recognized as the cradle of European civilization and, to the extent that law constitutes an essential part of the civilization, it should come as no surprise that the Greek law relating to the seller's liability for the existence of defects in goods sold also dates back to the years of classic antiquity. From the preserved legislative texts, the one considered the most important is the law of Avdira, which was found, though unfortunately only partly, on an inscription of about the middle of the fourth century B.C.[2] Avdira was a city of Thrace, built by the mouth of river Nestos, facing the Aegean Sea. It belonged to the Attic–Delian Alliance, so it is almost certain that the law of Avdira reflects Athenian law for defects in goods sold. According to this law, whoever sold, in a market, a slave or a beast of burden, should have told the buyer, in advance, whether there was any disease in the slave or the animal. In cases where no such declaration was made, and it was proven that the slave or the animal suffered from a disease, the buyer had a right of recourse within a certain time limit. The beginning of this time limit was the conclusion of the sale contract and its duration varied according to the severity of the disease. The right of recourse is known also from other philological texts[3] as the right of return of the slave or the beast of burden by the buyer to the seller for a refund of the price paid, but the refund was double the price paid if the seller was a professional, meaning a person

---

1   Lecturer in Civil Law, Faculty of Law, University of Athens, Greece. This article is, to a large extent, a published presentation of a paper with the same title submitted and orally presented by the author at the Regional Consumer Law Conference, which was co–organised by the International Association of Consumer Law and the Consumer Affairs Council of Malta and was held in Malta on 16 March 2006.
2   The archaeologist Michel Feyel found this inscription in 1937 near the Thracic city of Polystylos, which is situated on the ancient Avdira. For more about the law of Avdira see I. Triantafyllopoulos, *The real defects of the goods sold according to Greek ancient laws with the exception of Papyri*, (Athens, 1968), at p. 20 and following.
3   See Platon, *Laws*, (L. 916 a–d), see also Triantafyllopoulos, pp. 10–11.

experienced in such transactions, and the buyer was a private citizen, meaning a person inexperienced in such transactions.

The law of Avdira, as ancient Greek law generally, exercised obvious influence in the edictum of the *aediles curules*, which extended the liability of the seller of slaves or beasts of burden, beyond the existing liability for lack of specifically promised qualities (*dicta et promissa*), in adopting a special guarantee of liability of the seller for hidden defects, which were unknown to the seller and the buyer and which reduced the value of the goods sold. The basis of this liability was the notion of 'giving a guarantee', that is the idea that the seller is liable for the existence of defects although he/she did not assume a contractual obligation to warrant their absence.[4] Such liability was imposed by law, independent of the seller's fault, and the buyer was given the legal remedies of inversion (*actio redhibitoria*) and of price reduction (*actio quanti minoris*) with the edictum.

From this short historic review of the ancient Greek and Roman world, it follows that important goods, in the then prevailing market economy, were slaves and beasts of burden, and accordingly specific goods, for which it was, by nature, impossible to claim repair. For reasons of historic inheritance, this explains the absence of a right to repair as a stated legal remedy in the law of sale according to earlier Greek law,[5] prior to its alignment with Directive 99/44/EC.[6] The distinction between the sale of specific and generic goods constituted a fundamental aspect of the Greek civil law regarding the seller's liability for defects. In respect of the sale of specific goods, the seller was not, in general, contractually obliged to deliver to the buyer goods without defects or with the agreed qualities; it was considered that the seller fulfilled his contractual obligations by delivering the goods in the exact condition, as they were (*tale quale*). The seller bore, according to the Roman tradition, 'guarantee or inspectorate' liability, meaning that the seller was liable irrespective of his fault for a result (namely the existence of defect or the lack of quality), although he was not contractually obliged to prevent this.[7] Such guarantee liability of the seller in sales of specific goods resulted in the buyer's inability to claim repair (since a claim for repair would be a particular form of claim for correct and proper performance),

---

4   See A. Karabatzos, 'The seller's liability for the supply of defective goods in the system of contractual breach according to the Civil Code provisions applicable until now', in P. Papanikolaou, (ed.), *The New Law of the Seller's Liability*, (Athens, 2003), 33, at pp. 71–4.

5   The regulation of the seller's liability for real defects in the Greek Civil Code reflects the Byzantine–Roman law, that applied earlier, and the evaluations of the German Civil Code which has also Roman roots; see for further references in Karabatzos, 'The seller's liability for the supply of defective goods in the system of contractual breach according to the Civil Code provisions applicable until now', p. 71 at n. 123.

6   Council Directive 99/44/EC of the European Parliament and of the Council on Certain Aspects of the Sale of Consumer Goods and Associated Guarantees, OJ L171, 7 July 1999, p. 12.

7   See F. Doris, 'Introductory Remarks to Articles 534–562 of Civil Code', in A. Georgiadis, M. Stathopoulos, (eds), *Civil Code, Interpretation on an article basis, Volume III, Law of Obligations, Special Part*, (Athens, 1980), p. 124 at pp. 128–130, at numbers 14 and following.

except in the case where such a claim for repair had been specifically agreed between the parties (since such provision was concessive law) or was imposed by good faith as a consequential/collateral contractual obligation (Article 288 Greek Civil Code). Articles 540–4 of the Greek Civil Code gave to the buyer the right of inversion (=*Wandlung*) of the contract of sale or the right to demand a price reduction or damages.

In contrast, in the sale of generic goods, where the seller is obliged to deliver to the buyer goods of the generic type and of average quality (Article 289 Greek Civil Code), it was accepted that delivery of goods with defects (or without the agreed qualities) constituted defective performance of the seller's obligations. On this basis, it was further accepted that the law in Article 559 Greek Civil Code gave the buyer, in addition to the aforesaid rights, a right to replacement, and – although it was not specifically provided – also a claim for repair as a particular form of the claim for proper performance.

A common denominator in the Greek law of sale prior to Directive 99/44/EC was that the liability for the sales of specific and generic goods was formulated as a 'without fault' (strict) liability; fault was required only for the granting to the buyer of a claim for damages as an alternative to the other remedies. Reasons for the formulation of the seller's liability as 'without fault' were: (a) the need for speed and security of the transactions[8] and (b) the fact that, by supplying defective goods, the reasonable expectations of the buyer in the particular circumstances regarding the substance of the goods are not met. This disturbs the subjective balance between the supply of the goods and counter supply of the price to the buyer's detriment (such balance based on the estimations of the contracting parties) and creates the need, according to the idea of 'contractual justice', to protect the buyer. Such need is independent of (a) whether the emergence of the defect is attributed to the seller's fault or not or (b) whether the seller knew of or ignored the defectiveness of the goods.[9]

In summary, the Greek law regarding the seller's liability, prior to its alignment with Directive 99/44/EC:

- divided the sale of goods in sales of specific and generic goods;
- accepted guarantee liability of the seller in sales of specific goods and liability of the seller due to defective performance of his/her primary obligation to supply goods of average quality in sales of generic goods;
- did not require fault of the seller – irrespective of the nature of the goods – for the acceptance of the seller's liability, with the exception of specific cases related to the

---

8   This need imposed – again in harmony with the Roman tradition – the adoption, in Articles 554 and following Civil Code, of the shortest time limits for the exercise of the buyer's legal remedies: six months for movable and two years for immovable goods, commencing the time of the statute of limitation from the physical delivery of the movable goods and the physical or constructive delivery of the immovable goods, irrespective of whether the buyer discovered the defect later.

9   See P. Kornilakis, *Law of Obligations, Special Part, Volume I*, (Athens–Thessaloniki, 2002), at pp. 223–4; F. Doris, 'Comparative survey of the old and the new sales law', *Digesta*, (2003): 122, at 124–7.

buyer's claim for damages; and
- finally, did not recognize that the buyer had an *ex lege* right of repair of the defective goods, neither for the sales of generic nor of specific goods.

2. The *ex lege* Liability of the Seller Due to Non–Conformity of the Goods with the Contract

Law 3043/2002, which implemented in Greek law Directive 99/44/EC, amended: the provisions of the Civil Code, which cover the *ex lege* liability of the seller for defects and lack of agreed qualities (Article 534 and following); and Article 5 of l.2251/1994 for the protection of the consumer in the specific field of consumer sales.

The Greek legislator of l.3043/2002 considered that the provisions of the Directive 99/44/EC could be generalized and applied to sales of goods, whether movable or not, between any kind of contracting parties. Accordingly, the legislator preferred the amendment of the relevant provisions of the Civil Code, in order to avoid legislative incoherence in regulating similar problems. The provisions of the Civil Code are designed not only for contracts of sale concluded between professional sellers (natural or legal persons) and private citizens (consumers – only natural persons) – as is the case with the Directive – but also all other sales contracts concluded between professionals, or between private citizens, or even between private citizens as sellers and professional buyers, and irrespective of the qualification of the parties as natural or legal persons. As far as the objective scope of application of the provisions of the Civil Code is concerned, these refer to the sale of any type of goods, movable or not, with the exception of goods sold by way of execution, given that the Article 1017(2) of the Code of Civil Procedure specifically exempts the liability for real defects of goods sold by auction.

An important innovation of the new law of sales is a departure from the anachronistic influence of the Roman legal tradition with the establishment – in whole and with no differentiation depending on whether there is a sale of specific or generic goods – of the primary obligation of the seller to deliver the goods without defects and with the qualities agreed, namely goods which correspond to the purpose and terms of the sale. Accordingly, the liability of the seller due to defects is transformed from a guarantee liability, or liability for non–performance of the obligation to deliver a good of average quality, into a liability for non–fulfilment of the main obligation of the contract. In addition, the distinction between sale of specific and generic goods is abandoned, since it is now considered superfluous, as the legal consequences are the same in both cases.[10]

The Greek legislator, having complied with the requirement of Article 2(1) of the Directive, according to which 'the seller must deliver to the consumer goods which are in conformity with the contract of sale', recognizes from here on in every contract of sale as the primary obligation of the seller the obligation to deliver goods 'without defects and with the qualities promised' (Article 534 Greek Civil Code). The supply of goods without the qualities promised and with defects therefore

---

10   See the Explanatory Report of Law 3043/2002, under I.11.

constitutes a breach of a primary contractual obligation and creates liability due to non-performance of the contract,[11] which is again based on strict liability (Article 537(1) Greek Civil Code). For the first time the buyer is given the right to demand repair of the defective goods, as a special form of specific (*in natura*) performance of the contract (Article 540(1) Greek Civil Code). Whereas Article 534 Civil Code states the basic rule, Article 535 Civil Code, which transposes Articles 2(2) and (4) of Directive 99/44/EC, equates the obligation to deliver goods with no defects and with the qualities promised with the obligation to deliver goods that conform to the contract.[12]

In Article 535 Civil Code, there is an indicative list of the criteria for non–conformity of the goods with the contract, which basically reflect the criteria of Article 2(2) and the exemptions of Articles 2(3) and (4)(a) of the Directive, but with a more concise, simpler, and, therefore, legally more comprehensive wording in comparison to the wording of the Directive.[13] In contrast, whereas the Directive follows a positive declaration of the criteria of compliance to the terms of contract, the Greek legislator followed a negative wording, so that the buyer has just to prove the non–fulfilment by the seller, due to non–compliance of the goods with one of the

---

11   See also Explanatory Report of Law 3043/2002, under I.8, where it is mentioned that 'The need for higher protection of the buyer imposed the transformation of the guarantee seller's liability into a normal contractual obligation, which gives to the buyer as well the claim for fulfilment of the contract as the rights of contract inversion or damages, as it basically happens in the cases of impossibility of supplying, of debtor's delay, of defective fulfilment and of existence of legal defects. Within the purpose of sale, for responsible and reasonable contracting parties, corresponds the delivery of a good in such a quality and quantity that is proper for the use intended (conditions upon which the agreed price has been also paid), in other words the delivery of a good, which will have the agreed qualities and will lack real defects. This is from now on set as a primary obligation of the seller'. See also A. Pouliadis, 'The Directive on the Sale of Consumer Goods', *Critical Review Krit E,* 1 (2000):47, at 54–5.

12   In this way the terminology of the Civil Code for real defects and agreed qualities, which according to Greek legislator is preserved for reasons of tradition, is correlated with the terminology of the Directive for conformity of the goods to the contract of sale, so that the two wordings are considered as synonymous. See the Explanatory Report of Law 3043/2002, under II.3.

13   According to Article 535 Civil Code:
The seller does not fulfil its obligation that is stated in the former article, if the good delivered to the buyer does not conform to the contract and especially if: 1. It does not comply with the description given by the seller or does not correspond to the sample or model which the seller had presented to the buyer; 2. It is not fit for the purpose of the specific contract and especially for the according to this purpose special use; 3. It is not fit for the use for which the items of the same category are usually designated; 4. It does not have the quality or performance which the buyer reasonably expects from goods of the same category, taken into account also the public statements made by the seller, the producer, or his representative, particularly in the context of the relevant advertisement or labelling, except if the seller did not know or should not have known of the relevant statements.

criteria of Article 535 Civil Code, moreover he/she can prove the non–compliance even if all of the four criteria are met, as these are only indicative.

The conditions of the *ex lege* liability of the seller is that, first, a valid and active sale contract exists at the time when the buyer exercises his rights, and second there is a defect, or a lack of a promised quality, in the goods at the crucial time of the transfer of risk to the buyer (Article 537 Civil Code).[14] The crucial time for establishing the seller's liability is not the time of the good's delivery, as implied in Article 3(1) of the Directive, but the time when the risk is transferred to the buyer; this provision is in accordance with a permitted deviation by the Greek legislator from the Directive, given that in Recital 14 of the Preamble of the Directive, there is a specific provision that the national rules for the risk transfer are not affected.[15] The Greek legislator seems here not to address the problem created by Article 3(1) of the Directive whether 'delivery of the goods' has to be considered only the physical delivery (surrender) to the consumer-buyer, so that he is in a position to acquire physical power over the goods, or whether any kind of constructive delivery suffices, such as the delivery to the carrier after an agreement of the parties for dispatch of the goods.[16] The time of the risk transfer coincides with the time of delivery of the movable goods according to Article 522 Civil Code; however, delivery is not only the physical surrender of the goods by the seller, but also every way of constructive delivery, which is defined in Articles 977 and 978 Civil Code.

Furthermore, in Article 524 Civil Code, the time of the passing of risk precedes the physical surrender of the goods to the buyer and coincides with the delivery of the goods to the carrier, since, according to this article, if the seller, upon request of the buyer, sends the goods to a different place than the place of fulfilment of the contract, the buyer bears the risk after the goods have been delivered to the carrier for dispatch.[17] According to Article 320 Civil Code, if there is no different agreement between the parties or it cannot be otherwise concluded from the circumstances, the place of fulfilment of the non-monetary supply of the contract is considered to be the place of the professional installation of the debtor of the supply, which is in the case of a sale contract, the place of the professional installation of the seller. So, every time that a consumer-buyer wishes the goods be delivered to the place of his residence, but does not bother to agree in advance with the seller that the place of his

---

14   See A. Georgiadis, *Law of Obligations, Special Part, Volume I*, (Athens, 2004), at p. 80 and following and Kornilakis, p. 242 and following. According to Article 537(1) Civil Code 'The seller is liable irrespective of his fault, if the good, at the time of risk transfer to the buyer, has real defects or lacks the agreed qualities ...'.

15   See the Explanatory Report of Law 3043/2002 under II.4.

16   About this issue and the contrary views supported in Germany, see N. Reich and H.-W. Micklitz, *Europäisches Verbraucherrecht*, 4th edn, (Baden-Baden, 2003), at p. 656, whereas in the UK R. Bradgate and C. Twigg–Flesner, *Blackstone's Guide to Consumer Sales and Associated Guarantees*, (Oxford, 2003), at pp. 69–71, adopt the view that it would be more consistent with the Directive's underlying objectives of consumer protection and promotion of the Single Market to accept as delivery only the actual physical delivery of the goods into the buyer's possession.

17   About the time of risk transfer in a contract of sale with an agreement of dispatch, see Kornilakis, p. 328 and following; Georgiadis, p. 69 and following.

residence is also the place of fulfilment of the contract, the seller is not liable for a lack of conformity of the goods with the contract arising after the delivery to the third party carrier. In effect, this means that in every consumer sales contract concluded and/or fulfilled at a distance, the consumer-buyer will be obliged to pay the price to the seller, even if the goods are accidentally lost, or have deteriorated, during the carriage, and in addition any lack of conformity (defect or lack of promised quality) arising after delivery of the goods to the carrier will not give the consumer-buyer access to the legal remedies of Article 540 and following of the Civil Code. According to the Greek legislator, delivery to the third party carrier under Article 524 Civil Code is treated as delivery to the buyer, since it occurs upon his request, so the latter should bear the risk. Whether this view of the Greek legislator conforms to the protective intention of the Directive remains a highly controversial subject in consumer sale contracts.[18]

Finally, it is worth mentioning that the rebuttable presumption (presumption of the existence of a lack of conformity at the date of delivery) of Article 5(3) of the Directive has been transposed with the same wording in Article 537(2) Civil Code, whereas the two months notification period (notification period for the lack of conformity) of Article 5(2) of the Directive was not adopted by the Greek legislator, because it was considered that such a provision would be very burdensome for the buyer.

3. The Buyer's Rights

Article 540 Civil Code reflects, in a more concise way, Articles 3(2)–(6) of the Directive, since it has simplified the unnecessarily detailed regulation of the Directive. According to this article, in case of seller's liability for defects or lack of agreed qualities the buyer has one of the following rights at his discretion: (1) to demand the repair or replacement of the good with another free of charge, except if such an action is impossible or requires disproportionate expenses; (2) to have the price reduced; (3) to rescind the contract, except if the defect is minor. The seller must complete the repair or replacement in reasonable time and without any significant inconvenience to the buyer.

It is important to note first that, in Greek law, the rights of the buyer accumulate without any hierarchical ranking, without some of them having priority and others being subordinate.[19] This is in contrast to the Directive which foresees that the consumer should firstly claim for the repair or the replacement (Article 3(3)) and only if it is impossible or disproportionate or the seller does not complete it in reasonable time or without significant inconvenience to the buyer (Article 3(5)), the latter has the right to exercise his right of rescission or price reduction. The new Article 540 Civil Code grants to the buyer the right to demand a price reduction

---

18   It is worth mentioning that this deviation by the Greek legislator from the regulatory intention of the EU legislator of Article 3(1) of the Directive, has not been pointed out until today in the Greek literature.

19   This has been the intention of the Greek legislator of law 3043/2002; see the Explanatory Report of Law 3043/2002 under II.5.

or rescind the contract, even if the removal of a defect through the repair or the replacement of the good is possible without disproportionate expense for the seller. This choice of the Greek legislator is satisfactory to the extent that it results in higher protection of the buyer,[20] who is not obliged to accept a delayed proper fulfilment of the seller's obligation, but is left free to choose the legal remedy which corresponds best to the nature of the lack of conformity. Most of the legal remedies that are given to the buyer rank, according to the more accurate view of some authors, selectively among them. This means that the realization and not simply the selection of the legal remedy that has been chosen (that is the realization of the repair or replacement of the goods sold) excludes the remaining remedies, with the exception of the remedies of the rescission or the price reduction, which once exercised (that is with an extra-judicial declaration or a lawsuit) cannot be revoked.[21]

The rights of repair and replacement constitute a special form of the fundamental right of the buyer for a complete and proper performance. The seller is obliged, without any expense for the buyer, to repair the defective object, or to transfer property and deliver to the buyer another good that conforms to the contract, returning simultaneously the expenses incurred by the buyer in respect of the goods which are replaced (Articles 540(1) and 547(2) Civil Code). The rights of repair and replacement are restricted where such a repair or replacement is either, from a technical/realistic point of view impossible or disproportionate for the seller. Therefore, the repair of the goods is considered impossible when the goods are fully destroyed or have severely deteriorated due to the defect, so that their repair is not possible. It is also debatable whether replacement can be considered impossible in the case of a sale of specific goods.[22]

Despite the fact that the Greek legislator has been rather restrictive in enumerating the criteria according to which the restitution is considered disproportionate either in the form of repair or replacement, restricting himself to the criterion of

---

20　　See Kornilakis, p. 254 and n. 4, A. Bechlivanis, 'The amendment of Civil Code provisions on the sale – Comments on the Law 3043/2002 concerning the liability of the seller for defects and lack of agreed qualifications of the sold goods', *Business and Company Law, DEE*, 9 (2003): 620, at 626; contrary A. Pouliadis, *The seller's responsibility in the system of breach of contract*, (Athens-Komotini, 2005), at p. 121 and following, who concludes from the Article 540(2) Civil Code the existence of a hierarchical grading of the buyer's legal remedies according to the Directive and criticizes against the prevailing view in Greek literature.

21　　See Georgiadis, p. 113, Kornilakis, pp. 254–5, contrary Pouliadis, p. 133, who considers that also in the case of the formative rights of rescission and price reduction it should be accepted that the buyer is restricted in the right already exercised, only if the seller declares that he agrees to it or moves to its satisfaction or if a final judgment has been published, which accepts the relevant law suit of the buyer.

22　　The legal remedy of replacement is considered impossible in sale in kind according to Georgiadis, p. 99, Kornilakis, p. 257, whose arguments are also based on Recital 16 of the Directive, whereas K. Roussos, 'Characteristics and contents of the buyer's remedies in the new law of sale', *Chronicles of Private Law, ChrID*, 4 (2004): 577, at 580 and Pouliadis, p. 130 do not consider the right of replacement as incompatible with the sale in kind.

the 'disproportionate expenses', it has been accepted by some authors, that all the criteria of Article 3(2) and Article 3(3) of the Directive define the meaning of disproportionality. The wording of Article 3 of the Directive, however, is open to two different interpretations concerning the existence of disproportionality, and this difficulty lies in the ambiguity as to what is the alternative to repair or replacement as a form of cure: is the only alternative to repair, and therefore a comparable way of cure, the replacement of the goods and vice versa, or is any of the legal remedies so compared, including of price reduction and/or rescission?[23] In my opinion, the wording of Article 540 Civil Code has successfully circumvented this stumbling block. According to Greek theory, the principle of proportionality, which finds its expression in the aforesaid provision, functions on the one hand as a comparative criterion between the rights to repair and replacement and, on the other hand, sets the boundaries to the exercise of these rights from the exercise of the rest (price reduction, rescission, damages).[24] The remedy requested by the buyer (that is, replacement) is considered disproportionate, if in comparison to the alternative way of remedy (that is, repair), it results in an extremely high cost for the seller, such comparison not being restricted only to the comparison of the cost for the seller of both the two alternative possibilities, but also appreciating the market value of the goods, the nature and the importance of the defect, and the degree of inconvenience that would be caused to the buyer if another remedy were provided. All of the above criteria may lead to the exclusion of the right of repair or replacement, leaving the buyer with the possibility of exercising only the remaining rights of price reduction, rescission, and damages.

Further restrictions are also set by Article 540(2) Civil Code in respect of the realization of the remedy of repair or the remedy of replacement: These remedies should be provided in a reasonable time and without significant inconvenience to the buyer. The law does not specifically regulate the consequences of a total or partial failure of repair, but it is accepted by some authors, that it cannot be required from the buyer to accept more that one attempt at repair for the same defect, so that the right of repair should be considered to have been exercised and the buyer will be entitled to exercise another of the legal remedies provided to him.[25]

The right to price reduction is considered a formative right, since its extra judicial or judicial exercise from the buyer alters, from the one side, his legal relationship with the seller, the important element of the price, and creates, if the buyer has paid the price, the claim for return of the sum of reduction, with interest from the date when the price was paid. For the calculation of the sum of reduction, the method of relative calculation has prevailed: the market value of the goods in perfect condition is determined and their market value in defective condition. The ratio of the two

---

23   See for this issue and its solution in favour of the first, more narrow interpretation Bradgate and Twigg–Flesner, pp. 92–4.

24   See Georgiadis, p. 100.

25   See Roussos, 'Characteristics and contents of the buyer's remedies in the new law of sale': 579.

values is the ratio according to which the actual purchase price should be reduced in the given situation.[26]

Finally, the right of rescission is also formative, which is exercised by virtue of an extra judicial declaration, or a lawsuit, or an objection. Its exercise transforms the contract of sale in a relationship of liquidation, which is thoroughly described in Article 547(1) Civil Code. The buyer has firstly an obligation to return the goods to the seller, this is to transfer back to the seller the ownership and the possession of the goods free from any encumbrances which he or a third party may have added (that is, pledge or seizure) and, furthermore, to return to the seller any benefit he has gained from the goods, such a benefit is the value of use of the goods from the delivery to the buyer until their return to the seller. The seller has the obligation to return to the buyer the price paid with interest from the date that it was paid, and also the expenses for the conclusion and performance of the sale, as well as any sum that the buyer might have spent for the goods.[27]

It is clarified that also under Greek law the buyer does not have the right of rescission if the defect is only minor.

4. The Rights of the Buyer from the Provision of Guarantee

Prior to the Civil Code's alignment to the Directive, a guarantee was regulated only in the special case of an agreement to supply a guarantee period. With such agreement, the seller intended to protect the buyer against deficiencies in the goods, which manifested themselves within a specific time limit or within a specific duration of use, which was to be calculated according to the extent or the intensity of the use (that is for the first 5,000 km which a car will cover), such deficiencies not being necessary to exist at the time of transfer of the risk to the buyer (usually the time of delivery of the goods).[28] According to Article 556 Civil Code, if a term is agreed for liability of the seller for defects or lack of an agreed quality, this, in cases of doubt, meant that the statute of limitation for the defects or the lack of promised qualities, which were manifested within the time limit, began from the date of manifestation. The time of the statute of limitation was calculated to benefit of the buyer, since its commencement was transferred from the time of the goods' delivery to the time of the manifestation of the defect, subject to the obvious restriction, that it manifested within the guarantee period.

---

26   *Ibid.*, 584; Georgiadis, pp. 109–110, where it is also pointed out that the Greek jurisprudence seems to be divided about the issue of the crucial time for the estimation of these values (is it the time of conclusion of the contract or the time of risk transfer?). However, the method of relevant calculation is considered to be fairer, since it secures the respect of the intentions of the contracting parties regarding the price and also enables the buyer or the seller to maintain the profit from the initial transaction, see Kornilakis, p. 269.

27   See a further analysis in Kornilakis, p. 276 and following.

28   The regulation for this type of guarantee has remained intact and is still applicable today; see Pouliadis, pp. 299–303, Georgiadis, pp. 116–7, Kornilakis, pp. 309–10.

This provision was also maintained after the alteration of the Civil Code by l. 3043/2002, but to this was also added the provision of Article 559 Civil Code, which implemented Article 6(1) of the Directive. According to Article 559 Civil Code, if the seller or a third party has provided a guarantee for the goods sold, the buyer has, against the person who gave the guarantee, the rights that arise out of the guarantee statement according to the terms contained in it or the relevant advertising, without any effect on the rights provided by law. This provision was considered to have declaratory character, since it underlines the binding nature of everything stated in the guarantee document, an obligation that arises on any occasion because of the contractual character of the guarantee.[29] It has been additionally said – and I may add correctly – that even if the last sentence of the provision was missing, the rights of the buyer that arise from the law against his counterparty (the seller), would not be affected from the existence of a guarantee from a third party, whose guarantee could not alter or exclude the *ex lege* liability of the seller.[30]

However, the provision of Article 559 Civil Code has its own special importance: both because it is the only provision of the Civil Code which refers to the previously unregulated type of commercial guarantee given by third parties who are not in a contractual relationship with the buyer (for instance manufacturers, importers, commercial distributors), and also because it is the only provision that gives binding effect to the advertising statements of the sellers or third parties expressed in the pre-contractual stage.[31] As far as the method of conclusion of the guarantee contract is concerned, in the case that this (guarantee) is given by a third party, it has been accepted that such third party (this is the producer) makes an offer 'To Whom It May Concern' (proposal) and the seller simply acts as conduit for this declaration to the buyer, who usually accepts it silently. If the buyer is required to fill in its personal details and to send the guarantee card to the producer, the contract is concluded from the time of arrival of the acceptance of the buyer with the producer, otherwise it is considered that, according to the transaction's morals, the contract of guarantee is concluded solely with the buyer's silent acceptance (Article 193 Civil Code).[32]

In the case where the seller gives the guarantee, it will be usually collateral to the sale contract, and will alter, for the benefit of the buyer, the extent or the prerequisites of the remedies already provided by law, when the goods sold reveal deficiencies.[33]

---

29   See Kornilakis, p. 300.

30   See Pouliadis, pp. 311–2.

31   There are though contrary opinions on whether the advertising can, by itself, constitute a self-existent guarantee that is of the producer or whether it functions only supplementary within an already concluded contract of guarantee; in favour of the first view seems to be Kornilakis, p. 301, whereas in favour of the second view seems to be K. Christodoulou, 'Guarantee (Article 559 of Civil Code)' in P. Papanikolaou, (ed.), *The New Law of the Seller's Liability*, (Athens-Komotini, 2003), p. 533 at p. 554.

32   See about the way of conclusion of the guarantee contract with the producer, Pouliadis, p. 308 and following.

33   It is worth mentioning that the draft Directive required that any guarantee – independently by whom it is given – should place the consumer in a more advantageous position than that resulting from the rules governing the sale of consumer goods set out in the applicable national provisions; for further details on the Directive's proposal

However, when the guarantee is given by the producer, this may take the form of a guarantee of qualitative duration, or the form of provision of additional rights against the producer; in any case, though, it will contribute to the improvement of the legal position of the buyer, since he will have another subject against which he can sue in case of lack of conformity of the goods. Finally, the guarantee statements of Article 559 Civil Code are informal; they do not require manifest expressions, as long as the relevant intention of the guarantor to be legally bound by his offer is evident.

The provisions of Article 6(2)–(5) of the Directive, which refer to the principle of transparency of the guarantee provided, were incorporated as *leges speciales* for consumer sales in Article 5 of l.2251/1994 (Consumer Protection Act). An introductory remark about the scope of application of l.2251/1994 is necessary here: L.2251/1994 adopts a wide notion of consumer, since a consumer is considered not only the natural person that buys the product for personal, non-professional, needs, but also every natural or legal person that buys the good for satisfaction of his professional needs as far as it constitutes the final addressee of the product.[34] Accordingly, as a supplier for the purposes of Article 5 of l.2251/1994 is, by interpretation, accepted to be not only the seller and direct contracting party with the buyer-consumer, but anyone who makes a guarantee statement, either the seller himself or a third producer of the product (this is a manufacturer, importer into the EU territory, quasi producer and so on).[35]

Even prior to the alignment of the Greek law with the Directive, Article 5(3) of the Consumer Protection Act (l.2251/1994) imposed, specifically in respect of the contracts for supply of new products with a long term duration (permanent consumer goods such as domestic appliances, cars, furniture and so on), on the supplier an obligation to give a written guarantee with a reasonable duration dependent on the life expectancy of the product, or on the time for which it was expected that it would stay modern from a technology point of view, and a minimum legal context, corresponding to the rules of good faith and not revoked by excessive terms of exceptions (disclaimer clauses). Given that the suppliers usually took advantage of this guarantee as a way to disorientate the consumers and to make them believe that their only rights against them are the ones that arise out of the guarantee card, it was specifically provided in Article 5(5) that in any case the consumer preserves his rights according to the provisions of the Civil Code for the seller's liability for

---

see H. Beale and G. Howells, 'EC Harmonisation of Consumer Sales Law – A missed opportunity?', *Journal of Contract Law*, 12 (1997): 21 at 37–9. However, this requirement was not included in the final text of the Directive.

34   According to Article 1(4)(a) of law 2251/1994 (Consumer Protection Act) a consumer is considered any natural or legal person, for which the products are designated or the services offered in the market or which makes use of such products or services, provided he is the final addressee of them. Accordingly, supplier in Article 1(4)(b) of l.2251/1994 is every natural or legal person, which in the exercise of his professional or business activity, supplies products or services to the consumer.

35   Despite the fact that in Article 1(4)(b) of l.2251/1994 is explicitly mentioned that the producer as far as his liability for defective goods (product liability) is concerned falls under the notion of the supplier, it cannot be *a contrario* concluded that the producer does not fall generally within the meaning of the supplier.

defects of the goods, so that the consumer could not validly waive beforehand the protection provided by the provisions of the Civil Code.[36]

These provisions exist also today,[37] whereas Article 5(3)–(5) of l.2251/1994 has been amended in conformity to Article 6 of Directive as follows: In any occasion that a guarantee is given by the supplier to the consumer without the former being obliged to give such guarantee (non-permanent consumer goods), he should give it in writing or in another durable medium available and accessible to the consumer. Every guarantee must be given in Greek, should be in plain intelligible wording and set out the minimum legal contents referred in Article 6(2)(b) of the Directive, without the validity of the guarantee being affected in case of omission of the elements of the minimum content or the form of the guarantee. The 'essential particulars necessary for making claims under the guarantee' were omitted from the minimum legal context of the guarantee by the Greek legislator, an omission that is regarded as a defective implementation of Article 6(2)(b) of the Directive.[38] Furthermore, the guarantee must also set out the rights provided by the applicable law, but the Greek legislator omits to impose the obligation on the supplier to state in the text of guarantee that the legal rights of the buyer-consumer according to applicable law are not affected by the guarantee, an omission that is also considered to be a defective implementation of Article 6(2)(a) of the Directive.

Of importance is also the provision that in the case of replacement of the product or its spare part, the guarantee is renewed automatically for all of its duration as far as the new product or the spare part is concerned. Finally, it has been accepted that, because all of the terms of the guarantee are usually predefined for an indefinite number of future contracts and are not an object of personal negotiation with the buyer-consumer, they (the terms) are controlled according to Article 2 of l.2251/1994, which implemented Directive 93/13/EEC (Unfair Contract Terms Directive) into Greek law.

5. Conclusion

Directive 99/44/EC has been a source of inspiration for the Greek legislator and gave him the incentive to move forward, beyond the strict boundaries of consumer sales, to a thorough reform of law for the seller's liability in the Civil Code. It can be noted

---

36   See also Article 7(1) of the Directive.
37   For further details about the Article 5(3)–(5) of l.2251/1994 see I. Karakostas, *Consumer Protection Law,* L.2251/1994, (Athens 2004), at pp. 191–7; Christodoulou, 'Guarantee (Article 559 of Civil Code)', pp. 558–92; Georgiadis, pp. 142–4, and, prior to the modification of l.2251/1994; M. Avgoustianakis, 'Sale (after sale service)', in M. Stathopoulos, A. Chiotellis and M. Avgoustianakis, *Community Civil Law I*, (Athens-Komotini, 1995), p. 115 at pp. 115–20; E. Alexandridou, *Greek and Community Consumer Protection Law II*, (Thessaloniki, 1996), at pp. 125–35; K. Delouka–Igglesi, *Greek and Community Consumer Law*, (Athens-Komotini, 1998), at pp. 95–8.
38   This term of the 'essential particulars' of the Article 6(2) of the Directive is criticized as rather imprecise by Bradgate and Twigg-Flesner, pp. 177–8, who argue for a cleverer guidance by the EU legislator.

that the fact that in the sale of specific goods the seller who provided a defective product fulfilled his contractual obligation, contained certainly a contradiction and disturbed the harmony of the Civil Code,[39] reflecting, as we saw, anachronistic beliefs of the ancient Greek and Roman law. The fact that the Greek legislator needed the urge of the EU legislator to ensure that the law corresponds to the demands of the modern commercial life is surely unpleasant, nevertheless it is wrong to suppose that the dialogue between the national and EU legislator does not have two directions.

To conclude as I started, namely with the recognition of the value of humans, beyond a simple tradable kind, as my ancestors and our ancestors considered, allow me to mention to you, that the Greek legislator of the Civil Code had already, from the middle of the last century, included in the Civil Code a specific provision with which he protects the personality of every person against any illegal insult. As expressions of the right of personality are today recognized not only life, physical integrity, honour, esteem and human dignity, but also the protection of the person's private life, the protection of personal data, the use of environmental goods. The non-pollution, the preservation, protection and unhindered use of the environment are aspects that fall within the right of personality according to the Greek law of the Civil Code and according to established precedent rulings of civil courts. And this means that the EU legislator has, on his side, still a lot to learn from the national traditions of the Member States.

---

39   See instead of others P. Papanikolaou, 'Introductory remarks on the object of the study', in P. Papanikolaou (ed.), *The New Law of the Seller's Liability*, (Athens-Komotini, 2003), at p. 9 and following, especially at pp. 17–18.

11 The Effect of Information Based Consumer Protection: Lessons from a Study of the Irish Online Market

*Mary Donnelly and Fidelma White**

A review of European soft law and hard law throws up a number of types of European consumer; however there is no doubt that one type dominates: the well informed, confident consumer.[1] The creation of this well informed, confident consumer through the provision of information is a cornerstone of European consumer protection law and policy. Underlying this model of consumer protection is a concern to enhance the health of the economy as well as to protect the individual consumer.[2] The Commission in its Consumer Policy Strategy 2007–2013 states: '[t]he Internal Market cannot function properly without consumer confidence. Adequate consumer protection is necessary for growth and competitiveness.'[3]

Although information based consumer protection has dominated the European consumer policy agenda, the effectiveness of this method of protection has been questioned by commentators who have raised concerns about consumers' capacity to respond to information provided and expressed doubts about the linkage between information provision and consumer empowerment.[4] Many of these critiques have

* Senior Lecturers in Law, Faculty of Law, University College, Cork, Ireland. The research that underlies this paper was funded by the Irish Research Council for the Humanities and Social Sciences. We would like to thank Jane Mulcahy for her able research assistance on the underlying research project and the referee for the valuable comments provided.

1 Both case law and legislation subscribe to this stereotype. For instance, consumers have been described as 'reasonably well informed and reasonably observant and circumspect': see Case 210/96 *Gut Springenheideb GmbH* v. *Oberkreisdirektordes Kreises Steinfurt* [1998] ECR I–04657. See also Recital 18 of Directive 2005/29/EC, [2005] OJ L149/22 (the Unfair Commercial Practices Directive), which 'takes as a benchmark the average consumer, who is reasonably well informed and reasonably observant and circumspect'.

2 G. Howells, 'The Potential and Limits of Consumer Empowerment by Information', *Journal of Law and Society*, 32 (2005): 349, at 350.

3 Commission Communication, 'Healthier, Safer, more confident citizens – a health and consumer protection strategy', COM(2005) 115 final.

4 In addition to Howells, 'The Potential and Limits of Consumer Empowerment by Information', see also T. Paredes, 'Blinded by the Light: Information Overload and Its Consequences for Securities Regulation', *Washington University Law* Quarterly, 81

drawn on empirical data to provide support for the arguments made.[5] The importance of empirical work in this context is clear: it is essential to test the effectiveness of information provision in a practical way with reference to real consumers. As noted by Wilhelmsson, 'a functioning consumer protection needs to have a close understanding of the expectations of consumers and the prevailing consumer culture'.[6]

This chapter continues the work of examining the effect of information provision in providing consumer protection, drawing in particular on a study conducted by the authors into Irish consumers' responses to information provision in the context of the online market as required by Directive 97/7 on the protection of consumers in respect of distance contracts.[7] The study enables us to advance the debate regarding information provision in two respects. First, existing empirical data has become somewhat dated and furthermore, the data relates primarily to the provision of information regarding financial products, and in particular in relation to consumer credit.[8] At this point, it is so widely accepted that certain information will be given in this area that suppliers are largely compliant with the requirement and consumers are culturally attuned to information provision in this context. A study of the online market allows the effect of information provision to be considered in a fresh context,

---

(2003): 417; I. Ramsey, 'From Truth in Lending to Responsible Lending', in G. Howells *et al.,* (eds), *Information Rights and Obligations: A Challenge for Party Autonomy and Transactional Fairness* (Aldershot, 2005) p. 47; I. Ramsey 'Consumer Protection in the Era of Informational Capitalism', in T. Wilhelmsson *et al.,* (eds), *Consumer Law in the Information Society* (Dordrecht: Kluwer, 2001), p. 45, T. Wilhelmsson, 'The Informed Consumer v the Vulnerable Consumer in European Unfair Commercial Practices Law – a comment', in G Howells *et al.,* (eds), *Yearbook of Consumer Law 2007*, (Aldershot, 2006), p. 211; W. Whitford, 'The Functions of Disclosure Regulation in Consumer Transactions', *Wisconsin Law Review* 2 (1973): 400.

5   See in particular, Whitford's study of the effectiveness of 'truth-in-lending' legislation in 'The Functions of Disclosure Regulation in Consumer Transactions', which was based on empirical data collected shortly after the introduction of the legislation.

6   T. Wilhelmsson, 'The Abuse of the "Confident Consumer" as a Justification for EC Consumer Law', *Journal of Consumer Policy*, 27 (2004): 317, at 328.

7   [1997] OJ L144/19. For detailed discussion of this Directive and its companion Directive 2002/65 concerning the distance marketing of consumer financial services, see M. Donnelly and F. White, 'The Distance Selling Directives: A Time for Review', *Northern Ireland Legal Quarterly*, 56 (2005): 1. On Directive 97/7, see further T. Bradgate, 'The EU Directive on Distance Selling', *Web JCLI*, 4 [1997], http://webjcli. ncl.ac.uk/1997/issue4/bradgat4.html (last accessed 17 November 2006); A Cremona, 'The Distance Selling Directive', *Journal of Business Law*, (1998): 613; R. Brownsword and G. Howells, 'When surfers start to shop: Internet commerce and contract law', *Legal Studies*, (1999): 287; G Hornle, J. Sutter and I. Walden, 'Directive 97/7/EC on the protection of consumers in respect of distance contracts' in A. Lodder and H. Kaspersen (eds), *eDirective: Guide to the European Union Law on e–Commerce*, (The Hague, 2001), p. 11.

8   But see, for example, R. Hillman, 'Online Consumer Standard Form Contracting Practices: A Survey and Discussion of Legal Implications', in J. Winn (ed.), *Consumer Protection in the Age of the 'Information Economy'* (Aldershot, 2006), Ch. 2.

where the expectation that certain information must be provided may have less cultural resonance with either suppliers or consumers. Secondly, the study focuses specifically on Irish consumers. Previous work in this area has taken place in relatively developed consumer societies. For a range of reasons, discussed further below, Irish consumer society may be characterised as underdeveloped. Therefore, the results of the study enable us to investigate the linkage between the effect of information based consumer protection and the stage of development of a particular consumer society. With the expansion of membership of the European Union and the inclusion of less developed economies (and consumer societies) within the ambit of European consumer policy, it becomes increasingly important to undertake jurisdiction-specific investigations of the appropriateness of that consumer policy.

The chapter begins with a description of Irish consumer society, outlining the particular socioeconomic factors that have resulted in the relative underdevelopment of this society. It then sets out the background to the study before exploring in detail the ways in which Irish consumers have responded to information provision in the context of the online market and drawing conclusions about the effect of information provision in the environment studied.

1. Irish Consumer Society: An Overview

Despite unprecedented and continuous levels of growth in the Irish economy since the mid-1990s,[9] partly fuelled by a growth in consumer spending, Irish consumer society can be described as underdeveloped. In 2001, an OECD review of regulation in Ireland noted a poorly developed consumer culture and a policy bias in favour of producer interests.[10] Although it has long been recognized that consumers operate at a disadvantage in the market, and therefore are in need of protection by the state or by voluntary associations, the OECD found that, in Ireland, the 'consumer voice' (and particularly that of the domestic consumer) has been weak relative to producer interests.

A closer look at past and present policy frameworks in Ireland reveals that there are a number of reasons why the Irish consumer voice has been relatively weak. First, the 'Irish consumer' is of relatively recent vintage when compared with the United Kingdom, for example. Atiyah linked the rise of the consumer society in England with the Industrial Revolution of the nineteenth-century.[11] The new technology of mass production; new marketing techniques; a new range of goods; the existence of

---

9   For example, the Irish economy has grown at an annual average rate of over 7 per cent between 1997 and 2005. Unemployment has fallen from 10 per cent in 1997 to around 4¼ per cent in 2006, with long term unemployment of just 1.4 per cent, making Ireland's unemployment rate one of the lowest in the EU: Department of Finance, *Pre-Budget Outlook 2006*.

10   See further OECD, *Regulatory Reform in Ireland* (2001) available at www.oecd. org/dataoecd/48/35/2475450.pdf (last accessed 17 November 06); see also Consumer Strategy Group, *Make Consumers Count: a New Direction for Irish Consumers* (April 2005) available at www.irishconsumer.ie (last accessed 17 November 2006).

11   P.S. Atiyah, *The Rise and Fall of Freedom of Contract* (Oxford, 1979) pp. 572–81.

surplus income due to wage increases; and leisure time all combined to produce a consumer society. In Ireland, the development of a consumer society occurred later in time.[12] This derives in part from the absence of an 'industrial revolution' in Ireland.[13] Indeed, by the 1950s, Ireland was still largely dependent on agriculture. At the same time, high levels of unemployment and emigration resulted in a low standard of living.[14] The publication of the Whitaker Report in 1958,[15] heralded a major change in economic policy and has been identified by some as the origins of the 'Celtic Tiger' economy.[16] Accordingly, the Government turned its back on protectionist economic policy in favour of free trade and foreign direct investment was pursued to meet the country's employment needs. As a result, there was a continuous economic expansion from the late 1950s to the early 1970s. Total GNP almost doubled, the decline in population was arrested, living standards increased significantly and entry into the EEC in 1973 signalled the final stage in the reopening of the economy.[17]

Secondly, those charged with representing the consumer voice in Ireland have, to date, failed to deliver this protection. As is evident in the discussion to follow, this failure may be traced to inadequate legislative engagement with consumer issues and to the absence of mechanisms for bodies charged with representing the consumer voice to contribute to the development of public policy. In part, because of the late development of a consumer society in Ireland, the Irish legislature did not address the position of the Irish consumer until relatively recently. Legislation such as the Sale of Goods Act 1893 and the Hire Purchase Act 1946 applied to commercial and consumer purchasers/hirers alike and did not identify the particular needs of consumers.[18] It was not until the late 1970s, with the enactment of the Consumer Information Act 1978 and the Sale of Goods and Supply of Services Act 1980 that the Irish consumer was identified and specifically protected. This brief period represents the 'golden age' for the legislature and its consumer protection agenda. The 1980 Sale of Goods Act, with its provisions on guarantees and after-sales services, was described by the European Commission in its Green Paper on Guarantees for Consumer Goods as one of the most 'forward-looking national text

---

12   See further OECD, *Regulatory Reform in Ireland*; see also Consumer Strategy Group, *Make Consumers Count: a New Direction for Irish Consumers* (April 2005) available at www.irishconsumer.ie (last accessed 17 November 06).

13   There were pockets of industrial development, for example, the linen industry in the northeast, particularly Belfast, but nothing comparable to the Industrial Revolution in the rest of Great Britain at the time: see K.A. Kennedy, T. Giblin and D. McHugh, *The Economic Development of Ireland in the Twentieth Century*, (London, 1988), Ch. 1; R. Munck, *The Irish Economy*, (London, 1993) Ch. 1.

14   J. Blackwell, 'Government, Economy and Society', in F. Litton (ed.), *Unequal Achievement, The Irish Experience 1957–1982,* (Dublin, 1982), p. 43. See further T. Garvin, *Preventing the Future: why was Ireland so poor for so long,* (Dublin, 2004).

15   Department of Finance, *Economic Development*, (1958).

16   R. MacSharry and P. White, *The Making of the Celtic Tiger*, (Cork, 2000), Ch. 15.

17   See generally, D. O'Hearn, *Inside the Celtic Tiger* (London, 1998); Sweeney, *The Celtic Tiger,* (Dublin, 1998); MacSharry and White, *The Making of the Celtic Tiger.*

18   See also the Merchandise Marks Acts 1928–1970 and the Restrictive Practices Act 1953.

in this domain'.[19] However, shortly thereafter, the active legislative role of protecting the Irish consumer shifted to Europe.

Since the 1980s the vast majority of consumer protection legislation has emanated from the European Community, in the form of Directives. The Irish legislature's role in transposing these measures can be described as 'minimal' in character, for a number of reasons, thereby suggesting a lack of interest in the consumer protection agenda.[20] First, until recently, the bulk of Community Directives have been minimum harmonising Directives, as opposed to maximum harmonising Directives. In general, when transposing consumer protection Directives, Ireland has tended to harmonise to the minimum level only. The discretion to implement higher levels of consumer protection has usually not been considered in any meaningful way or pursued. Secondly, Irish measures transposing European Directives tend to follow closely the original wording of the Directive. Therefore, any uncertainties about the meaning of terms or omissions in the Directive are replicated in the Irish transposing measure. Thirdly, Directives are frequently transposed by the introduction of a standalone legal instrument, usually a statutory instrument. Any pre-existing legal rules often remain untouched by the transposing measure. As a result the relevant legal rules are located in a number of unconsolidated measures.[21] Such an approach is more likely to lead to inconsistencies and sometimes conflicts between the various rules.

In addition to inadequate legislative engagement, the opportunities for the consumer voice to impact on the broader development of public policy have been limited. The Consumer Information Act 1978 established the office of Director of Consumer Affairs (ODCA). [22] The ODCA's function was to support the legislation, which is essentially an extension of various nineteenth century Merchandise Marks Acts, designed to encourage higher standards of truthfulness in describing goods and services.[23] The functions of the Director, as set out in the legislation, included: keeping under review advertising practices; requesting traders to refrain from misleading advertising; requesting that criminal proceedings be initiated; applying to the High Court for an injunction prohibiting further misleading advertising; encouraging the adoption of codes of practice; and publicising consumer protection legislation.[24] Over time the remit of the ODCA extended beyond that of trade descriptions, consumer information and advertising to include labelling, prices, safety and the enforcement

---

19   'Green Paper on Guarantees for Consumer Goods and After-Sales Services', COM(93) 509 final, p. 96.

20   See further discussion of the approach to transposition of EC directives in Ireland in M. Donnelly and F. White, 'Regulation and Consumer Protection – A Study of the Online Market', *Dublin University Law Journal*, 28 (2006): 27, at 29–30.

21   See, for example, the Sale of Goods Act 1893, as amended by Part II of the Sale of Goods and Supply of Services Act 1980, and the European Community (Certain Aspects of the Sale of Consumer Goods and Associated Guarantees) Regulations 2003 (S.I. No. 11 of 2003).

22   1978 Act, s. 9.

23   This whole body of legislation has now been replaced with the Consumer Protection Act 2007 which seeks, *inter alia*, to transpose Directive 2005/29 on unfair commercial practices (see further text to n. 36 below).

24   1978 Act, s. 9(6).

of most EC consumer protection legislation. A survey of the ODCA's annual reports indicates that the emphasis has clearly been on enforcement of the legislation, albeit within a limited budget and other resources.[25]

In March 2004, the Minister of Enterprise, Trade and Employment established a 'Consumer Strategy Group' to develop a national consumer strategy. In their report, one area identified for change was the existing state structures, including the ODCA.[26] The Report identified five functions necessary for a national consumer policy: advocacy; research; information; enforcement; and education and awareness.[27] In contrast to the United Kingdom and the Netherlands where all five functions were found to be 'fully provided', in Ireland the Report found that only the enforcement function was 'fully provided'; the information, and, education and awareness functions were 'partially provided'; while the remaining functions of advocacy and research were 'not provided'. Moreover, the Report was critical of an enforcement system where no sustained effort was made to involve the consumer in protecting him or herself. In other words, the consumer voice was not being promoted by the state, in particular through the ODCA.[28]

The voluntary sector has also been largely unsuccessful in providing a voice for Irish consumers within the policy making process. Within this sector, the Consumer Association of Ireland (CAI), founded in 1966, is a largest and best known consumer organisation.[29] However, the CAI is clearly limited both by resources[30] and, equally importantly, by a lack of opportunity to directly influence the policymaking process. This lack of opportunity may be seen in relation to the social partnership agreements, of which there have been seven to date, and which many identify as being key to Ireland's economic prosperity.[31] The latest agreement, *Towards 2016: Ten Year Framework Social Partnership Agreement 2006–2015,* represents a negotiated agreement covering a range of issues, most notably a pay agreement for the private sector and the public service.[32] What is interesting to note is that among the

25   Annual reports, from 2002, can be accessed online at www.odca.ie (last accessed 17 November 2006).
26   See Consumer Strategy Group, *Make Consumers Count: a New Direction for Irish Consumers*, Ch. 15.
27   For more information on these functions see *ibid.*, pp. 64–5.
28   It should be noted that a variety of state organization, regulators and voluntary associations seek to represent the consumer interest in Ireland. However, the chapter on Structure Change focuses in particular on the Office of Director of Consumer Affairs.
29   Though its magazine *Consumer Choice*, the CAI provides information to its 8,500 members. It also operates a volunteer-staffed information line which in 2004 handled 8,000 calls. It is a member of the Bureau European des Union de Consommateurs (BEUC) and represents the consumer interest on a number of state and EU established boards and committees.
30   Its main source of funding are membership subscriptions and since 2001 a government subsidy of €63,000 per annum.
31   See commentators cited in n. 17 above.
32   The Partnership Agreement also addresses a number of related issues, including statutory minimum pay; partnership at the workplace; workplace learning and up-

plethora of interested parties who negotiated and agreed this document, including the Government, trade unions, employers groups, farming organisations, and the voluntary sector, nowhere was the consumer interest directly represented.[33]

There are indications that this domestic lack of interest in the Irish consumer is about to change. The Department of Enterprise, Trade and Employment has announced that it is in the process of a root and branch review of Ireland's consumer laws. Part of this review will involve looking at the law governing consumer contracts including the Sale of Goods and Supply of Services Act, 1980 as well as a review of all secondary consumer legislation.[34] Furthermore, following the recommendation of the Consumer Strategy Group[35] that a National Consumer Agency, independent of the relevant Government Department, should be established, an interim National Consumer Agency was created in May 2005. Legislation to establish the Agency on a statutory footing has now been introduced.[36] We can only wait and see whether this new state agency will succeed in representing the consumer voice and placing the consumer protection agenda closer to the heart of government than in the past. For present purposes however, the significance of the discussion above is that it establishes the underdeveloped nature of the consumer society within which the study, which provides the basis for this article, takes place.

skilling; and work–life balance. It also provides for a range of measures to protect employment standards in the context of a rapidly changing labour market.

33 This is all the more noteworthy when account is taken of the sheer range of negotiating parties which included the Irish Congress of Trade Unions (ICTU), Irish Business and Employers' Confederation (IBEC), Construction Industry Federation (CIF), Small Firms' Association (SFA), Irish Exporters' Association (IEA), Irish Tourist Industry Confederation (ITIC) and Chambers Ireland, Irish Farmers' Association (IFA), Irish Creamery Milk Suppliers' Association (ICMSA), Irish Co-Operative Organisation Society Ltd (ICOS), Macra na Feirme, Irish National Organisation of the Unemployed (INOU), Congress Centres Network, CORI Justice Commission, National Youth Council of Ireland (NYCI), National Association of Building Co-Operatives (NABCO), Irish Council for Social Housing (ICSH), Society of Saint Vincent de Paul, Age Action Ireland, The Carers Association, The Wheel, The Disability Federation of Ireland, Irish Rural Link, The Irish Senior Citizens' Parliament, The Children's Rights Alliance, and Protestant Aid.

34 For example, at the time of writing, the Department of Enterprise Trade and Employment has recently issued a consultation paper on EU price display legislation: http://www.entemp.ie/commerce/consumer/publications.htm (last accessed 17 November 2006).

35 Consumer Strategy Group, *Make Consumers Count: a New Direction for Irish Consumers*. The Report regarded this as the most appropriate way to fulfil all five consumer protection functions that it had identified. The recommendation also speaks in terms of the agency working in partnership with Government, regulators, business, consumer organizations, and unions in promoting the consumer interest.

36 See the Consumer Protection Act 2007 which established the National Consumer Agency from 1 May 2007.

2. The Study

As part of a larger project entitled *Consumers in the Electronic Marketplace*,[37] we investigated the pre-contract information provision requirements of Directive 97/7 which was transposed in Ireland by the European Communities (Protection of Consumers in Respect of Contracts made by means of Distance Communication) Regulations 2001 ('the 2001 Regulations').[38]

In brief, the Directive regulates all forms of distance selling, including online selling, utilising two main tools: the provision of information to consumers and the provision of a right of withdrawal.[39] There are two aspects to the provision of information obligations. First, Article 4 requires that the consumer be provided with specified information, in advance of contract formation, in a clear manner ('the prior information'). Secondly, Article 5 requires that some further confirmation or communication of the prior information (plus some additional information) be made available to the consumer in writing or in another durable medium during the performance of the contract and at the latest at the time of delivery of the goods ('post-contractual confirmation'). Lastly, Article 6 provides that the consumer has a period of seven working days to withdraw from the contract without having to give a reason.[40] As has been argued elsewhere,[41] the withdrawal right can be viewed as a form of information-based protection because it gives the consumer the opportunity to inspect the goods before making the decision to retain them. Therefore, the main protections in the Directive are underpinned by a view of the consumer as an autonomous actor in a free market who should be provided with sufficient information and then left free to make his or her own decision whether to enter the contract or not, and, whether to withdraw from the contract or not.

The study focused on the prior information obligations under the Directive and aspects of the right of withdrawal.[42] In practice, where goods or services are sold via

---

37   The research project was funded by the Irish Research Council for the Humanities and Social Sciences for a nine month period, between February–October 2005. See further M. Donnelly, J. Mulcahy and F. White, *Consumers in the Electronic Marketplace: an examination of information based consumer protection in the context of distance selling over the Internet* available at www.ucc.ie/law/faculty/staff/consumersdec05.pdf (last accessed 17 November 2006).

38   S.I. No. 207 of 2001, as amended by S.I. No. 71 of 2005.

39   Other protective measures in the Directive relate to the fraudulent use of payment cards, restrictions regarding cold-calling and the prohibition of inertia selling.

40   The withdrawal right is excluded in some circumstances (see Article 6(3)). These are where the performance of a service has already started; the price of the goods or services is dependent on fluctuations in the financial markets; the goods are made to the customer's specifications or are clearly personalized; the goods are perishable; audio or video recordings or computer software have been unsealed by the consumer; and in relation to newspapers, periodicals and magazines; gaming and lottery services.

41   See Howells, 'The Potential and Limits of Consumer Empowerment by Information': 353.

42   For a broader view of the online market in Europe see, the European Consumer Centre's study on *Realities of the European Online Marketplace* (2003) at: http://www.eccdublin.ie/publications/ecc_reports.html (last accessed 17 November 2006).

the internet, the prior information requirements are made available on the website, before or in the course of the ordering process. Therefore, the relevant information is accessible by browsing the net. The Directive sets out the information that must be provided before the contract is concluded. This information relates to:

(1) the identity of the supplier and, in the case of a contract requiring payment in advance, his or her address;
(2) the main characteristics of the goods or services;
(3) the price of the goods or services including all taxes;
(4) delivery costs, where appropriate;
(5) the arrangements for payment, delivery or performance;
(6) the existence of a right of withdrawal (except in the exempted cases);
(7) the period for which the offer or the price remains valid;
(8) where appropriate, the minimum duration of the contract.[43]

The Directive further requires that the commercial purpose of the information must be made clear and that the information be,

> ... provided in a clear and comprehensible manner in any way appropriate to the means of distance communication used, with due regard, in particular, to the principles of good faith in commercial transactions and the principles governing the protection of those who are unable ... to give their consent, such as minors.[44]

The study sought to establish how this information provision requirement operated in practice. To this end, we used two separate surveys.[45] The first ('the website survey') involved a close examination of 80 Irish based websites all of which were covered by the 2001 Regulations.[46] As part of this survey, we investigated levels of compliance with each of the prior information requirements. However, we sought to go beyond simple compliance issues and therefore we also investigated the methods employed in the websites to communicate information to consumers. This enabled us to develop a picture of how information provision operates in practice and provides useful supplementary data to inform the discussion of consumers' responses to information provision. The second survey ('the consumer survey'), based on 352 face–to–face interviews with consumers, was designed to ascertain Irish consumers' opinions and perceptions in relation to the provision of information. The interviews were conducted by the project researcher during the daytime in neutral, public areas

---

43   Article 4(1).
44   Article 4(2).
45   The surveys were drafted, piloted and finalized in March–April 2005; empirical data was collected May–July 2005; this data was reviewed, collated and analysed in August–September 2005.
46   The websites studied were drawn from large and small businesses, well known and more recently established businesses, selling goods and/or services. The researcher progressed to the checkout stage for every transaction so as to monitor the time and place of any pertinent information disclosure on the websites, taking comprehensive notes on the layout of the sites and the attempts made to convey information in a clear manner.

in a variety of geographical locations at different times of the day.[47] By way of background, 53 per cent of those interviewed had transacted online at least once,[48] of whom almost half had bought something between 5–20 times and 12 per cent had bought something more than 20 times.[49] As might be expected, the most common purchases were tickets (plane and concert); accommodation; CDs; books and downloadable materials.[50]

While this article explores the practical effect of information provision rather than the degree of formal supplier compliance with Directive 97/7, an appreciation of the degree of formal compliance is a necessary preliminary to the discussion of this broader question. Clearly, if suppliers do not comply with the requirement to provide information in the first place, this consumer protection mechanism can have no possibility of working effectively.

As is evident from the graph below, there was considerable variation in levels of supplier compliance depending on the nature of the information required to be provided. Thus, 100 per cent of sites surveyed provided information about the main characteristics of the goods or services and over 90 per cent complied with the requirement to provide information as to the identity of the supplier. However, almost 50 per cent of suppliers failed to provide adequate information regarding

---

47   Passers-by were stopped at random and asked if they would participate in the survey. By varying locations and times, the survey sought to ensure as balanced a demographic mix as possible, with regard to age, gender, educational background, consumer expectation and Internet buying experience.

48   This figure is considerably higher than the figure from an earlier Eurobarometer survey, conducted in 2003, which assessed levels of online transacting in Ireland at 1 per cent of Irish respondents (the EU average being 16 per cent of EU15): European Commission, *European Union Public Opinion on issues relating to business to consumer e–commerce* (2004) at: www.europa.eu.int/comm/consumers/topics/facts_ en.htm (last accessed 17 November 2006). The latest Eurobarometer survey indicates a slight increase in online transacting. For example, 19 per cent of consumers living in Ireland reported buying online from Irish websites and 12 per cent purchased from websites outside Ireland. Where respondents had an internet connection at home, the figure rose to 47 per cent (the EU average being 50 per cent of EU 25): European Commission, *Consumer Protection in the Internal Market,* (2006) accessible at http://ec.europa.eu/public_opinion/index_en.htm (last accessed 17 November 2006). Importantly, the purpose of our survey was not to assess levels of online transacting. Indeed, as part of our survey methodology, we purposely used locations likely to have higher numbers of respondents who had bought online and therefore our figure of 53 per cent is not intended to provide any definitive evidence regarding levels.

49   When broken down in demographic terms, 53 per cent male/47 per cent female had bought online; predictably, the most active age group was 25-39 at 71 per cent; but even the least active grouping 55+ scored 23 per cent – almost a quarter; in terms of occupation, the most active group were managers at 66 per cent and self-employed at 63 per cent; the least active groups were homemakers at 16 per cent and unemployed people at 11 per cent; in terms of residence, 57 per cent of respondents from cities and large towns had bought online and 54 per cent from rural areas and villages.

50   Notably, the two most common purchases (tickets at 84 per cent and accommodation at 55 per cent) are not covered by Directive 97/7.

payment, delivery or performance; over 30 per cent of suppliers failed to provide
adequate information regarding the consumer's right to withdraw; and almost 25 per
cent of sites failed to comply with the requirement to provide information relating
to price.[51]

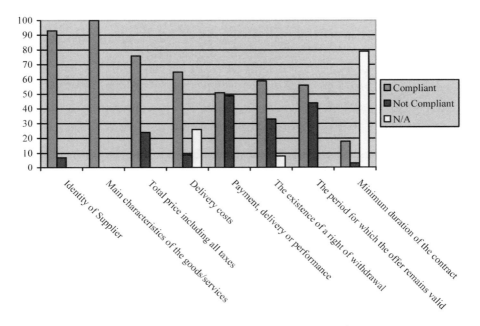

Figure 11.1 Supplier Compliance with Prior Information

We have argued elsewhere that, insofar as there was supplier compliance with the
information requirements, this may be attributed to commercial concerns rather than
effective regulation.[52] In areas of high compliance, we suggest that compliance was
largely commercially driven. A supplier must gain the consumer's trust in order to
persuade the consumer to transact online. Therefore, it is probable that, regardless
of legal regulation, information regarding the identity of the supplier, for example,
would be provided. However, where there is no direct benefit to be gained by the
supplier from the provision of the information (for example, information about
withdrawal rights), the levels of compliance were considerably lower.

A close look at the method of transposition of Directive 97/7 into Irish law suggests
why this may be the case. In transposing this Directive, the legislature adopted
the typical minimalist approach to transposition identified earlier in this article.[53]

---

51   The primary difficulty here related to the provision of information relating to whether
      or not tax was included in the payment price.
52   See Donnelly and White, 'Regulation and Consumer Protection – A Study of the
      Online Market': 35 onwards.
53   See text following n. 20 above.

As a result, the transposing Regulations fail to address difficulties regarding the interpretation of aspects of Directive 97/7. Many of the prior information provisions are ambiguous and hence it is arguable that this ambiguity is a contributory factor to levels of non-compliance.[54] Furthermore, the lack of meaningful enforcement methods[55] and the complete absence of mechanisms for supplier education[56] mean that many Irish suppliers are likely to be unaware of their obligations under the Directive and, if they are aware of their obligations, unlikely to feel legally compelled to comply with them.[57] In brief, the consequences arising from the absence of a sophisticated regulatory culture may be directly felt in the context of compliance with the information requirements of Directive 97/7. Bearing this in mind, it now falls to consider in more depth the effect of information provision on Irish consumers.

3. Information Provision: The Model and its Critics

An empirical investigation of the practical effect of information provision must take place against a background of the theoretical debate regarding the effectiveness of this form of consumer protection. On one side of this debate is the view, which clearly dominates the European consumer policy agenda that, once consumers are provided with sufficient information about a transaction, they will use this information in reaching a decision about whether or not to proceed with the transaction in question. Thus, information provision involves relatively minimal interference with party autonomy: from a supplier's perspective, all that is required is that information be provided and then the transaction may proceed without regulatory interference; from a consumer's perspective, the market remains fully open and consumer choice is unrestricted.

---

54   The website survey found three areas in which levels of non-compliance were especially high. These were in relation to the requirements to provide information relating to arrangements for payment, delivery or performance; the existence of the right to withdraw; and the period for which the offer remains open. Each of these requirements raises issues of interpretation. Yet, each requirement was transposed without any indications regarding appropriate interpretation: see further Donnelly and White, 'Regulation and Consumer Protection – A Study of the Online Market'.

55   The 2001 Regulations fall within a classic 'command and control' regulatory model, allowing for the imposition of very harsh penalties for non-compliance (including criminal sanctions) but leaving the task of enforcement entirely in the hands of the ODCA (now the National Consumer Agency). In light of the difficulties with the ODCA (discussed in text to n. 26 above) it is hardly surprising that there has not, to our knowledge, been a single instance in which proceedings have been taken by the ODCA under the Regulations.

56   See argument by C. Scott, 'Regulatory Innovation and the Online Consumer', *Law & Policy*, 26 (2004): 477, at 478 regarding the particular importance of regulatory innovation, including education provision, in the online environment.

57   The 2001 Regulations do not contain any provision regarding education. Contrast the express educative requirement in Regulation 29 of the UK Consumer Protection (Distance Selling) Regulations 2000 (S.I. 2334/2000).

An essential presumption underlying this view of consumer protection is that consumers will act in a rational way. As Ramsey notes, this approach does not presume that consumers will always seek out all the information relevant to a particular issue; they may prefer not to do so and instead choose to contract in a state of 'rational ignorance'.[58] However, the expectation is that consumers will perform a cost-benefit analysis in deciding whether to seek out and use a particular piece of information. The aim is to make the information available to consumers, should they choose to use it. Thus, under the simple version of this model, information provision is regarded as an unmitigated good.

A number of arguments are ranged on the other side of the debate. By and large, these arguments do not assert that information provision is inappropriate *per se*; rather, the main force of the arguments is that it is a less effective form of protection than its proponents assume and that attention needs to be paid to the detail of the way in which this form of protection works. Four sets of criticisms of the information provision model may be identified. First, at a very basic level, the information provided may never actually reach the consumer. This may be because the consumer cannot understand the information provided. Alternatively, the consumer might simply be too bored by the prospect of reading through the information provided. As aptly noted by Wilhelmsson, the communication of information depends on consumers 'investing time in very dull activities like reading standard form conditions instead of doing something more attractive'.[59] Thus, for these consumers, the fact that information is provided is unlikely to result in their becoming informed, empowered consumers.

Secondly, critics challenge the presumption that consumers act rationally on the basis of information received. Here, critics draw on insights deriving from behavioural economics which challenges assumptions of rational behaviour which underpin many aspects of the law.[60] In the context of information provision, it is argued that consumers do not necessarily respond rationally to information. Instead they tend to interpret information to support their own views[61] and to be overly optimistic in assessing risk.[62] Furthermore, the way in which the decision is framed and the way in which information in relation to the decision is provided have important impacts on the conclusion reached.[63]

Thirdly, insights from behavioural economics also lend doubts to the view that more information is better and suggest that too much information, or 'information overload', may decrease the individual's ability to make decisions. Commentators

---

58   Ramsay, 'From Truth in Lending to Responsible Lending': 52.

59   Wilhelmsson, 'The Informed Consumer v the Vulnerable Consumer in European Unfair Commercial Practices Law – a comment': 216.

60   For a general overview of this approach, see C. Sunstein (ed.), *Behavioural Law and Economics* (Cambridge, 2000).

61   See Howells, 'The Potential and Limits of Consumer Empowerment by Information': 360.

62   *Ibid.*, 360–1; Ramsey, 'From Truth in Lending': 52.

63   See further Ramsey *ibid*: 52–7; Howells, 'The Potential and Limits of Consumer Empowerment by Information': 358–62; Paredes, 'Blinded by the Light: Information Overload and Its Consequences for Securities Regulation': 434–43.

cite studies that show that as the mass of information provided reaches a certain point (generally accepted as somewhere between five and ten pieces or 'chunks' of information[64]), an individual's capacity to process this information begins to decrease.[65]

Finally, the information provision model adopts something of a 'one size fits all' approach and does not differentiate between types of consumer.[66] However, studies have shown that information provision may be most effective in the context of consumers from more 'privileged' socioeconomic or education backgrounds and that consumers from 'less privileged' backgrounds stand to benefit less.[67] Whitford's 'almost paradigmatic'[68] survey of studies following the introduction of 'truth-in-lending' legislation in the United States showed that the benefits of the legislation (greater consumer choice; greater competition through consumers 'shopping around') were concentrated in consumers in higher income groups. For consumers in lower income groups, information did not seem to be getting to the consumers.[69] Furthermore, the work of Crow *et al.* shows that, even if information were getting through to less privileged consumers, other (less rational) factors appear to be more influential on the decision-making process.[70]

---

64   Howells, 'The Potential and Limits of Consumer Empowerment by Information':
      360 cites a 1956 study which suggests that seven is the optimal number of 'chunks'
      while Paredes, 'Blinded by the Light: Information Overload and Its Consequences for
      Securities Regulation': 442 cites a series of studies to support the range between five
      and ten.

65   Parades, 'Blinded by the Light: Information Overload and Its Consequences for
      Securities Regulation': 441 presents reasons why this is the case. One explanation is
      that as people try to process information, they become overwhelmed and confused.
      Another explanation, based on decision theory, is that people adopt decision-making
      strategies depending on the complexity of the decision to be made. As the task becomes
      more complicated, the decision–making strategy will be correspondingly simplified.
      Because the provision of more information makes the decision-making task more
      complex, this has an effect on the decision-making strategy employed.

66   However, European case law has recognized that some consumers are not able to process
      more information, for example, Case 286/81 *Oosthoek's Uitgeversmattschappij* [1982]
      ECR 4575; and has taken into account the special needs of weak consumer groups, for
      example, Case 382/87 *Roger Buet* v. *Minister Public* [1989] ECR 1235.

67   See arguments made by Wilhelmsson 'The Informed Consumer v the Vulnerable
      Consumer in European Unfair Commercial Practices Law – a comment': 213,
      regarding why the term 'less privileged' is preferable to other frequently used terms
      such as 'vulnerable'.

68   As described by Wilhelmsson *ibid*: 215.

69   See the Federal Reserve Board studies cited by Whitford, 'The Functions of Disclosure
      Regulation in Consumer Transactions': 411 which showed that both the level of
      awareness of interest rates and the increase in awareness following truth in lending
      disclosure were substantially lower for residents of 'poverty areas' than elsewhere.

70   See I. Crow, G. Howells, M. Moroney, 'Credit and Debt: Choices for Poorer
      Consumers', in I. Crow, G. Howells, M. Moroney, (eds), *Aspects of Credit and Debt:
      Choices for Poorer Consumers* (London, 1993) p. 11.

4. Information Provision: The Practical Effect

In light of the ongoing theoretical debate outlined above, we were concerned to investigate the practical effect of information provision. While all of the critiques of information provision would benefit from more focused empirical work, we chose to concentrate on one issue in the specific context of an underdeveloped consumer society. Thus, we sought to investigate the extent to which the prior information required to be provided under Directive 97/7 was actually getting to Irish consumers and how Irish consumers were responding to this information.

In order to do this, we sought to evaluate three matters: first, how do Irish consumers assess their information needs? Second, how do Irish consumers respond to information when they receive it? And third, how much do Irish consumers actually know about their legal rights when buying online?

Consumers' responses on each of these matters, drawn from the consumer survey described above, will be outlined below and will allow a picture to develop of Irish consumers' needs and expectations. We supplement our reliance on consumer responses with the findings of the website survey, also described above and the findings of the European Consumer Centre's (ECC) Report, *Realities of the European Online Market*, (2003) which was based on a pan-European study of websites.[71] These surveys of websites can provide a degree of objective verification of consumers' perceptions[72] and also draw attention to the issues that arise in giving practical effect to information provision policy.

(i) Consumers' Assessment of their Informational Needs

Our evaluation of consumers' own assessment of their needs was based on responses to two questions, one unprompted, the second, prompted. The first question was whether there was any specific information that the consumer would typically check for before making a purchase online. Sixty per cent of respondents answered yes; however, the responses regarding what this information related to were extremely varied and made the identification of a pattern almost impossible. The only numerically significant response was that 31 per cent said that they would check security of payment on the site or search for the padlock icon.[73] In the second, prompted, question, respondents were asked to rate the importance of each of the prior information requirements set

---

71   Available at http://www.eccdublin.ie/publications/ecc_reports.html (last accessed 17 November 2006). This Report was concerned exclusively with cross-border online transactions. The project comprised three main parts: a shopping exercise whereby 114 orders were placed cross-border within the EU; an information quality examination whereby 262 EU based websites were checked; and legal and practical analysis of the cooling-off period.

72   However, in this regard, it should be noted that the sample for the website survey was not designed to correlate with the sites used by the consumers surveyed and which provided the basis for the consumer responses to the survey.

73   The next most significant responses were that 4 per cent said they would only buy from reputable companies; 4 per cent checked dispatch times and costs; 2 per cent checked refunds and returns policies.

out in Directive 97/7 in terms of importance.[74] Over 80 per cent of respondents rated all but one of the items required in Directive 97/7 as very important. Respondents were then asked if there was any other information that should be provided. Thirty-six per cent of respondents replied affirmatively, of whom almost one-third said that information on online payment security should be provided.

On the basis of these responses, it would seem that the designation of information as sufficiently important to require regulatory intervention in Directive 97/7 largely coincides with consumers' views regarding importance. However, insofar as this conclusion is based on responses to prompted questions, it should be borne in mind that respondents are more likely to answer in the affirmative when prompted. Therefore, the responses to the unprompted question may be more instructive regarding deeper consumer concerns. Nonetheless, consumer responses to the prompted questions do show consumers' appetite for information, at a theoretical level at any rate. Thus, while critics may question the effectiveness of information provision, information does seem to serve a consumer need and therefore, it would seem that information provision does contribute to building consumer confidence. In this regard, Directive 97/7 may be achieving at least one of its policy imperatives, namely, to develop consumer confidence in the online market and to contribute to economic growth in this way.[75] The degree to which this consumer confidence is well placed will be discussed further below.

While the information provided is generally welcomed by consumers, it is noteworthy that consumers' responses to both prompted and unprompted questions suggest the importance of one piece of information which is not currently legislatively required to be provided. This is information relating to online security.[76] However, although there is no legal requirement in this regard, the website survey found that over 80 per cent of websites did contain information relating to the technical security of online payment. This rate of information provision corresponds favourably with the compliance levels with some of the legal requirements.[77] It also confirms our view, discussed above,[78] that commercial concerns rather than regulatory intervention may provide the basis for information provision in an underdeveloped consumer society, such as Ireland. In addition to consumer concerns driving suppliers to provide this information at a risk of losing the sale, it is probable that credit card providers perform a kind of 'private' monitoring function in this context. The vast majority of websites which accept online payment will involve credit card payments and credit card providers are likely to insist on appropriate security mechanisms being in place before they will allow suppliers to avail of the service.[79]

---

74   For a list of these requirements, see text to n. 43 above.
75   See Recital 4 which presents the Directive as part of the 'attainment of the aims of the internal market'.
76   It should be noted that Article 8 of Directive 97/7 offers only limited protection as regards the fraudulent use of payment cards: see further Donnelly and White, 'Regulation and Consumer Protection – A Study of the Online Market'.
77   See text to n. 51 above.
78   See text to n. 52 above.
79   Donnelly and White, 'Regulation and Consumer Protection – A Study of the Online Market': 49.

However, while informal mechanisms, such as commercial concerns and private monitoring, may prove effective in pushing the information provision agenda in some contexts, when these factors are absent (for example in the context of providing information about what happens to advance payments in the event of supplier insolvency[80]), the formal regulatory framework must be able to fill in the gaps. It is at this point that deficiencies in the regulatory framework become problematic, in particular, in underdeveloped consumer societies, such as Ireland, where the consumer voice is weak.

(ii) Consumers' Responses to Information

Having ascertained that consumers tend to value information provision at a theoretical level, it next falls to consider how consumers respond to information which is actually provided. In order to do this, we used two approaches. The first sought to ascertain whether consumers actually read the information received; the second related to the difficulties consumers had encountered in relation to the information provided. In the first context, respondents were asked whether they read the terms and conditions before deciding to buy online. As is evident from the graph below, less than half (43 per cent) answered 'sometimes' and almost equal proportions answered 'always' (29 per cent) and 'never' (28 per cent).

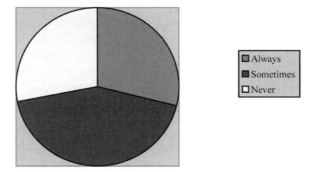

Figure 11.2   Responses to Question: Do you read the terms and conditions before buying online?

This finding shows that, while consumers may rank certain information as important in theory, actually checking that the information is provided in an individual purchasing situation is not a major priority for most consumers who buy online.[81] It confirms the claims discussed above that consumers do not necessarily take active steps in protecting themselves through reading information. This aspect of the

---

80   The website survey found that none of the sites surveyed provided information on the consequences of supplier insolvency.

81   There is no comparable Irish data in relation to whether consumers read information provided when transacting offline.

finding is hardly surprising and most readers will have little difficulty in finding anecdotal evidence that consumers do not always read the terms and conditions before transacting online. Indeed, it might be argued that the notable aspect of the finding is that 29 per cent of consumers claimed always read the terms and conditions and 43 per cent sometimes do so.[82]

From one perspective, this finding appears supportive of the effectiveness of information provision as a consumer protection mechanism. The fact that most consumers do not always read the terms and conditions might be explained on the basis that many online purchases are relatively low value and therefore that consumers may not feel the same need to protect themselves as, for example, in the context of loans or other financial services. Therefore it may be that consumers perform a traditional type of cost-benefit analysis and decide that it is not worth their time to read the terms and conditions when the consequences of the transaction are relatively unimportant. They choose to transact in a state of 'rational ignorance'.[83] For the relatively significant proportion of consumers who do choose to read the information, the information is available and, provided enough consumers do read the information to make a difference to suppliers at a general commercial level, the underlying policy goal of increasing competition between suppliers may be achieved.

However, viewing the matter from this perspective only may be overly simplistic. Stating that the consumer performs a cost-benefit analysis leaves one important variable unanalysed. This is the question of how great the cost is to the consumer. It is one matter to decide not to read accessible information and quite another not to take the trouble to locate and read information which is not accessible or not even available. Therefore, in order to assess consumers' responses to information provision, it is necessary to inquire into the difficulties encountered by consumers in using the information provided. This was the focus of our second inquiry into consumer responses to information provided. We began by asking respondents if they had encountered problems with information provided on a website. Thirty-six per cent of respondents had encountered such problems, 64 per cent had not. This appears quite a positive response. However, given that, as noted above, most consumers do not always read the information provided in the first place, this response is not necessarily such a positive an endorsement of information provision as first appears.

We then asked those respondents who had encountered difficulty about the nature of the problem encountered. This was a prompted question in that we provided a list of possible problems, although we did include an 'other' category, where respondents could include a problem which was not already mentioned. Our analysis is also supplemented by the findings of the website survey where we assessed the sites surveyed in terms of accessibility and other issues. Although not necessarily the same sites as those identified by the consumers, the combination of the two

---

82   In this context, some account should be taken of the fact that, in a face-to-face context, some respondents may have felt embarrassed to admit that they did not check terms and conditions and that this may have influenced responses somewhat.

83   See text to n. 58 above.

sources provides some indication of the issues that arise in the practical delivery of information in an online context.

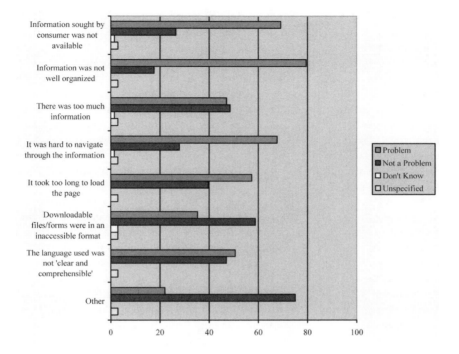

Figure 11.3 Problems experienced by consumers

As is evident from the graph above, the main difficulties encountered by consumers related to a lack of information or a lack of organisation of the information provided.

The most common problem related to the organisation of information on the website. Eighty per cent of those consumers who experienced difficulties (28.8 per cent of consumers overall) identified the organisation of information as a problem. This difficulty was also identified in the website survey, which noted a number of accessibility problems relating to organisation. This survey found that information that is legally required to be provided was accessible from each page of the site in only 60 per cent of sites. Of the remaining sites, in some cases, the information was accessible from all pages other than the front page while, in others, it was not accessible until the very last page where the consumer confirms the order.[84] While

---

84   We noted two other points regarding accessibility. First, a small number of websites used pop-up windows to provide information. As many computers have anti pop-up protection, this is not an effective way of communicating legal information. Secondly, in some websites, the legal information was linked at the very bottom of a page which must be scrolled down to and is not immediately obvious from the initial view of the screen.

technically compliant with Directive 97/7 (all that is required for compliance is that information be given prior to the contract), this method of information disclosure does not provide the consumer with information at the formative stage of the process in deciding whether to buy or not. In light of research which shows that individuals tend to interpret information to support the opinions they have already formed,[85] it is probable that the desire to purchase the chosen item or service will lead to negative information either not being sought or being disregarded if encountered.

The website survey also found that there was no uniformity in the way in which legally required information was described to consumers. Most sites surveyed provided the information under the heading 'Terms and Conditions' although a significant number of sites used other headings including 'Legal Conditions' or 'Frequently Asked Questions'. In other sites, the information was divided up into separate parts, such as 'Returns'; 'Payment Information'. This lack of consistency makes it more difficult for consumers to develop a strategy for locating information and makes the task of accessing information more difficult.

Moreover, the website survey found that most websites surveyed did not take active steps to bring information to consumers' attention. Only one-fifth of sites in the website survey required consumers to click a box to confirm that they have read the terms and conditions (sometimes referred to as a click-wrap system).[86] While the use of a click-wrap system does not guarantee that the consumer has actually read the terms and conditions, it does at least require some acknowledgement on the consumer's part of the existence of these terms and conditions and therefore increases the possibility of the information actually getting to the consumer. In short, the website survey confirms the view emerging from the consumer survey that there are accessibility issues which impede consumers in taking active steps to protect themselves.

The second most common problem encountered by consumers was that the information was not available, with 69 per cent of consumers who encountered difficulties identifying this as a problem. Again, this consumer concern would seem to be supported by the findings of both the website survey and the ECC Report.[87] As noted above, the website study revealed several areas in which a substantial number of websites failed to comply with the information requirements laid down in Directive 97/7.[88] This finding was replicated in the ECC Report, although the degree of non-compliance was less marked.[89] Furthermore, 26 per cent of sites in the

---

85   See Howells, 'The Potential and Limits of Consumer Empowerment by Information': 360.

86   The remaining sites either contained a statement that the consumer's use of the site constituted an agreement to the terms and conditions or were silent in this regard. The ECC Report (above n. 71, p. 29) found that 49 per cent of sites took active steps to bring terms and conditions to consumers' attention either through a click-wrap system or through having the terms and conditions automatically appear before the consumer confirmed the order.

87   Above n. 71.

88   See text to n. 511 above.

89   The ECC Report found (above n. 71, p. 17) that 32 per cent of websites failed to give information about the cooling-off period and 7 per cent of websites failed to give

website survey and 13 per cent of sites in the ECC Report did not contain any legal information relating to the contract at all.[90] Once again, it is notable that the results of the website survey (which focused on Irish websites only) showed considerably less compliance than the pan-European ECC study. This shows that, while insufficient information is by no means unique to Ireland, it seems to be a more extensive problem in the case of Irish websites. It would seem that the lack of meaningful enforcement mechanisms and the complete absence of an educative provision as part of the enforcement method results in consumers who use Irish websites encountering more of an information deficit than is the norm elsewhere.

The reverse problem of too much information was identified by almost half of the respondents. While this suggests that some consumers at least may feel something of an information overload, it is not possible to draw too definitive conclusions from this finding given the findings regarding the organisation of the information. Information that is badly organised may become overwhelming more easily than information that is presented in a more accessible way.

A further problem identified by approximately half of those respondents who had experienced difficulties was that the language used in the website was not clear and comprehensible. In addition to effectiveness issues, this also gives rises to compliance issues because, as noted above, it is a legal requirement in Directive 97/7 that the legal information must be given in a 'clear and comprehensible' manner.[91] Inevitably, the assessment of whether information is given in a clear and comprehensible manner requires a degree of subjective assessment. In particular, an issue arises regarding to whom the information must be clear and comprehensible. In other words, at what kind of consumer should the supplier direct the language used; can the supplier assume a certain level of education on the part of the consumer? The approach of the ECJ in other contexts has been to allow suppliers to assume that consumers have a reasonable level of comprehension.[92] In this context, the issue of less privileged consumers comes clearly to the fore. Because the focus of our study was on consumers in an underdeveloped consumer society rather than on specific groups of consumers, we did not attempt to link questions of clarity and comprehensibility with particular groups of consumers. This important question clearly merits further empirical study. The important lesson from our study, however, is that a relatively significant number of Irish consumers (half of those who experienced problems, which is 18 per cent of the total number of consumers surveyed) had issues with the clarity and comprehensibility of the information given.

---

information about the total cost of product or service (although it also found that only 33 per cent gave information about price in a 'truly convenient and accessible way').

90　Some of these sites contained a heading 'Terms and Conditions' or 'Terms of Use' but the information contained under this heading related to the use of the website and not to the underlying contract.

91　Article 4(2) of Directive 97/7.

92　See G. Howells and T. Wilhelmsson, 'EC and US Approaches to Consumer Protection – Should the Gap be Bridged?', *Yearbook of European Law*, 17 (1997), p. 207. The specific interpretation of the term in Directive 97/7 has not been considered by the European Court of Justice.

A number of lessons may be drawn from the discussion above. First, while many Irish consumers do not routinely take steps to protect themselves, a significant proportion of consumers do take such steps at least some of the time. This finding may be linked to the consumer responses to the earlier question where it was shown that Irish consumers have an appetite for information when contracting online. For those consumers who do take steps to protect themselves, there is evidence that the cost of the steps that they are required to take in order to do so is artificially high. In Ireland, at least, this can be seen to derive from the way in which information is communicated to consumers. Suppliers are often non-compliant with the requirements of Directive 97/7 and there are also problems in the organisation and accessibility of information. It is in this context that the underdeveloped nature of the consumer society becomes especially significant. Irish suppliers have had little or no guidance on either their legal obligations or on best practice in communicating legal information to consumers. Thus, the historic absence of a regulatory authority with a developed educative role has a clear impact on the extent of the protections available to consumers in an online context.[93]

(iii) Consumers' Levels of Knowledge

Having established in the previous sections that Irish consumers appear to have an appetite for information when contracting online and that they are ill-served by suppliers and by the regulatory structures employed in actually obtaining this information, it now falls to explore the final matter investigated in the study. Unlike the previous questions investigated, which were primarily focused on consumers' subjective experience, in our third investigation, we attempted an objective assessment of Irish consumers' levels of knowledge of their legal rights when buying goods or services online. In order to assess this matter, we used two separate test measures. First, we sought to assess consumers' general awareness of the existence of legal rights when they buy goods or services online and secondly, we utilised a case study relating to the right to return goods and asked consumers two specific questions through which we sought to test consumers' actual knowledge rather than their subjective views of their level of knowledge.

In the first inquiry, we asked all the respondents, that is, those who had bought something online and those who had not, whether they were aware of any laws that protect people when buying online. Seventy-eight per cent of the respondents

---

93   In this regard, it is instructive to review the website of the Office of Fair Trading (www.oft.gov.uk). The OFT website includes a downloadable business guide 'Home Shopping: Distance Selling Regulations' as well as detailed and accessible information directed towards consumers. Note also the efforts by the OFT to monitor levels of education among suppliers. An Office of Fair Trading study found that awareness of the distance selling regulations among business people was lower than awareness of other forms of consumer legislation. See: www.oft.gov.uk/News/Press+releases/2004/40–04.htm (last accessed 17 November 2006). The OFT responded to the findings of the study by initiating an information campaign to raise awareness of the legislation among suppliers.

were not aware of any such laws.[94] We then asked the 67 respondents who indicated that they were aware of laws protecting them when buying online to identify the protections available. The protections identified were very diverse and, by and large, inaccurate showing little awareness of the actual legal position. Thus, 3 per cent of respondents believed that the ODCA would protect them; 2 per cent believed that there credit card payments would be secure; and a small number identified sale of goods legislation. However, there was almost no awareness of the existence of the specific Directive or of the transposing Regulations.

The fact that consumers lack awareness of the legal protections available is hardly surprising in light of the findings of the website survey. It would seem that suppliers are making little attempt to draw consumers' attention to their legal rights. While a small proportion of sites (13 per cent) mentioned the existence of the legislation underlying consumers' legal rights in this area and some sites linked directly to the legal provision itself or to a consumer rights website, the norm was not to mention the legislation.

Consumers' lack of awareness of legal rights is confirmed by the responses to more specific questions explored through use of a case study relating to the withdrawal right arising under Directive 97/7 and specifically relating to the consumer's right to return goods bought online. The extent of the right is set out in Article 6. This Article states that '[f]or any distance contract the consumer shall have a period of at least seven working days to withdraw from the contract without penalty and without giving any reason'. Article 4 of Directive 97/7 requires a supplier to provide prior information regarding 'the existence of the right to withdraw'. Further details on the right must be given in a 'durable medium' after the contract has been concluded.[95]

We chose to focus the case study on the right to withdraw for a number of reasons. First, this right is an innovative aspect of Directive 97/7. Consumers do not have an equivalent right in the 'bricks and mortar' environment. Therefore, the right has little intuitive resonance for consumers. This means that an assessment of consumer knowledge of the right, allows, insofar as is possible, the provision of information to be assessed in a context where consumers are actually being informed about something that they do not already know. In this context, we were also struck by Brownsword and Howell's prediction on the enactment of Directive 97/7 that lack of consumer awareness of the existence of the right to withdraw might mean that 'despite strong paper recognition', the right would prove to be relatively weak in practice.[96] Secondly, it is clear from consumer responses that the matter of returns is to the forefront of consumers' concerns. Almost half of the respondents indicated that they always check the returns policy (as compared with only 29 per cent who always check the broader terms and conditions of the contract).

We asked consumers two questions relating to returns: first, how long do consumers have to return goods; secondly, in what circumstances may consumers

---

94   Of those who had bought online, 73 per cent were not aware of any legal protection
      while, of those who had not, 83 per cent did not know about any legal protections.
95   Article 5 of Directive 97/7.
96   Brownsword and Howells, 'When surfers start to shop: Internet commerce and contract
      law': 304.

return goods? Ten per cent of the respondents stated that consumers who buy online have up to seven days to return the goods. Most assumed that the time limit was longer with 34 per cent of respondents believing that consumers who buy online have a month in which to return goods.[97] The other noteworthy aspect of this survey is that only 6 per cent of respondents indicated that they did not know how long consumers who buy online have to return goods. Similar findings were recorded regarding the circumstances in which goods may be returned. Forty per cent of consumers knew that they had a right to return goods without giving a reason. Of the remainder, 40 per cent of consumers believed that the goods had to be faulty and 16 per cent gave another inaccurate response in this regard.[98] Once again, only 4 per cent of consumers indicated that they did not know the answer to this question.

The response to the case study confirms the more general finding that Irish consumers are not well-informed about their legal rights when buying online. Thus, it would seem that the aim of information provision, which is to produce well-informed and empowered consumers, is not being met in the online context. Directive 97/7 is not delivering as hoped. It is interesting however that, while Irish consumers lack information about their legal rights, this does not seem to lead to a great diminution in consumer confidence. A striking aspect of the consumer responses to the withdrawal case study was that very few respondents stated that they did not know the extent of their legal rights. While some of these responses may have been prompted by the respondents' embarrassment at admitting to not knowing the answer, the scale of the findings suggests that Irish consumers believe that they know their rights (even though they are frequently incorrect in this regard). It may be the case that Irish consumers' confidence derives in part from the fact they transact primarily with well known and reputable suppliers.[99] But this attitude of consumer confidence is also reflected in a broader context. For instance, in response to the *Eurobarometer Consumers Survey*,[100] approximately 66 per cent of Irish consumers regarded themselves as well protected, placing Irish consumers in the top half of EU15 member states in this regard.[101]

---

97   It should be noted that a significant portion of suppliers (41 per cent of those surveyed as part of the website survey) do allow consumers this longer period. However, consumers have no legal right under the Directive in this regard. The proportion of suppliers offering a longer period in which to return goods raised interesting questions about the relationship between market forces and legal rules. See also text to n. 52.

98   Some consumers thought that the right to return goods depended on the supplier's returns policy and others stated that the right of return varied depending on the jurisdiction from which the consumer purchased the products.

99   As part of the consumer survey, we did not ask consumers to specify the names of the websites with which they transacted and hence we cannot reach any definitive conclusions in this regard.

100   Flash Eurobarometer 117 *Consumers Survey* Results and Comments, January 2002, p. 33.

101   This compares with 21 per cent of Greek and Portuguese consumers (and 82 per cent of Finnish consumers).

5. Conclusion

This chapter has presented a 'snapshot' of the effect of information based consumer protection in the online market in Ireland. In this respect, it allows a number of specific conclusions to be reached in the context investigated. In addition, we consider that more general lessons can be learned from the study about the role of information provision in the development of European consumer policy.

In the specific context of the Irish online market, the study shows that information-based consumer protection is not working effectively. First, suppliers are not complying with the prior information requirements of Directive 97/7 and therefore at the very basic level, Irish consumers do not have access to the legislatively required information. While this is mitigated in some circumstances where suppliers are commercially driven to provide certain kinds of information, the underlying regulatory structure in Ireland does not persuade or compel suppliers to provide information when they would not otherwise have done so. Secondly, even where information is provided, it would seem that, for a number of reasons, the information is not reaching consumers. Consumers do not always read the information provided; information is frequently provided in an inaccessible or disorganised manner or using language that is not clear and comprehensible. Thirdly, Irish consumers have very little awareness of their legal rights when buying online.

The study also allows us to sketch a picture of the Irish consumer in the online environment. From the study, it appears that Irish consumers have an appetite for information at least at a theoretical level, even if they do not always take the steps to actually access the information in an individual purchasing situation. However, the study also suggests that the Irish consumer is badly informed. Irish consumers do not seem to know their rights. Notwithstanding this collective lack of knowledge, Irish consumers seem to have a high degree of confidence. Lack of information has not hampered the consumer spending which has fuelled the growth in the Irish economy and Irish consumers do not appear to think of themselves as lacking protection or information when transacting online. While this sketch is focused on the online environment, it may also describe Irish consumers in a more general context. Clearly, more empirical work would be required to establish a more general picture. And, this broader type of enquiry is vital in the development of Irish consumer policy.

Notwithstanding the specific nature of the study presented in this article, we consider that there are lessons for the development of European consumer policy and in particular, in the context of the ongoing review of the European consumer *acquis*.[102] The study shows the benefits of going beyond questions of member states' transposition of EC directives by looking at issues of enforcement, education and the ultimate effectiveness of the measure. While undoubtedly more time-consuming, this kind of research is an essential component of any full-scale review. One key lesson from the study is that a member state, such as Ireland, may have properly transposed a particular measure yet, because of the particular regulatory culture in the state in question, the measure may be, to all intents and purposes, ineffective.

---

102   See further: http://ec.europa.eu/consumers/cons_int/safe_shop/fair_bus_pract/cont_ law/index_en.htm.

Without jurisdiction-specific, in-depth research of the kind attempted in this study, the effectiveness of European consumer policy cannot be properly assessed.

Lastly, in light of this study, we believe that policymakers and legislators must be conscious of both the limitations of information based consumer protection and its use relative to the particular stage of development of the consumer society in question. The study shows that information based consumer protection is not operating effectively in Ireland, at a time when we would suggest Irish consumer society remains underdeveloped. That is not to say that information based consumer protection is wholly ineffective in underdeveloped consumer societies but that it may be less effective in this context.

In our view, the experience of Irish consumers shows that the linkage between information provision and consumer confidence is not inevitable. It suggests that consumers may be confident while, at the same time, being ill-informed. This may be a feature, which is unique to Ireland, or it may be a more general feature of underdeveloped consumer societies or indeed a feature of consumers in general. Further investigation would be required to ascertain how widespread a phenomenon the ill-informed, confident consumer actually is. However, if these findings are replicated elsewhere, they throw up some interesting questions about the dominant policy agenda underlying information based consumer protection. In particular, if the primary aim of EC consumer protection policy is the creation of confident consumers who will facilitate the development of the internal market,[103] this may be achieved notwithstanding the fact that information provision is not actually working in practice. However, if the aim is to genuinely empower consumers to make decisions, it is necessary to ensure that consumer confidence is not misplaced and that consumer protection is built on solid foundations rather than consumers' perceptions.

---

103   See Article 95 of the EC Treaty.

12 Class Actions for New Zealand Consumers

Kate Tokeley[1]

1. Introduction

This article examines the benefits of the class action for New Zealand consumers. It analyses the current operation of the New Zealand class action and recommends significant reform to expand the use of the class action and to give clear specific guidelines on its operation. Part 2 of the article defines a class action and gives some examples of when this procedure might be used in a consumer dispute. Parts 3 and 4 discuss the advantages of a class action procedure for New Zealand consumers and examine the concerns that are sometimes expressed about this type of procedure. The article concludes that these concerns are overstated and that fears of a US-style excess of litigation are unfounded. Part 5 examines 'opt-in' and the 'opt-out' approaches to the operation of a class action.[2] It is argued that allowing an 'opt-out' class action has significant benefits over limiting class actions to the more restrictive 'opt-in' approach. Part 6 analyses the specifics of the current New Zealand class action procedure. It examines the extent to which the class action rule and case law allow an 'opt-out' approach. The article concludes that the case law has restricted the class action to an 'opt-in' procedure in the case of damages claims. It is argued that this restrictive interpretation is unjustified and unnecessary. Part 7 suggests options for reform. It is argued that the current rule is lacking in detail and ought to be redrafted in order to provide more specific guidance on the operation of the procedure. In addition, it is suggested that the New Zealand rule should be expanded to provide expressly for an 'opt-out' class action. Finally, Part 8 considers the cost barriers associated with class actions. Several options for reducing the cost barriers are discussed.

2. What is a Class Action?

This article uses the term 'class action'[3] to mean any procedure that increases access to justice by allowing a single plaintiff (the representative plaintiff[4]) to bring an

---

action on behalf of persons with a common interest in the subject matter of the litigation. This procedure is used in New Zealand but not as liberally or to the same extent as in the United States, Canada or Australia.[5]

There are three main situations where a class action might be appropriate for consumer litigation:

- *A defective good or service causes economic loss.* For example, a number of consumers suffer loss due to purchasing a particular model of motor vehicle which has a common fault or because they are attending a University course where the teaching is inadequate. The economic loss in these cases is a reduction in the value of the good or service.
- *A misleading representation or misleading conduct in the marketplace causes economic loss.* For example, an error by a travel agent misleads a number of tourists about the cost of a particular holiday package or a representation in an advertisement misleads consumers about the specifications of a particular brand of computer.
- *A defective good or service causes personal injury or death.* This category of litigation is the one that is most often associated with the United States style of class action. It includes what is often referred to as mass tort litigation. Examples include the Dalkon Shield IUD and leaking breast implant litigation. In the case of services, litigation in this category could cover a rail disaster which kills or harms people. In New Zealand this type of litigation is generally prevented by the accident compensation legislation which bars claims for damages arising from personal injuries.[6] However, there are some exceptions. For example, it is sometimes possible to sue for disease that is caused by a product.[7] It is also possible to sue for exemplary damages in cases where the defendant has shown outrageous and flagrant disregard for the plaintiff's safety.[8]

---

the same interest in a proceedings. This article does not discuss the class action as used by a defendant. The focus is on the class action as a method of increasing access to justice for consumer plaintiffs.

5   Class Actions are available in American Federal Courts, see Fed.R.Civ.P. 23, and in all States but Mississippi and Virginia. Class actions are also available in Canada, see Code of Civil Procedure (Quebec), RSQ, c. C–25 (SQ 1978); Class Proceedings Act 1992 (Ontario); Class Proceedings Act RSBC 1996 c. 50 (British Columbia); Class Actions Act 2001 (Ch. C–12.01 of the Statutes of Saskatchewan, 2001); Class Actions Act 2001 (Newfoundland) (SNL 2001 Ch. C–18.1); Class Proceedings Act 2002 (Manitoba) (CCSM c. C130); Class Proceedings Act 2003 (Alberta) (Ch. C–16.5). Class actions in Australia are regulated by Pt IVA of the Federal Court of Australia Act 1976. These provisions were inserted by the Federal Court of Australia Amendment Act 1991 no. 181 and came into force in 1992. For discussion of the class action in Australian see S. Clark and C. Harris, 'Multi-plaintiff Litigation in Australia a Comparative Perspective', *Duke J. of Comp. & Int'l Law L.*, 11, (2001): 289 and G. Damian and K. Adams, *Class Actions in Australia* (Sydney, 2005).

6   Section 317(1) of the Injury Prevention, Rehabilitation, and Compensation Act 2001. The effect of this provision is that it is not generally possible to sue for personal injuries or death in New Zealand. See paras 4.2 and 4.3 for further discussion on how the accident compensation regime affects class actions.

7   See s. 26(2) of the Injury Prevention, Rehabilitation, and Compensation Act.

8   *McLaren Transport Ltd* v. *Somerville* [1996] 3 NZLR 424; *A* v. *Bottrill* [2003] 2 NZLR 721 (PC).

3. Benefits of the Class Action Procedure for Consumers

In his 1996 *Access to Justice* report, Lord Woolf had the following to say about the need for class actions:[9]

> It is now generally recognised, by judges, practitioners and consumer representatives, that there is a need for a new approach both in relation to court procedures and legal aid. The new procedures should achieve the following objectives: (a) provide access to justice where large numbers of people have been affected by another's conduct, but individual loss is so small that it makes an individual action economically unviable; (b) provide expeditious, effective and proportionate methods of resolving cases, where individual damages are large enough to justify individual action but where the number of claimants and the nature of the issues involved mean that the cases cannot be managed satisfactorily in accordance with normal procedure; (c) achieve a balance between the normal rights of claimants and defendants, to pursue and defend cases individually, and the interests of a group of parties to litigate the action as a whole in an effective manner.

There seems little doubt that there are significant benefits to a legal system incorporating some form of class action procedure. The benefits of such a procedure fall into three main areas: access to justice, deterrence and judicial economy. Each of these benefits will now be discussed.

(i) Access to Justice

New Zealand has an impressive array of consumer rights to protect consumers from harm caused by defective products, misleading conduct in the marketplace and oppressive credit contracts. These rights are contained in statutes such as the Fair Trading Act 1986, the Consumer Guarantees Act 1993 and the Credit Contracts and Consumer Finance Act 2003. Consumers also have rights under the common law of tort and contract. However, these legal rights have no meaning if, in practical terms, the remedies for breach of these rights are inaccessible. The class action device is one method of increasing the accessibility of these rights by making it easier for consumers to take a dispute to court.

Most importantly, the class action frees each consumer from individually having to spend money litigating the issue. For many consumers the financial cost of litigation is a significant barrier to accessing justice. Often, consumers simply cannot afford to hire a lawyer and take a claim to court. The problem of costs is particularly acute in consumer disputes because many of them involve relatively small amounts of money so that in many instances the cost of litigating the issue would exceed the amount recoverable if the litigation was successful.

Litigation is costly in terms of time as well as money. For many consumers it is simply unrealistic to spend the time necessary to resolve a consumer dispute through litigation, particularly when the dispute concerns only a relatively small sum of money. By joining together as a class, consumers who have suffered loss due to a

---

9   *Access to Justice*: *Final Report to the Lord Chancellor on the Civil Justice System in England and Wales* (London, HMSO, July 1996) Ch. 17.

defective product or unfair trade practice, are able to reduce both the time and cost of court action.

(ii) Deterrent Effect

Not only does the class action procedure have the advantage of making individual consumer redress easier, but it also has a corresponding deterrent effect on suppliers and manufacturers.[10] An effective class action procedure makes it less likely that manufacturers and suppliers will escape liability for their wrongdoings merely because they cause a small amount of harm to a large number of consumers. This point is well made by Chief Justice Bird in *State* v. *Levi Strauss & Co.*[11] '... without such actions defendants may be permitted to retain ill gotten gains simply by their conduct harming large numbers of people in small amounts instead of small numbers of people in large amounts'.

It may be tempting to conclude that because many consumer disputes are for petty amounts they are unimportant and should not be burdening the legal system. However, it is important to recognize the cumulative effects that many small harms can have on society. If a consumer has purchased a toaster and two weeks later the element does not work, the consumer may have only suffered a loss of $50, which is not a large sum of money. However, the manufacturer of this toaster may have sold hundreds of thousands of these defective toasters and the total loss that it has caused to consumers may be in the millions. If this manufacturer had caused a single person millions of dollars worth of loss, it would no doubt be sued and required to pay damages to that person.

There is no policy reason why a person who causes a little loss to a lot of people should escape liability whereas a person who causes the same amount of loss to a smaller number of people is liable to pay for this harm. As the former United States Vice President, Walter Mondale, comments:[12]

> Nothing is more destructive to a sense of injustice than the widespread belief that it is much more risky for an ordinary citizen to take $5 from one person at the point of a gun than it is for a corporation to take $5 each from a million customers at the point of a pen.

The class action procedure has been aptly described as an important means of achieving the goal of 're-conceptualizing little injustices as collective harms'.[13]

---

10   See H. Kalven Jr and M. Rosenfield, 'The Contemporary Function of the Class Suit', *U Chi. L Rev.* 8 (1941): 684. Kalven and Rosenfield argue that class actions are the only way to achieve deterrence and compensation where claims are small and not worthwhile litigating on an individual basis.

11   224 Cal. Rpt 605, at p. 612.

12   Vice President Mondale, Address to the Second Judicial Circuit Conference, 10 September 1977.

13   L. Nader, 'Disputing Without the Force of Law', *Yale Law Journal* 88 (1979): 998, at 1021.

(iii) Judicial Economy

Class action procedures are not only of benefit to individual consumers. They are also of benefit to society as a whole because it is less expensive and less time consuming for the justice system to deal with a set of issues once, in a single class action case than be faced with the same issues being heard repeatedly in hundreds of individual cases. The class action procedure results in a more efficient use of judicial resources.

4. Concerns about the Class Action

Critics point out several concerns about the class action procedure. These include the possible use of the procedure as blackmail, a floodgate of litigation, excessive fees for lawyers and massive damages awards for plaintiffs. Each of these concerns is now examined. It is concluded that these concerns are either invalid or overstated.

(i) Blackmail

Critics of the class action procedure claim that there is a danger that the procedure will be used as a form of 'legalized blackmail'.[14] In other words, it is feared that groups will threaten to sue as a class and use this threat as a way of forcing a settlement of a meritless claim. A potential defendant might be tempted to settle even if they feel they have done no wrong simply because they are concerned about the costs of litigating the issue, the likely bad publicity such a case would create and the possibility that the court may find against them and require them to pay out a large sum of damages.

This fear of legalized blackmail is largely unfounded. There is no evidence to suggest that the class action will be used in this way. In any event, current civil procedure requires that plaintiffs must be able to state a cause of action. If a plaintiff cannot state a reasonable cause of action, then the case will be dismissed at a preliminary stage. This avoids a defendant having to carry the full financial burden of defending a meritless claim and should go some way to alleviating the defendant's fears of litigation and therefore reduce the chances of a forced settlement. If the claim is not meritless then threatening to sue as a class is a legitimate form of pressure.

(ii) Floodgate of Litigation

Some critics of class actions are concerned not only about a potential increase in frivolous claims but are also concerned that a liberal availability of class actions will

---

14   See, for example, M. Handler, 'The Shift from Procedural Innovations in Antitrust Suits – The Twenty–Third Annual Antitrust Review', *Colum. L Rev.* 71 (1971): 1, at 9; F.G. Hawke, 'Class Actions: the negative view', *Torts Law Journal (Aus)* 6 (1998): 1, at 4.

result in a general floodgate of class actions overloading the court system.[15] The fear is that we will become an overly litigious society like the United States.

However, the New Zealand legal system is unlikely to ever be burdened to the same extent as the United States legal system because its accident compensation scheme prevents much of the mass accident type of litigation from proceeding to court.[16] In any event, even if a liberally available class action does significantly increase the number of legitimate claims brought before the courts, this is not a reason to abandon the procedure. Legitimate claims should be heard by the courts and therefore the legal system should aim to expand its capacity in order to be able to deal with these claims. Any procedure designed to increase access to justice will inevitably increase the use of the legal system.

(iii) Excessive Fees for Lawyers

Much of the dissatisfaction with the United States class action stems from the belief that class actions are only of benefit to the lawyers. There are plenty of stories of lawyers earning millions of dollars in class action cases where the plaintiffs receive only a small payout.[17]

The response to this fear is to point out that excessive lawyer fees are not an inherent part of a class action. Strict control over the level of both contingency fees and lawyers' fees for negotiating out-of-court settlements are both methods of ensuring that lawyers are paid a reasonable fee for their work. These suggestions are discussed respectively in paragraph 7(viii) below.

(iv) Massive Awards for Plaintiffs

A further concern about the adoption of a liberal class action procedure is that juries will award inordinately large payouts to plaintiffs. In the United States some massive awards have been made in class action jury trials. The fear is that these high awards will be overly punitive on defendants and possibly cause some defendant manufacturers or retailers to become bankrupt and lose their businesses.

There are three responses to this concern. First, is to point out that there are very few civil jury trials in New Zealand.[18] Civil trials, with the exception of defamation cases, are predominantly heard by the judiciary which has not, historically, granted massive awards to plaintiffs. Secondly, the New Zealand accident compensation regime prevents claims for damages arising out of personal injury by accident.[19]

---

15   See, D.J. Mullan and N.J. Tuytel, 'The British Columbia Class Proceedings Act: Will it Open the Floodgates?', *Canadian Journal of Insurance Law* 14 (1996): 30.

16   See s. 317(1) of the Injury Prevention, Rehabilitation, and Compensation Act 2001. The effect of this provision is that it is not generally possible to sue for personal injuries or death in New Zealand.

17   See J.M. Underwood, 'Rationality, Multiplicity & Legitimacy: Federalization of the Interstate Class Action', *S Tex. L Rev.* 46 (2004): 391, at 411–17.

18   The District Court has no juries in civil matters and the High Court has very few civil jury trials.

19   See s. 317(1) of the Injury Prevention, Rehabilitation, and Compensation Act 2001.

Therefore, many of the types of litigation that result in large awards in the United States would not be brought before the New Zealand courts. Admittedly, the possibility of suing for exemplary damages remains in personal injury cases. However, the courts have been careful to control the level of exemplary damages so that they reflect merely the goal of punishment and in no way attempt to compensate the plaintiff.[20] Thirdly, even if there comes a time in New Zealand where large compensatory awards are paid out, it is not fair to blame the class action as the cause of a defendant company going out of business. The cause of the defendant's downfall is its failure to adhere to legal standards of conduct thus causing harm to consumers.

5. 'Opt-In' and 'Opt-Out' Class Actions

There are two distinct ways in which a class action can operate. These are often referred to as the 'opt-in' class action and the 'opt-out' class action.

New Zealand case law has limited the class action to an 'opt-in' procedure for damages claims and even in other types of claim the 'opt-out' class action is rarely used. Paragraph 6 of the article examines in detail the extent to which the 'opt-out' class action is currently available in New Zealand and argues that the judicial interpretation of the class action rule has been unnecessarily restrictive.

At this point in the article it seems sensible to discuss the 'opt-in' and 'opt-out' approaches in the abstract before tackling the details of the New Zealand class action rule. What follows is an examination of how each of the two approaches works. It is then argued that the 'opt-out' class action has greater benefits than the more limited 'opt-in' procedure.

(i) How 'Opt-in' and 'Opt-out' Class Actions Operate

In an 'opt-in' class action the class only includes those who expressly give their consent to the action being pursued on their behalf. In contrast, an 'opt-out' class action includes any person who belongs to the class of potential plaintiffs unless he or she expressly opts out by a prescribed date. The 'opt-out' class action is used widely in the United States, Canada and Australia.[21] The more limited 'opt-in' class action is used in England and Wales.[22]

In an 'opt-out' class action an attempt is made to notify all class members of the proposed legal action, often, for example, by notices in newspapers and individual letters where possible. The class is likely to be described in general terms. For example, in a consumer dispute where the consumers are demanding a refund for a particular defective product, the class might simply be described as all those who suffered loss by reason of purchasing a certain product from the defendant between

---

20   *Auckland City Council* v. *Blundell* [1986] 1 NZLR 732 (CA).

21   See above n. 4.

22   See the English and Welsh Civil Procedure Rules, Part 19. For a critical discussion of the English and Welsh procedure see M. Mildred, 'The New Group Actions Rule in England and Wales: Issues for Access to Justice.', *NZBLQ* 8 (2002): 395.

particular dates. The court can decline to allow a class action if the class is not defined with sufficient particularity.[23]

All potential plaintiffs in an 'opt-out' action are deemed to be part of the class unless they individually inform the court of their opposition to being included. If the action is successful then public notices are published and sometimes the television or radio is used to invite those members of the class to come forward and claim their share of the damages.

(ii) The Advantages that an 'Opt-out' Action has over an 'Opt-in' Action

The 'opt-in' class action ensures that only those who clearly want to be part of the action will be bound by the court's decision. There is no chance that silent class members will be bound by a decision when in fact they would have preferred to take their own action rather than have the representative plaintiff take the action on their behalf. However, there are three problems created by an 'opt-in' class action which can be avoided by allowing an 'opt-out' procedure. First, the consent requirement is often cumbersome and sometimes impossible to satisfy. It will therefore severely limit the number of cases that are able to proceed as a class action. Secondly, in an 'opt-in' procedure many of the potential class members fail to join the class for reasons other than a desire to pursue individual litigation. Thirdly, the 'opt-in' procedure creates difficulties with latecomers. Each of these difficulties is examined below.

Cumbersome consent requirement   The main difficulty with allowing only an 'opt-in' approach is that it makes the class action extremely time consuming and difficult for the representative plaintiff. This is especially so in a consumer dispute where the class may be wide.[24] For example, a defective, mass-marketed product may have been sold to thousands of customers. It may be difficult for a representative plaintiff to individually identify a significant number of potential plaintiffs. Often it is the defendant trader who has a list of the people who purchased the defective product and this information is unavailable to the representative plaintiff.

In response to a proposal to add an opt-in requirement to the United States class action, one United States commentator has said:[25] 'Returning to an opt-in requirement for damage class actions would leave in place a vehicle for collective litigation, but the vehicle would be substantially under powered in comparison to the current model.'

---

23   See, for example, *Ryder* v. *Treaty of Waitangi Fisheries Commission* [1998] 1 NZLR 761.

24   The limitations of an 'opt-in' class action (called a representative action in the report) were discussed by the Australian Law Reform Commission in a report that recommended the introduction of an 'opt-out' class action procedure into Australian Federal Courts. See Australian Law Reform Commission Grouped Proceedings in the Federal Court, Report No. 46, 1989, pp. 40–45.

25   D. Hensler and T.D. Rowe, 'Beyond "It just ain't worth it": Alternative Strategies for Damage Class Action Reform', *Law & Contemp. Probs.* 64 (2001): 137 at 146.

Another commentator describes the 'opt-in' concept as:[26]

... a concept [which] cannot cope with the technology of everyday commercial transactions in today's society. We now have plastic cards, automatic tellers and electronic funds transfers which rely on computer technology and the microchip. A simple programming error may lead to claims by hundreds or thousands of consumers. To suggest that these consumers or their legal representatives might be able to identify a significant number of eligible claimants is sheer fantasy.

The 'opt-out' approach removes the difficult and often impossible process of identifying all those within a group of people who share a common interest in the proceedings. Consequently, an 'opt-out' approach is likely to result in a greater number of class actions being filed and an increase in their economy and efficiency.

In a general sense, the 'opt-out' approach therefore maximizes the power of the class action procedure to deliver the three benefits associated with a class action: increased access to justice, increased deterrent effect on wrongdoers and improved efficiency in the justice system.

Failure of potential members to join the class It should not be assumed that all those who fail to opt-in to an 'opt-in' class action have done so because they have decided to pursue individual litigation. There may be some people who would like to be part of the litigation but do not learn of the right to opt-in until it is too late. There may be others who are aware of the class action but are reluctant to join the class for other reasons. For example, they may be afraid of a backlash from the defendant, they may be immigrants with a poor understanding of English who may find the legal system intimidating or they may have low incomes and be concerned that they will be unable to contribute to the costs of legal action.[27]

In an 'opt-in' class action these potential claimants are excluded from the litigation, thus allowing the defendant to avoid being held liable for the full degree of damage caused by its conduct. The 'opt-out' class action has the advantage of increasing the number of aggrieved consumers likely to be awarded compensation. It is therefore more successful at achieving the deterrent function of a class action.

Difficulties associated with latecomers The 'opt-out' procedure also removes the difficulties associated with latecomers. In an 'opt-in' system, a consumer who wants to be a class member but misses the cut-off date presents a problem for the court.[28] Should the court refuse to allow the consumer to join the class and allow the

---

26   D. Nelthorpe, 'Class Actions: The Real Solution', *Legal Services Bulletin*, 13 (1988): 26, at 28.

27   See R. Mulheron, 'Some Difficulties with Group Litigation Orders – And Why a Class Action Is Superior', *C.J.Q.* 24 (Jan) (2005): 40, at 54 where Mulheron discusses the various barriers that may discourage a person from opting in to a class action.

28   *Taylor* v. *Nugent Care Society* [2004] EWCA Civ 51; [2004] 1 W.L.R. 1129 (CA (Civ Div)), a recent English case, illustrates the difficulty of dealing with latecomers within the framework of an 'opt-in' procedure. In *Taylor* the claimant missed the cut-off date for joining a class action dealing with claims for abuse in children's homes in the

consumer to instigate an individual claim or should judicial economy demand that a person who genuinely wants to be part of a class action not be refused membership to that class? The disadvantage of the latter approach is that it makes the notion of a cut-off date redundant and could lead to numerous latecomers having to be assessed for eligibility to join the class. However, the former approach could result in an inefficient outcome whereby several unnecessary individual proceedings go ahead, each dealing with the same set of issues as the class action.

The 'opt-out' approach removes these difficulties because everyone who fits within the description of the class is a member of that class unless they choose to opt-out. Although there is a danger with this approach that a person who would prefer to litigate individually fails to opt-out in time, there is equally some sense in encouraging the class members to cooperate with the efficient management of the proceedings as a class. The right to be a lone litigant comes at the cost of a reduction in the economy of the class action.

6. The Class Action Procedure in New Zealand

(i) Rule 78

The class action procedure in New Zealand is governed by Rule 78 of the High Court Rules which provides:[29]

> Where two or more persons have the same interest in the subject matter of a proceeding, one or more of them may, with the consent of the other or others, or by direction of the Court on the application of any party or intending party to the proceeding, sue or be sued in such proceeding on the behalf of or for the benefit of all persons so interested.

The Rule gives no further details to direct the Courts in the use of class actions. The class action procedure has therefore developed largely through case law interpretation of Rule 78 and its precursor Rule 79, which was substantially the same. The Rule was modelled on its English counterpart and so English case law has played a significant part in the development of the New Zealand procedure.[30]

1970s. He applied to become a member of the class but was refused, so he chose to continue with his individual claim. The defendant sought to have his claim struck out for abuse of process. The claim was initially struck out but was later reinstated by the Court of Appeal. The Court of Appeal held that the claimant was entitled to bring individual proceedings but that when dealing with the individual claim, the court was entitled to take into account the decisions in the group action. See also case comment on *Taylor* case by M. Mildred, 'Personal Injury – Civil Procedure – Group Actions – Group Litigation Orders', *J.P.I. Law C* (2004): 67.

29   The District Court Equivalent of Rule 78 is District Court Rule 80. The wording or Rule 80 is identical to that of Rule 78.

30   A more formal and detailed framework for the English representative action was not introduced until 2 May 2000 by way of a Group Litigation Order under Part III of the English Civil Procedure Rules. For Academic comment on the English rule see Mulheron, 'Some Difficulties with Group Litigation Orders – And Why a Class Action

(ii) Class Actions for Damages Claims

Interpretation of 'same interest' in damages claims　　One of the chief reasons why class actions have not been commonly used in New Zealand is the restrictive attitude taken by judges to the interpretation of Rule 78. For many years the phrase 'same interest in the subject matter of a proceeding' was interpreted as excluding claims for damages.[31] Class actions were considered inappropriate for damages claims because:[32] '[t]he relief which [the plaintiff] is seeking is a personal relief, applicable to him alone, and does not benefit the class from whom he purports to be bringing the action.' This was a severe limitation on the use of class actions particularly in relation to consumer disputes, which often involve claims for damages.

Admittedly, in many consumer claims for damages there may not be sufficient commonality in the interests of the class members to form a workable class action. For example, issues such as voluntary assumption of risk, contributory negligence and limitation periods are likely to depend on the particular facts of each individual class member's case. Also, issues of causation and quantum of damages may be different for each individual class member. In these situations, a class action may be unsuitable.

Nevertheless, the fact that the class action is inappropriate for many damages claims does not mean that it should be unavailable for all damages claims. There will be some situations where a group of consumers who wish to sue for damages do all have the same interest in the subject matter of the proceedings. There is nothing in the wording of Rule 78 or its English counterpart that prevents them from taking that claim as a class action. Even in circumstances where there are some issues that are not common it may still be possible to carve these individual issues off into separate hearings and deal with the common issue as a class action.

It was not until *R.J. Flowers Ltd* v. *Burns*[33] in 1986 that New Zealand broke new ground and recognized that some damages claims are able to satisfy the 'same interest' requirement under Rule 78. In this case a number of kiwi fruit growers had

---

Is Superior'; Mildred 'The New Group Actions Rule in England and Wales: Issues for Access to Justice'.

31　See *Markt Fletcher & Co.* v. *Knight Steamship Co. Ltd* [1910] 2 KB 1021 followed by *Take Kerekere* v. *Cameron* [1920] NZLR 302.

32　*Markt Fletcher & Co.* v. *Knight Steamship Co. Ltd* [1910] 2 KB 1021, at p. 1035. Later UK cases took a more flexible approach; see *Prudential Assurance Co. Ltd* v. *Newmans Industries Ltd* [1979] 3 All ER 507; [1981] Ch. 229; *EMI Records Ltd* v. *Riley* [1981] 2 All ER 838; [1981] 1 WLR 923. The High Court in Australia has also adopted a more flexible approach: see *Carnie* v. *Esanda Finance Corp. Ltd* (1995) 127 ALR 76.

33　[1987] 1 NZLR 260. Followed by *Andersen* v. *Capital Coast Health Ltd* [2000] 1 ERNZ 256. In *Taspac Oysters Ltd* v. *James Hardie & Co. Pty Ltd* [1990] 1 NZLR 442 the court mistakenly considered the principles set out in *R.J. Flowers* when assessing whether a case where the representative plaintiffs sought a declaration of liability should continue as a class action. There was no need for the court to have referred to the requirements in *R.J. Flowers* because these requirements apply only to damages claims not to other forms of relief such as a declaration of liability or an injunction.

contracted to have their fruit stored in Mr Burn's freezer. The fruit growers joined together as a class to claim damages from Mr Burns for negligently allowing the temperature of the freezer to drop to a level which was damaging to the fruit. Justice McGechan concluded that a class action is appropriate for a damages claim where four requirements are met:[34]

> ... the members of the class must have a common interest (with no defences applicable to only some members of the class); the representative action must be beneficial to all of that class; the class represented must cover all or virtually all potential plaintiffs; all represented members must consent to the payment of global damages to the representative plaintiff.

It might then be necessary for separate hearings to determine the split of this global award.

Requirement number 1 is not controversial in terms of the wording of Rule 78. Justice McGechan is simply repeating the 'same interest' requirement from Rule 78. However, his Honour's approach does represent a departure from the prior view of the courts that damages claims could never satisfy the 'same interest' requirement. Justice McGechan does not so much redefine 'same interest' as simply admit that in some cases involving a damages claim there will be enough of a common interest to come within the rule.

Requirement number 2, that the action must be beneficial to all of the class, is also simply a repetition of Rule 78. Rule 78 only allows the representative plaintiff to sue if it is on behalf of or for the benefit of all those who share this same interest. Requirements 3 and 4 need more careful consideration.

The class must cover all or virtually all potential plaintiffs   The third requirement provided for in *R.J. Flowers* for a damages claim is that the class represented must cover 'all or virtually all potential plaintiffs'. These words are not found in Rule 78 which provides that where two or more persons have the same interest in the subject-matter of a proceeding, the representative plaintiff may sue on behalf of or for the benefit of *all* persons so interested.

The phrase 'persons so interested' in Rule 78 is somewhat ambiguous. One possible interpretation is that it refers back to those who have the same interest in the subject matter of the proceedings. Accordingly, this group is referred to in *R.J. Flowers* as the 'potential plaintiffs' because they are able to sue the particular defendant due to their common interest. Under this interpretation, if a thousand consumers have purchased a defective camera they are all potential plaintiffs in a claim against the camera manufacturer. Justice McGechan rewrites Rule 78 so that it is sufficient that the action be brought only on behalf of or for the benefit of 'all or virtually all' of these one thousand camera buyers rather than 'all' of them as is required by Rule 78.

---

34   *R.J. Flowers*, above n. 33, at p. 270–271. McGechan J. adopts the category of claims for damages allowed in *EMI Records Ltd* v. *Riley* [1981] 2 All ER 838; [1981] 1 WLR 923.

The reason for this judicial creativity is understandable. If the Rule is interpreted as suggested above and 'all' means literally 'all' there are serious policy implications. If even one of the thousand camera buyers refuses to be a part of the class action then the class action will fail because the action does not meet the criteria of being taken on behalf of or for the benefit of all those with the common interest. This presents a serious limitation on the effectiveness of the class action procedure. Although it may not be efficient to persist with a class action where only a small number of those with the common interest are part of the action it nevertheless seems unnecessary to prevent a class action proceeding simply because there are just one or two individuals who refuse to join the class.

It should be noted that it is only express refusal to be part of the action that will pose this problem in the context of an 'opt-out' class action. In an 'opt-out' action the class is described in general terms and some class members will be silent as to consent. If these members do not expressly opt-out of the action it can still be assumed that the action is being taken on their behalf and for their benefit. In an 'opt-in' class action the problem created by the word 'all persons so interested' arises where consent is gained from only a portion of potential plaintiffs. The other potential plaintiffs may have refused to take part in the action or may not have been approached by the representative plaintiff.

The negative implications of requiring the action to be taken on behalf of all potential plaintiffs can be avoided in one of two ways. One option is to adopt the approach taken in *R.J. Flowers* and interpret 'all' as 'virtually all'. Even with this liberal interpretation many defendants will be protected from exposure to a class action. An alternative approach, that perhaps avoids manipulating the words of Rule 78 to the same extent, is to argue that the phrase 'all persons so interested' does not refer to all potential plaintiffs. Instead it can be read as meaning that so long as there are two or more people who have a common interest who are part of the class (either by consent in an 'opt-in' situation or because they have not expressly opted out in an 'opt-out' situation) then it is sufficient for the representative plaintiff to sue on behalf of or for the benefit of all of these persons. Under this interpretation 'all person so interested' does not include those who have expressly refused to be a part of an 'opt-out' class action or who have not given their consent in an 'opt-in' class action. It just includes those two or more people who have a common interest and are joining together as a class.

The preceding discussion demonstrates that Rule 78 needs to be reformed so as to remove uncertainty and avoid the negative effects of requiring the action to be taken on behalf of all potential plaintiffs. Rule 78 should be reworded to ensure that a class action is able to proceed despite the refusal of some persons to join the class. This reform would expand the use of the class action thereby reflecting the 'access to justice' goals underpinning the procedure.[35]

Consent requirement   The fourth requirement in *R.J. Flowers* for a class action in respect of a damages claim is that all represented members must consent to the

---

35   See s. 8.4 for further discussion of this suggested reform.

payment of global damages to the representative plaintiff.[36] Consent of this nature will only be available in an 'opt-in' class action. In an 'opt-out' class action, persons who fit within the class description are members of the class unless they expressly opt-out. With such an indeterminate and individually unidentified group of class members, it would be impossible to meet the requirement of consent to a global sum being paid to the representative plaintiff. The requirement of consent in *R.J. Flowers* therefore limits a damages claim to an 'opt-in' class action.

(a) Is consent necessary according to the wording of Rule 78?

The requirement of consent is not an inherent feature of Rule 78. In fact, the wording of Rule 78 suggests that consent is not always needed to commence a class action. The Rule provides for two alternative ways in which a class action can proceed. The first way that a class action can proceed is under the first limb of Rule 78, which requires the consent of class members. By requiring consent, this first limb provides for an 'opt-in' class action.[37] In other words, the class only includes those who expressly give their consent to the action being pursued on their behalf. The second way in which a class action may proceed under Rule 78 is by the direction of the court on the application of any party or intending party to the proceedings. This second limb is presumably to allow for the possibility of an 'opt-out' class action, which does not require the express consent of the parties.

The Employment Court in *Mitchell* v. *NZ Fire Service Commission* interpreted Rule 78 as including an 'opt-out' class action. Although the case involved an application for an interim injunction rather than a claim for damages, comments of the Court are nevertheless relevant:[38]

> It is not necessary to show that all members of the class wish to be parties to, or are aware of and have authorised the issue of the proceedings on their behalf. It may be sufficient that two or more persons have the same interest in the subject-matter of a proceeding and that the Court has directed that named parties should sue in the proceedings for the benefit of all persons so interested: High Court Rules 78.

In *R.J. Flowers* the plaintiffs had all consented to the class action. Oddly, this consent was not put forward as permitting the action and instead the plaintiffs applied for the direction of the Court under the second limb of Rule 78.

The decision in *R.J. Flowers* effectively eliminates the second limb for damages claims by making it essential in all damages claims that all the members of the class give their consent. Therefore, even if the representative plaintiff applies to the court for direction under the second limb of Rule 78 he or she will still need to obtain consent as is required under the first limb of Rule 78. Following the requirements of *R.J. Flowers* results in a prohibition on 'opt-out' class actions for damages claims.

(b) Could a class action for damages work without consent?

---

36   *R.J. Flowers* above n. 33, at p. 270.
37   The 'opt-in' class action' is described in detail above in s. 5.1
38   [1999] 1 ERNZ 206, at p. 211–12.

Having decided that the wording of Rule 78 does not require consent in all circumstances it is necessary to examine whether the nature of a damages claim itself necessitates a consent requirement. The question is whether it is either impractical or unfair to allow a damages claim without the consent of the class members. Considerations of workability and fairness may be the reason that the court in *R.J. Flowers* introduced a consent requirement to class actions for damages.

Where a global figure for damages is to be determined, it would be impractical in many cases to assess this figure accurately without input from the class members. In an 'opt-out' procedure the class members are not available to consult on this issue. Requiring consent to a global award and thereby restricting the class action to an 'opt-in' procedure makes it more likely that the assessment of a global sum will be accurate. So, in *R.J. Flowers* the kiwifruit growers would have been able to join together to determine the value of the damage done to their fruit. This was a sensible approach in the case as it ensured that the global award was reasonably accurate. The approach seems therefore to be grounded in considerations of fairness and workability.

The problem with the rule in *R.J. Flowers* is that it unnecessarily restricts *all* damages claims to 'opt-in' procedures where it is possible to gain consent to a global award. However, there are situations in which a damages claim could work in an 'opt-out' situation with no active consent from the class members. For example, it may in some cases be possible to assess accurately a global award without the consent of the class members. Evidence may be available about the number of faulty products sold to consumers and the reduction in the value of each product due to that fault. If the court is not certain of the exact global figure it could rule on a global upper limit amount and then make provisions for individual payment from this fund to be calculated in a particular manner.

Alternatively, it may be possible to frame a damages claim without reference to a global award. One way of achieving this would be to fix an amount each individual is entitled to and provide no specified global upper limit. In this scenario the court could decide that the defendant is liable to pay $x to each person who fits within the class description and comes forward to claim his or her award. A time limit could be ordered so as to avoid a situation where class members could come forward for many years after the case has been decided. In more complicated cases it might be necessary for the court to establish a formula by which individual class members can assess the amount of their entitlement. For example, in a case in which a holiday brochure has misrepresented the size and layout of some holiday apartments, a class member's entitlement could depend on whether they were staying in a one or two bedroom apartment and the number of nights of their holiday.

Requiring consent to a global award in all class actions involving a damages claim is unnecessarily restrictive. The analysis in *R.J. Flowers* should therefore be confined to the facts of that case which involved an 'opt-in' class action where consent of all members had been obtained. The requirement that consent should extend to all damages claims is obiter and is not persuasive.

Interestingly, in 2000 the High Court in *Registered Securities Limited (in liquidation)* v. *Westpac Banking Corporation* allowed a class action for damages to proceed despite the fact that the class members did not consent to the payment of a global award.[39] The representative plaintiffs in this case proceeded under the second limb of Rule 78 by applying for the direction of the court rather than by obtaining the consent of the class members. Curiously, the court professed to be following the principles in the *R.J. Flowers* case despite the fact that the consent requirement was not met.[40] The case focused instead on the existence of the requisite commonality of interest.[41]

c) Is a consent requirement desirable?

In a case such as *R.J. Flowers*, where the number of potential plaintiffs is small and easily identifiable, the requirement of consent does not present a problem. However, the vast majority of consumer disputes involve many consumers who are in no way linked to each other except that they all suffer damages because of purchasing the same defective product or being subject to the same misrepresentation. In these situations, the 'opt-in' approach will be unworkable because of the difficulties of individually identifying and gaining consent from all the potential class members.

The court in *R.J. Flowers* unnecessarily restricts the class action for damages claims to an 'opt-in' procedure with all its associated problems of identifying the individual members of the class and dealing with latecomers to the action. These difficulties are likely to dissuade plaintiffs from becoming representatives in a class action. Instead, the court system is left to deal with a series of individual claims all dealing with common issues. There are also likely to be a multitude of aggrieved consumers who do not access the court system at all. Without the option of an 'opt-out' class action for damages claims, manufacturers and suppliers are able to escape liability for causing harm to thousands of individuals. The requirement of consent greatly reduces the power of the class action to deliver the three benefits associated with a class action: increased access to justice, increased deterrent effect on wrongdoers and improved efficiency in the justice system.

(iii) Class Actions for Non-Damages Claims

A class action in a consumer dispute will not always involve a claim for damages. In some cases, the representative plaintiff will be seeking a declaration of liability with issues as to the establishment and quantification of damages left to individual actions. In other consumer class actions, an injunction or specific performance will be sought.

In non-damages claims there should be no difficulty in allowing a class action under Rule 78 wherever the class is adequately defined and where sufficient commonality of interest is established.[42] The requirement of consent identified in the

---

39   (2000) 14 PRNZ 348 (Robertson J, HC Auckland).
40   *Ibid.*, at p. 354.
41   *Ibid.*, at p. 353.
42   See, for example, *Ryder* v. *Treaty of Waitangi Fisheries Commission* [1998] 1 NZLR 761 where the representative plaintiffs in sought to take an 'opt-out' class action which challenged proposals of the Treaty of Waitangi Fisheries Commission as to the allocation of pre-settlement fisheries assets. The class was described in general terms

R.J. Flowers case will not apply.[43] Moreover, the second limb of Rule 78 does not require consent of the class members. Accordingly, an 'opt-out' class action where the class members are identified by a general description should theoretically be possible despite the lack of direction under Rule 78 about how such an action should be managed.

7. Reform of Rule 78

Rule 78 needs to be reformed in order to maximize the effectiveness of the class action and prevent its abuse. Consideration should be given to expanding the rule to expressly cover 'opt-out' class actions. In addition, the rule should establish a certain and principled approach to the difficulties of managing a class action. This needs to be coupled with more control over both contingency fees and fees for negotiating out of court settlements in order to ensure that only a reasonable fee is charged for the work done and the risk undertaken.

If a large scale reform of the New Zealand class action is adopted it may be better to enact a class actions statute rather than attempting to simply reword or expand Rule 78.

(i) General Lack of Detail

Rule 78 lacks detail. In comparison to other jurisdictions, the one paragraph direction given under Rule 78 is strikingly inadequate. Even the English rule, on which Rule 78 was based, has subsequently been redrafted into a much longer and more detailed set of rules.[44]

This lack of detail in Rule 78 leads to uncertainty and confusion. This is particularly so in respect of 'opt-out' class actions for which there are currently no clear guidelines. The following paragraphs examine various matters that could be incorporated into a set of rules governing class actions.

---

as all Maori who were unconnected with a particular traditional tribal group. The Court dismissed application for the case to proceed as a class action because the class was not defined with enough particularity.

43   In *Taspac Oysters Ltd* v. *James Hardie & Co. Pty Ltd* [1990] 1 NZLR 442 the court mistakenly considered the principles set out in *R.J. Flowers* when assessing whether a case where the representative plaintiffs sought a declaration of liability should continue as a class action. There was no need for the court to have referred to the requirements in *R.J. Flowers* because these requirements apply only to damages claims not to other forms of relief such as a declaration of liability or an injunction.

44   A formal and detailed framework for the English representative action was introduced 2 May 2000 by way of a Group Litigation Order under Part III of the English Civil Procedure Rules.

(ii) Clarification on the Legitimacy and Use of 'Opt-Out' Class Actions

Rule 78 fails to deal adequately with the position on the fundamental issue of whether a class action should be limited to an 'opt-in' procedure or extend also to 'opt-out' actions.

The second limb of Rule 78 appears to permit an 'opt-out' class action. It provides that a class action may proceed by direction of the court where two or more persons have sufficient commonality of interest. In contrast to the first limb of Rule 78, there is no requirement that the class members consent to the action. Rule 78 does not, however, expressly state that the Court will allow an 'opt-out' class action and to date there have been few 'opt-out' class actions taken in New Zealand.[45] Moreover, the decision in *R.J. Flowers* prohibits the use of 'opt-out' class actions in damages claims.[46]

Specifically allowing an 'opt-out' class action would greatly improve the usefulness of the class action mechanism to New Zealand consumers. The arguments in favour of allowing an 'opt-out' procedure are given above paragraph 5(ii). If the class action procedure were to be expanded in this way, the inclusion of an 'opt-out' procedure needs to be expressly stated. A class actions statute would also need to:

- provide that in an 'opt-out' class action the consent of class members is not required;
- require that the class be adequately defined or described but that there is no need to identify or name individuals;
- allow that a class member may opt out of the class by written notice within a specified period of time;
- require adequate notice to be given to the public about the commencement of the class proceedings.[47]

An alternative approach would be to restrict the use of an 'opt-out' class action to cases where the class is so large that individual suits or an 'opt-in' class action are impractical. This would avoid the use of an 'opt-out' procedure in a case where individual members could be easily identified and consent sought. This more cautious approach would minimize the risk of a person being unwittingly bound by the outcome of a class action and thus losing his or her right to take individual proceedings.

If it is decided that 'opt-out' class actions are inappropriate for New Zealand then Rule 78 needs to clearly prohibit such actions. At present, the rule appears to

---

45   The representative plaintiffs in *Ryder* v. *Treaty of Waitangi Fisheries Commission* [1998] 1 NZLR 761 sought to take an 'opt-out' class action which challenged proposals of the Treaty of Waitangi Fisheries Commission as to the allocation of pre-settlement fisheries assets. The class was described in general terms as all Maori who were unconnected with a particular traditional tribal group. The Court dismissed an application for the case to proceed as a class action because the class was not defined with enough particularity.

46   *R.J. Flowers Ltd* v. *Burns* [1987] 1 NZLR 260. See also para. 6.1 above.

47   See para. 8.3 below for a discussion of notice requirements.

allow 'opt-out' class actions but gives no express direction on the matter and fails to provide any guidelines on how an 'opt-out' class action should operate.

(iii) Notice Requirements

One of the chief criticisms of an 'opt-out' class action is that class members could become bound by a decision when they were not aware that they were a part of the class action proceedings. Therefore, if 'opt-out' class actions are to be adopted it is crucial that the rules on class actions provide for strict notice requirements.

The class action rule should require sufficient notice be given to potential class members and it should specify what satisfies sufficient notice. The Rule could require certain methods of notification to be used. For example, it might require that notification of a class action be given in newspapers, on the radio or television or on the internet. It might also be useful to create a court website that informs of current class action proceedings. Widespread notice will decrease the chances of a class member being unaware that they are part of the proceedings.

The cost of meeting the notice requirements might pose a problem for some representative plaintiffs. One solution to this is to set up a legal aid fund to pay the notice costs.

(iv) Requirement that Class Must Cover All Potential Plaintiffs

As has already been explained in paragraph 6(ii), Rule 78 requires the representative party to sue on behalf of or for the benefit of *all* persons with the same interest in the subject matter of a proceeding. This needs to be reworded so as to avoid the unsatisfactory possibility of a class action failing simply because one or two individuals refuse to be a part of the class action.

It may be sufficient to simply duplicate the United States requirement that the representative party fairly and adequately protects the interests of the class. This would retain the 'on behalf of or for the benefit of' element of Rule 78 but avoid the difficulties of requiring the action to be on behalf of or for the benefit of *all* potential plaintiffs. Reforming the Rule in this way would enhance the capacity of the class action procedure to increase access to justice.

(v) The Definition of 'Same Interest'

The cornerstone of any class action rule is the requirement that the class members share the 'same interest' in the subject matter of the proceedings. Rule 78 gives no directions as to how to determine whether there is sufficient commonality of interest. One issue to consider when reforming Rule 78 is whether more direction should be given on this issue and what form that direction should take.

One possibility is to require the common issues to be substantial issues. Another approach is to require that the common issues predominate over issues affecting only individual members. These two options are discussed below.

'Substantial common issue' requirement   It is unclear whether the phrase 'same interest' in Rule 78 means that the class members' interests have to be the same in all respects or whether there just needs to be some area of commonality. The Australian class action rule attempts to clarify this issue by requiring that all claims are 'in respect of, or arise out of, the same, or related circumstances and all give rise to *at least one substantial common issue or fact'*(emphasis added).[48]

The addition of a 'substantial common issue' requirement into the New Zealand Rule would give the court more direction in respect of the meaning of 'same interest'. However, the requirement is still somewhat imprecise. It is unclear whether the common issues need to be merely more than trivial or whether the rule goes further than this and requires the common issues to relate to a core or major issue.

The meaning of 'substantial common issue' in the Australian rule has been the subject of judicial consideration. The majority of the Full Federal Court concluded that the resolution of the issue in common must be shown to 'have a major impact on the litigation because it is at the core of the dispute'.[49] This decision was, however, overturned by the High Court that held it was not necessary for the common issue to be a major or core issue but was sufficient for it to be an issue that is real or is of substance.[50] This interpretation of the substantiality requirement is a wide one, which merely requires that the common issue not be trivial or superficial.

New Zealand would be wise to avoid the phrase 'substantial common issue' which has led to interpretation difficulties in Australia. It would be clearer if the rule were to require that there are 'common issues of substance' or 'common issues of law or fact that are neither trivial nor superficial'. This would allow the class action procedure to extend to all common issues of substance and after that require cases to be tried separately.

It might also be useful to include a specific provision that states that a class action should not be prevented from proceeding merely on the grounds that there are some issues which will require individual assessment after the determination of common issues. In other words, the fact that there are issues which are not common to the class should not prevent a class action being brought in order to resolve the common issues.

'Predominance' requirement   An alternative way of defining 'same interest' would be to require that there be common issues of law or fact which predominate over any questions affecting only individual members. This is the approach used in the United States.[51]

The justification for a predominance requirement is presumably based on the notion that if there are more issues that need to be determined individually than collectively then the efficiency of joining together as a class decreases. This argument is not particularly persuasive. It may be true that there are more efficiency gains in cases where the common issues predominate over individual issues. However, there

---

48   The Federal Court of Australia Act 1992, s. 33C(1).
49   (1998) 159 ALR 329, at p. 345.
50   *Wong* v. *Silkfield Pty Ltd* (1999) 199 CLR 255.
51   United States Federal Rules of Civil Procedure Rule 23(b)(2).

can still be efficiency gains in using a class action where there is a common issue of some substance even if there are also numerous individual issues which will need to be dealt with in separate proceedings. A rule based on the need for a common issue of substance is preferable to a rule based on a predominance requirement.

(vi) Provision for a Certification Process

A further matter to consider when reforming the law on class actions is whether to introduce a certification process. Unlike the United States class action procedure, the New Zealand class action procedure does not currently have a lengthy certification process. Under a certification process a class action must be certified as appropriate by the courts according to established threshold requirements.

In New Zealand a class action can proceed with little in the way of judicial approval. If the class action is commenced under the 'consent of the class members' limb of Rule 78 it will proceed as a class action unless a judge orders otherwise. Under the second limb of Rule 78, where a party applies for the direction of the court, the judge needs to decide that the elements of the rule are met. This generally only requires consideration of the 'same interest' requirement.

The United States certification process, by contrast, requires an action to satisfy four prerequisites before it can be formally certified as a class:[52]

1. Numerosity. The class must be so numerous that a simple joinder of all class members would be impractical. The courts have generally found 25 or more members to be numerous enough.[53]
2. Commonality. There must be a common question of law or fact.
3. Typicality. The claims of the representative must be typical of claims of members of the class in that they have the same general characteristics.
4. Suitability of representative. It must be shown that the representative party or parties will fairly and adequately protect the interests of the class.

In addition to these requirements, there are more general requirements in respect of the appropriateness of a class action.[54] For example, the court must find that questions of law or fact common to class members predominate over any questions affecting only individual members.[55] The court must also decide that a class action is superior to other available methods for the fair and efficient adjudication of the dispute.[56]

The disadvantage of a certification process is that it is time consuming and expensive. Courts are required to conduct lengthy certification hearings before the substantive case begins. The expense and delays are further exacerbated if the defendant or plaintiff is given the right to appeal the certification decision.

---

52   See the United States Federal Rules of Civil Procedure Rule 23(a).

53   See *Swanson* v. *Am. Consumer Indus. Inc.*, 415 F.2d 1326, 1330, n. 3 (7th Cir. 1969).

54   United States Federal Rules of Civil Procedure Rule 23(b).

55   United States Federal Rules of Civil Procedure Rule 23(b)(3).

56   *Ibid.*

Rather than introduce a certification process into the New Zealand class action it might be more effective to allow a class action to proceed whenever the 'same interest' test is met but permit the court to terminate inappropriate class actions later in the proceedings. Guidelines could then be established for determining when a class action will be considered inappropriate. One option would be to provide that a class action is inappropriate if it is found that allowing the case to proceed as a class action will not meet the objectives of access to justice, judicial economy and deterrence.[57] This approach would be more cost efficient than introducing a certification process that is undertaken with every class action. It might also be more effective because it may often be difficult to determine whether a claim is non-meritorious when it is first filed.

(vii) Rules for Out of Court Settlements

Settlement of the entire class action   Unlike the United States, the New Zealand class action procedure does not provide rules or principles in respect of judicial approval of out of court settlements of class actions.[58] Incorporating such rules into the New Zealand class action would reduce the likelihood of consumers being coerced into accepting a settlement that is not in their interests.

Rule 78 could require all out of court settlements or voluntary dismissal of class action claims to be approved by the court. The rule could also establish a set of factors that should be taken into account by the court when deciding whether or not to approve a settlement. Relevant factors could include:[59]

1. Whether the settlement was reached in good faith with no undue influence or coercion used.
2. Whether the settlement is in the best interests of the class members.
3. Whether the settlement is fair and reasonable taking into account:
   a. The stage of the proceedings at time of settlement;
   b. Likelihood of case being successful;
   c. The likely cost and duration of a trial.

It might also be desirable to state that the court has the power to approve or disapprove the settlement but is unable to rewrite the settlement. In addition, the rule should require that clear information about the details of any proposed settlement be

---

57   These guiding principles are used in the certification process in Ontario. See *Western Canadian Shopping Centres Inc.* v. *Dutton* [2001] 2 SCR 534 and *Hollick* v. *Toronto (City)* [2001] 3 SCR 158.

58   See United States Federal Rules of Civil Procedure Rule 23(e).

59   See *Re Domestic Air Transportation Antitrust Litigation*, 148 F.R.D. 297 (N.D. Ga., 1993) where the United States Federal District Court applied these factors when approving an out of court settlement in a consumer class action bought against the major United States airlines. For a discussion of this case, see W. Pengilley, 'The United States Class Action Airlines Settlement: Some Possible Lessons for Class Actions and Antitrust in Australia', *Competition & Consumer Law Journal*, 1, (1993–1994): 117.

communicated to the class members so that they understand what is being offered and can, therefore, effectively exercise their rights.[60]

Settlement of claims with individual class members   One Australian commentator has suggested that there should also be rules governing the principles and procedures for the settlement of claims with individual class members.[61] A rule on this matter could prohibit the practice of a defendant approaching individual class members directly with a view to settling that member's claim. The rule would prevent any class member from exiting the case after the initial amalgamation of claims and the cut-off date for opting-out has passed.

Alternatively, if a class member is allowed to enter an individual settlement at this stage, the arrangement could be subject to certain restrictions. For example, the rule could require all settlements to be judicially approved and require that all communications between the defendant and individual claimants be in writing in order to reduce the chances of undue influence.

Establishing rules about individual settlements entails the difficult task of balancing the freedom of the individual class member on the one hand and the protection of the interests of the group on the other.[62] On the one hand, it may seem undesirable to restrict the behaviour of individual class members. On the other hand, a defendant who attempts to settle with individual class members is arguably abusing the class action procedure. If enough class members secure individual settlements, the entire class action could collapse.

(viii) Special Rules Regarding Lawyers' Fees in Relation to Class Actions

One concern about the expansion of the class action procedure is that it will be accompanied by excessive fees for lawyers.[63] However, as has already been pointed out, excessive fees are not an inevitable part of the class action procedure.

Rule 3.01 of the *New Zealand Law Society Rules of Professional Conduct for Barristers and Solicitors* states that '[a] practitioner shall charge a client no more than a fee which is fair and reasonable for the work done, having regard to the interests of both client and practitioner'.[64] Lawyers are required to take into account

---

60   This requirement forms part of the United States rules on out of court settlements. See United States Class Actions Fairness Act 2005 s. 2(3)(c). See also J. Klusas, 'Saving the Class Action: Developing and implementing a model rule of professional conduct for class action litigation', *Georgetown Journal of Legal Ethics*, 16, Winter (2003): 353.

61   See V. Moratibo, 'Judicial Supervision of Individual Settlements with Class Members in Australia, Canada and the United States', *Tex. Int'l LJ*, 38, (2003): 663.

62   See R. Epstein, 'Class Actions: Aggregation, Amplification and Distortion', *U. Chi. Legal F*, (2003): 475. Epstein examines this dilemma of developing an appropriate balance between the desire for personal control of each individual class member and the need for coordination of claims brought under a class action.

63   Part 7 below discusses cost as a barrier to the use of class actions and explores ways in which this barrier could be reduced.

64   See Rule 3.01 of the *Rules of Professional Conduct for Barristers and Solicitors* (7th

all relevant factors when calculating a fair and reasonable fee including the skill and knowledge required, the time and labour expended and the complexity of the matter.[65] Clients that are concerned about the amount of a bill of costs can complain to an appropriate complaint service and the complaint will be referred to a Lawyers Standards Committee for review.[66] In addition, the Lawyers and Conveyancers Act 2006 defines 'misconduct' in relation to a lawyer as including the charging of grossly excessive costs for legal work.[67] A lawyer who is found guilty of misconduct could ultimately be suspended or have his or her name struck off the roll.[68] These rules alone should provide the representative plaintiff with reasonable protection against excessive fees.

The Lawyers and Conveyancers Act 2006 further protects the plaintiff from being charged excessive fees by setting some additional limits for the charging of contingency fees. A contingency fee is a fee for legal services that is only payable if the outcome of the case is successful. In the United States there have been cases of excessively high contingency fees calculated as a percentage of the client's recovery, whereby the fee charged has been far in excess of the time and effort the lawyer has invested in the case. The Lawyers and Conveyancers Act provides that a contingency fee arrangement is only legal if it is calculated either as a normal fee or a normal fee plus a premium.[69] The premium must not be calculated as a proportion of the amount recovered and it must be an amount that compensates the lawyer for the risk undertaken and the disadvantages of not receiving payments on account.[70]

A further problem with fees in United States has involved class actions that are settled by providing the class members with a coupon which is of little value and at the same time awarding huge fees to the lawyers. For example, in one consumer class action where manufacturers allegedly misrepresented the surface area of computer screens the court approved a settlement under which consumers received a $13 coupon that they could use toward purchasing a new monitor for which they would have to pay hundreds of dollars. The lawyers for the class received about $6 million in fees.[71]

In order to avoid this type of unfairness the guidelines under the Law Society's Rules of Professional Conduct for the assessment of a reasonable fee could include a requirement that a lawyer's fee for negotiating an out of court settlement must reflect

---

edn, New Zealand Law Society, 2004).

65   See the commentary to Rule 3.01 of the *Rules of Professional Conduct for Barristers and Solicitors* (7th edn, New Zealand Law Society, 2004).Other factors to be taken into account are the responsibility required, the value or amount of any property or money involved, the importance of the matter to the client and the results achieved, the difficulty or novelty of the questions involved, the urgency and the circumstances in which the business is transacted and the reasonable costs of running a practice.

66   Section 132 and 135 of the Lawyers and Conveyancers Act 2006.

67   Section 7.

68   Sections 241 and 242.

69   Section 333.

70   Section 334.

71   'Coupon Settlements Fall Short' *The Washington Post*, 12 September 1999.

the extent to which the lawyer succeeds in obtaining full redress for the alleged harm.

Inclusion of a class action procedure in disputes tribunal   A further issue to consider when reforming the law on class actions in New Zealand is whether to extend the use of class actions to cases heard in the Disputes Tribunal. At present, a large number of consumer cases are heard in the Disputes Tribunal. This is due to the fact that consumer disputes often involve a relatively small amount of money and the Tribunal offers a fast and inexpensive method of dispute resolution. The Disputes Tribunals do not hear class actions and therefore it is likely that in some areas of dispute the Tribunals are hearing many individual cases involving identical substantive issues. This is time consuming, inefficient and leads to potential inconsistency of results.

If class actions could be successfully executed in the Tribunals, the advantages would be the same as the advantages of a class action in a court setting: increased access to justice, improved efficiency in the justice system and a deterrent effect on wrongdoers. However, a class action in the Disputes Tribunals is probably unnecessary. Amalgamating many claims into a class action will often increase the monetary figure in dispute to a level outside the jurisdiction of the Disputes Tribunal.[72] Any claim outside the monetary limit would have to be heard in the District Court which already has provision for a class action.[73]

Attempting to extend the class action to Disputes Tribunals is likely to be fraught with difficulties. The Tribunals are presided over by referees not judges. The referees are not required to have legal training and are not required to follow the law. They are instead directed to determine the dispute according to the substantial merits and justice of the case having regard to the law.[74] It is arguably inappropriate to expect a referee to determine the difficult issues of whether there is a sufficient commonality of interest among the class members and whether in other respects a class action is appropriate in any given case. This is especially so given the current time constraints placed on referees.

(ix) Consumer Body as Representative Plaintiff

If it is decided that it is inappropriate for New Zealand to develop an extensive US style 'opt-out' class action, there is an alternative and less radical reform option. It entails the development of a rule which allows a consumer body to act on behalf of consumers who suffer loss by the same event, including situations where the individuals are not identifiable (that is, an 'opt-out'). The consumer associations allowed to take the class action should not just be a collection of injured consumers but legal entities suited to defending that group of consumers. The class action rule could list the approved bodies. The list might include such organizations as the Commerce Commission and the Consumers' Institute. Alternatively, there

---

72   The current monetary limit is up to $7,500 or up to $12,000 with the consent of both parties.

73   See District Court Rule 80.

74   Section 18(6) Disputes Tribunal Act 1988.

could be some degree of flexibility so that it would be possible for any appropriate organization to take an action. For example, a group such as Action on Smoking and Health (ASH) might take a class action against tobacco companies.

This approach would provide a powerful tool to protect consumers' interests. At the same time, it would limit the scope of 'opt-out' class actions so that they are more manageable. Providing the opportunity for an organization to take on the role of representative plaintiff would improve access to justice in situations where there is no individual class member willing to take on the representative plaintiff role due to the time and cost involved.

There is already a narrow scope for this type of class action under specific statutes such as the Fair Trading Act 1986 and the Credit Contracts and Consumer Finance Act 2003. These statutes provide that in certain situations the Commerce Commission can take proceedings on behalf of persons who have suffered loss or damage.[75] However, it is arguable that there should be a more general class action provision that allows class actions to be taken in any area of the law where requirements of 'same interest' and appropriateness are met.

8. Cost Barrier

Even if the New Zealand class action is expanded according to the suggested reforms discussed above, its use will still be potentially limited by the barrier of cost. This section of the article examines the problem of cost and offers some possible approaches to reducing the cost barrier.

The cost of a class action will, of course, be less than the cumulative cost of many separate court actions. However, the cost of a class action is likely, at least initially, to fall on the representative plaintiff. Many plaintiffs can hardly afford to bring regular actions let alone bring an action on behalf of others. Not only does the representative plaintiff have to pay lawyer's fees but he or she has to pay for the costs of giving notice to class members and may also be required to pay the other parties' costs if the case is lost.

The cost barrier is particularly acute in consumer disputes, as potential representative plaintiffs will be individual consumers who are often unable to bear the full financial burden of the action. Of course, if the action is successful then the representative plaintiff may be able to cover the costs from the winnings. Nevertheless, it is unfair that the members of the class are 'free riders' benefiting from a successful outcome without having to take the risk of spending significant amounts of time and money when the outcome of the litigation is inevitably uncertain.

The problem of costs is not, however, an inherent feature of the class action procedure. There are several possible solutions to the cost barrier.

---

75   See the definition of 'person' in s. 2(1) of the Fair Trading Act and the introductory words of ss 41 and 43 of the Fair Trading Act. See also ss 90 and 111(2)(c) of the Credit Contracts and Consumer Finance Act 2003.

(i) Share the Cost amongst Class Members

The most obvious and fair answer to the cost barrier is to require each member of the class to share in the costs of the procedure. This, however, means that the representative plaintiff has to know the contact details of the members and therefore this solution is limited to the 'opt-in' form of class action.

(ii) Civil Legal Aid

Another possible method of reducing the cost barrier is to expand the availability of civil legal aid. This could be done in one of two ways. One option is to introduce more generous qualifying standards. This would mean that more of the members of the class would be likely to qualify for legal aid. Another approach could be to introduce a special legal aid fund which is dedicated to financing class actions. Unfortunately, in the present political environment, such a fund may not be considered a priority and certainly there is little chance of unlimited sums being paid toward class action lawsuits.

(iii) Funding from Interest Groups

Another cost-saving option is for the representative plaintiff to approach a relevant interest group in the hope that it might fund the litigation. This is a useful approach in some consumer disputes. However, in other instances there will be no relevant interest group connected with the subject of the dispute, in which case the plaintiff must rely on alternative cost arrangements.

(iv) Contingency Fees

One of the most powerful strategies for reducing the cost barrier in a class action is the contingency fee arrangement. One commentator has gone so far as to say that:[76] '[i]f disapproval of contingent fees is not somehow relaxed, the options are limited and damage class actions are likely to be few.'

The contingency fee operates by reducing the financial barrier to litigation. As has been explained above a contingency fee is a fee for legal services, which is only paid to the lawyer in the event that the litigation is successful. If the case fails, the client is not obliged to pay the lawyer anything. Until recently, the legality of contingency fees has been somewhat unclear.[77] However, since the enactment of the Lawyers and Conveyancers Act in 2006 the matter has been resolved. The Act

---

76   T.D. Rowe Jr, 'Shift Happens: Pressure on Foreign Attorney-fee paradigms from Class Actions', *Duke J. Comp. & Int'l L.*, 13 (2003): 125, at 133.

77   In *Mills* v. *Rogers* (1899) 18 NZLR 291 the Court of Appeal held that contingency fee arrangements are champertous and therefore illegal. However, such fee arrangements are reasonably common in New Zealand and the commentary to Rule 3.01 of the New Zealand Law Society Rules contemplates the use of such fees. See *Rules of Professional Conduct for Barristers and Solicitors* (7th edn, New Zealand Law Society, 2004).

specifically states that, subject to some limited exclusions, the use of contingency fees in New Zealand is legal.[78]

The Lawyers and Conveyancers Act 2006 prohibits the calculation of contingency fees as a proportion of the amount recovered.[79] Nevertheless, it is probable that whether or not a contingency fee arrangement is adopted in any given case will depend on the size of the likely recovery. A higher recovery makes it more likely that the lawyer and representative plaintiff will agree to a contingency fee arrangement. In New Zealand the level of damages likely to be awarded in consumer disputes may be quite low and a contingency fee arrangement might therefore be unsuitable. This is in contrast to the high levels of damages awarded in some United States cases. The low level of damages awarded in New Zealand cases is partly due to the existence of the accident compensation scheme, which bars most claims for damages for personal injury by accident.[80]

Nevertheless, the combination of a class action and contingency fee arrangement will work well in some cases. In fact, without the use of a class action, a contingency fee arrangement will, in most consumer disputes, be an unrealistic option due to the relatively small sums of money involved. In a single plaintiff action, if the outcome is successful, the recovery will rarely be large enough to cover the lawyer's fees and would certainly leave nothing for the client. The use of a class action procedure results in a higher recovery from which the lawyer's fees can be paid.

(v) Reducing the Effects of the Cost Indemnity Rule

One significant cost barrier for New Zealand representative plaintiffs is the rule as to costs. If a plaintiff's claim is unsuccessful, he or she will generally be ordered to pay a significant portion of the winning side's costs.[81] The fact that claimants will incur such expenses if they lose may significantly reduce the attractiveness of a class member taking on the role of a representative plaintiff.

Short of abolishing this cost indemnity rule there are several methods of reducing this particular cost barrier. One option is to expand the contingency fee arrangement so that lawyers also agree to assume the risk of paying for the opponent's costs if the litigation is unsuccessful. Another option is to establish a legal aid fund that is used for the payment of adverse cost awards in class action cases. This is the approach taken in Ontario where there is a 'Class Proceedings Fund' from which all adverse costs in class action cases are paid. Australia has a different approach. A representative plaintiff in Australia may have a cost order made against them. However, if the representative plaintiff has insufficient finances to pay for the costs the rule expressly prohibits the costs being awarded against class members.[82]

---

78   See Clauses 305 to 308 of the Lawyers and Conveyancers Bill 2003.
79   Sections 333 and 334.
80   See s. 317(1) of the Injury Prevention, Rehabilitation, and Compensation Act 2001.
81   See Rule 46 of the High Court Rules and *Morton* v. *Douglas Homes Ltd (No. 2)* [1984] 2 NZLR 620.
82   See Federal Court of Australia Act 1976, s. 43(1A).

9. Conclusion

It is in the public interest to have some mechanism whereby consumers can sue as a class. Such a mechanism increases consumers' access to justice by decreasing the time and cost of court action. It also reduces the likelihood that manufacturers and suppliers will escape liability for wrongdoing merely because the large amounts of harm that they cause are spread thinly across the consuming public. Lastly, a class action improves efficiency in the justice system.

The current New Zealand class action mechanism is in need of reform. It lacks detail and therefore fails to guide the courts adequately in how the class action should operate. The restrictive interpretation that the courts have given to Rule 78 has resulted in a limited form of class action for damages claims. The rule on class actions should be reformed to specifically allow for an 'opt-out' class action. Rules must then be established so as to strictly regulate the class action in order to reduce the risk of it becoming unmanageable or abused. These rules should regulate such matters as the definition of 'same interest', the guidelines for terminating a class action, notice requirements, rules for out of court settlements and rules to reduce the risk of excessive lawyers' fees. This approach allows society to have the benefits of class actions but reduces the risks associated with the procedure.

13 Expanding the Use of Credit Reports and Credit Scores: The Need for Caution and Empiricism

Karen Gross[1]

1. Introduction

With the globalization of the consumer financial markets, increasing attention is being paid to the use of credit reports and credit scoring to determine which consumers should have access to credit and the price they should pay for the credit they obtain. Also, automated underwriting and the securitization of consumer receivables have both increased reliance on, and the impact of, credit reporting and credit scoring. Unfortunately, in nations such as the United States (US), where there are robust credit reporting and credit scoring systems, deep flaws exist in how these systems operate both to award and price credit.[2] Although there have been some efforts to ameliorate these issues through alternative approaches to both reporting and scoring and the creation of an entirely new scoring model, the problems have not been resolved – at least not sufficiently. Despite these concerns, there has been an expansion of the use of credit reporting and credit scoring to arenas beyond credit. Increasingly, these systems are being employed to determine access to, among other things, insurance and employment. Unfortunately, this expanded application of credit reporting and scoring exacerbates the already existing concerns about how these systems operate and, as such, multiplies the opportunities for unfair treatment of whole segments of the population. This essay is an effort to explain these risks and to urge caution before we make an existing problem worse through its application beyond its origins. In short, we are compounding concerns when insurers and employers make important financial and other life choices for our citizenry based on existing approaches to credit reporting and credit scoring. My suggestion is a simple one: Before the American approach to credit reporting and credit scoring is transported to other nations, we

---

1   Karen Gross is the President of Southern Vermont College in Bennington, Vermont. She is also a law professor at New York Law School. This paper is based on a three-part article series written by this author that appeared in both the Westchester County and Fairfield County Business Journals. These columns can be accessed online at www.westchestercountybusinessjournal.com or www.fairfieldcountybusinessjournal. com. My thanks to New York Law School student Rebecca Quatinetz, '08, for her fine research assistance.
2   For a comprehensive and thoughtful treatment of these issues, see E. Hendricks, *Credit Scoring and Credit Reporting: How the System Works* (Privacy Times, 2004).

should use the occasion to right the wrongs in the system. This may not solve all issues for those living in the US, when the systems are deeply entrenched, but it may help other nations and their citizens. There is some comfort in that.

2. Credit Reporting and Credit Scoring: The Present System

Since the approaches to credit reporting and scoring are most 'advanced' in the US, we begin with a description of that system. The US system involves the reporting of both positive and negative data about consumers; as such, it stands in contrast to other nations where the reporting of positive data is either non-existent or scarce. The positive/negative information is gathered and then reported primarily by three major repositories, Experien, Equifax and TransUnion, and is governed primarily (although not exclusively) by a body of federal law know as the Fair Credit Reporting Act ('FCRA'). To be sure, there are other credit reporting agencies, and there are other entities that collect data but seek to avoid characterization of themselves as 'credit reporting agencies' so that they can avoid the requirements of the FCRA.

The information contained in credit reports provides the main database upon which credit scores are calculated. In these scoring systems, the higher the score the better – unlike golf. Although there are a myriad of scoring models (and hence no one credit score for each consumer despite advertising and commentary to the contrary), there is a critical link between credit reporting and credit scoring. Until recently, the prime credit score was determined by *F*air *I*saac *C*ompany (and the score was known, not shockingly, as a FICO score), although two of the three major credit reporting agencies (TransUnion and Experien) used their own credit scoring models. Within the last year, the three major repositories teamed together to create a scoring model that is shared (although the inputted data are not) called a Vantage Score.[3] The relative value and utilization of the Vantage Score as compared to the more common FICO score (which can be calculated on the basis of a myriad of models that are presently in existence) is unknown. However, one can assume that both the Vantage and FICO scores are considered reasonable determiners of – proxies for – risk, at least in the eyes of creditors evaluating, offering and monitoring credit.

Currently, credit reports contain information about whether a person is paying his or her store, bank and gas credit cards, bank and finance company obligations and most student loans in a timely fashion. They will reveal the levels at which the consumer is borrowing and whether the consumer is close to maxing out available credit lines. The reports will show when the debt was incurred and a history of payments. These reports will display public records like judgments, liens and bankruptcies. They will show how often the consumer has applied for credit based on credit inquiries.

At first blush, this seems like worthwhile data for prospective creditors. If a consumer has not paid bills in a timely fashion, has over-extended him or herself and has been repeatedly the subject of collection actions, the likelihood of timely

---

3   See, for example, R. Smith, 'Viewpoint: Now It's Up to Creditors to Use a New Scoring System', *American Banker*, Vol. 171, 24 March 2006.

repayment is dubious. Conversely, repeated on time payments and low levels of borrowing signal that a new customer is likely to repay.[4] The new creditor can make two assessments: do I want to extend credit to someone who displays these characteristics, and if I do, at what price should I extend credit that takes into account the possibility of prospective non-payment? The future lender is engaging in an assessment of risk, and we live, at least in the US, in a system of risk-based pricing. At the theoretical level, this makes sense. Riskier borrowers pay more for the money they are lent than less risky borrowers. Of course, the system assumes some real correlations between risk and price, something that is clearly not in effect in the predatory and even sub-prime lending markets where lenders are overpricing for risk and for reasons that are too complex to explain or assess here, consumers are accepting credit through these lenders.[5]

There are several embedded assumptions in the system. First, there is an assumption that the collected data are accurate. Obviously, inaccurate data, particularly if it is negative data, would adversely affect a consumer's credit profile. Second, there is an assumption that all the data needed to make a credit assessment of risk are collected. If there are data that are not collected or revealed that could affect credit under an existing or an improved scoring model, then consumers could well be adversely affected. One more assumption that is noteworthy: the presumption that most consumers have a quality credit report in the first instance. Unfortunately, approximately 25 percent of all Americans have a thin or no credit file, making assessments difficult or impossible. Also, knowledge levels about credit reporting are strongly correlated, according to a recent study done by the GAO, to income, educative level, age, employment status, experiences with pre-existing loan transactions and race.[6] Stated another way, the vulnerable know less about this critical aspect of the consumer financial markets.

---

4   The accuracy of this statement can be questioned based on what are known as 'surprise bankruptcies', bankruptcy filings by individuals who did not appear to present a repayment risk. The development of a 'bankruptcy score', which is available to creditors but not consumers, is an effort to ameliorate this problem. For a recent discussion of this score, see Brigitte Yuille, 'Do You Know Your Bankruptcy Risk Score', available online at: http://www.bankrate.com/brm/news/bankruptcy/20060116a1.asp. See also a case study appearing in Viewpoints in September/October 2003 titled, 'Providian and INTRUST Bank Reduce Bankruptcies While Protecting Revenue', available online at: http://www.fairisaac.com/NR/exeres/68798B87-840C-4BCF-B8A3-25986719F23F,frameless.htm.

5   Why borrowers are not walking with their feet to better financial products is clearly a question worth investigating in greater detail, including whether the quality of, and access to, alternative financial products are sufficient.

6   The GAO issued a report titled 'Credit Reporting Literacy: Consumers Understood the Basics but Could Benefit from Targeted Educational Efforts' and it is available online at: http://www.gao.gov/new.items/d05223.pdf.

3. The Error Factor

The studies are clear: credit reports are replete with errors. While the estimates vary, studies show at perhaps as many as 70 percent of credit reports contain an error. The more important statistic is that up to 50 percent of credit reports contain the type of error that will hurt someone's credit score – that all important identifier of creditworthiness.[7] Some percentage of errors lead to total credit denial. There are also considerable inconsistencies in the data reported by the three major repositories; in other words, there are inconsistent databases that are used to create scores; this means that even if the same scoring model is employed across all three major repositories, the scores will be different.[8]

The errors on credit reports cover a wide spectrum. One study showed that 29 percent of credit reports contain false delinquencies – erroneously reporting that a consumer was late in making payments when that was untrue. A Federal Trade Commission study showed that revolving accounts (like a credit card) with positive information were frequently not reported to the credit bureaus and in some instances, credit limits (a key indicator for determining the ratio of debt to credit) were deleted, all of which makes the consumer look like a less appealing prospective borrower (except to the current lender) and produces a deflated credit score. Many credit reports contain outdated information, including items that should have been deleted as a matter of law. Identity theft, a rising crime, also leads to false information on credit reports. Divorce and death can also affect credit, and these changes in life situation are not necessarily collected nor reflected timely on credit reports.

The error problem would not be as serious if consumers knew about and then sought to correct the errors on their reports before entering the credit (or insurance or employment) process. A recent GAO report noted that even though many consumers apparently claim to understand credit scoring, fewer than 28 percent actually knew the scoring range and without that, the garnered information is useless. Even for those consumers who see their reports, correcting errors is often a nightmare – one of those instances in which the law on the books does not match the law in practice. In part, this is a problem of volume. The credit reporting agencies receive between 7,000–10,000 disputes per day, and it is estimated that the length of time spent resolving the average dispute is 1.66 minutes!

Here is the point: with so many errors, the judgments made about prospective creditors could be wrong – way wrong. The real financial condition of individuals may not be reflected on their credit reports and that, in turn, affects people's credit score and that, in turn, reflects the price they pay for the money they borrow.

---

7   For studies addressing the errors see, for example, A. Cassady and E. Mierzwinski, *Mistakes Do Happen: A Look at Errors in Credit Reports*, National Association of Public Interest Research Groups, (2004) June, available online at www.uspirg.org.

8   Consumer Federation of America and National Credit Reporting Association, *Credit Score Accuracy and Implications for Consumers*, (2002), 17 December, available online at http://www.ncrainc.org/documents/CFA%20NCRA%20Credit%20Score%2 0Report.pdf.

4. The Omission Factor

The information not contained in the traditional credit report issued by the big three repositories is as relevant as the data that is disclosed. Currently, the three major credit reporting agencies do not consistently report mortgage and utility payments, both likely indicators of credit worthiness. Other important information is missing – payments related to rent, childcare, parking, and use of storage facilities. Conventional credit reporting does not include regular payments made to one's home nation, instalment payments to doctors and hospitals, or alimony and child support.

What this means is that there are many people whose true financial lives are not reflected on existing credit reports, and creditors are judging people (negatively) on less than complete information. Obviously, if data are not reported and what are reported are limited or negative data, a person looks different from whom they actually are. In a sense, it is like taking a photograph of someone and leaving off the mouth and chin. Yes, it might be that person – but it is hard to tell and were the missing features inserted, they might appear quite different. Here is the point: with so much missing information, credit reports are an incomplete financial picture of a person and are telling an incomplete story. Stated another way, we may be inaccurately pricing for risk and whole segments of the population are overpaying for the money they borrow because the data used to determine their credit score is incomplete.

5. Why This Matters

Clearly, a system that overprices for credit harms certain populations more than others. Here is why. Credit reporting uses quite traditional and conventional data. This means that vulnerable groups in our society – including those with little previous credit history at least in the US – pay more to borrow. Thus, immigrants, students, newly divorced or widowed women, and minority populations are more likely to have less of the traditional credit information and hence lower credit scores, on average, than other segments of society.[9] And, there is no real proof, supported by empirical data, that these populations are, across the board, less worthy borrowers. It seems that most errors and omissions work to the detriment of most of the vulnerable populations.[10] Moreover, the problem is compounded by the fact that once someone has a low credit score and accesses credit through less than a prime lender, this deflates the credit score prospectively. Hence vulnerable people are hit twice: first, they get a deflated or no score and then they borrow from sources that even further lower their credit score which dooms them even further. In a nutshell, the more vulnerable the consumer, the more likely there are in credit scoring quicksand – they sink and cannot get out and can only sink in further. That cannot be right.

---

9   See, for example, K.R. Harney, 'Study: Mortgage Quotes are not always Colorblind', *Chicago Tribune*, 18 June 2006, Real Estate section.

10   R.B. Avery, R.W. Bostic, P.S. Calem and G.B. Canner, 'Credit Report Accuracy and Access to Credit', *Federal Reserve Bulletin*, (2004): 297–322, 321.

Were credit the only issue determined by credit reports and credit scoring, the situation would be problematic but perhaps remediable over the long haul. There have been recent efforts to reform credit reporting and credit scoring and the issue has captured the attention of a number of consumer groups and think-tank types – all of which are, from my perspective, positive developments.[11] There have been discussions of how credit scoring creates or reinforces discrimination; we deny opportunities to categories of individuals based on their credit score which becomes a stand-in for race, gender and ethnicity, all prohibited forms of credit denial.[12] Even some lenders, sensing that the conventional markets are tapped out, have been thinking about reforming credit reporting and credit scoring. I consider all of this good news.[13]

The bad news is that credit reports and credit scores are now used in many situations in addition to credit.[14] Insurers, landlords, utilities and employers are increasingly looking to make their decisions based on either credit reports and credit scores as conventionally calculated or, in the case of the insurance industry, on 'insurance scores' which are a variant of credit scores. In other words, whatever harms and risks are in existence in the context of the consumer credit markets, these are now being transported into other arenas. We can call this the new 'credit scoring influenza' – the application and extension of credit modelling to non-credit situations and it, like the real flu, is spreading. One might say we are experiencing or could prospectively experience a 'credit scoring pandemic' – and, like a possible flu pandemic, it should get us worried. Real worried. There are data to support this credit scoring pandemic. It is reported that the three major credit repositories generate one billion credit reports a year; of these, 'only' 16 million are distributed to consumers.[15] That means lots of other third parties are getting and using credit reports.

In thinking about the spread of credit scoring, the issue is whether there is a relationship between insurability and credit rating and between employability and credit rating and so on. Stated another way, the issue is whether one's credit score signals something more than credit worthiness or lack of worthiness. The question is whether credit riskiness is a proxy for other riskiness – the likelihood of filing for and obtaining high payment on an insurance claim or stealing monies from an employer or failing to pay timely rent. It is to these issues that I now turn.

---

11   Roundtable on Using Alternative Data Sources in Credit Scoring: Exploring Challenges and Opportunities. Report available online at: www.brook.edu.
12   See, for example, 'Credit Scores: What You Don't Know Can be Held Against You', *Consumer Reports*, August 2005.
13   D. DeZube, 'Giving Credit Where Credit's Due', *Mortgage Banking*, 66, (2005), 1 December.
14   See, for example, C. Stein, 'Credit-Scored for Life: Broader Uses Hurt Consumers', *Boston Globe*, 7 August 2005, s. D1.
15   *Supra* n. 6. at 298. An Experien fact sheet also notes the number of credit reports created annually. See online at: http://www.experian.com/consumer/ca_accuracy_report.html.

6. Insurance and Credit Worthiness

The problem starts with this reality: insurers of differing sorts are turning to 'insurance scores' (similar to credit scores) to determine consumer eligibility and price for a proffered product. Although some states are concerned about their citizens being denied insurance coverage on the basis of credit or insurance scoring and there has been litigation suggesting that denial of insurance on the basis of credit scores is discriminatory,[16] the data are ambiguous.[17] Some studies support a link between credit score and insurance claims filed, although the quality of these and other studies has been challenged.[18] There are studies showing that those with a weaker financial condition are under stress and are more likely to take risks.[19] This is a deadly combination for an insurer as it suggests these individuals may have an increased propensity to get into an accident or leave the stove on or fail to lock their home or set the alarm when departing. This means that those with lower credit scores will file and may recover on more claims. Some data from these studies are noteworthy: those with the lowest financial standing file almost double the claims of those with the best financial condition (as measured by credit scores).[20] The dollars recovered is another issue altogether.

But, not everyone agrees with these findings. Consider one counteracting piece of data. Those who seek bankruptcy relief – individuals in financial distress with deflated credit scores and suffering from the strain on over-indebtedness – are not more likely to file insurance claims. If this vulnerable population is not filing insurance claims in increased numbers, it is hard to suggest that economic vulnerability is correlated to insurance claims rates. Stated differently, there may be host of factors that explain the seeming correlation between insurance claims and financial status. To see the duelling arguments, visit this website: www.insurancescored.com.

7. Employment and Credit Worthiness

Despite the possible arguments for linking insurance and credit scoring (both having some financial linkage), employment is another situation altogether, and one that is

---

16   See A.P. Alert, 2 June 2006, 'Allstate, Minority Customers Reach Settlement in Texas', available online at Westlaw.

17   Testimony of Peter J. Molinari, Senior Deputy Superintendent of Insurance, before the NY State Assembly, 22 October 2003, available online.

18   See, for example, M.J. Miller and R.A. Smith, 'The Relationship of Credit-Based Insurance Scores to Private Passenger Automobile Insurance Loss Propensity', June 2003, available from EPIC Actuaries, PO Box 628, Minocqua, WI 54548; American Academy of Actuaries, *The Use of Credit History for Personal Lines of Insurance: Report to the National Association of Insurance Commissioners*, 15 November 2002, available online at www.actuary.org.

19   R.P. Hartwig, 'The Use of Credit Information as an Underwriting Tool in Personal Lines Insurance', New York State Assembly Standing Committee on Insurance, 22 October 2003; available online at www.iii.org.

20   Study conducted by the Texas Department of Insurance and issued December 2004 and January 2005 and available online from the Insurance Information Institute.

hardly comparable. Start with this realization. Employers want good employees, and hiring decisions are neither easy nor cheap. Even the best run searches can lead to mistakes, and remedying bad choices is both time consuming and expensive. It is no wonder, then, that employers look for credible ways to improve their hiring successes. One strategy being used with increasing frequency is obtaining and evaluating the credit reports and credit scores of prospective employees. The question is whether this is a good idea from a hiring and legal perspective.

Consider two job candidates. One has a credit score of 720 (which is the equivalent of 'A' credit and a credit report showing little borrowing. Another candidate has a score of 620 (on the cusp of sub-prime lending) and a credit report that shows considerable new credit card borrowing and an occasional late payment in the last year. Assume, just for the moment, that the employer has complied with all the required legal niceties under the FCRA with respect to use of credit reports (this involves getting the prospective employee's permission and adopting certain guidelines for notification of non-hiring).[21] Assume also that the candidates are, in all other respects, equal.

The choice seems easy. One candidate (the higher scored candidate) looks better than the other candidate (the lower scored candidate). Not necessarily so. Our son, a graduate student, has a better credit score than I do (by some 40 points). Since the score is not income based, one can get an excellent score by borrowing very little from one or two sources, paying on time and having access to considerable credit. My point: a good credit score may not indicate whether someone is financially sophisticated or is a good credit risk over the long haul.

Suppose that the prospective employee with the 620 score had a score of 720 the year before. But, in the intervening year, her marriage of 25 years fell apart; she had to purchase a new home and a new car. She had to obtain credit in her own name; she had to use her credit cards to make ends meet. My point: a low credit score does not necessarily indicate that someone is a bad credit risk over the long haul. It may indicate something else.

These examples show that high or low scores, in and other themselves, are not necessarily solid indicators of who is a good credit risk. One additional thing is known: certain groups within our society have lower scores than others. Women after divorce or widowhood, many young people, minorities and recent immigrants commonly suffer from deflated scores. Many people suspect that while scoring is not permitted to take race, gender, religion and ethnicity into account, some of the factors used to score (or omitted from the scoring model) are surrogates for these prohibited demographic variables. Hence, the argument goes, credit scoring and credit reporting do, in fact, discriminate. For those employers seeking to increase the number of women and minority employees, credit scoring will, generally speaking, undermine that effort. As to the possibility of discrimination in credit scoring, it looks to me like a lawsuit waiting to happen, particularly when there is seemingly

---

21   The Federal Trade Commission has a useful short report for employers on using credit reports. It is available online at: http://www.ftc.gov/bcp/conline/pubs/buspubs/credempl.htm.

no relationship between the employment role and access to money or confidential information.

But, these observations skirt another real issue: is there a correlation between poor credit reports (or a poor credit score) and being a less good employee. The embedded assumption in the use of credit scoring in employment is that a low credit score signals that an employee will be less reliable and less trustworthy. Stated differently, those who are fiscally troubled are, it is assumed, irresponsible. Asking this question is all the more important given the rise in the number of employers looking at credit reports.[22]

Even the insurance studies do not suggest that those with bad credit are more prone to being untrustworthy or unscrupulous with company money. So, the insurance debate (which is heating up and leading some states to ban or curb the use of credit scoring in determining insurance eligibility) does not answer the hiring question. A storeowner rightfully wants to know whether it can safely hire a cashier that has had or currently has financial woes. A company wants to know if it can comfortably hire an executive whose personal financial house in not in order.

To date, there have been very few studies of this issue, despite the growing trend among employers to use credit reports and credit scores. The studies that exist should make one pause – long and hard. Professor Jerry K. Palmer at Eastern Kentucky University and his colleague Laura Koppes looked at credit reports and employment in the financial services industry (which ironically included those employed as debt collectors).[23] They found no positive correlation between credit history and workplace performance or termination. Indeed, a weak negative correlation arose because the two employees with the greatest number 30-day late payments received high job ratings. Other commentators question the validity of credit reports and credit scores for determining employability.[24] Stated most simply, credit reports and credit scores have not proven themselves to be valid predictors – at least not yet.[25]

While awaiting further empirical assessment, there is another way of looking at this. An employee who needs money will work really hard for it and come to work – no matter what. The person entering or re-entering the workforce after a divorce or death may be grateful for the opportunity to work and will work extra hard to show her appreciation for the opportunity. A younger person or immigrant who sees

---

22   See T. Joyner, 'More Job Seekers Haunted by Past', *Palm Beach Post*, 27 April 2005, Business section.

23   See J.K. Palmer and L.L. Koppes, 'Investigation of the Credit History Validity at Predicting Performance and Turnover', presented at the Society for Industrial and Organizational Psychology, Chicago, IL. 3 April 2004; J.K. Palmer and L.L. Koppes, 'Further Investigation of Credit History as a predictor of Employee Turnover,' American Psychological Society, Atlanta GA 2003.

24   R.B. Avery, P.S. Calem and G.B. Canner, 'Consumer Credit Scoring: Do Situational Circumstances Matter,' *BIS Working Papers*, January 2004; L. Rosen, 'Credit Reports and Job Hunting', *Employment Screening Resources*, available online at: www.esrcheck.com/articles/article7.php.

25   L. Wasmer Andrews, 'The Nexus of Ethics: Many Experts Say a Person's ethics on and off the Job Cannot be Separated,' *Society of Human Resource Management*, Vol. 50, Issue 8. See also www.shrm.org/hrmagazine/05august.

a particular job as his or her first opportunity to succeed will feel a connection to the company that hired them. One thing credit scores do not measure is who will be loyal and who will work hard – things that really do matter in the workplace. This approach is strongly suggested by the work of Avery *et al.* in which they address the value of situational circumstances in interpreting credit scores.[26] Despite legal constraints (which are not insignificant), personal reasons do affect credit. This is an approach, however, that runs completely contrary to automated underwriting – at least as presently conducted because individualized decision-making has gone the way of the buggy whip.

8. Conclusions

In the absence of robust and conclusive empirical data, we should be cautious – extremely cautious – about expanding the use of credit reports and credit scores beyond the credit marketplace. Even within that marketplace, there are no shortage of issues and concerns. What worries me is a rush to utilization – the credit scoring pandemic. In the name of efficiency and access to credit and insurance and employment, we forgo an opportunity to get the algorithms right. Given whose ox is most likely to be gored by too swift application, we would do well to pause. America has a bad habit of exporting its worst habits and products. We would do well to stop that behaviour in this instance in particular and more generally as well. Other nations would do well to get credit reporting and credit scoring right in the first instance; it is vastly easier to get something right the first go-around rather than later when one has to correct entrenched modalities and established norms and practices. In short, there is time for some nations to get this right, and this essay is an effort to assist these nations in asking the right questions – before it is too late.

---

26   Above, n. 24.

Part 2: Hull Symposium: The Changing Face of Consumer Law

The Changing Face of UK Consumer Law

University of Hull, 11 April 2006

Opening Address by Professor Gerry Johnstone
Director, Hull Law School 2003–2006

A very warm welcome to the University of Hull. The Law School is delighted to host this symposium led by such leading authorities in the field of Consumer Law.

As you are aware, the Symposium has been organised to celebrate the contribution to Consumer Law scholarship of our colleague Deborah Parry, who retired from her post here at the end of 2005.

Participants in this conference will no doubt be aware of the significance of Deborah's contribution to this field. Her research is wide ranging, encompassing trade descriptions, fair trading, consumer credit, consumer safety, advertising, product liability, sale and supply of goods and services and codes of practice. She is co-author with Brian Harvey – one of our speakers today – of *The Law of Consumer Protection and Fair Trading* as well as an editor of *Butterworth's Trading and Consumer Law*.

Deborah has also employed her significant expertise to define and protect the interests of consumers in an area where such protection is especially needed: energy consumption. She was on the Yorkshire Electricity Consumers Committee of OFFER and the North of England Gas Forum. In 2001 her contribution was recognized through the award of an MBE for services to energy consumers in Yorkshire. She was also an academic member of the Department of Trade and Industry's Strategic Review of Consumer Protection Legislation.

Colleagues at the University of Hull are, of course, just as familiar with Deborah's many contributions to the academic work of the University of Hull Law School. As well as teaching Consumer Law, Deborah has – over a 30 year period – introduced our students to that remarkable institution: the Common Law. Over this period, her enthusiasm and knowledge have left their mark on goodness knows how many students.

There is one area of Deborah's work here which must, however, receive a special mention. Long before 'widening participation' became a fashionable political project, the Law School at Hull was providing Higher Education in Law on a part-time basis to significantly-sized groups of highly dedicated and enthusiastic local students whose circumstances would not have enabled them to study full-time. Deborah's work in coordinating this programme – and in particular in providing personal encouragement and support to these students – has without doubt changed lives for the better.

It is a mark of the esteem with which Deborah and her work is held that such distinguished scholars have agreed to present papers at this symposium, and that so many have come to Hull to participate in it.

I am very grateful to my colleague, Dr Christian Twigg-Flesner, for organising this event. Christian's presence here ensures, of course, that the reputation of Hull for its work in Consumer Law will continue, following Deborah's retirement. So without further ado, let us explore the changing face of UK Consumer Law.

Four papers presented at the conference are published in this volume of the *Yearbook of Consumer Law*. These papers have been largely left in the format of a conference presentation, except for minor editorial adjustments and the addition of references, as appropriate.

Sponsorship for the conference was generously provided by Domestic and General plc.

14 Trade Descriptions After the Unfair Commercial Practices Directive

Richard Bragg[1]

The Unfair Commercial Practices Directive is the first Directive requiring that no domestic legislation may be in force providing for stricter coverage than that in the Directive itself. This has consequences for the Trade Descriptions Act 1968.

This paper is postulated on two major premises, neither of which may turn out to be true. First, it is presumed that the Directive will be enacted with the same wording and coverage as it contains now. Second, it is presumed that the Trade Descriptions Act 1968 will be repealed. The purpose of the paper is to compare the current situation with that after enactment and to try to see what changes there would be in coverage. It does not concern itself with the remedies that might be applied under the new legislation. It is not intended to deal with prices legislation.

The Trade Descriptions Act 1968 (TDA) essentially prohibits false trade descriptions and false statements about services, but is wider than the Directive, which only applies to consumer transactions. The TDA covers inter-business transactions as well.

Article 3(1) of the Directive prohibits false and misleading conduct which deceives or is likely to deceive the average consumer. To this extent, it echoes the TDA. The requirement of the Act that the description is false to a material degree seems to be a reasonable person test. The classic test is the colourful one by Judge Gower QC, in *Burleigh* v. *Van Den Berghs & Jurgens Ltd*:[2]

> ... the court must be sure that ... [the description] was likely to mislead the average reasonable member of the public, and that means, of course, the shopping public. It is important that we should remember that we are dealing with the average person. It is not enough that we should be sure that an unusually careless person might be misled ... [or] a person who is dyslexic, illiterate, short-sighted, or less than average intelligence.

Thus the test would seem to be identical.

The Directive states that a factually correct statement that misleads is prohibited. That again echoes the TDA. In *Dixons Ltd* v. *Barnett*,[3] a telescope was described as '455 times magnification'. This was scientifically accurate, but in reality any magnification over 120 times was no more than an enlarged blur. Mr Justice Hutchinson laid emphasis that this was a sale to an ordinary lay member of the public

---

1   Senior Lecturer in Law, University of Manchester.
2   [1987] B.T.L.C. 337 at p. 339.
3   [1988] B.T.L.C. 311.

in a high street shop and ordinary members of the public would not understand what the scientific meaning was about. They were likely to be misled.

The biggest difference is between Article 6(1) and s. 2 of the TDA. Both these list a series of matters to which the false statement must relate. The coverage in the Directive is much wider, generally. However, there are some startling gaps. The Directive does not contain any requirements as to the name of the manufacturer (unless that is contained within the phrase 'commercial origin'). Since passing off generally and breach of copyright by sellers is rife, one would have expected a positive statement that this was covered. The Directive does, however, contain a reference to any statement or symbol in relation to the product, which may be wide enough to cover trader's logos and brand names etc. Article 6(2)(a) does cover marketing which creates 'confusion' with a competitor's products. There may not in fact be a gap here.

Section 2(1)(j) of the TDA covers other history, including previous ownership or use. This is, of course, the paragraph under which Trading Standards Officers have prosecuted the car traders who insist on 'clocking' cars. Unless this activity can be brought under the heading 'nature of the product' or 'usage', then it would not appear to be covered. The context of the word 'usage' suggests it means what the product can be used for, rather than how it has been used. Whether it would be possible to stretch the meaning or to enact separate domestic legislation under the Road Traffic Acts is unclear.

The Directive, however, contains references to a number of issues which are not within the scope of the TDA. These include:

(i) 'Availability'

There has been no successful prosecution, to my knowledge, of a trader who engages in switch selling under the TDA. The use of availability suggests that this might now be possible.

(ii) 'After-sales Customer Assistance and Complaint Handling'

This might have come under s. 14 TDA if it amounts to a promise of a service at the time of sale. In *Bambury* v. *Hounslow LBC*[4] a garage director offered a three month guarantee on a car he was selling. When the customer later tried to take advantage of that guarantee, the garage falsely pretended there was nothing wrong with the car. The Divisional Court upheld the decision of the justices that 'the original statement that they were entering into contractual relations was a false one'. It seems that, depending on the circumstances, where the statement is made before the performance of the service, the court can always consider whether there is falsity in the present. The problem is that the TDA does not cover mere promises of a service. The matter was clearly explained by Mackenna J. in *R*. v. *Sunair Holidays Ltd:*[5]

---

4   [1971] R.T.R. 1.
5   [1973] 2 All E.R. 1233, at p. 1236.

The section deals with 'statements' of which it can be said that they were, at the time when they were made, 'false'. That may be the case with a statement of fact, whether past or present. A statement that a fact exists now, or that it existed in the past, is either true or false at the time when the statement is made. But that is not the case with a promise or a prediction about the future. A prediction may come true or it may not. A promise to do something in the future may be kept or it may be broken. But neither the prediction nor the promise can be said to have been true or false at the time when it was made. We conclude that section 14 does not deal with forecasts or promises as such.

If that is correct then the Directive contains an extension. The notion that over optimistic advertising of a complaints handling service would become an unlawful goes way beyond the TDA, but will be welcomed by those sat on the end of telephones to engaged call centres.

(iii) 'Delivery'

It seems that broken delivery promises will become unlawful. This is probably not covered by the TDA at all.

(iv) 'The Need for Service, Part, Replacement or Repair'

Perhaps the classic example is *R.* v. *Bevelectric Ltd*,[6] where a firm of washing machine repairers regularly told customers that their machines needed a new motor, without any real attempt to diagnose the real fault. Lord Justice Staughton confirmed that a false statement about services already provided is within s. 14, if it was connected or associated with the supply of services in question. However, the Directive is wider, because it will cover promises made at the time of sale as to the durability of the product.

(v) 'Non-Compliance with a Code of Conduct'

Trade Associations' Codes of Practice have been seen under current legislation as voluntary and not therefore giving rise to offences. However, in the little known case of *V.G. Vehicles (Telford) Ltd*[7] an offence was proved under s. 14 of the Act where the firm displayed the standard notice that they were members of the Motor Agents Association and subscribed to its Code of Practice, but had in fact not complied with four clauses of the code. The Directive effectively upholds that decision.

Article 7 deals with misleading omissions. This is dealt with by the TDA in context, rather than explicitly. Exaggerated statements, which are not mere puffs, are clearly covered. *Sweeting* v. *Northern Upholstery*[8] is a clear prices example of an omission, where a generally advertised price for a suite in fact covered only a single colour. However, the Directive is wider since it includes a positive requirement to give information. Information mandatory under EU legislation is included, but there

---

6   (1992) 157 J.P. 323.

7   Noted (1981) 89 M.R. 91.

8   (1982) 90 M.R. 206.

appears to be a requirement to state the main characteristics of the product, the name and address of the seller and any other terms which differ from the norm.

Annex 1 of the Directive contains a series of things which are to be regarded as unfair in all circumstances. Most of these would currently be covered by the TDA or other legislation, but a few are new or would be borderline under the Act.

Bait and bait and switch are specifically included. As already noted this is dubious under the TDA.

Falsely stating that the product will only be available for a limited time is covered. It is doubtful if this is covered by the TDA at present.

False claims relating to the personal security of the consumer if he does not purchase the product. This is a breach of the Code of Advertising Practice, but would not amount to an offence under the TDA.

Pyramid selling schemes are banned completely. This appears to be much wider than the limited ban under the Fair Trading Act 1973. The TDA did not touch this.

Claims that the trader is about to cease trading or move premises where this is untrue. At last, we have a move to ban the permanent closing down sale. Section 14 of the TDA did not touch this. The courts refused to extend the word 'facility' to include what Woolf J. described, in *Westminster City Council* v. *Ray Alan (Manshops) Ltd*,[9] as 'shopping facilities'. Thus, the Divisional Court held that to advertise a 'closing down sale' when one is not closing down is not a statement as to a facility within s. 14.

Claims that a product is able to facilitate winning in a game of chance. Presumably this is limited to games were there is no element of skill whatsoever. Horace Batchelor would turn in his grave otherwise. There were no prosecutions of this nature under the TDA to my knowledge, and it is doubtful if the Act was wide enough to catch it.

Falsely claiming that a product is able to cure illness, dysfunction or malformation. Again this would be a breach of specific legislation, for example the Cancer Act, and the Code of Advertising Practice. Whilst it might come under fitness for purpose, it is doubtful if the TDA covered this. It is unclear how wide this prohibition is. Many advertisements for plastic surgery come close to this, since they are often misleading as to what may be achieved.

One area which is not covered by the Directive is false statements about 'accommodation'. This is explicitly covered by the TDA in s. 14 and indeed most of the prosecutions under that section have been about holiday accommodation. It is unclear whether the Directive intended to cover this aspect of consumer protection. Under EU legislation there are the provisions on package holidays, which are not really intended to deal with falsehood, but nothing more specific. It may be that this area falls outside the intention of the Directive and therefore s. 14 would not need to be repealed to this extent. It would, however, have to be amended to narrow the ambit of the section and, hopefully, this would include sorting out the unholy mess left by *Wings Ltd* v. *Ellis*.[10] If this is not the case and s. 14 has to go as a whole then it will leave a major gap in the coverage.

---

9   [1982] 1 All E.R. 771.
10   [1984] 3 All E.R. 577.

It should be stressed that the Directive is much wider than the TDA and goes on to cover many matters which the TDA was never designed to cover. These are not dealt with here. The main concern of this paper was to discover whether there were circumstances where a repeal of the TDA would lessen the coverage given by the Act. This brief review, which represents no more than work in progress, suggests that there are no major areas of the TDA that are not covered other than holidays.

15 (Mis)adventures of the Consumer in the Auction Room

Brian W. Harvey

1. The Glamour of the Auction Room

The sort of auction that one sees on television news bulletins involves a bejewelled company of bidders and tricoteuses of all nationalities, an auctioneer with a cut-glass accent and a cavernous, chandeliered room in London, Geneva or New York. We wait with baited breath the resolution between two or more members of the assembled company. Who will outbid the competition for a Renoir or Van Gogh or some other rare and valuable artefact, probably for a record price? When the lot in question is won, it is all rather a mystery how that happened since no one in the audience has apparently twitched an eyebrow, let alone *spoken* a word!

2. The Reality

But usually reality is less glamorous. There are about 300 auction firms throughout the UK, selling about 75,000 lots a week of which about 60,000 are actually sold. Lots vary from miscellaneous household clutter (some of which, no doubt, infringes the various EU-inspired safety regulations which are now legion) to motor vehicles (about 2.5 million per annum) plant and machinery, livestock, second-hand life insurance policies, fine art (where Sotheby's New York recently got £56 million for Picasso's *Garcon à la Pipe*), antiquarian books, postage stamps, musical instruments and so on). (The Internet is now being used as an adjunct to the traditional auction as well as a 'cheap and cheerful' standalone alternative, for example eBay, but, since the auction activities of eBay fanatics, by definition, take place online rather than in the auction room and raise many difficult, almost unexplored, points of their own, which lie outside our present enquiry, its existence will have to be noted and left.)

Traditional auction activity, involving a public sale and a saleroom on a specific day, is important economically, not least because it offers about the only feasible way to translate goods, (including plant and machinery) into often desperately needed cash on or by a specific date. At the lower end, 'Police Property' sales, government surplus sales and sales by bailiffs under distress warrants (or their close equivalents) take place throughout Europe, often pursuant to court orders, and explain why many continental auctioneers are primarily state or court employees or licensees, with a limited role and, perhaps, why the continental drafting of laws affecting auctions in European Directives, when they are remembered at all, is so deficient. The UK has similar statutory auction jurisdictions but does not licence or supervise auctioneers – anyone can set up as one with the minimum of formalities.

3. Some Fundamentals

It is important to understand some fundamental points about auctions before they can be effectively dealt with by modern consumer protection legislation, should that be desired. Some would say that the law governing them is really just an extension of the law of agency plus contract. The seller is the principal and the auctioneer his agent, employed by the seller to effect a sale to the highest bidder. This involves, finally, a contract between seller and buyer, out of which the auctioneer then drops, a mere 'conduit pipe'. Indeed, this over-simplified position statement is often a good starting point which litigators overlook at their peril, usually by suing the auctioneer rather than the apparently invisible seller, though both may in fact be liable under different heads, the one in contract and the other in tort, as will be mentioned later. But the picture is really a good deal more complicated even than that.

4. Seller, Buyers and Dealers

The *seller* can be a trader reducing stock, a private collector or a representative of a deceased estate or a trust; and the buyer a dealer planning to resell, a collector or an investor or someone buying for other non-business or trading purposes. Auctioneers all encourage members of the public to attend and the astute private buyer can certainly acquire second-hand goods at a fraction of their retail price, but with no guarantee of quality. Buying a pig in a poke may give you a bargain or you may have made an imprudent purchase. The dealer-seller gives you willy-nilly a much safer quality guaranteed product – so much may depend on how much you know about pigs.

Generally, all buyers of any experience accept that all is fair in love, war and auctions and expect no particular legal advantages. Auctioneers invariably supply 'viewing days' when the offerings can be carefully inspected and, if desired, individual condition reports obtained, and high and low estimates are given and usually published in the catalogue. Thereafter, if a buyer is of a nervous disposition, active participation in auctions should be avoided; otherwise no one can really complain if they pay too much or buy inadvisably.

It is surprising that all this activity is primarily governed by one section, s. 57 of the Sale of Goods Act 1979, stemming from the original 1893 Act unchanged.

5. Auctioneers' Responsibilities to Clients and Buyers

Before anyone rushes in to become an unregulated auctioneer, it is as well to remember that, in addition to his primary duties to his client, the seller, (for example not negligently to miss 'sleepers' consigned by uninformed clients), the auctioneer may also owe duties to a successful buyer, breach of which may entitle the buyer to claim damages. We saw a dramatic example of this recently in a case involving the sale, to a Canadian newspaper heiress, of the 'Houghton' porphyry vases for

£1.75 million – *Thomson* v. *Christies*[1] – where the issues were really two: were the two highly decorative vases materially misdescribed and misdated by Christie's (that is, were they sophisticated nineteenth-century copies) and, if so, were Christie's in breach of a duty of care (under the *Hedley Byrne*[2] tort principle) to the buyer, an enthusiastic and wealthy heiress, whose specific interest and custom had been exceptionally sedulously fostered by the auction house.

Most of the judicial and forensic effort here went into an analysis of the expert evidence as to whether the vases were genuine or copies. The case is unsatisfactory from the academic point of view because many of the interesting points – for example the validity of Christie's exemption clauses, and the position of the aristocratic owner (Lord Cholmondeley), who was arguably ultimately responsible for any misdescription or misrepresentation through his agents, the auctioneers, were untested. This was mainly owing to the lapse of time between sale and writ (more than six years). In the end Christie's won, the Court of Appeal taking the view that they had not materially misdescribed the goods since inevitably when and by whom they were made were matters of opinion – and expert opinion, though it clearly differed, supported, on the whole, Christie's attribution. So, provided reasonable care was taken in the circumstances, and in this type of case, this would presumably include getting reputable expert opinions justifying the catalogue description before the catalogue is finalized, there is no breach of a duty of care. The point whether this duty extended in the same way to *all* bidders, sedulously cultivated or not, was left rather open.

The auctioneer may also be liable in contract to a mere bidder if, as in the fairly recent case of *Barry* v. *Davies*,[3] the auctioneer advertises a sale or a particular lot to be 'without reserve' and then refuses to knock a relevant lot down to the highest bidder on the ground that this would have been too sacrificial a price. The case raised complex points of contract law left unresolved for almost 150 years. This breach of a 'collateral contractual offer' cost the over-conscientious auctioneer here over £27,000 in damages. The case also seems to confirm, that finding a collateral contract, and consequential consideration, is another way of binding auctioneer to bidders generally.

6. The Importance of Conditions of Business

So it looks as though the lot of an auctioneer may not always be a very happy one. What can be done to protect his own position? In fact nearly all these and other commonly arising problems, such as the auctioneer's nightmare of negligently failing to recognize a seller's consignment as a valuable article and allowing it to be bought as a 'sleeper' - see *Luxmoore-May* v. *Messenger-May Baverstock*,[4] – can either be eliminated or at least mitigated by well-drawn Conditions of Consignment (Seller to Auctioneer) and Conditions of Sale (Auctioneer to Buyer and other bidders) plus

---

1   [2004] All E.R. (D) 267.
2   *Hedley Byrne & Co. Ltd* v. *Heller & Partners Ltd* [1964] A.C. 465.
3   [2000] 1 W.L.R. 1962.
4   [1990] 1 All E.R. 1067.

an efficient insurance policy! These standard form Conditions are in fact absolutely vital to the governance of the auction sale and are often documents of considerable complexity.

7. Who is the 'Weaker Party'?

Now, having persuaded you, I hope, that the law of auctions is considerably more complicated than some would like to think, looking at the position from the consumer law reformer's perspective, the first question that ought to be asked is – 'who is the consumer in this scenario?' It is tempting to identify the buyer, because it is the buyer who is generally the consumer in relevant non-auction contracts of sale or supply of goods and it is to buyers that the law generally offers additional protection in respect of unfair contract terms.

Imagine, then, Auntie Sally who is widowed and owns an antique grandfather clock surplus to her requirements, particularly as it stopped in sympathy, 'never to go again', when her husband, Uncle Walter, died a few years back. She, therefore, consigns it to Sellem & Company the local auctioneers (established 1796), knowing nothing about it herself, but being delighted to learn that it was a good eighteenth-century clock in a mahogany case estimated at £1000–£1500 with a non-declared reserve (that is, the least acceptable price) of £700. Bill, an antique dealer, attends the auction and by suppressing the bidding of others interested by forming a 'ring' with his non-bidding colleagues, and having ascertained that the clock would cost little to restore, is the highest bidder at £700 exactly, plus, of course, buyers' premium! He later retails it, duly restored, for £2,800 (four times what he paid for it).

8. The Seller as Consumer

So, put another way, the question is this – when Adam delved and Eve span, who was then the gentleman? Or, who in our scenario is the consumer needing protection against roguish traders – the weaker party? Aunt Sally of course, but she is a seller, not a buyer of goods. But she is also in fact a consumer (and buyer) of the auctioneer's services.

9. The Buyer's Position

To add further to the complexities, no variety of buyer, even a private one like Miss Thomson, is to be regarded as 'dealing as consumer' for the purposes of the Unfair Contract Terms Act 1977 (UCTA) if he or she buys, at a public auction, 'second-hand' goods (UCTA s. 12, as dizzily amended by the EU-derived Sale and Supply of Goods to Consumers Regulations 2002[5]). In these circumstances, (that is, in 99 per cent of cases), buyers are not 'consumers' and the auctioneer is, therefore, free to exempt the seller from any statutory obligations arising under ss 13 and 14 of the

---

5   S.I. 2002/3045.

Sale of Goods Act 1979,[6] subject only to the requirement of reasonableness as laid down by s. 6 of UCTA (but apparently never formally tested in reported auctions litigation).

Whilst we may shed no tears for Dealer Bill, Aunt Sally gets no special protection either – her interests lie quite outside the remedial consumer legislation mentioned, but the question is – should the auctioneer be able to exempt himself effectively from possible negligence liability to her, subject only to the fall-back 'reasonableness test' applicable to the small-print exemption clauses in contracts between two businessmen under UCTA, s. 3 and still untested in the auction context authoritatively; or from an action based on his own material misdescription? And what about the pernicious 'ring'? It is surely highly desirable that, if protection is to be afforded to anyone in the saleroom, the Aunt Sallies of this world be properly looked after. It should be as sure as we can make it, that they are not fraudulently exploited by (in particular) hard-bitten dealers or (happily uncommonly) dishonest or negligent and unregulated auctioneers.

10. In Marches the Office of Fair Trading

The most recent important development is that the Office of Fair Trading (OFT) feels obliged, by virtue of Regulations 10 and 12 of the EU-derived Unfair Terms in Consumer Contracts Regulations 1999,[7] (UTCCR) when in receipt of a relevant complaint, to threaten to apply for an injunction against auctioneers or their professional bodies to suppress what it considers to be 'unfair' terms used or recommended; and also to disallow phraseology deemed to be impenetrable legal jargon, (and thus 'unfair'), in standard Conditions of Sale. The Regulations in question, we may note in passing, only apply to contracts involving a *consumer*, and say nothing specific about auction contracts involving buyers at a public auction. These are, therefore, deemed to be lumped in with the rest. A consumer is defined in these Regulations, in effect, as a private non-trading individual, but is a very rare bird in the auction room *for UCTA purposes*, even if a non-trader, as we have seen. Miss Thomson, for instance, would be a 'consumer' for purposes of the 1999 Regulations but a non-consumer for purposes of UCTA and therefore wide open to the 'reasonable' exemption clauses that are permitted (and try explaining that to an indignant client). In fact, an auctioneer will never know until, at the earliest, a successful bid is made whether the buyer is 'private' or 'trade', and the firm's conditions must therefore deal with either contingency.

At present, the OFT scrutinizes a number of auctioneers' printed conditions, about which they may receive a 'complaint', unless the complaint is deemed frivolous or vexatious. There is no 'clearance' procedure whereby a firm, or a professional association, can get its proposed contractual documentation approved in advance,

---

6   Implied terms of correspondence with description, satisfactory quality and fitness for purpose.

7   S.I. 1999/2083.

however *bona fide* it may be. All depends on someone first 'complaining', often, in practice, a local Trading Standards Officer![8]

Now this jurisdiction can be used admirably and should be applauded by all consumer lawyers when used to adjust, for example, standard form contracts offering 'warranties' of doubtful value to private buyers from second-hand car dealers. But auction Conditions are not of that ilk. Furthermore, the invitation in the Regulations to the OFT to crusade against 'legal jargon' in contracts can lead the two sides into arcane arguments as to, for example, the intelligibility of the word 'indemnity' to the ordinary person. The actual lay user of the Conditions in practice seems to be accorded the intelligence of a Caliban.

Instead, why not make it clear to the auctioneering profession generally what the OFT regards as acceptable in the way of, say, exemption clauses affecting private buyers, and what would be regarded as unfair, always depending ultimately on an injunctive court order? Auction contracts do not necessarily conform to the seller = dealer and buyer = consumer stereotype, as I have tried to show. Quite often the transaction is essentially business-to-business. The 'consumer' is then not remotely involved, but the documentation has to deal with *both* forms of status. It is not unreasonable to suggest that the OFT ought now to give the profession the benefit of its experience in negotiating with some major auction houses on their conditions.

As things stand at present, the OFT's processes can take a considerable time, certainly over a year, during which uncertainty prevails – never a good thing in commercial dealings. We might remind ourselves in passing that this power, for the OFT to obtain an injunction, applies in respect of a 'person' using suspect terms, is extended, in practice, also to any trade or professional body (such as the Royal Institution of Chartered Surveyors) which appears to be using or recommending use of an unfair term 'drawn up for general use in contracts concluded with consumers' (UTCCR, Regulation 10).

11. The Law Commission

The truth is that the ramshackle and predominantly Victorian structure of the law of auctions certainly needs remedial treatment. The Law Commission has being doing sterling work in rationalising the UK's confusing legislation on unfair contract terms,[9] but is understandably reluctant to take on a wider responsibility as to auctions, with all the prior consultation that any proposed reform would take, without a specific slot being made for it by the government. They have no recommendations as to the reform of auctions law, though the expression of it, as regards exemption clauses, has been improved. Briefly, then, what are the main items on the more radical reformist's agenda?

---

8   See OFT *Annual Report and Resource Accounts 2003-04*, 2004 H.C.P. 739.
9   See Law Com. No. 292, (2005).

12. Reforming the Law – Descriptions

On express and implied terms and exemption clauses there is a strong case for forbidding any attempted exemption from liability for misdescription under s. 13 of the Sale of Goods Act 1979 or otherwise. At present, the courts look to see whether there has been a breach of a general duty of care owed by auctioneers to buyers in respect of specific descriptions (as was alleged in the *Thomson* case) or a breach of a specific 'genuineness' anti-forgery guarantee often found in their General Conditions. But in an auction sale this should then be like Sale of Goods Act 1979 s. 12 (right to sell) which cannot be excluded in sale transactions at all. Accurate descriptions are at the core of the working of the auction contract and can vary according to choice from the extremely laconic to the luxuriant, so the auctioneer has little to fear if he plays his cards sensibly (as most do). Descriptions involving attributions remain matters of opinion but, if the opinion is one no reasonably careful auctioneer could hold, the shadow of the Trade Descriptions Act 1968 hangs over him in any case (and always has, contrary to belief in some quarters). Furthermore, auctioneers should take the *sole* civil law responsibility for their catalogue or written descriptions – it is no use relying on owners to be accurate and well informed about their chattels, or even knowledgeable about provenance, as any viewer of the Antiques Roadshow will appreciate. (Deliberate fraud by owners would of course remain a criminal offence.)

13. Reforming Quality Conditions and Exemption Clauses

On the other hand, the implied conditions for fitness for purpose and satisfactory quality should *never* apply in an auction sale. After all, if Aunt Sally had sold privately, (not being in business as an antique dealer), she would not give any such guarantee of quality, since s. 14 of the Sale of Goods Act 1979 only applies, by its own terms, to sales in the course of a business. (Auction sales are presently usually caught because s. 14(5) applies the quality guarantees to sales made by *agents*, unless it is made clear to the buyer that the principal/seller is private, (for example 'property of Lord Cholmondeley'– but this is uncommon in auction sales.) Nor does Aunt Sally pretend to know anything about the workings of grandfather clocks. Section 14 should, therefore, simply be excluded from operation in auction sales.

14. Codes of Practice

That leaves a number of other problems which are probably most practicably solved by a code of practice. For instance, it is axiomatic in agency law that agents must not make secret profits, but where an auctioneer delays payment to sellers and gathers significant interest on clients' money without accounting for it, this is objectionable. Clients' money should be kept separate from that of the auctioneer's firm – as is required by statute for estate agents, solicitors and so on – and any significant interest earned pending payment out should be accounted for.

Leaving commission bids with the auctioneer also needs strict self-control by the auctioneer, as there is an obvious conflict of interest and the procedure is potentially abusive. Nevertheless, this is a very popular device with bidders of all sorts who cannot attend, and seems, on the whole, to work well, so far as an outside observer can tell. Whatever is ascertained to be best practice here needs promulgation.

15. Protecting the Seller - The 'Ring'

Aunt Sally, you will remember, suffered from the scourge of 'the ring'. Rings were outlawed as long ago as 1927[10] but the relevant criminal legislation is hardly ever enforced – there are only two reported cases since the Act was passed. There are clear distinctions between informal buyers' partnerships to pool resources and criminal conspiracies which defraud owners of a part of the economic value of their property.

Probably rings have to be accepted as inevitable. Provided the auctioneer manages to get plenty of competing bidders and adopts a realistic reserve, Aunt Sally's interests should be reasonably protected.

16. Protecting the Consumer Interest

Auctioneers have been defined as 'rag and bone men in Saville Row suits'. But in over 25 years of close inspection, I have only very rarely found strong evidence of serious dishonesty. Nevertheless, in modern times the consumer interest (in broad economic terms) is sovereign and the auction, great or small, is subjected to much exposure on television. Those having responsibility for them must not only be honest, knowledgeable and efficient, but must be *seen* to be so. I suggest that modest law reform along the following lines, in addition to the points I have just made, is desirable in the interests of users of auctioneers' services.

17. The OFT's Powers

In the rush to protect the consumer as buyer, the interests of the private seller as consumer of an economically important professional *service*, should not be overlooked. And specifically, the OFT's overweening powers to threaten applications for injunctions in respect of auctioneers' standard form contractual conditions should be modified, to enable the OFT to give clearance in advance of auctioneers' (or other comparable professionals') Terms and Conditions of Sale and Consignment, or at least promulgate a 'model' set of key conditions. The present EU-derived system which involves trying to pick auctioneers off aggressively one by one never achieves consistency; it is illogical, economically inefficient and, in my opinion, ultimately indefensible.

---

10   Auctions (Bidding Agreements) Act 1927.

18. Reform Needed to be by Statute

But the main reform here suggested must be by statute, since primary legislation is affected. As already indicated, simple legislation is needed to forbid auctioneers contracting out of the civil consequences of making material misdescriptions under s. 13 of the Sale of Goods Act 1979 and to make that Act's conditions of fitness and satisfactory quality under s. 14 inapplicable to the auction sale. This would solve 'at a stroke' problems of reasonableness or otherwise of exemption clauses in this area, since none would be needed. And any reform should not be by way of afterthought, tacked on at the last minute in (usually) EU legislation aimed primarily at something else! 'Last minute.com' has no place in serious law-making.

19. *Floreat 'Caveat Emptor'*

The auction room is perhaps the last surviving exemplar of where the *caveat emptor* principle can be seen to work, as even the law-makers of the EU have had to accept, – but it also often promises legitimate and exciting rewards to the knowledgeable buyer willing to take a risk, and prompt compensation to the seller who needs cash. Some regulation is needed in the interests of both lay sellers and lay buyers, both in their different ways 'consumers'. But let the hand on the tiller be light. The auction flourishes on the virtues of speed, simplicity and non-bureaucratic efficiency - and long may this unique institution flourish!

16 The 'Oily Rag' of Enforcement

Roland Rowell[1]

1. Changing the Face of Trading and Consumer Law

A Time Lord has 13 lives; Dr Who is apparently into his seventh metamorphosis. In comparison, trading and consumer law is far more subtle, changing its face with chameleon-like regularity. The forces at play here, some would have the general public believe, are almost demonic originating from within that almost mythical place – 'Brussels'. In reality had the UK not signed the European Treaty we would have struggled as a trading nation. It is now strange to think that the UK traded with the world using a national currency that had 240 sub-units to the £1. That we weighed our goods using 16 ounces to the pound, of which there were 14 to the stone, making a hundredweight of 112 pounds or, conversely, 8 stones. Going in the 'other direction', we had 7,000 grains to the pound avoirdupois, or 5760 to the pound troy. It seems, therefore, somewhat outlandish that the country who gave us the avoirdupois system later produced the metric system.

2. Who Drives 'Change'?

The main driver for changing the face of consumer law is the 'Brussels machine', which has already reached and passed the point set for harmonization of Community laws. Nevertheless, there are still attempts, often generated by trade or national interests, by the Commission to make a challenge on the ground of a 'barrier to trade'. The persistent attack on hallmarking is an example of how the machine can be used to remove something that may not 'fit' the Brussels inspired market. Compulsory hallmarking of items of precious metal, required by some Member States, is an example. Even though such requirements operated as a consumer protection measure the challenge was that such regimes constituted a barrier to trade. The attack was intense and prolonged, being beaten back only after a spirited defence from those Member States who operate a hallmarking system. Brussels argued that Member States who did not currently require such marking were disadvantaged in their dealings in precious metals. In a situation such as this, it can be more cost effective to level up those lagging behind to a higher standard of protection rather than lowering them to the lowest common denominator.

---

1   JP, BA, LLM, LLD, FCMI, MTSI. A personal contribution to a symposium to mark the retirement from full-time academia of Deborah Parry MBE, Senior Lecturer, a colleague and co-editor, with Professor Brian Harvey, of Butterworths Trading and Consumer Law.

The argument was spurious due to the complexities involved in keeping precious metals untainted together with the 800 year pedigree that hallmarking in the UK has fostered. But the Eurocrats missed the point as under voluntary, *international* provisions,[2] the protection of hallmarking is widespread both within and beyond Europe. In European terms, however, the UK and other relevant Member States had already moved toward harmonization and unification of a far wider range of quality standards and the application of a set of unified European hallmarks following a judgment of the European Court.[3] Though the battle was won it is likely that a further attack will follow at some point under a different bureaucratic disguise.

3. The Example of Consumer Credit

Changing the face of consumer law could have no better example than consumer credit. The ground breaking Consumer Credit Act 1974 was borne out of the heady consumer-driven fervour of the 1970s.

Combining a framework of civil rights and criminal sanctions with an overseeing and licensing role under the, then brand new, Office of Fair Trading, it placed consumers on an entirely different footing from that previously enjoyed by credit providers. Things have also moved on. The Consumer Credit Act 2006 arrived on the statute book only days ago, the culmination of a wide-ranging programme of reform, outlined in the 2003 Consumer Credit White Paper. This Act forms the most wide-ranging overhaul of consumer credit legislation since 1974, boosting protection for consumers at a time when all forms of new communication are able to subject potential borrowers to 'easy' credit. Against the background of spiralling consumer indebtedness, coupled to a low threshold of understanding of credit, particularly on the part of young people, the reforms and the potential for redress when borrowing money are vitally important. By introducing major changes to the licensing of consumer credit businesses and with new powers, enforcers of the legislation should prove to be a vital force for changing the face of trading and consumer law in this increasingly important area of law.

4. Non-Statutory Forces for Change

Changes to law and practice are not brought about solely through legislation. The enforcers and the regulators have important roles to play. Credit laws provide good examples. Section 46(1) of the Consumer Credit Act 1974 addresses false or misleading advertisements: A garage advertised a car with zero percent finance, whilst implementing a lower sum on a part-exchange than would have been the case if the buyer had been a cash purchaser. It was held that an additional hidden charge for credit had been made, the Divisional Court rejecting the argument that there were two separate contracts involved, one for the sale of the customer's old

---

2   Convention on the Control and Marking of Articles of Precious Metals done at Vienna, 15 November 1972.

3   *Houtwipper* (Case C–293/93) [1994] ECR 1–4249.

car and one for the new car. The total amount payable on credit terms exceeded the cash price by more than £300[4] and was therefore misleading and illegal. That case arose out of ordinary dealings and was dealt with through the normal enforcement channels of a trading standards department. It is unlikely that many of the smaller trading standards departments that now exist would have in-house the knowledge, the determination and the support of their local authority to mount such an appeal. That is a significant loss to driving change.

The Office of Fair Trading has an overseeing role and exercised it in relation to the thorny issue of uniformity of credit card liabilities arising under s. 75 of the Consumer Credit Act 1974. Here liability exists for the creditor under a debtor-creditor-supplier agreement for breaches of the credit agreement made by the supplier – joint liability. The credit industry stance has consistently been that the section did not apply to transactions entered into outside the United Kingdom. The Court of Appeal has now held, overturning the decision of the High Court, that such transactions are caught by s. 75.[5] Though it is likely that even higher judicial authority will be brought to bear in this case, the stance of the Office of Fair Trading is a right one that, win or lose, will change the face of consumer law. It is right that there is a robust champion of consumer rights that is prepared to take on disproportionate industry interests. Should the case go to the House of Lords and, in the event of a finding for the industry, the OFT will not have 'lost'. They will have identified a serious failing in consumer credit law and Parliament will have to consider whether primary legislation is needed to remedy the situation. That robust and incisive action from a major regulator sends out a clear signal that they are operating from a position of strength.

5. Identifying 'Trading and Consumer Law'

(i) What is it?

The question then arises: 'what is trading and consumer law?' An enquirer will generally range from interested consumers through to lawyers working in what they regard as well defined 'traditional' areas of the law. Identifying 'trading and consumer law' is therefore rather more difficult to pin down – yet it affects everyone through each day of their lives. The old adage 'we are weighed on birth and measured at death' still holds good today. A glance at the 'sources stable' just within the Lexis-Nexis-Butterworths trading and consumer law series reveals: *O'Keefe – The Law of Weights and Measures*; *Butterworths Law of Food & Drugs*; Goode, *Consumer Credit Law and Practice*; Miller, *Product Liability and Safety*; and *Butterworths Trading and Consumer Law*. This collect discloses 23 large volumes containing the law and practice in this area identifying a quite discrete, yet wide ranging body of law. It differs from many other branches of law in the level of its technical content.

---

4   *Metsoja* v. *H. Norman Pitt & Co. Ltd* [1989] 153 JP 485, Q.B.D.
5   *Office of Fair Trading* v. *Lloyds TSB Bank plc. and Others* [2006] EWCA Civ 268.

(ii) Is it a New Area?

A popular misconception is that trading and consumer law is a recent phenomenon. Civilizations have acted over the millennia to protect their people from being cheated by those who would deal short weight and measure, adulterate their foodstuffs and water their beers wines and spirits. In 1215 uniformity was established in Magna Carta: 'Let there be one measure of wine throughout our Kingdom, and one measure for ale, and one measure for corn, and one width for cloth ... . Let it be the same with measures as with weights.' Gold and silver plate were protected by the use of assaying and hallmarking from as early as statutes of 1238 and 1300.

(iii) What is the Nature of the Law?

The law is an amalgam of both a public and private nature. The Trade Descriptions Act 1968 is a well-known public statute whilst the Sale of Goods Act 1979 is regarded as the cornerstone of a consumer's 'rights' in contractual situations. They are both 'consumer laws'. Consumer product safety provides a better example being controlled both by the public law under the General Product Safety Regulations 2005,[6] whilst a statutory tort of 'product liability' exists within s. 2 of the Consumer Protection Act 1987. The latter provides a useful private law remedy for damages arising where 'damage' is caused by a 'defect' in a product. The consequence is that the criteria for constituting on the one hand a criminal offence and, on the other, evidence of a civil wrong can arise from the same facts. A further feature of product safety laws is their emergence as European Directives, harmonizing two distinct, and yet essentially parallel, legal worlds. They serve also to underscore the importance of European harmonization in this field.

In short 'trading and consumer laws' regulate all matters relating to quantity; food and non-food quality and safety; description; price; credit; and contractual aspects of the goods and services consumed by a consumer. It can range from labelling requirements for a product to serious product counterfeiting activities that carry a maximum term of imprisonment for ten years.

(iv)The Trading Standards 'Service'

The role of the 'local weights and measures authority'   The trading standards service exits for one reason only – to carry out the duty placed by Parliament on the 'local weights and measures authority' to enforce a whole raft of legislation. This route has emerged due to the fact that inspectors of weights and measures have had a wider role during the last two centuries. The duty placed upon such authorities is mandatory. Failure to carry out that duty will be *ultra vires* the statute. There can sometimes be an overseeing role carried out by a specified body, but not in all cases. The somewhat arcane wording 'local weights and measures authority' is therefore long overdue for an overhaul. It indicates the 'peg' from which to hang the enforcement of trading and consumer laws. In what seems to be a 'first' a draftsperson has taken the adventurous

---

6   S.I. 2005/1803.

step of placing a duty to enforce upon the 'Trading Standards Authority'.[7] Whilst the London Olympic Games and Paralympic Games Act 2006 has broken the mould, that bold cross-heading then reverts to type by stating: 'A local weights and measures authority may enforce within their area the provisions of s. 8.'

A Service in reality? Though trading standards is referred to generally as a 'Service', it is no such thing. There is in fact little cohesion or coherency for within the UK there are 203 totally independent trading standards authorities. These are an eclectic mix of English Shire Counties, District Councils, Unitary Authorities, London Boroughs, Scottish Authorities, Welsh Authorities and Northern Ireland. An interesting feature is that the West Yorkshire Trading Standards Service is jointly run by a joint board of all the District Councils in that region which demonstrates that smaller local authorities can cooperate and join together to provide a more effective and efficient service across their combined geographic area. If plans to remove County Councils go ahead, the result will be yet a further increase in the number of ever-smaller units. As such the trading standards 'Service' is a myth. Government commitment to the formation of a new Consumer and Trading Standards Agency (CTSA) based upon the Hampton proposals was not strangled at birth it was simply aborted in the Chancellor's pre-budget speech last autumn.

Coordination? Since the elimination of the CTSA, there has been a greater focus on the Local Authorities Coordinators of Regulatory Services (LACORS). This organization came into being at the end of the 1970s. It was established on the back of the National Metrological Coordinating Unit, (NMCU) a statutory body created under the Weights and Measures Act 1979. Its establishment arose from the outcry from business that they were swamped by repetitive and suffocating demands from ill-informed officials in the trading standards service. There had to be a clearer way through and the concept of the Home Authority was devised and trialled in the West Midlands County Trading Standards Department. Using the NMCU secretariat LACOTS, as it was originally known, acted as an interface between business and the enforcers. Serviced by specialists from trading standards departments and a certain amount of in-house expertise it has disseminated advice to officers. This can be useful and decisions are generally respected. However, as a semi-formal body funded by local authorities, it cannot direct trading standards authorities operations and has no powers. It is hard to think of any other Service that operates in such a manner. Coordination is one thing – discharging a local authority's statutory duties is set upon an entirely different plane.

What is 'enforcement'? Enforcement of criminal law entails three things – prevention, detection and prosecution. In order to achieve those goals resources are need. The human aspects require officers to be trained and qualified in their respective disciplines. The scope of trading and consumer law is so wide that specialists having a narrower brief, but working at an enhanced level, are required. Smaller departments cannot meet that. This results in trading standards departments

---

7   London Olympic Games and Paralympic Games Act 2006, Schedule 3, para. 12.

being unable to fulfil the statutory duty placed on the local authority. In some areas, often those with high densities of population that carry the problems that go with it, they have the added difficulty of attracting and retaining staff.

Powers   Though the need for specialist equipment is a feature running throughout trading and consumer laws the basic 'tools' are the powers granted by Parliament. Without powers an officer would find it impossible to carry out the duties required. Though officers should be trained and qualified in what they do they must focus fully on what Parliament has granted them. Any deviation could result in the actions being *ultra vires* and an action for damages being mounted at a later date.

6. Using the 'Oily Rag'

Trading and consumer laws are therefore like a large and complex machine. Enforcing it is a combination of skills, training and experience that not only starts up the machine but also then makes it run efficiently. The skilled officer will know when to oil the moving parts and keep it tended with an 'oily rag'. Therefore, 'Oily Rag' is good; neglect is seizure and disaster. Yet officers are increasingly failing to use the oily rag approach. Whether that is because they are less well trained or experienced is unclear. But in such situations, their supervisors should be able to bring strength in depth. Prosecutions need to be taken against the background of the Enforcement Concordat and the Code for Crown Prosecutors. Just because a complaint has been made does not necessarily mean prosecution is inevitable – yet this seems to be the usual result in spite of the Court of Appeal in *Adaway*[8] making it plain that the Department's own prosecution procedure should be applied as well as those other procedures applying more generally.

7. Initiatives

There are few trading standards authorities that are able to plan and mount initiatives that address pressing problems. Loan sharking is one area and it is pleasing to see Birmingham Trading Standards having success using a special squad. Two successful high profile exercises have been concluded – but Birmingham is the largest local authority in the country. Such exercises should be routine. Loan sharking can occur in smaller towns and expertise needs to be spread about in particular the relationship with the police who are vital in executing the warrants, arresting and processing the suspects. The health and safety of the trading standards team is of paramount importance. Their expertise comes into play in assessing the evidence seized and working with the Crown Prosecution Service to ensure charges are brought that meet the seriousness of the activity. The new agency 'National IP Crime Group' coordinated by the Patent Office conducted its first operation, named 'Operation Dawn', at Wembley market on the weekends of 27 November 2005 to 18 December 2005. The National IP Crime Group is made up of enforcement authorities, including

---

8   *R.* v. *Adaway* (2004) 168 J.P., 645, C.A.

the police, HM Revenue and Customs, Trading Standards, Government agencies and a wide spectrum of private industry bodies. The results are awaited with interest.

North Yorkshire Trading Standards, a 'beacon' authority having decades of high quality enforcement work in their favour together with highly respected process and prosecution abilities, took the initiative recently to tackle the rather difficult area of itinerant builders. The Department secured heavy prison sentences in a particularly high profile case. Further, the Department has invested in the lengthy training of two senior officers in the Proceeds of Crime Act 2002. These skills have been brought to bear in pursuing the gains made by the accused in these cases. These are major initiatives that should be emulated elsewhere as a standard of good practice.

8. Office of Fair Trading

The OFT is a resurgent organization revitalized by the Enterprise Act 2002 and its restructuring. The appointment of a Director of Consumer Regulation Enforcement has taken the Office onto a different level. That has led to identifying and tackling national scams and European scams with closer collaboration with the USA. The success of the *Duchesne* case,[9] the first cross-border judgment, upheld by the Brussels Court of Appeal was ground breaking. Obtaining an injunction against the company in the commercial court in Belgium to stop the trader from making misleading prize notifications in connection with its home shopping catalogue business within the UK demonstrates what determination and innovation – backed up by good law can achieve. This is 'Oily Rag' with aplomb.

9. Conclusion

There is no trading standards 'Service' in the United Kingdom. There is localized, fragmented enforcement of relevant legislation. Whilst there remains pockets of excellence many departments are now so small, working at such a low level in the structure of their authority, that their contribution is minimal. There is lack of commitment from local and national politicians to remedy the situation as evidenced by the CTSA – a bird that never hatched. And perhaps that demonstrates that changing the face of trading and consumer law *enforcement* is unlikely to happen in the next ten years.

---

9   See *OFT Annual Report and Resource Accounts 2004–05*, 2005 H.C.P. 171, p. 32.

17   UK and EU Consumer Law[1]

Christian Twigg-Flesner[2]

1. Introduction

In choosing the topic for my presentation, I had to think about an aspect of consumer law in respect of which it is possible to identify significant changes over the last three decades. The landscape of consumer law has altered in so many different ways since 1975 that it was rather difficult to identify one specific topic. But there was one element of consumer law which saw the light of day in 1975 – which was, of course, the year that Deborah Parry started her academic career – and that is the influence of what is now the European Union on domestic consumer laws. What I intend to do today is to give a potted overview of the evolution of European consumer law and to consider how it has influenced UK consumer protection. Deborah herself wrote on this topic in 2000 in a collection of essays in honour of another distinguished consumer lawyer, Professor Brian Harvey.[3] Her views expressed in that paper and my own on this topic do not always converge, but we both share the view that EU legislation requires critical scrutiny in the same way as domestic legislation does, and that some of the European measures have not been massively useful for consumers in the UK.

2. The Early Days

My starting point is, of course, the *European Economic Community's Preliminary Programme for a Consumer Protection and Information Policy*.[4] Behind this rather grand title lie the origins of the EU's activities in the field of consumer protection. The purpose of this *Programme* was to put down a marker, to identify consumer protection as a component of the development of the common market – now, of course, known as the internal market. This document set out five basic consumer rights, which were:

---

1   The text of this chapter has not been changed from its format as a conference presentation (save for minor corrections to grammar and style). I have, however, added references to the footnotes.
2   Senior Lecturer in Private Law, University of Hull.
3   D. Parry, 'The impact of the European Community on the UK Consumer' in F. Meisel and P. Cook (eds), *Property and Protection: Essays in Honour of Brian W. Harvey*, (Oxford, 2000) p. 223.
4   (1975) OJ C92/1.

(a) the protection of health and safety
(b) the protection of economic interests
(c) redress
(d) information and education;
(e) representation.

The difficulty, however, was that there appeared to be no obvious basis on which the then EEC could develop a coherent legislative consumer protection programme, and very little of significance happened in the immediate aftermath of this programme. But the adoption of this programme was undoubtedly of immense symbolic value, because it confirmed that consumer protection was an area on which the EEC should focus some of its activities.

It would, of course, be wrong to say that the consumer had no place in the legislative framework of the EEC at that time. The consumer interest had, for example, been recognized in the context of the competition law provisions of the Treaty[5] as one of the matters to take into consideration in assessing whether a particular agreement, or practice, would fall foul of the prohibition on anti-competitive conduct. Moreover, in the context of the four freedoms, it had been accepted that some restrictions on the free movement of goods could be justified in the interest of consumer protection.[6] But these developments fell far short of anything resembling a coherent approach to consumer protection.

The 1975 resolution was therefore significant, because consumer protection was firmly put on the agenda. Nevertheless, it had to be acknowledged then that this objective could only be pursued within the confines of existing specific consumer policies. Consumer law could not develop as an independent policy at that time. Initial progress therefore was restricted to the rather more technical aspects of the law, such as legislation on foodstuffs or motor vehicles.[7]

3. Constitutional Matters

The development of a coherent European consumer policy was hampered by the absence of a suitable basis in the European Treaty, and any potential action in this field raised questions of 'competence'. A brief diversion into the realms of European Constitutional law at this point will explain why this is so significant: the European Community (as one should properly call the main law-making association at the European level) does not have unrestricted powers to adopt legislation. Its powers are limited to those areas which are mentioned in the Treaty itself. Moreover, even where a particular policy area is within the scope of the EC's legislative competence, the EC can only act where the particular objective could not be achieved at the domestic level (the principle known as 'subsidiarity'), and to the extent that the EC does have the power to act, it can do no more than is necessary to pursue a particular objective (proportionality). What is therefore needed for the EC to act is a legal basis

---

5   Articles 81 and 82 EC.
6   Case 120/78 *Cassis de Dijon* [1979] ECR 649.
7   S. Weatherill, *EU Consumer Law and Policy*, 2nd edn, (Cheltenham, 2005) p. 7.

in the Treaty. Without an appropriate legal basis, any binding act adopted is open to challenge before the European court on the grounds of invalidity.

Why is this important? Well, in the absence of a provision in the Treaty which gives the EC the power to legislate in the field of consumer protection, a desire to formulate a consumer protection policy that would go beyond the merely aspirational could not produce specific results.

So how could the EC adopt binding measures in the field of consumer protection? In the absence of a specific legal basis, the EC had to develop its activities in this area on a different legal basis, and the one that was eventually chosen was what is now Article 94, dealing with the 'approximation of [measures] as directly affect the establishment or functioning of the common market'. The argument for adopting legislation against the background of promoting the common, or internal, market is that consumers may be deterred by the differences in legislation from participating in cross-border shopping. If the laws of the Member States were sufficiently proximate, then consumers would feel more confident about shopping in another country. This, in turn, would benefit the internal market as a whole. This is not the time to subject this particular argument to detailed scrutiny – Thomas Wilhelmsson has done so in the *Journal of Consumer Policy*[8] – but it does seem rather unconvincing. It seems much more likely that consumers will be deterred from shopping across borders because of the practical difficulties of resolving problems, for example if goods bought from, say, Estonia fail to work once taken back to the UK. Nevertheless, the 'consumer confidence' argument is a major factor in the EU's consumer law.

Article 94 became the basis on which the Directive on Doorstep Selling was adopted in 1985. It was implemented in the Consumer Protection (Cancellation of Contracts Concluded Away from Business Premises) Regulations 1987.[9]

As far as consumer law is concerned, this was hardly an earth-shattering measure. Its main achievement has been to introduce a seven-day cancellation period for contracts concluded 'on the doorstep' when a trader had called without previous invitation by the consumer. The potency of this Directive has perhaps only come to light in more recent times: if a consumer has not been informed about his right of cancellation, then the start of the cancellation period is postponed until the point when this information is provided. The European Court of Justice (ECJ) has confirmed that there is no limitation as to time in such circumstances.[10] In subsequent directives, such as those on timeshare and distance selling, a longstop period of three months was introduced, but this does not apply in this context.

The rather simplistic reason for adopting this Directive was that the legislation on contracts concluded away from business premises in the Member States differed and that such differences would affect the operation of the common market. There can be little doubt that this reasoning would not stand up to scrutiny today and doubts

---

8   T. Wilhelmsson, 'The abuse of the "confident consumer" as a justification for EC Consumer Law', *Journal of Consumer Policy*, 27 (2004): 317.

9   S.I. 1987/2117, as amended.

10   Case C–481/99 *Heininger and another* v. *Bayerische Hypo und Vereinsbank AG* [2001] ECR I–9945; Case C–350/03 *Schulte and another* v. *Deutsche Bausparkasse Badenia AG* [2005] ECR I–9215.

about the EC's competence to adopt this particular directive have been expressed repeatedly. Nevertheless, at the time, all the countries which were then Member States of the EC agreed, and so the Directive has assumed the symbolic status of being among the first consumer protection measures.

4. Minimum Harmonization

One of the characteristics of this Directive – and of many other consumer related directives – is the existence of a so-called 'minimum harmonization' clause. The upshot of this provision is that whilst all the Member States are required to ensure that their legislation provides *at least* the level of consumer protection mandated by a directive, they are free to exceed this level of protection in their domestic law. Thus, if a country such as the UK already has legislation in a field on which a directive is adopted subsequently, and that directive falls short of the level of protection demanded by the domestic law, then there is no need to amend domestic law to lower the prevailing level of protection. There can be little doubt that the existence of such clauses has helped to bring about agreement on particular measures, because those Member States with a higher level of protection than that required by a particular directive were not obliged to reduce this.

The drawback to such minimum harmonization clauses is that there may still be a degree of divergence in the laws of the Member States, which might have the effect of undermining the aim of increasing consumer confidence.

In the context of doorstep selling, the minimum harmonization nature has enabled the UK to strengthen subsequently the protection introduced as a result of having to implement this Directive. Moreover, following a 'super-complaint' to the OFT, the DTI has consulted on further changes to the domestic rules to increase the protection offered to consumers. The fact that this directive is a minimum harmonization measure means that raising the level of consumer protection is permissible.[11]

A second measure adopted in 1985 was the Directive on Product Liability, implemented in Part I of the Consumer Protection Act 1987. This introduced strict producer liability for injury or damage caused by defective goods. A consumer who has been injured needs to show that the product was defective and that it caused the injury, or damage – but, unlike the tort of negligence, it is not necessary to establish that there exists a duty of care which has been breached by the producer. However, a number of defences in favour of the producer exist, and it has been suggested that these may undermine the strict-liability nature of this Directive. The most notorious of these defences is the so-called development risks defence. This enables a producer to escape liability if he can show that 'the state of scientific and technical knowledge at the time when he put the product into circulation was not such as to enable the existence of the defect to be discovered.'[12] The UK famously implemented this provision by altering the wording slightly, resulting in enforcement proceedings

---

11   See the two proposals announced in September 2006: DTI, *Doorstep Selling and Cold-calling* [http://www.dti.gov.uk/files/file33819.pdf].

12   Article 7(e).

before the European Court of Justice.[13] The UK prevailed at the time, primarily because there had been no reported cases on the application of the defence at that time. However, any hopes that the ECJ might offer clear guidance on the nature of the defence were dashed, and it remains uncertain where exactly the threshold lies for determining whether the state-of-the-art was such as to enable a defect to be discovered.

In her evaluation of the Directive in 2000, Deborah Parry queried whether 'the Directive [could] preclude the UK from, unilaterally, providing greater protection to its consumers at some future time'.[14] At that time, it was a reasonable question to ask. Since then, the ECJ has made it clear that such a possibility has been precluded, because the Directive does not contain a minimum harmonization clause and must therefore be regarded as not giving the Member States any freedom to depart from it, save in respect of the particular options included in that Directive.[15] This was a case against France. One of the issues related to the French implementation of Article 3(3) of the Directive, which specifies that each supplier of the product in question shall be treated as its producer where the producer/importer cannot be identified, unless the supplier provides the consumer with details of the producer or importer. In French law, however, a supplier would be liable in the same way as a producer, rather than only in the limited circumstances envisaged in Article 3(3). The ECJ held that France had been wrong to do so, because Article 3(3) had pre-empted France's right to impose greater liability on a supplier than under the Directive.

This ruling produced a rather unusual response from the Member States in that the Council of the European Union adopted a resolution in which it expressed its disagreement with the ECJ's position and called for the amendment of the Directive to allow Member States the right to choose whether to put the liability of a supplier on the same footing as that of producers under the Directive.[16] So far, this amendment has not been made.[17] Somewhat ironically, France was recently found guilty of having failed adequately to amend its law in response to the earlier judgment, and is currently subject to periodic penalty payments.[18] Deborah Parry's concerns about the restrictions this Directive has imposed not only on the UK legislator, but also those in all the other Member States, were therefore well-founded.

But let us return to the evolution of EU consumer policy. In 1987, with the entry into force of the Single European Act, a second legal basis was introduced into the EC Treaty. This is Article 95, which is the basis for measures 'which have as their object the establishing and functioning of the internal market'. Legislation adopted on the basis of this provision does not require the agreement of all the Member States, but only a qualified majority. Moreover, Article 95(3) acknowledges the role

---

13   C–300/95 *Commission* v. *UK* [1997] ECR I–2649.

14   Parry, at p. 232.

15   C–52/00 *Commission* v. *France* [2002] ECR I–3827.

16   Council Resolution 2003/C 26/02 of 19 December 2002, (2003) OJ C26/2, 4 February 2003.

17   The Commission has since announced, in its third report on the Directive, that it does not intend to put forward any proposals for amending the Directive (COM(2006) 496 final).

18   C–177/04 *Commission* v. *France* [2006] ECR I–2461.

of Article 95 as a basis for the adoption of legislation for the protection of consumers by mandating that 'the Commission, in proposals concerning ... consumer protection, will take as a base a high level of protection'. Article 95 soon displaced Article 94 as the basis for the adoption of consumer measures, and subsequent directives, such as the Package Travel Directive and the Directive on Unfair Contract Terms, were both adopted on this basis.

The scope of the EC's powers under this provision were clarified, and arguably curtailed, by the judgment of the ECJ in its '*Tobacco Advertising*' judgment in 2000.[19] This case is among the most significant decisions in EC law, certainly within the last decade or so. It would take too long to explore it in its full depth, and I shall confine myself to setting out its general relevance. In essence, the ECJ clarified when the EC may utilize Article 95 as a legal basis for the adoption of legislation. The Article does not give the Community a general power to regulate the internal market. A measure adopted on the basis of this provision must *genuinely* have as its object the improvement of the conditions for the establishment and functioning of the internal market (paragraph 84 of the judgment). Moreover, the ECJ held that a mere difference in domestic laws and the abstract risk of obstacles to the Treaty freedoms was insufficient to justify action on this basis. So the burden is on the Commission, as the initiator of legislation, to demonstrate that there is an appreciable obstacle which is causing real problems, before action in this area can be justified.

Although the full impact of this judgment is yet to be determined, it is clear that the adoption of consumer protection legislation on the basis of Article 95 will have to be based on much more substantial evidence of a real obstacle to the smooth functioning of the internal market. It remains to be seen whether this will bring about a major shift in the focus of EC action in this field, although we may get a clearer picture of the future of EC consumer law later on this year – more on this shortly.

Perhaps one further milestone in the evolution of EU consumer law was the introduction into the EC Treaty of a separate Article on consumer protection. This occurred in 1993 as a result of the Maastricht Treaty. Article 153, as it is now, makes consumer protection one of the policy areas of the EC, and puts this area of law on a firmer footing in the EC framework. According to Article 153(3), the EC may adopt legislation through:

(a) measures adopted pursuant to Article 95 in the context of the completion of the internal market; and
(b) specific action which supports and supplements the policy pursued by the Member States to protect the health, safety and economic interests of consumers and to provide adequate information to consumers.

So rather than making consumer protection an independent objective of the Treaty, it remains largely linked to the internal market, and measures will generally only be adopted to the extent that this would be necessary under Article 95 – and as

---

19   C–376/98 *Germany* v. *Parliament and Council (Tobacco Advertising)* [2000] ECR I–8419.

I have just explained, the threshold for this provision has been raised by the ECJ in *Tobacco Advertising*.

There is, however, a separate legal basis for 'specific action' supporting and supplementing Member States' policy on various matters. This has, however, only been utilized once for a directive on Unit Pricing (98/6/EC).

During the 1990s, the bulk of the current EC consumer law directives were adopted. Starting with a Directive on Package Travel, there were then directives on Timeshare and Distance Selling. All three directives have in common that they largely attempt to improve the position of consumers at the time of concluding a contract, rather than to regulate the substance of the particular transaction. These directives are also responsible for the rise in pre-contractual information obligations, which are now under review by the European Commission.

However, the EC has not limited itself to legislation in this area. In 1993, it adopted a directive on unfair terms in consumer contracts, requiring Member States to introduce a legal framework to combat the use of unfair terms in all pre-drafted consumer contracts. In the UK, the Directive is currently implemented in the Unfair Terms in Consumer Contracts Regulations 1999.[20] There can be little doubt as to its success here in the UK – before the Directive was adopted, the controls over unfair contract terms were rather limited. There were the common law control mechanisms, and the provisions in the somewhat grandly titled Unfair Contract Terms Act 1977 only assisted to control certain types of contract terms. The Regulations introduced the first comprehensive framework for dealing with unfair terms in consumer contracts. And the Directive introduced a whole new policing mechanism into domestic law: the power given to the Office of Fair Trading, and other bodies, to take action to prevent the continued use of unfair terms. Although there have been a dozen or so cases before the English courts (other than the county courts) where the Regulations were applied, it has been through the activities of the Office of Fair Trading that the real value of the Regulations can be seen. A quick glance at the Unfair Contract Terms Bulletins shows how powerful a tool these Regulations are.

One negative point about these Regulations is, however, that they were adopted to run alongside the Unfair Contract Terms Act 1977, with no thought given to dealing with the overlaps between these two measures. The Law Commission has proposed a consolidation of the two schemes, and I hope that the government will find the time to enact the Law Commission's proposals.[21]

A second measure dealing with substantive law is the Directive on Consumer Sales and Associated Guarantees, which – as some of you will know – has been of particular interest to me in recent years. This Directive introduces a general requirement that goods must be in conformity with the contract of sale – what we would describe as 'complying with the implied terms as to description, quality and fitness for purpose' – and makes available the remedies of repair, replacement, price reduction and rescission. It also makes voluntary guarantees legally enforceable.

---

20   S.I. 1999/2083.

21   Law Commission, *Unfair Terms in Contracts*, Report LC292; available at http://www. lawcom.gov.uk/docs/lc292.pdf.

This Directive was implemented by amending the Sale of Goods Act 1979 and related legislation, to balance the desire to give full effect to the Directive whilst retaining existing higher levels of protection. Although I welcome this approach as a good way of giving effect to directives, it has, unfortunately, not been particularly successful in this instance. It seems to me that the task that faced the government in trying to introduce the rules from the Directive into the existing legal framework was rather more complex than anyone could have imagined, and in its current form, the legislation is barely of satisfactory quality. I would hope that the Law Commission might be asked to consider improving the law in this area sooner rather than later.

Since the turn of the millennium, we have seen further legislation in the consumer protection field – a directive on distance selling of financial services, and an improved directive on Product Safety. We will hear more about Product Safety shortly, which I why I have not commented on this so far.[22]

Since then, the European Commission has announced its intention to move away from the minimum harmonization approach. Its first major piece of legislation is the Directive on Unfair Commercial Practices, adopted last year.[23] We have, of course, already heard how this might affect one long-standing area of domestic law.[24] The Department of Trade and Industry is now in the process of drafting the legislation for implementing the Directive. It seems likely that the landscape of domestic consumer law will change more than it has ever done before in response to an EC harmonization directive. Whether it will be for the better, we will only be able to tell with experience.

5. Impact on UK Consumer Law

I have already referred to several UK implementing measures adopted in response to an EC Directive. I would just like to say a few words about the challenges which the UK faces whenever it has to implement a consumer law directive.

A directive need not be transposed verbatim into domestic law. Sometimes, doing so could cause more problems that would be solved by following the language as closely as possible. However, the advantage of a 'copy and paste' approach to implementation is that the risk of 'gold-plating' is minimized. 'Gold-plating' is a phrase used to describe the situation where domestic law exceeds the demands of a particular directive. The Government is committed not to 'gold-plate' when implementing directives, although that policy is not applied where existing higher levels of consumer protection are at risk. Businesses are generally keen to avoid any form of 'gold-plating'. Attempts to make legislation 'fit' with existing domestic law may sometimes have the effect of 'gold-plating', albeit in a minor form. So at a technical level, there are challenges.

The post-implementation challenges are often also underestimated. It is not just the fact that there have to be domestic rules that mirror a directive, but the courts and

---

22   Professor Geraint Howells spoke separately at this conference about Product Safety.
23   Directive 2005/29/EC.
24   See Richard Bragg's paper on the effect of the UCPD on the Trade Descriptions Act 1968.

enforcement authorities must apply and interpret these rules in a 'European' fashion. That is easier where specific legislation has been adopted to implement a Directive. However, where existing domestic law is used, this is more complicated, because earlier case law might no longer be applicable. To give just one example: is the 'reasonable person' in the satisfactory quality test in the Sale of Goods Act 1979 now to be taken to be the 'European average consumer' when the legislation is applied in the consumer context? The Sale of Goods Act 1979 is the domestic legislation 'implementing' the Consumer Sales Directive.

The impact on domestic law is therefore quite often rather difficult to estimate.

6. The Future

This potted history of EU consumer law and its relationship with domestic law has shown that, whilst European consumer law had undoubtedly contributed noticeable to raising the level of consumer protection across the EU, its impact on UK consumer law has been mixed. In some instances, such as doorstep and distance selling, it resulted in legislation that might not otherwise have appeared, or at least not appeared as soon as it did. In the field of unfair contract terms, the 1999 Regulations (and their 1994 predecessor) have been a major success. On the other hand, whether the changes made in 2002 as a result of the Consumer Sales Directive have been of real benefit to consumers remains to be seen.

There have been several aspects which I have not had time to cover, but some of my colleagues this morning and this afternoon will deal with areas in which the European influence is strong.

Further major developments are underway. The Commission has commissioned research into the implementation of eight consumer law directives in all the 25 EU Member States. This project, the so-called 'consumer *acquis* review' is nearing completion and will give a comprehensive picture of how the Member States have transposed these directives, and to what extent differences remain in the areas subject to EC legislation. Such differences may be the result of the use of minimum harmonization clauses as much as the defects in the implementation in a particular Member State. The objective is then to review all these directives and consider whether these need to be improved. Some changes, particularly to increase overall coherence and consistency between these measures, are undoubtedly necessary. Variations in definitions, terminology, and even substantive rules such as different cancellation periods could be removed. But there is a further element to this *acquis* review, and that is the question whether the minimum harmonization clauses in these directives should be abandoned in favour of a total/maximum harmonization approach. This would considerably reduce the freedom of the member states to act; in particular, it would no longer be permissible to adopt legislation which would provide a level of protection higher than that demanded by a particular directive.

This review is linked to a wider project, which is the creation of a Common Frame of Reference on European Contract Law. This will initially be used to modernize the consumer *acquis*, and, hopefully, produce more coherent legislation. It will also, unfortunately, require fresh implementing legislation in the Member States, and it might exacerbate existing problems, rather than removing them.

In the medium-term, we might see a so-called 'optional instrument' on contract law, that is, an entirely separate system of contract law applicable to cross-border transactions. Although there has been talk of covering all types of contract, there are some who are calling for a limited 'cross-border consumer code'. Whether this will happen remains to be seen. What is clear, however, is that the European influence on consumer law is strong, and continues to grow.

Deborah Parry concluded that:

> ... the European influence has benefited consumers in the UK, but at some financial cost to those consumers and to manufacturers, retailers and enforcement agencies. For the future, care must be taken to ensure that European involvement does not stifle or delay national developments, place unwarranted burdens on business nor provide benefits only for well-informed and economically strong consumers.[25]

Six years later, these conclusions remain sound.

---

25   Parry, p. 244.

Part 3: Current Developments

18 Doorstep Selling

Richard Bragg[1]

In September 2006, the Department of Trade and Industry (DTI) published the Government's response to the public consultation on Doorstep Selling and Cold-Calling.

This document has an interesting history. It started in 2002, when the National Association of Citizens Advice Bureaux (since renamed 'Citizens Advice') published the results of research into doorstep selling and the consequent reported problems. After the passing of the Enterprise Act 2002, this report was presented in the form of a 'super-complaint' under s. 11 of that Act to the Office of Fair Trading (OFT). The OFT decided to act on the complaint. It undertook a wide study and published a report 'Doorstep Selling: A Report on the Market Study' in May 2004.

The OFT's Report recommended seven options for government consideration and recommended a full public consultation. This has been carried out by the DTI, which has now published a report and a Regulatory Impact assessment.

There is no doubt that there is a background of consumer problems associated with doorstep selling. Citizens Advice found much abuse. This ranged from bad workmanship and gross overcharging of required jobs, through high pressure selling and failure to advise of the cooling-off period, to downright fraud in pretending a job needed doing when it did not. Several firms associated with doorstep selling regularly appear on television consumer programmes. Trading Standards Departments also are clear that there is a problem. Many of the difficulties seem to relate to building and general household work. What makes this worse is that many of the traders involved seem to target the elderly, who may fail to appreciate modern selling techniques, and assume honesty.

It is worth noting that during the consultation period one tabloid newspaper ran a campaign to get readers to send in a coupon pushing one of the more extreme options. Some 2,500 did so, which suggests there is public concern.

Against this backdrop, it is perhaps a shame that the Government response is rather a damp squib, offering minimal change, although there are some good reasons for this. Of the seven options offered by the OFT, only two are thought worthy of legislation, with a third proposed for industry self-regulation.

The major reason given by the DTI for the minimal response is the adoption, in 2005, and proposed implementation, in 2007, of the Unfair Commercial Practices Directive (UCPD). The difficulty with this Directive is that it is a maximum harmonization Directive. Thus, Member States should not have legislation that goes beyond the requirements of the Directive. The author has always taken a robust view of this requirement, but the DTI seems to interpret it extremely widely. It seems to

---

1   Senior Lecturer, University of Manchester.

take the view that any legislation on which the Directive even remotely impacts should be repealed and no new legislation should be considered. A view might be taken that some legislation does not go beyond the Directive, but merely interprets it or gives it a content. This is not the DTI's view, which seems to be that it is solely a matter for the courts to interpret the Directive and to decide what falls within its purview and what does not. As the DTI takes the view that three of the OFT's proposals are within the ambit of the UCPD, its immediate reaction is that legislation is not possible or practical and has thus rejected those options.

The four rejected options will be dealt with first. The first two are essentially the same as they require a delay in (a) delivering goods or doing work and (b) taking money until the seven-day cooling off period under the Consumer Protection (Cancellation of Contracts Concluded Away From Business Premises) Regulations 1987[2] has expired. The DTI comments that these options received the least support, but their own figures only show that they attracted the least responses, with a healthy majority in favour and minimal opposition. What is perhaps more telling is the comment that 'it would put the direct selling sector at a significant disadvantage'. It is clear that the DTI is favouring trading interests over consumers. The argument that any legislation would need exemptions 'which would create another loophole open to exploitation by rogue traders and bogus callers' is a very weak one. However, it is true that the UCPD will impact on some of the abuses in this area and, if rigorously enforced, will prevent some of the abuses.

The third rejected option was to remove the requirement that, if the contract was performed so that the goods are delivered or the work commenced within the seven-day period, the consumer has to pay the cost of collecting the goods or undoing the work done if the contract is subsequently cancelled. It seems the trade took the view that this option was too much in favour of the consumer. The DTI seems worried that it could be abused by 'cowboy customers'. The rejection of this option ignores the fact that it is the rogue traders who are geared up to take most advantage of it.

The fourth rejected option was a general ban on cold-calling to offer property services with possible exceptions. The consultation evoked a newspaper campaign with 2,573 coupons in support sent in, but if these are discounted, the other support amounted to six, with 82 in opposition. This level of opposition is far greater than for any of the other options. The DTI concludes that the option would be 'a disproportionate response to the problem'. Again, it notes that the provisions of the UCPD would help in this area. It is difficult to see why this should be regarded as a disproportionate response. Legislation has been in place, for several hundred years, which prevents persons calling door-to-door in order to sell goods unless they have the necessary 'Peddlers Licence' from the local authority. Although these are relatively easy to obtain, they do form some control on cold-callers. Of course, they do not apply to mere canvassers or the providers of services and this major loophole allows most of the problematic callers to be legal. Again, it is clears that traders' interests are being preferred to those of consumers.

The options that the DTI will proceed with are those which are the most limited. Currently the 1987 Regulations only grant a cooling-off period where the visit is

---

2   S.I. 1987/2117.

unsolicited. It is often difficult to decide whether a visit is in fact unsolicited and whether the Regulations apply. The DTI has, therefore, accepted the proposal to extend the cooling-off period to solicited visits as well as unsolicited ones. Thus, the period will apply to all contracts signed off trade premises. Whilst, as the report notes, this may remove the incentive to solicit visits, this is not necessarily a bad thing. It may remove the increasing nuisance of telephone calls soliciting visits. It may mean, however, that more unsolicited doorstep calls may occur. Primary legislation will be needed for this option to be enacted. According to the DTI Report, this will be done at 'the earliest opportunity'.

The second option to be carried forward is to require notice of the cancellation period to be contained in the contract itself. At present, this can be done by giving the consumer a separate document. The requirement will be that the notice is 'of no less significance than the rest of the contract' rather than a particular prominence. There are to be no consumer credit style red boxes. This option will be introduced by secondary legislation. The cost to traders is minimal, as all it will require is redrafted contract documents.

The third option to be accepted is a general requirement for greater transparency on prices and a greater willingness to give written quotations. The DTI's view is that this should be done by extending the criteria needed to obtain an OFT accreditation for a code of practice. In itself, this is a positive move. However, it is limited. Rogues are rarely members of trade associations, and whilst it may limit the activities of rogue salesmen working for otherwise legitimate businesses, it will have only a very limited impact.

Overall, the outcome of this 'super-complaint' is very disappointing. The arguments used to deny action on the majority of the suggestions are often weak and there is clear pandering to the trading lobby. The reality is that most consumers would prefer it if no traders came to their door, legitimate or not. Whilst there was never much chance of a general ban on doorstep selling and canvassing; it is felt that the rejection of any real controls is an opportunity missed to enact some real consumer protection.

19 Restitution of Contributions to So-called 'Gift Communities' in Germany

André Janssen[1]

1. Introduction

In recent years, the German courts[2] have been increasingly faced with claims for restitution of payments to so-called 'gift communities' ('Schenkkreise'),[3] which have become widespread in Germany and whose economic damage is enormous. They mostly involve four-level hierarchical snowball or pyramid structures.[4] The

---

1   Assistant Professor, University of Münster, Germany. The author gratefully acknowledges the invaluable assistance of David Kraft in translating this essay from German.

2   Compare, *inter alia*, (in chronological order): *Amtsgericht (in this sense small claims court) Gütersloh*, judgment of 21 November 2003 – 14 C553/03; *Amtsgericht Cologne*, judgment of 18 February 2004 – 112 C551/03 (available at: www.nrwe.de); *Amtsgericht Springe*, judgment of 19 March 2004 – 4 C101/04 (III); *Landgericht (district court) Bielefeld*, judgment of 21 April 2004 – 22 S300/03 (available at www.nrwe.de), Berufung (appeal on points of fact and law) against the decision of the *Amtsgericht Gütersloh*; *Amtsgericht Altenkirchen*, judgment of 27 May 2004 – 71 C28/04; *Landgericht Bonn, NJW-RR (Neue Juristische Wochenschrift – Rechtsprechungsreport)* 2005, 490; *Landgericht Freiburg*, NJW-RR 2005, 491; *Oberlandesgericht (higher regional court) Cologne*, decision of 9 November 2004 – 24 U125/04 (available at: www.nrwe.de), decision according to § 522(1), second sentence ZPO (Zivilprozessordnung – Civil Procedure Rules) of *Landgericht Bonn*; *Oberlandesgericht Cologne, NJW (Neue Juristische Wochenschrift)* 2005, 3290; *Landgericht Bonn*, judgment of 23 June 2005 – 6 S220/04 (available at: www.nrwe.de).

3   These gift communities were regularly initiated as coffee mornings or as a kind of 'tupperware party'.

4   The problem of pyramid trading schemes which therefore invariably meant that new members would lose their money is not new and appeared a few years ago in the form of gaming schemes, such as for example as '*Life game*' (Oberlandesgericht Celle, *NJW* 1996, 2660), '*World-Trading-System*' (Bundesgerichtshof, *NJW* 1997, 2314) or computer system games '*Countdown 3000*' (Oberlandesgericht Bamberg, *NJW-RR* 2002, 1393). Their 'new guise' in systems entitled 'gift communities' particularly lure new participants with the notion that they are not part of a game, but rather should feel part of a special community (see on this point A. Goerth, 'Anmerkung zu OLG Köln,

members at the bottom level ('givers') pay contributions, which, depending on the individual scheme, can vary between €100 and €5,000, to members occupying the top level of the structure ('receivers'), who then drop out of the game.[5] The givers then move up a level, but for their own part must recruit new givers to constitute the level below them. This generally means that after each 'round' eight new givers must be found for each receiver. Thus, the number of new members to be recruited increases exponentially throughout the duration of the scheme. The ultimate consequence is that only the founders of these communities attain a guaranteed profit, whereas the subsequent members, by reason of the large number of new members to be recruited, barely have a realistic chance of making a profit themselves; rather, they inevitably lose their contributions.[6] A new member, who has already paid, can only maintain the (albeit merely theoretical) possibility of one day becoming a receiver himself, if he finds new victims.

In the cases which appeared before the German courts the victims, many of whom had subsequently grouped themselves together,[7] claimed restitution of the sums paid to the respective members above them in the pyramid structure. Some courts denied restitution of the contributions,[8] others, by contrast, allowed the victims' claims and thus enabled them to get their money back.[9] These contradictory judgments led to considerable legal uncertainty in Germany. This called for action by the Bundesgerichtshof (German Federal Supreme Court). In two identical judgments of 10 November 2005 the highest German civil court sided with the victims and allowed them to claim restitution of their money and thereby put an end to the conflict which had been smouldering for years.[10] Because of the significance of the judgments and the doctrinal issues they had to resolve, especially that of application of a bar on restitution where both parties are engaged in conduct which offends good morals according to § 817, second sentence BGB (Bürgerliches Gesetzbuch – German Civil Code), it is worth taking a closer look at the decisions and their reasoning.[11]

Urteil vom 6.5.2005, 20 U129/04', *VuR* (*Verbraucher und Recht*) 2006, 75 (75)).

5   On this problem area as a whole see the very informative documentary at www.mlm-beobachter.de/mlm/schenkkreise.htm and www.schenkkreise.org.

6   In this example 4,096 members would have to be recruited by the tenth round, and for the twentieth round this would total over 4 million. Compare, also S. Lorenz, 'Anmerkung zu BGH, Urteil vom 10 November 2005 – III ZR 72/05', *LMK* (*Lindenmaier-Möhring – Kommentierte BGH-Rechtsprechung*) 2006, Nr. 164413.

7   Such as for example the *Interessengemeinschaft der Schenkkreisgeschädigten (IGSG) (Syndicate of gift community claimants)*, founded in 2003.

8   Compare, for example, Landgericht Freiburg, *NJW-RR* 2005, 491 or Oberlandesgericht Cologne, *VuR* 2006, 73.

9   Compare, for example, Landgericht Bonn, *NJW-RR* 2005, 490.

10   Bundesgerichtshof, *NJW* 2006, 45.

11   See on this judgment also Lorenz, 'Anmerkung zu BGH, Urteil vom 10 November 2005 – III ZR 72/05'; M. Möller, 'Leistungskondiktion trotz beidseitiger Sittenwidrigkeit? – Die Einschränkung des § 817 S. 2 BGB durch den BGH', *NJW* 2006: 268; K. Schmidt, 'Anmerkung zu BGH, Urt. v. 10. November 2005 – III ZR 72/05', *JuS* (*Juristische Schulung*) 2006: 265.

2. The Cases Before the Bundesgerichtshof

The cases before the Bundesgerichtshof essentially corresponded to the illustration in the introduction. The claimants sought restitution of contributions paid to the defendants for the purpose of participation in a 'gift community'. The 'gift communities' were organised like a kind of pyramid. The members at the summit of the 'receiver community' received certain sums from the 'giver community' below them. Thereupon the 'receivers' dropped out of the game; those previously occupying 'giver' positions then took their place. This meant that enough participants then had to be found to constitute the new 'giver communities'. Their recruitment was the responsibility of the new members. In knowledge of this system, the claimants joined a 'giver community' and paid €1,250 to the defendants, who alongside others constituted the 'receiver community'. They wanted to remain in the game and later become 'receivers' themselves. It was only when this plan backfired that they demanded their money back from the 'receivers'. The subsequent claims were successful in all three instances.

3. Legal Assessment of the Decisions of the Bundesgerichtshof

(i) The Requirements of the Condictio Indebiti According to § 812(1), First Sentence, First Alternative BGB

In deciding the cases before it, the Bundesgerichtshof did not grapple with possible contractual claims from such a 'gaming arrangement', but proceeded directly from the principle of unjust enrichment, namely a *condictio indebiti* according to § 812(1), first sentence, first alternative BGB.[12] The requirement of this ground of restitution is that the defendant, by the performance of another, the claimant, has obtained something[13] without legal basis. That the defendants acquired ownership and possession of the money paid by the claimants as a result of the latter's performance[14] is unproblematic

---

12   § 812(1), first sentence BGB provides that: 'Anyone who obtains something by the performance of another or otherwise at his expense without legal basis is bound to make restitution to him.' Fittingly, the Bundesgerichtshof here did not consider a claim based on § 817, first sentence BGB, a *condictio ob turpem vel iniustam causam*. Its scope of application is very limited. The provision applies above all where the performance is received in circumstances forbidden by statute, without the causal transaction being void (such as for example acceptance of a benefit according to § 331(1) Strafgesetzbuch (Criminal Code), which does not affect the validity of the underlying gift). If, on the other hand, the causal transaction is void according to §§ 134 or 138 BGB, then § 812 BGB applies due to the absence of legal basis (compare Schmidt, 'Anmerkung zu BGH, Urt. v. 10 November 2005 – III ZR 72/05': 265; R. Schulze, *Handkommentar-BGB*, 4th edn, (Baden-Baden 2005), § 817 BGB para. 1).

13   'Something' in the law of unjust enrichment denotes any improvement in the recipient's pecuniary status (Schulze, § 812 BGB para. 3).

14   'Performance' in the law of unjust enrichment is defined as 'every conscious and purposeful addition to extraneous property' (compare Bundesgerichtshof, BGHZ 58, 188 or Bundesgerichtshof, *WM* (*Wertpapier-Mitteilungen*) 2002, 1560).

according to German law and therefore does not require any further discussion here. In respect of the requirements of the claim therefore, the Bundesgerichtshof only addressed in further detail the question of whether these performances occurred 'without legal basis'. The highest German civil court, in accordance with the wholly predominant view in case law[15] and literature,[16] proceeded on the basis that 'gift communities' were immoral snowball systems, and that the 'gaming contract' which constituted their basis was void as being contrary to good morals according to § 138(1) BGB.[17] The Bundesgerichtshof reasoned that the immoral character stemmed from the fact that '... the vast majority of participants – in contrast to the initiating "members", who (mostly) realise a guaranteed profit – necessarily did not make a profit, rather they merely lost their "contribution"' and that the "game" merely served to '...exploit gullible and inexperienced persons and persuade them to pay their "contribution" for the benefit of a few "members"'. Through this universally accepted immoral nature of such 'gift communities' and their consequent status as void the performances received by the defendants were without legal basis within the meaning of § 812(1), first sentence, first alternative BGB, so that each respective claimant had established a claim to restitution due to a *condictio indebiti*.

(ii) The Bar on Restitution According to § 817 Second Sentence BGB, Where Both Parties Are at Fault

This clearly established ground of restitution is also not excluded by § 762(1), second sentence BGB,[18] according to which anything given in the context of a bet or game cannot be recovered on the grounds that there was no obligation,[19] as also clarified

---

15   Compare, for example, Landgericht Freiburg, *NJW-RR* 2005, 491, Landgericht Bonn, *NJW-RR* 2005, 490; Oberlandesgericht Cologne, *VuR* 2006, 73.

16   Compare, for example, Lorenz, 'Anmerkung zu BGH, Urteil vom 10 November 2005 – III ZR 72/05'; Möller, 'Leistungskondiktion trotz beidseitiger Sittenwidrigkeit? – Die Einschränkung des § 817 S. 2 BGB durch den BGH'; Schmidt, 'Anmerkung zu BGH, Urt. v. 10. November 2005 – III ZR 72/05'.

17   § 138 BGB provides:
      (1) A legal transaction which offends good morals is void.
      (2) In particular, a legal transaction is void in which one party exploits the predicament, inexperience, lack of judgment or considerable weakness of will of another party, in order to cause pecuniary advantages to be promised or conferred onto him or onto a third party in exchange for a performance, whereby the pecuniary advantages are clearly disproportionate to the performance.

18   § 762 BGB provides:
      (1) No obligation is established by games and bets. Any performance pursuant to a game or bet may not be recovered on the basis that an obligation did not exist.
      (2) These provisions also apply to an agreement by which the losing party, for the purpose of meeting a gaming or betting debt, enters into an obligation towards the winning party, in particular an acknowledgment of debt.

19   The Bundesgerichtshof made no mention however of § 814 BGB. According to this provision, a performance made in pursuance of an obligation cannot be recovered inter alia if the performing party knew that he was not obliged to perform. However, as it turned out, this norm would probably not have been applicable anyway – it is not

by the Bundesgerichtshof in a few brief sentences. This provision only precludes recovery on the basis of § 762(1), first sentence BGB, that is by asserting that the stake was paid without a legal obligation to do so. If, however, the *causa* for the permission to retain the stake is defeated as void, such as by fraud, cheating or rescission, then a claim for restitution established on principles of unjust enrichment or tort cannot be precluded by § 761(1), second sentence BGB.[20] As the 'gaming contracts' in the present case were void according to § 138(1) BGB, then also the provision in § 762(1), second sentence BGB could not preclude restitution.

The clear emphasis of these judgments of the Bundesgerichtshof, other judgments[21] and comments in the legal literature[22] on the problem of 'gift communities' is the issue of the applicability of the bar to restitution where both parties are at fault according to § 817, second sentence BGB.[23] According to the wording of this provision there can be no restitution if both the party who has provided the performance as well as the party who received it were in breach of a statutory prohibition according to § 134 BGB[24] or acting contrary to good morals according to § 138 BGB.[25] This provision, which at first glance appears clear, is described by Karsten Schmidt[26] as 'one of the most puzzling and most discussed rules in the law of unjust enrichment'. The purpose of this rule has long been disputed: whereas it was previously regarded as

---

apparent that the claimants, at the time of performance, had *positive knowledge of the absence of obligation.* This includes, namely, not only knowledge of the facts which give rise to the absence of a legal obligation. Moreover, the performing party must also be aware of the legal situation to the extent that he knows he is not under any obligation. Even grossly negligent ignorance of the absence of a legal obligation does not lead to exclusion of the right to restitution (compare hereto, § 814 BGB para. 2; Schmidt, 'Anmerkung zu BGH, Urt. v. 10. November 2005 – III ZR 72/05': 266).

20   See on this point also Bundesgerichtshof, *NJW* 1962, 1671; Lorenz, 'Anmerkung zu BGH, Urteil vom 10 November 2005 - III ZR 72/05'; Schmidt, 'Anmerkung zu BGH, Urt. v. 10. November 2005 – III ZR 72/05': 266.

21   Compare, for example, Landgericht Freiburg, *NJW-RR* 2005, 491, Landgericht Bonn, *NJW-RR* 2005, 490; Oberlandesgericht Cologne, *VuR* 2006, 73.

22   Compare, for example, Lorenz, 'Anmerkung zu BGH, Urteil vom 10 November 2005 – III ZR 72/05'; Möller, 'Leistungskondiktion trotz beidseitiger Sittenwidrigkeit? – Die Einschränkung des § 817 S. 2 BGB durch den BGH'; Schmidt, 'Anmerkung zu BGH, Urt. v. 10. November 2005 – III ZR 72/05'.

23   § 817 BGB provides:
If the purpose of a performance was defined in such a way that by his acceptance the recipient violated a statutory prohibition or contravened good morals, the recipient is bound to provide restitution. Restitution is excluded if the performing party is also to blame for said violation or contravention, unless the performance consisted in the undertaking of an obligation; what has been performed in order to discharge such an obligation cannot be recovered.

24   § 134 BGB provides: 'A legal transaction which violates a statutory prohibition is void, unless a contrary intention appears from the statute.'

25   The only circumstance in which this does not apply is where the performance occurred to discharge an obligation (compare § 817, second sentence BGB).

26   Schmidt, 'Anmerkung zu BGH, Urt. v. 10 November 2005 – III ZR 72/05': 265.

establishing a form of civil punishment,[27] nowadays the main theory is of declining legal protection in the area of transactions contrary to good morals.[28] Whether the rule is at all sensible in terms of public policy is a subject of controversy,[29] but shall not and cannot be explored in further detail here.

The scope of application of § 817, second sentence BGB is extended in two respects (the so-called extension theory): First, the bar on restitution, contrary to the systematic relationship with § 817, first sentence BGB (*condictio ob turpem vel iniustam causam*) is also applicable to the 'general' right of restitution of § 812(1), first sentence, first alternative BGB (*condictio indebiti*). The Bundesgerichtshof, in both its judgments, does not explore this in any further detail, rather necessarily implies it. Second, *immorality solely on the part of the performing party* is sufficient for exclusion of restitution, which, however, due to the mutual fault of the parties, was of no significance here.[30]

This considerable extension of the scope of application did, however, once more prompt the need for limitations. Thus, it is also necessary (without the Bundesgerichtshof having to explicitly restate it due to the clarity of the facts),[31] in addition to an objective breach of statutory prohibition or good morals, that *the performing party was aware of the breach of statutory prohibition or immorality or at least tacitly acknowledged it*.[32] Courts have frequently attempted to circumvent the application of § 817, second sentence BGB in similar cases on the basis of this requirement, such as the Freiburg district court.[33] But even if this subjective component is fulfilled, this does not automatically result in immediate application of the bar on restitution according to § 817, second sentence BGB. Rather, as the Bundesgerichtshof already stated in a previous decision, § 817, second sentence BGB is 'in itself a rule foreign to civil law, which not seldom can lead to inequitable results', which is why 'pursuant to its purpose' it must be kept within certain limits.[34]

---

27   Reichsgericht, RGZ 105, 270 (271); Bundesgerichtshof, *NJW* 1983, 950. See hereto also the instructive comments in J. v. Staudinger/S. Lorenz, *Kommentar zum Bürgerlichen Gesetzbuch (§§ 812–822)*, (Berlin 1999), § 817 BGB para. 4; Schmidt, 'Anmerkung zu BGH, Urt. v. 10 November 2005 – III ZR 72/05': 265.

28   See hereto the instructive comments in Staudinger/Lorenz, § 817 BGB paras 4, 5; Schmidt, 'Anmerkung zu BGH, Urt. v. 10 November 2005 – III ZR 72/05': 265.

29   On the state of the controversy see Staudinger/Lorenz, § 817 BGB paras 4, 5; Schmidt, 'Anmerkung zu BGH, Urt. v. 10 November 2005 – III ZR 72/05': 265; Schulze, § 817 BGB para. 5.

30   On the extension theory see Staudinger/Lorenz, § 817 BGB para. 10; Lorenz, 'Anmerkung zu BGH, Urteil vom 10 November 2005 - III ZR 72/05'; Schulze, § 817 BGB para. 6.

31   The claimants in the present case at least tacitly acknowledged the immoral nature of such 'gift communities'.

32   Compare on this point Bundesgerichtshof, *NJW* 1994, 187 (188); H.G. Bamberger/H. Roth/C. Wendehorst, *Kommentar zum BGB*, (Munich 2003), § 817 BGB para. 16; Schulze, § 817 BGB para. 8.

33   Landgericht Freiburg, *NJW-RR* 2005, 492 (493).

34   Bundesgerichtshof, *NJW* 1980, 452. See thereto also Staudinger/Lorenz, § 817 BGB para. 10; Lorenz, 'Anmerkung zu BGH, Urteil vom 10 November 2005 – III ZR 72/05'.

Thus, for example in relation to remuneration for 'cash-in-hand' work – *inter alia* by reference to the principle of good faith according to § 242 BGB[35] – the court concluded that the bar on restitution in § 817, second sentence BGB was not applicable.[36] In the present case the court did not indirectly support its reasoning upon § 242 BGB, but rather directly upon the protective purpose of the sanction of nullity – in this case § 138(1) BGB – but likewise arrived at the conclusion that § 817, second sentence BGB is inapplicable. Fittingly, the court clarified that a bar on restitution would run contrary to the protective purpose of § 138(1) BGB, as the 'game' would not thereby be sanctioned at all. Indeed, a bar on restitution would be a de-facto legalisation and an invitation to the initiators of such 'games' to continue, if they could retain money obtained by immoral means – in spite of the nullity of the agreement constituting the basis of the 'game'. Just as with the remuneration of cash-in-hand work, the primary consideration is that the application of § 817, second sentence BGB should not and cannot lead to perpetuation of a state of affairs contrary to good morals or promote immoral conduct.[37] In this respect, the Bundesgerichtshof developed its case law consistently.

These decisions of the Bundesgerichtshof on the issue of 'gift communities' clearly show that the bar on restitution of § 817, second sentence BGB is based on a theory of general deterrence not wholly unfamiliar to German civil law,[38] which offers considerably more possibilities for just and soundly reasoned individual outcomes than the theory of declining legal protection.[39] In these terms, the decisions are ultimately sound: The members of so-called 'gift communities' cannot rely on being allowed to retain contributions, rather they must reckon with a claim for restitution at any time, thus removing a major incentive for participation in such schemes.[40] In the outcome, the approach of the Bundesgerichtshof founds a new exception to the clearly formulated norm of § 817, second sentence BGB, in that it interpreted it in a way which at least partly diverges from its express wording. Whilst this may be regrettable, it cannot always be avoided in a modern society.[41]

---

35   § 242 BGB provides: 'The obligor is bound to effect performance according to the requirements of good faith, taking into account accepted practice.'

36   The outcome was that the 'cash-in-hand' worker, despite the *Gesetz zur Bekämpfung von Schwarzarbeit* (Act to Combat Illicit Work), was entitled to compensation for the value of his work that accrued to the employer without legal basis, according to § 818(1), first sentence, first alternative BGB – admittedly no more than had been agreed, even in a void manner, and with a certain reduction to reflect the fact that he was not exposed to any claims with regard to conformity.

37   With an expressly different conclusion (no application of § 817, second sentence BGB) Oberlandesgericht Cologne, *VuR* 2006, 73.

38   See thereto, for example, also §§ 241 a, 661 a BGB.

39   In express agreement in this respect also Lorenz, 'Anmerkung zu BGH, Urteil vom 10 November 2005 – III ZR 72/05'.

40   In express agreement also Lorenz, 'Anmerkung zu BGH, Urteil vom 10 November 2005 – III ZR 72/05'; Möller, 'Leistungskondiktion trotz beidseitiger Sittenwidrigkeit? – Die Einschränkung des § 817 S. 2 BGB durch den BGH': 268. Probably also Goerth, 'Anmerkung zu OLG Köln, Urteil vom 6.5.2005, 20 U 129/04': 77.

41   Tentatively tending in this direction also Möller, 'Leistungskondiktion trotz beidseitiger

Moreover, case law and literature in Germany for their part are required to contribute to a responsible development of the law, by identifying the underlying theories in a manner which reflects the needs of legal practice, beyond the requirements of the individual case.[42]

4. Outlook

It can be assumed that the lower courts will follow the lead of the Bundesgerichtshof. Thus, in future, cases of immoral snowball systems in contravention of good morals will not, in relation to § 817, second sentence BGB, be won or lost on the issue of whether the participant paid his contribution in knowledge of the immoral nature of the scheme or at least tacitly acknowledged it. In respect of the so-called 'gift communities' the highest German civil court has paved the way for a general right of restitution of contributions. This is a welcome result. Time will tell though, whether injured parties will be in a position to successfully assert their claims and effectively realise them, as guilty parties regularly change their place of residence to escape the reach of the courts. The Bundesgerichtshof has, in any event, done its part and in its decision put the affected parties in a position successfully to defend themselves against the dubious machinations of 'gift communities'.

Sittenwidrigkeit? – Die Einschränkung des § 817 S. 2 BGB durch den BGH': 270.

42   Compare also Möller, 'Leistungskondiktion trotz beidseitiger Sittenwidrigkeit? – Die Einschränkung des § 817 S. 2 BGB durch den BGH': 270.

20 Current Developments – Malta: The Electronic Commerce (General) Regulations

Paul Edgar Micallef

On 24 October 2006 the Minister responsible for Competitiveness and Communications by virtue of his powers under Article 25 of the Electronic Commerce Act[1] ('E-Commerce Act'), enacted the Electronic Commerce (General) Regulations[2] ('E-Commerce Regulations'), which regulations came into force on the same date. The Regulations complement the measures already in place under the E-Commerce Act, and together with the measures under the E-Commerce Act, purport to implement the European Union ('EU') Electronic Commerce Directive,[3] the Electronic Signatures Directive[4] and the requirements under the EU Regulation on Consumer Protection Cooperation in so far as these relate to the Electronic Commerce Directive.[5] The E-Commerce Regulations also provide for procedural measures similar to the requirements of the EU Injunctions Directive[6] in so far as these relate to the Electronic Commerce Directive.[7]

1. Measures Preceding the E-Commerce Regulations

By way of a historical background, the process to have in place a comprehensive regulatory regime on e-commerce commenced in May 2000 when the Maltese Government issued a consultative document entitled the 'White Paper on the Legislative Framework for Information Practices' ('May 2000 White Paper') whereby

---

1   See Chapter 426 of the Laws of Malta.
2   As per Legal Notice 251 of 2006.
3   Directive 2000/31/EC of the European Parliament and of the Council of 8 June 2000 on certain legal aspects of information society services in particular electronic commerce, in the internal market.
4   Directive 1999/93/EC of the European Parliament and of the Council of 13 December 1999 on a Community framework for electronic signatures.
5   Regulation (EC) No. 2006/2004 of the European Parliament and of the Council of 27 October 2004 on cooperation between national authorities responsible for the enforcement of consumer protection laws.
6   Directive 98/27/EC of the European Parliament and of the Council of 19 May 1998 on injunctions for the protection of consumers' interests.
7   A proposal has been made to amend the Annex to the Injunctions Directive, extending the annex to other consumer protection related directives including the E-Commerce Directive.

Government submitted for public consultation a draft bill entitled the Electronic Commerce Act, 2000.[8] Until then there was no specific legislation regulating e-commerce and the rapid technological advances then taking place clearly necessitated legislative intervention in the short term. Consequently Government cognisant that the existing legislation did not regulate information services and prompted by the developments elsewhere including the imminent enactment of a Directive on E-Commerce by the EU, embarked on a project to enact a comprehensive legal framework, focusing primarily on the need to encourage and regulate electronic transactions whilst protecting the interests of the individual when his or her personal data is being processed. The Bill on e-commerce as proposed in the May 2000 White Paper sought to establish the legal basis for the safe but free conduct of electronic commerce, regulating various aspects underlying the effectiveness of electronic commerce including the validity of electronic communications and transactions, transmissions of electronic communications and the provision of signature certification services.[9]

In September 2000 Government after it took stock of the comments made by various interested parties further to the draft Bill on e-commerce it had proposed in the May 2000 White Paper, initiated a formal legislative process to have in place a law on e-commerce and published a Bill entitled the 'Electronic Commerce Act'. This Bill was subsequently approved by Parliament in January 2001 and came into force in May 2002. The Malta Communications Authority ('MCA') was subsequently nominated as the competent authority responsible for monitoring and ensuring compliance with this law.[10]

There were various changes to the law as proposed in the 2000 White Paper by Government, and as finally approved by Parliament.[11] These changes included more precise reference to the laws to which the provisions of the E-Commerce Act relating to legal requirements to electronic transactions and communications do not apply, amendments to the provisions relating to the use of an electronic signature and to the retention of information, documents and communications made electronically, and amendments when a party is deemed to have consented to an electronic contract. Significantly, changes were also introduced expressly protecting the interests of consumers in this context.[12] It is pertinent to note that when Government published the May 2000 White Paper, the EU was still in the process of determining the

---

8   This consultative document was published by the Office of the Prime Minister and included two other draft Bills entitled respectively the Data Protection Act and the Computer Misuse Act.

9   See *White Paper on the Legislative Framework for Information Practices*, May 2000, pp. 10–15.

10   As per Legal Notice 326 of 2005.

11   The Electronic Commerce Act was approved as Act III of 2001 and came into force on the 10 May 2002. It was initially published as a Bill in the Government Gazette on the 29 September 2000.

12   Under the draft Bill as proposed in the 2000 White Paper there was no explicit reference to consumers. Article 2 of the Electronic Commerce Act defines 'consumer' as meaning any natural person who is acting for purposes outside his trade, business or profession.

final provisions to be adopted in the Electronic Commerce Directive it eventually adopted.[13] Therefore to some degree Government was, in May 2000 when it first published its legislative proposals on e-commerce, charting new waters in deciding which measures to adopt to regulate electronic commerce in Malta.[14]

2. The E-Commerce Regulations

The E-Commerce Regulations makes requirements within the coordinated field[15] apply to the provision of an information society service by a service provider established in Malta, irrespective of whether that service is provided in Malta or in another EU Member State. Enforcement authorities are required to secure compliance with such requirements. Conversely, the requirements within the coordinated field are not applied to information society services provided by a service provider established in another Member State for reasons that fall within the coordinated field where their application would restrict the freedom to provide information society services to a person in Malta from that Member State.[16] There provisions do not apply to those fields set out in the Schedule to the E-Commerce Regulations.[17] However an enforcement authority may take measures exceptionally with regard to a given information society service where such measures are necessary for reasons of public policy, public health, public security, and the protection of consumers including investors, provided such measures are proportionate to those objectives.[18]

A service provider is required to make available to the recipient of the service,[19] and where appropriate or requested to the MCA or the competent enforcement

---

13   In May 2000 when the White Paper was published, the EU was still in the process of finalising its proposals on the various directives directly related to e-commerce. The E-Signatures Directive was approved some months earlier whereas the E-Commerce Directive was approved by the European Parliament and Council on the 8 June 2000.

14   Government in May 2000 in making its legislative proposals to regulate electronic commerce did not limit itself to EU legislation, but also referred to other sources including the United Nations Commission on International Trade Law (UNCITRAL) Model law on E-Commerce of 1996 and the laws of other jurisdictions notably those of Australia and Ireland. See May 2000 White Paper at p. 4.

15   'Coordinated field' is defined as referring to the requirements applicable to information society service providers or information society services, covering those requirements which the service provider has to comply with when taking up and in pursuit of the activity of an information society service. See Regulation 2, E-Commerce Regulations.

16   See Regulation 3, E-Commerce Regulations.

17   The fields listed in the Schedule reflect what is listed in the Annex to the Electronic Commerce Directive and include the freedom of parties to a contract to choose the applicable law, contractual obligations concerning consumer contracts, and the permissibility of unsolicited commercial communications by electronic mail.

18   See Regulation 4, E-Commerce Regulations.

19   'Recipient' is defined as any person who uses an information society service for the purpose of seeking information or making it accessible. See Article 2, E-Commerce Act.

authority, in a form and manner that is easily, directly and permanently accessible, certain information. Such information must include: the name of the service provider and the geographic address where he is established; his details including his electronic mail address; if he is registered in a trade or public register, the trade or other such register in which he is registered and his registration number or similar means of identification in that register; if his activity is regulated, the details of the supervisory public authority; where he is a member of a professional body a reference to it and to the applicable professional rules of that body and how these can be accessed.[20] If the service provider sends unsolicited commercial communications, details of how users can register their choice regarding such communications must be provided. Moreover, the service provider is expressly required to ensure that any unsolicited commercial communication sent by him is clearly and unambiguously identifiable as such.[21]

A service provider who intends to provide signature certification services is required to complete and file a notice with the MCA. Such notice must continue only such information as is necessary to enable the MCA to identify the service provider concerned and the services he provides. The MCA is required to keep a register of such service providers which register must be accessible to the public. Otherwise the provision of information society services by a service provider does not require any prior authorization. This however does not apply with regard to any authorization schemes that are not exclusively targeted at information society services.[22]

Electronic signature products which comply with the standards published by the European Commission in its Official Journal are presumed to be in compliance with the requirements of the E-Commerce Act, whereas the use of electronic signature products originating from outside Malta and which comply with the Electronic Signatures Directive are not subject to any restrictions.[23]

Certificates issued as qualified certificates to the public by a signature certification service provider established in a third country (that is outside the EU) are recognized as legally equivalent to certificates issued by a signature certification service provider established in the EU if either the said service provider fulfils the requirements of the Electronic Signatures Directive and is accredited under a voluntary accreditation scheme established in a Member State, or else a signature certification service provider in a Member State guarantees the certificate, or the certificate or signature certification service provider is recognized under a bilateral or a multilateral treaty between the EU and third countries.[24]

The MCA to ensure compliance with the provisions of the E-Commerce Act, may issue such technical guidelines as it may consider appropriate, and require a signature certification service provider to submit to it a statement concerning compliance with the Second Schedule of the Act relating to the requirements for qualified certificates or with the Third Schedule of the Act relating to requirements

---

20   See Regulation 5, E-Commerce Regulations.
21   *Ibid.*, Regulation 6.
22   *Ibid.*, Regulations 8 and 9.
23   *Ibid.*, Regulation 10.
24   *Ibid.*, Regulation 11.

for signature certification service providers issuing qualified certificates or with any technical guidelines. Such statement must then be verified by independent auditors approved by the MCA and paid for by the service provider.[25]

The E-Commerce Regulations provide for a dispute resolution process whereby consumers may refer complaints that they may have with regard to service providers in relation to any infringement of the E-Commerce Act or of the E-Commerce Regulations to the MCA. In doing so the consumer must *prima facie* show that he has been affected by the act or omission of the service provider allegedly in breach of the law and giving rise to his or her complaint. In resolving any such disputes the MCA may issue directives to the service provider concerned requiring that service provider to comply with any measure that the MCA may specify for the resolution of the dispute. Such directives may include an order requiring the service provider to make compensation payments to the consumer.[26]

A person aggrieved by a decision taken by the MCA under the E-Commerce Regulations, may contest such a decision before the Communications Appeals Board.[27] In doing so, he must demonstrate that he has a legal interest in contesting the decision of the MCA. Such a right of appeal extends also to the contestation of a compliance order issued by the MCA under the E-Commerce Regulations.

3. Enforcement Measures to Ensure Compliance with E-Commerce Legislation

The E-Commerce Regulations in line with the requirements of the EU Injunctions Directive and the Regulation on Consumer Protection Cooperation, empower the MCA to have recourse to various measures to ensure compliance with the provisions of both the E-Commerce Act and the E-Commerce Regulations. The MCA where it considers that it is 'reasonably appropriate or necessary for the protection of consumers', may either of its own initiative or else following a written application by a qualified entity,[28] issue a compliance order against any person including service providers.[29] In doing so, the MCA may require the person against whom the order

---

25   *Ibid.*, Regulation 13.
26   *Ibid.*, Regulation 14.
27   The Communications Appeals Board is an independent adjudicative tribunal appointed by the Prime Minister and is composed of a chairman and two experts versed in a communications sector.
28   Regulation 2 of the E-Commerce Regulations defines those entities which for the purposes of the Regulations are considered as a 'qualified entity'. These include consumer associations registered under the Consumer Affairs Act, independent public bodies which have a legitimate interest in ensuring the protection of the collective interests of consumers, organisations recognized by the MCA as collectively representing information society service providers and any qualified entity from any Member State which is included in the list of qualified entities. If the qualified entity is from another Member State, the MCA is required to treat the list published by the European Commission as conclusive proof of the legal capacity of the qualified entity in question to present an application in Malta for the issue of a compliance order.
29   Under the Regulations 'service provider' is defined any person established in Malta

is issued, to take those measures specified in the order, this within any timeframe stated in the said order. The MCA may also require a person to cease and desist from committing a breach of the Act or the Regulations.[30] In issuing a compliance order, the MCA is required to include information about the right to contest the order and to state its reasons for the issuance of the order. It is not required to prove actual loss or damage, or actual recklessness, negligence or fault by the person against whom the order is made.

If a qualified entity applies to the MCA for the issuance of a compliance order, the entity in question must first satisfy the MCA that it tried to achieve voluntary cessation of the alleged infringement in relation to which the order is being sought. The MCA may also seek voluntary compliance before issuing an order. It is at the discretion of the MCA whether to issue an order after an application from a qualified entity. If the MCA decides not to issue such an order the qualified entity may apply to the Communications Appeals Board ('Appeals Board') requesting that Appeals Board to order the MCA to issue the compliance order.

A compliance order when it is issued comes into force with immediate effect. The person against whom the order is made, has the right within 15 days from when he is notified with the order, to lodge an appeal with the Appeals Board asking for a revocation or amendment of the order. The MCA, and the qualified entity if the order was issued at the request of the latter, are also notified with the appeal and have the right to reply. Whilst the appeal is still pending the order remains in force unless the Appeals Board at the request of the appellant specifically orders that the order be stayed pending the outcome of the appeal.[31]

The MCA also has the faculty of issuing an order requiring a person to desist from acting in breach of the E-Commerce Act or Regulations or of any intra-Community infringement,[32] requiring that person to provide a written undertaking that he agrees

---

providing an information society service. For the purposes of Regulations 9 and 14 which respectively deal with notification requirements and disputes between such providers and consumers, the definition of service provider extends also to the services provided by a signature certification service provider.

30   See Regulation 15, E-Commerce Regulations.

31   The Appeals Board in staying a compliance order whilst an appeal is pending before it, may impose conditions and, or amendments as it may consider necessary. The Appeals Board is required to hear such appeals 'with urgency and as expeditiously as possible'. Any of the parties may also request the Appeals Board to abridge any of time limits established at law in relation to the proceedings before it.

32   Regulation 2, E-Commerce Regulations defines 'intra-Community infringements' as an act or omission contrary to the E-Commerce Act or the Regulations which take place in Malta and which harms or is likely to harm the collective interests of consumers residing in a Member State/s other Malta, or is an act or omission contrary to the E-Commerce Act or regulations by a seller or supplier established in Malta which harms or is likely to harm the collective interests of consumers residing in a Member State/s other Malta, or is an act or omission contrary to the E-Commerce Act or regulations which takes place in Malta and which harms or is likely to harm the collective interests of consumers residing in a Member State/s other Malta, or is an act or omission contrary to the E-Commerce Act or regulations which takes place in Malta and which harms or is likely to harm the collective interests of consumers residing in a Member State/s other than Malta where the evidence or assets pertaining to the act or omission are in Malta.

to cease and desist from committing such breach subject to any such conditions that the MCA may impose. A breach of such an undertaking so given, renders the person concerned liable to the imposition of an administrative fine not exceeding 10,000 Maltese liri and, or 200 Maltese liri for each day of non-compliance with the undertaking given.[33]

The MCA may for the better information of the public require the person against whom the compliance order was issued, to communicate at his expense in any manner which the MCA considers appropriate a copy in full or in part of the said order and, or a copy of an undertaking given, or of a corrective statement as may be required by the MCA in relation to any breach of the E-Commerce Act or of the E-Commerce Regulations.

---

33   Regulation 23, E-Commerce Regulations.

21 Protecting Consumer Telephone Records from Unauthorized Disclosure

James P. Nehf[1]

Computer giant Hewlett-Packard (HP) made headlines in September 2006 when its board of directors hired a private investigator who used pretexting — false pretenses — to obtain the telephone records of a director who was suspected of leaking sensitive company information to the press.[2] The pretexting worked (the director's communications to the press were confirmed in the phone records), but the resulting publicity focused more on the pretexting tactics than the director's breach of boardroom confidentiality. The scandal ultimately led to the resignation of the chair of the board at HP and the commencement of hearings in Congress to determine what, if anything, could be done to protect the privacy of consumer phone records.[3]

The news reports and hearings brought into public view what the Federal Communications Commission (FCC), the Federal Trade Commission (FTC), and consumer groups had known for years: there was a growing industry of data brokers that can obtain confidential consumer and business telephone records on just about any individual within hours or minutes, all for a relatively small fee.

Telephone companies (wireline, wireless, and Internet (VOIP)) maintain records of telephone numbers called, and the time and date of each call, which the FCC calls Consumer Proprietary Network Information (CPNI). Pretexting is the impersonation of an individual for the purpose of obtaining personal records such as CPNI. Federal law expressly prohibits pretexting for financial data (bank account and credit card numbers) under the Gramm-Leach-Bliley Act,[4] but the law does not cover telephone records, which are protected by a patchwork of state and federal laws governing

---

1   Professor of Law and Cleon H. Foust Fellow, Indiana University School of Law – Indianapolis.

2   G. Anders and A. Murray, 'Inside Story of Feud that Plunged HP Into Crisis', *Sunday Times* (London) 15 October 2006: 18.

3   *Ibid.*

4   The GLBA prohibits the use of false, fictitious or fraudulent statements or documents to get customer information from a financial institution or directly from a customer of a financial institution; the use of forged, counterfeit, lost or stolen documents to get customer information from a financial institution or directly from a customer of a financial institution; and asking another person to get someone else's customer information using false, fictitious, or fraudulent documents or forged, counterfeit, lost or stolen documents. 15 USC §§ 6821–6827.

identity theft, access to personal information in computer databases, and deceptive practices generally. While it is sometimes claimed that pretexting for telephone records is legal, it nearly always is not. The federal Telecommunications Act of 1996 requires carriers to protect CPNI from unauthorized disclosure,[5] and the Federal Trade Commission Act[6] and various state laws make it illegal to obtain telephone call records under false pretences.[7]

In 2005, the Electronic Privacy Information Center (EPIC) urged the FCC to investigate more than 30 online data brokers that openly advertise the ability to obtain CPNI.[8] The large number of brokers advertising the service indicated that the problem was widespread and that current laws were doing little to deter pretexting.

The FCC issued subpoenas to the more prominent online data brokers. The subpoenas sought details regarding how the brokers obtained CPNI and who their customers were. Unfortunately and not surprisingly, the companies did not answer the subpoenas. The FCC then sent letters of citation to the companies for their failure to respond and referred the matter to the Department of Justice for enforcement of the subpoenas. In addition, the FCC made undercover purchases of phone records from various data brokers.

In conjunction with the investigation of data brokers, the FCC met with wireless and wireline providers to discuss their security practices and efforts they have undertaken to protect CPNI from unauthorized disclosure. The FCC also asked carriers what employees within the company had access to CPNI and the procedures the carriers used to ensure that employees and third parties did not improperly access the information or disclose it to others.

The investigations revealed that pretexting typically occurs in one of three ways. The most common approach is bypassing telephone company security procedures by using personal customer information (name, address, Social Security Number, and so on) that is available in other data bases. Armed with this information, the data brokers impersonate the customer so the telephone company believes it is releasing

---

5   47 USC § 222.

6   The Federal Trade Commission has brought enforcement actions to prohibit telephone pretexting under s. 5 of the FTC Act, 15 USC §§ 45, which bars 'unfair or deceptive acts' in business practices. It has filed several lawsuits against companies that sell phone records on the Internet. See Civil Action No. EDCV06–0439 VAP (77 Investigations, Inc.); Civil Action No. 06CV105D (AccuSearch, Inc.); Civil Action No. 06–60602 CIV-Cohn – CEO Group); Civil Action No. 1:06–CV–01099-AMD (Information Search, Inc.); Civil Action No. 2:06–CV–241–RGD-JEB (E.D. Va.) (Integrity Security & Investigation Services, Inc.).

7   For example, the Georgia Telephone Records Protection Act, OCGA 46–5–230 to –232, makes it a felony punishable by up to $250,000 to knowingly procure, or try or conspire to procure, an individual or business's phone record by fraudulent, deceptive or false means. The law also bans selling or receiving such records without the phone customer's authorization.

8   Petition of the Electronic Privacy Information Center for Rulemaking to Enhance Security and Authentication Standards for Access to Customer Proprietary Information, Federal Communications Commission, CC Docket No. 96–115 (30 August 2005), available at http://www.epic.org/privacy/iei/cpnipet.html.

the information to an authorized person. A second way is to access phone records by cracking online account administration tools. Almost all phone carriers now give their customers the ability to view and pay their bills online. If this service has not been activated by the customer, the pretexting firm may attempt to activate it, create a password, and read the bill. The third approach is more direct: paying employees of the telephone company to release CPNI, typically by sharing the fee with the rogue employee.

Consumers can suffer substantial injury from the unauthorized sale of CPNI. Call records contain some of the most sensitive and private information an individual may have. Records can be used to track an individual's daily habits, to spy on a person's communications with others, or to stalk another person. Data brokers also offer location tracking services for wireless phone users, which allows an individual's movements and whereabouts to be monitored and reported. In addition, if online data brokers acquire information by accessing customers' online accounts, they may also have access to customers' billing address, credit card information, and other data. These items of personal information can be used in security verification for other services, so possessing the data gives the data broker additional opportunities for identity theft.

Some data brokers claim to be able to access a business phone record with only a phone number, name, and address. Given the prevalence of phones, both wired and wireless, used for business purposes, these services can be used for industrial espionage and other illicit business activities. Business phone records may yield sensitive information about client lists and contact information, resulting in privacy violations both for the businesses and the people whom those businesses have contacted.

In its complaint to the FCC, EPIC claimed that pretexting takes advantage of inadequate security procedures and urged the FCC to institute rulemaking procedures to mandate stronger procedures for carriers that are subject to its authority. In particular, EPIC urged the FCC to explore several possible security measures:

1. Strengthening password procedures so that CPNI cannot be disclosed without a password, or if the customer has forgotten the password, without the customer answering a series of personal questions that data brokers could not easily obtain. Password security procedures at telephone companies are often lax because customers frequently forget passwords and still want access to their accounts. The system used by a leading cellular company allowed an individual to specify a new password for online account access simply by submitting the billing zip code and the last four digits of the Social Security Number. Both identifiers are readily obtainable to online data brokers who maintain subscriptions to services that sell Social Security Numbers and other personal information such as home addresses and dates of birth. EPIC suggested that the FCC require a 'shared secrets' system in which the telephone company would ask the customer a series of pre-determined personal questions (for example mother's maiden name, favourite pet's name, and so on) before changing a password.

2. Creating audit trails that record all instances when a customer's records

have been accessed, whether information was disclosed, which employee disclosed the information, and to whom the information was disclosed. Audit trails can be used proactively to detect pretexting and internal company data breaches. For instance, statistical data showing how frequently a customer service representative accesses account records can be tracked. If a customer service representative is accessing an unusually high number of records, an investigation can be triggered. Under current FCC regulations, companies are only required to audit for specific types of disclosures involving marketing use of CPNI and disclosures to persons the company knows are not their customers (that is, known disclosures to authorized third parties, such as law enforcement agencies).[9] They do not have to maintain logs of disclosures to an apparent customer who may be a victim of pretexting. If pretexters know that a carrier has a strong audit practice, they may be deterred from pretexting against that carrier.

3. Mandating encryption of stored CPNI data. Encryption can make it more difficult for hackers to obtain CPNI by unauthorized access to databases. Moreover, through encryption, access to CPNI can be denied to employees of the telephone company who have not been given access to decryption technologies, thereby limiting the risk that rogue employees will release data for a price.

4. Putting time limits on data retention that require deletion (or archiving) of CPNI when the data no longer serve a legitimate business purpose. Telephone companies maintain that CPNI serves useful purposes for both the company and the customer, but the vast majority of those purposes dissipate over time. Older CPNI can be deleted or archived, with access to archived data restricted by narrowly delineated exceptions.

5. Requiring that companies notify customers when their CPNI has been disclosed or when the security of their CPNI may have been breached. While this information may come too late to prevent an unauthorized disclosure, mandatory notification can deter unlawful access because an informed customer may request an investigation. If an investigation shows who released the information and to whom, the customer or the company can take remedial action, including the instigation of criminal proceedings against the perpetrators. If pretexters think they might be caught, they are less likely to engage in the practice.

Compounding the privacy problem is a federal court decision that limited the FCC's ability to prohibit the release of consumer phone records by the telephone company to third-party marketers. The FCC had issued a rule that required telecommunications carriers to obtain the express written, oral, or electronic consent of customers before they could use any customer phone information to market services outside the existing service relationship with that company. A federal court struck down this 'opt in' rule as a violation of the First and Fifth Amendments of the Constitution, at least with respect to a carrier's sharing of information with affiliated

---

9   47 CFR 64.2009(c).

companies.[10] The FCC then modified the rule to take an 'opt-out' approach whereby a customer's phone records may be used by carriers, their affiliates, agents, and joint venture partners so long as the customer does not expressly withhold consent to such use.[11] Because few customers are aware of this 'opt-out' procedure, the ruling has resulted in broader dissemination of consumer phone records and thereby may have contributed to the proliferation of the unlawful practices of data brokers. If CPNI is found in numerous databases outside the telephone company, controlling access to the data is more problematic. The FCC has urged Congress to address this situation.

In response to the FCC rulemaking initiative, telephone carriers have objected to increased regulation. While they acknowledge that a problem exists, they maintain that existing laws make pretexting illegal, and if they are enforced more rigorously, the laws would be adequate. They also argue that the EPIC proposals for enhanced security would cost millions to implement. The carriers concede that internal security procedures at telephone carriers can be strengthened, but industry self-regulation would be more efficient and effective than regulatory mandates. To that end, several of the major telephone carriers are drafting a set of 'best practices' designed to tighten security and strengthen audit procedures, in hopes of forestalling federal regulatory control.

At the end of the day, EPIC and other privacy advocates prevailed. By the end of the year, Congress had approved the Telephone Records and Privacy Protection Act of 2006, which the President quickly signed into law. The law makes it a federal crime to engage in pretexting or trade in confidential telephone records, punishable by up to ten years in prison. In addition, the FCC issued new rules requiring passwords for customers who want to access their telephone records. Under the rules, telephone carriers will be required to notify customers if any of their personal information is changed or updated. The rules also mandate disclosure to law enforcement officials and customers when a breach of personal information occurs.

---

10   *US West, Inc.* v. *FCC*, 182 F.3d 1224 (10th Cir. 1999).
11   47 CFR. 64.2001 to 64.2009 (2006).

22 Private Law Control of Consumer Credit in the United Kingdom

David Kraft[1]

1. Introduction

The new unfair credit provisions of ss 140A–140B Consumer Credit Act 1974 (hereafter CCA) replace the extortionate credit provisions of ss 137–139 CCA. They constitute the primary source of private law protection for consumers in unfair credit relationships.

There is widespread consensus that the extortionate credit provisions have failed to provide adequate protection for consumers in unfair credit relationships.[2] As will be seen, this is due to, first, the wording of the provisions, second, the courts' restrictive interpretation of them and third, issues of access to justice. Despite an abundance of evidence on unfair practices in the consumer credit industry,[3] there have only been 30 cases in as many years of consumers seeking credit bargains to be re-opened on the basis of the provisions. In most of these cases the provisions were pleaded by way of defence to possession proceedings. In only ten cases have the courts actually re-opened the credit bargain.

The new provisions introduce changes in terms of scope, substance, remedies and procedure. The main changes are that:

- changes to interest rates and charges made after the agreement was entered into are now within the scope of review;
- the hurdle of 'unfair' is lower than that of 'extortionate';
- a wider range of remedies is available to debtors;
- a new alternative dispute resolution mechanism is established;

---

1   LL.B. (Hons) English & German Laws, Liverpool; Research Fellow (wissenschaftlicher Mitarbeiter), Centre for European Private Law, Münster.
2   I have not been able to find a single scholar who takes the opposite view. Rather than cite everything I have read, I cite merely the same claim made in G. Howells and S. Weatherill, *Consumer Protection Law*, 2nd edn, (Aldershot, 2005), p. 342 and the UK government: see White Paper 'Fair, Clear and Competitive: The Consumer Credit Market in the 21st Century', Cm. 6040, Department of Trade and Industry, (2003), para. 3.30, available at www.dti.gov.uk.
3   For example 'Daylight Robbery: The CAB case for effective regulation of extortionate credit', National Association of Citizens' Advice Bureaux (2000), available at www.citizensadvice.org.uk.

- where the debtor alleges the relationship is unfair the burden is on the creditor to prove it is not.

Arguably, the most significant aspect in assessing the fairness of a credit relationship are the rates of interest and charges. They are, therefore, subject to review under the unfair credit provisions and, to a certain extent, other sources of legal protection such as the Unfair Terms in Consumer Contracts Regulations 1999 and the common law on penalties. There are, however, no direct controls on interest rates or the cost of credit. In this respect the UK differs from most of civil law Europe and the common law world.

This chapter will set out the scope, substance, remedies and procedure of the unfair credit provisions by reference to existing law and identified needs for change. It will offer some thoughts and criticism of the new regulatory approach, in particular the highly vexed issue of direct controls on interest rates and the cost of credit.

2. Relationships to Which the Provisions Apply

The provisions apply to relationships based on a relevant credit agreement.

(i) Relevant Agreements

Relevant credit agreements are agreements between an individual (the 'debtor') and any other person (the 'creditor') by which the creditor provides the debtor with credit of any amount.[4]

'Individual' includes partnerships consisting of two or three persons not all of whom are bodies corporate, and unincorporated bodies of persons which do not consist entirely of bodies corporate and are not partnerships.[5] Small businesses thereby also fall within the scope of protection. The thinking behind this is that small businesses operate on a level more akin to consumers, so justifying giving them the same level of protection.[6] The weakness in this argument however is that small businesses are generally better informed about financial matters than consumers and have more affordable, ready access to legal advice, albeit not to the same extent as big business. An appropriate level of protection would, therefore, be somewhere between that given to consumers and that given to big business. In economic terms however, the solution can probably be justified as it avoids a complex regulatory framework and gives small businesses an advantage which helps them to compete better with big business. The change from the extortionate credit provisions limits the size of partnerships which can invoke the provisions to those with three members (this new limitation presumably better draws the line between big and small business).

---

4   Section 140C(1).
5   Section 189(1).
6   See 'Fair, Clear and Competitive: The Consumer Credit Market in the 21st Century', para. 3.66 and following.

The provisions also cover 'related agreements'[7] (as do the extortionate credit provisions). These are the component credit agreements consolidated under a new agreement, contracts of sale financed by the agreement, and security for the agreement.[8] This means that first, a lender will not be able to shield a number of unfair agreements from review by consolidating them into an agreement which, viewed in isolation, is fair. The particular mischief in mind here is the practice of 'rolling-over' existing loans into new loans to cash in multiple arrangement fees and even multiple early settlement fees (so-called 'churning'). Second, a credit transaction, which viewed in isolation is fair, will not escape review where it is concluded to finance the purchase of an item with an artificially high sale price to justify a higher loan (the so-called 'colourable cash price'). Finally, requiring a disproportionately high security (such as a second charge mortgage) is also caught by the test.

The provisions apply to new agreements from 6 April 2007 and existing agreements from 6 April 2008.[9]

(ii) The Reach of the Provisions into the Terms of a Relevant Agreement

All terms of the agreement and any related agreement are within the scope of review.

The extortionate credit provisions only apply to the terms of the agreement at the time it was entered into.[10] The change, therefore, permits the review of amendments to interest rates and charges made after the agreement has been concluded. These generally escape review under the extortionate credit provisions if such variations are clearly provided for in the agreement, the lender gives adequate notice, and they are not made capriciously.[11]

(iii) Scope of Other Significant Sources of Legal Protection

Unfair terms in consumer contracts regulations   The Unfair Terms in Consumer Contracts Regulations 1999[12] (hereafter: UTCCR) established a mechanism of judicial control of clauses in contracts concluded between businesses and consumers and have been held to apply to consumer credit contracts.[13] A 'consumer' within the meaning of the UTCCR is a natural person acting for purposes outside his trade,

---

7   Section 140A(1).

8   Section 140C(4).

9   See timetable for implementation of the Act, www.dti.gov.uk.

10   *Paragon Finance plc.* v. *Nash and Staunton* [2001] 2 All ER (Comm), especially para. [67]; see also *Broadwick Financial Services Ltd* v. *Spencer and Another* [2002] 1 All ER (Comm) 446.

11   *Paragon Finance plc.* v. *Nash and Staunton* [2001] 2 All ER (Comm).

12   S.I. 1999/2083. The Regulations implement Council Directive 93/13EEC of 5 April 1993 on Unfair Terms in Consumer Contracts, OJ L95/29.

13   *Kindlance Ltd* v. *Murphy* (1997) 12 December, Lexis: *Falco Finance* v. *Michael Gough* [1998] Tr L Rep 526; *Director General of Fair Trading* v. *First National Bank* [2001] UKHL 52 (25 October, 2001).

business or profession.[14] In this respect the unfair credit provisions constitute an extra source of protection for small businesses.

Whereas all terms of the agreement are subject to the unfair credit provisions, terms directly relating to the price or remuneration (core terms) are beyond the reach of the UTCCR, so long as they are written in 'plain, intelligible language'.[15] Core terms include the arrangement fee and, *generally*, the rate of interest of a credit agreement. I say generally for two reasons. First, the House of Lords in *Director General of Fair Trading* v. *First National Bank*,[16] the leading case on interpretation of the UTCCR,[17] has confirmed that this core terms exclusion must be given a narrow interpretation. This is appropriate because all contract terms relate to the balance of rights and interests of the parties and thus ultimately influence the contract price. This interpretation highlights the relevance of the term *directly* relating to the adequacy of the price or remuneration, without which the UTCCR would be redundant. It follows from this narrow interpretation that terms relating to default interest and charges are subject to review under the UTCCR.[18] The second reason interest rates *per se* are not excluded from review follows from the first. Where a credit agreement distinguishes between a concessionary interest rate and a standard interest rate, whereby the latter is considerably higher than the former and becomes payable if the borrower misses or is late in making a repayment, then it is really a default rate masquerading as a standard rate. In such a case the better view is that the 'standard' rate of interest is not a core term and is within the scope of review.[19]

---

14   Regulation 3(1).
15   Regulation 6(2). It is interesting to note that this core terms exclusion was not transposed in Austria, Denmark, Greece, Latvia, Luxembourg, Spain and Sweden (for a comparative law perspective see S. Camara Lapuente, *El control de las clausulas „abusivas" sobre elementos esenciales del contrato*, (Navarra, 2006).
16   [2001] UKHL 52 (25 October 2001).
17   In that case the House of Lords was interpreting the predecessor to the UTCCR 1999 enacted in 1994 (S.I. 1994/3159). The 1999 amendment merely extended the standing enjoyed by the Director General of Fair Trading to bring actions to prevent the continued use of unfair terms harmful to the collective interests of consumers to other 'qualifying bodies', including the Consumers' Association.
18   This is certainly the view of the OFT in relation to credit card and bank current account default charges: see OFT Press Releases 68/06 of 5 April 2006, 'Current credit card default charges are unfair', and 130/06 of 7 September 2006, 'Following success on credit card default charges – OFT turns attention to bank current accounts', available from www.oft.gov.uk.
19   *Falco Finance Ltd* v. *Michael Gough* [1998] Tr L Rep 526. Compare, however, the contrary view in *Kindlance Ltd* v. *Murphy* (1997) 12 December, Lexis, which relied on older cases (for example, *Astley* v. *Weldon* (1801) 2 B & P 346, 353 and *Wallingford* v. *Mutual Society* (1880) 5 App Cas 685, 702) supporting the proposition that a higher rate of interest which is reduced when payments are made promptly is not a penalty. The Judge also discussed *Lordsvale Finance plc.* v. *Bank of Zambia* [1996] QB 752, however that case was a commercial, and not a consumer dispute, and the uplift of 1 per cent was relatively modest. *Kindlance* has accordingly been subjected to stark criticism (see S. Bright, 'Attacking Unfair Mortgage Terms', *LQR*, (1999): 360 at 363).

Common Law on Penalties   The common law on penalties also applies to default interest and charges. The root principle of the common law is that contract law damages payable by one party should reflect the loss suffered by the other party as a consequence of the breach. Perfectly reconcilable with this principle are clauses which provide for the breaching party to pay a sum which corresponds to a genuine pre-estimate of those costs (so-called liquidated damages clauses). By contrast, a clause which aims to compel performance by providing for an exorbitant sum to be paid upon breach[20] is not. Therefore, exorbitant default interest and charges should fall foul of the common law on penalties.[21]

3. What Makes a Credit Relationship Unfair?

(i) Drawing Out the Meaning of Unfair

It helps to start by thinking about what we mean by unfair in this context. There is neither a statutory definition of 'unfair' nor any guidance in Hansard as to what Parliament intended the term to mean.[22] Whether a relationship is unfair is a matter for the courts to determine in view of the particular facts of each case.[23]

By contrast, a statutory definition of an *extortionate* credit bargain does exist. It is one which requires the debtor to make payments which are grossly exorbitant or otherwise grossly contravenes the ordinary principles of fair dealing.[24] The dictionary definition of 'exorbitant' is 'grossly excessive'; therefore 'grossly exorbitant' means 'grossly grossly excessive'.[25] If we assume for now that a breach of the principles of fair dealing (without this necessarily being a 'gross' breach) constitutes *unfair* dealing, and that 'excessive', or at least 'grossly excessive', payments are *unfair*, then the wording alone suggests that 'unfair' is a lower hurdle than 'extortionate'.

In determining whether a credit relationship is extortionate or unfair, under their respective provisions, the courts are directed to have regard to a number of matters

---

20   '[A] payment of money stipulated as *in terrorum* of the offending party': *Dunlop Pneumatic Tyre Co. Ltd* v. *New Garage & Motor Co.* [1915] AC 79, 86.

21   As also expressed by the OFT in respect of credit account and bank current account default charges. See OFT Press Releases 68/06 of 5 April 2006, 'Current credit card default charges are unfair', and 130/06 of 7 September 2006, 'Following success on credit card default charges – OFT turns attention to bank current accounts', available from www.oft.gov.uk.

22   Following the decision of the Court of Appeal in *Pepper* v. *Hart* [1993] 1 All ER 42, a court may, in certain circumstances, refer to Hansard as an aid to interpretation.

23   Compare the comments of Gerry Sutcliffe, Minister responsible for the Act: 'It is also important that the test does not constrain or impede the courts' ability to do justice in every case. That is why I will not try to define an unfair relationship. It is for the courts to determine such things according to the relevant facts of each case.' See House of Commons Hansard debates, 9 June 2005 (Pt 13), col. 1411, available at www. publications.parliament.uk.

24   Section 138 (1).

25   See 'Daylight Robbery: The CAB case for effective regulation of extortionate credit', National Association of Citizens' Advice Bureaux, (2000), p. 22.

or factors.[26] These are described in the extortionate credit provisions as including, on the one hand, the degree of risk accepted by the creditor, having regard to the value of any security provided, his relationship to the debtor, and whether or not the colourable cash price was quoted for any goods or services included in the credit bargain, and, on the other hand, the debtor's age, experience, business capacity and state of health and the degree and nature of financial pressure he was under when making the credit bargain. The unfair credit provisions essentially say the same thing, just with more brevity. The court is directed to have regard to any matters it considers relevant, including matters relating to the creditor and matters relating to the debtor. The word 'include' in the respective provision of the extortionate test denotes that the list is not exhaustive, as does the permission of the court to have regard to 'any other relevant consideration'. Under the extortionate credit provisions, the courts have trodden a safe path, interpreting the test restrictively, deferring to the creditor's assessment of the risk involved and being unsympathetic to the plight of debtors.[27]

What reason is there to believe the courts, in having regard to such matters, should be more debtor-friendly and less creditor-deferent under the unfair credit provisions than they have been under the extortionate credit provisions? The ordinary meaning of extortionate is stronger than that of unfair, as shown above. It should follow that the legal meaning of extortionate is stronger than that of unfair, even though no statutory definition of unfair exists. If it does, then the courts' consideration of the matters above should be more favourable to the debtor.

It is useful to contrast judicial pronouncements on the legal meaning of, on the one hand, extortionate and, on the other hand, unfair within the meaning of the UTCCR. Professor Goode's elaboration on the meaning of extortionate has been cited with approval by the courts:[28]

> (...) it seems clear that the concepts of extortion and unconscionability are very similar. Extortionate, like harsh and unconscionable signifies not merely that the terms of the bargain are stiff or even unreasonable but that they are so unfair as to be oppressive. This carries with it a notion of morally reprehensible conduct on the part of the creditor in taking grossly unfair advantage of the debtor's circumstances. ... the jurisdiction seems to me to contemplate at least a substantial imbalance in bargaining power of which one party has taken advantage.[29]

As to the meaning of unfair, in *Director General of Fair Trading* v. *First National Bank* Lord Bingham stated that: 'the supplier should not, whether deliberately or unconsciously, take advantage of the consumer's necessity, indigence, lack of experience, unfamiliarity with the subject matter of the contract [or] weak bargaining position.'[30] This contrast confirms that extortionate is stronger than unfair. To be extortionate, terms must not only be unfair, they must be so unfair as to be oppressive.

---

26   Section 138(3) and (4), s. 140A(2) respectively.
27   See generally L. Bentley and G. Howells, 'Judicial Treatment of Extortionate Credit Bargains', *The Conveyancer*, (1989): 164.
28   *Paragon Finance plc.* v. *Nash and Staunton* [2001] 2 All ER (Comm), para. 67.
29   In R. Goode, *Consumer Credit Law and Practice*, (London, 1999), para. 47.26.
30   [2001] UKHL 52 (judgment of 25 October 2001), para. 17.

A creditor is unfair if he takes advantage of the debtor's circumstances, either deliberately or unconsciously; to be extortionate he must take *gross* advantage.

Although the precise meaning of unfair within the meaning of the provisions cannot be definitively determined, at this stage it can certainly be said that it is not as strong as extortionate.

(ii) Interest Rate / Cost of Credit

There remains no interest rate above which a credit agreement is presumed to be unfair. The UK government has been opposed to direct controls on the cost of credit since the inception of the CCA.[31] The UK is pretty unique in this respect, as interest rate ceilings are a common feature across civil law Europe[32] and the common law world.[33] Thus the issue deserves some attention here. What follows is an outline of a

---

31   It repealed the Moneylenders Act 1927. That Act allowed the courts to re-open credit agreements which were harsh and unconscionable. It contained a presumption that interest rates above 48 percent were *prima facie* excessive.

32   For example, in Germany, s. 138 of the German Civil Code provides that transactions which offend good morals are void. It is settled case law that interest rates double the typical market rate are immoral and thus void. See Muenchener Kommentar zum BGB, s. 138(1), para. 116. In France, the limit is one third above the average market rate for similar products in the previous quarter. See D. Masciandaro, 'In Offence of Usury Laws: Microfoundations of Illegal Credit Contracts', *European Journal of Law and Economics*, 12, (2001): 193, at 196. In Spain the courts have interpreted the Ley de repression de law usura de 23 julio de 1908, which does not expressly provide an interest rate ceiling, to declare disproportionate an agreement which provided for a monthly interest rate of 5 percent (Tribunal Supremo, judgment of 12 July 2001). For contracts subject to the Mortgages Act, the Tribunal Supremo (judgment of 7 May 2002) decided that an interest rate of 29 per cent per annum considerably exceeded the threshold of reasonableness (limite razonable). For contracts subject to the Consumer Credit Act (Ley 7/1995 Credito al consumo), Article 19 para. 4 thereof prescribes an interest rate ceiling for current account overdrafts of 2.5 percent above the statutory interests rate (currently 4 percent: Ley 30/2005 of 29 December 2005). See J. M. Lete Del Rio and J. Lete Achirira, *Derecho des obligations, Volume II, contratos,* (Navarra, 2006), p. 475. The author expresses his thanks to Dr. M. Ebers for assistance on Spanish law, but naturally assumes responsibility for any errors or inaccuracies.

33   In Canada, § 347 Canadian Criminal Code makes it a criminal offence to impose an interest rate above 60 percent. It has however been noted that in practice the provision is rarely applied to 'payday' lenders, who often charge considerably in excess of this limit. See S. Lott and M. Grant, 'Fringe Lending and "Alternative Banking": The Consumer Experience', (2002) Public Interest Advocacy Centre, p. 61, available from www.piaac.ca. Ceilings also exist in several states of the USA, although commentators have noted that they are undermined by the fact that courts allow lenders established in non-ceiling states, to which law they are subject, to supply credit to customers in ceiling states. See M. Saunders and A. Cohen, 'Federal Regulation of Consumer Credit: The Cause or the Cure for Predatory Lending?', (2004) Working Paper Series, Joint Center for Housing Studies, Harvard University, BABC 04–21, pp. 7–8. Interest rate ceilings also exist in some Australian states, these cannot be circumvented in the same way as in the US (Clause 12 Australian Uniform Credit Laws Agreement 1993,

highly complex debate with contributions from lawyers, economists and sociologists alike; for a more comprehensive introduction the reader is referred to other works.[34] The debate concerns the harmful effects of high cost credit and the extent to which it is legitimate and desirable to seek to control market outcomes in this way.

The adverse effects of high cost credit on the individual, wider society and the economy, are easy to appreciate. As an increasing portion of the debtor's income is taken up to service debt he increasingly has to go without and has less money to place into the economy. Debt causes stress, people who are stressed are less productive and place more demands on health services. The problem is clearly more acute amongst the poor. Whereas higher income groups are more likely to use credit to acquire new assets or even finance investments (whereby the expected rate of return on the investments is higher than the rate of interest on the loan), the poor tend to resort to credit to meet unexpected financial shocks and even to pay bills and basic living expenses.[35] If they do so, it is only a natural progression that they will take on credit to finance existing debt; their existing inability to meet basic living expenses on their income alone is compounded by the costs of servicing debt. They are generally higher-risk borrowers, so that providers of cheaper, mainstream credit are reluctant to lend to them and, in the absence of social lending such as credit unions, they are forced into the hands of more expensive providers. Due to the higher rates charged in the 'fringe' credit market (the market for borrowers with low or insecure incomes or with impaired credit records), borrowers' ability to repay is reduced yet further, loans are increasingly rolled over and the spiral of debt is harder to break out of. There is an abundance of evidence on lenders abusing low income customers with morally reprehensible terms and practices (such as pressure selling and churning).[36] Expensive credit exacerbates the hardships of poverty and precipitate social exclusion and economic decline. Social and economic degeneration cause problems for all of us.

The main arguments employed by the UK government in rejecting direct controls on the cost of credit are the fear that interest rates would gravitate towards the ceiling,

---

available at www.creditcode.gov.eu). See N. Howell, 'High Cost Loans: A Case for Setting Maximum Rates?' (2005) Centre for Credit and Consumer Law Background Paper, Griffith University, p. 8, available at www.griffith.edu.au/centre/cccl.

34 A guide through the debate is Howell, 'High Cost Loans: A Case for Setting Maximum Rates?' especially pp. 22–32, available at www.griffith.edu.au/centre/cccl.

35 See G. Howells, 'Contract Law: The Challenge for the Critical Consumer Lawyer', in T. Wilhelmsson (ed.), *Perspectives of Critical Contract Law* (Dartmouth, 1993), p. 327 at p. 341.

36 Compare the following examples: A single mother on social security took out a loan of £800, repayable at £18 per week over 80 weeks. The total repayable is £1,440 and the Annual Percentage Rate (APR) is 132.5 percent. A low income client took out a loan of £300 to finance the deposit on rented accommodation. The APR is in excess of 200 percent. Another person took out a loan of £500. The total repayable is £1409.52 and the APR is 239.7 percent. A different loan for £500, repayable over 40 weeks at £20 per week, had an APR of 266 percent. Source: 'Daylight Robbery: The CAB case for effective regulation of extortionate credit', National Association of Citizens' Advice Bureaux p. 12.

and that it would exclude higher risk borrowers from the market and thus degenerate the market by stimulating demand for illegal moneylenders. The government supports its view on the basis of a study commissioned by the Department of Trade and Industry (DTI) in 2004 entitled *'The effect of interest rate controls in other countries'*. Before addressing the arguments in turn, it must be noted that the study has been subjected to stark criticism for its methodology and assumptions, which undermine its conclusions.[37] For example, it does not give any references for the mystery shopping, web- and telephone interviews, evaluations of court decisions, legislation, literature, research, industry and broker research it claims to have undertaken in France, Germany and the United States.[38] The study assumes that in liberal markets consumer choice for sub-prime (that is, not mainstream) products reflects consumer preference for these products.[39] This assumption is difficult to even entertain. Take the following real example:[40] someone borrowed £150. It was to be repaid within 28 days with an interest charge of £42. This equates to an Annual Percentage Rate (APR) of 1834.3 percent. If he could have borrowed the same amount from an overdraft facility, with, say, an interest rate of 1 percent per month, he would have paid £1.50 in interest. Are we to accept that he genuinely preferred to pay £42 instead of £1.50?

Now to the arguments. There is no empirical evidence that interest rates have gravitated towards the ceilings in countries which have them. The argument as to exclusionary and degenerative effects is founded on the assumption that the higher costs imposed on borrowers with low incomes or impaired credit ratings reflect higher costs to the lender (for example, they more frequently lend smaller amounts over shorter periods of time which can be just as expensive to administer as larger loans over longer periods of time; higher default rate). If the lender could not recover these costs through higher interest rates and charges then they simply would not lend to such groups, so the argument goes. This assumption is undermined by the excessive profits realised by fringe lenders.[41] Rather, the better view is that rates charged to fringe borrowers are the result of exploitation of market conditions.[42] It

---

37   U. Reifner, 'Comments on the DTI Study', (2004), available from www.debt-on-our-doorstep.com. The author wonders whether it is due to the force of the criticism it has attracted that the DTI commissioned study is no longer available on the DTI website.

38   *Ibid.*, p. 8.

39   *Ibid.*, p. 3.

40   Source: 'Daylight Robbery: The CAB case for effective regulation of extortionate credit', National Association of Citizens' Advice Bureaux, p. 13.

41   In North America see Lott and Grant, 'Fringe Lending and "Alternative Banking": The Consumer Experience'; C. Bruch, 'Taking the pay out of payday loans: Putting an end to the usurious and unconscionable interest rates charged by payday lenders', *University of Cincinatti Law Review* (2000): 1257.

42   Or, as Drysdale and Keeston state, 'simple opportunism': L. Drysdon and K. Keeston, 'The two-tiered consumer financial services marketplace: the fringe banking system and its challenge to current thinking about the role of usury laws in today's society', *South Carolina Law Review*, (2000): 589. For commentary on the UK market see D. Gibbons, 'Reducing the Cost of credit to Low Income Households: A case for capping credit charges', (2003) available at www.debt-on-our-doorstep.com; R. Murphy,

is thus both legitimate and desirable to impose direct controls on the cost of credit, to prevent unconscionable behaviour, to correct market failure, to combat social exclusion and economic decline.

Both the unfair and the extortionate credit provisions allow the court to consider the cost of credit. Under the extortionate provisions, the courts are only able to have regard to interest rates prevailing at the time the agreement was concluded.[43] They have been reluctant to intervene, with only ten instances of them reducing the interest rate payable.[44] The hurdle of 'unfair' is lower than that of 'extortionate', as demonstrated above,[45] so there is nothing to preclude the courts from determining that an interest rate which, at conclusion of the agreement, was not extortionate can never be unfair. Thus, if the unfair credit provisions do not deter lenders from charging unfairly high interest rates and do prompt more people to challenge high interest rates, then there is reason to believe that precedents will emerge from the case law which, if not *de facto* interest rate ceilings, will certainly provide guidelines as to maximum rates chargeable for particular types of agreements.

(iii) Undue Influence

A credit relationship may be unfair to the debtor if, as a result of undue influence exerted upon him (either by the creditor or, more commonly, the party for whom he is acting as guarantor), it cannot be treated as the expression of his free will.[46] In such circumstances the transaction can be set aside in equity. There are two broad classes of undue influence: *actual* (Class 1) and *presumed* (Class 2).[47]

A debtor can claim relief on grounds of *actual* undue influence (Class 1) if he can establish that such influence existed, that it was exercised, and that he entered into the transaction as a result. There are no further requirements.[48] A person can be under actual undue influence because of the trust and confidence he has reposed in another or because he stands in a relationship of dependency and ascendancy or dominion to the other. Thus, the classic case of actual undue influence is where the wife, under such influence from her husband, gives her signature to a mortgage on

---

'The case for an interest rate cap in the UK: A study based on Provident plc', (2003) prepared for Church Action on Poverty, The New Economics Foundation, and Debt on our Doorstep, available at www.debt-on-our-doorstep.com.

43   Section 138(2)(b).
44   For example *Barcabe* v. *Edwards* [1983] CCLR 11 (100 percent reduced to 40 percent), *Devogate* v. *Jarvis*, unreported (39 percent reduced to 30 percent). For other examples see references in Howells and Weatherill, *Consumer Protection Law*, pp. 342–3, n. 178.
45   See above, s. 3.1.
46   *Royal Bank of Scotland* v. *Etridge (No. 2)* [2001] UKHL 44 at [7].
47   *Barclays Bank plc.* v. *O'Brien* [1994] 1 AC 180.
48   Either of 'manifest disadvantage' to the debtor (*C.I.B.C. Mortgages* v. *Pitt* [1994] AC 200, disapproving *Bank of Credit and Commerce International S.A.* v. *Aboody* [1990] 1 QB 923) or that the transaction must be one which 'calls for explanation' (*Royal Bank of Scotland* v. *Etridge (No. 2)* [2001] UKHL 44 at [14]).

the marital home.[49] It is hardly conceivable that actual undue influence could arise between debtor and creditor.

Presumed undue influence arises where two basic facts are established.[50] Firstly, a relationship must exist in which one party has, in fact, reposed trust and confidence in the other. Such a relationship is takes as a matter of law to exist in certain types of relationship such as parent and child[51] and solicitor and client[52] (Class 2A relationships).[53] It is not taken to exist in relationships between husband and wife[54] (strange as it may sound) or banker and customer.[55] In relationships where trust and confidence is not taken as to exist as a matter of law, the person seeking relief must show that he had, in fact, reposed trust and confidence in the person benefiting from the transaction or that the person benefiting from the transaction had acquired 'domination' over him[56] (Class 2B relationships). The second fact that must be established is that the transaction is one which 'calls for explanation' or which 'is not readily explicable by the relationship between the parties'.[57] This will be so where the transaction is on terms more favourable to the person benefiting from the transaction than would normally be expected.

This presumption of undue influence can be rebutted if the person benefiting from the transaction can show that it was freely entered into.[58] This can usually be

---

49   For example, see the facts of *Bank of Credit and Commerce International S.A.* v. *Aboody* [1990] 1 QB 923; wife was absolutely submissive to husband's requests, never questioning him when he put documents before her to sign, one of which was an agreement to mortgage the marital home.

50   *Royal Bank of Scotland* v. *Etridge (No. 2)* [2001] UKHL 44, at [13].

51   For example, *Bullock* v. *Lloyds Bank* [1955] Ch. 317; *Cocking* v. *Pratt* (1749) 1 Ves. Sen. 400; *Powell* v. *Powell* [1900] 1 Ch. 243.

52   *Wright* v. *Carter* [1903] 1 Ch. 27.

53   This subdivision was first adopted in *Bank of Credit and Commerce International S.A.* v. *Aboody* [1990] 1 QB 923 at 953 and approved in *Barclays Bank plc.* v. *O'Brien* [1994] 1 AC 180 at 189–190. It is doubtful whether this subdivision has survived *Royal Bank of Scotland* v. *Etridge (No. 2)* [2001] UKHL 44; it is used here for ease of exposition only.

54   *Howes* v. *Bishop* [1909] 2 KC 390; *Gillman* v. *Gillman* (1946) 174 LT 272; *National Westminster Bank plc.* v. *Morgan* [1985] 1 All ER 821 at 838; *Kings North Trust* v. *Bell* [1986] 1 WLR 119 at 127; *Coldunell Ltd* v. *Gallon* [1986] 1 All ER 429 at 437; *Midland Bank plc.* v. *Shephard* [1988] 3 All ER 17; *Barclays Bank plc.* v. *Khaira* [1992] 1 WLR 623 at 632.

55   *National Westminster Bank plc.* v. *Morgan* [1985] 1 All ER 821; *Lloyds Bank* v. *Egremont* [1990] 2 FLR 351.

56   *Goldsworth* v. *Brickell* [1987] CL 378 at 404.

57   *Royal Bank of Scotland* v. *Etridge (No. 2)* [2001] UKHL 44 at [14] and [21] (the law previously required a 'manifest disadvantage': *National Westminster Bank plc.* v. *Morgan* [1985] 1 All ER 821).

58   '[F]ree exercise of independent will': *Inche Noriah* v. *Shaik Allie bin Omar* [1929] AC 127 at 136; *Mahoney* v. *Purnell* [1996] 3 All ER 61 at 85; *Naidoo* v. *Naidu, The Times,* November 1, 2000; *Royal Bank of Scotland* v. *Etridge (No. 2)* [2001] UKHL 44 at [7]: 'expression of (...) free will'.

established if the debtor was counselled by a competent advisor aware of all the relevant facts.[59]

Undue influence in relationships between husband and wife and banker and customer will thus be difficult to establish. A wife must show 1) that she reposed trust and confidence in her husband or was dominated by him and 2) that the transaction is one which calls for explanation. Whilst one would assume that it should not be too difficult to show that the wife had trust and confidence in her husband, that the transaction is one which calls for explanation or is not readily explicable by the nature of the relationship is more difficult to establish. It is in the nature of marital relationships that spouses support each other. Thus it is well conceivable that a wife would borrow money or stand as surety for the benefit of her husband, fully aware of what she was letting herself into. Undue influence in the relationship between banker and customer is even more difficult to conceive. A banker's interests are quite distinct from a customer's, and the customer does not generally repose such trust and confidence in the banker to look after his interests as though they were his own.

English lawyers are, however, familiar with the situation whereby they think the law is clear and settled; then along comes a case with three important characteristics. Firstly, the law as the lawyer thinks it is against the appellant. Secondly, the appellant is a poor old man (or more usually a woman). Thirdly, the presiding judge is Lord Denning, probably the cleverest and certainly the most creative judge in our history. The lawyer reads the case and realises that the law is not quite so clear cut as he thought. *Lloyds Bank v Bundy*[60] is such a case. It concerned a father who mortgaged his farm to guarantee his son's business debts. The relationship with the bank was long standing and, as stressed by Lord Denning, the bank was aware that Mr Bundy relied on it to provide him with disinterested advice. This gave rise to a duty of care which the bank breached when the assistant manager visited Mr Bundy at his home, explained the terms of the mortgage and persuaded him to sign, without advising him to obtain independent advice. Had Mr Bundy received independent advice, no doubt he would have been told to steer clear. The mortgage was not to secure new finance for his son, but for his son's existing debts; only the bank stood to gain.[61] This case was said to turn on its very special facts and there appears a reluctance to follow it again.[62]

(iv) Drawing Out the Meaning of Fair: Soft Law

There is good reason to believe that the courts may refer to sources of soft law[63] in applying the fairness test. Section 140D provides that the Office of Fair Trading

---

59   *Inche Noriah* v. *Shaik Allie bin Omar* [1929] AC 127 at 136.
60   [1974] 3 All ER 757.
61   See the opening of Lord Denning's judgment, in Denning's characteristic prose style: Broadchalke is one of the most pleasing villages in England. Old Herbert Bundy, the defendant, was a farmer there. His home was at Yew Tree Farm. It went back for 300 years. His family had been there for generations. It was his only asset. But he did a very foolish thing. He mortgaged it to the bank.
62   *National Westminster Bank plc.* v. *Morgan* [1985] 1 All ER 821, per Lord Scarman.
63   Soft law can be defined as: 'Rules of conduct that are laid down in instruments which

(OFT) shall publish guidance on how it expects the unfair credit provisions to interact with Part VIII of the Enterprise Act 2002, which empowers the OFT to take action to prevent the continuation of unfair terms and practices detrimental to the collective interests of consumers. A further factor is the courts' interpretation of the concept of fairness within the UTCCR. A term within the scope of the Regulations is unfair *inter alia* if it is 'contrary to the requirement of good faith'.[64] In *Director General of Fair Trading* v. *First National Bank,* Lord Bingham, following the passage quoted above,[65] stated that: 'Good faith (…) looks to good standards of commercial morality and practice'.[66] Sources of soft law provide a barometer for standards of commercial morality and practice.

Sources of soft law in this context are, primarily, the draft guidance of the OFT,[67] but also voluntary codes of conduct such as the Banking Code.[68] The Banking Code states that customers shall be fully informed of the nature and extent of his commitments under the credit agreement, both through advertising and promotional literature as well as individually, and that they should be dealt with sympathetically when they encounter financial difficulty.[69] The draft guidance of the OFT expressly refers to the Financial Services Authority's[70] 'treating customers fairly initiative',[71] which mentions six key themes illuminating what fairness requires in this context (given in italics; the elaborations thereafter are taken from Patient)[72]:

- *Give the customer what they have paid for:* ensure the customer fully understands the reality of the product sold.
- *Do not take advantage of the customer;* avoid pushy sales tactics; do not sell inappropriate products to customers; do not allow the priorities of the provider to unduly influence the sale of a particular product.
- *Offer the best product you can;* both initially and in the ongoing relationship.

---

have not been ascribed legally binding force as such, but nevertheless may have certain – indirect – legal effects, and that are aimed at and may produce practical effects.' (L. Senden, 'Soft Law, Self-Regulation and Co-regulation in European Law: Where do they meet?', *Electronic Journal of Comparative Law,* (2005): 1 at 23, available at www.ejcl.org).

64   Regulation 4(1).
65   Section 3(i).
66   [2001] UKHL 52 (judgment of 25 October 2001), para. [17].
67   OFT, *Unfair relationships – draft guidance – consultation document,* available at www.oft.gov.uk.
68   Available at www.bankingcode.org.uk. It sets standards of good banking practice for financial institutions dealing with personal customers, on a day-to-day basis and in times of financial difficulty – see Banking Code, para. 1.1.
69   Banking Code, para. 2.
70   The Financial Services Authority is an independent non-departmental public body and quasi-judicial body that regulates the financial services industry in the United Kingdom.
71   *Draft guidance,* para. 4.39.
72   J. Patient, 'The Consumer Credit Act 2006', *Journal of International Banking Law and Regulation,* (2006): 309 at 313.

- *Do your best to resolve mistakes as quickly as possible;* the provider should be prepared to acknowledge mistakes and make recompense where appropriate.
- *Show flexibility, empathy and consideration in dealing with customers;* use discretion where customers have made honest mistakes; judge each case separately; the provider should err on the side of generosity.
- *Exhibit clarity in all customer dealings;* terms and conditions should be as clear and as easy to understand as possible; changes or new features should be explained; messages should be consistent; avoid misleading language.

Where the OFT is dissatisfied with a creditor's conduct, it may issue a notice requiring it to do or refrain from doing anything specified in the notice.[73] Failure to comply with the requirements of a notice can be sanctioned by a fine of up to £50,000.[74]

Sources of soft law in this area will thus acquire a new significance. This is especially so in relation to voluntary codes of conduct, to which lenders are not obliged to subscribe,[75] those engaging in unfair practices least likely to do so.

4. Redress

The remedy available under the extortionate provisions is that the court can reduce the amount of repayment to what is 'fairly due and reasonable'.[76] In the few cases in which a remedy has been awarded, the courts have been very creditor-deferent in their interpretation of what is fairly due and reasonable.[77] Even if they were more debtor-friendly, as Howells and Weatherill note: 'simply to allow creditors to charge what would have been appropriate in the first place remains a weak sanction'.[78]

The unfair credit provisions by contrast equip the courts with a wider range of remedies. They may:
- require the creditor to repay anything paid by the debtor or a surety;
- require the debtor to do, not to do, or cease doing anything in connection with the agreement;
- reduce or discharge any sum payable by the debtor or surety;
- direct the return of any property provided by the debtor or surety;

---

73   Section 33A.
74   Section 39A.
75   The following financial institutions were not signatories to the Banking Code according to the Banking Code Standards Board's website, checked on 27 January 2007: Century Building Society, Harpenden Building Society, C Hoare & Co., Liverpool Victoria Banking Services, Penrith Building Society, Ruffler Bank plc., Weatherbys Bank. Application pending for ICICI Bank UK Limited, negotiations in progress for The Post Office.
76   Section 139(2).
77   For example the unsecured loan in *Barcabe* v. *Edwards* [1983] CCLR 11 was reduced from 100 percent to 40 percent; the secured loans in the unreported cases of *Devogate* v. *Jarvis* (1987) and *Prestonwell Ltd* v. *Capon* (1988) were reduced from 39 percent to 30 percent and 42 percent to 21 percent respectively. Source: Howells and Weatherill, *Consumer Protection Law*, pp. 342–3.
78   *Ibid.*, p. 344.

- set aside (in whole or in part) any duty imposed on the debtor or surety;
- alter the terms of the agreement;
- direct accounts to be taken.[79]

Such orders may be made notwithstanding that their effect is to place a burden on the creditor in respect of an advantage enjoyed by another person[80] (thus excluding any objection by the creditor based on arguments of unjust enrichment). One can safely assume that these sanctions will be more effective than merely reducing repayments to what is fairly due and reasonable, both in terms of the increased flexibility to do justice in the individual case and in their general deterrent effect.

To apply for a credit bargain to be re-opened under the extortionate credit provisions, the debtor or surety must endure the ordinary court process and bear the ordinary burden of proof in civil cases. This is a daunting prospect for most people and, evidence suggests, especially intimidating to the most vulnerable, who may also feel intimidated by the creditor.[81] Cost is a particular issue. People are not usually awarded public funding for these types of cases. Evidence suggests that even people with strong cases are thus deterred from claiming judicial protection.[82] Another matter, also related to costs, is the quality of legal advice available to debtors. Consumer credit law is a specialist subject of which most high street solicitors know little. The expert lawyers are generally retained by the lenders and have fees which correspond with their expertise. In the common law system, generally, 'costs follow the result', that is, if the debtor loses he will have to pay for the creditor's lawyers.[83] All in all, it is not surprising that practical, psychological and cultural barriers may prevent debtors from taking court action.[84]

---

79   Section 140B(1).

80   Section 140B(3).

81   See Financial Services Authority, 2002–2003 annual report, p. 211, available from www.fsa.gov.uk.

82   See the following case concerning a mortgage for £15,300. The clients obtained all information from a broker over the telephone. On that basis, the clients believed they would be repaying £150 per month over 20 years. The loan amount was increased by a broker's fee of £1,700 and payment protection insurance of £2,380, making a total loan of £19,380. It was in fact repayable at £305.24 per month over 20 years. The total payable was £73,257. At the time of signing the agreement the clients had suffered a family bereavement and did not pay proper attention to the terms. The matter was referred to the OFT and the CAB. The CAB commented: 'Whilst it is clear (...) that this (...) is (...) an extortionate credit bargain (...) to do anything about it will (...) cost (...) around £500 in fees alone.' Source: 'Daylight Robbery: The CAB case for effective regulation of extortionate credit', National Association of Citizens' Advice Bureaux, pp. 23–24.

83   The CAB report of one case in which the bill for solicitors, counsel, and expert witnesses in excess of £26,000 was awarded against the debtors. Source: 'Daylight Robbery: The CAB case for effective regulation of extortionate credit', National Association of Citizens' Advice Bureaux, p. 25.

84   See Financial Services Authority 2002-2003 annual report, p. 211., available from www.fsa.gov.uk.

The unfair credit provisions establish an alternative dispute resolution mechanism administered by the Financial Ombudsman Service, which will be available at no cost to the debtor and reverses the burden of proof.[85] This should encourage debtors to make use of the unfair credit provisions by addressing the barriers to court action identified above, and reduce costs for all concerned. It should also benefit fair creditors by deterring, and stimulating private enforcement against, unfair creditors, who enjoy an unfair competitive advantage.[86]

5. Concluding Remarks

The unfair credit provisions go some way to countering the deficiencies in the existing legal framework to protect consumers in unfair credit relationships. Most significantly, the level of unfairness which is required before the courts can intervene has been markedly lowered and any aspect of the relationship is relevant to its determination, whether it be the terms of the agreement or the conduct of the creditor. The courts have a greater armoury of remedies at their disposal to do justice between the parties, which should boost the deterrent effect of the provisions. The law only benefits consumers if they can actually use it and the alternative dispute resolution mechanism should enable them to do so to a greater extent than hitherto.

Perhaps the greatest deficiency of the reform is the refusal to introduce direct controls on the cost of credit. The basis for the government's continued opposition to them is highly questionable. The unscientific nature of the study on which this opposition is based, and its disappearance from the DTI's website following the compelling criticisms of Professor Reifner, invites suspicion. Suspicion that the government itself doubts the scientific basis of its position, suspicion that the conclusions of the study were written before the analysis was carried out, but also suspicion that the tide of government opinion may be turning.

Interest rates and charges are probably the single most significant factors in determining whether a credit relationship is unfair. The unfair credit provisions do leave it open to the courts to set precedents on what levels of interest and charges are unfair. Creditors who wish to continue imposing unfair interest rates and charges must realise that both the substantive and procedural rules for judicial intervention in credit relationships are now weighted considerably more in favour of the debtor. If they do not, and do not amend their rates accordingly, then the courts may well do so for them.

---

85   Section 140B(9).
86   For a full assessment of the costs and benefits of the new ADR system and the reforms
      of the Consumer Credit Act generally see 'Consumer Credit Bill, Regulatory Impact
      Assessment', DTI (2004), available at www.dti.gov.uk.

23 European Coalition for Responsible Credit – Principles of Responsible Credit

Udo Reifner (ed.)[1]

1. Why We Are Concerned

For today's consumers, *consumer credit* contracts now rank as high in importance as contracts for employment. But *over-indebtedness* has also become a similar threat in modern times to unemployment in the last century. Sustainable development therefore requires access to responsible credit products and services.

At the present time many consumer credit agreements are far from transparent, and involve terms and conditions that are at best confusing and at worst, deliberately misleading to consumers. These agreements often involve multiple firms, and anticipate that consumers will pay additional fees for unforeseen contingencies; many also require the purchase of linked services such as insurance of unpaid balances. The consequences for consumers who are unwilling or unable to pay attention to these details can be devastating.

Consumer Credit makes potential future income available for current spending on items such as consumption, education, starting a business, and paying for health care. As such, consumer credit is a basic element of participation in the economic life of modern society. The benefits of access to credit are many, including developing national wealth and meeting basic consumer needs. However, there can also be a dark side to consumer credit – in some cases, it can destroy families, and lead to the loss of valuable assets including homes. The continued extension of credit at high cost to people on inadequate incomes only serves to deepen the levels of poverty that they experience.

In Europe, most consumer credit is provided by private sector firms. If their activities are not tempered by moral institutions, public awareness, protective law and administrative supervision, firms might irresponsibly provide credit in the sole interest of gaining maximum profit. Borrowed money does not itself provide real wealth but only holds the potential to create that wealth. Vulnerable people can be harmed by greed, usury, exploitation and predatory lending, all leading to a lifelong

---

1   Institut für Finanzdienstleistungen. The principles have been developed in discussions among a steering group of ECRC (see http://www.responsible-credit.net). In the meantime they have been signed by numerous NGOs all over the world. The explanatory notes are not part of the signed principles.

entanglement in debt. This insight has become an integral part of the European legal tradition which bans usury, *laesio enormis*, extortionate credit, and the exploitation of need; this tradition goes on to require social responsibility and the exemption from seizure for some property and income.

Consumer credit is part of a cultural process of reproduction. Left unimpeded, market forces in the financial services sector tend to favour the rich and to discriminate against the poor. Trust in the 'invisible hand' has never safeguarded the interests of the disadvantaged –not with regard to poor countries and not with regard to poor people. Credit markets need rules that allow the benefits of credit provision to flow to all people and not just to the more fortunate, whilst rules are also required to protect those who are most vulnerable to exploitative lending practices. This balance, between providing access to credit whilst preventing the worst excesses of an unbridled market, is central to the concept of 'responsible credit'.

The EU, in Article 152 of the Maastricht treaty as well as in the proposed new constitution, acknowledges that the State must guarantee a high level of consumer protection and must actively oppose social discrimination. If the EU comes to see its primary goal as opening markets for the most influential (and sometimes also the most unscrupulous) lenders, without respect for national culture in credit regulation and morality, it will be seen as a threat to the idea of a unified Europe. Europe needs banking for, and not against, its people. Law and justice must therefore create a credit market that promotes the productive use of credit, including a consideration of social needs.

The current draft of the EU Consumer Credit Directive, which differs from previous versions, threatens consumers by allowing the sale, in all Member States, of financial services that will exploit the disadvantaged. The Directive includes virtually no consumer protections nor guarantees existing national protections, whilst it opens up the existing markets of all Member states to competition from lenders based in other countries. For this reason, the wider market for financial services threatens to undermine existing consumer protection laws in many Member States.

In order to uphold cultural diversity, to further social responsibility and 'good morals', and to keep up the *bona fide* principle of *ius commune*, the following requirements for a responsible European Consumer Credit Directive can be identified. The new proposal of a Consumer Credit Directive has been evaluated in the light of these principles. This evaluation shows that, at a minimum, the European Commission wants to apply significantly different principles to the European credit culture that have been in place thus far and we consider that to do so would be to the disadvantage of many consumers.

2. Principles for Responsible Lending

(i) Responsible and Affordable Credit Must be Provided For All

(a) Credit is an essential for full participation in society   In the industrialized society credit has become a service essential for full participation in society. By giving people access to their own future income, credit provides the opportunity

to obtain the use of advanced goods and services that require capital investments like cars, household appliances, permanent education or homeownership. Access to credit makes it possible to bridge variations in income and expenditure and thus provide the flexibility that modern labour markets require.

While credit may not currently be available in all countries, the creation of small business and self-employment requires capital everywhere. While individual capital is difficult to access, credit plays the role of seed capital in self-employment. Accordingly, providing access to credit realizes a human right to use one's own future resources properly. To this extent, credit has to be accessible for people in society irrespective of their social, biological, or cultural differences.

To realize this right requires the creation of banking facilities to be supported where no banking facilities are currently available, and needs people who are currently excluded from financial services to have access to banking facilities where they already exist or could be provided by the existing banking infrastructure. Regulation should under no pretext therefore prohibit access to the best and most affordable forms of credit under competitive conditions for all. This includes facilitating forms of Microlending and alternative credit institutions. But such alternative credit institutions which have lower technical and protective standards, and operate with less cost efficiency than existing banks should be used primarily as gateways to the general system of financial services provision.

(b) Banks should not discriminate and should provide real access   Banks have been trusted to administer the savings of their depositors and thus the monetary form of our wealth of nations. The public should monitor that they use this trust properly, without any discrimination, and that they reinvest it into our communities in ways that are ethical and which meet the needs of humanity across the world. Access to credit should empower communities, not leave them disenfranchised or open them to exploitation.

Developed banking systems under competitive market structures tend to exclude vulnerable consumers from their main business by providing direct or indirect services which do not meet their own standards. This is why markets require active state supervision and regulation to stir all providers of credit to accept poor or disfavoured consumers and communities by raising public awareness (e.g. through Community Reinvestment Legislation), creating obligations for inclusion (basic bank accounts, equal credit opportunities) or engaging in subsidies or support that can remove obstacles for these customers to be accepted (rate subsidies in fair housing finance, free credit and debt counselling, state guarantees etc).

(c) Credit to Consumers and Small Businesses must be supervised   The non-commercial use of credit requires active supervision, comprehensive protective regulation and the strengthening of good morals in order to protect the borrower's position in the market and from the market.

Consumer credit, housing finance and start-up credit is directly linked to the livelihood of families and their social wellbeing. Its use is not only a function of profitable calculations. Its users are often unskilled and have to manage unforeseeable events out of a weak individual market position. When they have to default, the rules of the market society alone cannot offer adequate answers. This is why from the very beginning of money societies debtors have been protected and modern legislation has enlarged these regulations in line with the extension of credit. Regulation does not replace consumer awareness and individual responsibility but has to strengthen it where this is required and needs to provide social solutions where the borrower is at a disadvantage in the marketplace.

(ii) Credit Relations have to be Transparent and Understandable

Two types of transparency should be delivered to potential borrowers to allow market forces to operate as intended. Competitive transparency gives consumers a chance to choose the cheapest and best product. But social transparency, indicating the potential impacts of credit on future household liquidity, is also necessary.

(a) Competitive transparency requires a standardized mathematically correct form of 'one-price' disclosure (the Annual Percentage Rate of Charge or APRC)   The APRC should include all credit related payments that will repay the borrowed capital. The calculation of the APRC must include all cost elements that will, in practice, burden household income in the future: payments on linked cross-selling products, endowments, brokerage fees, and fees associated with acquisition, risk coverage or debt collection. Such cost elements represent services for which alternatives exist and the existence of these alternatives should be disclosed in a form which makes comparison and exit easy. The lack of transparency on insurance costs also leads to a lack of price competition in this area and runs contrary to the aims of the Directive in opening up markets to deliver better outcomes through increased price competition.

(b) Social transparency requires a standardized pre-contractual payment plan   This pre-contractual plan should disclose the likely impact of future payments on consumers' household liquidity and future purchasing power, impacts that can be predicted by statistical analysis of past experience with similar contracts. Pre-contractual plans that demonstrate an ability to repay are the cornerstone of responsible lending but they rely on full disclosure of outstanding liabilities. The extension of credit that occurs without proper attempts to discover full outstanding liabilities (for example through credit card balance transfers and the unilateral raising of credit limits without borrower agreement) is a particular problem that must be addressed.

(c) Consumers should be provided with adequate time for reflection and with access to independent advice   The right to cancel an agreement exists only once a binding offer has been made. This system provides little time for reflection by the consumer or for independent advice to be sought. Where the amounts of the agreement are large, there should be improved systems to allow for advice to be taken and there needs to be facilities to provide advice to people who are in a particularly weak bargaining position.

(d) Consumers should have access to independent financial, credit and debt advice   Consumers and small businesses have most need of advice and help when

they are in difficult financial situations. This is the situation in which vulnerable consumers are most active information seekers and take the most disadvantageous decisions. In this situation they need to know about their legal rights, the economic and social consequences of their adjustments and help to cope with the effects of their problems on family, labour income and consumption. It is in this situation that the market cannot provide adequate services which require a consumer who has a free choice and adequate means to pay. Both are not available at this point. This is why credit and debt advice has to be provided at low cost by unselfish institutions monitored by society. To uphold such offers is a public task.

(e) Both parties in the credit markets have to take part in a mutually productive process of financial education Consumers need to understand and use financial services properly with respect to their potential and risks. But they also have to learn that products and services can be changed and made more adequate if they are able to voice concern, evade credit, and engage in a collective process to develop better market conditions. Equally, the process of financial education includes learning on the part of the creditors about the needs and necessities of borrowers in order to adjust their profit driven offers to consumer requirements. Banks are not the teachers of consumers but they can provide answers to their questions.

(iii) Lending Has at all Times to be Cautious, Responsible and Fair

(a) Credit and its servicing must be productive for the borrower Not every access to credit is productive. Especially in Europe and the US, lack of access is no longer the core problem. Credit is now offered to all through damaging forms of credit that are used for unproductive investments, increase the dependency of consumers, and lead to exploitation and over-indebtedness. This is why credit contracts have to be monitored and carefully regulated.

(b) Responsible lending requires the provision of all necessary information and advice to consumers and liability for missing and incorrect information Advice links consumers' needs with their future income and purchasing power and illuminates the impact that the provided services might have on the future lives of borrowers and their families. Responsible lending requires that lenders assume liability for misrepresentation, false advice or missing information as well as for the sale of services known to be inadequate, except where there has been a deliberate and malicious intent on the part of the borrower to defraud. Creditors must take all reasonable steps to validate information provided to them and must in particular share data on outstanding liabilities and repayment levels.

(c) No lender should be allowed to exploit the weakness, need or naivety of borrowers If markets encourage exploitation and dependency by favouring the rich and discriminating against the poor, the law must set minimum standards for the operation of those markets. Effective rate ceilings are a starting point.

There needs to be a social guarantee that lenders will not abuse their position when the borrower's circumstances worsen through no fault of their own. In these circumstances lenders should not be able to seek higher charges on default or to worsen the position of the borrower further. There also needs to be a more sophisticated understanding of risk and a proper consideration of risk across the credit portfolio rather than an attempt to identify an individual risk based price for each and every social group. The repayment of debts should be regulated so that early repayment is possible and so that refinancing conditions are closely regulated.

(d) Early repayment, without penalty, must be possible   Consumers should always have the right to repay their debts without penalty. It is unacceptable that profit-driven systems should be able to keep consumers indebted when economic efficiency suggests that debts can and should be repaid.

(e) The conditions under which consumers can refinance or reschedule their debt should be regulated   Refinancing is not the repayment of credit. It can often represent a deterioration of credit conditions at a time when the debtor is economically weak. Regulation should guarantee that this weakness is not exploited, and in particular limit the amortization of interest and other charges. 'Solutions' where future expectations are traded off for temporary relief should be controlled.

(iv) Adaptation Should be Preferred to Credit Cancellation and Destruction

If debtors experience adverse circumstances, changes in credit relations by adjustments and adaptation should be preferred to acceleration, cancellation and destruction of the credit relationship.

(a) There is a need for effective protection against unfair credit cancellation   Credit relations are as important as labour and housing rent contracts in relation to individual lives. The principles of protection against unjustified or premature cancellations in these relations should be extended to credit.

(b) Default charges should be adequate to cover losses only   Default charges should be regulated in a way that prevents lenders from recovering more than the true cost of the default and lenders should aim to ensure the speedy restoration of the original contract terms.

Default interest rates should not exceed the refinancing cost of the lender plus additional administrative costs.

(v) Protective Legislation Has to be Effective

It must cover any form of credit that is linked directly to the lives of borrowers and especially to credit provided for consumption, education, housing and the start-up of a small business. Exemptions on the basis of size of loan or type of loan only serve to confuse consumers and have adverse impacts on market behaviour.

(a) Credit regulation has to cover all non-commercial users It should include consumers, homeowners and individuals starting up small businesses (all hereafter called 'consumers').

(b) Credit regulation has to cover all commercial forms of credit provision Definition: Credit comprises all activities which bring people into debt through the commercial offer of purchasing power, irrespective whether this is done in the form of loans, deferred payments, leasing, rent or any other legal form and irrespective whether payments are called interest or fees.

(c) Credit regulation has to cover the whole process of credit extension as experienced by its users The economic development of suppliers has tended to divide the process of providing and servicing credit contracts into ever more distinct pieces, each undertaken by different types of firm. The impact of credit on consumer households, however, has become ever more integrated and unified. Credit was historically extended as part of one contractual relation in which a consumer bought goods and services through installment purchases. A singe institution was creditor, broker and debt collector and that institution was accessible for consumers' concerns. This relation was later split into two separate types of contract, one for purchases/ service agreements and one for loans. This has led to the creation of lenders who operate without any regard for the consumption purposes of the loan.

Cost efficiency, as expressed in the 'value chain' approach, drives suppliers into horizontal cooperation and into the development of a whole bundle of separate contracts. The provision of money, the acquisition of clients, the securing of debts and the servicing of credit contracts (and adapting them to the changing living conditions of the borrowers) and, finally, debt recovery have been put into different hands. Each player is solely focused on its own profit, freed from direct concern about consumers' employment problems and consumption needs. In addition, modern global competition among the most profitable multinational financial conglomerates has led to the increased exploitation of the dependency inherent in the creditor-debtor relations. Such institutions engage in the cross-selling of linked insurance, investment and financial products at above market rates. For consumers, there is only one process – getting money for present expenditures and paying it back from future income. Nonetheless, suppliers pretend to deliver hundreds of valuable services. It is an important task of our political culture to ensure a unified vision of the demand side as a leading perspective in law and to guarantee a market whose final goal should remain the satisfaction of the needs of the people.

(d) Credit regulation has to encourage efficient social and economic effects of credit extension Protective regulation has to adopt an economic and social language and should not use only legal language that is open to the manipulation by those who provide financial services. Providing legitimacy to usury through the device of 'borrowers' consent', for example, would ignore 1,000 years of experience in which credit contracts voluntarily undertaken by needy persons have led to their exploitation and dependency. Indeed we consider that usury, by definition, is undertaken with the borrowers' consent as it is precisely the desperation of the borrowers' financial

circumstances that drives them to seek out usurious loans. However, the extension of credit at usurious prices is not a solution to the problem of poverty and should not be entertained as such by credit regulation.

(vi) Over-Indebtedness Should be a Public Concern

Dealing with failed credit relations and over-indebtedness should be a public responsibility. The goal should be to rehabilitate and reintegrate consumers into the economic life of society.

(a) Profit-driven systems cannot cope with over-indebtedness   Refinancing, revolving credit, and predatory lending to economically over-indebted people, are not solutions to poverty. Instead, they can be a way into long-term poverty and dependence.

(b) Consumers should have a right to discharge   Consumers should have a right to a public procedure of discharge through which their duties to repay debts are adapted to the remaining productivity of the borrowed funds.
      Where credit no longer reflects a productive investment into the economic life of the borrower, a system of discharge and devaluation of debts is necessary. Firms vanish when they fail and their debts are written off in bankruptcy. Individuals, however, do not vanish and therefore their debt burden must be adapted to the value of their labour where this is the only source of income for repayment. Discharge is a fresh start for debtors and their families.

(c) Bankruptcy procedures should lead to rehabilitation and not to retortion   Discharge requires rehabilitation and reintegration into a productive life. It must involve independent advice, shelter from creditors, and help to readapt their income to their expenditures.

(vii) Borrowers Must Have Adequate Means to Defend Their Rights and be Free to Voice Their Concerns

(a) There should be adequate individual as well as collective legal procedures to enforce borrowers' rights   Creditors address legal matters strategically and calculate risks and cost with respect to the whole of their business. A single consumer, however, takes on an enormous risk when he or she sues a creditor. In practice, creditors dominate the selection of cases which come to the higher courts. It is therefore important to seek remedies for this strategic weakness of consumers in the process of further legal developments. In order to cover the financial risks *pro deo* procedures are especially important for credit law because the vulnerable poor are least likely to defend their rights in court. In theory, class actions are adequate remedies, if the state can guarantee funding for consumer organizations which effectively care for the rights of the poor. Ombudsman schemes, and other non-court based systems, whilst useful for individuals seeking redress should also be able to address broad issues within the credit industry where on the evidence of the number of individual

cases being dealt with it appears that these are apparent. This may be, by example, by placing a duty on ombudsman schemes to report to state regulators on the specific concerns arising on a regular basis.

(b) Critical public awareness is crucial for the development a fair and responsible distribution of credit Financial institutions exercise enormous influence within the media through their advertising budgets and through their investments in media firms. They can also use anti-defamation laws quite effectively to suppress critical journalism. In addition, most credit-related research in economics and law is partly financed by the supplier side. If the state does not counterbalance this enormous power, the prospects for critical responses are dim.

The provision of information on lending patterns of private sector lenders is critical to the development of public awareness and ensures that measures can be taken to address the unfair exclusion of lower income social groups from credit. The EU should therefore ensure that there is a standard obligation for lenders in the Member states to disclose information relating to lending patterns by social group and geography and that there is an affirmative obligation placed on lenders to address financial exclusion.

24 Product Safety Regulation Reform in Australia and Japan: Harmonising Towards European Models?

Luke Nottage[1]

The previous Yearbook outlined discussions underway in Australia about reforms to laws regulating the safety of general consumer goods, bringing its 1970s regime more into line with the EU regime inaugurated in 1992 and strengthened in 2001.[2] Part 1 of this Note outlines how those discussions have largely stalled, despite a related subsequent review that has already been quite critical of Australia's main peak standard-setting body, as well as several ongoing product safety incidents. The shadow of Australia's 'National Competition Policy', inaugurated in the mid-1990s,[3] is falling ever more sharply over consumer law.

By contrast, Part 2 contends that Australia's major trading partner, Japan, is developing more momentum towards comprehensive reform. Ironically, this comes out of an *annus horribilis* involving four major product safety incidents in quick succession from mid-2005. Another round of asbestos problems was followed by large scale problems with defective buildings; then problems with (mostly consumer) electrical goods regulation; then, with elevators made by Swiss-based Schindler.[4] Further incidents keep being reported too. Admittedly, tort law remains on an upward trajectory in Japan, and in parallel with economic deregulation since the late 1990s the government has been implementing civil justice reforms aimed to encouraging active pursuit of rights through the courts as a more indirect means of socio-economic ordering, in lieu of *ex ante* regulation by public authorities. However, many tort claims have been directed specifically against the government after World War II. Criminal prosecutions for professional negligence remain another salient feature of the way the Japanese legal system deals with safety issues. This underpins re-regulatory reforms underway or called for in specific areas, such as

---

1   Senior Lecturer and Co-Director, Australian Network for Japanese Law, University of Sydney Faculty of Law. For research support, thanks are due to Joel Rheuben and ARC Discovery Grant DP0450648.

2   2001/95/EC. Compare L. Nottage (2007) 'Consumer Product Safety Regulation Reform in Australia: Ongoing Processes and Possible Outcomes' 2 *Yearbook of Consumer Law* 327.

3   B. Morgan (2003) *Social Citizenship in the Shadow of Competition: The Bureaucratic Politics of Regulatory Justification* (Aldershot, Burlington, Vt.: Ashgate).

4   L. Nottage (2006) 'The ABCs of Product Safety Re-regulation in Japan: Asbestos, Buildings, Consumer Electrical Goods, and Schindler's Lifts', 15(2) *Griffith Law Review* 242.

asbestos products and construction. It also makes it easier to generate 'horizontal' reforms (covering all types of goods) like those enacted on 28 November 2006 for the Consumer Product Safety Law of 1973. As now in the EU, firms in Japan will generally need to report serious accidents to the authorities.

Nonetheless, the revised Law does not go as far as the new EU regime, and Japan's bureaucrats still try to retain their influence through sector-specific legislation. In addition, over 2001–2006 the Koizumi government accelerated deregulation, at least in some areas and certainly in the overall rhetoric of policymaking. Part 3 therefore concludes by highlighting the shared challenges faced by law reformers in our 'world risk society'.[5]

1. Product Safety Law Reform in Australia: Another Dimension

The Australian Government's Productivity Commission (PC) Final Research Report of February 2006 recommended at least some reforms to Australia's consumer product safety regime, which dates back to the 1970s and is very similar to Japan's.[6] However, the PC remained sceptical of imposing a general safety provision (GSP) on suppliers, requiring them to supply only safe products. The Commission contended that it remained to be convinced that the benefits outweighed the costs involved in making that move away from the present regime. That places the primary onus on the regulators to mandate safety standards, recalls or bans only if they consider products 'unsafe', although such action has become increasingly difficult in Australia's deregulatory environment since the 1990s. The PC also recommended only limited obligations to disclose possible serious risks to regulators.[7] By contrast, a disclosure regime combined with a GSP, strengthened in the revised EU Product Safety Directive regime,[8] seems more likely to generate optimal 'responsive regulation' between public authorities and private entities in this field.[9] Yet momentum to reform Australia's product safety system, along such lines, has fallen into a political black hole.

Nonetheless, the Australian Government did request the PC to undertake a study into the government's relationship with Standards Australia (SA) as well as the National Association of Testing Authorities (NATA). Both are private sector,

5   See generally U. Beck (1999) *World Risk Society*, (Malden, Mass: Polity Press).
6   See generally L. Nottage, 'Reviewing Product Safety Regulation in Australia – and Japan? Parts 1/2' (2005) 16 *Australian Product Liability Reporter* 100/126.
7   See the Report and other materials at <http://www.pc.gov.au/study/productsafety/index.html>.
8   D. Fairgrieve and G. Howells (2006) 'General Product Safety – A Revolution Through Reform?' 69 *Modern Law Review* 59.
9   I. Ayres and J. Braithwaite (1992) *Responsive Regulation: Transcending the Deregulation Debate*, (New York: Oxford University Press), elaborated on in L. Nottage (2006) 'Responsive Re-Regulation of Consumer Product Safety: Hard and Soft Law in Australia and Japan', forthcoming *University of Tokyo Soft Law COE Discussion Paper* <http://www.j.u-tokyo.ac.jp/coelaw/outcome.html> (also drawn on for more of this Part 1).

not-for-profit organisations that receive funding from the Government to represent Australian interests in key international standards writing and conformity assessment forums. The review of SA followed on from the problems identified by the PC both in its Building Regulation Review (2004, Chapter 8) and its Product Safety Review (Chapters 4 and 12). These included delays, unpaid and narrow participation in Committees, inadequate expertise, voting in Committees, and transparency more generally.

Specifically, the Treasurer's Terms of Reference announced on 2 February 2006 asked the PC to examine and make recommendations on:

(a) the efficiency and effectiveness of standards setting and laboratory accreditation services in Australia;
(b) the appropriate role for the Australian Government in relation to standard setting and laboratory accreditation;
(c) the appropriate means of funding activities of SA and NATA, which are deemed to be in the national interest;
(d) the appropriate terms for Memoranda of Understanding (MoU) between the Australian Government and its agencies and SA and NATA.

The PC was also required to have regard to 'the history of the relationship between the Australian Government and bodies that prepare standards and accredit laboratories, the cost impact on and benefits to business and the wider community of standards, including in regulation; and models in operation overseas'.[10]

The PC was required to present its final report by 2 November 2006. To this end, it released an Issues Paper in March, and called for a first round of Submissions by 21 April, with a view to releasing a draft report by the end of June and holding roundtable forums on this report over August and September. By the end of September, over 180 Submissions had been uploaded on the PC's website. They indicated widespread interest, particularly in SA.[11] Most came from business interests, but some were from individuals or other stakeholder groups. Indeed, some appeared to be worried that the Government was seeking justifications simply to reduce or even abandon its residual funding of SA, leaving the organisation even more open to 'industry capture' and broader 'self-regulation'.

My own Submission (No. 52) argued that the standard-setting system operated by SA had become dysfunctional and needed substantial reform, because it represents a key site of governance in Australia's deregulating polity. First, SA acts as a delegated *legislator*, most clearly when setting many standards that promptly or eventually become mandatory. Most remarkably, s. 65E of the *Trade Practices Act* (Cth) allows the Minister to adopt SA Standards without having to show that it was 'reasonably necessary to prevent or reduce risk of injury to any person', which is the requirement if the Minister mandates a standard instead under s. 65C(2).[12] This

---

10 <http://www.pc.gov.au/study/standards/tor.html>.
11 The Issues Paper, Submissions and other resources are available via <http://www. pc.gov.au/study/standards/>.
12 *BMW Australia Ltd* v. *ACCC* [2004] FCAFC 167 (28 June 2004) (freely available,

may assist consumers if the adopted SA Standard promotes optimal safety levels, but SA's processes and resource constraints increasingly make it more likely that its Standards do not adequately promote consumer safety. In addition, SA legislates more indirectly by generating 'soft law' through 'voluntary' standards that *de facto* must be followed in a particular field, or which may prevent or minimise the superimposition of mandatory standards via s. 65C(2). A recent example appears to be aerosol cans.[13] Secondly, SA can also act as a de facto regulatory *enforcement* agency, particularly when it provides (directly or via subsidiaries) services to certify that important standards are being met by firms and other organisations. Thirdly, although less frequently and obviously, SA can even act like a *court*. This may occur when it reconvenes and directs Committees to redraft standards (e.g. for aerosol cans) after disputes arise over interpretation and/or technological changes.

Compared to such governance bodies, however, SA operates largely free of important constraints, such as participation, transparency, and potential for 'appeal' or challenge. This vacuum also contributes to the inefficiencies of its processes. In short, my Submission contended, SA's current system is unlikely to generate optimal (*efficient*) standard levels; it is *ineffective* in promoting other values (such as participation, transparency, accountability and good citizenship); and it is certainly not *cost-efficient* in both those respects. This situation calls for considerable rethinking of the government's role and relationship with SA, including its MoU with the Government and its funding of SA.[14]

---

along with other Australian case law and legislation, via <www.austlii.edu.au>). However, the Court did mention (obiter, paras 30–31) several considerations that might limit such deference to the SA, or indeed other 'expert' standards: whether or not they were developed by varied Committee members, after considering a range of issues and information sources, and have been subjected to periodic review.

13   An Australian inventor, Peter Nardone, has developed a capping device to make them tamper-evident as well as much more difficult to refill (<www.aerocanlok.com>). This promises benefits in terms of consumer safety (minimising foreseeable misuse), as well as economic loss to consumers (through cans releasing contents before sale) and to property owners (through more opportunities for graffiti), and enhanced national security. However, there exists an Australian Standard AS–2278 for aerosol cans which, although 'voluntary', has been what the big players in the industry work off. This Standard was quite quickly renamed – no longer described as for 'refillable' cans – after that was pointed out to be misleading. However, the Aerosol Association of Australia remains negative towards such an invention like Mr Nardone's (Ben Cubby, 'Inventor Wants to Put a Cap on Graffiti', *Sydney Morning Herald*, 2 September 2006). This makes it unlikely that a second-stage review of the Standard will lead to more substantive changes requiring better tamper-proofing and measures to prevent refilling, or even warnings labels. If the Standard is changed, manufacturers will come under more pressure to adopt such technological improvements, but this will mean a (small) increase in costs. The inventor has accordingly withdrawn from the SA Committee undertaking the review of the Standard, to which he had been eventually appointed as the representative of the Australian Consumers' Association (ACA).

14   A revised version was published in L. Nottage (2006) 'Reviewing Standardisation in Australia: Another Dimension to Product Safety Regulation' 17 *Australian PL Reporter* 65, including footnote references to some of the Submissions that had been uploaded

Predictably, however, the PC's draft report released on 25 July 2006 was more muted and tactful. It argued that: 'In general, Australia's standard setting and laboratory accreditation arrangements are working effectively, but there is scope for improvement'. For SA, nonetheless, this meant:

processes can be made more efficient and effective by ensuring:

- systematic consideration of the costs and benefits prior to any decision to develop or revise a standard, and publication of reasons for such decisions;
- balanced stakeholder representation;
- barriers to volunteer and public participation are addressed; and
- improved accessibility, transparency and timeliness, including an improved appeals and complaints mechanism.

There is also a case for increased accreditation of other standards development organisations and partnering arrangements between Standards Australia and others. *Most importantly, governments should undertake rigorous impact analysis before referencing a standard in regulation, to ensure it is the minimum necessary to achieve their objectives.* The Australian Government should continue to support, with some reallocation of funding and possibly at an increased level overall, Australia's participation in international standardisation activities and the role of the Standards Accreditation Board. Funding should also be extended to cover the development of, and to enable lower cost access to, regulatory standards.[15]

As the Australian Consumers Association proclaimed after the PC's Discussion Draft report on product safety was released in mid-2005, once again the PC has got it 'half right'.[16] Although Government funding to SA now seems unlikely to be cut altogether, in exchange for the organisation making more substantial improvements in transparency and efficiency, the deregulatory urge is evident in many parts of this Standard-Setting Report – including the italicised 'key point' above.

The PC's policy penchant, presumably with a keen eye to federal politics despite its independent status, is also underpinned by a request on 11 August 2006 to 'undertake a study on performance indicators and reporting frameworks across all levels of government to assist the Council of Australian Governments (COAG) to implement its in-principle decision to adopt a common framework for benchmarking, measuring and reporting on the regulatory burden on business'.[17] On 15 August,

---

by the PC as of 21 April 2006. Some other mostly critical Submissions include those from Professor Ben Selinger (No. 2), Dr Richard Aynsley (No. 39), the ACA (No. 62), the Consumers' Federation (No. 77) and Mr Nardone (No. 116). However, consumer advocates cannot really be too critical of SA, otherwise the Government is likely to cease or diminish support, leaving standard-setting more completely to industry interests.

15 <http://www.pc.gov.au/study/standards/draftreport/keypoints.html> (emphasis added).

16 Cf. ACA, 'Consumer Product Safety: Productivity Commission Gets It Half Right', 9 August 2005 press release: <http://www.choice.com.au/viewPressRelease.aspx?id=10 4862&catId=100202&tid=100010&p=1>.

17 See <http://www.pc.gov.au/study/regulationbenchmarking/index.html>.

the Treasurer also announced that the PC's (already powerful) Office of Regulation Review would take on additional roles and responsibilities as the 'Office of Best Practice Regulation', 'facilitating the Government's strengthened Regulatory Impact Statement (RIS) processes which will include, where appropriate, a requirement for enhanced cost-benefit and risk analysis'.[18] This was one Government response to the report of the Government's *Taskforce on Reducing the Regulatory Burden on Business*, to which the Chairman of the PC (but not the Commissioner in charge of its Product Safety Review) was appointed on 12 October 2005.[19]

Overall, the Australian experience does illustrate an awareness of the need to realign areas of law impacting on consumer product safety, especially an appropriate balance of public regulation versus tort law, given the nationwide 'tort reforms' restricting claims in negligence implemented since 2002.[20] Yet it is clearly increasingly difficult to persuade policymakers to experiment with more 'responsive re-regulation' involving better information flows and backup enforcement potential by public authorities, or even closer oversight of peak (mainly industry) bodies like SA. This is consistent with a broader 'meta-regulation' that has developed in Australia particularly since the 1995 'National Competition Policy'. That has required Government at all levels to systematically review hundreds of laws and regulations to assess not only their costs and benefits, but also whether they sufficiently promote competitive markets.[21]

Thus, even if the possibility of some stricter rules impacting on product safety can still be put on the agenda, Submissions tend to be reframed to appeal to this paradigm of economic rationalism. An example is my own Submission (No. 42) to the PC's Product Safety Review. While this may allow more stakeholders to participate in the reform process and even have more impact on policy outcomes in the short run or in that particular sector, such strategies also make it difficult to go beyond this discourse of 'technocratic citizenship' towards a more expansive one seeking to revitalise 'social citizenship'. Nonetheless, Submissions like mine (No. 52) to the PC's Standard-Setting Review can attempt to broaden the frame of reference by developing distinctions, raised rather differently by the PC itself, as to 'efficiency' and 'effectiveness'.

Thus, some headway can and probably will be made towards re-regulating Australia's consumer product safety system, even if it does not end up going as far as the EU. This would be consistent with observations that 'social regulation' has had more chance of surviving compared to regulation primarily of economic activity, even in Australia and also on a more global scale.[22] As Australia looks

---

18   See <http://www.pc.gov.au/orr/index.html>.

19   The Taskforce reported in April 2006: see <http://www.regulationtaskforce.gov.au/index.html>.

20   See the 'Ipp Report' and aftermath via <http://www.lawcouncil.asn.au/tortreform.html>. More generally, cf. H Sarumida (1996) 'Comparative institutional analysis of product safety systems in the United States and Japan: alternative approaches to create incentives for product safety', 29 *Cornell International Law Journal* 79; P. Cane (2002) 'Tort Law as Regulation', 31 *Common Law World Review* 305.

21   Morgan, above n. 2.

22   *Ibid*; and J. Braithwaite and P. Drahos (2000) *Global Business Regulation*, (Cambridge;

beyond multilateral institutions like the OECD and the WTO, and begins building up bilateral Free Trade Agreements (FTAs), particularly with diverse Asia-Pacific nations that have now weathered the 1998 Asian financial crisis, the prevailing discourse may become even less monolithic. That is, despite the rhetoric of 'free trade', the debate may not be dominated by those demanding drastic deregulation. This seems particularly likely for product safety, where the principles set by the WTO and hence FTAs remain quite porous, and where diverse areas of law interact in different ways in different countries.

2. Re-regulating Japan

A particularly promising possibility may come from an unexpected direction: Japan. It has long been Australia's major trading partner, and both governments have recently concluded a Feasibility Study broadly favouring a bilateral FTA.[23] Australia's experience with a longer standing FTA with New Zealand,[24] and even more so the EU example, shows how consumer law issues can creep into a 'business law' harmonisation agenda that may be superimposed on FTAs. Even linked by some harmonisation agenda pursuant to a future FTA, Japan may seem an unlikely impetus for consumer safety law improvements in Australia, as Japan has long been considered to be a 'producers' paradise'. Yet consumer activism and influence on policymaking has grown steadily in Japan, accelerating over the last decade despite – and, indeed, partially because of – considerable deregulation.[25]

As in many other industrialised democracies, *ex ante* regulation by public authorities has been wound back in favour of more indirect socioeconomic steering through more functional civil and criminal justice systems providing *ex post* compensation or other sanctions following infringements. Enactment of Japan's Product Liability Law (No. 89 of 1994), modelled on the EU Directive, provides a good example of this shift.[26] Nonetheless, the possibility of a re-regulatory reaction in Japan remains generally higher than in Australia, since its deregulation rhetoric and practice has developed more recently and less extensively. If Japan can take the lead in 'remodelling' responsive regulation in consumer product safety, this may

---

Melbourne: Cambridge University Press).

23   See <http://www.dfat.gov.au/geo/japan/fta/index.html>.

24   For its most recent Review, see <http://www.dfat.gov.au/geo/new_zealand/anz_cer/ anz_cer.html>.

25   See generally e.g. P. Maclachlan (2002) *Consumer Politics in Postwar Japan: The Institutional Boundaries of Citizen Activism*, (Columbia University Press), and L. Nottage (2006) 'Nothing New in the (North) East? The Rhetoric and Reality of Corporate Governance in Japan', 01–1 *CLPE Research Paper* <http://ssrn.com/ abstract=885367>.

26   L. Nottage (2004) *Product Safety and Liability Law in Japan: From Minamata to Mad Cows*, (London: Routledge Curzon), and L. Nottage (2005) 'Comparing Product Liability and Safety in Japan', in H. Scheiber (ed.), *Emerging Concepts of Rights in Japanese Law*, (Berkeley: UC Berkeley – Robbins Collection).

open up possibilities also for current and potential FTA partners such as Australia.[27] This scenario becomes more likely following a suite of large scale product safety incidents since mid-2005, which have prompted an awareness that tort law, insurance and other more market-based forces still often remain inadequate substitutes.

(i) 'Vertical' Re-regulation: Asbestos, Buildings, Electrical Goods and Elevators[28]

The latest and most serious chapter in Japan's asbestos saga opened in June 2005 when Kubota, a leading machinery and materials manufacturer, announced that 79 of its employees had died of asbestos-related diseases over recent decades. This disclosure was linked to more attention being paid recently by major Japanese firms to Corporate Social Responsibility, as well as sensitivity to environmental pollution since the 1970s. Investigations by other firms and the government quickly confirmed that many more hundreds of employees had filed for workers' compensation nationwide, and that asbestos remained widely used in private and public facilities.

A picture emerged of 'creeping regulation' since the 1970s. The Japanese government generally delayed the implementation of measures even after broad international consensus had been reached about the need to control certain types of asbestos, giving firms more time to wind down their usage and develop less profitable substitutes. Patchwork responses were also related to jurisdictional tensions among Japanese regulators, since asbestos raised health issues for what is now a combined Ministry of Health, Welfare and Labour, Environmental Agency (now a Ministry), and the Construction Ministry (now the Ministry of Land, Infrastructure and Transport or MLIT). After the disclosures prompted by Kubota's announcement in mid-2005, the government was forced to re-regulate more comprehensively and decisively, accelerating a total ban on new asbestos use as well as introducing measures to facilitate safe disposal of existing stocks.

A state compensation scheme was also inaugurated from January 2006. This occurred in the shadow of lawsuits brought against the government as well as private firms, pressure brought by some local governments, and a general election held on 11 September 2005. The scheme extended certain entitlements to employees not covered by workers' compensation, as well as family members and residents in areas where factories had used large quantities of asbestos. The model was said to be social security schemes, like earlier schemes for side effects from drugs or nuclear accidents. The asbestos scheme is funded by the central government (50 per cent), but also local governments (25 per cent), and industry as a whole (25 per cent) via extra levies alongside workers' compensation levies – with firms like Kubota with

---

27   On Japan's slow but quite steady socioeconomic transfiguration particularly over the last decade, see S.K. Vogel (2006) *Japan Remodeled: How Government and Industry Are Reforming Japanese Capitalism*, (Ithaca, N.Y.: Cornell University Press) and J. Kingston (2004) *Japan's Quiet Transformation: Social Change and Civil Society in the Twenty-First Century* London; New York: Routledge). On muted free-market rhetoric despite growing consumer activism, see also P. Maclachlan (2004) 'From Subjects to Citizens: Japan's Evolving Consumer Identity', 24 *Japanese Studies* 115.

28   In much more detail on the following four case studies, see Nottage, above n. 3 (available at <http://ssrn.com/abstract=929941> or on request from the author).

high levels of asbestos-related problems contributing more. It remains to be seen whether funding will be adequate, and whether the amounts of compensation and the coverage offered by the scheme will be sufficient to dampen ongoing tort claims. Meanwhile, the government has also allocated an enormous budget to remove asbestos from public facilities.[29]

Two journalists from the *Asahi Shimbun*, the most progressive of Japan's nationwide daily newspapers, suggest that initial concern about asbestos in the mid-1980s – and, one might add, the mid-1990s – petered out partly because although the risks were apparent, large scale deaths had not yet occurred.[30] Another difference this time was that copious information began to flow from both firms and government agencies. Relatedly, they point out that asbestos came to be seen as involving widespread environmental pollution, rather than workers' compensation, making it more difficult to pin blame on specific companies like Kubota. The media also toned down initial claims that the government had acted irresponsibly, as it reacted remarkably quickly this time and pointed to some earlier measures, such as relaxation in September 2003 of the standards to claim asbestos-related diseases under workers' compensation.

The authors conclude that the scheme, although an improvement, remains unsatisfactory. First, they contend that the asbestos scheme's entitlements, set also in light of the compensation amounts that the central government agreed on in 1996 to settle the tailend of the infamous mercury poisoning in Minamata Bay,[31] have ended up too low. Payouts even to those not or no longer covered by workers' compensation are less generous than those covered by that regime; and payouts to residents are even less attractive, so only a few companies have agreed to pay more. However, it should be added that litigation is still possible and indeed ongoing.

Secondly, and more persuasively, they argue that the Japanese government is still struggling to stop playing 'catch-up', to the benefit mostly of business interests, and adopt a more preventative approach to safety and other social issues. The authors contrast the historical analysis and recommendations in the European Environmental Agency's 2001 Report entitled 'Late Lessons from Early Warnings'.[32] It can be added that a precautionary approach was also lacking and is now more evident in Japan's regulation of BSE (mad cow disease). However, it is politically easier to achieve in that context given the added protectionist impulses of Japanese farmers, vis-à-vis large volumes of US beef imports.[33]

---

29   Further helpful outlines of the legislative package are provided (in Japanese) in 1767 *Toki no Horei* (August 2006).

30   K. Takeuchi and T. Yasuda, *Media kara mita asbesuto mondai [The Media's View on Asbestos Issues* in Kenji Morinaga *et al.* (eds), Asubesuto Kansen to Kenko Higai [Health Problems from the Spread of Asbestos] (Nihon Hyoronsha, Tokyo, 2006) 193–208.

31   See further e.g. T.S. George (2001) *Minamata: Pollution and the Struggle for Democracy in Postwar Japan*, (Cambridge (Mass.): Harvard University Asia Center: Distributed by Harvard University Press).

32   Available via <http://reports.eea.europa.eu/environmental_issue_report_2001_22/en>.

33   Compare L. Nottage with M. Trezise (2003) 'Mad Cows and Japanese Consumers' 14 *Australian Product Liability Reporter* 125 and Editorial, 'Keep An Eye on U.S. Beef', *Japan Times Online*, 3 August 2006.

Despite such ongoing concerns, light was beginning to emerge at the end of Japan's asbestos tunnel towards the end of 2005. From November, however, another major safety issue generated further social and political furore. Revelations emerged of around 100 defectively designed and constructed hotels, condominiums (especially around Yokohama and Tokyo), and other buildings spread around the country. As with asbestos, the reaction has involved funding from the Government, partly in the shadow of lawsuits claiming it should have checked and uncovered earthquake resistance data falsified by architectural firms pressured by construction companies and consultants, as well as the bankruptcies of several large firms. Again, state authorities were forced to react quickly, belatedly coordinating investigations and responses within and across many branches of government, with additional pressure coming (quite unusually) from a parliamentary committee. Civil litigation among private parties has also emerged, along with pervasive media attention. However, a major difference from asbestos is that criminal prosecutions have already been brought. As mentioned in the introduction and discussed further in Part 3 below, prosecutions are also comparatively quite frequent in many other areas involving accidents in Japan, both collective (e.g. pollution) and individual (e.g. traffic accidents and medical malpractice).[34]

By early 2006, a series of legislative amendments had been introduced. Changes to 'hard law' strengthened coverage and sanctions for building standards, architects, real estate brokers and construction companies. 'Soft law' initiatives encouraged more retrofitting of earthquake-prone buildings, and means for consumers to check more prior to purchasing condominiums. However, the government has been slower to suggest mandatory home warranty insurance. This is due to insurance industry opposition, and the variety of schemes operating around the world, making it harder for advocates to identify the clear 'global standard' so persuasive still in Japanese policymaking processes.

Then, from late February 2006, Japan's third large scale product safety controversy broke out. A distinctive feature was that this arguably involved over-regulation, rather than under-regulation putting consumers at risk. Indeed, some suggested that the re-regulation was driven by large manufacturers keen to put pressure on the second-hand industry (a growth business over Japan's 'lost decade' of economic stagnation, until recently). Yet this incident also help sustain wider interest in consumer safety law. In the late 1990s, the Ministry of Economy, Trade and Industry (METI) had amended legislation (now known as the Den'an Law) to allow outsourcing of certification for certain high risk electrical goods. This was consistent with the government's deregulation programme (and outsourcing of building inspections, now considered to be one cause of the defective buildings saga). However, it also involved a new 'PSE' Mark being affixed, initially only by manufacturers of new goods. METI failed to adequately publicise that as of 1 April 2006, other suppliers would have to test many electrical goods and affix a PSE Mark before being able to sell them. When

---

34   See e.g. R.B. Leflar and F. Iwata (2006) 'Medical Error as Reportable Event, as Tort, as Crime: A Transpacific Comparison', 12 *Widener Law Review* 195, and L. Nottage (2007) 'Product Liability and Safety Regulation', in G. McAlinn (ed.), *Japanese Business Law*, (The Hague: Kluwer).

it announced reminders in February, METI had to back down in the face of a loud adverse reaction from second-hand dealers, fans of older musical equipment, and others. The Ministry created an exception for certain 'vintage' goods, and adopted such an expansive definition of 'lease' (not covered by the legislation) that second-hand goods markets had promptly recovered by May 2006.

A fourth story then unfolded from July. Media attention turned to deaths from doors closing incorrectly and other problems caused by elevators made by the Swiss-based Schindler conglomerate, which had been making inroads into the Japanese market from its new manufacturing base in China. Once again, police and regulators quickly became involved. On 22 August 2006, an advisory panel created by MLIT recommended the introduction of a recall system similar to that strengthened in recent years for automobiles, requiring full disclosure of accidents and costless repairs or replacement of unsafe elevators.[35] However, linking this 'doors' case to, a successful Chinese businessman based in Japan has warned in his regular newspaper column not to forget 'self-responsibility' – including choosing products that may not be the cheapest, but may promise more safety. He drew a parallel between the 'doors' cases involving Schindler's lifts, which had been priced competitively to break into the Japanese market, and the ongoing scandal involving 'livedoor', whose investors had made large gains through the company's takeovers until the recent prosecution of its high profile young president and political hopeful.[36]

(ii) Heaters, Shredders, and 'Horizontal' Product Safety Re-regulation[37]

Despite a few such calls for caution, therefore, these four major incidents maintained public attention on consumer safety problems from mid-2005 to mid-2006, and underpinned mainly sector-specific re-regulation. They have also subsequently prompted the more comprehensive reassessment of consumer product safety regulation that seemed obviously necessary from a comparative perspective.[38]

This new sub-chapter opened with reports from late July 2006 of dozens of deaths and other injuries from gas water heaters manufactured since the early 1980s by Paloma, a large Nagoya-based family firm.[39] There were several uncanny

---

35   'Erebeta ni rikorusei, shibo jiko uke ... kokko-sho hoshin [In response to fatal accidents ... the Land Ministry's policy for elevator recalls]' *Yomiuri Online*, 23 August 2006.

36   'Gakeppuchi ni wa chikazukana – erebeta jiko de omou "seizoku-sekinin" to "jiko-sekinin" [Don't go near the "edge" – the manufacturer's responsibility and personal responsibility of the elevator accidents]' *Nikkei Net*, 19 June 2006. On the livedoor saga, see further Nottage, above n. 24. For a technological perspective from Japan on safety problems involving doors, see generally Y. Hatamu (2006) *Kikengaku no Susume – Doa Purojekuto ni Manabu [An Invitation to Risk Analysis: Learning from the Doors Project]* (Tokyo, Kodansha).

37   Citations have been kept to minimum from a large volume of newspaper articles on the following further case studies, in both English and Japanese, available in PDF format on request from the author.

38   Cf. Nottage, above ns 5 and 25.

39   See e.g. 'Safety tweaks led to nine of 28 poisonings: Paloma', *The Japan Times*, 1 August 2006.

resemblances to the Schindler saga, suggesting that xenophobia was not the major factor behind the collective responses in that case. First, investigations into Paloma were pushed along by the Tokyo metropolitan police, due to persistent complaints by some residents that incomplete combustion had led to carbon monoxide poisoning of their loved ones. Second, Paloma initially responded by blaming unauthorised tampering with the gas heaters' electrical circuits. It soon emerged that some of these maintenance services had been provided by its own associates. More importantly, the need for repairs had arisen because of a design defect, soldering that cracked particularly in colder areas of Japan. Third, Paloma was also blamed for a lack of sincerity in responding to consumers' concerns, particularly by belatedly presenting a report to METI without contacting them first.[40]

Finally, the response by the regulators was sharp, even though METI has long been the bastion of industrial policy. During August 2006, the Ministry requested an additional report, raided Paloma's offices searching for further information, and eventually issued a mandatory recall of tens of thousands of gas heater units – judging that the 6,000 units voluntarily recalled were insufficient to avert further serious injuries. Rather like some politicians in the defective buildings saga, METI Vice-Minister Nikai realised the risks of fallout – but also perhaps some opportunity for political gain. He apologised for the lack of intra- and inter-Ministry coordination that had hampered information-gathering and disclosures, particularly to consumers.[41] Other gas heater manufacturers got the message, and began reviewing their product lines.[42]

Further, when ordering the Paloma recall, METI admitted that a better review of its files, and those of other government agencies collecting accident and complaint statistics, revealed problems with many other products that had not been adequately followed up. These are summarised in the following Table:[43]

---

40   See e.g. 'Paloma offices searched in water-heater probe', *Asahi Shimbun*, 8 October 2006. Unlike the Schindler case, however, a group of Osaka-based lawyers and others promptly organized a free-dial line to collect further information about problems with Paloma heaters, leading to a product liability claim being brought as well. See e.g. 'Paroma higai-bengodan o kessei, songai baisho shinkyu mo kento [Creation of Paloma victims defence team, also considering seeking damages]', *Nikkei Net*, 8 August 2006.

41   See e.g. 'METI tells Paloma to resubmit heater report', *The Japan Times*, 2 August 2006; 'Ministry orders Paloma heater recall', *Asahi Shimbun*, 29 August 2006; 'Coordination key to product safety', *Daily Yomiuri*, 30 August 2006.

42   See e.g. 'Toshi gasu kakusha, Paroma seihin no 8-wari-kyo no tenken kanryo [Metropolitan gas companies complete investigation of over 80% of Paloma products', *Nikkei Net*, 30 August 2006; 'Keiyo gasu, gasu kiki kokan o sokushin, Paroma mondai kanren de [Keiyo Gas recommends changing gas apparatus in connection with Paloma problem]', *Nikkei Net*, 6 September 2006; 'Toho gasu, kyushiki no furogama nado 30 oku-en toji shitadori [Toho Gas to spend 3 billion yen replacing old bath heaters]', *Nikkei Net*, 9 September 2006; 'Tokyo Gas to use 10 billion yen to replace old water heaters', *The Japan Times*, 8 September 2006.

43   Translated from 'Seihin anzen, gyosei ni shikaku … "Paroma" uke, keizaisho sotenken [Bureaucracy in a tight corner over product safety … METI's general investigation in response to "Paloma"' *Yomiuri Online*, 29 August 2006. See also 'Coordination key to product safety', above n. 40.

Table 24.1 Results of METI product accident inspections (excluding Paloma-manufactured water heaters)

Item	Details of incident	Response of METI, etc
Industrial steamer	August 2004 in Wakayama Prefecture: death due to carbon monoxide poisoning.	Warning issued to manufacturer.
Industrial fryer	Carbon monoxide poisoning incidents from December 2003 to May 2004.	
Industrial air conditioner	August 2003 in Ehime Prefecture: fire caused by faulty wiring.	
Gas kitchen stove	July 2006: information provided about gas leak from joint in pipe.	No problem with item.
Shredder	Incidents in March and July 2006 involving small children losing fingers in Irisohyama and Carl office shredders.	Requested investigation by industry group. Considering revising technological standards.
Lithium-Ion battery	Incidents globally involving spontaneous combustion of Sony batteries installed in Dell notebooks. Incidents in Japan from October 2005 to June 2006.	Demanded reports from both companies; investigated other manufacturers. Established a safety investigatory committee.
Electric floor heater	October 2004: incident involving flooring being scorched by JBH floor heater film.	Inspections involving 11 221 items. Completed after 896 inspections and repairs.
Solar power system connection main	February 2001: Nitto-manufactured circuit board scorched.	1083 out of 2491 units shipped out inspected and repaired.
Internet modem	July 2006: sparks released from cord joint in Softbank Broadband modem. 7 similar incidents.	Early investigation into cause; instructions for preventing repeat incidents.
Gas bath heater	109 incidents of carbon monoxide poisoning over 21 years until 2005. 89 deaths.	Strengthening technological standards; recommending further use of carbon monoxide warning instruments. Demanded manufacturers investigate corrosion.
Gas exhaust pipe	71 incidents of accidents caused by faulty connection and corrosion over 21 years until 2005. 38 deaths.	

Bathroom dryer/ ventilators (all-in-one heater, clothes-dryer and ventilator)	• Electric system: 24 incidents of scorching from 2001 due to improper soldering to electrical output. • Radiator system: 5 incidents of fires at hot water mains over 1 year until August 2006 in Osaka Gas, Tokyo Gas, Noritz and Harman-manufactured units.	• Demanded publication of product information, inspection and repair. • 4 companies are currently independently inspecting 124 860 units. 2 incidents of fires in August 2006 during inspections.

One category that drew particular media attention comprised paper shredders. Several brand items had mangled fingers of several small children in early 2006, but were not followed up until June, when the National Consumer Affairs Centre (NCAC) warned METI of the probable risks. Sales of shredders had ballooned in 2005, as – ironically – the Personal Information Protection Law 2003 came into full effect. New models had 'migrated' from the workplace to the home – a problem addressed by the revised EU Directive, which includes such items within its definition of consumer goods. Under the predecessor to the Den'an Law, in 1975 METI had issued informal 'administrative guidance' requesting reports of any injuries. However, by the 1980s such guidance was increasingly recognised as depending on voluntary compliance, and as Japan's economy slowed over the 1990s the pressures grew on firms not to disclose risks and make costly recalls. METI had also asked some industry associations to report problems, but it failed to ask others comprising the manufacturers of the newer shredders since they belonged instead to associations of manufacturers of stationery and plastic products.[44]

Another major category of concern belatedly revealed by METI comprised ceiling units functioning as combined heaters, ventilators and clothes dryers, particularly units made by Mitsubishi Electric for prefabricated bathrooms. It had learned from manufacturers that 24 fires had broken out since 2001, probably due to inadequate soldering or insulation when the units were installed, but the Ministry had not dealt adequately with this information. The division responsible for defective products had not shared information with that responsible for installation services – let alone notified consumers of likely hazards, until June 2006. Again, the revised EU Product Safety Directive begins to extend coverage to certain services associated with the supply of goods, and the Australian Government's Review also identifies this as a common problem area.[45]

---

44   See e.g. 'Kids lose fingers: shredder safety probed after mishaps', *The Japan Times*, 24 August 2006; 'Caution sounded on shredders over mutilated fingers', *Asahi Shimbun*, 24 August 2006; 'Ricoh reveals seven accidents with its shredders', *The Japan Times*, 25 August 2006; 'Ministry in call to home appliance makers to report all accidents', *Asahi Shimbun*, 26 August 2006; 'Shureddaa de yubi setsudan – "soteigai" jiko kyuso [Fingers cut by shredders – accidents increase "beyond expectation"]', *Yomiuri Shimbun*, 29 August 2006.

45   See '89 bath-heater deaths due to poor ventilation', *Asahi Shimbun*, 30 August 2006. Compare the PC's final Research Report via <http://www.pc.gov.au/study/

Other controversial products highlighted in Japan recently include rechargeable electric shavers, and whirlpool baths where long hair can get caught – a problem which has recently caused a fatal accident in Australia.[46] Since such revelations in late August 2006, newspaper reports and editorials have begun urging a new regulatory regime to overcome the compartmentalised bureaucratic approach still evident in Japan, and require better information disclosure by both regulators and firms in order to give higher priority to consumer safety.

METI announced plans to create a better database of accidents, both among its divisions and across government agencies; to amend the Consumer Product Safety Law by the end of 2006 to make firms disclose serious safety risks; and to promptly disclose detailed information including manufacturers' names – as it did, belatedly, for the shredders.[47] A better disclosure system is also a key feature of the strengthened EU regime.[48] Commentators generally welcomed the Japanese government's initiatives; but queried whether METI deserves this role given its historical mission to advance specific industry interests, and its recent failures. Another possible candidate for this central role under a strengthened regulatory regime as would the NCAC, under the aegis of the Cabinet Office.[49] However, wresting such authority away from the still mighty METI appeared a big test of the Koizumi administration's five-year campaign to centralise more authority in the Cabinet Office, as well as of the weight to be given to the consumer voice in policymaking and enforcement.[50]

3. Reforming Consumer Product Safety Law in a Deregulating World

Intriguingly, some commentators supported a new accident disclosure regime for general consumer products by pointing to a similar longstanding regime in the US, administered by the Consumer Product Safety Commission.[51] Is this further evidence of 'the Americanisation of Japanese Law', like Japan's PL Law of 1994?[52]

---

productsafety/finalreport/index.html>, pp. 153–53.

46   See 'Long Hair Cost Amanda Her Life', *Sydney Morning Herald*, 12 September 2006, <http://www.smh.com.au/news/national/long-hair-cost-amanda-her-life/2006/09/12/1 157826922171.html>.

47   See e.g. '89 bath-heater deaths due to poor ventilation', above n. 44.

48   On notifications among regulators within the EU, see the RAPEX system at <http:// ec.europa.eu/consumers/dyna/rapex/rapex_en.cfm>.

49   See e.g. 'Economic Forum: product safety being neglected', *Daily Yomiuri*, 5 September 2006; L. Nottage (2006) 'Consumers Beware! Comparative Product Safety Re-regulation', *New Zealand Law Journal*, forthcoming.

50   See e.g. J.A. Amyx (2005) 'Symbolic Politics: Postal Privatization and Institutional Change in the Liberal Democratic Party', book chapter manuscript dated 12 September 2005 (on file); Maclachlan, above n. 24; and S. Kozuka and L. Nottage (2007) 'Re-regulating Consumer Credit in Japan: The Politics and Economics of Contemporary Law Reform', paper presented at the Law and Society Association's Annual Meeting, Berlin, 11 August 2007.

51   Above n. 48.

52   R.D. Kelemen and E.C. Sibbitt (2002) 'The Americanization of Japanese Law', 23 *University of Pennsylvania Journal of International Economic Law* 269.

Aspects of the strengthened EU Directive have also been described in the UK as Americanisation.[53] Yet appeals in Japan to policy changes following the US model appear more *tactical*: if even the *laissez-faire* US imposes such reporting obligations on firms, Japan should be able to too in spite of its ongoing deregulation. From a broader *strategic* perspective, Japan's pattern of economic liberalisation and other changes to its sociopolitical environment retain closer parallels to (continental) Europe, and this 'gradual transformation" is likely to continue in the field of consumer law, including product safety re-regulation.[54]

The strengthened EU Directive differs from the US system, for example, in its overt recognition of the precautionary approach – increasingly highlighted and urged in Japan, as in the asbestos saga. The Product Safety Directive also provides persuasive precedents for shared areas of controversy such as:

- second-hand goods;
- related services;
- reasonable systems for reporting serious risks; and
- the definition of 'safe' products (overlapping with the definition of 'defect' under the PL Directive and PL Law) – including the role to be accorded to standard-setting organisations (such as SA or its Japanese equivalent, the Japanese Standards Association).[55]

More broadly, the EU's horizontal Product Safety Directive operates in the context of stronger consumer voice in vertical (sector-specific) standard-setting and regulation, and an expansionary trajectory for consumer policy in general.[56] The US differs from Japan in these respects, as does Australia.

On the other hand, Australia's more neo-liberal approach in recent years risks encouraging a 'reverse course' in Japan, if the two countries draw closer together from a legal as well as economic perspective under a possible FTA. After all, particularly since 2001 Japan anyway has been pursuing a reform agenda under the banners of deregulation and revival of the civil justice system. Re-regulation of consumer product safety involved a strong possibility of METI expanding its coordinating role rather than the NCAC, since METI has adeptly redefined itself as the main Ministry pursuing an overall deregulatory agenda in a bid to revive Japan's flagging economy.[57]

---

53   Fairgrieve and Howells, above n. 7, at 65.
54   Above ns 24 and 26.
55   Fairgrieve and Howells, above n. 7.
56   G. Howells (2000) 'The Relationship between Product Liability and Product Safety: Understanding a Necessary Element in European Product Liability through a Comparison with the US Position', 39 *Washburn Law Journal* 305, and G. Howells and S. Weatherill (2005) *Consumer Protection Law*, 2nd edn, (Aldershot; Burlington, VT: Ashgate) (especially Ch. 1).
57   See generally e.g. M. Elder (2003) 'METI and Industrial Policy in Japan: Change and Continuity', in U. Schaede and W.W. Grimes (eds), *Japan's Managed Globalization: Adapting to the Twenty-First Century*, (Armonk, N.Y.: M.E. Sharpe).

Indeed, amendments to Japan's Consumer Product Safety were enacted on 28 November 2006 that left METI alone with jurisdiction. Manufacturers and importers are now obliged to report to METI when they become aware of a 'serious accident'. However, this obligation does not extend to situations where the cause is clearly not a defect in the goods. Such distinctions mean that conscientious firms should monitor the safety of their products even after supply to consumers, as well as providing non-defective goods as judged at the time of supply in order to avoid civil liability under Japan's Product Liability Law. Nonetheless, the revised Product Safety Law failed to add a GSP, so regulators cannot sanction firms for supplying unsafe goods – only for not reporting serious accidents. Other differences from the revised EU Safety Directive are the lack of mention of the precautionary principle, no extra guidance on product-related services or second-hand goods, the weight to be given to voluntary standards, and so on. Nonetheless, the new reporting obligations in the revised Law raise the bar for manufacturers and importers in Japan. This should also have direct ripple-on effects on firms abroad dealing with the Japanese market, and its increasingly demanding consumers backed up by a legal system that has been considerably remodelled particularly over the last decade. The recent revisions to the Consumer Product Safety Law may also still influence the course of reform debates in increasingly integrated countries like Australia's.[58]

This horizontal re-regulation primarily directed by METI may end up favouring some of the specific business interests in Japan that it still is charged with supporting. Other Ministries, still jealous of their traditional areas of socioeconomic influence, may also prevail in keeping product safety re-regulation more sector-specific. Either way, re-regulation seems much more likely than in Australia due to other features of government-business relations, society, and law in Japan. In particular, recent events highlight the continued importance of criminal prosecutions in dealing with accidents. This also characterises some European states (e.g. France) more than others (e.g. the UK). The spectre of state liability, also important in Japan, varies considerably in the EU as well.[59] Thus, consumer product safety re-regulation in Japan will not be 'Europeanised' in any straightforward manner, but it is even less likely to be 'Americanised'. Developments in Japan in this field, and even in the US, should maintain pressure on Australia to undertake more comprehensive reforms. However, the setbacks being experienced there illustrate the challenges to consumer law posed by over a decade of strong deregulatory rhetoric in politics, and perhaps Australia's broader retreat from following global consensus and multilateral initiatives.[60]

---

58   L. Nottage, (H. Nasu trans), (2006), 'Shihoseikatsuyohin no Saikisei in mukete – Nihon, Osutoraria, Oshu o torimaku Kaikaku no Arashi [Towards Consumer Product Safety Re-regulation: The Law Reform Tempest Enveloping Japan, Australia and Europe]' 847 NBL 4–7.

59   D. Fairgrieve, (2003), *State Liability in Tort: A Comparative Law Study*, (Oxford, England: Oxford University Press).

60   See e.g. Australia's continued support of the occupation of Iraq, and refusal to sign the Kyoto Protocol against global warming.

25 Recent Judgements of the European Court of Justice and the Elusive Goal of Harmonization of Product Liability Law in Europe

Magdalena Sengayen[1]

1. Abstract

A lot has happened in the area of product liability in the European Union over the last two years. This short paper focuses upon the recent judgements of the European Court of Justice (ECJ)[2] and also provides a brief overview of other developments which inform the product liability discourse across the European political, legal and academic scene. During the past two years, the ECJ considered a number of cases involving interpretation and application of the Product Liability Directive. Whilst these cases demonstrate the fact that the Directive is becoming quite well established within the civil liability regimes of the Member States, they also illustrate the intricacy and to some extent lack of maturity of the new liability regime. The judgements of the Court express its continued emphasis upon the 'maximum harmonization' nature of the Directive and provide guidance on application of some key concepts which the Directive left undefined. In spite of the overwhelming conviction on the European and national level that the Directive ought not to be amended, one may expect further cases concerning the complex liability regime it established. Inaccuracies in implementation of the Directive still continue coming to the fore, and national courts have problems with applying the often unclear provisions to cases before them. The interaction between national civil liability laws and the provisions of the implemented Directive is not always easy to discern. Increasingly, questions about

---

1   Research Programme in European Civil Liability Systems Centre for Socio-Legal Studies, Oxford University.

2   Cases mentioned in this paper are: Case C–52/00 *Commission of the European Communities* v. *French Republic*, 25 April 2002, *ECR 2002 I–03827;* Case 177/04 *Commission of the European Communities* v. *French Republic*, 14 March 2006, ECR 2006 I–02461; Case C–154/00 *Commission of the European Communities* v. *Hellenic Republic* ECR 2002 I-03879, Case C–183/00 *Gonzalez Sanchez* v. *Medicina Asturiana* ECR 2002 I-03901, Case C–203/99 *Veedfald*, ECR 2001 I–3569), Case C–402/03 *Skov AEg* v. *Bilka LavprisvarehuscA/S* and *Bilka Lavprisvarehus A/S* v. *Jette Mikkelsen, Michael Due Nielsen*, OJ C 48/4 10 January 2006; Case C–127/04 *Declan O'Byrne* v. *Sanofi Pasteur MSD Ltd, Sanofi Pasteur SA*, OJ C 86/09 9 February 2006.

the role and mechanisms of harmonization of product liability on the European level appear in academic and political papers. The Directive is no longer seen as the sole mechanism ensuring such harmonization. As the European Union embarks on the journey towards a greater harmonization of civil law and justice systems on the one hand and a greater synchronization of laws concerning markets on the other, the role and shape of product liability within Europe are changing.

2. Product Liability Directive, its Aims and Effects

(i) Introduction

It may appear at first sight that the Product Liability Directive and its 'strict'[3] liability of 'producers'[4] for 'damages'[5] caused by 'defective products'[6] are here to stay in an unchanged shape. In spite of some suggestions of reform,[7] the Directive has now become quite firmly established within the civil liability regimes of the Member States. The ECJ confirmed on numerous occasions what is already clear in the Preamble: the Directive is to establish a balance between the interests of consumers and businesses.[8] Its substantive provisions ascertain this balance by establishing 'liability without fault'[9] of 'all producers involved in the production process'[10] for defective products, by providing for compensation for death and personal injury as well as certain types of property damage, by granting producers several defences,[11]

---

3   For a critique of the regime of the Directive, and in particular its 'strict' liability standard – see for instance: J. Stapleton *Product Liability* (London, 1994); or G. Howells and S. Weatherill *Consumer Protection Law*, 2ⁿᵈ edn, (Aldershot, 2005) pp. 240–253.

4   Article 3 of the Directive.

5   *Ibid.*, Article 9.

6   *Ibid.*, Article 6.

7   The most prominent call was the Council Resolution of 19 December 2002 *on the amendment of the liability for defective products Directive* (OJ C26, 4 April 2003, pp. 2–3), where the Council suggested that the Directive might be amended to allow the national law to provide for liability of suppliers to be the same as the liability of the producers under the Directive.

8   The Preamble talks about a 'fair apportionment of risk between the injured person and the producer' (Recitals 2 and 7). The Report from the Commission to the Council, the European Parliament and the European Economic and Social Committee *Third report on the application of Council Directive on the approximation of laws, regulations and administrative provisions of the Member States concerning liability for defective products (85/374/EEC of 25 July 1985, amended by Directive 1999/34/EC of the European Parliament and of the Council of 10 May 1999).* Brussels, 14 September 2006 COM(2006) 496 final, hereafter called the 'Third Commission Report' refers more precisely to the balance between claimants, manufacturers and their insurers (p. 8).

9   Preamble – Recital 2.

10   Recital 4. The definition of producers is wide, and includes manufacturers of finished products and raw materials as well as quasi-producers and importers.

11   Article 7 of the Directive.

by providing that liability of suppliers is only subsidiary,[12] or by establishing time limits for claims.[13] According to the recent activities focused on the Directive: the Third Commission Report, the Lovells and Rosselli Reports,[14] meetings of expert groups, and the jurisprudence of national courts,[15] the prevailing view is that the desired balance was satisfactorily achieved. This is the climate in which the ECJ adjudicates on various questions concerning practical application of this legislative instrument. The Court very strongly emphasizes the 'complete harmonization' argument and strives to interpret the key concepts used by the Directive in the spirit of such harmonization because it is seen as ensuring that the producers-insurers-consumers balance is preserved. On the other hand, opinions that the Directive is unable to accomplish the aims it has set out to realize can increasingly be heard. Present day harmonization of European substantive and procedural laws involves greater coordination and search for consistency between various civil liability regimes and their practical application. A more inclusive approach to market regulation can be seen in the spirit of improving competitiveness and 'better regulation'. These phenomena accompany and inform the efforts to ensure harmonized approach to product liability cases throughout Europe. Below is an assessment of the recent jurisprudence of the Court, followed by a short evaluation of how the judgements tie in with these other developments affecting product liability in the European Union.

(ii) Shortcomings in Implementation – the Dilemma of Supplier Liability

The issue of supplier liability surfaced once again to show lack of uniform implementation among the Member States in spite of the clear judgement of the ECJ in the case against France (C–52/00). The primary defendant under the Directive is the 'producer' (defined in Article 3.1), with the suppliers' liability being merely subsidiary. The latter is conditional upon two circumstances: that the producer cannot be identified and that the supplier does not inform the injured person of the identity of, wherever applicable, the producer, the importer, or his own supplier within reasonable time (Article 3.3). The motives for the limitation of suppliers' liability

---

12   *Ibid.*, Article 3.3.
13   *Ibid.*, Articles 10, 11.
14   Lovells, *Product Liability in the European Union*, A Report for the European Commission, February 2003, MARKT 2001/11/D; Fondazione Rosselli *Analysis of the Economic Impact of the Development Risk Clause as provided by Directive 85/374/EEC on Liability for Defective Products* Study for the European Commission, available on: http://ec.europa.eu/enterprise/regulation/goods/docs/liability/2004-06-dev-risk-clause-study_en.pdf.
15   The jurisprudence in the area of product liability on the national level is assessed by a number of professional and academic research journals and projects: the European Product Liability Review (Lovells), the Product Liability Database (Tort Law Centre of the British Institute for International and Comparative Law, for members of the Product Liability Forum), and the European Tort Law Series (here the focus is on tort law in general) – Tort and Insurance Law Yearbook (edited by the European Centre of Tort and Insurance Law – Koziol/Steininger, Vienna, New York – Springer).

can be found in the statement of reasons for the proposal of the Directive.[16] Although it was considered simpler for an injured person to be able to sue the supplier, the consequences of this simplicity: higher prices of products resulting from the cost of liability insurance premiums paid by suppliers were deemed to outweigh its benefits. Further, the reason which was reiterated in the further judgement against France (C–177/04) and in *Bilka* (C–402/03), both analysed below, was that liability of suppliers at the same level as the producers' liability could lead to multiplicity of actions which the Directive is trying to avoid.[17]

In the aforementioned judgement against France (C–52/00) the ECJ declared the incompatibility of the French Civil Code (Article 1386–7) with the Product Liability Directive. France breached the Directive by having provided in the law implementing it – its Civil Code – for suppliers of defective products to be liable to the same extent as the producers.[18] France amended the Code following the judgement, but it has done so after the Commission commenced an Article 228 EC action (concerning lack of compliance with Article 226 EC judgements of the ECJ). As a result of the amendment by *Loi No* 2004–1343 *de simplification du droit*,[19] Article 1386–7 of the Civil Code provided that 'the vendor, hirer, except a lessor under a hire purchase agreement or a hirer assimilable thereto, or any other supplier in the course of business shall be liable for safety defects in his products on the same basis as the producer only if the latter is unknown'. This, as pointed out by the Commission, meant that the supplier would still be liable even if he advised the victim within reasonable time of the identity of his own supplier, as long as the producer was unknown. Thus, the European Commission considered the amendment insufficient and continued with the action.[20] The ECJ did not agree with the arguments of the French government that the remaining discrepancy between the text of the Code and the Directive would have virtually no practical implications as cases where the producer was unknown were rare. According to the Court, and following the opinion of the Advocate General in the case, whether or not the discrepancy with the text of the Directive could have adverse effects was irrelevant.[21] By providing that the supplier was liable to the same extent as the producer, if the latter could not be identified, France failed properly to transpose the Product Liability Directive. The Court ordered France to pay a daily penalty of €31,650 from the day of the

---

16   Document COM(76) 372 final; OJ 1976 C241, p. 9, referred to in the ECJ judgement
      C–402/03 *Bilka* paras 27–8.
17   Case 177/04 para. 53; Case 402/03 para. 28.
18   The French regime also included damages below the threshold of €500 prescribed by
      Article 9b of the Directive (Article 1386–2 of the Civil Code) and required producers
      wishing to benefit from the development risk defence or regulatory compliance defence
      (Article 7(d) and (e) of the Directive – Article 1386–12 of the Civil Code) to prove
      they have taken 'appropriate steps to avert the consequences of a defective product'.
      These two inconsistencies were rectified by *Loi* No. 2004–1343 *de simplification du
      droit* - Law of 9 December 2004, JORF of 10 December 2004, p. 20857.
19   Law of 9 December 2004, JORF of 10 December 2004, p. 20857.
20   Case C–177/04.
21   Case C–177/04, para. 52.

judgement until the day of compliance. Following the judgement, France amended Article 1386–7 of its Civil Code by *Loi* No. 2006–406 to read:

> ... if the producer cannot be identified, the seller, the hirer, with the exception of a finance lessor (...), or any other professional supplier, is liable for the lack of safety of a product in the same conditions as a producer unless he discloses the name of his own supplier or producer, within three months as from the notification of the claimant.

A similar approach to suppliers' liability can be seen in the Danish preliminary reference case which involved salmonella poisoning caused by eggs sold by Bilka and produced by Scov.[22] Denmark transposed the Directive into its legal system by Law No. 371 of 7 June 1989.[23] In this Law the supplier was referred to as an 'intermediary' and made liable directly to 'injured persons and subsequent intermediaries in the distribution chain'.[24] The Law followed that after satisfying the claim of the injured person the intermediary would take over the latter's rights against any operators higher in the distribution chain. A Danish district court found the eggs to be defective and ordered Bilka (the 'intermediary' in the case) to compensate the victims. Scov was ordered to reimburse Bilka for this compensation. The regional court which heard the appeal referred a set of questions to the ECJ. These essentially focused upon two main issues: whether the Directive precluded national law from extending the producer's strict liability onto intermediaries (which is what happened in the Law implementing the Directive), and whether it precluded it from extending producer's fault liability onto them (this was the position before the implementation of the Directive).[25] The Court held that while Member States could not extend producer's strict liability onto the supplier, the Directive did not preclude such extension in case of fault liability. Again, the Court stressed the complete harmonization of the liability system introduced by the Directive.

(iii) Supplier Liability in Other Liability Systems – Effects of Complete Harmonization

It may appear that the approach of the Directive to the issue of supplier liability has now been fully clarified. Further, the judgements concerning this notion contributed to elucidating the relationship between the implemented provisions of the Product Liability Directive and the national civil liability regimes also regulating supplier liability (those of a legislative nature and those established by case law). The focal issue has been the interpretation of Article 13 of the Directive which permits

---

22   Case C–402/03.

23   Amended by Law No. 1041 of 28 November 2000.

24   Case C–402/03, para. 12.

25   To be precise – suppliers were liable for the liability of economic operators placed further up the production and distribution chain (Case 402/03 para. 9). With regard to the latter – although in theory producer's liability was based upon the general fault liability provisions, it was indicated in the ECJ judgement that the developments in the case law meant that sometimes the producer was liable even he was not at fault (para. 9). See below for a short assessment of the implications of these developments.

Member States to retain any rules of contractual and non-contractual liability or a special liability system existing at the time when the Directive was notified.[26] The ECJ interpreted Article 13 strictly to mean that Member States' discretion to regulate strict product liability 'is entirely determined by the Directive itself and must be inferred from its wording, purpose and structure'.[27] Harmonization of laws, regulations and administrative provisions in the matters regulated by the Directive is complete and no provision of national law based on the same ground as the Directive may provide for greater advantages for injured persons. The Court stressed that the Directive provides a compensation for victims of products if they prove the defect, damage and causal link, but it does not preclude the 'application of other systems of contractual or non-contractual liability based on other grounds, such as fault or a warranty in respect of latent defects'.[28] While it has been clear for some time that Member States cannot, in measures implementing the Directive, extend strict producers' liability onto suppliers,[29] the matters were less straightforward as regards supplier liability based upon other rules of civil liability, deriving from statute or case law. Before the latest ECJ judgement in *Commission* v. *France* and the judgement in *Bilka*, Whittaker pointed out that it was still possible for Member States to render suppliers strictly liable for defective products – either by renaming them, by reclassifying their liability, by placing the liability in a law other than the mechanism implementing the Directive, or basing it on other legal grounds.[30] His view was that such a situation made 'little practical sense and no sense at all from the point of view of the harmonising effect of the Directive'.[31] *Bilka* seems to have provided an answer to his concerns. It indicates that Article 13 covers liability regimes *other than strict liability for defective products*. The only question which may still present itself is: would it also cover a liability system based on fault but interpreted by courts to create a system where fault did not need to be proven? Such systems have been present in some Member States, for instance France,[32] Hungary[33] and, indeed, Denmark. Obviously if one considers the spirit of complete harmonization and its aims, such court-made strict liability could not prevail. The judgement of the ECJ in *Bilka* recognized these developments within the case law of Danish courts.[34] It may therefore be assumed that the Court does refer to both – the written provisions

---

26 Here the Preamble refers directly to a special liability system in the pharmaceutical products' sector – Recital 13.
27 *Bilka*, Case C–402/03, para. 22.
28 Case C–154/00 para. 18; Case 52/00 para. 22; Case 183/00, para. 31.
29 Case C–52/00, Case 177/04, Case C–402/03.
30 S. Whittaker, *Liability for Products. English Law, French Law, and European Harmonisation*, (Oxford, 2005), p. 443.
31 *Ibid.*
32 Whittaker.
33 M. Sengayen, 'Product Liability: The Perspective of New Member Countries', in D. Fairgrieve (ed.), *Product Liability in Comparative Perspective*, (Cambridge, 2005).
34 'Developments in the case-law had the result (…) that in certain cases the producer was held liable even in the absence of fault. The supplier was answerable for the liability of the economic operators further up the production and distribution chain.' (Case C–402/03, para. 9, also para. 41).

of Danish law (the Law implementing the Directive) and the established case law – when it concludes that 'a national rule under which the supplier is answerable, beyond the cases listed exhaustively in Article 3(3) of the Directive, for the no-fault liability which the Directive establishes and imposes on the producer' is precluded by the Directive.[35] This conclusion is in line with the approach of the Court to the idea of maximum harmonization as well as to the understanding of the role of national courts in the enforcement of EC law. National courts are a key element of the enforcement mechanism within the European Union – the ECJ stressed their obligation to follow EC law, even in spite of the existence of contrary provisions of national law.[36] In *Centrosteel* the Court concluded that: 'when applying national law, whether adopted before or after the directive, the national court that has to interpret that law must do so, as far as possible, in the light of the wording and the purpose of the directive'.[37] By including national court-made liability systems in its definition of 'national rules' of liability in *Bilka* the ECJ continued this train of thought. National courts enforce the wording and purpose of the Product Liability Directive. They are not only to interpret the national provisions implementing the Directive in the spirit of the latter, but also they must retract from their own progressive interpretation of national general tortious liability rules whenever it would contravene the Directive. The potential problems with this approach touch upon the most crucial features of the EU law enforcement system. Its necessary reliance on cooperation between national courts and the ECJ creates a potential for incoherence and mistakes in interpretation of law.[38] In the light of the inconsistencies in interpretation of the Directive which are already being noted, the process of harmonization of European product liability law will necessarily require further guidance from the ECJ. This guidance enables the practice of product liability in Europe to realize the postulates of proper balancing of interests of businesses and consumers – the necessary element of 'maximum harmonization'.

(iv) 'Putting the Product into Circulation' – ECJ Dealing With Complex Corporate Structures

The need for the balance of interests of businesses and consumers prevailed also in another judgement where the Court interpreted the Directive – the preliminary

---

35   Case 402/03, para. 45.

36   Case C–106/89 *Marleasing SA* v. *La Comercial Internacional de Alimentacion SA* [1990] ECR I–04135 (doctrine of indirect effect), Case 6/64 *Costa* v. *ENEL* [1964] 12 CMLR 425, Case 11/70 *Internationale Handelsgesellschaft* [1970] ECR 1125, Case C–231/89 *R* v. *Secretary of State for Transport, ex parte Factortame (Factortame II)* [1990] 3 CMLR 867, Case C–48/93 *R* v. *Secretary of State for Transport, ex parte Factortame (Factortame III)* [1996] ECR I–1029 (supremacy of EC law). For a further analysis of the issue see for instance: S. Weatherill, *Cases and Materials on EU Law*, 6th edn, (Oxford, 2003), pp. 159–166; I. Maher, 'National Courts as European Community Courts', *Legal Studies* 14/2, (1994): 226–243.

37   Case C–456/98 *Centrosteel Srl* v. *Adipol GmbH* [2000] ECR I–6007, para. 16.

38   Maher, 'National Courts as European Community Courts': 234–242.

reference in the case of *Declan O'Byrne*.[39] It focused on the notion of 'putting the product into circulation',[40] which is very important in the regime established by the Directive. It is a determining factor for producers' liability; it is the activity upon which liability depends,[41] the point from which liability commences, and a starting point for the ten-year cut-off period for an action under the Directive. The notion is quite typical of measures of the European Community law concerning safety of products, with many product safety regulations referring to 'placing on the market'.[42] In the Commission's *Guide to the Implementation of Directives based on the New Approach and the Global Approach* it is indicated that the passing from the stage of manufacture to the stage of distribution is the key moment.[43] The fact that the Product Liability Directive refrains from defining this notion causes particular difficulties in cases where, as it often happens, producers distribute their products to branches or sister companies instead of independent wholesalers or distributors. The ECJ dealt with such a situation in *O'Byrne*, where it seems to have attempted to achieve some consistency with the interpretation of 'placing on the market' in regulatory law.[44] The case involves severe brain damage allegedly caused by a vaccine produced by Aventis Pasteur SA (APSA) in France and supplied in September 1992 to its sister company Aventis Pasteur MSD (APMSD) in the UK. APMSD subsequently supplied the vaccine to a hospital which in turn supplied it to a surgery where it was administered to the claimant. The case was initially brought against the APMSD in the mistaken belief that they were the producer. The issue was the exact time of introduction of the vaccine into circulation because when the action was finally brought against APSA, the defendants claimed that the ten-year cut-off period for claims under the Consumer Protection Act 1987, Part I had passed. The Court of Appeal referred a number of questions to the ECJ, including an inquiry as to the exact moment of 'introduction into circulation' in the context of the ten-year period for expiry of claims under the Directive. The main aim of Article 11, which introduced the cut-off period, was held to be securing 'legal certainty'. It is clear, however, that this provision mainly protects the interests of producers in setting the time limits for their liability. Yet, as stressed by the Advocate General Geelholed, 'a producer should not be able to manipulate the length of the liability period by way of its internal organization'.[45] 'Outsiders' may be unaware of the internal structure of

---

39 Case 127/04.

40 The ECJ already explored the notion in Case C–203/99 *Veedfald*, but it was in the context of Article 7(a) (defence of the producer) and no definition of a general nature was given there.

41 It is one of the exonerating circumstances provided by Article 7(a) for producer to show that he did not put the product into circulation.

42 C. Hodges, 'Case comment. Product liability: suppliers, limitation and mistake', *Law Quarterly Review*, 122 (2006): 393–8.

43 http://ec.europa.eu/enterprise/newapproach/legislation/guide/document/1999_1282_en.pdf. European Commission *Guide to the Implementation of Directives based on the New Approach and the Global Approach*, 2000, pp. 18, 19.

44 Hodges, 'Case comment. Product liability: suppliers, limitation and mistake': 396.

45 According to the Advocate General, such manipulations could take place if companies transfer the products to sister companies where they can be stored for quite some time

the manufacturing company and it may be difficult for them to know when exactly the delivery to a subsidiary took place – 'intra-group relations are often too opaque to be useful in this respect'.[46] This appeared to have been the major concern of the Advocate General when he declared that the notion 'introduction into circulation' ought to be understood as leaving the control of the group and entering the chain of distribution. Although the Court agreed that the moment of 'introduction into circulation' should not be dependent upon the internal structure of the producer, it focused on the activities conducted with relation to the product, delivering what could be seen as a more balanced conclusion. It held that the product is introduced into circulation when it 'is taken out of the manufacturing process operated by the producer and enters a marketing process in the form in which it is offered to the public in order to be used or consumed'.[47] Thus, it was left to national courts and subject to the circumstances of a case at hand whether the internal structure within the chain of distribution is of consequence or not. In principle, the links within the chain of distribution are not relevant; and it is of no importance whether two distinct legal persons are involved or even whether the subsidiary receiving the product must pay for it. However, the Court indicated that the link between a producer and a subsidiary company might need to be considered by national courts in so far as it resulted in the subsidiary being involved in the manufacturing process.[48] Although some level of clarity has been achieved, the judgement in *O'Byrne* should not be seen as the last word on the issue of 'introduction into circulation'. The Court of Appeal which referred the questions in *O'Byrne* has not yet decided on the issue of introduction into circulation in this particular case.[49] Hodges suggested a number of questions which still remain unanswered: can it be implied from the judgement that more than one company may be the 'producer', should a company which merely dealt with packaging or some other minor activity be 'producer', and what about products which are altered by an intermediary (doctor, pharmacist, installer)?[50] Considering that complex distribution structures are common in the corporate world of today, one may expect further cases where doubts will arise in these matters.

(v) The Ten-year 'Long Stop' and Substitution of Defendants – Lack of Clear Response from the ECJ

The Directive very clearly sets out the time limit for expiry of claims. The ten-year 'long stop' period starts from the moment of introduction of the defective product into circulation. Its existence in the Directive is justified by the need to provide legal certainty, mostly in the interests of the defendants. One of the dimensions of

---

thus reducing the period of strict liability (para. 42 of the Opinion of Advocate General Geelhoed to Case 127/04, delivered on 2 June 2005).

46   Paragraph 50 of the Opinion.

47   Case 127/04, para. 32.

48   Case 127/4, para. 29.

49   So far only the question of substitution of defendants was settled by the Court of Appeal – *O'Byrne* v. *Aventis Pasteur MSD Ltd* [2006] EWHC 2562 (QB), [2006] All ER (D) 252 (Oct). See below for an analysis.

50   Hodges, 'Case comment. Product liability: suppliers, limitation and mistake': 395.

this rule was explored above. The *O'Byrne* case presented a very difficult situation which may arise in product liability cases, with a potential to disrupt the protective effect of ten-year 'long stop' for defendants. The issue is defendant substitution. The need for a substitution may arise for various reasons – not least because of an honest mistake on the part of the claimant or his solicitors. The mistake may also be caused by the fact that the claimant or the solicitors did not research the identity of the defendant with sufficient diligence, or that they were misled by the person whom they originally sued or by another person. While the law may need to provide protection for claimants who commenced proceedings against the wrong defendant, this needs to be done with the importance of the ten-year cut-off period in mind. The ECJ, when faced with the question concerning substitution of defendants in *O'Byrne*, did not provide an exhaustive or indeed an unambiguous indication of the desired approach in cases of substitution. The circumstances in *O'Byrne* were quite complex. The first case was brought against APMSD in 2000 and it was only in the late 2002 that the claimants realized that APSA was the producer. Even then, however, the claimants' solicitors did not attempt to substitute defendants but rather tried to join APSA to proceedings against APMSD, to which the former did not agree.[51] Following this, action was brought to substitute APSA for APMSD as producer in the action for damages based upon the Consumer Protection Act 1987, Part I (which implemented the Directive). The provision at issue was in fact s. 35 of the Limitation Act 1980. This section specifies conditions for party substitution. It stipulates that substitution is possible if it is necessary for determination of the original action, and continues that substitution is necessary if the party originally named was given in mistake for the new party's name. It is not the purpose of this paper to analyse in detail the meaning and implications of s. 35. Suffice it to say that this section was already interpreted in the United Kingdom for the purposes of product liability litigation in the case of *Horne Roberts*.[52] The Court of Appeal held there that it was possible to substitute one party for another after the expiry of the ten-year period established by the Consumer Protection Act 1987. Because of the peculiarity of the facts of *O'Byrne*, however, it was not clear whether there was in fact a mistake and thus whether the substitution was necessary for the determination of the original action. The defendants submitted that there could be no question of necessity because there was no mistake – at the time the relevant limitation period passed the claimants were aware of the identity of the true producer but chose not to substitute then. In the light of the Directive being silent on substitution, the ECJ provided only very broad guidelines. It held that national courts must take into account the 'personal scope' of the Directive when deciding on the admissibility of an action to substitute.[53] The Directive aims to achieve complete harmonization in the matters it regulates and thus no substitution is possible if it would involve persons not covered by Article 3 of the Directive. Upon receipt of the answer of the ECJ, the Court of Appeal did not agree with the defendants that it was to be implied from the judgement that

---

51   See description of facts in *O'Byrne* v. *Aventis Pasteur MSD Ltd* [2006] EWHC 2562 (QB), 20 October 2006.

52   *Horne Roberts* v. *SmithKline Beecham plc.* [2002] 1 WLR 1662.

53   Case 127/04, para. 38.

substitution should not be decided lightly. It did take into account the suggestion to consider the personal scope of the Directive. It also considered the importance of the ten-year expiry period. Substitution was allowed, based upon a number of findings. First of all, the Court stressed that APSA must have known of the original claim (both companies were linked), and thus should have considered the possibility of substitution. The Court found no prejudice to APSA caused by the delay in making the application to substitute. While the defendants suggested that courts should not endorse solicitors' failures to conduct enquiries as to the identity of the producer, the Court of Appeal did not acquiesce to their calls. It acknowledged inadequacies in the conduct of the claimant's solicitors, only to reply that 'mistakes which give rise to an application to substitute will often be the result of a failure of some sort and the jurisdiction exists to remedy such mistakes'.[54]

The position of the ECJ on the issue of substitution and, indeed, any other procedural issue which the Directive leaves to the Member State law, is justified. The jurisdiction of the Court in the area of product liability is limited by the scope of the Directive. Further, the leading model of the European legal order still remains the dependency of European substantive law on national procedure.[55] While this approach may well help greater assimilation of European law within national legal orders,[56] one cannot help noticing that it leads to significant discrepancies in application of such crucial provisions of the Directive as the ten-year expiry period. It is by no means certain that the *O'Byrne* case would produce similar results in France, Germany or Poland. Again, the discussion comes back to the role of national courts in enforcing and interpretation of the Directive, mentioned above. Although some evidence of involvement of the ECJ in building a 'European procedural primacy' was already observed,[57] no clear signs of this tendency can so far be seen in the area of product liability. Where does this leave the ultimate goal of the Directive? What is this goal and can the Directive achieve it?

---

54   Paragraph 43(ii) of the Court of Appeal Judgement in *O'Byrne*.

55   J.S. Delicostopoulos, 'Towards European Procedural Primacy in National Legal Systems', *European Law Journal*, 9/5, (2003): 599, at 599; Maher, 'National Courts as European Community Courts': 232.

56   Maher, 'National Courts as European Community Courts': 232 indicates that 'despite the problems that the application of national rules can cause, national judges are more likely to entertain a Community law point as a matter of course, if no extraordinary procedures are required'.

57   This can be seen in the ECJ judgements in *Factortame* (n. 36) – Maher, 'National Courts as European Community Courts': 239–242. See a more detailed analysis of the tendency to build 'a more subtle combination of national procedural competence and European procedural primacy' – Delicostopoulos, 'Towards European Procedural Primacy in National Legal Systems': 599.

3. Harmonization of Product Liability in Europe

(i) The Goal of the Directive

While, as indicated by the Third Commission Report, the Directive 'works by and large in a satisfactory way',[58] it is much more difficult to ascertain whether the Directive in fact achieved the main purposes which it set out to achieve. In fact, it is argued that it is unable to achieve these purposes. The Preamble makes it clear that the 'strict' liability regime is to prevent distortions of competition and obstacles to free movement of goods on the one hand and to eliminate differences in the degree of protection of the consumer on the other (Recital 1). Studies on the effect of the Directive in Europe found no proof that the remaining national divergences in interpretation of crucial elements of the regime such as 'defect', causal link, or the development risk defence (and these are still significant) actually inhibit intra-Community trade.[59] On the other hand, questions whether differences in legal approaches to product liability ever in fact inhibited trade to an appreciable extent continue to appear in academic literature.[60] It is also very unlikely that the sole existence of the Directive can ensure equal degree of protection for consumers with regard to damages caused by defective products. Their legal position in this context is determined by the whole array of measures of substantive law (contract law, for instance rules on warranties, tort law, and rules establishing various compensation schemes), a large number of regulatory measures, the applicable procedural rules, as well as their own perception about adequacy of protection provided to them. The Eurobarometer Survey 2006, which sought to determine the level of cross-border shopping and consumer confidence within the internal market, found that the level of consumer confidence in legal remedies available to them in case they do shop cross-border is still relatively low.[61] The means to achieve the aim of eliminating barriers to trade and ensuring equal level of consumer protection seem to reach beyond the scope of the Directive. Some academic writings and policy documents indicate the fact that the Directive itself is unable to provide the level playing field for businesses and consumers across the European Union.[62]

---

58   Third Commission Report at p. 4.
59   Lovells Report.
60   Whittaker, p. 439, continuing Stapleton's discourse on the weak legal and theoretical basis of the Directive (1994); G. Howells, 'Product liability – a history of harmonisation', in D. Fairgrieve (ed.), *Product Liability in Comparative Perspective*, (Cambridge, 2005). pp. 202–217.
61   European Commission *Consumer protection in the Internal Market* Eurobarometer Special Report 252, http://ec.europa.eu/public_opinion/archives/ebs/ebs252_en.pdf.
62   See Whittaker; Lovells Report indicates that issues outside the scope of the Directive – such as consumer protection law in general, civil procedure (in particular its reforms aimed at improvements in the widely understood 'access to justice'), developments in the area of product safety regulation – have the potential of affecting product liability law and practice and thus may affect this 'level-playing field'. These findings were presented in the Third Commission Report.

(ii) Complete Harmonization – an Elusive Goal?

On numerous occasions the Court stressed the need to retain the balance between different interests including: 'guaranteeing that competition will not be distorted, facilitating trade within the common market, consumer protection and ensuring the sound administration of justice'.[63] The Directive was adopted on the basis of the former Article 100 (now 94) of the EC Treaty which allows adoption of directives 'for the approximation of such laws, regulations or administrative provisions of the Member States as directly affect the establishment or functioning of the common market'. There is no doubt that one of the aims of the Directive is protection of consumers.[64] Essentially, however, the Directive is a market integration measure. Fairgrieve and Vaqué put forward a view that the ECJ preferred the 'internal market argument' when it declared the Directive a 'maximum harmonization measure'.[65] In view of the contemporary approach to market integration demonstrated by the Lisbon Agenda[66] and in particular the Better Regulation goal of the European Union[67] it appears that this course of action may no longer be an expression of preference of one set of interests over another. The approach to market regulation has shifted towards a more inclusive view of the interactions between consumers and businesses. The goals of enabling businesses to 'get on with their business' and making sure consumers 'get the full benefit of the internal market' are placed side-by-side in strategic documents

---

63   See in particular: Case 154/00 *Commission* v. *Greece* para. 29; see also case 183/00 *González Sánchez*.

64   The Preamble to the Directive mentions 'protection of the consumer against damage caused by defective product to his health or property' (Recital 1). A number of Recitals justify the introduction various provisions by the requirement of 'protection of the consumer': for instance liability of 'all producers', possibility of claiming compensation from any one of them, the definition of 'defect' focused on consumer expectations, compensation for death and personal injury as well as damage to property, or no possibility of exclusion of liability.

65   D. Fairgrieve, L.G. Vaque, 'Introduction', in D. Fairgrieve (ed.), *Product Liability in Comparative Perspective* (Cambridge, 2005), p. 3. See judgements of the ECJ: Cases C–183/00 and C–52/00.

66   Ten-year strategy adopted by the Lisbon European Council, the aim of which was initially to 'make the European Union the most competitive and dynamic economy in the World', Special Eurobarometer No. 215, *Lisbon* European Commission 2005 http://www.ec.europa.eu/public_opinion/archives/ebs/ebs_215_en.pdf). See also *Extracts from Presidency Conclusions on The Lisbon Strategy by Theme. European Councils: Lisbon (March 2000) to Brussels (June 2004):* http://ec.europa.eu/growthandjobs/pdf/thematic_lisbon_conclusions_0604_en.pdf. On the revised strategy see Communication from the Commission to the Council and the European Parliament *Common Actions for Growth and Employment: the Community Lisbon Programme* SEC[2005] 981, Brussels 20 July 2005, COM(2005) 330 final.

67   Communication from the Commission to the Council and the European Parliament *Common Actions for Growth and Employment: the Community Lisbon Programme* SEC[2005] 981, Brussels 20 July 2005, COM(2005) 330 final, pp. 7–9; also http://ec.europa.eu/growthandjobs/areas/fiche03_en.htm.

of the European Community.[68] Consumer protection policy is seen as an integral part of market integration policy, and the existing European consumer protection law is being reviewed for its impact on the internal market.[69] Such an approach also entails a more comprehensive outlook on the harmonization of product liability in Europe. Thus, although the target of complete harmonization pursued by the ECJ remains in line with this approach to market harmonization policy, the same approach reveals how far indeed the European Community is from achieving the ultimate goals set by the Product Liability Directive.

Surely, what is required from the regime aiming at 'complete harmonization' introduced by the Directive is greater clarity and consistency. The clarity and thus predictability of the law can bring benefits for both consumers and businesses. As far as the position of the latter is concerned, predictability impacts risk assessment in the context of the relevant insurance premiums. The manner in which the Directive is enforced and interpreted throughout the European Union, essentially based upon the cooperation between the European Court of Justice and national governments and, more importantly, national courts entails great difficulties in achieving such predictability. Because of the realization of the inevitability of these difficulties, the 'complete harmonization' is becoming, instead of some steady future goal, a process where the goalposts are being moved gradually – towards deeper and wider harmonization of law and procedure.

4. Deeper and Wider Harmonization?

The Directive is increasingly seen to be merely opening 'the way towards greater harmonization'.[70] This view, reiterated in the Third Commission Report, may be seen to concern solely the area of product liability or may be taken even further to relate to product liability law as a trendsetter (and a cautionary tale) within the process of harmonising the European civil law. On the other hand, developments within European substantive law and civil justice system are bound to affect the manner in which product liability law functions in Europe. The political and academic climate is changing towards recognition of the need to see the Product Liability Directive as a component of wider 'patterns of liability'.[71] This tendency may well be a reflection of the fact that Europe is now in a better position to harmonize its civil liability laws than it was at the time when the Directive was drafted. However, it has appeared in

---

68   See the explanation of the main thrust of the Better regulation strategy: http://ec.europa. eu/growthandjobs/areas/fiche03_en.htm. See Howells and Weatherill, for an academic view on consumer law as part of law of the market.

69   Review of Consumer *Acquis*: Commission Communication on European Contract Law and the revision of the *acquis*: the way forward (COM(2004) 651 of 11 October 2004).

70   This role was indeed stressed in the Preamble – Recital 18.

71   Whittaker. For first indications see: Stapleton's arguments on whether product liability ought to be distinguished from general tortious liability regime at all; with regard to tort liability in general P. Cane, *Atiyah's Accidents, Compensation and the Law*, 6th edn, (London, Edinburgh, Dublin: 1999).

recognition of the realization that the Directive itself is unable to harmonize product liability law in Europe because of other areas of law and procedural issues which directly or indirectly affect product liability law and practice. On the substantive law side – the existence of un-harmonized systems of contractual and tortious liability within the legal systems of the Member States may well distort the effect of the Directive.[72] The process of harmonising these rules of contract and tort law has already begun within the European Union and it is bound to affect the practice of product liability. The work on the Common Frame of Reference and the related review of Consumer *Acquis* aim to create a basis for future codification of European contract law.[73] The work on harmonization of European tort law, although less advanced, is also gradually progressing.[74] Some research undertakings emphasize the interdisciplinary links between various strands of civil liability and the importance of recognition of these links for the effective harmonization of European civil liability.[75] On the procedural side, issues such as access to justice, funding of litigation, existence or non-existence of class actions and other collective enforcement mechanisms may produce different effects of even the most precisely harmonized rules of substantive law. As indicated in the Lovells Report, procedural matters, access to justice and 'litigation culture' may well constitute a barrier to trade of a much greater strength than any differences in substantial laws of liability. The European Community recognized the importance of access to justice for consumers in the Green Paper *Access to Justice* and in the European Commission Plan of Action.[76] Civil procedure and access to justice play an increasingly important role on the European Community level[77] – with the work of the Directorate General for Justice, Freedom and Security,

---

72   Whittaker recommends seeking 'patterns of liability' which link product liability with other civil liability systems (contract law – consumer sales and guarantees, general tortious liability rules) as well as with criminal or administrative rules.

73   Communication from the Commission to the European Parliament and the Council: A More Coherent European Contract Law: An Action Plan COM(2003) 68, 12 February 2003; Communication from the Commission: *European Contract law and the revision of the acquis: the way forward* COM(2004) 651, 11 October 2004.

74   See for instance – the draft of the 'Principles of European Tort Law' developed by the European Group on Tort Law, published in H. Koziol, B.C. Steininger, *European Tort Law 2002*, (Vienna, New York, 2003), pp. 562 – 571. See also H. Wagner, 'The Project of Harmonising European Tort Law', *Common Market Law Review* 42, (2005): 1269–1312. The developments within European substantive law concerning consumers are explored by C. Hodges in (forthcoming), 'Europeanisation of Civil Justice: Trends and Issues' *Civil Justice Quarterly* (2007): 396.

75   C. von Bar, U. Drobnig (2002) *Study on Property Law and Non-Contractual Liability Law as they relate to Contract Law* Submitted to the European Commission – Health and Consumer Protection Directorate General SANCO B5–1000/02/000574.

76   Green Paper: *Access of consumers to Justice and the settlement of consumer disputes in the single market* COM(93) 576, 16 November 1993, *Action Plan on Consumer Access to Justice and the Settlement of Consumer Disputes in the Internal Market* COM(96) 13 final, 14 February 1996 (follow-up to the Green Paper).

77   See Action Plan of the Council and the Commission on how best to implement the provisions of the Treaty of Amsterdam on an area of freedom, security and justice – Text adopted by the Justice and Home Affairs Council of 3 December 1998, OJ C019,

establishment of the EJ-Net which hosts comprehensive information about the judicial systems of the Member States,[78] the Community framework of activities to facilitate the implementation of judicial cooperation in civil matters,[79] and several pieces of hard law which have so far been enacted.[80] Various European Community consumer protection Directives contain enforcement mechanisms involving possible action by consumer organizations as representatives of collective interests of consumers.[81] The interest in civil procedure extends also upon funding of litigation, with the Legal Aid Directive harmonising legal aid in cross-border proceedings.[82] Community may well be prompted to extend its activities in the area of civil procedure and access to justice by the growing interest on the Member State level in this area. Member States recognize the importance of enforcement of law, civil procedure and access to justice and they are reforming their civil procedure rules, enacting class actions or other types of group or representative proceedings.[83]

This need for a more complex approach to civil liability is increasingly becoming prominent on the political and academic agenda.[84]

23 January 1999; and Tampere European Council 15, 16 October 1999 – Presidency Conclusions (http://www.europarl.europa.eu/summits/tam_en.htm#top).

78   See the Council Decision of 28 May 2001 *establishing a European Judicial Network in civil and commercial matters*, OJ L174/25, 27 June 2001.

79   Council Regulation No. 743/2002 of 25 April 2002 *establishing a Community framework of activities to facilitate the implementation of judicial cooperation in civil matters* OJ L115/1, 1 May 2002.

80   See for instance: European Parliament and Council Regulation 805/2004 *creating a European Enforcement Order for uncontested claims* OJ L143 of 30 April 2004. See also proposals: Proposal for a regulation of the European Parliament and the Council establishing a European Small Claims Procedure COM(2005) 87, 15 March 2005: (http://ec.europa.eu/justice_home/doc_centre/civil/doc/com_2005_087_en.pdf). Amended Proposal for a Regulation of the European Parliament and the Council creating a European order for payment procedure COM(2006) 57 final, CEC 7 February 2006: (http://europa.eu.int/eur-lex/lex/LexUriServ/site/en/com/2006/com2006_0057en01.pdf).

81   See in particular – Directive 98/27/EC of the European Parliament and of the Council of 19 May 1998 *on injunctions for the protection of consumers' interests* OJ L166/51, 11 June 1998.

82   Directive 2002/8/EC of 27 January 2003 of the European Parliament and of the Council *to improve access to justice in cross-border disputes by establishing minimum common rules relating to legal aid for such disputes* OJ L026, 31 January 2003.

83   Hodges, 'Europeanisation of Civil Justice: Trends and Issues'.

84   For further information about these issues see: Whittaker; J. Stapleton, 'Bugs in Anglo-American products liability' in D. Fairgrieve (ed.), *Product Liability in Comparative Perspective* (Cambridge, 2005) p. 295, at p. 295. The Third Commission Report mentions the findings of the Lovells Report indicating problems with procedure, access to justice and culture of litigation.

5. Conclusions – the Way Ahead

Interesting times are ahead for those dealing with product liability. On the one hand, although judgements of the ECJ provide general guidance on the interpretation and application of important concepts used by the Directive, they often raise new questions and lead to diverse understanding. Crucial elements of the regime, which the Directive established but did not define, continue to leave scope for widely differing interpretation by the national legislatures and courts. On the other hand, the developments which only recently started appearing on the political and academic arena are sure to impact the Directive and its interpretation by the ECJ.

Naturally, clarity and the resulting increase in uniformity of interpretation of the rules established by the Directive are beneficial for businesses and consumers. The ECJ continues on its course to elucidate the meaning of the concepts used by the Directive, and the examples of such efforts are assessed in this paper. However, the more complex look at harmonization of product liability law and practice in the European Union might well soon impact product liability law and practice. Thus, while the conviction that the Directive should not be amended is strong, changes are ahead, both within the legislative framework and the practical application of product liability law in Europe. The Third Commission report indicated several areas within the product liability system which may need to be monitored, not least in the light of the potential 'opening the way towards greater harmonization': these are the burden of proof, the concept of defect, the development risks defence, the regulatory compliance defence, the minimum threshold, and the issues related to novel products, design defects and failure to warn.[85] This may mean a closer coordination between various pieces of Community legislation – for instance by recognising links with company law (the concept of producer, or introduction into circulation in the context of complex corporate structures), contract law (in particular consumer sales and liability of suppliers there), or product safety law (the notion of defect or the possible regulatory compliance defence).[86] In the light of the overwhelming resistance to changes within the substantive content of the Directive, such links could be recognized by either providing a set of guidelines on interpretation of the existing law,[87] or through judicial decisions. The role of the ECJ would obviously be significant in this process. An even more extensive development may be ahead with regard to enforcement and procedural aspects of product liability. Again, with a view to recognize the links between various strands of civil liability and regulation and to preserve the balance between consumers and businesses, harmonising European procedural rules needs to be a comprehensive exercise reaching beyond specific legal issues. Although the ECJ is constrained by the scope of the Product Liability Directive, which clearly indicates autonomy of Member States with regard

---

85   Third Commission report at pp. 9–11.

86   Such tendency for greater coherence and consistency can already be seen in the development of Common Frame of Reference in the area of contract law (part of which is the review of Consumer *Acquis*, or work of the *Acquis* Group).

87   A set of guidelines for interpretation of these concepts may well be adopted by the European Commission – Third Commission Report, p. 12.

to procedure, the growing involvement of Community law in this area will surely affect the way in which the Court interprets its existing provisions.

26 Consumer Protection Law and Policy in Serbia: The Current State and Projections for the Future

Tatjana Jovanic[1]

1. The Existing State of Consumer Protection in Serbia

Consumer protection has become a reality in all countries and economies and globalization makes it difficult for a single country to escape from this common trend. In the former decade, consumer protection has become one of the main areas of the fundamental reforms in Central and Eastern Europe.

Consumer protection remains strongly related to the overall level of economic development. The existing situation in Serbia owes much to the negative impact of economic sanctions, tariff protection, the low level of major retail investments, unemployment and decline in the consumer purchasing power. The production of goods, although improving, may not be of a high quality because of lower standard products being put into circulation, even if purchased for relatively high prices. On the other hand, low purchasing power incites consumers to buy goods that are not too expensive but of a poor quality, sometimes illegally put on the market. Moreover, some foreign companies do not hesitate to take benefit from the inadequate legislation to use some aggressive sales methods.

As it was the case with all markets in transition, the Serbian situation is also characterized by huge information deficits: low education of the population on consumer issues, lacking or inadequate indication of prices, incomplete labelling of products, absence of instructions and warnings, lack of information about contract terms, warranty conditions and consumer rights in general, weak independent consumer information systems, non existing or limited comparative testing and so on. Other deficits relate to the lack of effective redress mechanisms to solve consumer disputes: difficulties in accessing law itself and legal expertise. Costs are likely to constitute a most decisive barrier, while collective redress mechanisms remain exceptional.

2. Stabilisation and Association Process – The Need to Harmonise Consumer Law

Due to political constraints, the Serbian process of Stabilisation and Association with the European Union is rather slow. However, during the previous couple of

---

1   MA, LL.M, PhD Candidate. Lecturer, University of Belgrade School of Law.

years, many new laws have been enacted. Chapter 23 of the Annex to the 1995 EU White Paper on the Preparation of the Associated Countries of Central and Eastern Europe for Integration into the Internal Market of the Union[2] is precise regarding the approximation of laws to be carried out by the associated countries in the consumer field in preparation for accession to the European Union. Key measures concern: product safety (both general and sectoral measures), consumer sales and warranty obligations, denomination, classification, labelling and packaging of products destined for the consumer, indication of prices of food and of non-food products, misleading and comparative advertising, consumer credit, unfair terms in consumer contracts, package travel, contracts negotiated away from business premises, distance contracts (including e-commerce), trade practices and marketing methods, the protection of purchasers in contracts relating to the purchase of a right to utilise one or several immovable properties on a timeshare basis, actions for injunctions and alternative dispute resolution schemes. The White Paper also stresses the conditions which are held as necessary in order to operate consumer legislation properly.

The State Union of Serbia and Montenegro had entered the negotiations for Stabilisation and Association Agreements (SAA) in October 2005. With the SAA, the legal harmonization process represents the basic legal instrument of the relationship between EU and Serbia. It may be presumed that the EU/Serbia Stabilisation and Association Agreement will include consumer protection commitments similar to those undertaken by Macedonia and Croatia. Those commitments are medium term or 'soft' commitments in the SAA, and this level of commitment is likely to be insisted upon by the EU and its Member States, based on the Macedonian and Croatian SAA benchmarks and the level of political commitment already in place between the EU and Serbia.

Under the SAA concluded between the EU and both Macedonia and Croatia, consumer policy is given an important place. It seems likely that specific medium term commitments will feature in the EU/Serbia SAA, in line with Article 74 of the Interim EU/Croatia SAA of May 2001 and Article 94 of the EU/Macedonia SAA.[3] In these agreements, the parties declare, as a point of principle, that 'effective consumer protection is necessary in order to ensure that the market economy functions properly, and this protection will depend on the development of an administrative infrastructure in order to ensure market surveillance and law enforcement in this field'. They then agree to 'cooperate in order to align the standards of consumer protection in the Balkan country concerned with those of the EU' and, specifically, to encourage and ensure: 1. The harmonisation of legislation and the alignment of consumer protection to EU standards; 2. A policy of active consumer protection including the increase of information and development of independent organisations; 3. Effective legal protection for consumers in order to improve the quality of consumer goods and maintain appropriate safety standards.

Similar prerequisites for Serbia are already underlined in the Council Decision 2004/520/EC of 14 June 2004.[4] The European Commission acknowledged the

---

2   COM(95) 163, May 1995.
3   Annexes 2 and 3 set out these provisions which are identical in both Agreements.
4   Council Decision 2004/520/EC on the principles, priorities and conditions contained

developments in the legal framework of consumer protection, but has also warned the Serbian legislator that institutional framework of consumer protection had been weak and that administrative capacities must be strengthened.[5] The EU officials and the Serbian Government have recently signed a Memorandum of Understanding regarding financial aid for strengthening the Consumer Policy. The European Agency for Reconstruction (EAR) is about to launch 2 million Euro CARDS Programme in 2007 as a support to the first National Consumer Protection Programme.

(i) The Existing Legal Framework

Until 2002, consumer protection in Serbia was in the domain of a Federal Legislator and primarily based on the Federal Trade Law.[6] The relevant provisions of this Law were repealed and replaced by the Federal Law on Consumer Protection prepared by the Federal Ministry for Economy and Internal Trade and adopted on 2 July 2002.[7] This represented the first milestone in the reform of consumer law in Serbia and Montenegro. The Federal Law on Consumer Protection of 2002 regulated only selected issues in a very general way, without taking into account the EU Directives on consumer protection. Subsequently, with the adoption of the Constitutional Charter, the Federal Republic of Yugoslavia was converted into the loose State Union of Serbia and Montenegro and consumer protection was no longer a matter for a Federal legislator.

The Serbian Law on Consumer Protection was enacted on 15 September 2005.[8] It was the first attempt to harmonize national legislation with the EU Consumer Law framework. It is worth mentioning that, in the same period, two other relevant laws were enacted: Law on Advertising and Law on Prices which also took effect in September 2005.

In terms of Consumer Law harmonization, from a comparative law perspective we may differentiate three main regulatory models in Central and Eastern Europe.[9] The Serbian legislator has chosen a segmented regulatory approach, which means that, although there is one Law on Consumer Protection which specifically deals with these issues, there are several other laws which represent a specific legal framework for selected issues. This Law is a kind of codification in the field of consumer rights protection since it integrated new consumer rights. In many of the provisions of the

---

in the European Partnership with Serbia and Montenegro including Kosovo as defined by the United Nations Security Council Resolution 1244 of 10 June 1999, Official Journal No. 227, pp. 21–34.

5   European Commission: Serbia and Montenegro – 2005 Progress Report, COM(2005) 561 final, p. 38.

6   Official Gazette of the Federal Republic of Yugoslavia No. 32/93, 50/93, 41/94 and 29/96.

7   Official Gazette of the Federal Republic of Yugoslavia No. 37/02.

8   Official Gazette of the Republic of Serbia No. 79/2005.

9   For an extensive overview of the regulatory approaches see publications of the Centre de droit de la consomation, Université catholique de Louvain, Series on 'Consumer Institutions and Consumer Policy Program' and Series on 'CICPP Compendium' (published by the Centre in the context of the *Phare Program*).

Law on Consumer Protection, the Serbian legislator referred to over 20 laws, often using the same phrase 'in line with the relevant law regulating this issue'. Some of them are existing (such is for example the Law on Advertising, the Law on Tourism), while some are still lacking. It is natural that certain provisions about consumer protection had to remain in other legislative acts (Law on Obligation Relations, Law on Standardisation, Law on Sanitary Protection of Food, Law on Protection of Food, Law on Environmental Protection, Law on Trade, and so on). For this reason, the Law on Consumer Protection is to be applied together with the laws applicable to various other sectors.

This 'umbrella' Law on Consumer Protection contains 81 articles in its ten sections. The Law governs fundamental consumer rights, the manner in which such rights may be exercised, protection of consumer rights, and application of ethical principles. In the first Section (Main Provisions), the Law formulates general principles and consumer rights. The fundamental consumer rights are enumerated in Article 3: the right to satisfy elementary needs; the right to safety; awareness and availability of information; freedom of choice; consumer voice; the right to compensation; consumer education and the right to a healthy environment. The Law is lacking interpretative provisions, as it only defines the statutory concept of a 'consumer' and a 'vendor'. Therefore, many relevant concepts mentioned in the Law, not to mention the EU consumer legislation, are not defined, which makes its practical implementation difficult. Moreover, in defining 'consumer', Serbian Law is not in line with the EU *acquis*. In Article 2(2) of the Law, apart from a natural person who purchases products or obtains services for their own needs or household, 'consumer' is considered to be 'a company, enterprise, other legal entity or entrepreneur, when they are purchasing products or obtaining services for their own needs. A vendor, for the purposes of this Law, shall be a company, enterprise, other legal entity or entrepreneur, when they are selling products or providing services to a consumer...'.

Consumer life, health and safety protection is briefly regulated in Section Two, which contains only six articles and is very elementary, mostly of a declaratory nature. More specifically, it deals with safety of products and packaging, protection of minors, notification about quality of water and air and there is just one sentence on genetically modified products. Several articles in the Third Section on the protection of consumers' economic interests are dedicated to the main forms of consumer protection, as well as main obligations of vendors or service providers. Further to this, a few provisions deal with the prices of goods and services, packaging material, invoice issuing, guarantee, delivery of the product, selling of technical products, discount sales, customer complaints and so on. Also, this section regulates distance selling, but in a very basic way. Only two provisions (Articles 29 and 30) relate to consumer credit, not to mention the other financial services.[10]

The Fourth Section (Articles 36 to 43) relates to the public utility services and services in general. It generally enumerates the obligations of a service provider, introduces principles of price setting for the services, and contains several provisions

---

10   However, the National Bank of Serbia issued an Ordinance on the calculation of effective annual interest rate and calculation of the total costs of a credit transaction.

on products and services of a public interest, timesharing and real estate. However, the legislator just declares special forms of consumer protection related to services without deeper immersion into the protective regulation. The Fifth Section relates to contracts of adhesion, and with only two articles (which even in the first look are not enough to harmonize this complex issue with the EU standards) attempts to transpose the Directive 93/13/EEC on unfair terms in consumer contracts. The main deficiency of this approach is a failure to enumerate situations or contractual terms which are considered to represent unfair clauses.

The following Section is about informing and educating the consumer. It promulgates the principle that information and data about the characteristics of products and services and the conditions of their sale must be truthful, comprehensive, well founded, unambiguous, clear and timely. Consumers are entitled to be informed, in an understandable manner, about the characteristics of the products or services they are obtaining and, in particular, about: the composition, sanitary safety, quality, mode of payment, manner of maintaining the product, and about any hazards that might arise if not properly used. This section also contains provisions related to advertising and product declaration.

The Seventh Section of the Law regulates the compensation for damage. First, it should be stressed that its provisions are not in line with the EU standards and the objective responsibility of the producer for the defect. The law says that a consumer shall be under an obligation to prove that he has suffered damage caused by the flaw in the product or service obtained, if: 1) the product is not suitable for the intended purpose and cannot be used in the usual fashion; 2) the consumer was misled in respect of the date of production and period of use; 3) the consumer suffered damage due to other flaws in the product or service he has obtained. Moreover, redress mechanisms are not envisaged.

However, shortcomings of this approach are corrected to a certain degree with the enactment of the Law on the Responsibility of a Producer for Defect Products of 21 November 2005,[11] which introduced the objective responsibility of producers. In addition, relevant provisions of the Law on Obligations of 1979 are applicable. This section also contains few declaratory provisions on the court and out-of-court mechanisms of consumer protection.

The Eighth Section relates to the National Consumer Protection Programme and the Consumer Protection Council within the Ministry of Trade, Tourism and Services. Among subjects in charge of Consumer Protection, one of the provisions (Article 68) enumerates the main functions of consumers' organizations. Consumers' organizations are entitled and asked to: 1) ensure the protection of individual and common interests of the consumers; 2) provide consumers with the information, advice, and other kinds of aid related to exercise of their rights; 3) organise education of the consumers; 4) notify consumers about prices, quality, control, and safety of products and services in the market; 5) conduct independent control over quality and safety of the products or services offered; 6) report to the competent government authorities, enclosing the evidence about products and services which do not conform to the prescribed quality and other prescribed requirements; 7) notify

---

11   Official Gazette of the Repubic of Serbia No. 101/2005.

consumers about possibilities of non-judicial settlement of disputes; 8) file charges with the competent court with the purpose of consumer rights protection; 9) take part in the activities of the competent authority when consumer related issues are being considered; 10) establish cooperation with counterpart authorities and organisations, in the country and internationally.

Two final Sections (Ninth and Tenth) are dedicated to market supervision and penal provisions. The Ministry exercises inspection supervision through market inspectors and tourism inspectors. Consumer protection tasks are also exercised by the Ministry in charge of health issues; the Ministry in charge of agriculture; water management and forestry related issues; the Ministry in charge of energy issues; the Ministry in charge of transportation, telecommunications, planning and construction related issues; and the Ministry in charge of environmental protection. Relevant administrative laws strengthened the independence of these administrative organs in relation to the Government.

3. The National Consumer Protection Programme

The National Programme for Consumer Protection includes five years objectives for the protection of consumers in the Republic of Serbia, the manner for attainment of such objectives, the manner of educating and informing the consumers, incentives related to consumption, and other elements of relevance for the exercise of consumers' rights. The National Programme is currently in the form of the Final Draft, proposed by the Ministry of Trade, Tourism and Services and is about to be adopted by the Government of the Republic of Serbia. In drafting this Programme, to be operative in the period between 2007 and 2012, the officials of the Ministry of Trade, Tourism and Services carefully analyzed and relied upon similar Programmes in the region (notably Slovenian, Croatian and Macedonian) and took into account the relevant EU framework and various acts of the regional and international organizations of consumers.

The Programme clearly sets out the main shortcomings of the existing Law on Consumer Protection and the current state of protection in selected fields (for example, distance sale, financial services) and enumerates relevant EU legislation which should be taken into account. The Programme stresses the problems of coordination among various administrative bodies which deal with selected consumer issues, especially the need to create an effective IT system which would, among other, enable Serbia to join the RAPEX system.

The National Consumer Protection Programme contains operative targets and tasks projected for the period between 2007 and 2012, aiming at the creation of a uniform and effective consumer protection framework. One of the main segments of the National Consumer Protection Program is the Framework Programme on the use of financial means for the fulfilment of the National Programme. A constitutive part of the Programme is a detailed table with a set of 'to do' actions and an overview of the main tasks, subjects in charge of them and the financial means in the period 2007–2012.

In line with the existing Law, the Programme further describes duties of the competent authorities and civic organizations. One among them should be particularly mentioned here. Pursuant to the Law on Consumer Protection, the Consumer Protection Council of the Minister is set up within the Ministry for Trade, Tourism and Services as the advisory/consulting body. The Council is headed by the Minister and members of the Council are prominent scientists and experts in the field, as well as representatives of consumers' organisations.

The Programme initialized the establishment of the Educational Centre for Consumer Protection, with the aim to educate people who will perform an advisory role in relation to consumers. Six Advisory centres are planned to be established (the main will have a seat in Belgrade, followed by four regional centres seated in regional centres), and it is expected to have eleven centres established by the end of 2008. These centres would serve as a link between consumer organizations and the public administration. As such, they would not represent consumers in disputes, but provide help to consumer organizations which are entitled to represent consumers.

The Programme reveals the problem of consumers' organizations which suffer from a 'Balkanization' syndrome. Namely, there are over 40 consumers' organizations, which are still not united within a national association of consumers' organizations, and therefore experience difficulties in international cooperation. Exactly because of this 'Balkanization' syndrome and attempts to establish several alliances with the prefix 'national', the authors of the Programme decided to diverge from the usual concept known in a comparative law and to suggest the proliferation of a State administration in the national association. The Programme also suggests that Consumer Advice Bureaus should be structured in several levels: both regional and local consumer centres would incorporate civic initiative backed with the help of a public organ, while independent consumers' organizations would initiate the procedure on the protection of consumer interests. Withdrawal of public bodies is envisaged once consumers' organizations become stronger and more credible.

(i) The Course of Action to Develop the Efficient Consumer Protection System in Serbia

In the first place, Serbia must develop the concept of consumer protection, as it is obvious that the concept itself is not well developed. In order for the concept of consumer protection to emerge, the Serbian legislator must develop a concise and user oriented functional regulatory framework of consumer protection. Part of it has been undertaken by enactment of the Serbian Law on Consumer Protection of 2005, but this needs to be further developed and strengthened. In order to pave a way to the EU, this Law needs many amendments. Therefore, a better solution would be to enact a new and up-to-date Law on Consumer Protection.

The new Serbian Law on consumer protection, although imperfect, if amended with several core amendments, could serve as a good framework for the legal and institutional harmonization with the EU *acquis*. Practice of the newly accessed EU Member States shows that the first phase of adjustment of a national legal framework may only be partial. Hence, in the first phase the main principles of the EU Law should be introduced together with main instruments for their implementation.

Further, in order for the regulatory framework to be functional, the awareness of citizens on their rights as consumers must be upgraded. The concept of 'consumer protection' still doesn't really exist, because consumers are not yet aware of their rights. That is why raising public awareness on consumers' rights and legal redress seems crucial for the development of an effective consumer law framework.

One of the nagging amendments relates to the effective mechanisms of out-of-court settlement of disputes, in line with the relevant EU standards. Among institutional preconditions, one is to strengthen market inspection and its infrastructure (including laboratories for product testing) and to interlink all state administrative bodies which deal with issues related to consumer protection. Civic consumer organizations must be developed, especially their role in the formulation of the consumer policy. Their role will be crucial in the development of the sustainable system of consumer protection in Serbia in the following ten years.

A no less important concern relates to the choice of the State organ in charge of consumer protection. Currently, this organ is the Department for Consumer Protection and Prices within the Ministry of Trade, Tourism and Services with only four people responsible for all issues (market inspectors are not included). There was a doubt whether to merge the Antimonopoly Department with the Consumer Protection Department, but it was concluded that the 'two-tracks' system should be kept, especially due to the increasing number of tasks given to the Consumer Protection Department.

4. Conclusion

Although the existing Serbian legal framework on consumer protection deserves to be criticized, the point should not be lost that – at least from a purely legislative standpoint – the new Law indisputably advances the legal base and framework for consumer protection in Yugoslavia. The main concern is to ensure that the new Law on Consumer Protection is enforced, that it is developed further and that there is the necessary political and administrative commitment and capacity to generate positive and tangible reform benefits for Serbian consumers.

The present position of consumer protection in Serbia is under-developed. Put simply, consumers in Serbia are insufficiently prioritized in the overall economic reform process and this, by definition, has wide social implications. While the basic political will to advance consumer protection is evident from the very existence of the new Law, this can be seen only as a baseline situation and a starting point for real progress. Whatever the exact focus, timetable and direction of future reform in this sector, a sustained and strategically driven effort will be required for the effective development of this sector in Serbia.

While the Stabilisation and Association Process generally anticipates the gradual approximation of laws and practices in the Balkan region with EU legal and policy norms (the 'EU *Acquis*'), there is still no particular reason to expect strong commitments in Serbia's forthcoming Stabilisation and Association Agreement (SAA) in the field of consumer protection.